FOUNDATIONS OF ETHICAL PRACTICE, RESEARCH, AND TEACHING IN PSYCHOLOGY AND COUNSELING

SECOND EDITION

FOUNDATIONS OF ETHICAL PRACTICE, RESEARCH, AND TEACHING IN PSYCHOLOGY AND COUNSELING

SECOND EDITION

Karen Strohm Kitchener
Sharon K. Anderson

Routledge
Taylor & Francis Group
New York   London

Routledge
Taylor & Francis Group
270 Madison Avenue
New York, NY 10016

Routledge
Taylor & Francis Group
27 Church Road
Hove, East Sussex BN3 2FA

© 2011 by Taylor and Francis Group, LLC
Routledge is an imprint of Taylor & Francis Group, an Informa business

Printed in the United States of America on acid-free paper
10 9 8 7 6 5 4 3 2 1

International Standard Book Number: 978-0-415-96541-5 (Hardback)

Library of Congress Cataloging-in-Publication Data

Kitchener, Karen S.
   Foundations of ethical practice, research, and teaching in psychology and counseling / by Karen Strohm Kitchener, Sharon K. Anderson. -- 2nd ed.
     p. cm.
   Includes bibliographical references and index.
   ISBN 978-0-415-96541-5 (hardback : alk. paper)
   1. Psychologists--Professional ethics. 2. Psychology--Moral and ethical aspects. 3. Psychology--Research--Moral and ethical aspects. 4. Psychology--Study and teaching--Moral and ethical aspects. I. Anderson, Sharon K. II. Title.

BF76.4.K58 2010
174'.915--dc22   2010021219

Visit the Taylor & Francis Web site at
http://www.taylorandfrancis.com

and the Routledge Web site at
http://www.routledgementalhealth.com

To Richard Frank Kitchener—for his competence, support, and inspiration

Karen

To my students—for our lively and wonderful conversations about ethics—
I am a better and more ethical teacher and supervisor because of you!

Sharon

Contents

Preface

The ethical issues and dilemmas confronting psychologists and counselors are becoming increasingly more numerous and complex. Managed care has forced practitioners to consider and reconsider issues of confidentiality and what it means to offer competent treatment. Practitioners are faced with questions of when and whether to break confidentiality in light of clients' dangerous behavior. Researchers need to consider the meaning of true informed consent and how to study socially significant behavior, such as child abuse, while protecting participants' privacy. University faculty members struggle with their responsibilities to enhance students' intellectual and personal development while at the same time maintaining reasonable standards that protect the public from inept and unqualified psychologists and counselors.

Furthermore, the cultures in which these problems occur are also changing. In the United States, the populations that psychologists and counselors treat, study, and teach are increasingly diverse. This growing diversity within and among cultures demands that practitioners, researchers, and faculty take the time to reflect upon and reconsider the underlining assumptions of concepts like consent, confidentiality, boundary issues, and justice in different cultural contexts. In addition, the growing diversity within our clients and students raises questions about competence in the provision and availability of psychological services, approaches to research, and training.

The increase in the complexity of ethical issues psychologists and counselors face and the cultural contexts in which they are embedded is taking place in a society that is also increasingly litigious. Ethical issues and decisions have become difficult to separate from legal ones and, when they can, psychologists and counselors often have to weigh both the legal and ethical implications of their actions.

When the first author of the book began writing on ethics in 1984, she introduced the concept of principalism to psychology. Now it is difficult to read anything on ethics in psychology and even counseling without coming across the concept of ethical principles. Still they are sometimes misunderstood or misapplied. Thus, as in the first edition, the first section of this book is spent on a discussion of ethical decision making that is based on ethical principles. This edition goes further, however, in discussing how principles and ethical decision making are related to ethical theory and metaethics (Kitchener & Kitchener, 2008). In addition, it adds a chapter on acculturation to the profession. The ethical principles and ethical issues with which new trainees in particular are faced require them to rethink the values of their family of origin, perhaps, their religion, and their responsibilities to others. All of this and more involves acculturation profession.

Anyone who is familiar with the first edition to this book will note several changes in the second edition. First, the current edition is written for a broader audience including both psychologists and counselors. Many of the issues that confront those working in these professions are similar. As professionals they all deal with issues of informed consent, justice, dual role relationships, and so on. Further, the model of ethical decision making introduced in the book and the acculturation process to the profession applies to both professions. In order to do both professions justice, Sharon Anderson, PhD, member of the counseling faculty at Colorado State University, has joined me to coauthor this edition. In addition, Randi Smith, PhD, a faculty member at Metropolitan State College in Denver was added as a coauthor of the chapter on confidentiality. Her membership on the Colorado Psychological Association's Ethics Committee brought up-to-date experience with particularly thorny problems in legal and ethical issues in therapy and supervision.

The second change is that this edition is neither tied to a particular code of ethics nor have the codes been included as appendices. Although we have not identified specific codes in the text, all the references to ethics codes apply to current as well as future versions. The most current version can be downloaded for free from the Internet site for each profession. To download the current Ethical Principles and Code of Conduct for the American Psychological Association (APA) go to http://www.apa.org/ethics/code/index.aspx. To download the Ethics Code for the American Counseling Association (ACA) go to http://72.167.35.179/Laws_and_Codes/ACA_Code_of_Ethics.pdf. In addition to this change, we have added some resources as pdf files via the Web site for our book: http://www.routledgementalhealth.com/foundations-of-ethical-practice-research-and-teaching-in-psychology-9780415965415. These resources included: American Psychological Association Guidelines on Multicultural Education, Training, Research, Practice, and Organizational Change for Psychologists; American Psychological Association Guidelines for Psychotherapy with Lesbian, Gay, and Bisexual Clients; American Psychological Association Guidelines for Psychological Practice with Older Adults; and Guidelines for Psychological Practice with Girls and Women.

One goal of the first book was to illustrate that there was more to acting morally than information and decision making by using James Rest's model as a template. In brief summary, based on a review of the psychological literature on moral behavior, Rest identified four components that were necessary to produce moral action. These are: Component 1, sensitivity to moral issues; Component 2, critical decision making; Component 3, valuing moral behavior over other values like money or success; and Component 4, ego strength. With the exception of the three chapters committed to ethical decision making and the role of ethical virtues addressed in Chapter 4, the first edition did not attend carefully to the other components. In addition, readers were not asked to consider their own moral values. Consequently, the third change in this edition is that at the end of several chapters, discussion questions, case scenarios, and/or other activities will be suggested. These sections are included to help readers: increase their sensitivity to the ethical issues in their own work or to practice; promote their ethical thinking processes; enhance their ability to make tough ethical decisions; challenge their ethical justifications; and consider which of their personal values interfere with the professional ones.

Fourth, the order and names of some of the chapters have been and the material in them has been updated and expanded. For example, the chapter on competence has been moved to the beginning of the book since all ethical choices and decision making depends on the competence of the professional. The chapter on multiple role relationships and conflicts of interest has been retitled.

The fifth change in the second edition is the addition of three chapters. Chapter 4 discusses the practicalities of ethical decision making. Chapter 6 looks at the importance of self-knowledge and ethical acculturation to the professions. The material on competence has been divided into two chapters. In the first chapter (Chapter 7), general issues of competence and self-care are discussed. In Chapter 8, the meaning of competence in therapy, research, supervision, and so on are discussed within the multicultural content of psychology and counseling. In addition to these new chapters, we have expanded each chapter to include implications for supervision.

One important issue to highlight that distinguishes our ethics book from others and remains the same for the same second edition is the format. The book is organized around ethical issues such as informed consent, competence, confidentiality, multiple role relationships, and so on. We took this organizational approach because the book's structure encourages an in-depth discussion of the reasons why these are ethical issues. Other ethics text are organized around roles that psychologists and counselors play, for example, therapist, educator, researcher, and each chapter will have a section on informed consent, confidentiality, multiple role relationships, and so on. In going through material presented this way, students will often memorize the rules around these issues, but fail to understand what makes the issues critical in their everyday professional responsibilities. In this book, each chapter begins with a discussion and the reasons why the issue is important and the ethical principles that provide the foundations for the issues are articulated. The chapter's focus is then applied to the different roles that psychologists and counselors play. For example, we follow each of the issues to its application in practice, research, teaching, and supervision. Each section is clearly titled. This not only provides the foundation for understanding why different ethical issues are important, it avoids redundancy.

If instructors want to use the book in a more traditional manner, they can begin by having students read the sections of each chapter that provide the rationale for why the issues are important and then follow with having them read the sections on practice or research or supervision and so on. Since the sections on these topics are clearly titled in each chapter, the instructor could have students read, for example, all of the sections on practice at one time adding any material they think the book has failed to highlight.

Goals of the Book

As noted in the Preface to the first edition, the primary purpose of this book is on ethical reasoning and ethical behavior. The assumption is that in the current climate, formal codes of ethics and even ethics texts that try to cover the full range of ethical issues in psychology and counseling, cannot address all of the concerns and conflicts that professionals in the field face. Consequently, one of our goals is to help readers develop the thinking skills necessary for solving ethical dilemmas so they can then analyze the new issues as they arise.

A second goal of the book is to show that more is involved in behaving ethnically than applying ethical rules or making ethical decisions. Since some models of moral behavior (Rest, 1994) suggest that sensitivity to ethical issues, moral motivation, and ego strength are all critical principle- and rule-bound ethical strategies are incomplete. Accordingly, the importance of ethical character and the role of ethical virtues and ideals in supporting ethical behavior are discussed; this is then related to acculturation to the professions. Here, the goal is to help psychologists and counselors reflect broadly on what it means to be an ethical professional as well as on how to train future professionals who value being ethical.

A third goal of the book is to point out the ways in which psychologists and counselors as individuals and the professionals need to ponder their responsibility to society as a whole. Thus, the last chapter is devoted to questions of social justice, such as who should pay for mental health services and who should bear the burdens and reap the benefits of mental health research. The hope is that it will stimulate future and current professionals to think about their ethical responsibilities in the widest possible context.

This book does not attempt to be a treatise on the law and ethics. Other authors have tackled this task. But in some situations, legal and ethical issues are closely interrelated. Legal decisions often rest on ethical premises, and sometimes ethical understanding can be clarified by legal definitions. In other situations, legal decisions like the *Tarasoff* case have raised ethical issues for professionals in the fields of psychology and counseling. In such situations, although the focus remains on ethics, legal issues are also discussed.

Cases Presented in the Book

Cases are used throughout the book to illustrate particularly difficult ethical problems, ethical errors, and sometimes laudatory ethical behavior. These cases derive from ethical issues that real professionals have faced; however, several procedures have been used to protect the privacy of the people involved. These procedures include integrating material from more than one real-life case, changing the gender, location, and names of people involved, and/or focusing on one aspect of a particularly complex case or expanding on one aspect of a less complex one. Exceptions are cases taken from newspaper accounts of events that are public information or from books that describe the real-life experiences of particular people. In these cases, information may be condensed; however, we did our best to represent the events in question as accurately as possible.

It is always difficult to decide what kinds of names to use for the individuals in ethics cases. Different authors have used several alternatives. One alternative was to use bland descriptors, such as "Dr. X;" however, some students found this distracting and noted that it masked gender and ethnicity when they were important. Consequently, we often refer to the professional only as a psychologist, counselor, or mental health practitioner. When we do use names to clarify the role, gender, or ethnicity of the people involved, we use short surnames, none of which have any resemblance to the names of the real people involved in any of the cases from which ideas were drawn.

Because cases may illustrate more than one point, they may be cited in more than one place in the book. All of the cases are included in Appendix E to make the cases easily accessible and provide a resource that allows discussion of particular cases out of the context of the text itself. Instructors, for example, may want students to think about one or two of the cases prior to reading a chapter to prime them for the material they will read at a later time.

Dr. Karen Strohm Kitchener
Dr. Sharon K. Anderson

Acknowledgments

We want to thank Elizabeth Zuckerman and particularly, Allison Cashwell for the research they did that provided much of the recent literature on many of the topics we discuss. Allison was particularly helpful in the last stages of organizing the book, creating the Table of Contents, and double checking references. Her dedication to good scholarship cannot be underestimated. We only wish her well in her search for a position in academia because she will make an outstanding teacher as well as researcher.

We also both had support systems that kept us going when we tired of the project and feared our own incompetence. Karen wants to thank her husband, Richard, whose professional competence in philosophy added immeasurably to the contents of the book and his moral support was ongoing and unyielding. He has always made her life richer in ways that can never be enumerated and will always be valued. Sharon wishes to thank her many students in the counseling program! The countless conversations and intellectually stimulating dialogs about ethics and "being ethical" still play in her mind. Thanks for helping me become a better and more ethical teacher!

Authors

Karen Strohm Kitchener, PhD, a former chair of the Ethics Committee of the American Psychological Association (APA), is Professor Emeritus of the Counseling Psychology program at the University of Denver. She worked with a revision of the 1992 APA Ethics Code and with the APA Office on AIDS on a casebook illustrating ethical issues dealing with HIV-positive clients. She wrote an article on ethical issues and practice in research for the third edition of the *Handbook of Counseling Psychology* (John Wiley & Sons, 2000). Recently, she coauthored an article on social science research ethics for *The Handbook of Social Science Research Ethics* (2009), and is currently coauthoring an article on the ethical foundations of psychology for the *APA Handbook of Ethics and Psychology*. She also wrote an article on the foundations of ethics in psychology for the fourth edition of the *Corsini Encyclopedia of Psychology* (Wiley, 2010). In addition, her extensively funded research on the development of reflective thinking in adolescents and adults has resulted in numerous publications, including a book on the development of reflective judgment. She is a recipient of the Ralph Birdie award from the American Counseling and Development Association, the Contribution to Knowledge award from the American College Personnel Association, and received the first Lifetime Achievement award from the Colorado Psychological Association in 2006. In addition, she received the 2010 APA Ethics Educator award.

Sharon K. Anderson received her PhD in counseling psychology from the University of Denver in 1993. She is currently an associate professor of counseling and careers development in the School of Education at the Colorado State University. Dr. Anderson is well versed in the area of psychotherapy and passionate about ethical and legal issues in psychotherapy. She has professional experience as a licensed psychologist and currently maintains a small practice in life coaching. Dr. Anderson has been described by students as being "wickedly enthusiastic" about ethics. For several years, she was one of the few professionals recognized by the State of Colorado to provide workshops on mental health law for all mental health professions. Dr. Anderson's writing and research agenda includes issues such as the ethics of multiple relationships and the ethical sensitivity and decision-making of psychologists and other professionals. She has published numerous articles and book chapters on the theory and practice of professional ethics in psychotherapy. Dr. Anderson is a successful writer with three books in print and/or in press and is most pleased with the recent book coauthored with Dr. Handelsman titled *Ethics for Psychotherapists and Counselors: A Proactive Approach* (Wiley-Blackwell, 2010) and a 2nd edition coedited book titled *Explorations in Diversity: Examining Privilege and Oppression in a Multicultural Society* (Brooks/Cole Cengage Learning, in press).

Ethics*
What It Is and What It Is Not

Psychologists and counselors, irrespective of their roles, are increasingly faced with situations in which values conflict. Take the following cases as examples.

Case 1-1

A married man with two small children enters into therapy with a therapist. In the course of treatment, he reveals that he is bisexual and is HIV positive. He fears he will develop the symptoms of AIDS but does not wish his wife to know of his HIV condition unless the AIDS symptoms actually develop. After multiple attempts to by the therapist to reason with him, he still refuses to tell his wife. The only source of comfort for the therapist is the indication from the client is that most of the time he and his wife use condoms as a form of birth control.

Case 1-2

A professor generally gives a similar assignment to his graduate seminar each year. It involves designing a study to explore a particularly difficult problem that the class has studied. When the papers are turned in, he notices that one of the papers is remarkably like a paper he received the previous year. He confronts the student with the possibility that she has plagiarized the information from another student's paper. The student explains that there was a recent death in her family and that she was having difficulty concentrating. As a result, she read a former student's paper to get herself thinking about the task. She claims that she designed the study herself and really did not think the paper she read influenced her work. When the professor points out the similarities, she seems genuinely surprised at the amount of overlap. The professor is perplexed by the student's actions because he has always found her to have a great deal of integrity and to be one of the best students in the class.

Case 1-3

A medical researcher has received a large multiyear grant to study the use of gene therapy to alleviate the symptoms of Parkinson's disease. No one has systematically asked whether the therapy improves the patients' perceived quality of life or that of the family. The principal investigator (PI) hesitantly agrees to allow a psychologist to add a prepost questionnaire to the battery of tests that will be given to the research participants. The medical consent form notes the medical risks; however, it does not mention the occasions when confidentiality may need to be broken, such as when a patient is a danger to self or others. The PI believes that the consent form is adequate to cover the psychologist's research but indicates that if the psychologist does not believe that is sufficient, the psychologist can drop out of the project.

Each of these cases presents a difficult choice for the professional involved. The first case involves balancing two potential harms: harm to the client and harm to the therapeutic relation-

---

* Selections of this chapter are based on the findings by Kitchener (1984a).

ship. If the therapist breaks confidentiality against the client's wishes, the therapeutic relationship may be broken or at least damaged to where trust of the therapist is in question. If the therapist does not break confidentiality, it may bring harm to the wife and, ultimately, to the children because if the wife contracts AIDS, the children may lose both parents to AIDS. The second case involves deciding what it means to cheat and whether this student actually engaged in an action that could be called plagiarism. Furthermore, it means deciding whether to judge the student's behavior on her intentions or her actions, whether her general character ought to influence the decision, and whether using the situation to educate her on ethical responsibility is a viable alternative. Ultimately, the professor must decide what action, if any, should be taken, balancing the responsibility to society not to graduate a student who is academically dishonest with a genuine concern for the student. In Case 1-3, the psychologist must weigh the importance of gathering data against the need for adequate consent and the rights of patients to make informed decisions about participation. Most psychologists and counselors would agree that each case involves some kind of an ethical issue, but trying to define the nature of the ethical problem and work to come to an ethical conclusion is more difficult.

In fact, multiple studies (Barnett, Cornish, & Kitchener, 2008; Hubert & Freeman, 2004; Pope & Vetter, 1992; Sherry, Teschendorf, Anderson, & Guzman, 1991) found that psychologists and counselors struggle with a variety of ethical issues some of which were reflected in complaints received by Ethics Committees and some of which were not. In some of these studies, many participants state that they were truly perplexed by what to do. In addition, many students reported problems in supervision with their supervisor's competence, but did not recognize it as an ethical issue (Barnett et al., 2008).

Ethics Defined

When confronted with the question of what makes something an ethical issue, people will often respond that it involves a determination of right and wrong. However, when considering the above cases, it becomes apparent that ethics involves more than just judgments about whether an act is right or wrong. In Case 1-2, for example, in which the professor is faced with deciding whether the student's actions were wrong, the professor must define what "wrong" means as well as decide what his obligations are to the student and to the society. In Cases 1-1 and 1-3, the professional is faced with deciding between competing moral obligations or between competing claims about what is "right." In each case, the professional faces an ethical dilemma, a problem for which no choice seems completely satisfactory, since there are good, but contradictory reasons to take conflicting and incompatible courses of action. The cases illustrate the inevitability of having to make ethical choices as a psychologist or counselor.

Ethics is a branch of philosophy that addresses questions of how people ought to act toward each other, that pronounces judgments of value about actions (e.g., whether someone ought to be praised or blamed for those actions), and that develops rules of ethical justifications (e.g., how we can justify holding one set of values over another). Philosophers (Frankena, 1963; Hospers, 1961; Taylor, 1978) frequently refer to ethics as the philosophical study of morality.

Some philosophers have tried to distinguish ethics from morality. Frankena (1963) described ethics as philosophical thinking about "morality, moral problems, and moral judgment" (p. 3). Morals are what people believe about what is right and wrong or good and bad about character or conduct (Rollin, 2006). In other words, morals are one of many values that humans hold and use as guides for their behavior. Morals are unique; however, because they sometimes impose requirements on human conduct that take precedence over other values, including self-interest (Gewirth, 1978). A good example is the obligation of psychologists or counselors in private practice to terminate therapy when it is in the patient's best interests, even though the practitioner would benefit financially from further sessions.

Because morals are a part of the human value system they can be studied as they are or as they exist (i.e., as they are defined and understood in different various cultures) or as they ought to be (i.e., is as they prescribe how people should ideally act). The study of morals as they exist is called descriptive ethics and has usually been the domain of disciplines like psychology, sociology, and anthropology. These disciplines study how people actually make moral decisions or what ethical values they hold.

By contrast, the attempt to identify what moral values people ought to hold has been the domain of philosophy and has been called normative ethics. It not only asks what moral ideals people hold but what moral ideals are better than others, and why they are better (Hospers, 1961). In other words, normative ethics involves judgments about what values are worth holding or "pronouncing judgments of value upon human behavior, not just describing that behavior" (Hospers, 1961, p. 6). It confronts questions of moral responsibility, such as when people should be praised, blamed, or punished for their behavior. Frankena (1963) pointed out that normative ethics also entails studying both general questions of what certain groups of people are obligated to do and particular questions of what certain individuals are obligated to do. For example, later in this book, the argument is made that psychologists and counselors are obligated by their roles to help others and not to harm them. However, as seen in Case 1-2, the professor's dilemma may be deciding what exactly ought to be done to honor this obligation.

In summary, differentiating between descriptive and normative ethics directly confronts what has been called the *is–ought distinction*. Descriptive ethics focuses on what *is*, and normative ethics evaluates what *ought* to be. As Hospers (1961) has said, normative ethics is "concerned not only with what a certain individual or group considers right but what is right" (p. 6). Normative ethics does not merely describe moral ideals held by human beings but asks which ideal is better than others, which ideal is more worth pursuing, and why.

The philosophical study of morality also includes metaethics, in which questions are asked about the meaning of ethical words and the logic of justifying moral decisions. For example, philosophers engaged in metaethical analysis ask questions such as "What does it mean to say that something is right or good?" In some ways, by raising the question of what it means to cheat, the professor in Case 1-2 is engaged in a metaethical activity.

The focus of this book is a fourth domain—applied or professional ethics. Generally, applied ethics involves using the principles and insights from normative ethics and metaethics to resolve specific moral issues and problematic cases or to define what it means to have good or bad character in practicing a profession. Although this book focuses on the issues that arise for psychologists and counselors who assess and treat clients, teach, supervise, and do research, other professionals such as lawyers, nurses, physicians, and teachers face similar concerns. Applied or professional ethics involves much more than the mechanical application of insights from other fields of philosophy to practical problems (Callahan, 1988). It often raises questions that require further elaboration of moral principles and generates a deeper understanding of what constitutes morality. Similarly, information from descriptive ethics can inform normative values. For example, evidence that sexual relationships between therapists and clients caused grievous consequences led the American Psychological Association (APA) and the American Counseling Association (ACA) to define these kinds of relationships as unethical (APA, 1981; American Personnel and Guidance Association [APGA], 1981).

If the distinction between morality and ethics were consistently maintained, it could be said that morality refers to the human belief structure and ethics to the philosophical study and evaluation of that belief structure. Applied ethics would be the study and evaluation of moral beliefs and actions within a given professional setting. However, the distinction between morality and ethics does not always hold. Thus, some sources use *ethical* as a synonym for *moral*, the term *moral philosophy* is frequently used as another term for *ethics* (Taylor, 1978). Since the terms *moral* and *ethical* are often used interchangeably, they will be used that way in this book. The distinctions among descriptive ethics, normative ethics, and metaethics remain important.

Applied Ethics in Psychology and Counseling

The question that immediately arises when considering ethical issues in the practice, research, and teaching of psychology or counseling is, "What ethical insights ought to guide the thinking and actions of these professions?" Many individuals are content to believe that adhering to a code of ethics that governs their professional behavior can solve all ethical issues. Closer scrutiny, however, reveals inherent contradictions and gaps in codes of ethics give the professional minimal guidance when faced with some decisions of ethical consequence. Take Case 1-1 for an example. Here, the therapist is faced with the decision of whether or not to disclose to the patient's wife that the patient is HIV positive. Considering the facts that HIV is sexually transmitted, that the sexual partner is placed at risk, and that a child conceived by HIV-positive parents may be born with the disease, the professional is confronted by the potentially lethal consequences of the client's behavior (see Chapter 10). Additionally, the client's children could be left without either parent to raise them. However, ethics codes are not always clear and sometimes the codes of different professions contradict each other. For example, the ACA code and APA codes provide different advice about such cases. The ACA code (2005) indicates that members are justified in breaking confidentiality if someone is that a high risk for contracting the disease. Even with this guidance there rages a debate about the level of responsibility counselors hold to warn and protect a third party (Anderson & Barret, 2001; Stanard & Hazler, 1995). Contrastingly, the APA code (2002) permits disclosing such information if it is mandated or permitted by law to protect others from harm. Because this rule is permissive (gives a psychologist permission to break confidentiality) and not prescriptive (requires a psychologist to break confidentiality), several authors have argued that neither a legal nor ethical obligation follows (Lamb, Clark, Drumheller, Frizzell, & Surrey, 1989; Melton, 1988; Stevenson & Kitchener, 2001) to disclose to someone that his or her partner is HIV positive. Their arguments revolved around the meaning of "harm" and the consequences of acting on the rule that psychologists should always disclose information to the client's partner that the client is HIV positive. Additionally, because the law is equally ambiguous, it offers little direction (Burris, 2001). Currently, there is only one state (Utah) that imposes a legal obligation on mental health practitioners to warn and protect those at risk of HIV exposure (Glosoff, Herlihy, & Spence, 2000).

Although the duty to warn in HIV cases is discussed in more detail in later chapters, it suffices to illustrate the caveat that ethical codes do not always provide complete guidance when psychologists and counselors are faced with tough ethical decisions. As Hospers (1961) argued, there is often a large "twilight zone of cases" (p. 13), where it is unclear whether or how ethical codes apply, and still other cases that the codes do not address at all.

Psychology and counseling are growing fields that are consistently expanding their boundaries and are being influenced by external forces that cannot always be anticipated. New techniques and applications are introduced yearly (Goodyear & Sinnett, 1984). In addition, new issues are addressed within the code. For example, the 2005 ACA code addresses counselors' work with clients dealing with end-of-life issues and the use of technology (i.e., internet online counseling). Consider the fact that the 1992 APA ethics code added an entire section on forensic work that had not been addressed in earlier codes. Because an increasing number of psychologists had become involved in this specialty and because it offered unique ethical challenges, it was a critical area to be addressed. Nevertheless, the field often changes more rapidly than the code itself; consequently there will always be concerns about which the code offers little guidance.

Further complicating matters, professionals often belong to more than one organization, each of which may have its own code of ethics. Sometimes these codes give contradictory advice.

Additionally, psychologists and counselors often work with health professionals from other fields. How are they to understand their own ethical responsibility when the codes of physicians or physical therapists give them different and sometimes contradictory advice as was true in Case 1-3? How are they to talk about their ethical responsibilities in treatment or research with professionals who do not share the same ethical standards? In the next chapter, we argue that what is needed is a broader conceptualization of ethical responsibility that allows dialogue across professional lines, that allows counselors and psychologists to make ethical choices when codes are silent, and that affords guidance when codes give contradictory advice. In addition, in Chapter 5, we suggest that exclusive focus on decision making, without nurturing the character traits that support good judgment and that provide the motivation to act morally, is insufficient.

Ethical issues become problematic when there are no existing guidelines to give direction to professionals as they act. Often these problems involve ethical dilemmas. They arise when there are good moral reasons for taking different and sometimes conflicting courses of action (Beauchamp & Childress, 2001). In such situations, some psychologists or counselors rely on their personal values and judgments, but not all value judgments are considered to be equally valid or good by colleagues (APA, 2007, 2008, 2009; Hubert & Freeman, 2004; Kocet & Freeman, 2005), society, or courts of law; nor are all values moral ones. In the real world, people sometimes allow values such as self-interest, financial gain, or power to trump moral considerations. A moral solution must be defended with moral reasons for taking one action over another (Baier, 1958; Brandt, 1979).

In light of the limitations of ethical codes and the fact that there are real ethical dilemmas that involve deciding between competing ethical obligations, it is particularly important that counselors or psychologists develop a deeper understanding of ethical decision making. This is particularly true at a time when these fields are coming under increasing scrutiny and criticism by the law and society at large. As Tymchuck et al. (1982) argued,

> [The profession] needs to attend more closely to decision-making processes and develop decision-making standards that can be applied to situations as they arise. What may be most useful for the profession are broader and more basic decision-making standards rather than specific rules that attempt to define behavior as "right" or "wrong." (p. 240)

Some Critical Distinctions

Before describing a model of applied ethics, some basic distinctions are necessary. Because psychologists or counselors are seldom trained in the language of ethics, some confusion may exist between the relationship between ethics and the law and between ethics and values.

Ethics and the Law

Often when we present Case 1-1 and ask people to make an ethical decision about what to do, they suggest that the psychotherapist has a responsibility to inform the client's wife about the client's HIV status citing the "duty to warn" as the reason for their decision. When we ask where this so-called duty comes from, they point to the *Tarasoff* decision (*Tarasoff v. Regents of the University of California*, 1974). Then when we point out that *Tarasoff was* a legal decision and does not necessarily specify an ethical obligation, some appear to be surprised.

It is not difficult to illustrate the point that ethics and the law are not necessarily identical. First, laws frequently are concerned with behavior that has little or nothing to do with ethics. Second, they may differ from city to city or state to state. Thus, in one state it may be legal for a girl to marry without consent of her parents at the age of 16 years whereas in another state, the legal age is 18 years. Similarly, states differ on whether it is legal to make a right-hand turn on a red light. It would not make sense to say that because a girl married at the age of 16 years, she was moral in New Hampshire but that if she moved to New York her action would become immoral. A similar statement could be made about the morality of making a right-hand turn on a red light. Further, arguments can be made about laws being unfair, unjust, or immoral. For example, in the 1960s one of the arguments against laws that discriminated on the basis of race was that they were immoral and, therefore, ought to be changed. By contrast, some laws may be evaluated as "just," and these are the ones in which ethics and the law usually overlaps. Evaluating laws as moral or immoral suggests there is another perspective, an ethical one, from which they may be judged.

Similarly, as there are concerns that the law addresses issues that do not directly derive from moral responsibilities, so are there ethical questions about which the law is silent. For example, although society legislates actions that parents may not engage in with their children, such as incest or abuse, there are many positive ethical responsibilities that parents have toward their children about which the law is silent. Moreover, many states now have laws forbidding certain acts between psychotherapists and their patients, but few, if any, legislate the positive responsibilities that a professor has to his or her students.

Some of the difficulty in distinguishing what is legal and what is ethical derives from the fact that laws define which acts are right and which are wrong from the perspective of the body that established the law, for example, legislature. Because ethics is also involved in evaluating whether acts are right or wrong, there is an overlap of subject matter. As legislative bodies further attempt to control the work of psychotherapists through laws, the overlap will only grow. For example, since the early 1970s, the courts have taken an intense interest in the possibility that psychological tests lead to discriminatory practices against minorities, women, and individuals with disabilities (Bersoff, 1983). These court decisions often refer to some concept of fairness or justice embodied in the law which is an ethical argument.

The overlap is further complicated by the fact that when judges are setting precedent or interpreting laws, they frequently give ethical arguments for their positions. As an illustration, both the majority and dissenting opinions in *Tarasoff v. Regents of the University of California* (1974) were argued from an ethical perspective. In fact, Levine (1988) suggested that "At its best law reflects society's concepts of ethical duties both positive ('thou shalt') and negative ('thou shalt not')" (p. x). However, as already illustrated, the law does not always meet the ideal and may, in fact, regulate some areas of life that do not call for ethical evaluation. Because professional ethics and the law have areas of common concern as well as divergence, they can probably best be conceptualized as two overlapping circles that share a common intersection, as illustrated in Figure. 1.1.

Law is defined as a rule of conduct prescribed or recognized as binding by a controlling authority (*Webster's Ninth New Collegiate Dictionary*, 1988). If that is the case, then the codification of ethical rules by a profession gives it the standing of law for that profession. Furthermore, if laws may be evaluated as moral or immoral, the possibility must also be considered that the ethical rules for the profession—in this case the rules explicated in a professions ethical code can also be evaluated as moral or immoral. In other words, by the higher standard suggested

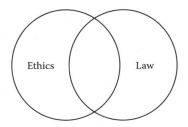

Figure 1.1 The relationship between ethics and law.

here, an action may be unethical even though it does not explicitly violate a section of the ACA or APA ethics codes. For example, although the APA and ACA ethics codes allowed limited bartering, some have argued that bartering for services is always unethical because the practitioner enters into a dual relationship with the client that might negatively impact his or her objectivity.

These statements, as with earlier ones, should not be interpreted as advocating a rejection of codes of ethics. Rather, the intent is to differentiate the "ethical" from the "legal" and to emphasize the continuous need to evaluate the ethical validity of a code that a profession endorses.

Ethics and Values

As already noted, when faced with difficult ethical decisions, people sometimes argue that one should fall back on one's own values or sense of personal obligations. But which values should be relied on, and are everyone's values equally acceptable? Part of the problem in identifying appropriate values is that the term *value* is used in multiple ways, so that what constitutes a value is often unclear.

When value is used as a noun, at least eight different realms of values have been distinguished (Frankena, 1963). These include morality, art, science, religion, economics, politics, law, and customs or manners. When value is used as a verb, it means to prize or esteem and can extend to anything liked or desired. For example, someone may say he or she values ice cream, sex, a blue sky, and so on. Rollin (2006) calls this area "personal ethics" and suggests most of these can be left to the discretion of the individual. Like law personal values have areas that overlap with ethics and are distinct from them. This is particularly true of religious values many of which, like promote the welfare of others, would overlap with both the law and professional ethics. On the other hand, there may be areas in which a professional's personal values conflict with the ethics code, the profession's culture, or the law. For example, a student in training may hold personal values based on spiritual or religious beliefs that conflict with law (i.e., abortion) or the core values of the profession (i.e., that gay or lesbian relationships are wrong). One of the authors of this book had a student approach her with a complaint that her practicum supervisor, without any discussion, would not assign her gay, lesbian or bisexual clients because she was Catholic. What the supervisor did not take into consideration was that the student differed from the church on these particular issues. The practicum supervisor automatically assumed that the student would be pro life and from a spiritual perspective, opposed to same gender relationships. If in fact the religious values of the student would conflict with the client's goals, it is best for the student to excuse him or herself from the case, however, in this case the supervisor's bias may have denied the student an important learning opportunity.

When it is said that an ethical decision should be based on personal values, it needs to be clear that these are not just any values; rather, they are moral ones. Other values, like money, the desire for success, or the need for inclusion in a group, can compete with ethical concerns when people are faced with moral decisions, but they do not necessarily lead to choices that would be considered moral (Rest, 1983). Although this may seem like an abstract idea, sometimes such conflicts are everyday occurrences as is clear in Figure 1.2.

The question of whether there are specific ethical values that therapists ought to hold is the cause of considerable debate. Most practicing psychologists or counselors, for example, learn that tolerance of a client's values is one of the most basic assumptions of psychotherapy and that they are not to impose their values on a client. Others argue that professionals in the field have a right to hold and act on their own values. Certainly this argument has some merit particularly with regard to values that do not directly influence professional decisions. However, as already noted, there are some values psychologists or counselors ought not to hold and there are some things that people esteem or value that are not moral. As an illustration, few would argue that

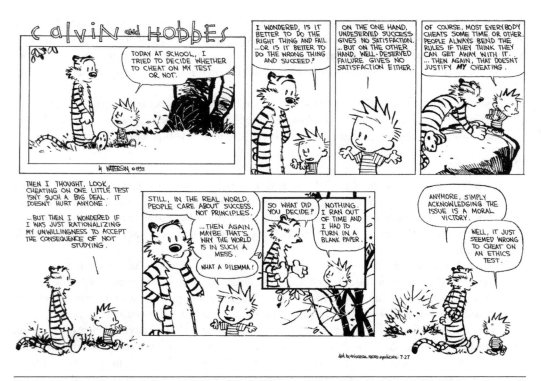

Figure 1.2 (Reprinted from Calvin and Hobbes ©1993 Watterson. Distributed by Universal Uclick. With permission. All rights reserved.)

professionals ought to value deliberately torturing clients or research participants. In other words, there are limits to the values that a profession can tolerate its members holding.

Individuals freely choose to enter the professions of psychology or counseling. Once they have made that choice, it is presumed that they hold the values promoted by the profession and denounce ones that are antithetical to it. Idealist philosophers such as Bradley (1951) have made similar points. Bradley argued that once people have made a choice to participate in a particular system, certain moral obligations follow from it. Veatch (1981) called these obligations "duties of station" (p. 84). In other words, certain ethical responsibilities are acquired when one assumes a professional role. The acts or behavior of members are then evaluated by the standards that are acquired with that role or profession.

For example, typically the introductions to ethics codes in the helping professions provide a common set of values, which are expected to guide the work of the members of that profession when they are acting in a professional capacity whether that capacity is practice, research, or teaching. These values are not optional. Rather, they represent the core values of the profession. Typically, one of those values used to enhance the welfare and development of the individuals and groups with whom those professionals work—a point that is further elaborated on in Chapter 3. In other words, abhorring the idea that psychologists or counselors might deliberately torture their clients or research participants derives, in part, from a fundamental value of the profession, which is to promote the welfare of others. We can judge the behavior of a psychologist or counselor who engages in behavior that violates this value as unethical.

Ethics, Values, and Conscience

When it is said that an ethical decision ought to be based personal values, what someone may have in mind is something like "Let your conscience be your guide." In fact, conscience is defined as "the sense or consciousness of the moral goodness or blame worthiness of one's own conduct, intentions, or character together with a feeling of obligation to do right or be good" (*Webster's Ninth New Collegiate Dictionary*, 1988, p. 278). According to Beauchamp and Childress (2001) conscience "is a form of self-reflection on and judgment about whether one's acts are obligatory or prohibited, right or wrong, good or bad. It is an internal sanction that comes into play through critical reflection" (p. 38). In other words, in contrast to acting on personal values, acting on conscience implies that one is guided by moral values which one is considered in relationship to the situation at hand.

On the other hand, in some cases, one's conscience is erroneous. The maxim to follow one's conscience does not imply that conscience is either a sufficient or infallible guide for moral action. In fact, claims of acting on conscience may merely be rationalizations for immoral acts. Further, sometimes our conscience may fail to give us any direction at all. Again, this does not imply that people should act in a way that they believe is wrong but that conscience, too, can be informed by a critical evaluation of ethical values.

The critical question that psychologists and counselors must ask is, "What are the ethical values that psychologists or counselors ought to hold, and how can they be justified?" Often the initial answer to this question is that those values are identified in the ethics code of that profession. On the other hand, the argument has already been made that codes are not infallible and that they, too, are open to criticism. Thus, professionals should also ask, "What are the ethical values that the profession ought to hold and entail in the ethics code, and how can they be justified?"

Value conflicts cannot be avoided in most professions and is particularly true in psychology and counseling. Often these value conflicts lead to difficult ethical choices and force professionals to ask questions regarding the "right thing to do." Sometimes this involves considering whether the right ethical choice is consistent with the law. Although in some cases ethics and the law overlap, there are many professional issues that the law does not address and occasions when the law and ethical reasoning may lead to different conclusions.

It would be reassuring if a professional ethics code could solve all such conflicts, but codes are fallible, open to interpretation, and limited in the situations they can address. Furthermore, as the profession develops, new situations and arenas of practice arise. Because ethics codes are revised only periodically, new ethical challenges often do not get addressed until the next revision. Some would like to believe they could rely on their value system in these situations, but, as already noted, not all values are equally justifiable in a professional setting. This observation leads to the question of what values are consistent with the science and practice of psychology or counseling. Additionally, following one's conscience does not necessarily lead to an ethically defensible decision. Consequently, counselors and psychologists need to understand the foundational ethical principles on which their professions stand, how to apply these in concrete situations, and how to critically evaluate their own conclusions.

Conclusion

In summary, by becoming a member of the profession, a psychologist or counselor forgoes the right to hold certain values by virtue of his or her place in a larger system. One way that both APA and ACA legitimize this process is by stating to prospective members that by submitting an application they are agreeing to uphold the profession's code of ethics. If individuals become members and act on values that are antithetical to psychology or counseling in their professional capacity, the profession can judge their behavior to be unethical and revoke their membership.

The following chapter provides a framework for ethical decision making and describes how ethics codes fit within this framework. Chapters 3 and 4 attempt to answer the following questions, "Which ethical principles provide the foundation for ethical choices?" and "What kinds of values should psychologists or counselors hold?"

Questions for Discussion or Consideration

1. Identify an ethical problem that is arisen in your work as a psychologist or counselor and explain why it is an ethical problem.
2. Was there a legal issue involved? If so, explain the difference between the legal and ethical aspects of the problem.

2

Thinking Well About Doing Good

As noted earlier, psychologists or counselors sometimes face ethical problems for which no choice seems completely satisfactory. These ethical dilemmas often pit good but contradictory values against each other. Take the following cases, for example.

Case 2-1

A 52-year-old developmentally delayed adult who has been institutionalized most of his life has recently been tested by a new psychologist in the institution. The psychologist determines that the retardation is not as severe as previously thought and on examining the case file believes that the client has suffered from incompetent assessment as well as neglect. The psychologist recommends moving him to a community care home where he may develop some life skills that promote more independence and a different kind of life for him. This will save the state about $50,000 a year and relieve overcrowding on the ward. In a preplacement interview, the client tells the psychologist that the institution is his home and he begs not to leave it. As the date of his transfer nears, he begins to exhibit symptoms of a severe depression.*

Case 2-2

A female student in a counseling program is in her internship. This is her last semester of training. She shares with a faculty member a legal problem. During Christmas break she was arrested for shop lifting while under the influence. She decided to tell the faculty because of her fear that the program would find out about her arrest in the newspaper. She also shared that prior to her eighteenth birthday a similar situation had occurred. As a student she received very good reviews on the work at her internship site and she performed well in all her classes. The program faculty decided to meet to determine if she should be required to go through substance abuse treatment before she could graduate.

In the first case, should the psychologist insist on the client's placement in a community care home on the basis that a less restrictive environment may allow the client to live a more normal life and at the same time benefit the institution? Or should the client's wishes be respected and a recommendation made that he be allowed to stay in the institution considering his past history? In the second case, the faculty is faced with a decision about the character of the student in question. Should and can the faculty consider her in illegal conduct that apparently has not affected the student's work in the program? Has information about the effects of illegal activity on progress in the program been published in student handbooks or entry material? These kinds of problems pull reasonable psychologists or counselors with good moral values in different directions.

With the goal of providing a basis for ethical decisions like those just described, the material and discussion of the model that follows addresses three important points: (1) The model distinguishes between two levels of moral thinking: the immediate level and the critical-evaluative

---

* This case is based on the one written by John Keller, which was initially published by Kitchener (1984b).

level (Hare, 1981); (2) The model suggests that the APA and ACA ethics codes and more general ethical principles, such as "do no harm," constitute the foundation for the critical-evaluative level of reasoning in psychology and counseling; and (3) The model offers suggestions for justifying ethical decisions when there is ethical conflict. In Chapter 5, this model of ethical justification is supplemented with a discussion of virtues, such as caring and responsibility (Beauchamp & Childress, 2001; Jorden & Meara, 1990; Meara, Schmidt, & Day, 1996), which provide the motivation for taking moral action.

Overview

Figure 2.1 diagrams the model (Kitchener & Kitchener, 2009). The diagram is arranged to suggest that there are different levels of moral reasoning and that they are hierarchically related. According to the model, at the immediate level, judgments and actions are based on information about the situation and an individual's ordinary moral sense. One's ordinary moral sense is based on a combination of what a person has learned about being moral over a lifetime and his or her moral character. In ideal circumstances, one's ordinary moral sense presupposes an individual to act in morally appropriate ways and leads to sound ethical choices; however, in ambiguous or confusing scenarios and cases, it may not. When ordinary moral values fail to provide guidance, the components of the critical-evaluative level can be called on to help in decision making. The critical-evaluative level is composed of tiers of increasingly general and abstract forms of justification that can be drawn upon ethical rules, foundational ethical principles, ethical theory, and metaethics (Kitchener, 1984b; Kitchener & Kitchener, 2009). If the first tier does not provide insight for the issue at hand, the second can be consulted, and so on. The following sections explore the model in depth.

The Immediate Level of Moral Reasoning

Individuals have ethical beliefs and emotional responses to problems. These ethical beliefs or "ethics of origin" (Anderson & Handelsman, 2010; Handelsman, Gottlieb, & Knapp, 2005) are the result of early learning from parents, teachers, and society about what individuals ought

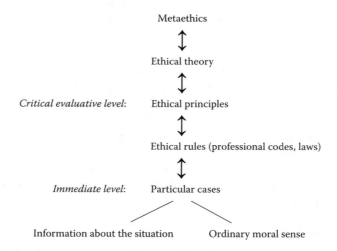

Figure 2.1 A model of ethical justification (From Kitchener, K.S., *The Counseling Psychologist*, 12 (3) pp. 43-55. ©1984 by Division of Counseling Psychology of the American Psychological Association (reprinted by Permission of SAGE Publications) and revised from Kitchener, K.S. & Kitchener, R.F. (2009). Social science research ethics: Historical and philosophical issues. In D.M. Mertens & P.E. Ginsberg (Eds.), *The Handbook of Social Research Ethics* (pp. 5-22). Thousand Oaks, CA: Sage.)

and ought not to do. As people grow older and become more educated, they typically develop the capacity to reason about their moral beliefs. It's important to note, that this capacity to reason about their moral beliefs is likely influenced by personal values, motivations, and needs (Anderson & Handelsman, 2010). As that capacity becomes mature, their ability to understand moral problems potentially becomes more complex (Fischer & Pruyne, 2003; Rest, 1983). Thus, prior learning and ethics of origin; the complexity of individuals' reasoning; and personal values, motivations, and needs provide the foundation for their ordinary moral sense.

Typically, the immediate response to a problem is based on beliefs, moral character, knowledge about the problem, and the circumstances surrounding the issue. One's gender, culture, racial and ethnic background, and sexual preference, among other characteristics, color one's perception of the immediate problem. In other words, individuals have an immediate, prereflective response to an ethical situation on the basis of the sum of their prior ethical knowledge (ethics of origin) and experience. This response forms the basis of their ordinary moral judgment. This ordinary moral sense is the basis of, for example, the typical psychologist's outrage when a colleague seriously abuses a client or research participant. For example, it may be the basis on which the psychologist in Case 2-1 might be upset that the adult with limited intelligence suffered from incompetent assessment and neglect in the first place.

However, there is a second component of the immediate level of moral reasoning that is often ignored in discussions of moral justification and that is an assessment of the information available about the situation. An erroneous understanding or misperception of events, and their consequences for the people involved, can and often does lead to poor moral choices. Both a person's ordinary moral sense and information about the situation are discussed in detail in the following sections.

Ordinary Moral Sense

As already noted, under ideal circumstances an individual's moral character built around their ethics of origin provides the foundation for his or her ordinary moral sense and includes beliefs about his or her ethical responsibilities in a particular case. These immediate moral beliefs are critical to everyday ethical actions. In fact, as psychologists or counselors work with students, clients, and research participants or as expert witnesses or administrators on a day-to-day basis, their moral character may be more important than a particular set of ethical rules or principles. Under most circumstances, the ethical professional does not need to be told that he or she should tell the truth when providing forensic testimony. It is an ethical assumption that is an intrinsic part of what it means to offer such services. In other cases, such as when deciding whether to intervene in the life of a suicidal client or to continue an experiment in light of ill effects to a participant, there may be little time for conscious and explicit reflection. In such crises, Hare (1981) argued that "firm moral dispositions have great utility" (p. 34). That is, a firm set of ethical values (such as honesty) and beliefs (such as "saving a life is more important than keeping a promise") has a great deal of moral utility because it may allow a psychologist or counselor to take immediate action. It seems that these "firm moral dispositions" are what compose our ordinary moral sense.

Some might argue that people need to be more critical in their everyday moral decisions. However, because of time constraints this is not always possible. Although psychologists or counselors can, with ethics training and by continually reading about ethics cases (Herlihy & Corey, 1996; Nagy, 2001; Pope & Vetter, 1992), anticipate and think through many of the common ethical issues that they may face, some ethical problems will still arise that could not have been foreseen. In such situations—situations in which the ethical implications were not previously considered, in which an immediate decision is necessary, and in which there are no convenient rules on which to rely—our moral "good sense" is critical. In fact, Hare (1981) suggested that in these situations one's moral intuition is more than a convenient and timesaving mechanism: it can help identify an appropriate moral response. Often professionals are more likely to err ethically by abandoning their ordinary moral standards than by observing them. Take the following case as an illustration.

Case 2-3

After being in therapy for about 6 months, Ms York expressed concern that she was feeling sexually attracted to her psychotherapist, Dr. Evans. Dr. Evans informed her that such feelings were a normal part of the therapy process, called *transference*, and that acting out these feelings was not only unethical but inadvisable therapeutically. Therapy proceeded with appropriate gains being made by Ms York; however, she continued to maintain that she was very attracted to him. Dr. Evans became increasingly aware that he had similar feelings toward Ms York. The feelings did not abate even after discussing them with a colleague. One late afternoon when Dr. Evans was meeting with Ms York, who was his last patient for the day, his secretary informed him that she had to leave on an emergency. As Ms York was leaving, she again professed her love for him, and he, again, repeated his ethical responsibilities. However, Ms York was caught in a sudden downpour on her way back to the bus. Cold and wet, she decided to return to the counselor's office. As he offered her towels to dry herself off, she tried to embrace him and professed her love for him. Again, he gently turned down her requests and suggested they needed to discuss the issue further in the next session. Later, he told his colleagues that in the heat of the moment, he was grateful that he had internalized the strong prohibitions against such behavior in the ethics code.

Hare (1981, p. 35) pointed out that it is frighteningly easy to be deceived by the "special pleading" of clients or others that our ordinary moral beliefs do not apply in a particular situation or to be confused by conflicting values. To illustrate this point, Rest (1983) cited the case of Dean (1976), advisor to President Nixon. Dean wrote in *Blind Ambition* (1976) that he knew his actions were wrong in regards to the Watergate break-in to the Democratic National headquarters during Richard Nixon's administration, but he wanted the President and the others in the administration to know that he could play hardball like the other staff.

Consider situations in which therapists do become involved in sexual intimacies with their clients. It is probable that they, like Dr. Evans, are aware that such acts are professionally unacceptable and violate the professional ethics codes but convince themselves that ordinary moral standards do not apply to their particular situation. In some instances, psychologists and counselors terminated therapy with their clients before it was explicitly prohibited by both APA and ACA and then immediately engaged in sexual relationships with them rationalizing that they were no longer in a dual role. Both organizations now provide explicit standards about how soon after termination such relationships might be ethical and then also have standards that require the therapist to prove that the new relationship was not influenced by the therapy. Both standards are used to evaluate the ethicality of such relationships because of their potential for harm caused by issues like ongoing transference.

Their ordinary moral sense is what people refer to when they suggest that they should fall back on their own moral values in the face of hard ethical decisions. However, it is not difficult to establish that one's immediate moral response to a situation may not be sufficient. As already noted, in some cases, the situation may be so unusual that one may not have a sense of which direction to take. Furthermore, an immediate moral response cannot always be trusted to lead to good ethical decisions. This is because personal values, motivations, or needs may be in conflict with those of the profession (Anderson & Handelsman, 2010). Take Case 2-4 as an example.

Case 2-4

Students repeatedly approached the head of a graduate program complaining about a particular faculty member. The faculty member reportedly was doing research on emotional responses to disasters. According to the students, she had accumulated a series of excessively gruesome pictures of both auto and plane accidents that she apparently enjoyed flashing at students in the hall to see their reaction. One student complained that he was so upset by the pictures that he vomited; another complained that she went home and cried, and the others indicated that the pictures had given them nightmares. When the faculty member was confronted, she indicated that it was "no big deal" and that she no longer had the pictures; however, after a brief hiatus, the complaints began again. Frustrated that the faculty member may have been deceiving him and sincerely concerned that students were being harmed by the harassment, the department chairman used his master key to enter the faculty member's office and search the faculty member's desk for the pictures.

In this case, the department chairman's ordinary moral sense failed him. His concern about the students and possibly his motivations and values led him to enter the faculty member's office, without permission, thus violating her privacy. The maxim "two wrongs don't make a right" would have probably offered him better guidance in this case. One has only to review the ethical complaints against psychologists or counselors that are filed with the professional organization or state grievance committees to find other examples. Not everyone has moral intuitions that lead to defensible ethical choices. No one would argue that Adolf Hitler's ordinary moral sense was as valid as Mother Teresa's.

As professionals mature, as they consider the ethical problems they encounter in practice, teaching, or research, and as they critically reflect on these problems and their own decision making, their ordinary moral sense ought to become more sophisticated. The moral values they learned as they were growing up and through their professional education will be supplemented by a deeper understanding of both their professional roles and their professional obligations. However, for this to occur, they must engage in thoughtful reflection on the ethical problems they face and on the underlying moral values, personal motivations, and personal needs that impact their decision-making process. Some of this will occur by reading and understanding the profession's code of ethics and using the code as a way to expand their ordinary moral standards. However, as already noted, moral codes themselves must be open to evaluation and grounded in foundational moral principles.

Information About the Situation

To act ethically, psychologists and counselors also need clear information about the situation. Relevant information may range on a continuum from what is clear-cut to what is open to interpretation. For example, whether a client is pregnant or not is an objective piece of information whereas the client's psychological diagnosis might be open to different points of view. Sometimes practitioners make ethical errors because their understanding of specific circumstances or details about the issue is incomplete or erroneous.

Case 2-5

Jabar, a Middle Eastern student, entered treatment with a psychologist complaining that he was lonely and had difficulty developing interpersonal relationships. Treatment commenced and continued for the 3 months prior to Christmas. Knowing that she was going to be absent for the holidays, Dr. Jones arranged with another professional to cover her practice and discussed her absence with her clients. Jabar initially seemed particularly despondent because he had not been too successful initiating relationships with others. During the last session prior to her departure, the therapist assured Jabar that she would be returning and that she would look forward to seeing him when she returned. She noted that the client seemed particularly pleased when she said this. As the client left, she touched his shoulder and reminded him of the back-up psychologist. She sent all of her clients a brief holiday greeting reminding them she would be home in January. Because she had been concerned with Jabar, she penned a short note at the bottom of the card reassuring him that she was looking forward to seeing him after her vacation. After receiving the card, Jabar called the back-up psychologist reporting that Dr. Jones was in love with him and asking what he should do. He pointed to the card and the time she touched him on the shoulder as proof. When the back-up psychologist indicated that he did not think those were necessarily indications of Dr. Jones' "love" for him, the client filed a complaint with the local ethics committee alleging he had been misled and deeply hurt by Dr. Jones.

When Dr. Jones was asked about her actions she responded that she had no idea that Jabar was interpreting her actions this way and that he had never indicated to her that he had been misinterpreting what she was intending to communicate. In fact, she claimed that her intention was merely to indicate her concern and that she had gone out of her way to do so. She perceived her actions as virtuous. Thinking that her work with the client ought to be valued, she expressed dismay that the ethics committee questioned her.

In this case, Dr. Jones may have blundered because she did not have all of the facts regarding how the client was interpreting her actions. This is particularly important in multicultural relationships and speaks to the importance of multicultural competence (APA, 2003). Whether Dr. Jones was culpable in this case (i.e., whether she bore some moral responsibility for hurting the client) would also depend on how the facts of the case were interpreted. For example, should she have anticipated that this particular client with his cultural background would misread her physical touch and her card? Although ethics codes (APA, 2002; ACA, 2005) emphasize the importance of understanding multicultural differences, they do not give Dr. Jones explicit guidance about what to do other than seeking consultation or supervision. Had she done so prior to treating Jabar, she might have learned critical information about Middle Eastern customs and the outcome might have been quite different.

In addition, sometimes what appear to be disagreements about ethical questions are really disagreements about factual matters. For example, in Case 1-1 the client, who is HIV positive, refuses to tell his wife about his illness. A psychologist and counselor both evaluating the case could agree that the professional has a duty to break confidentiality if the client's conduct foreseeably endangers someone and has life threatening consequences. On the other hand, they might disagree on whether confidentiality ought to be broken because they could disagree on how certain it is that the client's conduct would endanger his wife's life. In fact, the probability of transmitting HIV is a complex empirical question (Lamb, Clark, Drumheller, Frizzell, & Surrey, 1989; Melton, 1988; Stevenson & Kitchener, 2001). Answering this question depends on having up-to-date information about the transmission of HIV. It also depends on the standards set for the probability of harm occurring. In other words, a clear understanding of the information surrounding the situation is essential to a sound moral judgment.

It should be noted that gathering information about the situation often means stepping back from the pressure to make an immediate decision. Taking time to consider the issue carefully can often help the professional consider alternatives that are not immediately obvious and to identify information that may help solve the problem.

The Critical-Evaluative Level of Moral Decision Making

Moral rules, such as those stated in the ethical codes of various professional organizations, compose the first tier of the critical-evaluative level. These ethical codes are grounded in foundational ethical principles, which compose the second tier. The problems stemming from the inadequacy of professional codes, being too broad in some cases and too narrow in others, may sometimes be resolved by reference to these higher level norms or foundational principles (Beauchamp & Childress, 2001; Drane, 1982; Veatch, 1981). Ethical principles are more general and fundamental than moral rules or codes and serve as their foundation. Principles may provide a more consistent framework within which cases may be considered. In other words, these ethical principles may help psychologists and counselors think well about doing good when the ethics code is silent. Further, they typically provide the rationale for the choice of directives or guidance in the code itself.

Although some (Beauchamp & Childress, 2001; Engelhardt, 1986; Meara et al., 1996; Ross, 1930; Veatch, 1981) have suggested slightly different sets of foundational principles, those that seem central to thinking about ethical problems in psychology or counseling are beneficence (do good), nonmaleficence (do no harm), respect persons (individuals should be treated as autonomous agents and those with diminished capacity need protection), justice (be fair), and fidelity (keep promises, do not lie, be faithful) (Kitchener, 1984b). These five principles articulate distinctions that are used in ordinary moral discourse in the mental health professions and articulate core ethical norms that are central for clinical practice, teaching, supervision, and research.

The American Psychological Association is the first social science organization to recognize these principles or ones that are closely similar as providing a foundation for the standards in their code. Although the APA ethics code combines beneficence and nonmaleficence, there are good reasons for keeping them separate since they lead to very different recommendations. In general, the duty not to inflict harm (nonmaleficence) includes not inflicting intentional harm nor engaging in activities which risk harming others. In other words, it forbids certain activities. In contrast, beneficence suggests there are positive obligations like helping others and maintaining confidentiality to the greatest extent ethically and legally possible.

In some cases, foundational principles themselves may conflict and offer contradictory moral advice. For example, a counselor might be faced with deciding whether to break the confidence of a client to protect the physical well-being of the client's child. Although the facts of the case may be clear, the counselor's ordinary moral sense may fail her. At the first step in the critical-evaluative level, the counselor may reach a decision grounded in the ACA ethics code which gives her permission to break confidence if the law mandates or allows it in order to protect others from harm. In turn, this rule can be justified by the ethical principle of allowing no harm to come to others.

If someone challenges this judgment and points out that breaking confidence destroys trust, the counselor must be prepared to reason further about the problem. At this point, ethical theory is consulted, and a decision might be justified on the basis of something like the golden rule—act in such a way toward others as you would wish them to act toward you or others you love. The decision to breach confidentiality might also be made from a utilitarian perspective of doing the least amount of unavoidable harm. In this particular case, the balance probably falls on breaking confidence because children are vulnerable and protection of a vulnerable population is seen as a priori. (Needless to say, it is also legally sanctioned in all states through child abuse laws.) Thus, although foundational ethical principles provide further clarification and guidance about ethical problems, they are not panaceas for good ethical reasoning. Ethical reasoning must be guided by ethical theory and reasoned judgments about where the weight of the argument lies. These ideas are articulated further in Chapter 3.

At the last critical-evaluative level, conflicts about ethical theory or ethical principles may require metaethical reflection. Here, the meaning of words like "harm" and "benefit" may need to be clarified. Furthermore, additional reflection may help clarify which principle or ethical theory seems more relevant in the context of a particular case (Kitchener & Kitchener, 2009).

The critical-evaluative level of moral reasoning is called on when psychologists or counselors face issues for which their ordinary moral sense provides no answers. In the following section, the first tier of the critical-evaluative level, ethical rules are discussed. An exploration of foundational ethical principles, ethical theories, and metaethics is reserved for Chapter 3.

Ethical Rules and Ethics Codes

For mental health professionals, the first resource in evaluating tough ethical decisions ought to be the ethics code of the profession. An ethics code attempts to bring together in one document the cumulative wisdom of the profession about acting morally toward those with whom they work. Basically, it formulates a set of ethical rules or action guides that function to tell professionals how to act in specific circumstances. Ideally, these rules should be written from what K. Baier (1958) called the "moral point of view," that is, from the point of view of reasonable and objective people concerned with identifying how psychologists or counselors ought to act toward others. These rules should provide answers to many of the everyday ethical questions that the professionals face and provide a standard against which others, both in the profession and outside of it, can judge their actions.

Fisher (2003) argues that ethics codes serve four functions. First, they establish integrity for the profession. Adoption of a code reflects the core values of the discipline and provides the discipline with an assessment of what is or is not morally acceptable. Doing so enhances public confidence that individuals have been trained to meet the standards and identifies for the members of the profession their responsibilities and duties to others. Second, she argues they serve an educational and professional socialization role. It helps those who are teaching the next generation of professionals by providing guidance regarding the kinds of behavior they ideally will promote in their students. In addition, it should deter students and other professionals from actions that may harm those they are obligated to help. Third, she suggests it incurs public trust because professionals can be held accountable for actions that do not meet the standards addressed in the code. Last, at least in psychology and counseling the standards serve an enforcement value. Members of the professions can be held accountable by the associations for their actions based on the standards and they are often used by the public in developing licensing requirements as well as legal sanctions. In some ways, they provide the backbone for the profession saying that by following the standards members will do good well.

Ethics Codes: A Historical Perspective

An important antecedent to ethical codes in the social sciences was federal regulation of biomedical research which was stimulated by the atrocities committed by the Nazis during World War II. These concerns were first fueled by several controversial research cases in medicine. For example, there was public outrage over the Thalidomide drug tragedy (1961) and the horrendous Tuskegee syphilis study (1972). Although these were medical cases, the need for social sciences to develop self-regulating standards became clear because of several controversial studies like the Wichita jury trial (1953), Zimbardo's prison study (1973) as well as others. These cases led to several regulations which were applied to both medical and social science research. First was the Nuremberg code of ethics, which identified morally acceptable and unacceptable conduct when doing research with humans. Eventually, this led to the creation of Institutional Research Boards (IRBs) and the Belmont report (1978) (Childress, Meslin, & Shapiro, 2005) which formulated fundamental ethical principles like beneficence, justice, and respect for persons that provided the philosophical basis of the federal guidelines and later those in the social sciences.

APA was one of the first social sciences to be explicitly concerned about ethical standards. In fact, it received and adjudicated ethical complaints against psychologists prior to actually having an ethics code (Golann, 1970; Sanford, 1952) and prior to the tragedies of World War II. In

1940 the association established a committee to consider charges of unethical behavior against its members, but the committee found that making decisions about particular cases without further guidance was "tenuous, elusive, and unsatisfactory" (Sanford, 1952, p. 427). As a result, the association appointed a committee to begin the task of developing an ethics code.

In response to the difficulties of adjudicating cases and federal guidelines, all members of APA were polled using the critical incident technique. Members were asked to describe from firsthand experience situations that they faced that had ethical implications. On the basis of the replies, the committee identified the following six areas of concern (Golann, 1970):

1. Public responsibility
2. Client relationships
3. Teaching
4. Research
5. Writing and publishing
6. Professional relationships

These areas of concern provided the foundation for the first APA ethics code, which was adopted in 1953. The first ethics code raised a variety of important moral questions with which the association had to struggle. For example, some asked (Sanford, 1952): Whether the code, by establishing institutional authority for ethical behavior, would undermine the importance of individual conscience? Whether the association needed a code to be able to handle ethical problems? Whether the code would benefit society? These are important questions that need to continue to be asked.

Although the original code was hailed as an important contribution to professional ethics (Committee on Ethical Standards of Psychologists, 1958; Golann, 1970), several problems were immediately identified. For example, it codified many common courtesies along with standards that had ethical implications (Committee on Ethical Standards of Psychologists, 1958). A new code was written that has guided subsequent revisions of the code. It identified as few standards as possible that would allow coverage of key concerns and be certain to be applicable to all psychologists regardless of their specialty. In addition, an attempt was made to retain what the revision committee called the "hard core of ethical issues" (Committee on Ethical Standards of Psychologists, 1958, p. 267). They defined these as the problems that could result in a case being brought against a psychologist. These criteria have remained important for subsequent committees.

After the initial APA code was written, a major concern became its usefulness in adjudicating complaints against psychologists (Fisher & Younggren, 1997). The majority of the code described minimal standards against which the behavior of psychologists might be judged. These standards were attempts to establish a "threshold of behavior" below which psychologists' conduct should not fall (Nagy, 1989, p. 5). Pope and Vetter (1992) pointed out recent codes had not used a critical incident method to evaluate the ethical issues that troubled current psychologists, so it missed many dilemmas that psychologists were facing. Consequently, for the 2002 revision the task force charged with revising the code collected a broad range of scientific and professional critical incidents that troubled members (Fisher, 2003). In addition, they established an open call for comments from APA members, licensing boards and the public regarding drafts of the new code. The goal was to write standards which were broad enough so that they could apply to psychologists in a variety of roles and work contexts (Fisher, 2003). The standards in mental health ethics codes should reflect underlying moral principles. To some extent, the 2002 APA ethics code addresses this by identifying five aspirational principles. While they are not enforceable in and of themselves, they should provide members with guidance as they try to understand the standards and make decisions based on them.

The ACA ethics code had a similar beginning to the APA code (Allen, 1986; Herlihy & Corey, 2006; Talbutt, 1981; Walden, Herlihy, & Ashton, 2003). The American Counseling Association was originally known as the American Personnel and Guidance Association (APGA) and was formed in 1952. A year later, the president of APGA, Donald Super, established a committee called the Ethical Practices committee to develop the organization's first code of ethics. The main purpose for establishing this first code was to bring legitimacy to the profession of guidance and student personnel services. In 1959 the code was presented for review by the membership and formally adopted in 1961. In the early 1970's, the APGA membership recognized the need for a revised ethics code and the new code was adopted in 1974. Less than 8 years later, the APGA Ethical Standards was revised again in 1981.

During the early 1980's the organization changed its name to the American Association for Counseling and Development (AACD). The new organization developed and adopted its own ethics code in 1988. In the early 1990's, the organization (AACD) saw the necessity of a major revision of the code with three goals as the focus: the development of ethical standards that were more comprehensive, at the same time develop a document that was useful or relevant, and implement the revision process in a manner that provided opportunities for the membership from all of the divisions to share their views and opinions. The end result of this process was the 1995 Code of Ethics and Standards of Practice. The most recent version of the code, the 2005 ACA Code of Ethics and Standards of Practice, came in response to call for the code to address more clearly issues of multiculturalism, diversity, and social justice. In addition to being more responsive to multicultural concerns and issues of social justice, the 2005 code encourages the professional to practice their craft from an aspirational ethical stance. The committee that worked on the revision strove to find a balance between "prescriptive" guidelines (so that ethical cases could be adjudicated with clarity) and the call to aspirational ethics where professionals are encouraged to use reflection and good ethical decision making for complex issues.

Using the Ethics Code to Enlighten One's Ordinary Moral Sense

As already noted, training about the ethics codes is one way to initiate new students into the profession and provide guidance for members of the profession as well as the public. Failing to conform to these standards could lead to a psychologist or counselor being sanctioned by the profession, by state or local organizations or by other legal bodies that use ethics codes as a basis for judging the competence of mental health professionals.

It is important to differentiate between ethical responsibilities and legal mandates, since different rules may apply in each case. In general, ethics codes establish that in cases when the code sets a higher standard than does the law, professionals are bound to follow the higher ethical standard. This is important because some states regulations or laws do not address the legality of the posttherapy sexual contact between psychologists or counselors and their clients. By contrast, the 2002 APA ethics code established a 2-year minimum and the 2005 ACA code established a 5-year minimum before such contact can occur. In addition, both codes have criteria that a professional must meet before engaging in sexual contact that would be applied even after the 2- or 5-year time lapse. As a result APA or ACA members could be held accountable by the profession for not upholding the higher standards enunciated in the codes despite the law.

Some professionals have at best only a cursory familiarity with their ethics code. One might hope that even this cursory familiarity enlightens their ordinary moral sense. However, our experience has been that many psychologists and counselors do not use their code for the rich resource that it might be. Despite criticisms of the limitations of ethics codes like failing to help professionals work out difficult issues such as in Case 2-1 or 2-2 (Bersoff, 2003; Hadjeslavropeoulous & Molloy, 1999; Kitchener, 1984b, 1996a; Pope & Vetter, 1992), ethics codes address a wide variety of professional issues and are rich resources that are often misunderstood and unappreciated. We share the following example as a case in point. Several years ago, one of us was taking one of our children to a music lesson. The music teacher had recently graduated from a master's degree program in counseling and in a casual conversation prior to the lesson, she found out the mother was a professor who taught professional ethics. The music teacher asked without any embarrassment, "What is this confidentiality stuff all about?" After getting over the shock of her lack of information, the concept was explained as clearly as possible and it was mentioned that the importance of confidentiality was discussed in detail in the ACA code. She said she knew about the ethics code, but found it long and sometimes confusing.

On another occasion, one of us spoke to a group of psychology students at a university where she was not affiliated. She had provided them a copy of the APA ethics code to read prior to that meeting. Before beginning to speak, she asked the students to list a set of questions that they would like her to address. Questions ranged from whether they should discuss confidentiality with children who were their clients to how authorship should be decided on a multiple-authored publication. What was interesting was that all of their questions were addressed more or less specifically in the ethics code.

In both cases, the students had likely read their ethics code but at least two factors prevented them from really understanding what they read. First, as already noted, the codes are very detailed. As a result, the professional who does not read the code carefully may have difficulty recalling specifics. Second, even when a specific section of the code is identified that may be relevant in a particular case, it may be difficult to figure out exactly how it applies to other cases.

Given these difficulties, authors such as Canter, Bennett, and Jones (1994), Fischer (2003), and Nagy (2000), have written books offering explicit interpretations of each of the APA standards. Unfortunately, we are not aware of a book that does the same for recent ACA ethics codes. These books, as well as other available interpretations can provide insight on how the more ambiguous standards might be applied. On the other hand, there are sections of the codes of both professions, such as the prohibitions against sexual intimacies with current clients or plagiarism that are quite explicit and need little interpretation.

Criticisms and Limitations of Ethics Codes

Historically, the development of ethics codes was partially driven by the need to protect professions from federal regulation and to increase the status of the profession (Barber, 1982). However, ethics codes themselves have been criticized. For example, the 1992 APA ethics code was criticized for being more protective of the profession than of the consumer (Vasquez, 1994) and for being overly "lawyerly" (Bersoff, 1994). In other words, it was more concerned with protecting the psychologist from legal liabilities than with instilling ethical ideals. Other limitations of ethical codes include not addressing several important ethical concerns. For example, questions of justice, such as "What constitutes a fair distribution of or access to psychological or counseling services?" are generally neither covered, nor are issues regarding the rights of consumers or research participants other than that involving informed consent. It should be noted, however, that the ACA code was revised in 2005 specifically because of the need to address social justice issues. Issues of truth telling and promise keeping are dealt with in a peripheral manner although the 2002 APA ethics code suggested these are "ethical ideals."

Since 1958, a major focus of the APA code has been to establish standards that are enforceable when psychologists are accused of unethical behavior. It may be that this focus on identifying "prohibited" activities has distracted the association from attending to more positive ethical responsibilities. Attention to the aspirational principles, as in APA's 2002 code may help to balance this effect although the 2005 ACA code did not offer such a balance since it does not include ethical principles.

In some cases, reasonable people disagree about specific details or aspects of standards included in the code. For example, during the 1992 revision of the APA code there was a consensus about the need for a standard to be written regarding sexual intimacies with former clients. On the other hand, there was considerable debate about the language of the standard and whether the prohibition of such intimacies ought to be absolute or not (Vasquez, 1991). The controversy did not abate after the publication of the code (Bersoff, 1994; Gabbard, 1994). Although the 2002 code clarified the circumstances under which posttherapy sexual relationships might not be unethical, the controversy over whether there should be an absolute standard has not changed.

Conceptual criticisms that were leveled at earlier versions of APA's ethical standards (1977) also remain pertinent despite several revisions (Kitchener, 1996a). For example, Sinclair, Poizner, Gilmour-Barrett, and Randall (1987) criticized earlier codes for failing to have a consistent conceptual framework. Although the specifics of these criticisms differ, their point remains well-taken. For example, in the APA's 2002 code there was not a consistent framework for organizing the standards. Some standards were listed by areas of practice, such as therapy or assessment although important areas of practice like supervision, which were covered in detail in the ACA code, were completely missing. Others were listed by general ethical concerns such as confidentiality and privacy. Furthermore, neither the ACA nor the APA code provides any justification for the standards they adopted. Although the inclusion of fundamental principles in the 2002 APA code was helpful, their inclusion was confused by the introduction that said they did not represent obligations. The ACA code is subject to most of the same criticisms.

Members of both associations are sometimes faced with other complications. The codes sometimes address different topics and as already noted, they do not always offer the same advice. As a result, individuals who are members of several associations may find themselves offered different advice by the different codes. When this happens, we recommend taking the most ethically cautious position that is consistent with the law. As will be discussed in the next chapter, ethical principles and theories can help think through such situations.

Value of Professional Ethics Codes

None of the above should be taken to imply that professional codes are not important. Despite the criticisms noted, the ethics codes continue to make an important contribution to the practice of psychology and counseling as practitioners, researchers, and faculty try to identify how to be ethical. The codes provide one level of ethical justification for taking or not taking certain actions. The ethics codes can promote a sense of professional trust and loyalty. To return to a point made earlier, firm moral rules, such as those explicated in the codes, are particularly important when professionals are tempted by their own weaknesses or by the weaknesses of others (Hare, 1981). When a professor is sexually attracted to a student in her class or a client in her current care, the clear prohibitions in the codes regarding becoming sexually involved with either provide important protection for the consumer.

In addition to providing firm moral rules, the ethics code provides a means by which the profession can reprimand those who transgress the guidelines. Generally, state boards and professional associations report similar complaints against mental health professionals. For example, between 1983 and 2000 the Association of State and Provincial Psychology Boards reported that the top two reasons for disciplinary action were: (1) sexual or dual relationships with patients, and (2) unprofessional or negligent practice (Reeves, 2000). Similar to this earlier report, the 2007 and 2008 reports by the APA Ethics Committee indicated that sexual and nonsexual dual relationships were the second most frequently opened cases in the prior year and inappropriate professional practice such as in child custody cases or in a crisis situation were the most frequently opened cases.

Although it appears that there are few repercussions for breaking the codes, in fact, the opposite is true. When states adopt the ethics codes as the basis for legal action related to licensure and action is taken against the mental health professional, it can lead to loss of licensure. Such a loss can have severe financial consequences. Additionally, when applying for professional insurance, questions are typically asked regarding ethics complaints and an affirmative answer can lead to being turned down for insurance. While insurance is not required in most states, it is financially risky to practice without it. In addition, even having a malpractice case filed against a psychologist or counselor can lead to the professional feeling a loss of self confidence, depression, anger, frustration and an increase in illness and somatic symptoms. In addition, it takes both time and money to defend oneself. This is true even for defendants who ultimately were not found guilty of the complaints filed against them (Schoenfeld, Hatch, & Gonzalez, 2001). Consequently, ethics codes are not to be taken lightly.

Conclusion

This chapter has attempted to establish the need for a decision-making model for psychologists or counselors to use if they are to think well about doing good in their interactions with students, research participants, clients, or colleagues. The professional ethics codes are one part, but only one part, of that decision-making process. As mental health professionals, we need to be concerned with developing an ordinary moral sense that will allow us to have a reliable moral response to ethical situations when they arise. In addition, we need to have the tools to evaluate decisions as well as to guide us as we reflect on moral problems at those times when our immediate moral judgment abandons us.

Ethics codes offer some firm action guides and aspirational values that can, in some cases, provide professionals with clear moral guidance and, in others, help them frame the issue they are facing from a moral point of view. We argue that the principles of beneficence, nonmaleficence, autonomy, justice, and fidelity suggest that each person and each problem ought to be considered from a perspective that would offer the appropriate respect for people's rights and dignity, including their privacy, confidentiality, and autonomy. (These principles differ slightly from those in the APA code, but we suggest that they are foundational for all mental health professions.) In addition, these principles suggest that each relationship into which a psychologist or counselor enters should be characterized by integrity (i.e., being honest and fair). Similarly, they suggest that when psychologists and counselors enter professional relationships, a high priority should be placed on contributing to the welfare of those with whom they work.

On the other hand, ethics codes are limited by the use of cautious language, the failure to address some important questions, the lack of a balancing principle that would allow psychologists or counselors to give priority to certain standards over others when there is a conflict, and some inherent conceptual problems. An additional limitation is the nature of ethical codes. Most professionals can see them only as rules to be followed but do not reflect on how their own ethics of origin match the profession's ethics. It is because of these weaknesses that psychologists and counselors need to turn to the foundational ethical principles and theories and acculturation to the profession, issues that are addressed in the next few chapters.

Questions for Discussion or Consideration

Consider the ethics case you described at the end of Chapter 1.
1. As you reflect on this case, use the ethics code of your profession to identify the ethical standards that might apply.
2. Based on these standards you have identified thus far, what do you consider to be the most ethical course of action?

3
Foundational Principles and Using Them to Think Well

In the previous chapter, ethical principles were introduced as general norms that provide a rationale for the standards in the ethics codes of most health professions. These principles, nonmaleficence, beneficence, autonomy, fidelity, and justice, are derived from the "common morality" (Beauchamp & Childress, 1994, p. 102) that undergirds the practice of psychology or counseling. In other words, when professionals from these fields are conducting research or therapy ethically, these are the implicit principles they share. Similarly, they appear to be the principles that tacitly guided the practice of ethical counselors or psychologists prior to the writing of the first ethics codes. In other words, they were common norms. In this sense, they provide the foundation or justification for all subsequent codes, including the current ones. If, for example, a standard was written that advocated or led to injustice, we could judge it to be a poor standard because it violated the principle of justice. In the following pages, each of these principles is articulated in greater detail and its foundational nature further explored.

Although some might argue that these are universal ethic principles and provide the foundation for ethics across contexts and situations (Ross, 1980, 1988), this may or may not be true. Rather, the argument made here is not whether they are universal, but that they are the norms which provide the foundation for behavior in the helping professions, particularly in the United States and Canada.

As noted in Chapter 2, foundational principles are not a panacea for solving all ethical problems. This should not be a surprise to a profession like psychology that counts problem solving as an area of critical investigation. Those writing in the area of problem solving (Churchman, 1971; Simon, 1976; Wood, 1983) have long acknowledged that there are some "real-world" or "ill-structured" problems that are difficult to solve and that require complex judgment that goes well beyond the use of deductive logic (King & Kitchener, 1994, 2002; Kitchener & Kitchener, 1981). Accordingly, Chapter 4 provides a discussion of using ethical principles and ethical codes to make reasoned judgments in light of the uncertainty involved in ethical decisions in the real world where decisions may also be influenced by the law and personal values.

Foundational Ethical Principles

Nonmaleficence

Nonmaleficence means not causing others harm. It finds its roots in the history of medical practice. Although popularized as *primum non nocere* (above all do no harm) and attributed to the Hippocratic Oath, it is not cited as such in the oath. Rather, the closest expression comes in a strained translation of a single Hippocratic passage "at least do no harm" (Beauchamp & Childress, 2001, p. 113). However, Beauchamp and Childress claim the Hippocratic Oath clearly expresses both the obligations of nonmaleficence and beneficence. It also appears in both Hindu and Buddhist teachings and has been recognized by modern ethicists as central to medical ethics (Beauchamp & Childress, 1994; Ross, 1930; Veatch, 1981) both in Eastern and Western cultures.

In general, the duty to not inflict harm on others includes neither inflicting intentional harm nor engaging in actions that risk harming others. It forbids certain kinds of activities, in contrast to the principle of beneficence, which suggests that there are certain positive obligations, such as helping others. For example, given the evidence (Pope & Bouhoutsos, 1986) that sexual contact between therapists and clients often has devastating effects on clients, engaging in those activities violates the principle of nonmaleficence and provides the foundation for forbidding such activities in both the ACA and APA codes.

The principle of nonmaleficence need not be considered absolutely binding if it is in conflict with the other moral principles, such as in the case of self-defense, where one's own right to life is being violated. On the other hand, many ethicists (Beauchamp & Childress, 1989; Frankena, 1963; Ross, 1930) have suggested that, all other things being equal, not harming others is generally a stronger ethical obligation than benefiting them. Returning to the concept of role obligations, if the focus of psychology and counseling is to promote human welfare, harming another would not only prevent achieving this goal, it would undermine it. Identifying nonmaleficence as fundamental suggests that if professionals must choose between not harming someone and benefiting another, the stronger obligation could be summarized as "In trying to help others, at least do not harm them."

Most ethics codes in psychology and counseling recognize this responsibility and have standards that forbid their members to harm others or at lease take reasonable steps to avoid harming with those whom they work or teach and to minimize harm where it is foreseeable and unavoidable. The problem with such standards, as with the principle of nonmaleficence, is that the concept of harm is ambiguous. The difficulty lies in defining what constitutes harm. For example, how does one distinguish the discomfort and stress that are frequent temporary side effects of clinical treatment from the long-term harm that is, in some cases, an outcome of therapy (Lambert & Bergin, 1994)? Harm might also be difficult to determine or define when it comes to multicultural differences. What a counselor or psychologist from one culture sees as beneficial may be seen by a client or student from another culture as harmful (Goodman et al., 2004).

Generally, to harm someone means that the interests or the well-being of another person has been reduced in a substantial way. In psychology or counseling, harm can be either physical or psychological. Thus, for professionals in these fields, the principle of nonmaleficence leads to ethical concerns, such as how much discomfort is justifiable in therapy or research and whether it is justifiable to use high-risk treatments with clients when there is little or no research confirmation of their benefits.

Beauchamp and Childress (2001) point out that the concept of harm needs to be distinguished from the justification for harm, meaning that just because harm occurs does not mean it is morally wrong. Sometimes harm may be justifiable, albeit regrettable. For example, the harm to the therapeutic relationship that sometimes accompanies breaking confidentiality can be justified when there is a higher ethical obligation like protecting a child who is being abused. Furthermore, the discomfort and distress experienced by the client during therapy is unlikely to be defined as unethical. By contrast, a therapist whose treatment leads to client deterioration would be violating the principle of nonmaleficence if a reasonable standard of care was not met in the treatment. Similarly, the faculty member in Case 2-4 who showed students gruesome pictures, which seriously disturbed some students, violated the principle of nonmaleficence.

Arguments about the ethics of assessment and diagnosis can also be understood in terms of psychologists' and counselors' ethical responsibility not to harm those in their care (Reich, 1981; Szasz, 1961). It is not difficult to establish that misdiagnosis can harm a client. One need only consider the role of diagnosis in mental competency hearings (Fitting, 1986) to understand the importance of responsible diagnosis. Sometimes this problem has resulted in the maligning of psychological tests. However, as Bersoff (1983) pointed out, most psychological tests are ethically neutral. It is *how* they are used that has ethical consequences. He argued that tests have been used as

> exclusionary mechanisms to segregate, institutionalize, track and deny access to coveted and increasingly scarce employment opportunities. As this use of tests increased, so did their potential for causing unjustified negative consequences. (Bersoff, 1983, p. 41)

An awareness of the negative consequences led the legal system in the 1970s to scrutinize particular testing practices to determine whether individuals or classes of individuals were harmed. The perception of the courts was that these practices were sometimes used to deny access to education and employment, resources that were critical to the well-being of individuals in our society.

Clearly, this was a major concern underlying the decision of the San Francisco Federal District Court in the *Larry P. v. Wilson Riles* (1972) case. In this historic case, the judge ruled that intelligence testing, as practiced in California, placed African American children in an undue proportion in programs for the mentally retarded. The consequence, the court claimed, was to potentially stigmatize these children for life. As a result, the judge ruled that the State Board of Education could no longer use these tests for the purposes of placement. The implication was that the diagnostic label led to psychological harm for the child and that this harm was substantially greater than the benefit that accrued from the testing or placement in special classes. In the judge's opinion, harm occurred that was not justifiable.

The legal concept of negligence is also derived from the principle of nonmaleficence (Beauchamp & Childress, 2001). Negligence involves risking or causing the harm of others by practicing below what is considered to be a reasonable standard of care or by acting carelessly. Typically, the legal standard involves four aspects: (1) the professional has a duty to the person(s) harmed through an implicit or explicit contract, for example, informed consent; (2) the professional has broken the contract or failed in his or her duty; (3) the person experienced harm; and (4) the harm was caused in some way by the professional's failure to perform his or her duty (Beauchamp & Childress, 2001; Bennett, Bryant, VandenBos, & Greenwood, 1990; Curd & May, 1984). Duty is often determined by assessing what the professional community considers to be a reasonable standard of care. For example, if a counselor or psychologist was sued for negligence by the relatives of a client who committed suicide, the court would try to determine whether the professional followed procedures that were recognized as standard by others in the field. Did the professional recognize the symptoms that are often associated with suicidal behavior? Did the professional respond to those symptoms in an appropriate manner? Similarly, the duty to act responsibly with consumers, supervisees, students or research participants derives in part from the principle of nonmaleficence because irresponsibility can be considered negligence if it leads to harm.

Some might argue that the maxim "above all do no harm" should be the most central ethical responsibility in applied psychology and counseling. However, such an absolutist position can have a conservative effect on a profession: it can lead to the absurd position that no one should be treated because a positive outcome cannot be guaranteed and because there is a risk of harm in all treatment (Veatch, 1987). In general, the position taken here is that as the risk and magnitude of potential harm increases, ethical prohibitions and limits on the treatment, supervision or research procedure also increase. In fact, this was the position taken in the 2002 APA Ethics Code which stated that "when conflicts occur among psychologists' obligations or concerns, they attempt to resolve them in a reasonable fashion that avoids or minimizes harm." Similarly, the 2005 ACA ethics code required its members to "minimize or to remedy unavoidable or unanticipated harm." However, the risk of harm must also be balanced with other ethical principles.

Beneficence

Beneficence means doing good or benefiting others. At their very core, psychology and counseling are committed to contributing to the health and welfare of others. As noted earlier, the introduction to both of the ethics codes (ACA, 2005; APA, 2002) identify improving the welfare of society, individuals, and others with whom they work as a primary goal for the members of these organizations. They do so through research, teaching, supervision, counseling, consultation, and so on. This theme was reiterated in the 2002 APA code under the aspirational principles "beneficence and nonmaleficence" as well as "fidelity and responsibility" which urges responsibility to society and the importance of contributing some other professional time for little or no compensation.

Even more basic than ethics codes, the term *helping profession* underscores this obligation. Whereas, philosophers may argue about whether people in general have a duty or help others, psychologists and counselors have accepted it as their raison d'être. It is the primary role obligation associated with being a professional within these organizations. Although this may not be apparent for some researchers, ideally the outcome of studies will lead to benefits for others at least at another point in time.

What this moral obligation means in practice is more difficult to define. Does it mean, for example, that professionals should benefit others at the expense of their own health and welfare? Does it mean providing clients with money and shelter when they are without resources so as to provide them for themselves? Does it mean that a counselor should try to help others even when they do not want the counselor's help?

The principle of beneficence has two aspects (Beauchamp & Childress, 2001). The first requires providing benefits to others by acting in ways that furthers their general well-being. The second characteristic obligates a psychologist or counselor to balance the potentially beneficial consequences of an action against the potentially harmful ones (Beauchamp & Childress, 2001). In other words, they should do a risk–benefit analysis. Unfortunately, in a world as complex as it is today, there is often a price to pay for accruing benefits. This issue may be most familiar to research psychologists and counselors who work with institutional review boards (IRBs). IRBs must evaluate whether the benefits that may follow from a proposed research project outweigh possible negative consequences of the research. The problem also appears in therapy. For example, clients may have to balance the need for treatment against limits on confidentiality that may arise from using a managed care provider or when therapy itself involves some kind of mental anguish such as uncomfortable thoughts and feelings during treatment. Case 1-3 regarding research with Parkinson's patients, illustrates the need to balance harm and benefits (among other ethical principles) in research. Similarly, in Case 2-1, the psychologist is called on to balance the potential harms and benefits that might arise from transferring a patient who had been wrongly assessed to a community care home.

Doing good for others, just like not harming them, has its limits as an ethical principle. Many people want the freedom to choose the course for their own lives even if some kind of objective observer, like a therapist, does not think that their choice is a good one. If beneficence were accepted as the therapist's primary ethical principle, psychologists or counselors could always trump clients' wishes as long as they were acting in the client's "best interests" even if it meant deceiving the client. This problem raises the issue of parentalism,* which is revisited later in this chapter.

There are also multicultural issues involved in both what constitutes beneficence and nonmaleficence. Take the following Case 3-1 as an example.

---

* The word parentalism is substituted for parternalism to avoid the latter's gender-specific connotations.

Case 3-1

The parents in an East Asian family that has immigrated to the United States use extreme physical punishment of their children to ensure the obedience and conformity to their standards, including a high level of respect for elders. A child protective service worker who has investigated complaints from the psychologist cannot prove that the incident meets the legal definition of child abuse, although she suspects that abuse really does occur. At the very least the discipline techniques represents very substandard parenting according to Western standards (Knapp & VandeCreek, 2007, p. 660).

In this case, the parents appear to believe their type of punishment benefits their children while the case worker and psychologist (using Western standards) believe the children are being harmed. Multicultural issues and this case will be revisited later in the chapter and throughout the book.

Respect for a Person's Autonomy

The core idea of autonomy is that of self-rule, "remaining free from both controlling interference by others and personal limitations, such as inadequate understanding, that prevent meaningful choice" (Beauchamp & Childress, 2001, p. 58). Generally, autonomy has been understood to include both freedom of action and freedom of choice. Freedom of action means doing what one wants to do with one's own life as long as it does not interfere with the similar actions of others. Freedom of choice means making one's own judgments. Like beneficence, it has two aspects. First, it includes the right to act as an autonomous agent, to make decisions, to develop values, and so on. The second follows from a reciprocal responsibility. If people wish to be treated autonomously, they must treat others in the same way. This reciprocity presumes a fundamental respect for the rights of others to make choices even when their beliefs may appear to be mistaken, unless their choices infringe on the rights of others.

Many philosophers have held that the field of ethics requires the concept of an autonomous person. In contrast, many theorists in psychology, from Freud to B. F. Skinner, have argued for some kind of determinism that presumes the actions of people are determined by biological, psychological, and/or historical events. However, if people's actions are determined, then it follows that they are not responsible for their actions, nor can they be held morally culpable. Thus, it becomes impossible to talk about actions as being good or bad or right or wrong. Morality, by contrast, assumes that people are responsible for their own actions, and this in turn requires that they have some ability to freely choose those actions. As Veatch (1981) observed, for people to accept moral responsibility, they must at least believe they are free.

Social contract theorists argue that morality develops out of an implicit contract between people acting rationally. Fundamental to this contract is respect for the choices that others make. Without this respect, the alternative would be to force others to believe as we do (Engelhardt, 1986). To live in a society marked by peace rather than force, people agree to respect the opinions of others even if they do not agree with them. As Rawls (1971) suggested, individual liberty must be "compatible with similar liberty for others" (p. 60). That is, although liberty is fundamental, it is not absolute and must be limited when it infringes on the liberty of others, because not to do so would be disrespectful of others' similar rights. Hence, autonomy does not mean unlimited freedom.

From this perspective, cases that involve breaking a therapeutic confidence to warn another person of impending danger can be seen as an ethical conflict involving different rights deriving from autonomy. When clients are a danger to others, the conflict often entails the right to privacy and confidentiality (based on the respect due to autonomous persons to decide who hears information relevant to their life) versus the restriction that autonomous rights do not permit infringing on the autonomous rights of others. For example, if a client is HIV positive and having unprotected sex with his wife, who has no reason to believe that he is HIV positive, the client's actions could irrevocably infringe on the rights of his wife and an unborn child. Thus, one can argue that, other things being equal, the husband does not have a right to expect the information about his HIV status to be kept in confidence. (These issues are discussed in greater detail later in this chapter and in Chapter 10.)

In psychology or counseling, respect for autonomy as a foundational moral principle has sometimes been confused with autonomy as a personality characteristic or type. Feminist authors such as Gilligan (1982) have, for example, criticized the personality ideal of autonomy conceptualized as separateness and individuation, arguing that, although it may be a characteristic of the development of many men, it does not characterize the development of many women. From Gilligan's perspective, the development of many women is characterized by a greater concern for attachment and relationship. Similarly, in the multicultural literature, authors have argued that an emphasis on autonomy reflects a bias toward an individualistic perspective that may not be appropriate in collectivist cultures (Pedersen, 1995).

By contrast, respect for autonomy as a moral principle imposes the moral requirement that we respect others including their choices and desires, regardless of their personality type or characteristics. In fact, respecting others' choices is a central feminist value (Kitchener, 2000; Lerman & Porter, 1990) and is at the core of tolerance for different cultural values (Burn, 1992; Cayleff, 1986). Respect for autonomy should remind psychologists and counselors that individuals with different racial and ethnic background and who are at different points in their racial identity development may choose to balance their self-interest with the interests of their family and cultural group in ways different from the majority culture. To honor autonomy, the counselor or psychologist would respect these choices.

Autonomy as a moral principle is embedded in many of our political institutions and in the law, and it provides the foundation for many concepts in psychology or counseling. For example, the ideas of unconditional worth and tolerance for individual differences imply a respect for others' rights to make their own decisions. Similarly, mutual respect, which many see as a basic ingredient of the therapeutic bond, implies a relationship between two people, both of whom are regarded as free agents. In fact, respect for a person's autonomy was explicitly included in the 2002 APA Ethics Code under the principle, *Respect for People's Rights and Dignity.*

Worries about protecting clients' rights to privacy (Everstine et al., 1980) can be understood as concerns about issues of autonomy. The right to privacy follows from the assumption that autonomous individuals have the right to make decisions about their own lives and the information relevant to it, including to whom that information is confided. Thus, for example, although students and supervisees may not have the right to confidentiality in a strict sense (because they may not have an implicit contract that promises it), when they confide information to professors or supervisors, they do have a right to expect that the information will be treated with respect and kept private to the extent that it is possible (see Chapters 9 and 10 for a further discussion). Similarly, the faculty member who was harassing students with violent pictures in Case 2-4 had a right to expect that her office was private and to make decisions regarding who had access to it. Professionals accrue several responsibilities from the right to privacy. These include limiting disclosures of private information to what is essential, discussing confidential information only for professional purposes, and establishing limits on when confidential information may be disclosed.

Both the professions' commitments to informed consent in research and practice also follow from concerns with respecting autonomy. Requiring psychologists and counselors to inform consumers or research participants about aspects of therapy or research that may influence their willingness to participate in the activity safeguards the right of individuals to make autonomous choices about their own lives when they are capable of doing so. Recent discussions of supervision strongly recommend that a similar process be used with supervisees (Barnett, 2007b). (See Chapter 9 for a further discussion of informed consent.)

It is important to reiterate that there are limits on considering others as autonomous agents. Beauchamp and Childress (2001) argued that autonomous choice involves acting intentionally with understanding and without undue controlling influences. Intentionality presumes that the person involved is able to consider information and make decisions rationally. Thus, if someone is unable to understand a choice, as might be the case if that person were under the influence of drugs or alcohol, that person's choice would not be fully autonomous. Similarly, a prison environment, which by definition restricts choice, would limit the autonomous nature of the choices made by prisoners. Thus, whether or not a professional ought to respect an individual's choice may depend on the extent to which the decision-making process is a rational one and the person is allowed real choices. For this reason, the choices of irrational suicidal clients can be seen as essentially nonautonomous, and thus not honoring them can be ethically justified. (See Chapter 10 for a further discussion of confidentiality and rational suicide.)

Although the distinction between those who are autonomous and those who are not autonomous is useful, perhaps some of the most ethically difficult cases in psychology and counseling involve individuals who are not fully competent or totally incompetent. Consider cases in which a person has limited intelligence or is periodically psychotic. Should such a person be accorded the right to make his or her own decisions even when the practitioner believes that person to be mistaken? Macklin (1982) reasoned that it would be ethically unacceptable to violate individual freedom and interfere in others' lives against their will if they are competent. On the other hand, it would be equally unacceptable to allow "harm, destruction, or even death to befall an innocent helpless human who is unable to make a reasonable choice" (Macklin, 1982, p. 337).

Part of the difficulty lies in the fact that competence and incompetence are not absolutely dichotomous concepts: the ability to understand choices lies on a continuum. In this regard, the concepts of limited and intermittent competence (Beauchamp & Childress, 2001) are particularly useful for clarifying this issue. *Limited competence* is usually applied to people who are not fully capable of rational decision making. Consider, for example, the ethical concerns that would arise where in a group living home two residents with limited intellectual ability wished to marry and have children. Are the individuals involved competent enough to make these decisions and understand their ramifications?

A person with *intermittent competence* is one who at times experiences periods of lucidity and at other times is incapable of rational choice. Someone in the early stages of Alzheimer's disease might, for example, be intermittently competent. With people of limited or intermittent competence, restrictions on autonomy ought to be proportional to the limits on their ability to understand the issues involved and their ability to act as free and rational agents on the basis of those choices.

It should be noted that there are no absolute criteria, including psychological or legal ones (Macklin, 1982), for determining rationality or competence. Age clearly plays a critical role because, in the average person, competence is closely linked to cognitive development and cognitive decline. To the extent that the development of formal operational thinking allows an individual to think about abstract consequences (e.g., death is forever), to think ahead, to think logically about hypothetical possibilities or impossibilities, it may be one criterion for determining rationality. This is an important consideration for psychologists and counselors who work with adolescents and college students, given that some studies (King, 1986; Neimark,

1982) have found that even college students cannot pass some formal operational tasks. On the other hand, Powell (1984) pointed to evidence suggesting some adolescents may be as competent decision makers as are adults. These concerns are revisited in Chapter 9 on informed consent.

Conflicts between Nonmaleficence, Beneficence, and Autonomy

The three principles of nonmaleficence, beneficence, and autonomy are at the core of many ethical decisions as well as many ethical disputes in counseling and psychology because there are some inherent tensions between the principles of beneficence and nonmaleficence on one side and the principle of autonomy on the other (Engelhardt, 1986). With regard to the first two principles, Engelhardt suggested that applications of the principles of beneficence and nonmaleficence are more likely to be justified in terms of their teleology or consequences. It does not make sense to say that there is a principle to do good and then not be concerned if a particular ethical standard led to more harm than good. However, he argued that the principle of autonomy is not consequence oriented. Mutual respect should not be offered because it leads to a good outcome, but rather because it is a condition for morality itself. As a result, standards regarding informed consent in research or practice, which are based on autonomy, cannot be disregarded just because disregarding them might lead to good consequences. Similarly, a therapist cannot override the wishes of a rational client, other things being equal, even if the therapist believes that a client is making a poor choice and the client's choice will lead to poor consequences in the long run. Thus, the principle of respect for autonomy should serve as a check on psychologists and counselors who believe that they know what is in the best interests of their client and act on that belief against the wishes and without the consent of their clients.

On the other hand, can someone's liberty ever be constrained for his or her own good? This is the issue of parentalism that was briefly addressed in the section on beneficence. Parentalism literally means acting like a parent toward a person. It presumes that an authority has knowledge of what is good for an individual and undertakes to regulate that person's behavior according to what the authority believes to be in the person's best interests. Because professionals, such as psychologists or counselors, have superior knowledge and training, it is easy to presume that they also know what is in the best interests of their clients or supervisees.

Parentalism is the ethical stance underlying the involuntary commitment of self-destructive clients. These extreme cases are not ethically troublesome, however, because they frequently involve individuals of limited or intermittent competence who either are nonautonomous or are making choices that are not substantially autonomous. Take Case 3-2, for example.

Case 3-2

Janet enters treatment for depression. She has no family. She has recently been promoted to a new position that she finds meaningless. After several months of cognitive therapy, she remains substantially depressed. She indicates to her therapist that she may not return for the next session and thinks about committing suicide because life seems so hopeless.

Intervention in this case would be considered weak parentalism (Beauchamp & Childress, 1989). Weak parentalism is justified when the person's action is substantially nonvoluntary or when an intervention is necessary to determine whether the action is voluntary or not. In this case, because of Janet's depression, there is good reason to believe that if she acts on her suicidal ideology, her decision would not be autonomous. As Beauchamp and Childress (1989) argued, it "could be callous, uncaring, and wrong to allow such persons to die through their own decisions when certain conditions substantially reduce the autonomy of their actions" (p. 221). Most mental health professions allow (but do not require) a weak parental stance when someone with whom a psychologist or counselor has a confidential relationship is potentially dangerous to themselves.

Weak parentalism can be contrasted with strong parentalism, which allows those with superior knowledge and authority to intervene against a person's wishes in order to provide some kind of beneficial outcome even if the person's choices are informed and voluntary. Beauchamp and Childress (2001) concluded that strong parentalism is a dangerous moral position because the potential for abuse is strong. They suggest that it can be justified in only rare cases, particularly if the person is at risk of serious harm and the action would prevent it. Furthermore, the potential benefits should outweigh the risks, there should not be a feasible alternative to the paternalistic action, the infringement should be minimal, and the action should involve the least infringement on the life of the person that is possible.

Fidelity

The principle of fidelity is at the core of the fiduciary relationship between psychologists or counselors and consumers of their services or participants in their research. *The Oxford English Dictionary* (1989) offers two definitions that are useful in understanding the meaning of fidelity. The first focuses on the quality of faithfulness or loyalty, and the second on honesty and trustworthiness. Both aspects reflect core components of human trust. Strangely, although not explicit, the first definition was implied by the principle of fidelity and responsibility in the 2002 APA ethics code, but the second definition was included under the definition of Integrity, which we argue is a virtue since it describes more of a personality characteristic than a principle.

Although often attributed to Beauchamp and Childress (2001), they did not explicitly identify fidelity as a moral principle. Although they talk about many aspects of fidelity under the general topic of professional–patient relationships, the term fidelity can be traced back to Ross (1930), who used fidelity to describe the responsibility to keep promises and be truthful. Although others (Meara, Schmidt, & Day, 1996) have argued that veracity (truthfulness) is a separate principle, Ross understood it to be a part of the responsibility involved in promise keeping. In other words, to say "I promise to keep the information you give me in confidence" and then to break the promise means that the original statement was not truthful.

According to Ramsey (1970), the principle of fidelity, which includes faithfulness, promise keeping, and truthfulness, is basic to all helping professions. Issues of fidelity arise when individuals enter into some kind of a voluntary relationship, such as the relationship between a psychologist or counselor and a client or research participant or between a supervisor and supervisee. The fact that two people freely consent to participate in a relationship implies an ethical commitment that involves certain obligations for both parties. At a more fundamental level, fidelity can be seen as the core of the bond between people (Ramsey, 1970; Ross, 1930). If people lied, were untrustworthy, and regularly broke promises, no meaningful human relationships could exist.

The principle of fidelity seems especially critical in counseling and psychology because honesty and promise keeping are basic to trust. Although trust is vital to all human relationships, it is particularly vital to therapist–patient, researcher–participant, supervisor–supervisee, teacher–student, and consultant–consultee relationships. Each of these relationships is based on an implicit contract between the participants that require certain role obligations for each. Honesty and promise keeping are important commitments on the professional's side of the contract. Educational institutions would likely be empty if students believed that faculty made a practice of lying to them. Similar statements could be made about each of the relationships mentioned above.

Clients, other consumers, and research participants also have role obligations derived from the principle of fidelity. If clients regularly did not keep their promises to pay their bills, psychology as a consultative profession could not exist (Bayles, 1981). Similarly, if research participants made a habit of falsifying the information that they give to scientific investigators, psychology as a scientific discipline would for the most part be impossible.

It can also be argued (on the grounds of utility) that lying, deception, and failure to be trustworthy have serious consequences for all professional relationships and ultimately for the profession itself. They destroy faith in the therapist, instructor, or supervisor to be helpful; they destroy faith in the mutuality of relationships in general; and they destroy faith in the benefits that psychology or counseling can offer to the public. If lying and deceit were perceived as the norm for professional relationships, clients and research participants alike would be suspicious of a professional's motives and would feel no obligation to be truthful in turn. This is one reason why deception in research is so ethically troublesome (Diener & Crandall, 1978).

Similarly, supervision is based in the assumption that supervisees are reporting truthfully about their clients Case 3-3, based on a highly publicized case in Colorado, illustrates what can happen if that does not occur.

Case 3-3

A clinical psychology student was being supervised by psychologist, who was deeply concerned about one of her supervisee's clients who were being seen more and more frequently. The client was a law student who entered therapy because she was having difficulty concentrating and motivating herself. The supervisor and supervisee would discuss the case with the supervisor making recommendations for treatment, but the client continued to deteriorate, dropped out of law school and was becoming increasingly suicidal. Finally the supervisor insisted on seeing the client with the supervisee. The supervisee admitted she had not been following the supervisor's instructions and was using "regression" therapy which included nursing the client. Eventually, the client brought a lawsuit against the therapist, the supervisor and the University for malfeasance.

The supervisee had been lying to the supervisor about the whole case. In essence, the supervisee was blatantly violating the principle of fidelity. This type of scenario emphasizes the need for supervisors to occasionally do *in vivo* supervision or at least review audio or video tapes of sessions. It may also be wise for supervisors to ask for copies of tapes of cases that the supervisee is not discussing.

Although confidentiality and informed consent can be understood as deriving from the rights of autonomous persons (Beauchamp & Childress, 2001), they can also be understood as deriving from the principle of fidelity. As already noted, implicit or explicit contracts between therapists or researchers and consumers typically include the promise of confidentiality. Similarly, a supervisor–supervisee relationship includes the promise to keep information about the supervisee private as long as it does not have implications for the supervisee's training and needs to be divulged to other staff members. Failure to keep promises such as these destroys the trust necessary for human, as well as the trust necessary for professional relationships.

In other words, confidentiality can, to some extent, be understood as a special obligation that psychologists or counselors incur when they enter into a relationship with a client or a research participant. Because confidentiality involves promise making and assumes that the mental health professional is not lying, the ethical obligations surrounding it derive in part from fidelity.

Similarly, Ramsey (1970) argued that informed consent is a statement of fidelity between a professional and the client or consumer because it explicitly establishes the nature of the relationship and the requirements on both parties that define the relationship. For this reason, consent is particularly critical to the ethical practice of psychology or counseling, regardless of whether the practice involves supervision, consultation, therapy, or research.

Justice

Justice involves both the individual relationship between the mental health professional and a consumer or research participant and how to distribute goods, services, and burdens in a human community. The latter is a deeply critical social issue, as illustrated by the debate over limiting the services that the state can provide to illegal immigrants. The question is whether services should be limited to those that are required in an emergency situation or should include equal access to health care and education. Both proponents and opponents argue their case on the basis of what is and is not "fair." Proponents argued that it is not fair to taxpayers to use tax money to provide services for people who are in the country illegally. On the other hand, opponents argue that immigrants need the services, and therefore, it is not fair to deny them access to these services. Both of these views represent different concepts of justice.

Many ethicists have argued that justice in its broadest sense means "fairness" (Benn, 1967a, p. 298). Justice concerns arise, according to philosophers such as Hume and Mill, because in society sometimes goods and services are scarce. In these situations, there are conflicts of interest over who should have access to them because human benevolence is limited. Thus, in order to live together with minimal strife, people must develop rules and procedures for adjudicating claims and distributing goods and services in a fair manner. Because society frequently takes the responsibility for deciding what is fair for all concerned, questions involving justice often involve the law.

In general, the problems associated with proportioning goods and services involve distributive justice. In psychology and counseling, they include how the benefits and burdens associated with the profession ought to be distributed. The benefits involve the services that derive from the knowledge base derived from the research and how they ought to be distributed to others; the burdens include things like participating in research studies. In the social sciences, the issue is critical since science has been criticized for testing white males and then assuming the results could be generalized to women and people of color or on the other hand, burdening those who have little power, like college freshmen or the poor, with participation in research with little hope of accruing any benefits. In addition, because counseling and psychology are helping professions and because to some extent the issue of justice can be seen as an extension of beneficence or trying to do good (Engelhardt, 1986; Ross, 1930), psychologists and counselors need to be concerned with wider issues of social justice. Social justice may be focused at the individual level, like whether children have warm winter clothing or helping individuals recognize social constraints in therapy, but also involves identifying whether they are inadvertently acting in ways that reinforce the status quo.

The formal meaning of justice has been traced to Aristotle (Beauchamp & Childress, 2001; Benn, 1967a), who argued that justice involved treating equals equally and unequals unequally but in proportion to their relevant differences. In the words of Beauchamp and Childress (1989), rules, actions, or laws are "unjust when they make distinctions between classes of persons that are actually similar in relevant respects, or fail to make distinctions between classes that are actually different in relevant respects" (p. 263). It is not by chance that justice is portrayed with a blindfold, implying that the judgment of relevant and irrelevant characteristics in a particular case should be done impartially or, as Rawls (1971) said, behind a "veil of ignorance" (p. 136).

It is on the basis of the principle of justice that ethics codes in the helping professions, for example, forbid professionals to unfairly discriminate on the basis of cultural issues like age, gender, race, ethnicity, national origin, religion, sexual orientation, disability, socioeconomic status, and so on. For counselors or psychologists, these personal characteristics should be considered irrelevant when it comes to the administration and distribution of psychological services and they should be trained to recognize other own biases interfere with how they work with others who are not white and middle class.

Considerations of how to distribute psychological services often lead to debates between the justice of merit and the justice of need. The justice of need dictates that to the extent that people need mental health services, they ought to be provided, even though the recipients cannot pay for the services. Here, need would imply that people would be hurt or affected negatively if they did not receive services. By contrast, the justice of merit holds that mental health professionals have spent years in school and that they deserve a reasonable compensation for their services. From this perspective, services ought to be distributed according to a person's contribution to society. It is on this basis that substantial fees for services have been justified. The consequence of this second position is, of course, that there is an inequality in responding to need, thus, there are substantial numbers of people who do not have access to psychological services. Many debates in political campaigns have hinged on which concept of justice is endorsed. In order to balance these two aspects of justice, mental health professionals are urged to do some *pro bono* work.

There are those who may ask why psychologists or counselors should be concerned with problems of social justice. In answering the question of why people in general ought to be concerned with justice, Rawls (1971) argued that reasonable people must be committed to justice by the fact that they are engaged with others in activities designed to promote their common interests. If they expect others to be fair and respect their interests, they must treat others fairly in return. He suggested that a concern with fairness is a requirement of people engaged in a society that assumes social cooperation.

Generally, psychologists and counselors ought to have a commitment to being fair that goes beyond that of the ordinary person. To the extent that they agree to promote the worth and dignity of each individual, they must work to ensure that people have access to a decent minimum of goods and services, such as education. Consequently, to the extent that mental health is deleteriously affected by unequal treatment, such as employment discrimination, psychologists and counselors must be concerned about fairness. It would be inconsistent with this commitment to fairness if psychologists or counselors focused their efforts only on particular groups, such as the White middle class, and condoned or promoted the unfair treatment of others. Therefore, it would seem that the commitment to reduce unequal treatment of people on the basis of age, gender, race, ethnicity, national origin, religion, sexual orientation, disability, language, or socioeconomic status would be strong. (See Chapter 13 for a further discussion.)

In fact, the Feminist Therapy Group (Brabeck & Brown, 1997), although focused on the oppression of women, argue that when an ethical person becomes aware of a wrong against any person or group, he or she is obligated to work for social justice. This may involve working within existing social structures or changing them if they're not amenable to a just social order (Brabeck & Ting, 2001). In other words, justice goes beyond what is fair for individuals and requires seeking solutions that affect entire communities. It may involve advocacy and intervention at the community and policy levels (Goodman et al., 2004). (See Chapter 13 for an expanded discussion.)

This discussion of justice has focused on some abstract societal issues; each mental health professional must decide how to fairly distribute the benefits and burdens associated with his or her position. Clinicians must decide whom to treat, how much to charge for services, and under what circumstances they would provide services at low or no cost. Because many practitioners are aware that not everyone has equal access to psychological services, they often contribute a portion of their time to help those who have limited resources. For example, one faculty developed a list of local clinicians who provided services for students at very low cost since the mental health center on campus had practicum students that would have been their peers.

Furthermore, once therapists have accepted a client for treatment, they must decide what kind of treatment is fair. Is it fair, for example, to provide brief therapy for someone who was sexually abused because that is what her health maintenance organization (HMO) is willing to pay for? Is it fair to treat a middle-class African American woman using the same techniques and theoretical stance as used in treating a Euro-American woman struggling with poverty? These are very real issues of justice with which clinicians must struggle daily.

Similarly, faculty members often have to make decisions regarding which students should receive assistantships or invitations to work on special projects. Should an assistantship be given on the basis of need (to a student who is struggling but who might benefit from the special attention) or should it be given on the basis of merit (to a student who has excelled and who may contribute more to the professor's project)? What would be fair? Again, although the profession has a general obligation to justice, psychologists or counselors need to consider how issues of justice are relevant to their work whether it involves teaching, supervision, therapy, research, or other forms of practice.

Ethical Theory

In discussions of moral principles, the question of how decisions should be made when ethical principles conflict always arises. Although Beauchamp and Childress (1979) originally argued that moral principles followed from ethical theory and it provided guidance when ethical principles conflicted, they no longer hold this view (Beauchamp & Childress, 2001). Our own view (Kitchener & Kitchener, 2008) is that although ethical principles do not precisely follow from ethical theory, ethical theory does serve as a heuristic and aids in reflecting on ethical principles and helping to make decisions when they conflict.

Three answers are often given to the question of how ethical principles should be followed. First, some argue that principles are absolute and ought to be followed unconditionally in all circumstances. Second, others argue that moral principles are not valid at all. Morality is relative to the individual, and therefore no principles can guide behavior because morality is subjective. The third answer is that moral principles are prima facie valid (Ross, 1930). Those who take this view argue that moral principles are neither absolute nor relative but are always ethically relevant and can be overturned only when there are stronger ethical obligations. Good judgment is required to weigh and balance the principles in a particular situation in order to arrive at the most reasonable solution. In the following paragraphs, each of these claims is considered and the argument is made that the moral principles described in the previous section ought to be considered prima facie valid and that there needs to be good reasons both for how these principles should be balanced and for overturning them.

Single-Principle Theories

Some argue that certain moral principles should be followed without exception or without regard for circumstance. For example, if being truthful is an absolute principle, then it ought to be followed even in cases in which telling the truth might lead to the death of an innocent person, such as revealing the location of a Jew in Nazi Germany.

Two major moral theories have been proposed that identify a single, absolute principle as a guide to moral action. Although it is beyond the scope of this book to articulate the subtleties of these theories, short sketches of each follow. The first, often called *deontological theories* draw from the work of Immanuel Kant, the late-eighteenth century philosopher. From this perspective, ethical decisions should be based on reasons that can generalize to others who are in similar situations and that can be universalized as norms of conduct (Abelson & Nielsen, 1967); however, following the Kantian principle absolutely can some time lead to bad ends. Using the above example, if we universalize the rule of not lying, it should be applicable to all members of a group without exception, thus, lying would always be wrong even if it meant saving a life (Hospers, 1961). Another way of understanding the categorical imperative was to treat all humans, whether others or yourself, as an end and not just a mean to that end. In other words, one should never exploit people but treat them as intrinsically valuable.

The second theory is *utilitarianism*, which states that decisions are morally correct if they find the best balance of good over bad consequences. Some philosophers have suggested that this means doing the least amount of avoidable harm under the circumstances (Toulmin, 1950). The idea of trying to do the least amount of harm seems particularly compelling in psychology or counseling. Knowing that counselors and psychologists can and do sometimes harm research participants, students, supervisees and clients, it is tempting to embrace "above all do no harm" as a primary moral commitment. As has already been discussed, however, this would lead to a very conservative position that might undermine the innovation and scholarly explorations that have been essential in the field's expansion. Therapists would be limited to using the therapeutic intervention that would be least likely to harm clients, without considering the balance between possible harms and possible gains. In fact, although the ACA and the APA ethics codes acknowledge the importance of avoiding harm when it is possible and minimizing it when it is foreseeable but unavoidable, they do not establish nonmaleficence as an overarching principle.

Although the idea of finding the greatest balance between doing the least amount of avoidable harm and doing good may seem to provide a simple solution to difficult decision making, problems with utilitarian theory have been identified. There may be times when finding the greatest balance of good over bad consequences could lead to committing immoral acts (Beauchamp & Childress, 2001). Take, for example, psychological research that may benefit many people in the long run but causes pain and suffering to the research participants. Most would intuitively suggest that such research was not ethical unless the participants knew about the possible consequences ahead of time and agreed to participate anyway. In other words, the potential positive consequences are not enough to ethically justify causing harm. This observation leads to the second criticism of utilitarianism; it pays little attention to individual rights or the rights of minorities and can lead to the trumping of the rights of individuals for the good of society. Furthermore, there are difficulties both in measuring and defining pleasure and pain especially in multicultural contexts (Knapp & VandeCreek, 2007).

Many contemporary moral philosophers (Abelson & Nielsen, 1967; Hospers, 1961) have argued that following a moral principle without exception would sometimes lead to immoral acts, such as in the case of lying noted earlier. Furthermore, information about a particular situation, the first level in our model (Kitchener & Kitchener, 2009), may influence which moral principles are most relevant or important. In addition, as noted in the preceding sections, there are many cases in which it is impossible to act on one moral principle (e.g., beneficence) without violating another (e.g., autonomy). Attempts to provide an absolute ordering of principles have not been particularly helpful because circumstances may lead to slightly different interpretations of the principles and their application. To argue, for example, that the principle of autonomy always trumps the obligation to help others or to prevent harm would lead to the conclusion that mental health professional should never intervene to save a person's life against his or her will—a position that seems intuitively unethical. For these reasons, most contemporary ethicists find single-principle theories untenable without some modification.

Ethical Relativism

One of the reasons that the social sciences, in general, have rejected ethical absolutism has been because of the recognition of and an ethical commitment to tolerance of diversity. Anthropological and sociological observations have confirmed that people, cultures, and values differ as illustrated in Case 3-1. This view has been used to support the claim that what is ethical, true, good, or right depends on one's culture and/or situation and, therefore, that there are no general moral principles. This claim, however, confuses descriptive and normative ethics. Just because moral values differ (a descriptive observation), it does not follow that all values are equally good (a normative claim).

Part of the difficulty in evaluating the relativist's argument is assessing the level of disagreement about cultural values. For example, there are certainly different religious and social practices among groups when and under what circumstances they safeguard human life. However, at a fundamental level, most religions and cultures of the world accept the protection of human life as a basic principle (Brandt, 1967). If it had not been a fundamental principle, humanity would not have survived. Others have pointed to the universality of principles such as nonmaleficence, beneficence, and so on. In other words, at least some principles seem universal, although the way they are observed may differ because of cultural differences (Knapp & VandeCreek, 2007).

Kohlberg (1971) argued that social scientists frequently confuse relativism with tolerance. For example, some psychologists might claim that a person's beliefs and values ought to be respected because they are understandable in the context of that person's life; therefore, values are relative to a particular context. However, if all values are relative, and tolerance is a value, then we can choose to be tolerant or not. It follows from this perspective that being intolerant (i.e., devaluing people just for holding different beliefs or being different) may be acceptable in some situations. This claim would, however, be inconsistent with the professions' assumption that intolerance is antithetical to the commitment to respect human dignity and promote human welfare and is thus ethically unacceptable.

The general issue of ethical and epistemological relativism is a complex one (Gifford, 1983; Krausz & Meiland, 1982). Accepting it as an ethical framework, however, would lead to the position that if someone thinks an action is right, then it is right and what is moral depends totally on the situation. As has already been noted, this position does not work ethically or legally. In fact, no profession could set forth an ethics code if it was accepted that the "situation" completely dictated the relevant considerations in making an ethical choice or if morality were simply a matter of individual taste. Further, as Kitchener (1980) has argued, an "even more dangerous consequence of such a view is the belief that moral decisions in therapy do not have to be justified because they cannot be justified" (p. 6).

In summing up the problems with relativism, Rollin (2006) identifies two points. First, relativism is self-defeating. If all positions are equally true or valid, then this is also true of relativism. In other words, relativism is no truer than any other position. Second, although it is true that there are cultures which hold different ethical positions, it does not mean their values are equally valid. As Brabeck and Ting (2001) argue, relativism supports the status quo in a world where oppression is rampant. From a relativistic stance there would be no way to argue that acts like torture, female genital mutilation, and stoning women who commit adultery are wrong.

Principles as Prima Facie *Binding and the Common Morality*

It was suggested earlier that the moral principles of autonomy, nonmaleficence, beneficence, fidelity, and justice arise from what Beauchamp and Childress (1994, p. 102) called the "common morality." In this case, the common morality of psychology and counseling justifies the relevance of the five principles as has been argued in previous pages.

If, however, these ethical principles are neither absolute nor relative, then we still must determine how they should be used when we face moral problems. Early in this century, Ross (1930) argued that ethical principles should be considered to be prima facie binding. For Ross, this meant that although a principle did not establish an absolute requirement, obeying the principle "tended" to be a duty.

The core concept of prima facie comes from the law, where it means that a contract establishes an obligation unless there are special circumstances or conflicting and stronger obligations. In ethics, prima facie implies that a principle must be upheld unless it conflicts with another principle or unless there are extenuating circumstances that throw it into question (Beauchamp & Childress, 1989). In other words, although ethical principles are not absolute, they are always morally relevant and give consistent guidance about which moral issues need to be considered. In this sense, the principles are conditional duties (Abelson & Nielsen, 1967). The conditions under which they may be overturned must, however, be morally relevant ones, such as when there are stronger moral obligations. Ethical principles, therefore, provide a standard framework within which to consider ethical questions. Although one principle might be weighed more heavily in certain circumstances, such as valuing life over truth telling in the case of saving a person from Nazi death camps, this does not mean telling the truth is not an important principle. Rather, there are morally relevant reasons for not acting on it. As Beauchamp and Childress (1989) noted, moral principles "count even when they do not win" (p. 52).

Ethical Justification—Finding the Best Balance

Ross (1930) argued that when faced with the competing demands of two or more prima facie valid principles, the best balance between right and wrong should be found. Each of the principles should be considered, and reasons should be given for why one principle is weightier in the particular situation than another. In some cases, however, there may be no single right decision because good but not absolute reasons can be given for more than one action (Beauchamp & Childress, 2001).

When faced with an ethical dilemma, Engelhardt (1986) argued for finding the greatest balance of benefits over harms for each potential alternative with the constraints set by respecting autonomous decision making. That is, one should find the best balance of value over disvalue. From this perspective, precedence should be given to respecting others' decisions about their own lives over making decisions about how to help them. Psychology and counseling have taken a similar position with regard to informed consent for research and therapy. Participants must give consent before the positive consequences of research or therapy can be considered. In effect, the professional ethics codes make respect for autonomy a stronger obligation than beneficence, but they do not ignore the consequences of the research or therapy in terms of their potential benefits.

Another approach to the problem of making good moral choices in the face of competing principles has been called the good reasons approach (Baier, 1958). This position argues that the best choice is one that is supported by the best reasons generated from the moral point of view and that takes into consideration accurate information about the situation and the relative weight of other considerations. Adopting the moral point of view implies acting reasonably and impartially even when making decisions that concern one's own welfare.

Because moral rules or principles are meant for everyone, they must also be applicable across different circumstances, without exceptions made for one's self. This is a modification of Kant's categorical theory that implements the concept of universalizability. In this case, while a

Figure 3.1 (Reprinted from Calvin and Hobbes ©1992 Watterson. Distributed by Universal Uclick. With permission. All rights reserved.)

rule may be identified, the rule itself may specify particular exceptions. An example might be "Never lie except when a life it at stake."

The *Calvin and Hobbes* cartoon in Figure 3.1 illustrates the problem when moral standards fail to be universalized. Universalizability does not mean that everyone should be treated the same way but rather that others in similar circumstances ought to act or be treated in a similar manner. Thus, in considering a person's circumstances one would have to consider that person's cultural background, ethnicity, gender, and so on because even deciding whether an action would harm or help someone would depend on the cultural meaning given to that action. An example of how the idea of universalizability might be applied as illustrated in Case 3-4.

Case 3-4

A counselor admitted somewhat sheepishly that she had some concerns about a decision she had made regarding a client who was suffering from an unusual disease. A friend of hers happened to be suffering from a similar disease and she thought the client might benefit from talking to someone with similar symptoms. With the friend's permission, she gave the client the friend's telephone number. Her intentions and the consequences were clearly beneficent, and the client did benefit from the consultation with the therapist's friend. Further, no one's autonomy was violated because the client had the choice to call the friend or not. Nevertheless, the counselor seemed uncomfortable with her decision but was unclear why she felt that way. When she was asked whether she would recommend that other therapists introduce their clients to their friends, she said that she could not because counselors could not always control the outcome of such interventions. Friends are not trained as helpers, and clients can become confused by the lack of clarity in boundaries between themselves and their therapist when they are interacting with a therapist's friend.

In other words, the risk of harm is probably greater than the possibility of benefits occurring if such actions were generalized. The counselor conceded that she probably should not have excused herself from the warnings about multiple-role relationships. This was particularly true in her case because although there were no support groups available for people with this particular disease, there were other resources, such as books or others in the community that the counselor could have tapped before asking for her friend's help. These alternatives could have provided similar help for the client without having risked potential harmful side effects.

Baier (1958) also argued that in deciding the best moral course of action, one must also ask whether the decision would be the same if one was on the giving or receiving end. That is, the decision must be "reversible." From our perspective as parents, an equally telling question is whether we would want our children or loved ones treated in a similar manner. In some ways, it is the essence of the golden rule. Do unto others, as you would have them do unto you. Although the golden rule in and of itself could be used in a self-serving manner to rationalize treating others either well or poorly, but by balancing it with impartiality and universalizability one hopes that good moral decisions will be formed.

Ideally, committees write or revise professional ethics codes by taking the moral point of view. They attempt to arrive at a balance among ethical principles that can be applied in particular cases. It is when the profession moves into new areas that are not anticipated by such committees that professionals must arrive at their own well reasoned balance. In these cases, it is important to consult with other reasonable people, both professionals and lay people, about how they would consider and resolve the conflict before making a final decision because consultation sometimes helps identify whether a particular blind spot is obscuring the most ethical choice.

In the end, however, even reasonable people acting from the moral point of view may not agree on a solution to every moral problem. Some moral problems may be insoluble because of a lack of clarity of facts or principles (Engelhardt, 1986). This is not too surprising. Even in the intellectual domain, psychologists have identified what have been called "ill-structured" problems (Churchman, 1971; Wood, 1983). These types of problems cannot be solved with a high degree of certainty. Sometimes facts are unavailable, potential alternatives are unknown, or the utility of outcomes is unclear. Considering that moral problems are even more complex and involve balancing complex values, it is not surprising that sometimes even experts may disagree about solutions. As Beauchamp and Childress (2001) said, "We regard disunity, conflict and moral ambiguity as pervasive features of the moral life" (p. 390).

This does not mean that all solutions are equally good; rather, there may be more than one solution that can be defended from the moral point of view. These solutions would have to consider relevant ethical rules; the five principles enumerated above, and would need to be defended as universalizable, impartial, and reversible. In such circumstances, Engelhardt (1986) concluded that the best one may do is "to act so as to lose as few goods as possible and to violate as few rights as possible" (p. 99). Even so, the best moral solution may involve overriding one moral directive, such as to "keep promises," because of a stronger ethical obligation such as "save a life." In such cases, we are left with what Nozick (1968) called "moral traces," or a sense of regret at having to make such a choice. Sometimes this sense of moral regret can lead the truly virtuous professional to move beyond the ethics of obligation to supererogatory actions in an effort to make up for violating a less central moral consideration. This issue is pursued in greater detail in Chapter 5.

In a more recent book, Beauchamp and Childress (2001) argued for what Rawls called "reflective equilibrium." This shared source of judgments begins with the principles that seem fundamental to all people and are certainly central in the mental health professions, in other words, the principles just articulated. They argue that a particular judgment is acceptable if it maximizes the coherence of the overall conclusion that is developed based on reflection. Although their view is very abstract, it seems to be supported by everyday moral thinking.

Metaethics

In some ways metaethics should not be at the top of our ethical decision-making model since it is a tool that is used throughout the decision-making process. In philosophy the subject matter of metaethics is concerned with the meaning and justification of ethical statements (Kitchener & Kitchener, 2008). In fact, to some extent the section on ethical theory was dealing with questions of metaethics. First, it deals with questions like is there a single ethical theory or principle that is adequate for ethics in psychology and counseling. We have clearly argued for pluralism in which all principles have something to offer when thinking about ethical issues whether it's in science, practice or supervision. The second question and the one that is most difficult, addresses the question of which theory should guide our ethical decisions since they are not all compatible. Kitchener and Kitchener (2008) argued for a "balancing approach" which suggests that all are valuable and, in a particular situation, they must be balanced to get the best overall combination. Again, this is the position we are taking here. The third issue deals with the question of what the appropriate method is to use in applied ethics. "If particular cases are at the bottom and abstract general principles are at the top, then the question is whether one proceeds in a top-down fashion or in a bottom up fashion" (Kitchener & Kitchener, 2008, p. 19). Although there are a variety of answers to this question the standard model in bioethics in psychology is "principlism." From this perspective ethical principles are self-sufficient and do not need justification by higher ethical theory; they do, however, justify ethical rules like confidentiality. Although ethical theory is a useful tool in making a decision, as already noted, it does not deductively identify an absolute decision about which principle takes precedence. There are at least two alternatives to principlism. First, the existence of a moral rule with no higher order set of ethical principles. This seems to be the position that the ACA code of ethics takes. The second is the existence of ethical theory from which ethical rules are directly derived. Clearly, the argument made here is that the rules are derived from principles and theories are useful heuristics when it comes to balancing the principle.

Applying Moral Principles to a Multicultural Case

As Case 3-1 illustrated not all clients in the multicultural society in which we live share the same values as the majority culture. Knapp and VandeCreek (2007) raised the question of whether the principles just discussed are universal or are influenced by the Judeo-Christian ethical tradition which is then applied cross culturally. First, it seems important to clarify that the claim made here is not that they are universal moral principles (although some would make this claim). Rather, the claim is that these are the principles on which the ethical codes of at least the American and Canadian mental health organizations are built.

This section will show how to apply the model even when working with people from minority cultures. First, it is critical to understand the facts of the situation. As Knapp and VandeCreek point out, we should not assume that what clients or supervisees from minority cultures present as normative is necessarily the case as they say, "cultures are always changing and never stagnant ... and that similar conflicts exist when treating patients from Western backgrounds" (p. 661). For example, the values of children and their parents may be quite different no matter what culture in which they are raised. They also point out that certain behaviors are "normative" in the sense of being common but are not necessarily culturally acceptable. For example, about 25% of American women are sexually abused or assaulted (Dube et al., 2005). This does not mean the American culture sees this as ethically acceptable. Furthermore, opinions may vary within cultures as to what constitutes acceptable behavior-like corporal punishment of children. In addition, it is very difficult to identify cultural groups. Hispanics and their cultural values vary considerably depending on whether their background is from Puerto Rico, Mexico, Cuba, or other Latin American countries. As in America, people from the same country may also have different values. In Mexico, people of Mayan dissent may have very different values then descendents of the Spaniards. In other words, psychologists and counselors have to look beyond cultural stereotypes in identifying the real problem. In Case 3-1, for example, the parents may have sought out counseling because their current methods of disciplining their children aren't working and are seeking alternatives. In this case, it would be critical to know the parents' values and perhaps, how they fit with the teachings of their religious or world view.

Assuming that what the therapist knows about the parents' behavior does not meet the state's requirements for reporting abuse, the therapist needs to identify the best way to help the family while avoiding the least amount of avoidable harm. As Kitchener (1984b) has argued a good therapeutic solution is most often a good ethical one.

Knapp and VandeCreek (2007) suggest select clarifying cultural values throughout the therapy process. Doing so would allow the clinician to discern whether the parents perceive violence as an "instrumental or absolute" value (p. 663). Beneficence would suggest the therapist clarify the parents' values and offer alternative tools of parenting. If this does not work, the therapist needs to gather additional information on the nature of the discipline actually occurring. If in fact they discover that the parents are severely abusing the children, as a last resort they would need to take a week parentalistic stance and report the parents to social services. In this case, it would amount to allowing the principles of nonmaleficence and beneficence to temporarily override the parents' autonomy.

In summary, Knapp and VandeCreek argue for what is called a "soft universalistic" position (Rosenstand, 1994). It argues there are some overarching ethical values, but also acknowledges that different cultures may differ on the particulars. In other words, they may interpret or define the general principles in culturally specific ways, an issue of metaethics. From this perspective, mental health professionals would uphold certain minimal standards of conduct that are consistent with the principles and allow for culturally specific expressions of those values without falling into stereotypes of what those values may be. They emphasize clarifying the client's specific values through respectful dialogue. Based on the principle avoiding harm, they recommend that therapists seek supervision if they have little or no knowledge of the particular cultural group with whom they are working.

Conclusion

When ethical codes are silent or ambiguous, the principles of do no harm, do good, respect others, be faithful, and be fair provide a foundation for thinking about the moral problems faced by professionals, whether they are academicians, practitioners, or researchers. They allow psychologists and counselors to frame the ethical problems they face in a common vocabulary and think carefully about issues, even if they are not addressed by an ethics code. Furthermore, they provide a vocabulary with which to discuss moral issues with others in the health care professions like doctors or physical therapists.

The foundational principles are not panaceas, as Case 3-1 illustrates. They must be balanced with each other, evaluated in light of a particular case, integrated with the law, and used to develop an ethically defensible plan of action. Decision making in the real world involves more than ethical principles and theories. As in the case of the Asian family, sometimes the law prescribes actions that counselors or psychologists need to be aware of and attend to. The next chapter addresses decision making in the real world where ethical rules, principles, and theories are only part of the decision-making process. In either case, psychologists and counselors need to consider carefully the options available and the potential consequences of acting on each of them. On some occasions, they need to consult with others to check on their own biases and potentially erroneous thinking. Additionally, they need to be aware that there may not be a perfect ethical solution. The decision they make should, however, be ethically defensible, given the circumstance, and provide the best possible balance of ethical harms and benefits while protecting individual rights.

Questions for Discussion or Consideration

1. Identify a difficult ethical problem you faced as a professional. What issues were at stake?
2. What advice did your ethics code give?
3. What ethical principles would have helped with your decision making?

4

The Practicalities of Ethical Decision Making

In Chapters 2 and 3 we discussed the critical issues of ethical reasoning and laid out a model for justifying ethical decisions. This information is an important foundation for making ethical decisions in a larger, real-life context that involves personal values and stresses, administrative responsibilities, the law, and numerous other impinging events. With this being the case, practitioners need access to a useful procedure or process that helps to identify the ethical issues, sort out the competing ethical and legal obligations, and clarify who they are accountable to and for what. Although there are many models (Bersoff, 2003) for coming to a decision about how to do good when faced with a moral quandary, we have found the following to be particularly helpful. As noted earlier, it is critical that psychologists and counselors (ACA, 2005) have one to two with which they are familiar so they do not panic and make hasty ill-formed choices when faced with such problems. Furthermore, there is evidence suggesting that those who are trained using an ethical decision-making system and a problem-solving approach are significantly more skilled at the decision-making process (Gawthrop & Uhlman, 1992).

The first model (see Table 4.1) is adapted from one that arose in discussions with a group of practitioners who were concerned with making good ethical decisions in HIV-related practice (Barret, Kitchener, & Burris, 2001). This process has nine steps and encourages the professional to be reflective at different points along the way and to consider or develop optimal decisions. The first three steps help fill out the immediate level of moral reasoning while Steps 4–6 highlight the critical evaluative level of moral reasoning presented in Chapter 2.

Model 1: Reasoning About Doing Good Well

1. Pause and Think About Your Response   Take time to pause and sort through what is frequently a complex set of personal and professional reactions to the situation. This may include identifying how your beliefs and values are coloring your response. Although ethical decisions may feel like they require immediate action, taking time to carefully consider the issues can lead to clearer thinking and can help identify your ordinary moral response to the situation. Of course, there may be real emergencies that require immediate action, but sometimes the stress involved in the situation may prompt a premature response.

2. Review the Available Information   Review the information that is available about the situation. If this is a clinical situation, identify the client's diagnosis, presenting problem, and other contextual information. If this is a research question, consider the literature regarding how similar designs have affected participants, and what the alternatives are. In fact, both the ACA (2005) and APA (2002) ethics codes, as well as prior ones, warn against using deception research practices unless alternatives are not feasible and the study is justified by its scientific merit. Both presume thorough examination by alternatives prior to planning the research. If it is a teaching or training situation, remember that working with students and supervising trainees have two competing obligations: one to the student and the other to the public. Remembering these considerations may help clarify what are informational questions and what are ethical ones. Psychologists and counselors often deal with events that have different probabilities, so

Table 4.1 Reasoning About Doing Good Well

Step 1	Pause and think about your response.
Step 2	Review the available information.
Step 3	Identify possible options.
Step 4	Consult the Ethics Code.
Step 5	Assess the foundational ethical issues.
Step 6	Identify legal issues and agency policy.
Step 7	Reassess options and identify a plan.
Step 8	Implement the plan and document the process.
Step 9	Reflect on the outcome of your decision.

what appears to be a moral issue may actually be a disagreement about the relative probabilities of events, such as harming participants in a study involving deception or the frequency with which an HIV positive mother may transmit the disease to the fetus.

3. Identify Possible Options   Generate alternative plans. Again, these may be alternative research designs, alternative clinical plans, or remediation for the student depending on the situation. This is a good time to consult with colleagues who may help identify other possibilities.

4. Consult the Ethics Code   As prior chapters have suggested, at the critical evaluative level the first step is to review the ethics code of your profession. Ethics codes may provide clear guidance and help limit some alternatives you are considering. If the code provides clear advice, follow it unless a greater harm would occur from doing so than not doing so. If it is an absolute dictum, like the prohibition against having sex with clients, research participants, or students, do not excuse yourself from following it. If no single alternative emerges evaluate the options using the following steps.

5. Assess the Foundational Ethical Issues   Using the foundational ethical principles (i.e., nonmaleficence, beneficence, and justice) assess the ethical questions and balance the principles involved in each option. Remember the facts of the case may influence which principles are most viable. Ethical theory may help in balancing the principles, for example, "do the least amount of avoidable harm." This step includes the second and third tiers of the critical evalutive level presented earlier. Identify the option that is most justifiable from a moral point of view.

6. Identify Legal Concerns and Agency Policy   One's ethical decisions may have legal implications, or the law may highlight ethical issues that have not been considered. Legal questions may be identified by consulting a lawyer; the legal literature; national, state, or local professional organizations; or colleagues. In this case, the professional should consider the legal consequences both for him or herself and for the person or people receiving services or participating in research. Although it may seem farfetched, that there may be any legal consequences for a research participant, there have been cases when research data have been seized by law enforcement officials to identify whether there has been illegal activity by participants (Seiber, 1992). Many times psychologists and counselors are working for agencies that have their own policies. These too must be taken into consideration. The well-informed ethical professional may sometimes find these policies do not support the most ethical option. In this case, an

intervening step may be to help challenge and change internal policies (Hanson & Goldberg, 1999 for an extrapolation of these issues).

7. Reassess Options and Identify a Plan   By moving through the first six steps, a plan may have emerged or it may be clear that one's original plan has some important ethical flaws. Consider possible outcomes if the plan is initiated, ask what the short- and long-term consequences may be for the individuals involved as well as the community. Ask if the greatest balance of value over disvalue that respects individual rights has been found.

8. Implement the Plan and Document the Process   Implementing the plan may involve talking to the people involved, such as clients, supervisees, or students, and helping them understand your decision. Their input may require you to back up and reconsider your decision if you have based it on faulty information or have failed to consider a critical ethical issue. Once the plan has been put in place, it is important to document in writing the rationale for your decision and the process of making it.

9. Reflect on the Outcome of Your Decision   Once the decision has been made, the consequences will emerge sometimes in ways that might not have been anticipated during the decision-making process. Once this happens, the information may be used to enlighten your ordinary moral sense in the future, so that when similar issues arise you can draw on that additional information.

As professionals who have had many years of experience with making ethical decisions and consulting with other psychologists and counselors who face ethical quandaries, we still find this process helpful. We carefully consider the relevant information, review the ethics codes, consider what the foundational principles imply, consult colleagues, and often find ourselves reading and rereading the law. At this point in our careers, the process is automatic. But to someone who is a novice, the process may feel clumsy and time-consuming. Practice using it, however, will make it more natural. That practice does not always have to come with firsthand experience but may be supplemented by reading about and thinking through difficult cases ahead of time. The application to the case of Jerry that follows after Model 2 serves as an example.

Model 2: Acting Ethically—An Ethical Choice Making Process

The second process (Anderson & Handelsman, 2010) is an adaptation of an ethical choice making process by Anderson, Wagoner, and Moore (2006). Anderson et al. (2006) decided to use *choice* to highlight the action part of implementing an ethical decision and word *process* to suggest the nonlinear and interactive nature of the model. New information or insight at any point in the process can influence other points along the way. The centerpiece of the model draws upon Rest's (1984) four components of moral behavior in which he argues that acting morally is a multifaceted phenomenon that involves more than decision making. Rest's model was developed based on a thorough review of all the psychological literature on moral behavior available at the time. It still, however, seems to capture the major components of moral behavior today. Model 1 describes the processes underlying the second component of Rest's model. Model 2 fleshes out the other aspects of moral action embedding moral decision making among them.

In 1994, Rest defined the four components as "the major determinants of moral behavior" (p. 22, 23–24) and identified them as follows:

Component 1—Moral sensitivity   Interpret a situation as having ethical implications meaning that one's decision will impact someone else.

Component 2—Moral decision making   Evaluate potential actions or decisions based on moral reasoning and identify the most ethically ideal solution.

Component 3—Moral motivation   Identify other values, for example, money, success, etc., that compete with ethical values. It has to do with the importance given to moral values in light of the other values and decide whether or not to fulfill one's moral ideal.

Component 4—Moral character   Implement the ethical ideal through "ego strength, perseverance, backbone, toughness, strength of conviction, and courage" (Rest, 1994, p. 24).

According to Rest (1994) all four components must occur for moral action or behavior to be the outcome. These components do not happen sequentially. In fact, Rest suggested that there is a complex interaction between the four components.

To highlight each of the components and illuminate the process within each one, Anderson and Handelsman (2010) and Anderson et al. (2006) developed representative questions for the professional to consider. These questions tap into the professional's thinking, motivations, values, needs, and possible conflicts of interest. In addition, the questions show the importance of perspective taking. We have added or modified questions to encourage the psychologist and counselor to seek input from the others including clients, students or colleagues at appropriate times.

Component 1—Ethical Sensitivity   The following questions encourage the psychologist and counselor to develop sensitivity to the issues at hand and how alternative choices will affect others positively and negatively:

> What strikes me as strange or makes me uncomfortable?
> What demands my attention?
> Who is involved in this situation?
> What makes me think, "Uh-oh, this doesn't feel right?"
> What makes me think, "Yes, this feels good or right?"
> What are their issues related to diversity that need my attention? What are the demographic differences between me and others involved in the dilemma? Are there issues of oppression or discrimination?
> How does my point of privilege or value set affect my sensitivity to this issue?

Component 2—Formulating an Ethical Plan   As previously mentioned, this component is exemplified in Model 1. The focus here is to identify a good plan by using the ethics code, law, and ethical principles. With the exception of the last question, the rest of the questions reflect the process already described in the first model.

> What do I know about the situation? What are the facts of the case?
> What else do I need to know?
> What does the ethical code have to say about this situation?
> What ethical standards conflict in this situation?
> What ethical principles are involved? Is ethical theory helpful in resolving ethical dilemmas?
> What are the legal issues involved?
> With whom should I consult?
> What do I need to explain to or share with the consumer or research participant about the ethical issue?
> If I were the consumer or research participant, what would I hope my psychologist or counselor would do?

From what I know right now, what choices would be the most positive, and what would be closest to an ethical decision or action?

Component 3—Ethical Motivation and Competing Values These questions call for the psychologist or counselor to identify conflicts of interest and personal motivations and values that compete with professional values:

What are my personal values and motivations in this situation?
What are my professional obligations in this situation?
Is there a match between the two or is there a conflict?
What new value or values do I need to cultivate?
If there is a conflict between my personal values and professional values, can I express my values and motivation in a different way?
If there is a conflict, how can I reorganize or reprioritize my personal values?
With whom might I consult to see the conflicts as clearly as possible?
What core values (personal and professional) are being stretched?
What core values (personal and professional) are being strengthened?
How does my client, student, or research participant benefit or be harmed, depending on the course of action?

Component 4—Ethical Follow-Through These questions encourage the psychologist or counselor to seek out support for and implementation of the choice:

To whom or what (e.g., the law) must I be accountable? To whom do I want to be accountable?
Who in my professional circles can and will encourage or support me to do the right thing?
What personal and professional values do I need to draw upon?
What do I need to let the client, student, or research participant know?
What action(s) do I need to take and what is the timeline for implementing them?

Making an Ethical Decision: Using the Case of Jerry

Case 4-1

Jerry is a Euro-American, HIV-positive, gay man with anxiety and depression. He has been in a relationship with another man for several months and has told him of his HIV status. Subsequently, his partner expressed fears about dealing with Jerry's HIV status and they had many arguments about Jerry's illness and their relationship. Jerry is afraid that his partner will make him move out, that he will never have another relationship because of his HIV status, and that he will die alone. When he gets highly anxious and angry, he visits gay bars and picks up other men. He admits to engaging in anal intercourse with these men and not using a condom. He says that such encounters help him forget his problems and adds angrily, "That's the way I got HIV, and anyone stupid enough to have sex with me deserves what they get!" (Barret et al., 2001, p. 139).

Using Model 1: Reasoning About Doing Good
Step 1—Pause and Think About Your Response When faced with a client like Jerry, a therapist's immediate response may be one of ethical confusion because of a concern both for Jerry and his anonymous sexual partners. Because Jerry's partners are unknown, the therapist may be unsure about what might be done to protect the men with whom Jerry is engaging in a risky sexual practice and to what extent Jerry's disclosures should be kept confidential. His angry

statement at the end may be particularly troublesome. It may raise a variety of emotional reactions from the therapist, from empathy to anger.

Step 2—Review the Available Information   To sort out the ethical confusion, the next step would be to evaluate the information surrounding of the case. This might include learning something about the probability of acquiring HIV from a single sexual encounter, identifying what may be motivating Jerry to engage in one-night stands, Jerry's diagnosis, and considering what treatment options might be available. In addition, the therapist must consider to whom a report might be made if Jerry's confidentiality were to be broken and what laws might be relevant.

Step 3—Identify Possible Options   Because Jerry's partners are anonymous, directly informing them is not an option. Two possibilities are informing the public health department or the police although this may or may not be legal or required in his state. On the other hand, the therapist might choose to work directly with Jerry, trying to educate him about the dangers of such behavior for himself and his partners. He knows Jerry can act responsibly since he does so with his partner, so he might have him sign a safe sex contract. The therapist would need to consider the clinical and ethical implications of doing each one. Consulting with a colleague or someone more knowledgeable about HIV-related practice may be particularly helpful in identifying options.

Step 4—Consult the Ethics Code   The wording and numerical ordering of standards change with changes in the codes. For purposes of illuminating the strengths and weaknesses of ethics codes, in cases like Jerry's, we choose the 2002 APA and 2005 ACA Ethics Codes as examples. As should be clear in the following paragraphs, careful reading of the exact wording of the codes is necessary before an accurate application can occur. In this case, the issue of confidentiality is the critical point and maintaining confidentiality, if ethically possible, is the primary obligation. However, both the APA and ACA ethics codes have traditionally indicated that there "may" be times when there are exceptions to maintaining confidentiality and require that those exceptions are highlighted in the consent process.

For example, the 2002 APA code identified when psychologists may break this "primary obligation." The most relevant part of this standard stated that "Psychologists disclose confidential information without the consent of the individual only as mandated by law or permitted by law for a valid purpose such as to (1) provide needed professional services; (2) obtain appropriate professional evaluations; and (3) protect the client/patient, psychologist or others from harm" (Std. 4.05b). The 2005 ACA code addressed the issue as follows: "When clients disclose that they have a disease commonly known to be both communicable and life threatening, counselors may be justified in disclosing information to identifiable third parties, if they are known to be at demonstrable and high risk of contracting the disease. Prior to making a disclosure, counselors confirm that there is such a diagnosis and assess the intent of clients to inform the third parties about their disease or to engage in any behaviors that may be harmful to an identifiable third party" (Std. B. 2.b.).

Although both codes permitted disclosure under some circumstances, they do not require it. In Jerry's case, in terms of APA the therapist is limited by what is required or permitted by law. The ACA standard is really irrelevant because there is no identifiable third party.

One 2002 APA standard offered some additional guidance in this case: Standard 3.04, avoiding harm, required that psychologists "avoid harming their clients/patients" and "minimize harm where it is foreseeable and unavoidable." This standard was by a principle from the aspirational section of the code, which suggested that when conflicts occur among psychologists' obligations or concerns, they should attempt to resolve them in a way that avoided or minimized harm. Both of these statements seem to underline the importance of nonmaleficence in making a decision about how to deal with Jerry.

Different standards that address informed consent to therapy, and the limits of confidentiality, should also remind Jerry's therapist that prior to beginning treatment, clients should always be informed about the parameters surrounding confidentiality. A discussion about the limits to confidentiality will help clients understand the circumstances under which confidentiality may be broken.

Where, then, did the ethics codes leave Jerry's therapist in regards to how to handle Jerry's case? First, they stressed the importance of both informed consent and confidentiality; second, they emphasized the importance of balancing potential harms and third, the APA Code *gave* the therapist permission to break confidentiality if it was legally required or permitted. Neither code *required* breaking confidentiality. Finally, both codes remind the therapist that any intrusions on privacy should be minimal.

Step 5—Assess the Foundational Ethical Issues As noted earlier, to some extent, protecting confidentiality rests on the principle of respect for autonomy since it involves allowing the individual the right to make decisions with whom private information is shared. On the other hand, under some circumstances, people forfeit their right to have their autonomous choices respected. One of those circumstances is when they infringe on others' rights to make similar choices. Because Jerry is engaging in unprotected sex with other men without informing them of his HIV status and because it is potentially life threatening, he is infringing on others' rights. As a result, other ethical principles may trump Jerry's right to keep the information confidential. Similarly, the principle of beneficence should remind psychologists and counselors that they have a responsibility to society. This responsibility sometimes involves protecting others from harm. Consequently, there is an additional argument based on beneficence for intervening in a way that protects Jerry's partners. In addition, when engaging in unprotected sex, Jerry is at risk for contracting opportunistic infections from his partners that can seriously threaten his ability to ward off full-blown AIDS. Thus, on the basis of beneficence, there may be an obligation to protect Jerry, although this would be a paternalistic stance that would need further justification.

On the other hand, there is a question of whether breaking confidentiality in this case would offer any protection for his partners or his own health. In other words, would breaking confidentiality honor the principle of beneficence—to do good for Jerry and those he is sexually intimate with? Helping him process his motivations and fears in therapy might be more effective in changing his behavior. If Jerry has been tested for HIV in the state where the event occurs, the Public Health Department may already have a record of his HIV status and in this case could do little more than the therapist to inform Jerry's partners. Informing the police would be the most intrusive option available to the therapist and certainly the one that would probably lead to the most harm for Jerry and, unless he were jailed, would not offer additional protection for his partners. Thus, it is unclear which action would be more beneficent and save more lives in the long run, although maintaining confidentiality and working directly with Jerry seems like it has the greatest potential for being effective.

The principle of fidelity offers another perspective on the ethical relationship between Jerry and the therapist because it highlights the fiduciary relationship between them. If the therapist chooses to violate confidentiality, it would mean breaking his promise to Jerry about the privacy of the information he shares and undermine the trust of the therapeutic relationship.

The principle of nonmaleficence should remind the therapist that breaking confidentiality might have a variety of harmful consequences for Jerry. It may also destroy his faith in the therapist, as well as in other mental health professionals. If this occurred, there would be no opportunity for the therapist or others to use therapeutic or educational interventions in the future that might successfully change his behavior. Finally, the principle of justice should remind the therapist that Jerry should be treated fairly and should not be discriminated against because of his HIV status or sexual orientation.

What kind of ethical conclusion can be defended in this case? Clearly, whatever the therapist decides, the choice should do the least amount of harm possible. The most ethical course of action would be one that allowed the therapist to both respect Jerry's confidentiality and provide some protection for his partners. It appears that unless Jerry is jailed, little or no protection for Jerry's partners will be gained by breaking confidentiality and the potential to harm Jerry will be high. In these circumstances, it would be better to maintain confidentiality and work with Jerry on his motivations for acting out and his impulse control.

Needless to say, this is not a perfect solution. It does not offer an absolute guarantee of safety to Jerry's anonymous partners. On the other hand, it can be defended as a reasonable alternative that probably provides the most benefit and does the least amount of avoidable harm, under the circumstances, to Jerry and others. Despite this conclusion, the therapist may be left with a sense of moral regret that he cannot find a better solution.

Step 6—Identify Legal Concerns   The therapist might want to consult a lawyer regarding the legal implications of the options he is considering. A lawyer might point out that although the laws vary in most states there are no laws requiring that Jerry be reported. Burris, an expert in HIV law, (Barnett, Kitchener, & Burris, 2001) says, "Fifteen years into the HIV epidemic, there has yet to be a judicial opinion anywhere in the United States ruling that a psychotherapist is responsible to warn sexual or needle sharing contacts of patients with HIV, and I for one do not expect there ever will be one" (pp. 145–146).

In an excellent chapter that reviews the privacy laws in every state protecting information about a person with HIV status, Burris (2001) points out that the laws prohibit releasing any information except in very narrow circumstances. Furthermore, these notification laws apply almost universally only to physicians. In fact, at least two cases have held that strict HIV confidentiality laws override any duty a health care provider might have to warn even a patient's spouse of his HIV infection. In other words, privacy laws would protect Jerry's confidentiality. Consequently, there seem to be few viable options other than working with Jerry directly because informing the police would be a clear violation of privacy. The lawyer might also argue that the legal risk seems slight in this case. If Jerry's sexual partners are having anonymous sex with partners they identify in public places, it would be difficult for them to prove that Jerry transmitted the virus to them.

Step 7—Reassess Options and Identify a Plan   On the basis of the ethical analysis and legal advice, the therapist may conclude that both lead to a similar conclusion: the best option is to keep working with Jerry in an educative way, helping him to understand his behavior and the risks he is posing both to himself and others. In the long run, this approach may be the most protective of society as well as Jerry.

Step 8—Implement the Plan and Document the Process   The therapist may deem it clinically appropriate to inform Jerry about his own moral quandary as well as challenge Jerry's attitude and destructive behavior. He may also want to help Jerry find an HIV support group and educate him about opportunistic infections as well as transmission. The therapist might also engage Jerry in resolving the dilemma by saying something like, "Jerry, I find myself in an ethically awkward position. I worry about your welfare, and I also worry about your anonymous partners.

Can you help me resolve this?" Such an intervention may offer some protection for Jerry's partners and avoids the potential harm to him that could occur if trust were violated. Further, it does not add to the existing distrust between mental health professionals and those who have HIV, keeping open the possibility of intervening with other HIV-positive clients in a similar manner in the future.

Step 9—Reflect on the Outcome of Your Decision   The therapist should consider the effect of his intervention on Jerry and his behavior. These reflections may lead to new moral directions.

Model 2: Acting Ethically—An Ethical Choice Making Process

Although the above model focuses on decision making in Jerry's case and would fit with the second component of Rest's model. Model 2 fills in the other components which lead to acting morally. Below it is applied to Jerry's case.

Component 1—Ethical Sensitivity   In this component the practitioner is addressing the facts of the case, why the case is ethically problematic, how issues of diversity impact the choice making process, and personal values that may be impacting the professional's sensitivity to the issues. The therapist may do well to ask him or herself some of the following questions to increase ethical sensitivity: Does the information that Jerry is sharing with me cause me to feel uncomfortable? If I feel uncomfortable, does this hinder me from being as affective a therapist as I need to be and as sensitive to all the issues involved that exists? Am I overreacting or under reacting to Jerry's behaviors or choices because I want to be sensitive to the fact that Jerry is a gay man or because I am fearful or lack knowledge about the HIV virus? What are the issue of oppression and discrimination I need to recognize? Are my personal values or biases getting in the way of truly helping Jerry think through his choices at this time of perceived crisis in his mind?

Component 2—Formulating an Ethical Plan   In this component the practitioner is utilizing the facts to identify possible courses of action. In addition, questions in this component encourage perspective taking.

The psychologist begins to identify the key ethical issues. In this case the primary issue involves Jerry's sexual behavior (unprotected sex) that could result in other men being infected with the HIV virus. As previously stated, Component 2 is well addressed in the first model with the exception of two issues or questions. These two questions have to do with perspective taking. In this case the psychologist or counselor would do well to take a couple of minutes to think through: What should I share with Jerry about my decision? And, if I were Jerry what would I hope my therapist would do to assist me in an ethical manner? As previously discussed in the first model, there is no legal obligation in this case to report Jerry's behavior or breech his confidentiality. It appears that the greatest course of assistance that Jerry's psychotherapist can offer is to work with him on his emotions which appear to be driving his behavior.

Component 3—Ethical Motivation and Competing Values   These questions call for psychotherapists to identify conflicts of interest and their personal motivations and values that are competing with professional values in Jerry's case. This component might call into view the most difficult part of this scenario for the psychotherapist. The counselor or psychologist might have personal values or motivations that seem in conflict with the professional values. For example, the psychotherapist might hold personal values that sees that Jerry's behavior as reprehensible and must be stopped. But from a professional stance, the psychotherapist must find a way to work with Jerry in a compassionate and therapeutic way and uphold the professional value of confidentiality and ethical principles of autonomy and fidelity. There may be other conflicts within the psychotherapist that he or she is not initially aware of. One of the questions in this component works to uncover any subconscious conflicts: With whom might I consult to see the conflicts as clearly as possible? In exploring this question, the psychotherapist may become more aware of how personal values are impacting work with clients such as Jerry. Discussing the case with another professional and being honest about any personal conflicts will help uncover any of these concerns or values that may interfere with being an ethical professional. Finally, if there are multiple courses of action possible, the psychotherapist will do well to assess how Jerry will be harmed or benefit from each.

Component 4—Ethical Follow-Through The questions related to this component help the counselor or psychologist put in place the necessary supports to implement the ethical plan he or she developed in the second component. Whatever the plan is that the psychotherapist has made he or she can establish a timeline of what will be done by when. A trusted colleague may be helpful in remaining accountable. It may be that with good work and caring confrontation by the psychotherapist that Jerry will see his choices are actually fueling his feelings of anger and fear. It might also be that the psychotherapist can draw out Jerry's sense of compassion and empathy for others and help him make other choices that do not put others at risk.

Conclusion

Although the ethics codes and ethical principles provide guidance when people are faced with ethical problems, they are not panaceas as Jerry's case illustrates. In addition to being aware of the ethical issues, legal ones further complicate the process as do one's values and biases. In fact, the psychologists or counselors may need to consult with others about their own biases and erroneous thinking. Professionals need to carefully consider the options available and ask themselves what the consequences would be of acting on each. Even so, there may not be a perfect ethical solution. The decision they make should be ethically defensible and they must document each step they take and why they have taken it. Ultimately, their decision should provide the best balance of ethical harms and benefits while protecting individual rights.

Questions for Discussion or Consideration

1. Take the case you described earlier or one from the book and apply the first and second decision-making models to it.
2. How do the two decision-making models overlap? How do they complement each other?
3. How would you have handled the case of Jerry? Did you come to a similar conclusion or was your different? If different, why?

5

Beyond Ethical Decision Making

As discussed in Chapters 3 and 4, sometimes decisions need to be made that violate one ethical principle in order to uphold others or when it otherwise not possible to achieve an ethically perfect resolution. This often leaves us with a sense of moral regret as if we failed in some way. These feelings may lead us to question our decisions, and in some cases they will lead us to try to compensate for our less-than-perfect solution or for violating one ethical principle in order to uphold another. In response to a case like Jerry's (Case 4-2), one psychologist reported that although he decided to maintain his client's confidentiality for the reasons already articulated, he had a strong emotional reaction that led him to take further action. First, he met with his "Jerry" and expressed his concerns. Although his "Jerry" agreed to examine his behavior and sign a safe sex contract, the psychologist still felt uncomfortable. His observations follow:

> When I saw my first "Jerry," I struggled with finding peace with myself as I continued to provide him treatment. While his behavior did become more responsible, I was not sure when or how often he "slipped." So, I began to identify other options I could pursue that would help me feel better about what I was doing. First, I approached the local health department and asked them to post information about risky behavior and safe sex in adult bookstores and other areas of sexual activity. I got in touch with a local reporter who covered HIV issues in our community. She agreed to write a story that featured risks that many were taking as they engage in unprotected intercourse. One point of her study featured sex between men in public places (Barret, Kitchener, & Burris, 2001, pp. 151–152).

How do we understand this therapist's actions? We suspect most of us would agree that there was something special about him. He went beyond what is typically expected in a therapist's role and exhibited what sometimes gets called the highest standards of the profession. He exhibited compassion for his client and a responsibility to others in the community. At the same time he came to terms with his own values and was able to integrate them with his professional responsibilities. He exhibited the kind of behavior that we believe many of us would like to emulate but often fall short of exhibiting in our daily activities.

This example illustrates the limitations of a model of ethics that is based on ethical codes and ethical principles alone. If the psychologist had only acted upon the ethical codes and principles, he would not have felt obligated to contact the health department. Not only did he take the right action based on the code but he went further with his actions, he achieved what some have called "ethical excellence" (Anderson & Handelsman, 2010). By contrast, it is not difficult to identify situations in which psychologists or counselors knew the "right" thing to do but failed to act on that knowledge because of what might be called a "weakness of will." Take Case 5-1 as an example.

Case 5-1

Dr. James, a psychologist, is asked to supervise a new practitioner trying to accumulate hours for licensure. Although Dr. James is already very busy he agrees to do so, telling the supervisee to bring in any insurance forms for him to sign. Dr. James also tells the supervisee to keep track of his own hours and that he will sign off on them for licensure. The only time Dr. James sees the supervisee is when he comes in to sign insurance forms. Most often their meetings last less than 15 min, even though the state law calls for weekly supervision for a minimum of 1 h to discuss and review all of the supervisee's cases. When Dr. James is later confronted about his lax supervision, he admits that he was "cutting corners," but he defends his actions by saying that everyone knew the supervisee was a good psychologist, so he really did not need supervision.

Principle ethics alone cannot account for why some people know the right thing to do but fail to do it or why psychologists like the one in Case 5-1 cuts ethical corners, nor can it account for Barret's response to his first client like Jerry. Principle and rule bound ethics fail to address questions of moral character (Beauchamp & Childress, 2001; Fowers, 2005; Frankena, 1963; Hansen, 2008; Meara, Schmidt, & Day, 1996; Stewert-Sicking, 2008).

Virtue Ethics

In the past few years questions of character have been increasingly discussed in relationship to the professions of psychology and counseling under the rubric of virtue ethics (Fowers, 2005; Jordan & Meara, 1990; Meara & Day, 2003; Richardson, 2003; Tjeltveit, 2003). Meara et al. (1996) argued that virtue ethics, which attends to motivation, emotion, character, and ideals, presents "a more complete account of the moral life than actions based on rules or principles which can be applied detached from individuals, their aspirations and their communities" (p. 24). Some have argued that good moral character is more important than conformity to rules because a virtuous person is more likely to understand the principles and rules on which he or she acts. It is more likely that someone of good character will follow moral rules and principles than someone with bad character. In fact, Jordan and Meara (1990) have argued that character is critical, meaning that an ethical professional develops from being a virtuous person. To use an analogy borrowed from Brown (1994b) in another context, if you plant a seed in polluted soil the plant growing from the seed will probably be deformed. Consequently, if you try to teach someone of poor moral character to be ethical, what may grow is a deformed sense of ethical responsibility. Again, although this is an abstract idea, even Calvin from the *Calvin and Hobbes* comic strip understands that moral character is important in motivating people to be "good" (see Figure 5.1).

Annas (1993) suggested that modern ethics, principle ethics being one example, has been overly concerned with questions of "obligation, duty, and rule-following" (p. 4), whereas ancient virtue ethics focused on the intrinsic goodness and worth of the person. In other words, principle ethics focuses on the question of what I ought to do, whereas virtue ethics focuses on the question of what kind of person I should be (Meara et al., 1996; Pence, 1991) and it involves the person not just in their professional role but in their life as a whole. Although this difference is a subtle one it is not unimportant.

In fact, as the interest in virtue ethics has grown, so has some disillusionment with ethics based on rules and principles alone. As the last two chapters illustrated even when there are rules to follow and decision-making guides, many situations remain ambiguous, rely on good judgment or what some virtue ethicists, following the lead of Aristotle, call practical wisdom (Fowers, 2005).

Similarly, Noddings (1984), a feminist ethicist, has argued that current moral theory has focused too much attention on moral reasoning. In fact, she has rejected the ethics of principle as too ambiguous and unstable, suggesting that it leads to the false belief that there is more consistency in moral decision making than is the case. She argued that one must perceive the uniqueness of human encounters and conditions in order to act morally and that the moral person ought to focus on "how to meet the other morally" (Noddings, 1984, p. 4).

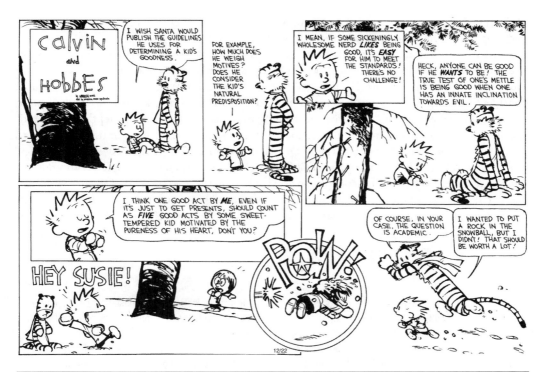

Figure 5.1 (Reprinted from Calvin and Hobbes ©1992 Watterson. Distributed by Universal Uclick. With permission. All rights reserved.)

It may be true, as Bersoff (2001) has argued that virtue ethics is irrelevant when an ethics committee adjudicates cases and that principle ethics is a valuable tool for resolving ethical dilemmas. On the other hand, although principles and rules can help decide whether an action is right or wrong, they cannot fully address whether a person is good or bad or what a fitting consequence should be for making an error. Take the student described in Case 1-1 as an example. Objectively, on the basis of moral rules she did not give appropriate authorship credit where credit was due, thus, objectively speaking, she was plagiarizing. Therefore, one could judge her actions as "wrong." The professor's dilemma, however, is not in judging the student's actions but in deciding how to respond in that particular situation. Because the student has typically exhibited integrity and good character in her interactions, he is troubled because she apparently had no intention of cheating. Undoubtedly, the professor would have been less perplexed if the student was someone who had a reputation for dishonesty or lack of integrity.

In the experience of the first author, sometimes similar considerations affect the outcome of the adjudication of ethics cases, both at the national and state level. Ethical errors that on the surface appear alike (e.g., two cases that involve breaching client confidentiality) do not always lead to similar sanctions even though the same rules or laws apply. Sometimes the circumstances, such as the defendant's remorse (or lack of it), work at remediation, or denial of responsibility justified the differences in sanctions. That is, judgments about a defendant's moral character sometimes appeared to make a difference in the sanctions that the committee imposed.

Although some (Foot, 1978; MacIntyre, 1981) have argued that principle-based ethics have to be abandoned, that is not what is being argued here. Principles and rules provide a common vocabulary to make moral decisions and to use when thinking through tough situations. However, as the above example illustrates, they may not be sufficient in evaluating the character of the person involved, in accounting for what it means to be an ethical professional, or even in deciding how to respond to a particular situation.

According to Beauchamp and Childress (2001), someone who has a virtuous moral character is predisposed to understand which moral choices should be made and more likely to act on moral ideals. Often people who are trusted to do what is morally right are ones who would be considered to have a strong or virtuous moral character. Others may know moral rules and in most cases adhere to them, sometimes begrudgingly, but seem to lack an in-depth understanding of what it means to be moral. Furthermore, they may cut corners even in their response to professional requirements, as was true of Dr. James, who failed to adequately supervise a new practitioner (Case 5-1). Beauchamp and Childress (2001) suggested that people's willingness to trust health care professionals depends to a great extent on their assessment of the professional's competence and character and that the rise in malpractice cases may reflect an erosion of trust in the character of professionals. Character goes deeper than memorizing rules or principles as the following case illustrates.

Case 5-2

During doctoral dissertation orals, a student was defending a dissertation that focused on developing a measure that would assess incest trauma. In the course of the defense, a committee member asked a question regarding the ethical problems involved in treating women who might have repressed memories in light of the controversies surrounding both the existence of such phenomena and the treatment of possible victims. The student had been taught the ethics code of her profession and the ethical principles articulated in Chapters 1–3. In the discussion, the student was able to articulate an approach to clinical work that was defensible ethically but failed to mention any of the ethical principles and only a few standards from the ethics code. Initially, the committee member was upset since she had been the instructor of the ethics course and despaired at her failure as a teacher as well as the student's failure to articulate the principles underlying her practice. Later, after sharing this concern with her, the student indicated that she had learned an attitude toward clients in the program that presumed she would act ethically. From the perspective of principle ethics, she had failed to defend her position, but from the perspective of virtue ethics, she had developed a good moral character.

What, then, do we mean by virtue ethics and virtuous character, and what does it add to principle ethics? As already noted, principles are normative generalizations that we have a prima facie obligation to uphold. They try to answer the question "What is the right thing to do?" When psychologists or counselors are unclear about their ethical responsibilities, ethical principles can be invaluable tools for sorting out rival ethical demands and obligations. They do not; however, answer the question of the nature of good moral character and how it develops.

According to Fowers (2005), "virtue ethics has a clear focus on the pursuit of goodness, the character strengths that make that pursuit possible, and the practical wisdom that guides ones seeking what is good" (p. xi). Unlike professional rules and principles, it involves the whole person—both professional and personal—since character is not something one leaves at the laboratory or office. We would not find someone of good character treating colleagues with genuine kindness and generosity and then going home and beating his or her children.

Although virtues and what Tjeltveit (2003) notes is the related term, character, have been defined in a variety of ways, he suggests they have to do with who a person is and the excellence of their qualities. In particular they have to do with the ethical qualities of people and what we see as particularly praiseworthy. Even though some in the behavioral sciences have tried to eliminate the ethical dimensions of character, to do so Tjeltveit argues, would omit essential characteristics of the person like honesty and courage.

Virtue ethics presumes that psychologists and counselors with good character will be better able to understand the moral dilemmas they face and to make good decisions about them. It involves questions about "what a 'good person' would do in real life situations?" (Pence, 1991, p. 249). A virtue from this perspective is a disposition to do the morally right thing and to have feelings and emotions that are consistent with it (Annas, 1993). As mental health professionals, we are concerned with the dispositions that are central to being a "good" or ethical professional. Although theses dispositions may be somewhat different for therapists, researchers, supervisors, or teachers, the position suggested in the following pages is that there is a strong commonality. Furthermore, codes of ethics acknowledge that we are committed to "goodness" in the very assertion that one goal of the professions is to advance human welfare (ACA, 2005; APA, 2002). If that is the case, advancing human welfare implies some concept of what the good life is (Tjeltveit, 2003).

The concept of a disposition or character trait implies a relatively stable set of characteristics that lead people to act in particular ways. These concepts should be familiar to psychologists because character traits derive from personality structure, and the study of personality has a long history in psychology (Drane, 1994). Unlike some personality theories, however, virtue ethics does not assume that a person's character is a given. That is, people are not born with a virtuous or vicious moral character. Although these qualities may build on inborn personality traits, they develop over time with practice, modeling, feedback, and teaching (Annas, 1993; Gert, 1988; MacIntyre, 1981) in a developing community (Fowers, 2005). From MacIntyre's (1981) perspective, people develop virtue by understanding the moral tradition from which they come but then criticize those traditions and adjust their understanding accordingly. Good community values can remind us of what we aspire to become as moral persons. Through critical reflection on community values, people develop an overall picture of what it means to be moral. Others have suggested that this process is somewhat like reflective equilibrium (Annas, 1993), where people act and then reflect on their actions; character develops during the process.

On the other hand, some community values may not be worth idealizing. As Friedman (1989/1992) noted, "many communities are characterized by practices of exclusion and suppression of nongroup members, especially outsiders defined by ethnicity and sexual orientation" (p. 106). What is important, she argued, is to identify community expectations and obligations "that are not oppressive or exploitative" and that fit our "radically heterogeneous modern society" (Friedman, 1989/1992, p. 107). In other words, we need to identify virtues that have been essential to the community of psychology or counseling, with an eye for values that do not exploit others. Meara and Day (2003) note that pluralism or multiculturalism, both of which mental health professionals embrace, provide challenges for the development of virtuous communities. This is because they by definition involve differences among people, including values and worldviews. These values and world views are not always consistent with each other leaving the person with a sense of uncertainty about which set of values, he or she should emulate. Fowers (2005) argues that it is practical wisdom that allows people to discern what values are praiseworthy and those that use erroneous and convoluted reasoning to justify practices like exclusion and oppression or worse still murder as was the case with the Nazis.

Although it is important to ask which virtues are central to the practice of psychology and counseling, it is also important to remember that a person's character consists of more than a set of particular virtues. Someone might exhibit a certain virtue such as courage or dependability, but still not be someone we consider having good moral character. To have good character means striving to be ethical in one's practice and in life. Although being perfectly virtuous is an ideal to which people can only aspire, all psychologists and counselors can work to develop a stronger moral character.

To reiterate a point made earlier, even people of high moral character sometimes fail to perceive what they ought to do when faced with a moral crisis (Beauchamp & Childress, 2002). As a result, even those with a virtuous character need principles and rules to provide important guidance in deciding the best moral action in difficult situations. Furthermore, as Beauchamp and Childress (1989) noted,

> public rules remind us of the moral minimum expected of everyone, and sanctions may both deter morally good (but imperfect) persons from succumbing to temptations to cut moral corners and prevent morally untrustworthy persons from immoral conduct. (p. 383)

These observations do not diminish the point that character plays an essential role in identifying what it means to be an ethical psychologist or counselor.

What Moral Virtues are Essential to Psychology and Counseling?

Although many psychologists and counselors would probably agree that having good character is important for ethical behavior, it may be more difficult to agree on how that character should be described. In fact, it is sometimes easier and leads to greater clarity to identify what is considered bad character (Gert, 1988; Pence, 1984). For example, there would probably be little disagreement that someone who was deceitful, cruel, dishonest, and untrustworthy was not exhibiting the characteristics of a morally good professional.

Beauchamp and Childress (2001), Frankena (1963), and Gert (1988) have suggested that because virtue or character is linked to the motivation for moral action, most principles have a corresponding character trait that predisposes a person to act on that principle. Thus, for Frankena, the two overarching principles are beneficence and justice and the corresponding virtues are benevolence and being just. Beauchamp and Childress added that respectfulness is necessary to uphold respect for autonomy and that nonmalevolence is necessary to uphold the principle of doing no harm. Similarly, we could argue that faithfulness, truthfulness, trustworthiness, and honesty provide the foundation for upholding the principle of fidelity. This is not to say, however, that all virtues correspond to moral principles. We might argue, for example, that psychologists and counselors ought to be kind; however, there is no moral principle that corresponds with kindness.

The issue becomes whether there are qualities that are internal to the practice of psychology or counseling that are essential to the character of a moral professional or whether there are some qualities that need special articulation. Meara et al. (1996) identified key characteristics of virtuous individuals like those in professions such as psychology and counseling. Some of these characteristics include the motivation to take the right action because it appears to be the correct action to take, the professional is not motivated out of obligation or fear; sensitivity and compassion for others who are hurting; and self awareness that alerts the professional to biases or assumptions that impact the work with others. It is difficult to identify all of the traits that are central to being a good professional without coming up with what sounds like a laundry list of virtues. Beauchamp and Childress (2001), for example, focused on compassion, discernment, trustworthiness, conscientiousness and integrity as being particularly important to medicine, and Meara et al. (1996) identified prudence, integrity, respectfulness, and benevolence as being basic to moral character in psychology. By contrast, based on Aristotle, Fowers (2005) argues that practical wisdom is the central virtue. He notes that one of the most difficult parts of virtue ethics is the almost complete absence of rules for acting because circumstances vary so widely. This is why we must rely on people's ability to choose wisely.

However, in keeping with Meara et al.'s (1996) analysis, the virtues of prudence (or practical wisdom), integrity, and respectfulness (or being tolerant) are emphasized here. Our analysis departs somewhat from theirs in also advocating trustworthiness and compassion (or care).

We see these virtues as being important for the practice of psychology and counseling when they are considered broadly to include science, clinical practice, and teaching. Of course there may be other important virtues but the question that really needs to be answered is, "What kind of character is essential for being a good psychologist or counselor?"

Practical Wisdom or Prudence

Aristotle and other ancient Greek philosophers (Annas, 1993) agreed that to be virtuous one must have *phronesis*. *Phronesis* is a Greek word that has no direct translation. It has been variously translated as practical reasoning, wisdom, practical wisdom, intelligence, discernment, or prudence (Annas, 1993). Although somewhat of an archaic term, the concept of prudence or practical wisdom captures what is meant in the discussion that follows. Partially an intellectual characteristic, prudence refers to the ability to reason well about moral matters and apply that reasoning to real-world problems in a firm but flexible manner. Annas (1993) suggested that whatever else it is, "it is the disposition to make right moral judgments" (p. 73). Whatever it is called part of being an ethical psychologist or counselor involves acting carefully and with good judgment, but also with the right emotional intensity.

> Calling it a prudence, Meara et al. (1996) suggested that it involves appropriate restraint or caution, deliberate reflection upon which moral action to take, an understanding of the long-range consequences of the choices made, acting with due regard for one's vision of what is morally good, and a knowledge of how present circumstances relate to that good or goal. (p. 39)

They also suggested that prudence implies knowing when and how to apply principles to a particular case and recognizing and accepting the uncertainty of ethical questions (Meara & Day, 2003).

Beauchamp and Childress (2001), calling a similar virtue "discernment," emphasized the judgment component, suggesting that it includes the ability to understand a situation and make a good judgment about it without being unduly influenced by extraneous pressures. They associated discernment with practical wisdom suggesting that a practically wise person knows how to act with the correct intensity of emotions at the right time and in the right way. They understand how rules and principles should be applied and have the courage to apply them.

Fowers (2005) suggested practical wisdom involves being able to respond well and fittingly to one circumstances as one seeks what is good. It allows the person to know what goods are worthwhile and have the strength to pursue those aims. For Fowers it involves three components: moral perception of what is at stake, deliberation about what is possible, and reasoning among choices to decide which is the best course of action. Moral perception involves discerning the essential components or features of the situation. It is not limited to seeing what is right or wrong but rather what is most important and valuable. A person of good character is able to perceive the moral dimensions of the situation. Second, deliberation involves reflecting on how to ascertain the best goods given the circumstances and it involves the ability to respond well in situations of uncertainty. Last reasoned choices involve a reflective capacity. This sense includes considering what the results of one's actions might be. The point is that it has a social component as individuals reflect with others about the best course of action, not just to protect themselves, but to understand the consequences of their actions for individuals and the community.

Following Fowers (2005), we will primarily use the term "practical wisdom" because it is intuitively more understandable than "discernment" or "prudence." There is a psychological literature on wisdom that may help in understanding its nature and how it develops. Last, it doesn't carry some of the more negative connotations of words like "prudence" which for example, can be confused with "prudery" or someone who shows excessive concern with modesty. In addition, Fowers points to other negative connotations like "caution, calculation, and frugality" (p. 107).

Fowers keeps the concept of goodness open-ended because the historical community's ideas about the nature of goodness evolve over time as new circumstances and contacts with other cultural groups evolve. However, good and goods refer to accomplishments that are worthwhile. He argues that people in reasonably coherent societies are guided by a more or less shared of understanding of what is good, thus, mental health professionals taken as a community hold certain values in common. He points to honesty as one such value that cuts across all the roles that mental health professionals play. It takes practical wisdom, however, to know when honesty is called for and when it is not.

As a psychological construct, practical wisdom or prudence is interesting because it overlaps with many concepts studied in psychology under the general rubric of judgment or decision making. Although it is beyond the scope of this book to explore these links, counseling and psychology may have an important contributions to make in understanding how practical wisdom develops and operates in the real world. As an example, some extent distinctions that Fowers makes are similar to the categories that Rest (1994) identified as the psychological components of ethical action that were discussed in the last chapter. For a discussion of the literature on wisdom and judgment see Fowers (2005) and Sternberg (1990).

Meara et al. (1996) argued that the concept of prudence (practical wisdom) underlies much of the language of ethics codes because terms such as ordinarily, reasonable, feasible, and when professionally appropriate are used throughout to modify the applicability of the standards. Although Bersoff (1994) and Koocher (1994b) have criticized such language as providing loopholes for the person of poor moral character, from Meara et al.'s perspective, the language provides the occasion for the operation practical wisdom in ethical judgment. They argued that such language recognizes that there are few absolutes in the ethics of daily life and that application of standards to particular situations involves good judgment. They also emphasized that practical wisdom is necessary for operating in complex multicultural situations in which it is important to recognize that others may be operating with a different understanding of the situation or with a different worldview of what a good outcome might be. The prudent professional acts carefully and wisely in such situations, considering the feelings and perceptions of other parties.

Even if practical wisdom or prudence is the central virtue, there are character strengths that cut across the roles that psychologists and counselors play. Fowers (2005) agrees that there are some that are central. He uses honesty as an example pointing to its necessity in research, practice and teaching noting, however, that practical wisdom is necessary to know when it is appropriate to be honest and at other times misguided. For example, although honesty is important in therapy this does not mean a therapist should blatantly say everything he or she is thinking. It takes wisdom to know when the right moment is for honesty and how it should be expressed. What follows are those characteristic strengths that we see as necessary for the many roles played by psychologists and counselors?

Integrity

As noted earlier, it is sometimes easier to identify the absence of particular virtues than their presence. Such is the case with integrity. It is probably easier to describe the characteristics of someone who does not have integrity than someone who does. For example, we might identify those who are insincere in their promises or cannot be counted on to uphold their moral values as lacking integrity. Beauchamp and Childress (1994) added to this list those who are hypocrites, those who act in bad faith, and those who deceive themselves about their motives. Each of these examples, they suggested represents a break in the connections between "a person's moral convictions, actions, and emotions" (Beauchamp & Childress, 1994, p. 472). They argued that the most fundamental deficiency in people with a lack of integrity is the absence of core values. Such people fail to exhibit a commitment to any moral position or are inconsistent. They waiver and waffle under the influence of other's directions.

The word integrity comes from the Latin word *integri* which means something acts as a whole (Halfon, 1989). In current usage, to say someone has integrity suggests a characteristic of his or her whole life. However, this definition does not capture completely what is meant by integrity as a moral virtue because even the life of someone who had poor moral character could have a wholeness or consistency to it.

A second definition of integrity is a "firm adherence to a code of, especially, moral or artistic values" (*Webster's Ninth New Collegiate Dictionary*, 1988). This is closer to what is meant by integrity in this context. Halfon (1989) suggested that "persons of integrity characteristically maintain a consistent commitment to do what is best especially under conditions of adversity" (p. 8). Here, "doing what is best" implies "doing what is morally best." Although ideally, it could be clearly defined by the principles and rules articulated in the earlier chapters, in fact, as Fowers (2005) points out doing what is morally best involves a judgment, informed by practical wisdom.

To have integrity means that we uphold standards even when upholding them might not be popular and may be difficult for other reasons (related to Rest's last component of moral follow through). For example, psychologists and counselors who are tempted to look the other way when a colleague is behaving on ethically but choose instead to confront the colleague have integrity even though the confrontation could cause stress in the relationship. Similarly, Beauchamp and Childress (1994) pointed to C. Everett Koop, the U.S. Surgeon General under Ronald Reagan, as a man of integrity. His belief in the sanctity of human life led him to both oppose abortions and to promote the use of condoms to help combat the spread of AIDS. The first position was condemned by liberals and the second by conservatives, but from his perspective, both positions were consistent with his commitment to saving human lives. His actions fit both definitions of integrity. They had a wholeness or overall consistency, and they reflected a commitment to a consistent set of moral principles, which he upheld in the face of much political criticism. In fact, when we refer to someone as having integrity, we typically mean that it is a characteristic moral stance toward others or objects that is maintained over time.

To use a more recent example, this chapter was written in the early days of Barack Obama's presidency. In his acceptance speech, his speech about African Americans, and in his inaugural address, he emphasized the importance of working together, of overcoming party loyalties and listening to what others have to say, of community, and of hope. It was interesting that some of the political commentators noted that at his inauguration there was true joy in the crowd. It seems like, at least at that point, there was a belief that we had finally elected a man of integrity, a man of moral principles who would uphold them even in the face of criticism.

As Meara et al. (1996) pointed out the 1992 APA ethics code identified integrity as one of the primary aspirational goals for psychologists. It implored psychologists to promote integrity "in the science, teaching and practice of psychology," implying that psychologists should act on justifiable moral values, such as honesty and respectfulness, in all aspects of their work. The same was true in the 2002 APA code which added that psychologists should not "steal, cheat, or engage in fraud, subterfuge or deliberate misrepresentation of the facts."

Several authors (Beauchamp & Childress, 1994; Halfon, 1989; Meara et al., 1996) have noted that the downside of integrity is rigidity. There is a fine line between being consistent in upholding important moral values and failing to compromise when compromise is appropriate. It may be that deep moral values, like the commitment to help and not harm others, should not be sacrificed, but compromise may be necessary when considering how they are implemented with a particular cultural group or with different individuals. This is when practical wisdom becomes important. Halfon suggested that a person of integrity does not have a blind commitment to act on particular principles but rather has a commitment to do what is best when all things are considered. It is also important that the individual believes that he or she is pursuing a morally justified course of action. If the person believes that he or she is acting immorally, integrity is compromised.

The question of when and under what circumstances moral principles can and should be compromised is a complex one and beyond the scope of this chapter. It is, however, important to recognize that caution needs to be exercised in blindly adhering to moral principles. This observation underscores the importance of the interrelationship between integrity and practical wisdom. Whereas integrity emphasizes commitment to moral values, to know how to interpret it requires good judgment. Taken together, both help provide the basis for serving the public in a morally defensible way. As Meara et al. (1996) argued, "professionals who demonstrate prudence and integrity will make good ethical decisions, develop sound ethical policies and deservedly enjoy public trust" (p. 43).

Respectfulness

The third virtue that Meara et al. (1996) argued was central for the character of psychologists is respectfulness. Most accounts of respectfulness suggest it is an attitude that is marked by a willingness to take into consideration particular concerns of others, especially when our actions might affect them (Darwell, 1992). That is, we should consider others' wants or points of view. Again, to choose a negative example, lack of respectfulness may lead to racism, sexism and any of the other negative "isms" because the fundamental respect to which individuals are due is not given.

Darwell (1992) suggested that there are two kinds of respect. The first, appraisal respect, is directed toward people or features that exhibit some kind of excellence; thus, we might respect someone for being an excellent behavior therapist. The second, recognition respect, involves giving moral recognition to some aspect of a person, such as racial background, gender, or disability, or to an object, such as the law or social institution. It does not specify, however, how we should treat people or social institutions.

It is respect in the second sense that seems particularly important in psychology. Darwell (1992) argued that respecting individuals in this sense involves regarding them in a way that restricts our moral behavior toward them, thus, being respectful would restrict us from acting in a, for example, sexist or racist way toward them. It is for this reason that Meara et al. (1996) argued that respectfulness is critical for psychologists who operate in a culturally diverse society. They pointed to an account by Darou, Hum, and Kurtness (1993) of an incident in which a native Canadian group, the Crees, ejected several researchers because they failed to respect the Cree culture, its authority structure, and its expectations with regard to conducting research. The incident illustrates that the meaning of respectfulness may vary depending on the culture in which the person is embedded and may extend beyond the individual to social or cultural institutions.

On the surface, respectfulness is linked to being tolerant of others, however, tolerance implies a sympathy for beliefs or practices that are different from our own and allowing those practices and beliefs to continue without interference. Respectfulness implies we must do something more than simply tolerate people's differences. It implies that we see the person as having value just because they are living being.

Again, both APA (1992, 2002) and ACA (2005) ethics codes have acknowledged the importance of respectfulness; the APA codes specified that psychologists respect the "fundamental rights, dignity, and worth of all people." They also specified how psychologists should be respectful: they should respect the rights of individuals to privacy, confidentiality, self-determination, and autonomy, as well as be aware of cultural, individual, and role differences. Although slightly less explicit, the 2005 ACA ethics code required counselors to "respect dignity" of clients when promoting their welfare. On the other hand, although the codes mandate that all psychologists and counselors act respectfully, it cannot require that they develop an attitude that makes such behavior more than conformity to rules. Thus, one must attend to virtuous character as well as to principles and rules. It also underscores the relationship between the virtue of practical wisdom and respectfulness. Practical wisdom may be necessary to discern the way respect should be expressed.

As Beauchamp and Childress (2001) noted respectfulness can be taken to an extreme and become an excuse for blind obedience to authority or for an unwillingness to be reasonably critical when criticism is important. As with integrity, respectfulness taken to the extreme may become a vice.

Trustworthiness

Trustworthiness is central to every role psychologists or counselors play. To trust someone implies that we can rely on his or her character, truthfulness, ability to get something done, strength of character, and so on. We have confidence in that person. Beauchamp and Childress (1994) observed that, "trust is a confident belief in and reliance upon the ability and moral character of another person. Trust entails a confidence that another will act with the right motives in accord with moral norms" (p. 469). Baier (1993) argued that trustworthiness is at the core of the virtues that women such as Gilligan (1993) see as absent from much of current moral discourse. Trustworthiness, she suggested, is what binds relationships between parent and child, teacher and student, and so on. Trustworthiness is certainly central for the researcher. If they are not trustworthy then their results are not either. Consequently if the results cannot be trusted then it undermines the basic foundations of the science of psychology or counseling.

Trusting someone always involves taking a risk because when trust is given we make ourselves vulnerable. Therefore, appropriate trustworthiness suggests that others' trust in us will not be misplaced (Baier, 1993). This is clearly an essential trait for therapists because therapy is dependent on the client's trust of the therapist. A similar argument can be made for teaching and research, however. Students trust their instructors to provide them with accurate information and reasonable insight, and research participants trust researchers not to harm them needlessly.

Ethics codes are almost strangely silent on issues of trust, although it was mentioned briefly in the 2002 APA Ethics Code under the principle of fidelity. In fact, it appears that codes provide rules to take the place of a trustworthy character, establishing rules regarding deception in research, not lying to the public about research results, not stealing others' ideas through plagiarism, forbidding sexual relationships with clients and former clients, and being accurate and objective in teaching. All are protections against untrustworthy psychologists or counselors. It is possible that the codes are silent because of an assumption that trustworthiness is included in the ethical virtues of respect and integrity.

Care or Compassion

Beauchamp and Childress (1994) argued that compassion for others is vital for the character of health professionals. Similarly, Drane (1994) argued that people of all ages and cultures "expect their healers to be gentle, caring and concerned primarily for them" (p. 301). If compassion is defined as deep concern and empathy for another's welfare and sympathy or uneasiness with another's misfortune or suffering (Beauchamp & Childress, 1994), it has much in common with the concept of care as described by Gilligan (1982, 1993). From a multicultural perspective, compassion, or care, has also been identified as critical to the character of helping professionals. Ratanakul (1994) argued that from a Theravada Buddhist point of view, the importance of compassion supersedes all principles because it involves the obligation to enhance the well-being of others and to alleviate their suffering just because they are human. He calls such compassion "loving care" (Ratanakul, 1994, p. 127). Furthermore, from a Latin American perspective, dos Anjos (1994, p. 133) urged those in health-related fields to allow themselves to feel solidarity with those who suffer and see with their heart.

The ethics of care has been much debated in feminist psychology and philosophy (Brabeck, 1989; Larrabee, 1993). Noddings (1984), who has provided one of the most complete discussions of care, argued that to be ethical we must be caring in our relationships with others. She argued that ethical caring arises from our experience with natural caring, those instances when people naturally respond out of love. It is a special kind of love, however, because it requires a commitment from the "one-caring" to act on behalf of the other person or to at least reflect on what should be done. In other words, it requires a kind of practical wisdom to know when acting on behalf of someone would be helpful and when it would not.

To act out of care is not to respond in terms of fixed rules or principles but out of affection and regard for another who is in a particular circumstance. The goal is to promote the well-being of the other; thus, in Noddings' terms, the "one-caring" should act in such a way as to bring about a favorable outcome for the "cared-for." Unfortunately, many psychologists who meet the moral minimum in their work never treat a student, research participant, or client with kindness or care (Kitchener & Anderson, 2000).

Care, as Noddings (1984) conceived of it, is not a simple notion. It requires a mental toughness that allows the "one-caring" to decide what to do for the other person as well as to care for oneself, and it requires never sacrificing a person for a principle. Elaborating on this idea, Churchill (1994) noted that principles can be abused when they are valued above the concerns of real people. In his words, it is an error to deify principles, so that they have an "intrinsic value, as things to be protected, rather than a means to respect and protect persons" (Churchill, 1994, p. 326). Thus, principles should never be used as an excuse to treat someone without care or as an object. To do so, Noddings (1984) suggested, would diminish the ethical ideal because being ethical depends "upon the will to be good, to remain in caring relation to the other" (p. 103).

The virtue of care, or compassion, should remind counselors and psychologists that fulfilling role responsibilities and acting on rules need to be moderated by an awareness of the people with whom they are dealing. For example, even if the professor in Case 1-2 decides that the student cheated on her paper, the responsibility to treat the student with care remains. Acting with care or compassion would mean trying to understand the student's pain, to perceive the situation through her eyes doing some perspective taking, and to make an initial commitment to remediation. As Noddings (1984) maintained "an ethic of care is likely to be stricter in its judgment, but more supportive and corrective in following up its judgment, than ethics otherwise grounded" (p. 93). This does not mean that the professor should abrogate responsibility to consider whether the student has a serious defect in her character that would undermine her ability to be an ethical professional. As a faculty person, one of the responsibilities is that of a gatekeeper to the profession and this means balancing the obligation to the student and to the public the student will eventually serve (Anderson & Handelsman, 2010). In this particular case the professor should act in a way that preserves the possibility of future care until that alternative is no longer available. Remediation could be offered as an alternative to severing the ties with the student, which would occur if she were dismissed from the graduate program. This provides a way to preserve the possibility of caring. If, however, the student makes a similar error in the future or in some other way leads the professor to believe that she cannot become an ethical and competent professional, then there may be no alternative than to dismiss her from graduate study (Kitchener, 1999). Ultimately, the lack of an alternative, according to Noddings, diminishes the ethical ideal but would not rescind the responsibility of the professor to act. Similarly, a caring or compassionate response to the institutionalized adult described in Case 2-1 would require receptivity to that person's pain and fear about leaving the only home he has known as well as a responsibility to respond to him in a caring way, no matter what decision is made about his placement.

As with other virtues, caring, when taken to an extreme or conceptualized in a self-serving manner, can be a vice. When taken to an extreme, care can lead to parentalism, the view that "I know what is best for you." As discussed in the previous chapter, this view can seriously undermine people's rights to make their own decisions and is often disrespectful. When caring is conceived in a self-serving way, it can also "cloud judgment and preclude rational and effective responses" (Beauchamp & Childress, 1994, p. 467). For example, consider Case 5-3.

Case 5-3

A psychologist admits falling "in love" with one of her patients, a man who has recently lost his job. Because she has a spare room, she invites him to live in her home for a few weeks, excusing herself from the rule on avoiding multiple-role relationships by rationalizing that she should respond to the particular circumstances of her client. Eventually, her life becomes increasingly entangled with his and they enter into a sexual relationship. After several years, the former patient, now lover, terminates the relationship and files a complaint against the psychologist claiming that he has been irrevocably harmed by the therapist's actions. When confronted, the therapist claims that she did nothing wrong because she "cared for" her patient and continues to do so.

The psychologist in this example has lost her objectivity and ability to enter a rational-objective mode in order to decide how to act on behalf of her client. She uses caring as an excuse to meet her own needs and loses sight of his well-being. Fowers (2005) would argue and we would agree that it takes practical wisdom to know how and when to act compassionately. Perhaps because people are vulnerable and can lose touch with their natural impulse to act on behalf of the other, Noddings (1984) suggested that moral principles, such as those described in Chapter 3, can provide guidance.

On the other hand, Noddings (1984) also warned of the dangers of moral principles: "Too often, principles separate us from each other. We may become dangerously self-righteous when we perceive ourselves as holding a precious principle not held by the other" (p. 5). Hence, ethical principles and rules can sometimes be used as clubs to force others into submission and can become an excuse to forgo caring about or acting on behalf of another. When this happens, the ethical ideal is diminished. In fact, in the experience of the first author with ethics committees and grievance boards, this is their greatest weakness. It is easy for them to fall into a self-righteous stance when others have failed to uphold ethical standards or laws and treat them as objects. It is difficult, perhaps impossible, to reprimand someone and still remain in a caring attitude toward the person who has made the error. This is particularly true when the acts they have committed have been egregiously harmful. However, when ridicule, scorn, sarcasm, and other attributions of evil are heaped on those who have made ethical errors, it undermines the ethical ideal and, ultimately, diminishes a caring, ethical attitude in psychology or counseling.

We have also noticed that when students initially become acquainted with ethics, they sometimes develop an attitude of superiority toward others and their failings. It is important to remind students, "Unethical behaviors are not restricted to a type or class of psychotherapist. We are human with complex motivations …. Consequently, we are all capable of unethical behaviors" (Anderson & Handelsman, 2010, p. 87). Thus, it is important that they be reminded not to lose touch with ethical virtues such as caring, kindness, and humility.

From this perspective, ethical virtues in general, and the virtue of care or compassion in particular, are not antithetical to an ethic based on principles and rules; rather, they complement it.

Considerations of both moral principles and virtues make it possible to have a more comprehensive view of what it means to be an ethical psychologist or counselor who upholds the highest standards of the profession. A belief in the importance of care, for example, may be combined with recognition that people who are caring may sometimes not know what to do and may suffer from weakness of will. As Veatch (1981) observed, "the trick is knowing what the loving thing to do is in the crises of a situation" (p. 42). Further, the virtue of care or compassion may remind psychologists and counselors steeped in rules and principles that acting without care may lead to a sterile and sometimes dangerous application of those principles.

Virtue Ethics in Practice, Research, and Teaching

A comprehensive discussion of the application of virtue ethics in practice, research and teaching would require an entire book. However, some brief introductions may be helpful. Although Fowers (2005) discusses how practical wisdom is central to these three tasks, his examples aren't ethical per se but focus on wisdom as it is used in counseling interventions or in wisely choosing research topics. Perhaps that is what he means when he says virtues are both personal and professional and make up the core of the person. The next section will focus on some particularly difficult ethical issues that occur in psychotherapy, teaching, and research.

Psychotherapy

Even choosing goals for clients is an ethical decision. Some therapists may choose the same basic goals for clients assuming as Tjeltveit (2000) notes that the "goodness, rightness and/or virtue of these goals applies to all clients" (p. 208). However, goals may need to be tailored to cultural contexts, the issues at stake, and others who may be influenced by those goals like the children, spouse, and friends. For example, a particularly good marriage and family therapist in the vicinity refuses to see clients whose immediate goal is to get a divorce. He argues that he knows too many in the community in addition to the couple, may be harmed by that choice. He needs to know it is a beneficial decision for all involved and kindly refers them to other therapists.

Several authors have noted that the traditional goals of Western psychotherapy that emphasize autonomy and independence may not be appropriate for those of a nonWestern background. Richardson (2003) argues that it takes openness and personal strength to engage in dialogue with those of different backgrounds in order to establish goals or to discern what point of view makes better sense in terms of the motives and circumstances with which someone else struggles. On the other hand, Tjeltveit argues that some goals may in fact be universally applicable ethical truths like the need for safe parental care for children but these ethical truths need to be altered to some degree to meet individual needs and backgrounds.

Richardson argues that modern psychotherapy has bought too heavily into the liberal individualistic view of things and may perpetuate some of the problems it addresses in the suggestions it has for curing them. "It offers yet more liberation, personal self-realization, and empowerment to people who often hunger, in part, for more lasting social ties, a wider sense of purpose, greater modesty and simplicity, and perhaps a credible spiritual sense of life" (p. 449). He points to the increased isolation of people as they withdraw into their private lives and hand over many social problems to various kinds of experts like psychologists or counselors. To some extent, he is suggesting that psychotherapy may be part of the cause of the rampant self-centeredness and egocentrism that seems to permeate our culture.

We propose that virtue ethics does not offer rules or principles for conducting therapy or what to do with clients, but rather it asks questions about the very foundations of the process. That is not to say it does not have something to offer when considering issues like confidentiality or informed consent. As already noted, psychotherapy could not be successful without wisdom, trustworthiness, compassion, respectfulness or integrity. What client would sign a consent form without trusting the person to whom he or she is giving consent? Similarly, how could clients divulged innermost secrets to someone they did not trust or who did not have some compassion for them?

Research

Two of the primary goals of the university are the creation and dissemination of knowledge through teaching and community service. These goals which bind the academic community have some particular ramifications in psychology and counseling and have implications for the virtues expected of academicians, both researchers and instructors. Meara and Day (2003) identify four. First, the subject matter of psychology is personal in the sense that it touches on issues that are of particular importance to human beings like intelligence, emotion, interpersonal relationships, gender issues, race relations and family dynamics to name a few. Each of these can carry implications for both students and their professors and may evoke personal comparisons and other emotional reactions some of which may be beneficial and others not. Second, although all scientific findings have some degree of uncertainty, because of the probabilistic nature of psychological findings and statistical methodologies, psychological science is particularly subject to the uncertainties of science. They note, for example, individual differences make psychological measurement particularly difficult and the findings open to more than one interpretation. Third, the diverse theoretical perspectives from humanistic to behavioristic that can be brought to bear on data add to the uncertainty in the interpretation of research findings. Last, because the culture of the United States places a great deal of confidence in the ability of experts to solve difficult social problems and because psychology often focuses its attention on social issues, psychological research and psychologists are often asked to provide opinions on a wide range of social issues which may have important policy implications. Consequently, those involved in the psychological research enterprise have a particular responsibility to the ethical in their pursuits as scientists.

There are many temptations in academia to stretch data, to over interpret it, or to deviate in the description of the methodology because of the tenure system, the incitements of fame, and even the page limitations in journals. However, to succumb to such temptations undermines the goals of the university and the creation of knowledge. Furthermore, they may mislead the public into making policy decisions that are erroneous or harmful. This is why the virtues of trustworthiness and honesty are so important in science.

Here, practical wisdom is also essential in the creation of truly innovative ways to investigate issues of importance that do not harm the participants and lead to new insights about important issues. Good ethical scientists need to be sensitive to the issues at hand which allow them clarity about what issues and questions are important to investigate. Deliberation is a characteristic of any good science particularly in defining research questions, choosing the appropriate statistical techniques to analyze and interpreting the data. Fowers (2005) argues that accomplished researchers use wisdom naturally, knowing how to capture what is lacking in the literature and the courage and clarity to pursue it. Sometimes academicians get caught up in counting publications and the endless publication mill rather really evaluating the importance of the questions they are asking. It takes integrity to both avoid the temptations that undermine the creation of knowledge and it takes practical wisdom to astutely ask and answer questions that will produce work of significance.

Although respectfulness and compassion do not necessarily seem central to research, it should be remembered that in most psychological research, humans are volunteering their time and energy to participate in projects that may not provide them with any immediate benefits. As Meara and Day (2003) have said, "respectfulness goes beyond the Western notion of respect for autonomy and includes understanding of, and being sensitive to, others' definitions of the situation and how they would like to be regarded, treated, and appreciated" (p. 468). Similarly, in studies using animals, there are few excuses for treating them cruelly.

Teaching

Trustworthiness and honesty are as important in the classroom as they are in the creation of knowledge. As Fowers (2005) has pointed out trustworthiness and honesty are critical in providing a balanced point of view of the subject matter and allowing students to question whether the supervisor's or instructor's points of view are accurate without fear of repercussions. Furthermore, they teach students about the importance of truth in psychology and in counseling. These are not always easy virtues to model since sometimes they reveal our weaknesses and our blind spots. They do however encourage dialogues with students about sometimes difficult or painful issues since honest feedback about performance is not always easy to give or to get. Yet, for the graduate student to develop into an excellent researcher or psychotherapist both are necessary. For example, sexual feelings in psychotherapy are difficult issues for students to discuss even though data suggests they are quite common (see Chapter 12). Consequently, one of the authors would sometimes share her experience the first time she felt a sexual attraction to a client. Whether or not to share of the information was dependent on timing, the nature of the class, and wisdom about whether or not it would help or harm the discussion. Sometimes her honesty and sense of integrity about the issue allowed students to talk more freely about the issue.

Practical wisdom is also essential in knowing how and when to intervene with students both in the classroom and in supervision. Because the subject matter of psychology or counseling is uncertain but also can be very personal to students, what is said in the classroom can sometimes be mistakenly over generalized to others or to the self (Meara & Day, 2003). Even in casual conversations with administrators, colleagues, or students, academic psychologists or counselors may be ask for their advice on a variety of personal matters. It takes wisdom to know how to handle such situations without leaving someone with misinformation or incorrect interpretations. In addition, even in choosing classroom assignments professors must be careful about boundary issues both because of multicultural issues and because some assignments may lead students to reveal personal information that they might later regret. A professor must also consider carefully with wisdom both what and how material is presented, so that is fully understood and not misunderstood. Questions should be answered respectfully and with care since students are often hesitant to share their points of view for fear of being seen as foolish or uninformed. This is not always easy since students, especially those who have less investment in being or staying in college, are not always respectful of professors—walking out in the middle of lectures, whispering in the back row, texting with friends, and so on. Ethics codes have nothing to say about such situations. It takes a wise professor to know how to handle such situations discreetly. Sometimes the students resist any interventions and the best a professor can do is to ask the student to leave class because of his or her disruptive behavior. As Noddings (1984) has noted this may diminish the ethical ideal, but it does not excuse the professor from acting.

Integrity is particularly important in the teaching of psychology because of its subject matter. As already noted, it can be a highly personal subject and individuals may generalize it to themselves or others whether or not it is applicable. Consequently, Meara and Day (2003) point to the importance of integrity to both the credibility and reliability of what academics teach their students. Because the substance of psychology may be so important, it is particularly critical to remain current in the field and be sensitive to one's audience. They point to the clarity of presentation around issues of empirical justification and the importance of separating empirically supported information from one's personal perspectives. Furthermore, integrity and trustworthiness are required given that academicians, no matter what their discipline, have tremendous power over students. They have power not only in terms of deciding what material is presented but also in terms of evaluating students and providing them with references. This evaluative nature of the academic enterprise makes integrity and trustworthiness critical values of the university.

Conclusion

Considering questions about virtue will, we hope, help the reader think about what kind of psychologist or counselor he or she wants to be. Counselors and psychologists can probably stay out of trouble from licensing boards and ethics committees by adhering to the standards in the ethics code; however, developing the traits of practical wisdom, trustworthiness, integrity, respectfulness, and compassion may help them develop a truly ethical attitude toward those with whom they work. As Welfel (2006) suggests from the writings of Meara et al. (1996), "Virtuous professionals believe so strongly in the ethical values of the profession that they hold themselves accountable even when others do not" (p. 345). Integrating those virtues with the personality and character that new graduate students bring to academic programs can sometimes be traumatic because it involves the whole person not just their professional life and will be the focus of Chapter 6.

Understanding the relationship between ethical decision making and moral character is not easy. If the critical-evaluative level of moral decision making provides the content on which good moral judgment operates, then good character provides the foundation for being sensitive to the moral components of one's work, being motivated to act morally, and having the ego strength to do the right thing when it is called for. It is the basis for the individuals "ordinary moral behavior" and the intuitive level of moral reasoning. Just as there is more to the psychology of moral behavior than moral judgment, there is more to being a good psychologist than following principles and rules.

If character development is important for becoming an ethical psychologist or counselor, and if it is related to the psychology of moral behavior, then the data on moral behavior ought to inform discussions about how to promote ethical character. The data that are currently available suggest that ethics education is minimally meeting this goal (Kitchener & Anderson, 2000). For example, weak evidence suggests that ethics training may improve compassion as it is related to moral sensitivity. Other data suggest that good judgment is malleable at least into the early adult years and that graduate education can have a profound influence on it (Kohlberg, 1984; King & Kitchener, 1994; Rest, 1994). Consequently, understanding the psychology of moral behavior and the data on it may be critical in helping students become ethical professionals. From this perspective, what educators model and teach both implicitly and explicitly is essential if they take seriously the task of helping students develop a strong moral character.

Questions for Discussion or Consideration

1. What does the concept of virtue ethics add to your understanding of being an ethical professional?
2. Would ethical principles and codes suffice in handling ethical problems in your work in teaching, practice, research, or supervision?
3. What virtues do you think are particularly important? Why?
4. Choose one of the problems you have discussed earlier or one from the book, what would ethical virtues add to your understanding of your responsibility if you were the psychologist or counselor involved?

6

Professional Ethical Identity
The Foundation for Doing Good Well

In Chapters 1 through 5, we covered ethical reasoning and decision making, and pointed out that methodological ways of processing ethical decision making are important tools for the professional. In addition, we discussed the importance of ethical virtues and how counselors and psychologists need to develop and embrace these be an ethical professional. We pointed out that virtues involve the whole person not just in their professional role. However, developing one's ethical identity and becoming an ethical professional involves more. It includes the purposeful reflection on the intersection between the values, motivations, and needs of the individual and the values and ethical perspective of the profession, in other words, the integration of the personal and the professional (Anderson & Handelsman, 2010). This reflection and integration process is a critical issue to address.

Professional Ethical Identity and the Professional Cultures of Psychology and Counseling

New professionals entering the academic training of psychology or counseling are faced with several developmental tasks. Some of these tasks include gaining an understanding of psychological theories, therapeutic techniques grounded in theory, the current research in the field, and how this research needs to impacts practice. In mastering these developmental tasks, psychologists and counselors develop skills that allow them to offer important services to society. Society supports the counseling and psychology professions because of these services and in return expects that professionals will "adhere to an exemplary code of conduct, observe fiduciary relationships with their clients as well as the community at large, and act beyond their own self interest" (Meara & Day, 2003, p. 459). In order to meet these expectations in a consistent manner, psychologists and counselors need to look within—to their core character and values—and use these along with the knowledge and skills they have learned to provide good service, develop meaningful research and to make ethical decisions. In order to do so, they must develop an ethical identity.

Becoming a professional who understands, appreciates, and commits to being an ethical practitioner, researcher, professor, and/or consultant takes more than just knowing about ethical principles, ethical codes, and having access to a decision making model. There is still the task of developing one's "professional ethical identity" (Handelsman, Gottlieb, & Knapp, 2005, p. 59). One's "professional ethical identity" is where the personal part and professional part of the person intersect and what professionals draw upon to be ethically sensitive, motivated, and committed to carry out ethical responsibilities in their day to day professional duties. In other words, it is the part of the individual that helps him or her actualize the components in Rest's model of moral action and is the well spring for virtue ethics. In this chapter, we address the intersection and development of one's professional ethical identity through an acculturation process (Anderson & Handelsman, 2010; Bashe, Anderson, Handelsman, & Klevansky, 2006; Handelsman et al., 2005).

Ethical Acculturation and the Professional Cultures of Psychology and Counseling

Every profession has its own culture; its own way of operating and being in the world (Anderson, Wagoner, & Moore, 2006). This culture can and does change as the profession evolves and as it welcomes new professionals into its membership. Reading the history of APA and ACA's ethics codes and the foundational ethical principles of these codes provides an introduction to part of the professions' culture. Learning about ethical principles, guidelines and standards of practice may enlighten the intellectual side of the new professional or student, but ethics and values of origin as well as motivations and needs of the individual are important to explore in light of the new professional culture and the ethical virtues it carries with it (Anderson & Handelsman, 2010). Entering a profession is in many ways like entering a new country. This new country/profession has its own distinct set of values and ways of operating in society and the new psychology or counseling student (immigrant to continue the analogy) has an acculturation task in front of him or her (Handelsman et al., 2005).

In the cross cultural psychology literature, Berry (1980) and Berry and Sam (1997) discussed the idea of "acculturation" as individuals enter a new ethnic culture and confront the task of adapting or not adapting to the new cultural context. During the adjustment process, the individual is faced with two tasks: "cultural maintenance" and "contact and participation." The resulting behaviors and attitudes from these two tasks indicate or suggest the type of acculturation strategy the person will employ as they live in the new culture. Taking this idea of adaptation to a new culture from the multicultural literature, Gottlieb, Handelsman, and Knapp (2002) proposed that adjusting or adapting process the psychology or counseling student goes through could also be considered as an acculturation process. In a subsequent writing Handelsman et al. (2005) furthered the concepts of "ethical acculturation" and a "professional ethical identity." It is important to note that these two tasks are neither sequential nor are they necessarily done in a conscious fashion. In the worlds of psychology and counseling, it may seem that being an ethical professional and developing an ethical identity starts and ends with knowing about the ethical principles and being familiar with the ethical guidelines and standards (Anderson & Handelsman, 2010; Bashe et al., 2006). However, this is only a part of developing into an ethical professional and building a professional ethical identity Learning about ethical principles, guidelines and standards of practice may enlighten the intellectual side of the new professional or student; however, there is still the other part of the individual, the personal ethics, values, and motivations, that needs to be explored in light of the new professional culture and its ethical virtues (Anderson & Handelsman, 2010). Working through the intersection between personal values, ethics, and the professional culture is an acculturation process just as living in a new country involves acculturation. In the following sections of this chapter we provide an overview of the ethics acculturation model as proposed by Handelsman et al. (2005), discuss the four acculturation strategies using case scenarios, and address the topics of teaching and supervision which are two key professional responsibilities for future psychologists and counselors.

The Ethical Acculturation Process

As previously stated, the newcomer to a different culture is faced with two tasks. The first is "cultural maintenance." Here the new comer is asking, is it "of value to maintain cultural identity and characteristics" from my culture of origin in this new culture (Berry & Sam, 1997, p. 296)?

Applying the "cultural maintenance" task to ethical acculturation, as the students or new professionals become aware of differences between their personal views and values and the counseling or psychology culture they will ask, "What of my personal ethics and ethics of origin will I keep as I enter this profession and what will I let go?" The personal ethics and morals may be based on ethnic background, religious upbringing, or previous career. Note the following case.

Case 6-1

As Dr. Kirk explained the ethical decision making model, the students in the doctoral class soaked up every word. They knew there would be ample opportunities to use the model with intriguing ethical dilemmas toward the end of class time and throughout the semester. Dr. Kirk presented a case where a pregnant teenager was using therapy to decide whether or not to pursue an abortion. Questions were asked and Dr. Kirk responded with either an answer or another question that prompted more dialogue and deeper reflection by students. One particular student, Sarah, sat quietly and listened to each of the responses wondering to herself, "Isn't there a Big E in ethics? Isn't there a final or absolute of ethical and unethical, a right and wrong?" Sarah had been raised to see "right" and "good" from a certain lens and in the case being discussed she was hoping the therapist would encourage the young teenager to see abortion as wrong. Another student, Frank, was dealing with a similar quandary but from a different perspective. He'd been raised to see a woman's choice for abortion as a legal right. Frank believed the therapist should encourage the client to see an abortion as the right choice and help her find a doctor. Both students were clear about their personal ethics and wondered how the others in the class could even spend time deliberating the case. Finally, neither Sarah nor Frank could stand the internal tension any longer; their hands shot up in the air. They both had the same question: "Where's the absolute here? Isn't there a Big E in ethics?"

In Case 6-1, both students were trying to make sense of how the "absolutes" they grew up with and their personal code of ethics fit the profession's ethical principles and guidelines. Sarah's personal values might stem from a strong, conservative, religious background which saw abortion as killing an innocent baby. She was struggling with the idea that to be ethical is to present and discuss with the client all the possible options regarding her pregnancy, abortion included. Frank is struggling too. He believes the most ethical action is to focus in on abortion and forget about looking at other options. Both students must consider how to keep their own ethics and values and yet not impose them on this client who is contemplating a course of action that is "right" for her.

As previously stated, there is a second task of acculturation. This task is "contact and participation" (Berry & Sam, 1997). At the same time newcomers are figuring out what to keep of their culture of origin, they are evaluating the new culture and deciding what to embrace or adopt as their own. This task of "contact and participation" is just as important as "cultural maintenance" and is expressed by the question, "Is it considered to be of value to maintain relationships with the dominant culture?" (Berry & Sam, 1997, p. 296).

As explained by Handelsman et al. (2005), new professionals and students in psychology and counseling are also faced with this task. They are assessing what they see as worthwhile in the professional culture. In essence they begin to ask, "What do I see as valuable and worth connecting with in the professional culture?" This assessment process includes looking at the ethical guidelines and rules as well as the virtues and principles of the profession and making some judgments about their value and usefulness. Note the following case.

Case 6-2

Dr. Freeze, a new faculty person, was sitting across the table from his former colleague who still worked in the business world. Dr. Freeze was bemoaning the status of his current research project; he needed at least 50 participants and thus far only 25 students had signed up. Rita Blanch looked at Dr. Freeze with a perplexed expression. After the first five minutes Rita piped up with, "Scott, I can't believe you're making this into such a big problem. Don't you remember what we use to do at Company X to get folks to try a new product? We'd give them an incentive. So, tell each student who signs up that they'll get a free beer for every student they recruit for the project." Dr. Freeze liked the idea. "That would sure make it easier" but then he had a second thought. "No, I better not. I haven't gotten that process approved for the IRB. I don't want to get into trouble and besides, I'm not sure that providing students incentives like this is really the ethical thing to do."

In this case, Dr. Freeze is assessing what values and ethics of his current professional culture he wants to embrace and implement. It is interesting to note the differences between professional cultures, in this case the culture of marketing and the culture of psychology. In another professional culture certain activities may be seen as ethical and just a matter of practice. But in psychology or counseling there may be a different view of the same activity. An important point here is what the student and/or new professional brings with them from other professions that then influences the second ethical acculturation task. One of the authors remembers the surprise of a student during a discussion about informed consent and the information a therapist needs to provide the client. In this student's former career such openness with a business client would have been unnecessary and in fact possibly a hindrance to getting the job done from her organization's perspective.

Four Ethical Acculturation Strategies

The adaptation process or working through the two tasks, cultural maintenance and contact and participation, results in one of four acculturation strategies: integration, assimilation, separation, and marginalization. It is important to note that it is the attitudes toward the two tasks and the resulting behavior that result in the individual's acculturation strategy (Berry & Sam, 1997). According to Handelsman et al. (2005) the tension for the individual in the new professional culture is between the person's own values and ethics and those of the organization to which he or she is adapting. The resolution of this tension not only suggests the acculturation strategy but also the development of the professional's ethical identity. Figure 6.1 shows these strategies in one of four quadrants (Berry & Sam, 1997; Handelsman et al., 2005).

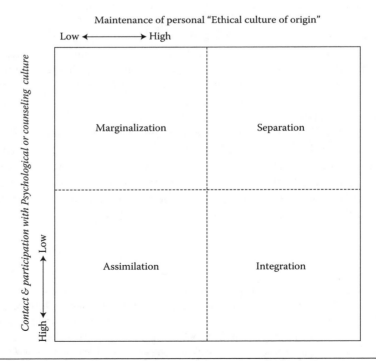

Figure 6.1 Strategies of ethical acculturation. (Reprinted from Anderson, S. K., & Handelsman, M. M. (2010). *Ethics for psychotherapists and counselors: A proactive approach.* Malden, MA: Wiley-Blackwell. With permission.)

Integration Strategy   The integration strategy represents the greatest congruence between the ethics and values of the individual and those of the professional culture. In this strategy the person is able to maintain their personal ethics and values set while simultaneously adopting those of the profession.

It is important to note that integration does not mean bending the ethical guidelines to match personal values or motivations (Anderson & Handelsman, 2010). Integration has more to do with the attitude toward the ethical guidelines and the resulting behaviors when confronted with an ethical issue. When a professional is truly integrated with the profession there is a good fit between who the person is and what the profession professes. This is not to say that the process of ethical acculturation is tension free. It is likely that individuals will feel some acculturation stress at times between their personal and professional ethics; however, in the process these individuals will seek to resolve the tension in a way that fosters even more integration between self and profession (Handelsman et al., 2005). In returning to Case 6-1, both Sarah and Frank have a conflict or tension between their personal ethics and those of the profession. Although each of them may personally want to encourage the client to accept their personal view, the most ethical way would be for them to discuss with equal attention all the possible options with the client and honor the client's right to autonomy; the right to make her own decision.

Integrating one's personal and professional ethics leads to "good *ethical* adaptation" and would likely result in "becoming and staying ethically excellent" as a professional (Anderson & Handelsman, 2010, p. 55). Anderson, Waggoner, and Moore (2006) state it this way: "The more the individual can adapt to the new culture … with its values, philosophy, and traditions while retraining aspects of one's ethics of origin or personal ethics, the better the fit, and the more likely the individual is to have a coherent professional ethical identity" (p. 48). Berry and Sam (1997) discuss the evidence of a positive relationship between healthy "psychological adaptation" and the use of integration as an acculturation strategy (p. 298). Although the research Berry and Sam discuss is in the area of "cultural acculturation" we would propose that this same positive relationship exists between integration and psychological adaptation in the process of ethical acculturation. Possibly this is what the student was explaining to her dissertation committee member in Case 5-2. The student had integrated the essence and practice of the ethical principles to where it was in her practice "a given" for how she would be with clients and other people using her professional services.

Assimilation Strategy   The student or new professional who operate from the assimilation strategy has adopted the ethics of the profession possibly to the exclusion of their own ethics. Anderson and Handelsman (2010) discuss several reasons why people choose to implement this strategy. One key reason could be that individuals entering a new profession haven't taken time to reflect on their ethics of origin and which ones they will work to integrate with those of the profession. Note the following case.

Case 6-3

Craig, the practicum student, sat there confused about how to respond. This was his second meeting with the client and he felt like the connection thus far was strong. Teresa, a single mother of two, wanted to know more about him personally, "Are you married? Do you have any children?" Just last night in a social setting he was asked the same two questions. In that context he responded with, "No, I'm not married. I got divorced last year and have a three year old daughter." Now in a therapy session he wasn't sure what to say. Craig ached to respond in an open and honest manner which fit his usual way of communication. Craig believed more self disclosure would only deepen the therapeutic relationship. But he felt like he should be more circumspect but wasn't sure why. He recalled the ethics class when the group discussed the timing and purpose of therapist self disclosure with clients. At the time he hadn't paid much attention but he did recall the instructor giving a word of caution about boundaries. He felt flustered and decided to respond with a short comment of, "I'm sorry Ms Gaines. I can't really share that information. It wouldn't be appropriate."

In this case, we might assume that part of Craig's confusion was due to not seeing how to integrate the ethics about therapist self-disclosure and boundaries with his value in being spontaneous, open, and honest in communication. As result he responded in a way that over emphasized the perspective of little to no self-disclosure which he believed articulated the profession's ethical view. It could be that little or no disclosure was ethically appropriate but Craig could have responded to the client in a way that honored therapeutic boundaries and his value of open and honest communication.

A second reason new professionals and students might use the assimilation strategy is because they do not see the usefulness of their own ethical values in the profession (Anderson & Handelsman, 2010). They struggle to see how their ethics of origin (possibly from a religious or cultural background) match with that of the profession and when they don't see a way to integrate the two they give up the personal part of themselves. For example, in Case 6-1, Sarah is trying to make sense of the absolutes of right and wrong that she grew up with and the profession's value of client autonomy which might lead to an abortion. If in the end, Sarah believes she must let go of her own values to become an accepted part of the profession, her acculturation strategy would be one of assimilation.

Individuals may also adopt the assimilation strategy because they believe being ethical is just a matter of taking on a professional persona and they have a limited personal ethical foundation (Anderson & Handelsman, 2010). The attitude of the individual might be one of, "Just tell me the rules and I'll follow them. I don't want to get into trouble." However, there is no deep commitment or understanding on the person's part of ethical principles or codes because of the good that comes from ethical behaviors or choices.

At first glance, the assimilation strategy may appear to be less problematic than the integration strategy. Assimilation behaviors may look similar to or even identical with integration behaviors. However, the attitude with this choice may be the most problematic place to start the developmental task of becoming an ethical professional. In the short term the person might be able to meet the ethical demands of their new role. However, over the long haul when ethical issues become more pressing or issues in their personal life become overwhelming, the professional might become frustrated with the profession (Anderson & Handelsman, 2010). As a result, the professional may choose unethical behavior. Note the case below.

Case 6-4

Terry called his friend Fred, who was also on internship. Terry was struggling with a supervision issue and thought Fred might provide some good consultation. Fred was the star student who got the better grades and was always one step ahead of everyone else. He'd even landed the prized internship in the region. Within the first five minutes of the conversation Terry could tell something was wrong. Terry asked what was up and Fred blurted out, "Look, stop badgering me. I'm fine, everything is fine. I mean, ok ... I'm a little lonely and under some stress of my own." Terry was shocked by Fred's outburst. He'd never heard him be so abrupt and angry. Then he remembered that two weeks before leaving for his internship, Fred had signed divorce papers. After what seemed like a long minute of silence Fred said he needed to go. A month passed and Terry heard that Fred had been dismissed from his internship. Fred had been dating a client and the client's former partner complained to Fred's supervisor.

There could be multiple reasons for Fred's unethical behavior. As humans, psychologists and counselors are capable of ethical lapses especially when dealing with personal issues. It may very well be that Fred had a high level of commitment to his personal and professional ethics and these were initially integrated, but in the throes of a recent divorce and the stress and strain of a doctoral internship he gave into the temptation of meeting his personal needs for companionship. However, it could also be that on the surface he appeared to understand and appreciate the professional ethics of psychology but he was really only playing out an expected role or persona. In all actuality the ethical guidelines and rules were not integrated into Fred's character. During internship with personal and professional stress this persona was not able to help him make ethical decisions or to steer clear of crossing boundaries with clients. As was addressed in Chapter 5 on virtues, moral character along with knowledge and appreciation for ethical principles provides a firm foundation for consistent and thoughtful ethical decision making and action.

The developmental task for individuals who are using an assimilation strategy is to begin integrating their personal ethics and values with those of the profession. To grow an coherent professional ethical identity, it is important individuals have as clear a sense of who they are and what personal ethics they bring to the profession and how these relate to the ethics of the professional culture (Anderson & Handelsman, 2010; Gilley et al., 2008). He needed to grow a stronger foundation of personal ethics which could be integrated with the ethical principles and standards of the profession.

Separation Strategy   When individuals choose to use their personal ethics and values to the exclusion of those of the psychology or counseling profession they are using the separation strategy. The attitude and resulting behavior may come from seeing the ethical guidelines as impersonal or too restrictive. For example, Craig, the practicum student in Case 6-3, spontaneously hugs people as a way of showing care and concern. In addition, he's been known to offer financial assistance to others in need. Let's suppose that during the second session with Teresa he not only shares about his divorce and young daughter but also hugs Teresa at the end of the session. He does this because he sees these behaviors as a way to deepen the relationship and regards the ethical guidelines about boundaries as petty and too limiting for his personal style as a therapist.

Individuals might also use the separation strategy because of "well-developed ethical sense from their own upbringing, or the values of other professions to which they may have belonged" (Handelsman et al., 2005, p. 61). An example of this could be seen in Case 6-1 if either Sarah or Frank impose their values on the client. If Sarah only talks with the client about adoption after the baby is born and if Frank only talks with the client about abortion and calling a doctor to make an appointment, they would be acting on their personal ethics over that of the profession. In essence they would be choosing to impose their values on the client.

Research in the medical field supports the notion that students in training use the separation strategy. Bucher and Stelling (1977) completed a longitudinal study of students who participated in professional training programs in disciplines such as psychiatry, biochemistry, and internal medicine. Students who appeared to struggle with the expectations of the training program were identified by the researchers as *socialization failures*. Socialization failures were those students who, for various reasons, did not match with what was expected in their training program. One key characteristic of these students was their inflexible commitment to the values and personal ethics they brought with them upon entering the training program. Handelsman et al. (2005) suggested that these students had adopted separation strategies when confronted with a difference between their values and professional expectations. It is also very likely that although these individuals had positive and good intentions about the future and the profession, they could not identify with or connect with the professional culture. Bottom line, ethical work whether it is with a client, student, or research participant cannot occur with just good intentions. As Handelsman et al. (2005) said:

> Although they may have a very strong personal code of ethics and be very well intentioned, these students may also be unaware of the potential harm that may come from acting on a set of principles or virtues that are inconsistent with the professional context. (p. 61)

There remains at least one more reason why students might operate from the separation strategy. At the beginning of psychology and counseling training, students are not acquainted with or understand the ethical expectations of the profession. One of the authors remembers an interesting class discussion about relationship boundaries with clients and the ensuing look on a student's face. After some minutes the student raised his hand and said something to the effect that he had wished this class discussion would have occurred a week earlier. During the previous week he had given a client some money for a phone bill and offered her a ride home. In this case the student inadvertently operated from a separation strategy because he didn't know the ethical issues to consider. His choice to give the client money and a ride home was solely based on this generous, well meaning personality and personal ethic of care.

The developmental task for individuals using the separation is to explore how they might implement their personal values and still honor the professional ethical principles and codes. For example, Craig, in Case 6-3, could draw upon his value of honest communication that honors both the client's question and the ethical consideration of maintaining appropriate boundaries. He could have asked Teresa about her question, "These are two good questions for a client to ask a therapist. They might suggest that you are wondering if I have the personal knowledge of marriage or parenthood or even more so if I understand your experience as a single parent. Is this accurate?" This statement and question by Craig acknowledges the client's questions, explores her reason for asking them and matches his style of direct and hones communication.

Marginalization Strategy   The attitude and then subsequent behaviors of one using the marginalization strategy is similar to a rudderless and anchorless ship on the sea drifting along with no mechanism to guide its course nor does it have a heavy object (anchor) to provide stability (Gilley, Anderson, & Gilley, 2008). A student or new professional who does not have a base of personal ethics or has lost the connection with his ethical compass and has no real commitment to professional ethics is likely to exhibit the marginalization strategy. "Those exhibiting marginalization will obey ethical standards out of personal convenience rather than a sense of moral commitment" (Handelsman et al., 2005, p. 61) to the profession or themselves. In these cases, acting ethical is seen as a part to play rather than a way to be or live out the professional life with students, clients, colleagues, research participants, and so on. There is no real appreciation for ethical virtues of the professional culture or the underlying principles on which the codes are based (Handelsman et al., 2005). To demonstrate this attitude and resulting behavior we continue Case 6-4.

Case 6-4 (Continued)

Four months after Terry had heard about Fred's dismissal, they happened to see each other at an airport. Terry shared that he was headed to an interview for a psychologist position. Fred mentioned that he was headed home for a friend's wedding and then to Chicago to work. Fred said he was "glad to be out from under the program and psychology altogether." He'd had enough "with all the rules and do's and don'ts." He was training to be a stock broker.

Fred's declaration at the airport about "all the rules and do's and don'ts" of psychology give us another possible explanation for Fred's unethical choice with dating a client during his internship. Although he appeared during his preinternship training to have a good ethical foundation and promise as an ethical psychologist, it was possible that his commitment to ethics was superficial at best and that his behavior was more for appearances. Before the internship, Fred appeared to the faculty and his fellow students as a model student. He knew the ethics code and responded well on paper to ethical dilemmas. However, this superficial adoption of the ethical identity was out of a motivation for a good appearance. He had no deep commitment to ethical behavior. When multiple stressors came his way there was no foundation of professional or personal ethics on which to draw. The following is another case that highlights a professional using a marginalization strategy.

Case 6-5

Dr. Hardy had a wall filled with plaques and certificates from various counseling organizations. Kathy, her client, was impressed by all she saw and had made a decision to work with Dr. Hardy right then and there. At the end of session three, Kathy again asked Dr. Hardy for the insurance forms so she could get reimbursed by the insurance company. Dr. Hardy quickly filled out the forms and wrote in four sessions. When Dr. Hardy gave Kathy the completed forms Kathy was pleased. But as she looked at them Kathy's smile turned to a frown. "Dr. Hardy, we've only met three times so far. You have four sessions down here and I don't think these are even the right dates." Dr. Hardy waved her hand and said, "Oh really? Well let's just go with it this time. I'm sure the insurance company won't miss a few dollars."

Both Fred and Dr. Hardy demonstrate an attitude which suggests a lack of integrity and commitment to behaving ethically. As was addressed in Chapter 5 on virtues, moral character along with knowledge and appreciation for ethical principles provides a firm foundation for consistent and thoughtful ethical decision making and action.

Acculturation Issues for Teaching and Supervision

In the role of teacher or supervisor, there are at least two important issues to be addressed. First is the issue of teacher's or supervisor's own acculturation process. In the classroom and in supervision the teacher and supervisor are influencing students' understanding of ethics and what it means to be an ethical professional. It sends a mixed or double message to students when faculty and supervisors state one thing and do another. Modeling would suggest that students follow in or make similar choices as their supervisors when it comes to unethical behavior. The teacher and supervisor who more times than not operate from an integration strategy in their professional activities will be sending a clear message to students and supervisees that commitment to the ethical principles and guidelines as well as ethical virtues are critical to a professional ethical identity.

At the same time, teachers and supervisors need to recall what we stated in Chapter 2. Becoming a professional in the world of psychology and counseling does not guarantee perfection. When a teacher or supervisor makes an ethical error or violates the ethical principles or codes the ethical virtue of humility is necessary. Admitting the mistake and taking corrective or restorative action is called for. As faculty who teach about ethics we have discovered the benefits for sharing with students our own ethical mistakes as well as ethical successes. This type of appropriate disclosure by faculty and supervisors communicates to students and supervisees importance of self reflection and honesty as well as the human factor of the profession.

In addition to the necessary attention due to their own acculturation process, faculty need to provide students and supervisees opportunities to explore who they are, their ethics of origin and whether he these match those of the profession. As faculty provide students these opportunities for self exploration, several key issues about ethical acculturation are important to highlight. First and possibly the most important issue is that the acculturation process is just that, a process or journey that never ends (Anderson & Handelsman, 2010). As students and new professionals address new ethical situations and challenges they will uncover or better understand (with some purposeful reflection) how their personal values and ethics are impacting their view of and ability to act on what is ethical. The ethical acculturation journey never ends since the professional culture changes. For example, a current debate in psychology is importance of evidence based therapy. Some psychologists believe that therapist should only offer types of psychotherapy that is supported by research. Other psychologists believe that this approach to therapy is limiting and suggests a narrow positivistic approach to a working with people. Five to eight years ago this issue was not an issue; now the professional culture of psychology is dealing with possible change.

Instructors and supervisors also need to be sensitive to the experience of acculturation stress which is that internal discomfort (Handelsman et al., 2005) that individuals feel at different points in the acculturation journey. Anderson and Handelsman suggest ethical acculturation stress occurs for several reasons. First, there the student or new professional needs to consider the ethical expectations and obligations associated with the professional role of psychologist or counselor which may be different than their own. Second, there could be what Berry and Sam (1997) refer to as "cultural distance" (p. 307) between the skills, values, and virtues individuals bring with them and those required by the professions of psychology and counseling which then suggests "cultural shedding" is a necessary. Cultural shedding is defined as "the unlearning of aspects of one's previous repertoire that are no longer appropriate" (Berry & Sam, 1997, p. 298). Ethical acculturation stress may also occur because ethical codes are sometimes vague and may even appear contradictory. Both of the authors have seen the frustration of students who struggle with the "it depends" factor of ethical decision making. For example, a therapist is ethically and legally required to report child abuse but would be seen as violating confidentiality when reporting other types of crimes such as burglary. Last, entering and integrating with the professional culture may prompt a shift in personal relationships. The fields of psychology and counseling encourage self exploration and self growth. These professional values will then impact the interactions with family members and friends. In exchange, family members and friends will begin to treat the new professional and student differently. Faculty and supervisors' need to address these acculturation stress possibilities with the students to prepare them for the internal conflict.

Conclusion

Although there is no research at this time to suggest that all students in training go through this cultural maintenance task, it is easy to assume that most if not all students are challenged to make sense of who they are and how this matches or mismatches with the professional culture. For example, one of the authors had a Native American student ask her, "How can I be a warrior and a psychologist?" This psychology student was trying to make sense of how he could bring his two worlds together, the one world as a Native American "warrior" and the other a "psychologist" in many ways is built on western European world view. A key point here is the importance of making conscious the unconscious experience of this acculturation process. Without some purposeful reflection on the individual's part, this acculturation experience can feel psychologically confusing and unproductive resulting in unethical choices or half hearted compliance with the ethical guidelines to stay out of trouble and possibly lead to dissatisfaction with the profession (Anderson & Handelsman, 2010). The more that the new professional can embrace the psychology or counseling profession while keeping or maintaining his personal ethics and values, the more likely the new professional will be better able to draw upon the ethical motivation needed to implement ethical action.

To move the process from unconscious to conscious, authors (Anderson & Handelsman, 2010; Bashe et al., 2006) have suggested ways for students and new professionals to explore their personal ethics, values and motivations and how these compare and contrast to those of the profession. For example, students and new professionals can write an ethics autobiography. The autobiography could include answering questions that explore: motivations for entering the profession, personal needs they hope are met while in the profession, personal ethics and values they've retained as an adult and how these impact their professional work, conflicts or challenges they anticipate because of perceived differences between their personal values set and the values of the profession. Anderson and Handelsman (2010) propose that purposeful reflection results in a better, more psychologically healthy adaptation to the profession and a coherent professional ethical identity. We end this chapter with a case that revisits one of the people in Case 6-1. Sarah, now Dr. Sanders, demonstrates the use of integration strategy and highlights a coherent ethical identity.

Case 6-6

Sarah, now Dr. Sanders, listened to her client explain the confusion around the pregnancy. The client was not sure whether she wanted to do. Should she have the baby? Should she get an abortion? If she had the baby, should we keep it? Or should she give it up for adoption? "What should I do, Dr. Sanders?" the client was asking. Dr. Sanders needed to bring herself back, she had been day dreaming. For a split moment she was back in Dr. Kirk's class listening to the class debate what the therapist should do with a client who didn't know what steps to take after finding out she was pregnant. Dr. Sanders remembered her clear reaction to the issue: "Do not discuss abortion as an option and encourage the client to have the baby." Now she was faced with same issue. She still did not agree with abortion, yet she understood that her client was an autonomous individual and respected her right to choose. The client asked again, "Dr. Sanders, what should I do? I mean, if you were me what would you do?" Dr. Sanders had thought about this scenario several times and felt prepared to offer a response that now came from an integration strategy. She replied, "It is a wonderful thing that you get to decide what you wish to do. I'll be here to support you in your process." As Sarah leaves her office that day, she feels good about the work with clients especially the one who was faced with a pregnancy. She was able to work with the client in a way that helped the client make the decisions based on the client's values while still being clear about her own.

Questions for Discussion or Consideration

1. What do your personal ethics say about right and wrong behavior and where do these come from?
2. What personal ethics and values are you bringing with you as you enter training as a psychologist or counselor?
3. What messages did you get from your family about groups of people different from yourself (ethnically or culturally) and how they see right and wrong behaviors?
4. When you compare and contrast your personal values with those of the profession, where is the match and where is the mismatch? What cultural shedding might you need to do?
5. What personal morals are most important to you and how do they align with or conflict with the professional ethics code?

7

Competence

Doing Good and Avoiding Harm

To incompetently engage in research, practice, or teaching is a violation of the fundamental obligation to benefit those psychologists and counselors have agreed to serve and can lead to substantial harm. Additionally, disparity in services to a particular group because of incompetence is a fundamental violation of the principle of justice. In research, incompetence can lead to false claims and the waste of valuable and scarce resources. As Swenson (1997) suggested, psychologists "should be fully trained, keep up-to-date, and be good at what they do. Otherwise they should stop doing it" (p. 64). Undoubtedly, the same maxim should be applied to counselors. The basic tenant should be that if you are not competent to adequately fulfill the responsibilities associated with your role, do not perform your role unless you are under the supervision of someone who is competent.

Competence is a critical milestone for psychologists and counselors to obtain. In fact Kaslow et al. (2007a) called competence the cornerstone of ethics. Because competence provides the foundation for ethically fulfilling all of the roles psychologists and counselors play, the ethics codes of the professions have had standards that focus on competence and its importance in practice or research for many years. Both the 2002 APA ethics code and 2005 ACA ethics code spent considerable space spelling out the need for counselors and psychologists to practice within the boundaries of their competence and to take steps to continually monitor their effectiveness as professionals. Generally, the codes emphasized that psychologists or counselors should perform their roles within the limits of their competence, which is based on education, training, supervised experience, or other appropriate professional experience. In addition, when they move into new areas, they should seek further education, training, supervision, and/or consultation from others who are already competent in those areas in order to develop and maintain their competence. The burden of responsibility for maintaining competence in areas of existing expertise and developing competence in new or emerging areas always remains with the psychologist or counselor (Canter, Bennett, Jones, & Nagy, 1994). By contrast, incompetence increases the risk of harm and minimizes the potential for benefit to occur.

Over the last 10 years there has been increased attention, particularly in psychology on competence-based practice although increasing multicultural competence has been an important emphasis in ACA. As Rubin et al. (2007) have said "psychology education, training, and credentialing are on the brink of a major paradigm shift in culture toward an approach that is devoted to providing outcomes-based education and training; defining benchmarks of specific competencies; ascertaining how to most effectively attain these competencies; developing and implementing reliable, valid, and high-fidelity measurements of outcomes; and offering remediation and enrichment for individuals whose performance is not consistent with expected outcomes (p. 459)." Although it is not possible to provide the complete historical background of the competency movement as Rubin et al. (2007) have done, it is important to note that a conference was held in Scottsdale Arizona in 2002 sponsored by the Association of Psychology Postdoctoral and Internship Centers (APPIC), APA, several education and training groups under the leadership of the Council of Chairs of Training Counsels (CCTC), and ethnic minority psychology organizations. The purpose of this conference was to define the core competencies for professional psychologists. The eight competency domains identified were: ethical and legal issues, individual and cultural diversity, scientifically minded practice, psychological assessment, interventions, consultation and interprofessional collaboration, supervision, and professional development. The conference was followed by a task force appointed by the American Psychological Association to identify guiding principles and recommendations for the assessment of competence (Kaslow et al., 2007a). Some of the outcomes of this conference will be discussed in Chapter 8. Although generally the focus has been on competence in practice, other events have occurred that suggest a growing concern with competence in teaching and research. As Kaslow et al. (2007a) have summarized "failing to provide competent services falls outside the bounds of what is acceptable because the risk of harm is so great and the likelihood of benefit is so small" (p. 487).

What Does It Mean to Be Competent?

Even though ethics codes emphasize the importance of competence, it is easier to require psychologists or counselors to be competent than it is to define what competence means. As with other ethical constructs, competence is sometimes easier to identify in its absence than it is to clearly specify what a proficient level of practical or scientific competence or expertise involves. Take the following case as an example.

Case 7-1

Mr Austin hired Dr. Dale in a bitterly contested child custody case. Prior to the case, Mrs Romero, Mr Austin's former wife, had custody of their sons, aged 9 and 11 years. Dr. Dale evaluated Mr Austin and his current wife as well as the children. A psychologist whom Mrs Romero hired reviewed the testing materials and indicated that the choice of tests was a good one and that they appeared to be fairly interpreted. At the trial, Dr. Dale stated that Mr Austin and his wife would be better parents and should have custody of the children and that Mrs Romero should have limited visitation rights. Dr. Dale, however, had never evaluated either Mrs Romero or her current husband. All of his information about them was gained secondhand. Dr. Dale said that the boys preferred their father to their mother. The psychologist Mrs Romero hired pointed out that prior to the trial, Mrs Romero had custody and Mr Austin saw the boys infrequently. When he was with them, they only did fun things like go to ball games and he bought them toys. Mrs Romero had to do all of the disciplining, and her financial resources were limited because Mr Austin paid his child support infrequently. Furthermore, Dr. Dale ignored the fact that Mr Austin was an alcoholic and was probably still drinking. Dr. Dale had information about the prior drinking problems because Mrs Romero sent him copies of hospital records.

Mrs Romero lost custody of her children as a result of the trial. She then began to get letters from her sons telling her that their father was drinking heavily. He also beat his second wife, which was similar to the behavior that led Mrs Romero to divorce him in the first place. Mrs Romero is an Anglo, but her current husband is a Mexican American. She sometimes wonders if that affected Dr. Dale's evaluation of them.

Most psychologists and counselors would recognize that something was wrong in this scenario. Dr. Dale appears to have violated several standards in both the 2005 ACA and 2002 APA Ethics Codes regarding the competence and assessment. Dr. Dale drew conclusions about Mrs Romero and her husband without evaluating them. Furthermore, he apparently ignored data that were available to him about Mr Austin's prior history of alcoholism. As in many cases of incompetent practice, the consequences were dire for Mrs Romero and her family.

What can we learn from this example about competent practice? Did Dr. Dale lack the knowledge and skill that would allow him to do a competent forensic assessment? Was it less a case of lack of knowledge and skill but really one of laziness? Was he simply being devious in ignoring information about the person who was paying him for the assessment? Were conscious or unconscious prejudices about race and ethnicity operating when he made comments about Mrs Romero and her new husband? It may be that all were involved. According to the psychologist Mrs Romero hired, Dr. Dale had the skill and knowledge to competently choose and interpret tests. It may be, however, Dr. Dale lacked the skill and knowledge to work in the forensic area or his ability to apply his knowledge was limited by his own biases.

As professional associations and state legal bodies struggled with how to define *competence*, they developed ethical standards, standards of practice, and licensing laws that attempted to define *incompetent* practice. Competence was often equated with practicing at or above the customary standard of care; although professionals are not expected to be perfect in everything they do, they are expected to perform at least as well as the average psychologist or counselor who is well trained (Bennett et al., 1990; Swenson, 1997). Recently, however, some consensus has been reached about the meaning of competence (Rodolfa et al., 2005). Rodolfa et al. (2005) suggest that competency "is generally understood to mean that a professional is qualified, capable, and able to understand and do certain things in an appropriate and effective manner" (p. 348). Epstein and Hundert (2002) define it as "habits of mind, critical thinking and analysis, professional judgment in assessing situations and ascertaining appropriate responses, in evaluating and modifying decisions via reflective practice" (p. 227).

Typically, as Case 7-1 suggests, being competent involves having the knowledge, skills, values, and abilities to perform one's professional role and the self-awareness to recognize when one's knowledge, skills, and abilities are inadequate or impaired. If skills are inadequate or impaired, alternatives need to be considered, such as removing oneself from the situation, referring to someone who can perform competently, or seeking consultation, therapy, or treatment (Bennett et al., 1990; Swenson, 1997). Competent practice also involves the willingness to use one's *knowledge, skills*, and *abilities* for the benefit of the consumer; that is, the professional needs to be motivated to do good.

Although knowledge, skills, and abilities are closely related, each contributes a different connotation to the construct of competence. Knowledge involves having the requisite facts or ideas to complete the task successfully. These are usually acquired by study, investigation, or experience (*Webster's Ninth New Collegiate Dictionary,* 1988). Knowledge is the foundation of competence. In research, it would include basic information about research design, statistics, interpretation of data, and ethical treatment of participants. In assessment, it would include information about relevant measures and their reliability and validity for different purposes and populations. In forensics, it would mean knowing about the legal system, legal precedents, civil rights, the role of the psychologist or counselor in the court room, and the difference between the legal system and the rules of science (Anderten, Staulcup, & Grisso, 1980; Committee on Ethical Guidelines for Forensic Psychologists, 1991). In other words, for each role the professional plays, there is a body of knowledge that competent practice presumes. Take Case 7-2 as an example that illustrates a lack of competence based on lack of familiarity with fundamental information.

Case 7-2

A faculty member reported that one of her colleagues knew so little about statistics that he referred his students to consultants or other faculty for even the most basic information. When he tried to assist a student with the statistics on her master's thesis, so many errors were made that the student failed her orals (Goodyear et al., 1992).

In 1972, Dubin estimated that the half-life of psychological knowledge was 10–12 years. As knowledge continues to accumulate at a faster and faster pace, to remain competent, professionals must remain familiar with current literature and research and be able to translate that new knowledge into competent performance (Jensen, 1979). Therefore, a commitment to competence means that psychologists and counselors must also have a commitment to continuing education, whether it is formal or informal. In fact, one of the themes that ran through all of the reports from the Scottsdale conference was that competence was developmental and that it did not end with licensure.

Although skills are based on knowledge, they involve the capacity to use knowledge effectively in performing a task (*Webster's Ninth New Collegiate Dictionary,* 1988). Thus, for example, psychologists may have knowledge of psychological testing derived from a class on personality assessment; but if they have never given a psychological battery under supervision (where feedback about performance can be provided), it is unlikely they would be skilled in psychological assessment. Similarly, students could learn about statistical procedures, but if they never had to apply them to data analysis, they would probably be unskilled in doing so.

Case 7-3

A woman entered a therapy group on the advice of her therapist, whom she had found very helpful in individual therapy. The therapist argued that it would be helpful for her to find out that others had similar problems to hers and to develop better social skills. The client found her therapist to be remarkably different in the group setting. Instead of providing structure and support, the therapist was passive and seemed to lack confidence. In fact, the group seemed out of control. When the client was aggressively belittled in front of the group and the therapist neither intervened nor helped the woman process the incident, the client confronted him. He admitted that although he had a class in group process, he had never led a group in graduate school or under supervision. He pointed out, however, that he did have a license to practice and that it did not limit him to individual sessions.

As Case 7-3 suggests, in professional practice, textbook learning is often insufficient for a professional to begin a new area of practice unless supervision is provided so that the professional can get feedback about effectiveness. Additionally, it highlights the fallacy that licensure in and of itself guarantees competence. Although licensure in most states has been established to help ensure a decent minimum of services, it does not guarantee that professionals are competent in all areas of practice.

Abilities involve the physical or mental capacity to perform a task. In this respect, they involve the fitness to perform a professional role. Individuals may have the knowledge and skill to perform a task, but because of mental or physical limitations they may be unable to use the knowledge and skills competently. Sometimes psychologists or counselors can compensate for these disabilities; however, to do so presume they are knowledgeable about their own limits and willing to accommodate for them. In some cases, individuals may also lack the ability to learn basic psychological information or use particular skills. Although abilities were not specifically identified as critical by the Scottsdale conference, Cases 7-4 and 7-5 illustrate some of the problems that can occur when a problematic behavior interferes with competent performance. Furthermore, Rodolfa et al. (2005) pointed out that competency requires action and that the professional's behaviors are consistent with the values of the profession. In other words, their actions benefit rather than harm the public. Action would not be possible if professionals did not have the abilities to take action.

Case 7-4

A graduate research assistant complained to the department chairperson that his supervisor, a psychologist, often came drunk to the lab. As a result of the supervisor's apparent alcoholism, the student alleged that the supervisor had botched data collection on a particularly rare strain of mice. In addition, because of his carelessness when he was under the influence of alcohol, he had endangered the mice by compromising their care; in fact, several had died as a result of mishandling.

Case 7-5

After she went through a difficult divorce, Dr. Quin decided to close her practice in one part of the state and move to another city about 200 miles away where she could work for a mental health agency. However, she continued to act as the supervisor for several master's-level practitioners. Because she was so far away, she could not meet with them. She did talk with them by phone every 2 weeks and sign their insurance forms, which were mailed to her. When one of the master's-level therapists was charged with having sexual intimacies with a client, Dr. Quin was also charged with inadequate supervision. She indicated that as a result of the divorce she was having severe emotional problems that interfered with her professional judgment.

Even though the psychologist in Case 7-4 may have had the knowledge and skills to adequately run a lab and conduct experiments, the intake of alcohol interfered with competent performance. Similarly, in Case 7-5, Dr. Quin's ability to make professional decisions was negatively affected by her own emotional problems and may have led to incompetent supervision.

Because of the link between personal problems and competence, counselors and psychologists should recognize when they have personal problems and refrain from undertaking an activity when they know or should know that their personal problems are likely to harm to a person to whom they may owe a scientific or professional obligation. They should be alert to signs of personal problems and get assistance for them before they negatively affect performance, and they should take appropriate remedial measures and get consultation to help them decide whether they should limit, suspend, or terminate their work-related duties. However, this is easier said than done since incompetence often brings with it an inability to be objective about one's own abilities. Here, it is important to have a peer group or colleagues that can provide honest feedback when they become aware of such problems even if it means contacting the licensing board or talking with faculty about the issues.

In some cases, it is perfectly clear that a psychologist or counselor may lack knowledge, skill, or ability. In other cases, as in the following example, it may be more difficult to discern which is missing.

Case 7-6

Students repeatedly complained to a department chairperson about a professor's teaching. They said that they had no doubt that he was "smart" and knew a lot about the subject matter (he was highly published and had an international reputation), but he could not communicate it. He often talked over their heads, and his lectures were poorly organized. Additionally, he never made eye contact with anyone in the class and talked so quietly they could barely hear him.

Even though department heads often get complaints about faculty teaching, it is clear that knowledge of the subject matter is not enough to make a competent instructor. Both skills and abilities are also important. In Case 7-6, it may be that the professor lacked a skill that could be developed or that he had some fundamental personal problems that limited his ability to perform in this area.

Values provide the motivation to "do good" and consider how one's actions might cause harm. The values described in Chapters 2 through 5 provide the foundation for considering the well-being of clients, research participants, supervisees and so on. Clearly, the professor in Case 7-6 did not have the practical wisdom to be aware that his teaching was substandard and that he needed guidance in how to improve his ability to communicate with students. He had to value the impact that his lectures were making on students enough to do something about it.

Rodolfa et al. (2005) summarize competency to mean that "a professional is capable (i.e., has the knowledge, skills, and values) to practice the profession safely and effectively" (p. 349). Furthermore they identified several functional domains of competency (e.g., assessment, research, supervision, and interventions) that should be required of all individuals seeking to practice as psychologists in the United States or Canada and pointed out that there is a different set of knowledge, skills, values (and we would add "abilities") that are required for competency in each domain. Furthermore they suggested there were foundational competency domains that provided the building blocks of what psychologists do in every functional domain. These included reflective practice or self-assessment, knowledge of research methodology and a respect for the scientific basis of the functional domains, application of ethical and legal issues regarding the practiced activities, and awareness of and sensitivity to the cultural diversity of the individuals, groups, and communities with whom they work. They argued that the functional and foundational domains are orthogonal to each other and that they differed with each stage of professional development. In fact, almost all the groups that were describing the basic skills and training necessary for working in the foundational domains argued that competency is a developmental process with different skills, abilities, knowledge, and values necessary at each step of development from practicum student to practiced professional.

As noted earlier, knowledge, skills, and abilities are only one part of the competence equation. Competence also involves knowing when one has reached one's own limits and a willingness to use one's knowledge, skills, and abilities for the benefit of the consumer. Having a virtuous character probably plays a role in both self-assessment and motivation. To make good moral judgments about one's own capacity to fulfill responsibilities, a psychologist or counselor must be prudent. Furthermore, acting with a sense of moral integrity and respectfulness toward students, clients, or research participants helps to guarantee that knowledge and skills are applied in a thorough way.

Students in training frequently struggle with feelings of incompetence and have questions about whether they are, by definition, unethical because they are not completely trained. If they were fully competent, however, they probably would not be in a graduate program. Much of the burden for assuring students' competence falls on the shoulders of faculty. It is faculty members' responsibility to evaluate whether students have sufficient background and knowledge to begin new scientific or clinical activities and to provide the supervision experiences that ensure that their skills are, at least, minimally competent. Clinical role-plays, practice assessments, and acting as an assistant on a research project may be low-risk first steps to developing competence. Furthermore, faculty members have the responsibility to monitor progress and to evaluate whether students have the ability to competently use the knowledge and skills that they have acquired. In fact, APA-accredited doctoral programs are mandated to provide regular evaluations of all students (Forrest, Elman, & Gizara, 1997). Supervision plays a key role in this and while the APA Ethics Code provides little direct attention to supervision, the ACA Ethics Code offers clear guidelines. These issues will be developed later in this chapter.

Negligence: The Failure of Competence

Negligence is a concept from civil law. Although the focus of this book is on ethics, as already noted some concepts like competence may be better understood in their absence. Understanding negligence, which is a failure of competence, may be useful in this regard.

Tort law is a branch of civil law involving deliberate or careless acts that harm others (Burris, 2001). The tort of negligence involves "the failure to use the care a reasonably prudent and careful person would use under similar circumstances or the doing of something that a reasonable person would not have done" (Swenson, 1997, p. 463). In the U.S. legal system, if psychologists practice below what the courts consider to be a reasonable standard of care, they can be accused of negligence. If they are found guilty, they can be liable for the harm that resulted from their negligence (Bennett et al., 1990; Swenson, 1997).

Because psychologists and counselors are professionals who offer their services for a fee and are paid for work that is dependent on their competence, they owe the consumers of their services or their research participants a certain duty of care (Bennett et al., 1990). This duty is typically measured by identifying the level of care that an ordinary psychologist or counselor would exercise under similar circumstances. In other words, incompetence is defined as practicing below the level of other reasonable counselors or psychologists with similar training and a similar theoretical orientation. For a professional to be found guilty of negligence, the plaintiff must prove that the professional had a professional relationship with the plaintiff and therefore incurred a duty of care. Further, the plaintiff must prove that the psychologist or counselor's actions fell below the standard of care and that the plaintiff was injured as a result of those actions (Bennett et al., 1990; Herman & Burris, 1993). Typically, courts will develop a consensus about the standard of care by interviewing expert witnesses with similar training and orientation. Other times they will use standards established by professional ethics code or guidelines for practice.

Issues of negligence and malpractice do not mean that counselors and psychologists should never try new or experimental techniques. They do, however, mean that appropriate precautions should be taken when they do so (Swenson, 1997) and that supervision should be sought when they move into new areas. Concerns about negligence should also caution psychologists and counselors to inform consumers if they are using methods that are experimental and offer other alternatives (Pope & Vasquez, 1991). Ultimately, negligence and malpractice are reminders that the practice of counseling in a clinical setting or the practice of psychology, whether in a clinical setting or laboratory, is serious business and that counselors and psychologists have a strong duty to consumers to be competent at what they do.

Professional Competence Problems: The Precipice of Harm

Sometimes competent psychologists and counselors become incompetent for a short or extended period of time. They may suffer a profound personal loss that clouds their ability to process information or make decisions clearly, as was true in Case 7-5. They may become incapacitated by drug or alcohol abuse (see Case 7-4). Depression may lead to thoughts of suicide or otherwise incapacitate them (Pope & Tabachnick, 1994). Yet it has only been in the past 20 years that psychology and the mental health professions in general have begun to focus attention on questions regarding professional incompetence (Stadler, Willing, Eberhage, & Ward, 1988). Most of that focus has been problems with professional competence in clinical practice (Layman & McNamara, 1997; Schoener & Gonsiorek, 1988).

In the prior edition of this book, problems with competence were lumped under the term "impairment." However, although the term has been widely used both in psychology and in other professions including medicine, nursing, and law as well as others, many problems with the term have been identified in the literature (Elman & Forrest, 2007; Kaslow et al., 2007b). The primary one is that the term impairment has a specific legal meaning in the Americans with Disabilities Act (ADA, 1990). As a result according to Falender, Collins and Shafranske (2005), when it is used carelessly in a professional setting it creates legal risks for faculty and supervisors. Because the ADA defines someone who has a disability as having a physical or mental impairment that interferes with or substantially limits one or more daily activities, they prohibit discrimination against such individuals and require employers to make accommodations for them (Falender et al., 2005). In fact Kaslow et al. (2007b, p. 481) emphasize that "impairment should only be used in conjunction with disabilities and not when addressing other aspects of professional competence." Consequently, those doing evaluations, like faculty and supervisors, need to understand the legal ramifications when they use the word impairment. Elman and Forrest point out that in addition to the legal problems the term has been used inconsistently in psychology and therefore lacks clarity.

In psychology, impairment had come to mean a broad set of concerns that included personal distress, decreased professional functioning, and ethical violations (Forrest et al., 1997). Stadler (1990) describes impaired counselors as professionals who "have lost the ability to transcend stressful events" (p. 178). The term *impaired professional* had even been used to describe psychologists who committed boundary violations (Orr, 1997). It should be noted, however, that despite the problems with the use of the term impairment much of the literature still uses the term.

Generally, there was little professional consensus on how to clearly distinguish between incompetence, impairment, and unethical behavior. In psychology, Laliotis and Grayson (1985) defined impairment as "interference in professional functioning due to chemical dependency, mental illness, or personal conflict" (p. 84). Although this definition was frequently referenced, impairment generally means a decline of abilities from a prior level of functioning (*Webster's Ninth New Collegiate Dictionary*, 1988). In psychology or counseling, the decline refers to a decrease in professional functioning (Nathan, 1986). Several authors (Kutz, 1986; Nathan, 1986; Schwebel, Skorina, & Schoener, 1994) recommended this meaning of impairment; that is, impairment was a deterioration or decay in professional abilities from a prior competent level. By contrast, *incompetence* they suggested meant the professional never achieved a reasonable standard of competence or failed to maintain it. They argued that failure to maintain competence may occur because the professional had not remained current with scientific knowledge or professional practice or was impaired (Forrest et al., 1997; Guy, Poelstra, & Stark, 1989). In other words, *impairment* has been used to meet a variety of things in different settings. Elman and Forrest (2007) summarized the problems with the term impairment:

> the current uses of the term impairment create legal and conceptual problems suggesting that the field cease using the term to describe trainees who are not meeting minimum standards of professional competence. We recommend retiring the term because it (a) overlaps with the ADA definition, (b) creates three kinds of legal risk, (c) comingles diminished functioning with competence never achieved, (d) mixes descriptions with explanations or potential causes of problematic behavior, and (e) is viewed as insensitive and disrespectful from some students' frame of reference. (p. 503)

They later go on to point out that the problems apply to the use of the word impairment when talking about the problems of mature professionals. Providing a clearer definition of incompetence is critical if it is going to be assessed and assessment of incompetence is critical because failing to provide competent service or for that matter failure to do competent research has already noted violates the principles of beneficence, nonmaleficence and justice.

Although the assessment and remediation of problems with professional competence is in its infancy, Kaslow et al. (2007b) identify eight proposals that might provide initial basis for assessment and remediation. First, it is important to establish benchmarks for performance and develop a schema for categorizing essential competencies. Benchmarks should identify the minimal level of competency for each stage of professional development. Among other things they should be "teachable, observable, measurable, containable, practical, derived by experts," (p. 480). In addition, they need to be categorized based on origin, for example, are they situational, developmental, or are they interpersonal problems, and on their severity and chronicity. Furthermore, is there potential for remediation? Second, policy should be in place to ensure due process and these should be communicated in advance to everyone in the system. Third, self-assessment should be encouraged. For example, the book by Anderson and Handelsman (2010) provides a primer with exercises that encourage self-assessment. Fourth, when competence problems are assessed remediation strategies should be in place that are clearly disclosed and developmentally appropriate. Fifth, attention to diversity is critical when assessing competence problems. The assessor should consider his or her own beliefs, values and attitudes about the individual and how they might be perceived and influence the choice of remediation strategies. Sixth, competence problems should be clearly communicated across levels of training and there should be more direct communication between internships and training programs. For example, the current norm for letters of recommendation in the United States rarely includes negative qualities (Megargee, 1997). Pressure to do so comes from a variety of sources, for example, accreditation of a program in psychology often takes into consideration where and how many students have been placed in internships. Seventh, protection of confidentiality should be consistent with current ethics codes. For example, the 2002 APA ethics code provided guidance about when personal information about a student could be disclosed. Information about when it might occur should be included in program materials as well as information used to evaluate to evaluate or assist a student whose personal problems affected their competence or they posed a threat to others. Last, ethical, legal, and regulatory implications need to be considered when assessing competence. The article by Kaslow et al. provides much more detail about each proposal and should be considered carefully by anyone concerned about problems with competent students to mature professionals.

Questions about the incidence of incompetence among psychologists and counselors are difficult to answer, although journalistic exaggeration has led to claims that most psychotherapists are "wounded" or "crazy" (Maeder, 1989, pp. 37–38). Because most estimates rely on survey data that are dependent on how questions are phrased, how impairment is defined, and who are surveyed (Deutsch, 1985; Gilroy, Carroll, & Murra, 2002; Guy et al., 1989; Mahoney, 1997; Norcorss, Strausser-Kirtland, & Missar, 1988; Thoreson, Miller, & Krauskopf, 1989), estimates vary widely. The same problem exists when trying to estimate the incidence of student impairment (Forrest, Elman, Gizara, & Vacha-Hasse, 1999). Surveys have reported that between 20% and 82% of psychologists indicate they have relationship and/or marital problems, 13%–57% suffer from depression, 12%–35% have episodes of anxiety, and 9%–11% have difficulties with substance abuse. Pope and Tabachnick (1994) reported that 29% of the psychologists they surveyed indicated that had felt suicidal and 4% disclosed at least one suicide attempt whereas Deutsch (1985) found that 2% of her sample had attempted suicide. If these figures are accurate, Layman and McNamara (1997) suggested that the incidence seems to exceed the rate of mental problems for the general population reported in the *Diagnostic and Statistical Manual of Mental Disorders* (4th ed. [*DSM-IV*]; American Psychiatric Association, 2004).

Additionally, between 26% and 43% of practicing psychologists report sometimes struggling with issues related to their effectiveness at work (Guy et al., 1989; Mahoney, 1997). These include episodes of emotional exhaustion, concerns about the size and severity of their caseload, doubts about their own therapeutic effectiveness, and feelings of disillusionment (Mahoney, 1997). In one study, 26% identified themselves as having been impaired at some point in their lives (Coster & Schwebel, 1997). More recently Gilroy, Carroll, and Murra (2002) found 62% of counseling psychology members of APA identified themselves as depressed and 42% had experienced suicidal ideation or behavior. These rates are higher than those reported by Deutsch (1985).

These problems may sometimes negatively impact consumers. For example, in a study of members of the psychotherapy division of APA, Pope et al. (1987) found that 71.2% admitted that they had worked when they were too distressed to be effective and 5.9% had done therapy under the influence of alcohol. In a parallel study of academic psychologists, Tabachnick et al. (1991) found that 77.2% had taught when they were too distressed to be effective, 4.6% had taught while under the influence of alcohol, and 0.8% had taught while under the influence of illegal drugs.

Although a particular figure may not be reliable, taken together the data suggest that psychologists and counselors are not unlike other people. Sometimes they become too emotionally upset to be effective in their work and in other aspects of their lives. On the other hand, we know very little about the frequency with which psychologists and counselors meet the ADA definition of physical impairment, although Thoreson et al. (1989) indicated that 10% of their sample had recurrent physical problems and Guy et al. (1989) found that over 14% of their sample reported stress from physical illness. Just like other people, psychologists suffer strokes, get diseases, break bones, and suffer from dementia. These too can be sources of deterioration in both physical and psychological functioning. Clearly, being a professional does not insulate one from problems of professional competence or impairment. Furthermore, being a psychologist or counselor does not mean that they are all willing to seek therapy for their problems (Deutsch, 1985; Smith & Burton, 2009).

O'Connor (2001) asks how do we reach professionals who are distressed or incompetent and give them the care they need, and how should the profession handle the potential for harm to the public? First, he points to the professional role of the professional as the reason for some of the problems. He points out the roles are complex and often emotionally exhausting. Sometimes psychologists or counselors move from being an administrator to a therapist to a teacher to a supervisor with little time to process what happened in the prior hour. Furthermore the role of clinician requires a heightened sensitivity to the emotional needs of others, a willingness to put their needs before one's own, and the ability to withhold one's own emotions in the face of reported trauma and the client's intense emotional experiences. In addition practitioners often work environments that are isolating. Information conveyed in them is confidential and reciprocal relationships with clients are not allowed. Not only must dual relationships be avoided but personal needs must be kept out of the treatment room. O'Connor asks although these are a necessary part of the therapy process, in what other professions are individuals required to repress such basic human responses to such a degree?

Knapp and VandeCreek (2006) have argued that that vicarious traumatization and compassion fatigue have been noted in helpers of trauma survivors. In addition client may act out in frightening ways. They may be aggressive toward the therapist physically, emotionally, and legally. Knapp and VandeCreek give the following example:

Case 7-7

The female patient of a psychologist is furious when she was referred to another provider. Although the referral was therapeutically indicated and handled tactfully, the psychologist's car was vandalized, a rock was thrown through his office window, and his wife received a letter falsely accusing him of having an affair with another woman.

O'Connor reports a study by Pope (1994b) that found one in five psychologists have been physically attacked by a client, four and five have feared an attack and 97% have feared that a client would commit suicide. One of the authors had the personal experience of having a client tell her she had a gun in her backpack. Her only thought was how to get between the client and the door. Luckily, her supervisor was in the building and she was able to express her fear to him in a safe environment and they were able to come up with a plan to help the student without endangering her.

Because as Pope (1994a) has noted, there is a conspiracy of silence some which surrounds professional distress and impairment, psychologists and counselors often try to insulate themselves from incompetent or unethical colleagues. This often results in an adversarial approach to those individuals charged with a violation. On the other hand, the American Psychological Association first publicly addressed the need for assistance and intervention for distressed and impaired psychologists at the 1981 convention (Smith & Moss, 2009). Although early efforts focused on substance abuse and dependence, the goals of the committee have shifted to education, prevention, and treatment. However, as noted later, state, provincial and territorial associations are still significantly lacking in structured assistance for impaired professionals (Barnett & Hillard, 2001).

Furthermore there is no consistent approach to assessing the problem psychologist or counselor. The ethical acculturation model (Anderson & Handelsman, 2010; Handelsman et al., 2005) introduced in Chapter 13 could be of great help along these lines. Is this a counselor or psychologist who is behaving from a separation strategy? Does his or her attitude come from seeing the ethical guidelines as too personal or restrictive? By contrast, the psychologist or counselor may be someone who was truly integrated into the profession, but because of changes in the profession is experiencing acculturation stress. Assessing where an individual is in terms of their ethical acculturation to the profession might provide a way to decide who may be good candidates for rehabilitation and who may not be. In addition, it would provide a starting point for an intervention. Certainly research is necessary both on the model and its implications for rehabilitation.

As noted earlier, some state psychology boards operate primarily to protect the public, but fail to identify ways to help the practitioner in the process. O'Connor (2001) points to the California Board of Psychology which does not support a diversion program for psychologists despite the fact that the state medical board has an active diversion program for physicians. Certainly some offenses might preclude diversion because the risks to the public would be too great. For example, sexual involvement with a client or student may be an offense to dangerous to risk reoccurrence. Certainly monitoring, supervision and costs of running a diversionary program are significant but they have been addressed in other fields like medicine (Smith & Moss, 2009). In fact Barnett and Hillard (2001) examined the availability of colleague assistance programs among state and provincial psychology boards between 1998 and 1999 and found that 69% of them had no formal program for impaired professionals. Furthermore, 61% reported no plans to develop a program that 54% believed that such a resource was not needed. Furthermore several boards reported having prior programs which were now defunct primarily because of lack of use. Although they no longer offer these services some had resources available to assist impaired psychologist like providing referrals. Smith and Moss (2009) hypothesized that the lack of use might be due to misinformation about the services or the fear of negative consequences resulting from using an assistance program, for example, personal embarrassment, loss of status, or restricted or loss of license. On the other hand, they pointed out that private therapy is an important option for psychologists and that is possible that may choose this over assistance programs affiliated with state associations because of the fear of negative consequences.

O'Connor has several recommendations that might improve psychologists' approach to the impaired professional and at the same time protecting the public. Although too lengthy to include here, a few more critical ones will be mentioned. First, demonizing those who are distressed or impaired is counterproductive and fails to acknowledge that as psychologists and counselors, under certain circumstances, we can all be vulnerable to distress and even inappropriate or impaired behavior. We all have life crises and we need to admit they sometimes influence our work with students, colleagues, and clients. At the same time, we need to acknowledge that impairment does not negate consequences for unethical behavior or incompetence. As O'Connor says:

> The business of our profession is delicate and complex. The dangers for the consumer and occupational hazards for the practitioner are very real. In so far as the person of the psychologist is used as a therapeutic tool, both client and professional must be alert, and have effective alternatives, to ensure that this very important work is managed carefully, responsibly, and you mainly for all parties. (p. 350)

The Incompetent Trainee

A great deal has been written over the last 10 years about incompetent trainees. Although initially the term impairment was used to describe trainees with competence difficulties, for the reasons already articulated an attempt is being made to change the vocabulary to one of competence since it provides clearer definitions and descriptions of a problematic behavior and avoids problems with the ADA (1990). For example, it can distinguish between students who have reached an acceptable level of professional competence which has been reduced in the wake of personal distress, like a particularly contentious divorce, and students who have not yet reached or are unable to reach a minimal level of professional competence (Gizara & Forest, 2004). As Elman and Forest (2007) point out, professional competence that is lost may be more remediable than competence that has never been attained, particularly if the person has demonstrated a basic inability or unwillingness to do so, perhaps someone who is using an ethical acculturation separation strategy to form his or her professional identity.

In a thorough review of the identification, remediation, dismissal and legal issues surrounding the incompetent trainee, Forest, Elman, Gizara, and Vacha-Haase (1999) found that most studies of trainee impairment or incompetence provided very limited empirical information because of the way the surveys were structured, the statistics used and the methods for reporting results. They did note that at that time not all programs conducted annual evaluations of their students or they did not evaluate them one critical aspects of professional functioning like assessment, ethical conduct, and interpersonal skills. Those that did were not consistent in reporting the results either verbally or in written form to their students suggesting that some graduate programs were not in compliance with accreditation or ethical standards that require written notification as a part of due process. Furthermore, little information was available about the criteria that programs used to evaluate students progress. To summarize they found that the most common forms of impairment identified across the studies were clinical deficiencies, interpersonal problems, problems in supervision, and personality disorders. They found no studies within psychology that specifically addressed impairment and research conduct. On the other hand, they reported a study of students' exposure to research misconduct in graduate programs in chemistry, microbiology, engineering, and sociology. Andersen et al. (1994) reported that the average student was exposed to 2–5 episodes of research misconduct by faculty or students. In a more recent study that examined faculty's perception of students' emotional difficulties that impacted learning and performance with clients, Huprich and Rudd (2004) found the more common problems reported were adjustment disorders, alcohol problems, anxiety and depression, or personality disorders. It's important that similar data is gathered in counseling.

Based on the studies reviewed, Forest et al. (1999) concluded that most academic and internship programs reported having at least one incompetent trainee during the last five years. In other words every academic and internship program is regularly dealing with at least one case of incompetence or unethical behavior. Dealing with such students can take an emotional and time toll on faculty. The following case is an example.

Case 7-8

Beginning with his first year in the program the faculty recognized that the student was problematic despite the fact he had glowing recommendations from his master's program and had a publication. The other students did not want to work with him and he failed his first practicum and his grades in his coursework were weak. The faculty spent numerous hours counseling the student and at faculty meetings trying to decide the best course of action. He was required to repeat his practicum and faculty worked very close with him in the program's own clinic. Although his skills were minimal, the clinic director decided that based on his progress he deserved a B in the class. He went on to do an off-campus practicum at a site that the program had not used before. The supervisor gave him glowing reports. Furthermore, during this practicum the student worked on a research project and had a second publication. When it came time for him to apply to internships, he was very careful in picking the people to write letters. The supervisor from his last practicum site was one. With some reservations, the internship coordinator recommended him for internship emphasizing his strengths believing that the internship site would recognize problems if they looked at his transcript. He got an internship at an APA approved site but failed it at the midyear evaluations. When he returned to campus, he was counseled out of the program and got a degree in educational psychology. Later, the program faculty found out that he had completed another internship that was not APA approved and was able to get licensed in the state.

Forrest et al. point out that one of the possible reasons that focusing on trainee incompetence is so stressful is that as psychologists or counselors prefer roles with students to be positive. We prefer to provide support rather than to be punitive. Yet as Vasquez (1999) points out we have the responsibility to face the complex and emotionally stressful dilemma of the trainee who is demonstrating some kind of incompetence. She points out from a feminist perspective that supervisors should be proactive in analyzing power dynamics and differentials between the supervisor and supervisee and model the use of power in the service of the supervisee. At the same time she points out the realities of the power imbalance in the therapeutic relationship and reminds psychology and counseling faculty that they have responsibilities to the students' future clients.

Forrest et al. also point out that one of the barriers to dismissal in the studies they reviewed included the fear of legal reprisals by students. They reviewed several notable court cases which indicated that when appropriately handled through due process, the courts have supported the reasonable decision by faculty in training programs and that courts include interpersonal skills as part of academic requirements. As Vasquez (1999) points out it's important to be aware of one's state laws since some require a right to a hearing in the due process involved in dismissals while most states do not.

Despite the fact that faculty decisions are usually upheld in legal cases as long as due process has been followed, Johnson (2008) has recently pointed out that programs, internships, supervisors play the "hot potato game" with incompetent supervisees passing them on to the next person hoping that person or site will fail the student. He provides three definitions of competence: professional competence refers to the psychologist's ability to carry out certain tasks appropriately and effectively. It includes having the knowledge, technical skill, and clinical training for use with the individual or community being served. He points out that what Elman and Forrest (2007) described as problems the professional competence, such problems are often connected with insufficient training or to difficulties with moral character or psychological fitness. By moral character he refers to virtues such as honesty and integrity in which are critical to maintaining public trust. These are the virtues discussed in Chapter 5. Third, he distinguishes psychological fitness as the emotional or mental stability of a professional and is highly relevant to the person's capacity to provide services safely and effectively. These three issues are critical to the gatekeeping obligation of faculty which he calls *an ethical imperative.*

As Kitchener (1992) has said, "There is a specific ethical obligation *not* to graduate those who, because of their incompetence or lack of ethical sensitivity, would inflict harm on the consumers whom they have agreed to help" (p. 190). Turning a blind eye to trainee competence problems not only endangers the public but also damages the public's image of counseling and psychology. Johnson points out that there is a tension between trying to foster growth and objective and accurate evaluations. He calls this the *advocacy-evaluation tension* and provides several suggestions to manage this tension. First, he calls for actively preparing faculty members and supervisors for their roles and especially managing the advocacy-evaluation tension. Second, ensure that all psychologists or counselors who work with trainees are familiar with the ACA (2005) or APA 2002 ethical principles and standards that are relevant to the gatekeeping obligation. In Case 7-8 the profession as a whole had failed in its gatekeeping function despite the fact that the internship failed him and he was counseled out of his academic program. Third, ensure that all psychologists who are engaged in training are competent to detect problems of competence and to provide the necessary but difficult corrective feedback. Fourth, recognize that competence is neither a dichotomous nor static construct. Trainees may be highly competent in some areas and yet lack the ethical virtues allow them to provide safe and honest service. Fifth, training programs should try to develop strategies to separate the mentoring and evaluator roles with trainees reducing the burden on specific individuals. Sixth, develop strategies to prevent grade inflation which affects student evaluation and letters of recommendation. Clearly, not all students can be in the top 10% and yet looking at letters of recommendation, sometimes it appears that way. Seventh, routinely provide formative and summative evaluations for all trainees and carefully document these evaluations. Eighth, work with professional organizations and accrediting bodies to develop standardized, valid and reliable measures of competence. Clearly a work that is already underway. Last, consider both formal and informal mechanisms for enhancing communication and cooperation among psychologists or counselors working in graduate training programs internship sites, and state licensing boards.

Forrest, Miller, and Elman (2008) add to this an ecological model based on Brofenbrenner (1995) that directs attention to the interconnection among settings rather than a single person or a single setting. The model moves from the individual's direct interaction with peers, supervisors, and instructors to cultural beliefs about being a professional as well as other factors such as attitudes about race and ethnicity, gender, sexual orientation, and disability. They argue that development is a function of the person psychological resources and liabilities and their capacity to engage with the environment. A critical assumption is that planning and policies need to be present at all levels before there is a problem with a specific trainee as was true of Case 7-8.

Maintaining Competence

Reducing the incidence of events that harm consumers, research participants, trainees, or other professionals is preferable than to wait until a trainee is so stressed or incompetent that they fall over the precipice. To do so involves two processes: becoming aware of the risk factors that lead to the vulnerability and result in incompetent behavior and engaging in self-help behaviors that provide support and decrease the sense of isolation and fear of reprisals. Smith and Moss (2009) identify several occupational factors associated with the risk for burnout and other causes of incompetent behavior. They include managing many roles in the work environment and the expectation to shift rapidly from one role to the next several times throughout the course of a single day and maintaining a high level of performance in each. Derived from the work of Rupert and Morgan (2005), they added decreased control over work, longer work hours, greater time devoted to paperwork word, administrative duties, and negative client behavior.

Certainly the pressures from managed care have added to the potential for burnout among therapists. In fact the nationwide study of psychologists and clinical practice, Sherman and Thelen (1998) found that malpractice claims and a change to work situation where the most troublesome work events.

Smith and Moss point to other more personal characteristics which can contribute to the risk of incompetent behavior, for example, relationship problems and personal illness or injury. They point out that it one sample of psychologists these were the factors that contributed most to stress and burnout. Certainly, as current events have illuminated, financial problems and loss of income have increased the risk for suicide. These added to other personal concerns like relationship strain with a spouse or partner, and loss in financial status, all may lead to feelings of inadequacy.

Sherman and Thelen (1998) found that these were the work and personal pressures that were reported most frequently as leading to feelings of distress and "impairment." They found that respondents who experienced a greater number of life events and/or work factors were also most likely to report a greater amount of distress or impairment. Barnett (2007a) points out that numerous data exists to suggest that psychologists have life histories that place them at increased risk for distress and impairment. For example, women mental health professionals are more likely to have histories of childhood abuse, parental alcoholism and dysfunction in their family of origin as well as being more likely to have experienced the death of a family member than women from other professions (Elliott & Guy, 1993). He suggests that as a result mental health professionals may be more attracted to their profession because it allows them to continue as caregivers and because it also allows them to resolve earlier patterns of difficulty and dysfunction.

By contrast, because counselors and psychologists are "mental health professionals" they are expected to have it together, to be the ones that other people come to for help, and not the ones who need help themselves. These beliefs add to the fear of or embarrassment about asking for help themselves. We believe this is especially true of trainees, who have not yet developed a clear sense of professional identity, but may act on false beliefs about a profession about which they still know little.

By contrast, Barnett (2007a) argues that psychologists and counselors must look out for and avoid the use of negative coping strategies that may further compound their difficulties. For examples, self-medicating with substances such as drugs, alcohol or food and seeking emotional support or gratification from clients rather than providing them the support they need.

Due to the fact that professional distress if ignored or left untreated can lead to professional incompetence, the possibility of ethical violations, and real harm to the consumer, Barnett, Johnson, and Hillard (2006) call the pursuit of inter- and intrapersonal wellness and ongoing self-care an ethical imperative. Barnett (2007a) pointed to several sections of the 2002 APA Ethics Code that support this stance. Similarly, the 2005 ACA Ethics Code also had several standards that require counselors and counselor trainees to engage in self-care and seek help. Ultimately, these requirements are based on the principles of beneficence, nonmaleficence, and justice. As already noted, the incompetent professional can cause great harm whether through supervision, therapy, or research ignoring the basic principle of the professions which is to help others. The principle of justice basically meaning fairness cannot be fulfilled when the professional is incompetent since consumers are basically cheated out of the services or information, they contracted to receive.

Baker (2007) suggests that prevention should begin with graduate training. She suggests training modules should be developed for use in graduate programs as well as continuing education programs that focus on personal and professional aspects of self-care across the professional lifespan. Elman and Forrest (2007) suggest that is edification and intervention with trainees who are having problems should begin at the level of graduate training. The focus should be on students who are having problems developing professional competence or whose behavior indicates a lack of self reflective thus, self-awareness in self-care. Generally faculty and supervisors have no models for addressing these challenges and often they do not model them. When they do not model the value of self-care for themselves or convey that is respected as much his hard work and scholarly productivity, it is difficult for the trainee to admit they need help. Baker (2007) aptly calls professions like psychology or counseling a "culture of silence" (p. 609) and points out a culture such as this does not tend to foster conversations between faculty or supervisors with the trainees.

Self-Care

Data suggest that professionals actually engaged in substantial amounts of self-care behavior. Mahoney (1997) found that four out of five practicing psychologists read for pleasure, engaged in a hobby, took time off for vacations, and/or went to movies, museums, or concerts for enjoyment. Additionally, three out of four engaged in physical exercise and got together with peers for support. He concluded that the average practitioner is a healthy and happy individual who enjoys working and takes active steps to cope with his or her own personal problems. For the majority, this also included seeking personal therapy when it was appropriate. In fact, Coster and Schwebel (1997) found that 74% of psychologists are well functioning and that social support was rated as one of the key components of their success. Thoreson et al. (1989) also concluded that the majority of the psychologists they surveyed were healthy and satisfied with their work and interpersonal relationships.

Coster and Schwebel (1997) also investigated the kinds of experiences psychologists think are critical to function well. Their data, along with Mahoney's (1997), indicate a pattern of coping mechanisms in which psychologists can engage to safeguard their psychological well being, avoid impairment, and protect consumers.

- *Develop and nurture a strong interpersonal support system with family, friends, and other companions.* Family and friends can be a wellspring of support when the stressors involved with work seem overwhelming.
- *Develop a close, cooperative relationship with a group of peers to share the frustrations and excitement that surround your work.* These people can provide objective feedback when necessary, confront stressors when they see them arise, and help problem-solve before stressors begin to overwhelm effective coping. Knowing that others are struggling with similar problems can help relieve stress. Hearing their solutions may unlock some for you.
- *Take time to nurture your personal well-being.* One psychologist said the following words should hang on every psychologist's wall: "Rest, relaxation, physical exercise, avocations, vacations" (Coster & Schwebel, 1997, p. 11). These words and Mahoney's (1997) data suggest the importance of developing and maintaining a balanced lifestyle that allows time for fun and physical activity as well as work. As Sommers-Flanagan & Sommers-Flanagan (2007) suggest, the most valuable tool the professional has is his or herself and this makes self care critical. Osborne (2004) adds the importance of developing stamina both on the job and off the job. It would help the professional maintain their disposition of wonder and curiosity that may have led them into the field initially. Rather than promoting a deficit model by referring to burn out, mental health professionals should be encouraged to focus their attention on and engage in activities that prioritize endurance, resilience and stamina.
- *Stay involved in professional development activities.* This can involve continuing education activities, workshops, supervision, and more. They can help avoid incompetence from failing to stay up with current literature and a sense of isolation.

- *Monitor yourself and seek help, including therapy, if your own efforts at remediation fail.* Because so much of what psychologists and counselors do involves working with consumers or others whose welfare often lies in their hands, as already noted, it is essential that they are vigilant about their own weaknesses. Through honest self-assessment and recognition of the danger signals described by Elliott and Guy (1993) and Barnett (2007a).
- *If personal problems persist, remove yourself from professional activities that could lead to harm for consumers or research participants.*

This last recommendation is consistent with the ACA and APA ethics codes for several years. It is likely that the emphasis on self-care and protecting the public from incompetent and unethical professionals will only increase. Many professionals are aware of the stresses in their lives and how they affect their work and their need to engage in self-care behaviors. Take the following case based on one by Knapp and VandeCreek (2006, p. 67).

Case 7-9

A psychologist underwent a series of personal tragedies. Within a two-year period four deaths of significant others had occurred in his life. One death involved his father which left him substantial problems with the estate that needed to be handled. In addition, his wife became ill and had to undergo numerous treatments and his son was hospitalized as a result of a serious traffic accident. He recognized that the events had exacted a substantial emotional toll. He appropriately reduced his workload so he could meet his own responsibilities at home and he entered therapy to help him deal with the stress and anxiety. In addition, he started a regular exercise routine.

In other words, he appropriately engaged in self-care following the requirements of ethical standards.

On the other hand, sometimes "professionals can be their own worst enemies" (Kilburg, 1986, p. 25). Psychologists or counselors, like other professionals, learn to be and are rewarded for being independent thinkers and for handling situations on their own. Asking for help may threaten their identity. Yet battling incompetence alone may be destructive because it may lead to a loss of perspective (Kilburg, 1986). When facing evidence of incompetence or feelings of profound distress, psychologists and counselors should remember that many of their peers have faced similar challenges and that they have an ethical responsibility to get help.

When professionals fail to seek help, they may inadvertently or intentionally harm consumers or research participants. One of the most difficult ethical questions facing the profession involves whether professionals who have committed unethical acts as a result of incompetence should be treated and allowed to return to their professional positions, whether they should be punished, or both (Brown, 1997b; Gonsiorek, 1997; Layman & McNamara, 1997; Orr, 1997; Remely & Herlihy, 2010). Part of the difficulty in answering this question seems to be confusion about the causes of unethical acts that can be remediated and those that cannot be. There is a difference between a professional who is incompetent due to insufficient training and supervision, one who is incompetent because of an inability to achieve the expected level of a professional, one whose moral character is sadly deficient, and one who is incompetent because of psychological problems.

When ethical violations occur, assessing the cause of those violations is critical in determining the consequences for the violator (Schoener & Gonsiorek, 1988). For example, if unethical behavior results from chemical dependency or personal stress that interfered with professional functioning, there might be a possibility for remediation. However, protection of the consumer needs to be balanced against the responsibility to save the livelihood and possible social value that a remediated professional might make (Gonsiorek, 1997; Layman & MacNamara, 1997; Orr, 1997). Although, mental health professionals have a responsibility to treat colleagues with care and compassion and allow them a fair hearing (Welfel, 2010), firm guidelines or limits on future professional activities must also be set in order to protect the consumer (Orr, 1997). In addition, there is a social responsibility to the victim or victims, who may want nothing more than a sincere apology and admission of responsibility from the offending person (Brown, 1997b). If, however, unethical acts are due to bad character, meanness of spirit, maliciousness, or a need to exert power over a woman or other vulnerable persons, impairment is probably not an issue and rehabilitation should probably not be considered. It is hard to imagine, for example, that Dr. Julius H. Masserman—a psychiatrist who allegedly raped at least three female clients under the influence of Sodium Amytal, which rendered them unconscious, and who apparently violated other female clients over a 30-year period—could be considered impaired, or forgiven even if he was (Noel & Watterson, 1992).

Conclusion

Competence has received a great deal of attention in the literature in the last few years. Undoubtedly, it is because it is the foundation for ethical behavior in the mental health professions. It does no good to provide good informed consent, keep information confidential, and avoid multiple relationships if the professional is basically incompetent. Internship sites, academic programs, and professional organizations are working together to define what it means to be a competent professional as will be clear in Chapter 8. It seems clear, however, that incompetence has many causes. There are differences between a professional who is incompetent because of insufficient training, one who is incompetent because of the intellectual or psychological inability to reach the expected level of competence that a mature professional has, one who has a moral character lacking in the virtues necessary for a competent professional and one whose psychological fitness may be limited temporarily, for example, as a result of alcoholism, and one whose psychological fitness is too limited for a career in counseling or psychology.

Luckily, most professionals do not fall into one of the categories that suggest they cannot be remediated. On the other hand, as already noted the professional responsibilities of psychologists and counselors are often stressful and can lead to temporary incompetence. Professionals must remain vigilant about their own mental health and how it is affecting their students, clients, supervisees, and research participants. In these cases, as Barnett, Johnson and Hillard (2006) have said, it is an ethical imperative that mental health professionals remain competent and consequently engage in self-care. The suggestions enumerated in this chapter should help.

Questions for Discussion or Consideration

1. What stressors are you facing in your own life?
2. Are you engaging in any self-care behaviors? If so, which do you find of most help and why do you think they are so helpful?
3. What keeps you from engaging in self-care behaviors?
4. Are you worried about your competence in any area? If so, how are you handling it?

8
Competence in Practice, Research, and Teaching

Although competence in general as discussed in Chapter 7 applies to any area in psychology and counseling, each area requires specialized competencies that allow ethical practice, research, or teaching to occur. This chapter discusses those specifics. In addition, specialty areas like working in schools, in forensics, in industrial or organizational settings each require specific knowledge, skills, attitudes, and values. Anyone wishing to venture into the specific settings will find it ethically necessary to develop those qualities that make competent service possible. However, overarching all areas is the need to develop knowledge about individual differences. You simply cannot treat, supervise or do research with an aging Japanese population the same way you might work with White, young, gang members. Everyone is not the same and for too long psychology treated white, middle-class males as the standard against which everyone was judged. Consequently, this section begins with a rather detailed discussion of individual differences since they're so critical in every role that counselors and psychologists play.

Competence and Individual Differences

The professions of psychology and counseling in the United States exist in a rapidly changing world with substantial demographic shifts. According to the projections by the U.S. Census Bureau, Whites of European descent will be in the minority by 2042 whereas racial and ethnic "minorities" will represent the majority of the population and by 2050, Whites are projected to be only 46% of the population, making them the minority. In fact, by the time the baby boomers retire, the primary groups who contribute to social security will be racial and ethnic minorities (Sue, Arredondo, & McDavis, 1992). While this has been called, the "diversification of America" (Sue et al., 1992), a second trend called the "graying of America" is happening concurrently (Cavanaugh, 1997). In 1900, older adults represented 4% of the population. By 2030, older adults will account for 21% of the population (Cavanaugh, 1997) and most of these older adults will be women (Rybash, Roodin, & Hoyer, 1995). Again according to a report released in August of 2008 by the Census Bureau, the older population is expected to more than triple between 2008 and 2050.

One implication of these social and demographic changes is that mental health professionals will have to continually update their skills, challenge their biases, and remain knowledgeable in order to serve and study changing populations without harming them out of ignorance or being disrespectful of their decision making. This is particularly true since only 6% of the psychologists are people of color (American Psychological Association, 1997). As a result, the likelihood of a person of color receiving services from someone who is White is very high. Furthermore, because people are living longer and are often providing care for their grandchildren (Jimenez, 2002), it is more and more likely that psychologists and counselors will be seeing older adults. Consequently, one of the essential competencies identified by the 2002 Scottsdale conference was individual and cultural diversity competency (Daniel, Roysircar, Abeles, & Boyd, 2004). They focused on increasing self-awareness about three isms—racism, hetero sexism, and ageism.

Daniel et al. (2004) pointed out that while each group has unique characteristics in terms of "visibility, stigmatization, marginalization, and social activism," they all have stereotypes that frequently lead researchers, therapists, instructors, and supervisors to hold attitudes and express behaviors based on biases and unwarranted assumptions (p. 757). In addition to guidelines on sexism and racism (Appendices D and A, respectively), the APA Council approved guidelines on ageism (The Guidelines for Psychological Practice with Older Adults, APA, 2004; Appendix C) and heterosexism (The Guidelines for Psychotherapy with Lesbian, Gay and Bisexual Clients, APA, 2000; Appendix B). Since the therapist's persona is critical to the development of the therapeutic alliance and the therapeutic alliance is critical to successful therapy, the therapist must be open to self-examination of their own privilege and reactions to race, gender, sexual orientation, and ageism (Anderson & Middleton, 2011; Daniel et al., 2004).

Psychologists began to recognize the need to respond to changing demographics and cultural differences in the late 1960s and early 1970s. These concerns culminated in the Vail Conference in July 1973 (Korman, 1974). Out of the conference came an ethical commitment to the recruitment, retention, and graduation of minority students as well as a recognition that all psychologists need to be prepared to function in a culturally diverse society (Korman, 1974). Eventually, this led to an increased emphasis in APA accreditation policies on social responsibility as well as on knowledge of and sensitivity to cultural and individual differences (APA, 2002; APA, 2005). Similarly, the multicultural counseling movement has represented a revolutionary force that has taken center stage in the counseling profession (Cartwright, Daniels, & Zhang, 2008; D'Andrea & Heckman, 2008). Both APA and ACA have advocated for increased research on these populations. In addition Sue et al. (1992) formulated a set of 31 multicultural competencies. In the same year, these competencies were endorsed by the Association for Multicultural Counseling and Development and affiliate of ACA. These guidelines along with the ethics codes of both ACA and APA call for increased research on racial/ethnic minority groups as well as older populations and increased training to combat the continuing discrimination and prejudice that is day-to-day reality in the lives of many marginalized groups and impacts their access to institutions such as healthcare resources (Collins et al., 2002; DHHS, 2001).

Competence with Racial and Ethnic Minorities

Despite the written attention to the needs of marginalized groups and the changes in policy, Carter and Forsyth (2007) point out that there is minimal availability of research that focuses on or includes racial or ethnic minority groups. Consequently, this leads to serious questions about the ability of psychology or counseling to ethically provide adequate and competent services to these populations. The immediacy of these concerns was identified by the National Institute of health (1994) and the 2001 Surgeon General's report (U.S. Department of Health and Human Services [DHHS], 2001) on race, culture, ethnicity and mental health in the United States. The Surgeon General's report indicated there were serious disparities both in the access to and quality of mental health services available to racial/ethnic minority groups as compared with Anglo-Americans and that the scientific basis to provide such services was inadequate (DHHS, 2001). If this research is not conducted, it may render psychology and counseling obsolete to substantial portions of the United States and Canadian populations.

Carter and Forsyth (2007) pointed out that a number of studies have analyzed the content of various psychology and counseling journals since 1976. They conclude that although there has been a general increase in the number of articles that focus on racial/ethnic minority groups, even when a focus on racial/ethnic groups is broadly defined the percentage of articles that actually focus on these groups is disproportionately low. Despite the guidelines from ACA, APA and NIH, there appears to be little progress over the past 20 years in many specialty areas in adequately addressing issues of race and culture in the research literature.

The treatment and integration of racial and ethnic minorities in psychology and counseling create complex dilemmas for the professions. In addition to the lack of research literature, because the Euro-American male culture is so dominant in the western view of psychology and counseling, it is difficult for those who were raised in that culture to recognize their own encapsulation (Wrenn, 1985). According to the concept of cultural encapsulation, many mental health professionals define reality according to the set of cultural assumptions and beliefs that they learned growing up. In addition, there has been little within the mental health literature that encourages professionals to examine their own points of privilege and how this lack of self awareness impacts work with clients, students and colleagues who are different from the professional (Anderson & Middleton, 2011). Thus, those in the majority culture are often insensitive to cultural variation and their own privilege and assume others view and experience the world as they do. These assumptions also include unreasoned beliefs about others who are different that are accepted without proof. The heterogeneity within particular groups adds to its complexity. Because the beliefs are assumed, there is little motivation to change them (Wrenn, 1985). Nevertheless, data (Carter, 1991) suggest that there are profound differences in cultural values, both between and within different racial and ethnic groups. This has led some to suggest that "a serious moral vacuum exists in the delivery of cross-cultural counseling and therapy services because the values of a dominant culture have been imposed on the culturally different consumer" (Pedersen & Marsalla, 1982, p. 498). This is probably why individual and cultural-diversity was included as one of the core competencies in the 2002 APA conference (Daniel et al., 2004).

Despite the explicit commitment to diversity, behavior and attitudes have been slower to change, perhaps because changing attitudes and behavior implies that mental health professionals need to examine their own biases. Self-assessment to identify attitudes and behaviors that reveal racial insensitivity may include self-report standardized measures, journaling, process notes, self reflective skills, critical incidents, and supervision (Daniel et al., 2004). Such self-evaluations can be painful, as they may reveal attitudes that are not consistent with the self-concepts of people who see themselves as healers, helpers, and students of human behavior. At the same time, such self-examination is essential if psychologists or counselors are going to avoid rigid, limited, monocultural perspectives and to honestly evaluate the transcultural applicability of the theories they use to conceptualize clients as well as research (Katz, 1985). Such an evaluation can help avoid the kind of harm that occurred in the following case.

Case 8-1

John Jones, a 40-year-old, single, African American parent, joined a parenting-education group. He reported needing help to cope and communicate with his 13-year-old daughter, who had recently become difficult to control and uncommunicative. He was feeling significant stress because of his parenting problems. As the only African American in the group, Mr Jones felt somewhat uncomfortable. This was exacerbated when, prior to the second session, several of the group participants began to question him about the fact that several male African American high school students were beginning to date White girls in the community. Mr Jones indicated he had no particular insight into the issue. The psychologist overheard the interchange but ignored it, choosing to redirect the group to the preplanned topic for the evening. Mr Jones did not return to the group after that session (Burn, 1992).

The therapist neglected to consider the cultural implications of her decisions by putting Mr Jones in the group without considering the effect on him and other group members, by failing to deal with cultural differences after the initial group meeting, and by failing to confront racism when it occurred. By pretending to be color-blind, the therapist was guilty of racism. Although it was probably unintentional, this kind of racism not only failed to help Mr Jones with the problem for which he entered therapy, but it also may have reinforced the belief that therapy is a White discipline and offers little help to those who do not fit the monocultural perspective. The case highlights the importance of understanding not only the cultural values of clients but also the history of racial and ethnic relations in this country (Sue, Zane, & Young, 1994; Zeter, 2011). The role of racism in the lives of both Whites and ethnic and racial minorities can hardly be ignored.

Ethical responsibilities to be responsive to cultural differences derive from principles of beneficence and nonmaleficence, as do other issues of competence. In this case, they overlap substantially with issues of justice, given that justice is concerned with fair treatment when the rights of one group are balanced against the rights of another group (Cayleff, 1986). Fair treatment implies that particular characteristics, such as a disability, a disease, sexual orientation, or racial or ethnic identity, should not be used as criteria to condone providing less competent services to some people than are provided to others. As Daniel et al. (2004) point out since the therapist's persona and self-awareness are crucial to the therapeutic alliance therapists must understand their clients' worldviews. They point out that the types of cultural knowledge that persons of color identified as important included knowledge of family relationships and expectations, racism and discrimination, sexism and gender role issues, communication styles, cultural beliefs about counseling, cultural issues related to sexual orientation, ethnic and cultural identity, and norms for behavior. They encourage therapists to examine their own reactions to race, sexual orientation, and ageism and must assume that biases are part of their worldview.

In addition to cultural sensitivity, working with persons of color requires knowledge and skill. Data suggest that therapists (Fuertes, Mueller, Chauhan, Walker, & Ladany, 2002) who know Helms' (1990) racial identity theory and are aware of its role in their clients' lives are more able to make accurate statements about their clients' racial identity. Furthermore they are better able to describe their clients' interpersonal concerns at how they are related to racism, homophobia, and poverty. These therapists reported that they had better rapport, better intimacy and more self-disclosure from their clients. Furthermore, they reported more overall improvement in clients' involvement in therapy as well as gains for their clients.

Perceptions of cultural insensitivity may contribute to the underuse of mental health services by racial and ethnic minorities (Beutler et al., 1994). Research suggests that cultural responsiveness improves therapists' credibility with minority clients, clients' willingness to return for counseling, and client satisfaction and depth of self-disclosure (Atkinson & Lowe, 1995). Cultural responsiveness has been found to be an important variable with African Americans (Pomales, Claiborn, & LaFromboise, 1986; Poston, Craine, & Atkinson, 1991; Thompson, Worthington, & Atkinson, 1994), Asian Americans (Ginn, Atkinson, & Kim, 1991; Sodowsky, 1991) and Mexican Americans (Atkinson, Casas, & Abreu, 1992). Furthermore, Daniel et al. (2004) report that there are many studies that show that training in multicultural counseling has an important impact on developing interracial comfort as well as promoting positive Caucasian racial identity.

According to Atkinson and Lowe (1995), research supports the use of ethnically similar dyads. They argued that other things being equal, most ethnic minority clients prefer an ethnically similar counselor over an ethnically dissimilar counselor, and some ethnic minority clients express greater willingness to see an ethnically similar counselor and benefit more from therapy (p. 405). Research by Jerrel (1995) would support Atkinson and Lowe's assertion; however, more recent research presents a different picture. A review of several studies by Maramba and Hall (2002) suggests that ethnic matching of the therapist and client has little effect on therapy outcomes. The clear ethical point here is that whether or not ethnic matching between the therapist and client is a critical variable in therapeutic outcome, the therapist needs to be competent in working with the client (whatever ethnic group he or she represents).

This book has been based on the assumption that the general ethical principles of benefi-cence, nonmaleficence, justice, autonomy, and fidelity are no less valid with racial and ethnic minorities than they are with members of the majority culture (Pedersen, 1995). However, the understanding of, for example, what constitutes harm and what constitutes a benefit may need to be modified depending on the cultural group. As LaFromboise and Foster (1989) noted,

> accepting goods for payment, attending a client's special event, accepting services in lieu of a fee, accepting client gifts, asking for favors from clients, and lending money to a client are behaviors that might be considered unethical in one context (Hall & Hare-Mustin, 1983), yet culturally appropriate in another context. (p. 127)

When assessing the potential for harm or benefit that may arise from multiple relationships, cultural context needs to be considered. Clearly, the virtues of respectfulness and caring need to guide understanding of both general ethical principles and the association codes when it comes to the treatment of members of different cultural groups.

The 2003 APA Multicultural Guidelines focused not just on practice but also on culturally sensitive research which entails specialized knowledge in order for designs and data interpreta-tion to be competent and fair. Behavior associated with the White middle class has often been presumed to be "normal," and behavior and beliefs associated with ethnic and racial minorities or the poor and the elderly have been considered deviant. Culturally sensitive research involves respect for the culture and a careful evaluation of the potential harms and benefits from the perspective of the cultural group being investigated (Tapp, Kelman, Triandis, Wrightsman, & Coelho, 1974).

Tapp et al. (1974) developed a set of ethical guidelines for cross-cultural research. Although the guidelines were intended to apply to international cross-cultural research, the themes they identified are also relevant to culturally sensitive research wherever it takes place.

1. Significant involvement of members of the culture being studied is important and desirable in evaluating the research and its implications. This is particularly true in defining harm because what is stressful, embarrassing, or humiliating may differ in different cultural contexts.
2. Freedom to participate or to decline to participate should be honored. This includes using informed consent; however, criteria for informed consent should be determined in each cultural context.
3. Although the ultimate responsibility for the ethicality of the research lies with the investigator, colleagues from the culture being studied as well as others should be con-sulted to help identify potential harm, define criteria for consent, and consider benefits that might accrue from the culture's perspective.
4. Investigators have a special responsibility to enrich the individuals participating in the research and the community in which it is being conducted.
5. The host culture should be respected, and behavior that violates cultural norms or that reflects a culturally biased perspective should be avoided.
6. Honesty should characterize communication, with special attention being paid to clear communication given the cultural and linguistic barriers.

Because of the history of racism both in the United States and in the social sciences, psy-chologists and counselors have a particularly strong ethical obligation to be competent in their work with groups that are culturally dissimilar from themselves. This includes becoming knowledgeable about and sensitive to cultural differences, as well as similarities, and being thoughtful in how they use that knowledge when providing services and when doing research. (For further discussion, see Chapter 13.)

Unfortunately, research on multicultural counseling in some ways is still in its infancy. It is been 25 years since Sue et al.'s (1982) original model of multicultural counseling competencies (MCCs) was published and many psychology programs have incorporated the model into their graduate training. Yet, as recently as 2003, Atkinson and Israel noted the relatively little empirical research has actually validated the model. Although several researchers (Perez et al., 2000; Pope-Davis et al., 2001) have conducted content analyses of both APA and ACA journals, the most comprehensive has been done by Worthington, Soth-McNett, and Marino (2007). They point out that the most basic question remains unanswered: "Do counselors who possess these competencies evidence and proved counseling outcome with clients across cultures?" (Ponterotto et al., 2000, p. 641). Their study analyzed all empirical research on MCCs between 1986 and 2005. They found that empirical research on MCCs has consistently increased over the past 20 years; however, they found that 72% of all the research had been done by a small number of scholars. However, even among the top 10 contributors only a few articles were typically published. Most studies used surveys and very few studies use some form of objective assessment. It should be noted, however, that several studies that included observer rated MCCs (Constantine, 2001; Worthington, Mobley, Franks, & Tan, 2000) have produced results consistent with the model. Worthington, Soth-McNett, and Moreno concluded that counselors who possess MCCs appear to have improved counseling and process outcomes with clients who have racial and ethnic differences. Clients perceptions of counselors, client outcomes attrition and self-disclosure were all improved. Although they did not find any studies that demonstrated negative findings, one exception was published after their article. Cartwright, Daniels, and Zhang (2008) compared the results of surveys assessing the multicultural competence with observer ratings. Observer mean ratings were significantly lower than the self-report scorers although there was some improvement (not significant) after students participated in a course. Clearly more research needs to be done on this question.

Homophobia

Brown (1996) argued that all psychotherapists must assume that they have heterosexist and homophobic biases. Furthermore, they need to explore their own sexual identities and beliefs before practicing psychotherapy with or teaching about gay, lesbian, bisexual, and transgendered clients (GLBT). As is true with exploring beliefs about racism, data suggests any course or workshop should have an affective-attitudinal component (Philips, 2000; Whitman 1995). Since surveys of licensed psychologists have shown that most practitioners will work with one or more GLBT client, there is an obvious necessity for training about GLBT issues (Daniel et al., 2004). This is especially true since many students and professionals report feeling in adequate for working with GLBT clients and make errors like treating same sex couples with models developed for heterosexual ones. However, trainers themselves must be knowledgeable since courses often omit bisexuality, have pathologized it, or denied its existence. In one study half of those supervised about GLBT issues reported that their supervisors had limited or inadequate knowledge (Murphy, Rawlings, & Howe, 2002). Consequently, they tried to search the literature for adequate knowledge. However, in the 1991 survey by Tabachnik, Keith-Spiegel and Pope about 23% of the respondents reported treating homosexuality as pathological at least sometimes. This lack of unfamiliarity can have serious consequences in therapy as the client deals with the coming-out process, the effects of discrimination, and the process of identity formation.

Considerably less has been written about competency issues with GLBT clients than about racism, although a literature is developing (Barnett & Anderson, 2001). On the other hand, Murphy et al. (2002) reported that that a search of mainstream clinical and counseling journals found that articles with a significant focus on GLBT issues represented only 8–2.11% at a given period of time. Considerably less has been written about bisexual and transgender issues.

Students or professionals who seek out information in the literature have scarce resources to turn to. Daniel et al. (2004) argue that training should be structured with three basic areas of focus. First, the interface between GLBT clients who live in a heterosexist or homophobic society needs to be covered. Although sometimes professionals are naïve enough to think that GLBT individuals are accepted by society, in the last month, one of the authors has read in local newspapers about two incidents that reflected the deep hatred and fear that some people have toward GLBT individuals. In one case, a bisexual woman was brutally killed and in another a lesbian student was bullied by her classmates. Second, trainees need to understand the interface between sexual orientation and community resources. Third, they need to explore the interaction between feelings, attitudes, and sexual orientation of the clinician (particularly their own) and the client (Cashwell, 2011). Add to this the interactions of racism and sexism with homoprejudice. Furthermore whether they are psychologists or counselors, they need to be familiar with the Guidelines for Psychotherapy with Lesbian, Gay and Bisexual Clients (Appendix B) published by the American Psychological Association in 2000 and other resources such as Competencies for Counseling with Transgender Clients established by Association for Lesbian, Gay, Bisexual, and Transgender Issues in Counseling (ALGBTIC, 2009). It has been emphasized that a safe learning environment is essential before training about these issues can occur, so that individuals can feel free to explore their feelings and attitudes (Buhrke & Douce, 1991; Phillips, 2000).

Ageism

Robert Butler claimed he first used the term "ageism" in 1968 when he was chairman of the Washington DC committee on aging. He defined ageism "as a systematic stereotyping and discrimination against people simply because they are old just as racism and sexism accomplish this with skin color and gender" (U.S. Congressional Senate, 2003, p. 15). He claimed ageism derived from a general fear of growing older and no longer being able to take care of oneself. Negative stereotyping has resulted in discrimination practices in the workplace and elsewhere including elder abuse. Some commonly held beliefs about older adults include that they are isolated, depressed, unable to cope, and have to depend on others (Daniel et al., 2004). The truth is that many older adults remained remarkably active at least through their 70s. One of the authors knows an older adult in his 70s who leads hikes in one of the national parks. Others are active in singing groups, golf, volunteer work and some are even starting businesses. Furthermore, according to the U.S. Census Bureau over almost 89% of those aged 65 years and older live in households with their spouses or partner, 53% remain married and have never been separated and another 31.6% are married or were once. In addition, almost 14% remain employed.

Gatz and Pearson (1988) argued that many practitioners do not hold globally negative stereotypes, but they have specific misconceptions that lead to less than quality service to older adults. For example, some practitioners may believe they may not warrant long-term therapeutic interventions or that depression is just a part of aging consequently it doesn't warrant treatment. Because Alzheimer's disease has had a great deal of recent publicity many practitioners believe that complaints about memory imply the presence of early Alzheimer's. In fact, Gatz and Pearson (1988) previewed several surveys conducted with some younger, some older populations. All tended to overestimate the prevalence of Alzheimer's disease. Even some professionals contributed to this by estimating 20% of those over 80 have Alzheimer's but that figure represents all of dementia. By contrast, data consistently show that many memory problems of older adults can be reversed and avoided if they remained active intellectually. Daniel et al. (2004) suggests that practitioners believe that older adults who perform well, are the exception rather than typical.

Based on a survey Palmore (2001) found that ageism is common in the United States both in respondents over 75 and under 75 years of age. By contrast data suggests that the negative effects of ageism can be prevented by increasing exposure to older adults and providing knowledge about the impact of physical and mental changes as aging occurs (Edelstein & Semenchuk, 1996; Peila-Shuster, 2011). In fact one of the authors taught a class in adult development in which two older adults were videotaped talking quite freely about their sex lives. After getting over the shock, the students mostly in their 20s and 30s discussed their surprise and indicated they felt more positively about growing older. Abeles et al. (1998) pointed out that older adults develop coping mechanisms that assist them despite any age-related physical or cognitive changes. B. F. Skinner, in one of his last speaking engagements at the annual meeting of the American Psychological Association, talked about using hot spices in his food, pornography, and other mechanisms to cope with senses that were less keen than they used to be.

Whitbourne and Sneed (2003) proposed a model of identity accommodation that occurs in older adults that assumes they attempt to view themselves as ethical, positive and competent. This accommodation, however, has the risk of buying into social stereotypes of aging and lead individuals to internalize negative stereotypes that make life more painful as these attitudes become self-fulfilling prophecies. A positive accommodation could take place if the individual becomes actively involved in activities that help them adjust more adequately and realistically and seek services if and when they are needed.

Gender Issues and Competence

Issues of gender in psychology and counseling have also had a blemished history. It is hard not to read Freud, for example, without being aware that he treated a preponderance of women. Despite this, he failed to consider the social political issues that were oppressing them and affecting their mental health (Brown, 1994b). Early work in psychology often ignored differences between men and women and generalized theories that were developed on men to women. When women failed to operate as predicted, they and their differences in behavior, attitudes, and feelings were often characterized as inferior.

With the rise of feminism, sensitivity to women's issues and the special needs of women in both practice and research became the focus of discussion (Brodsky, 1980; Brodsky & Hare-Mustin, 1980; Chesler, 1972; Hare-Mustin, 1983). Out of this discussion came the recognition that society is not neutral in its treatment of women and that the experiences of women need to be understood in the larger social context, which frequently trivializes or ignores their concerns.

In response to these concerns, APA (1975) established a task force to examine the issue of potential gender-bias and gender-role stereotyping of women in psychotherapy. Four general areas of bias were identified: (a) therapists values were often sexist, and their knowledge of women's biology and psychological process was limited; (b) therapy often fostered traditional gender roles; (c) therapists often used outdated psychoanalytic concepts that devalued women; and (d) therapists sometimes treated women clients as sex objects (which sometimes included seducing them). In response, principles for competent service to women were developed both by the task force and by the Ad Hoc Committee on Women of Division 17 (1979). Although they served as an initial first step, they failed to recognize the diversity among women. Later, a feminist therapy code of ethics (Feminist Therapy Institute, 1990) was developed that brought attention to the power differential in therapy, the interaction of gender and diversity issues, the problems of oppression, and the importance of working toward social change. It argued that gender is an important issue of women's oppression but it interacts with other issues of oppression including things like ethnicity, culture, class, age, sexual orientation, ability, and linguistic status (Brabeck & Ting, 2000a, b). In other words feminist ethics ought to enhance the human condition and create a more just and caring world. Consequently, a new set of guidelines on practice with women and girls that recognized cultural diversity were developed and accepted by APA Council (APA, 2007).

Research practices also came under scrutiny since the science of psychology is as value laden as is the practice of psychology. Sexism could and can enter research in a variety of ways, from the choice of methodology to the interpretation of results. McHugh, Koeske, and Frieze (1986) argued that the inadvertent gender bias has resulted in a substantial social and scientific loss to women. On the other hand, controversy continues to surround the interpretation of gender differences (Buss, 1995; Eagly, 1995a, b; Hyde & Plant, 1995; Marecek, 1995). In fact, Eagly (1995b) claimed that the feminist movement overly sensitized reviewers and authors to see political dangers associated with gender differences and has led to a new bias that underestimates gender differences. Whether her point is correct or not, it is clear that the politics of gender is strongly linked with the science of gender (Eagly, 1995a; Maracek, 1995). To remain competent both clinicians and researchers need to remain up-to-date on the literature on women and gender differences.

In addition, feminists have offered is distinctly different take on the obligations of researchers toward participants. For example, Fisher (2000) has argued that the scientist has a special relationship and subsequent moral obligations toward research participants. She argued that a participant-oriented ethics in which the concerns of research participants are valued need to be balanced with the benefits of science to society. She also argued that the scientist needs to take final moral responsibility for the ethical procedures selected in research since there is clearly an asymmetric power differential that is inherent in research projects. This is true even if participants are viewed as moral partners and consulted on the construction of ethical procedures (see Chapter 13).

Women's experience and that of other oppressed groups is often one of being powerless. Many of the conflicts with which they struggle, like low self-esteem, are intimately related to the roles they play in society and their experience of oppression (Langer, 2011; Lerman & Porter, 1990). Fear of violence from men is a normal part of women's experience as his fear of whites a normal part of the lives of people of color. Prevalence figures suggest that 15%–22% of women have been raped sometime during their lives, many by people they trusted (Gidyez & Koss, 1990; Koss & Burkhart, 1989). Similarly, most working women have been sexually harassed. Women in nontraditional careers have particular problems with harassment (Gutek, 1989).

Take Case 8-2 as an example of how gender socialization may affect a counseling or therapy relationship.

Case 8-2

Amy Martino, a Latina, chemical engineer, entered therapy for bereavement issues. She told the therapist that in the past year both her mother and her sister had died. She felt down most of the time and lacked energy. As the therapist gathered background information, he discovered that Ms Martino had two children for whom her husband was the primary care taker because he did not work outside of the home. She indicated that she and her husband had a good relationship and that neither he nor the children were the focus of her concerns. Despite her disclaimer, the counselor asked her several times about her marital relationship. When he probed similar issues in the second session, Ms Martino decided not to return to therapy. Because she was still feeling down, several weeks later she went to another therapist who focused almost entirely on her grief and guilt about the deaths in her family since family is central in the lives of Latinas. As her depression lifted, Ms Martino wondered to what extent her gender and ethnicity played a role in her treatment by the first counselor.

The first therapist in Case 8-2 appears to have been biased against women of color and men in nontraditional roles. Data suggest that therapists' gender assumptions can exert a subtle but profound impact on how therapy is conducted and diagnoses are made. For example, Robertson and Fitzgerald (1990) found that practicing counselors and therapists were more likely to diagnose a man in a homemaker role as more pathological than one in a more traditional role. Often times the disorders used to diagnose women, for example, histrionic and borderline personality disorders, have been conceptualized as exaggerations or stereotyping of traditional female gender roles. This is particularly true when the client's problems and behaviors are inconsistent with social expectations, such as when an Asian woman, assumed to be meek by stereotype, reacts to discrimination with anger.

Feminist psychologists have argued that competent work with women must confront the dominant patriarchal norms that condone violence against women and inequalities based on race and gender (Brown, 1994b). To do less, they have argued, is to condone the system that victimizes women and ultimately helps maintain a culture in which the voices of women, as well as those of other oppressed groups, are obscured or diminished (Lerner, 1993). The new 2007 APA Guidelines for Psychological Practice with Women and Girls are important given that the majority of those seeking mental health services continue to be female (Rhodes, Goering, To, & Williams, 2002). Furthermore, they recognize that contemporary social forces interact with gender and other social identities to create unique issues for the treatment of women. Competent practice with women regardless of their racial identities or age will have to be aware that social forces change and practice and research need to change with them.

Although the task force writing the Guidelines (APA, 2007) recognized that many social forces could be identified, they focused on four. First, the increasing prevalence of global terrorism, violence, and war in which women are particularly victimized. As already noted, this includes rape, assault, and poverty. Second, the media has an incredible effect in popular culture. It typically portrays women as thin, White, sexualized and victimized. It continues to convey cultural stereotypes regarding gender, race, ethnicity, age, and sexual orientation. This has led to an increased preoccupation with weight, shape, and appearance particularly among White women and Asians (APA, 2007). Third, the biopsychosocial aspects of reproduction have always been relevant to the lives of girls and women. The social identities of girls and women are often related to their perceptions of menarche and reproduction (Durkin & Paxton, 2002; Stice & Bearman, 2001). Therapists must be particularly sensitive to the biopsychosocial aspects of women's lives. Understanding the resources and difficulties women face is likely to contribute to a more competent practice. The therapist who says to a pregnant woman: "you must be so happy" may completely misunderstand the implications of pregnancy for her client's cultural group, age, and self-image. And fourth, the increasing lifespan with an aging population consist mostly of women. Although women in general, experience more good years of health then men (Altman, 1997), they are also more likely to live with chronic illnesses like fibromyalgia, arthritis, migraine headaches and so on (Misra, 2001; Schmaling, 2000). One of the authors lives with a chronic illness which has affected her self-concept, activities, and general lifestyle. Once seeing herself as independent and strong, she has had to become increasingly dependent and carefully limits her activities—a difficult adjustment.

Individuals who seek out the services or expertise of psychologists or counselors have multiple identities. They have both a gender identification and a racial/ethnic background. In addition, they are of different ages, different socioeconomic background, and differently abled. Prudent judgment, respectfulness, and care are required to understand and adequately respond to these and other individual differences. Although sometimes it is tempting to ignore the cultural complexity with which psychology and counseling are embedded, in the end it undermines scientific and professional integrity and does a disservice to both professions and the public.

Competent Therapy Practice

Oftentimes the kinds of incompetence in therapy that comes to the attention of ethics committees and regulatory agencies involve fairly clear-cut incompetence, as was true in Case 7-3 where the psychologist claimed competence in group therapy despite having had little or no training in it. Psychology and counseling have attempted to limit this kind of gross incompetence by setting out the standards that appear in ethics codes. As noted in the last section, APA and ACA have also set out a series of specialty guidelines for practice with underrepresented groups and women (see Appendices A through D). The intent is to help psychologists and counselors define the meaning of competent practice and research with these groups. Generally, psychology and counseling rely to a great extent on appropriate education and supervised experience as the major criteria for determining competence (ACA, 2005; APA, 1981b, 1987b, 2002). Yet, most counselors and psychologists know other professionals who have been educated at the best schools and who have appropriate credentials, but to whom they would not refer a client.

Although competence can be defined as being smart, being well trained, and not making "dumb mistakes," more fundamental questions about competence in psychotherapy can be linked to questions of whether psychotherapy benefits the client. Given that empirical studies have shown that, on average, psychotherapy is effective when practiced by competent professionals (Lambert & Ogles, 2004) we need to ask what characteristics effective therapists have and what techniques lead to positive outcomes. At the same time, it may be even more important to ask what therapist characteristics, techniques, and practices lead to client deterioration and negative outcomes.

The group from the Competency Conference that focused on becoming a competent clinician provided one definition of the competencies that would avoid client deterioration and lead to interventions that would benefit clients (Spruill et al., 2004). The members of the working group clearly identified that competency was a developmental and lifelong learning process and that competency needed to be judged according to the developmental level of the person making interventions. The group identified six basic foundational competencies that cut across all developmental levels.

Importantly, the first competency listed was the scientific foundation of practice. It included knowledge of both theoretical models and of evidence-based interventions for the problem in question and the ability to make an informed choice of the best intervention based on the data available. Based on the concept of the "science–practitioner," there was agreement that no matter in which specialty the practitioner was being trained or practiced, all clinicians needed to know theoretical models of intervention, what works best for which type or problems and, use the scientific literature to choose the best intervention for treating a particular individual. There is evidence that practitioners say that they value research and their clinical practice should be augmented by research findings, but what they say and what they do are quite different. They suggest the profession as a whole needs to reaffirm the integration of science and practice and develop a series of validated procedures for interventions that balance the scientific foundation of psychology and particularly the use of empirically validated treatments with the day-to-day applications of science and practice The importance of evidence-based practice (EBP) has become more important since APA appointed a task force in 2006 on EBP (APA Presidential Task Force on Evidence-Based Practice, 2006). This issue will be elaborated later in this section.

The interpersonal and communication skills of the clinician and their appropriate application to the particular client taking into consideration age, ethnicity, race, gender, and so on were the second set of skills emphasize. Under the heading of the therapeutic alliance the skills of warmth, empathy, genuineness, and respect for patients have a long history in the research literature of being foundational for good therapy (Martin, Garske, & Davis, 2000). The task group noted that to some extent these are qualities that students bring to their training program; however, they must be educated in how to develop a therapeutic alliance and to further develop their relationship skills. Not surprisingly, therapist skill has also been positively associated with outcome. In fact, Lambert and Ogles (2004) have argued that the therapeutic relationship is vitally important and that training programs should emphasize the development of the therapist as a person as well as the acquisition of therapeutic technique.

The third skill identified was the ability to communicate effectively with the patient or client on many levels. They pointed out that communication skills are one of the most important of the relationship building skills and facilitate or hamper the development rapport with the client. Communication, they argued, included not just talking but also listening to both what is being said and what is not being said. It means being attentive to body language and cultural differences. They pointed out that this is sometimes called "listening with the third ear."

In both APA and ACA, recent literature has focused on the "culturally competent" psychotherapist, thus the fourth skill identified involved knowledge of individual and cultural differences as were discussed in the last section. The fifth area of knowledge about which therapists should be competent is ethics. In addition they should be knowledgeable about state and federal laws relating to practice in their particular area. In particular, therapists should be knowledgeable about the ethical codes of their particular profession.

Last, the group (Spruill et al., 2004) emphasized importance of critical thinking or as articulated in Chapter 5 on virtues as practical wisdom. They defined critical thinking as the ability to listen and evaluate or judge all aspects of the situation, problem, or issue. It includes evaluating the therapist's own practice and intervention skills throughout the therapy relationship. They emphasize that it is the kind of thinking that is based on training as a scientist that ensures that critical thinking is brought to bear on the therapeutic process. They go on to identify some of the components necessary to critically plan and evaluate interventions. These include assessment, case formulation, and selection of the best strategies for intervention. They point out that in the era of managed care, treatment plans have taken on new importance as goals and objectives need to be spelled out in outcomes should be measurable and measured by the clinician. One of the assumptions of this book is that the ability to do "good" well is dependent on having the necessary knowledge base and the ability to think well about it. Critical thinking or the virtue of practical wisdom is part of that.

Evidence-Based Practice

Only naïve readers would fail to notice the importance placed on scientifically based practice in the recommendations of the task force. As already noted APA appointed a presidential task force in 2006 to evaluate and make recommendations about EBP. As a consequence, "the evidence-based practice movement has been embraced by organized psychology as a key strategy for promoting effective psychological services" (Hunsley, 2007, p. 113). Increasingly practitioners are being faced with having to decide how EBP applies to their own clinical setting. McCabe (2004) points to several independent reports describing problems in the American health system including those in the behavioral health area. These reports concluded that there is a chasm between the quality of care patients could receive and that which they do receive. We know that some practices are effective but the difficulty is how to generalize the knowledge gained in research to typical clinical practice. On one hand, the intrapersonal characteristics of the client like age, ethnicity, gender, their feelings of self confidence, and their need and readiness for change all play a role in how and whether EBP applies. In addition as McCabe (2004, p. 575) says "the tendencies of scholars, scientists, and clinicians to dismiss research findings that are not congruent with their values and belief systems is well recognized the phenomenon has been called "therapeutic imperialism" (Nathan, 1998). Although there have been sweeping condemnations of EBPs, the question McCabe asks is, "If not evidence, on what should clinicians base their practice?" (p. 572).

Hunsley (2007) addressed the question of how EBPs should be used in practice. He argues that applying patient knowledge gained from treatment studies across all patients would result in more benefit than harm, but sometimes the complexity of the patient's characteristics like age and ethnicity may lead the clinician to believe the research is not relevant. He however encouraged clinicians to ask themselves whether their client is really so different from those of the research studies. After doing so the clinician should tailor what has been gained in the research studies to fit the patient's clinical presentation and life circumstances and then closely monitor the impact of treatment. Second, he asked whether the participants in treatment studies are clinically representative and therefore limited in their generalizability. He concluded treatment studies have not systematically excluded all difficult cases. Third, he questioned whether the range of evidence-based treatments is sufficient for clinical practice. He points to two reviews of the literature. Hunsley and Lee (2006) concluded there were a multitude of treatments for adults with anxiety disorders, eating disorders, mood disorders, substance abuse disorders, somatoform disorders, sleep disorders, sexual disorders and marital/couple conflicts. A second study by Schiffman, Baker, and Daleiden (2006) examined child and adolescent mental health services from the Hawaii Department of Health. They concluded that 89% of the youth had a primary diagnosis for which an EBP was identified. Hunsley also refers to recent meta-analytic evidence (Lambert et al., 2003) that "strongly indicates that, regardless of clinician orientation or patient condition, improvement rates can be increased and deterioration rates decreased by implementing treatment monitoring strategies to gauge how patients are progressing in treatment and using the resulting data to modify treatment" (p. 117). The last issue Hunsley raised is whether evidence-based treatments really work in the real world. Although the area has been criticized for the fact that there are few effectiveness studies (ones that try to maximize external validity while maintaining an adequate level of internal validity), Hunsley and Lee (2006) reviewed the treatment effectiveness literature and found that more than 75% of the patients followed the course of treatment to completion which was substantially greater than the 50% completion rate usually reported for treatments provided in clinical settings. Furthermore, the outcome in most of the effectiveness studies was comparable to or superior to the results obtained in typical efficacy studies (those that try to maximize the internal validity of the study). They concluded that in terms of completion and outcome the results are very encouraging and seem to indicate that EBP can be transported to regular clinical practice.

Hunsley and Lee (2006) acknowledge that it may not always be easy for clinicians to receive training in EBP because of institutional barriers like the lack of financial support and heavy caseloads. In addition, they reiterate the point that EBP requires practitioners to adopt a self-critical stance that may be unsettling at times. Neither psychology nor counseling can afford what Nathan (1998) called "therapeutic imperialism." Avoiding evidence because it doesn't fit with the therapist's pet theoretical orientation can lead to negative consequences for the client but it is clearly unethical. The principle of beneficence requires therapists to use the best tools available both in order to help their clients and avoid harming them. As Stricker (1992) wrote, "Although it may not be unethical to practice in the absence of knowledge, it is unethical to practice in the face of knowledge. We must all labor with the absence of affirmative data, but there is no excuse for ignoring contradictory data" (p. 544).

On the other hand, Wampold and Bhati (2004) pointed out that some types of psychotherapy like cognitive behavioral lend themselves more easily research designs, thus, there are more studies designed to evaluate their efficacy. Furthermore they argue that meta-analyses have shown that no particular treatment or approach is demonstrably superior to another across disorders or within disorders. They argue that little evidence is available that shows the treatments work through the mechanisms that are hypothesized. For example, when the cognitive components of CBT for depression are not included, the treatment is as effective as CBT with all components included. They argue that well-designed meta-analysis studies indicate that whether one add or remove the critical components of efficacious treatments does not attenuate the benefits. In fact strict adherence to a particular protocol seems to detract from the therapeutic alliance and lead to poorer outcomes. They suggest there is strong evidence that factors common to all therapies are responsible for the benefits of those treatments that are considered efficacious. Therapeutic alliance between a psychologist and the patient has been the most researched common factor and has been found to be the most robust predictor of outcome even when measured early in therapy. They fear that researchers have focused on the type of therapy delivered and have ignored the most important source of variance that matters and that is the psychotherapist.

Even the American Psychological Association's (2006) Presidential Task Force on EBP acknowledged that it requires an understanding and appreciation of multiple sources of scientific evidence. They conclude that "psychologists of good faith and good judgment may disagree about how best to weigh different forms of evidence; over time, we presume that systematic and broad empirical inquiry in the laboratory and in the clinic will point the way toward best practice in integrating best evidence …. The scientific method is a way of thinking and observing systematically, and is the best tool we have for learning about what works for whom" (p. 282).

In other words, competent therapists need to stay up with current scientific work and incorporate it as best they can into their practice. At minimum, practitioners have a responsibility to remain knowledgeable about the research on psychotherapy process and outcome. Additionally, they should read beyond their focused theoretical interests. Focus on a particular area of interest may blind therapists to evidence that other interventions may be more effective and/or efficient for a particular client with a particular problem. Finally, if psychologists and counselors remain ignorant of the empirical literature, they will be unable to take basic responsibility to inform clients about the limits of their treatment and reasonable alternatives.

In addition, beneficence requires that therapists take responsibility to choose the best treatments that they can identify for their clients. The identification of empirically validated treatments should contribute to that goal. If, however, empirically validated treatments are misused by insurance companies or managed care organizations to prescribe treatments for clients with little consideration for the particular person involved, practitioners may face other ethical issues, such as deciding how and when to fight for their beliefs about appropriate treatment alternatives. This is especially true for clients, with multicultural backgrounds. Although Hunsley (2007) argued that therapists need to ask themselves if their clients are so different from the one this in the treatment groups, sometimes the answer may have to be "yes." (See Chapter 13 for further discussion.) If this occurs, it further emphasizes the importance for therapists to be equipped with the evidence of the treatment efficacy for alternative methods.

Emotional Competence

Pope and Vasquez (2007) point out that intellectual competence is only one aspect of competent therapy. Competence also requires knowing oneself or what they call emotional competence. Therapists need to know their own emotional strengths and limits. Sometimes therapists have very strong emotional reactions to clients or their problems. Based on three national surveys they identify several emotional reactions that therapists have had to their patients like being angry or even feeling hatred toward a patient to the point that they may raise their voice because of their feelings. Therapists even report telling clients they were angry or were disappointed with them. All therapists at some point in their career are going to face clients whom they fear will commit suicide and they fear that they will be incompetent to deal with them. Suicidal or homicidal clients can be some of the most challenging clients and may provoke strong emotions in the therapist. Similarly, sexual feelings toward a client are also not uncommon (see Chapter 12) and can be confusing, frightening as well as challenging. Pope and Vasquez provide the following case as an example of one that might evoke strong emotions of the therapist.

Case 8-3

A new client shows up at your office for an initial session. The person says: "I have felt so incredibly edgy all week. I don't know what's wrong with me. But I feel like I want to smash someone in the mouth, like I want to get my gun and blow someone's brains out. I don't even know who, but it's like something's building up and it just won't be stopped" (Pope & Vasquez, 2007, p. 171).

The first question a therapist needs ask when confronted with an issue like this one is: "How do they feel?" and then "Are they competent to deal with it?" It is times like these when therapists need to ask themselves whether they need to consult with a colleague or supervisor.

Nonmaleficence requires the therapist take ethical responsibility for being aware of their own attitudes and feelings toward their clients. Sometimes this may mean admitting that there are clients with particular problems that they simply cannot work with and need to refer them to other competent therapists. Pope and Vasquez point to a study by Pope and Feldman-Summers (1992) that indicates that almost one-third of male therapists and over two-thirds of female therapists have experienced various kinds of abuse during childhood, adolescence, or adulthood. These experiences cannot help but effect therapists. Whether they negatively influence a therapist's emotional competence is a very individual matter.

Pope and Vasquez argue that ethical responsibility requires self-awareness especially during difficult or challenging periods. These times may be brought on by clients or by events in the therapist's current or past emotional life. Since we know the therapeutic alliance is critical to client improvement, if the therapist is emotionally distraught they may be unable to form that alliance which limits the ability to benefit the client. They point to several other potentially damaging consequences when the therapist is "distressed, drained, or demoralized. These common consequences include disrespecting clients; disrespecting work; making more mistakes; lacking energy; using work to clock out on happiness, pain and discontent; and losing interest" (p. 50).

Unfortunately, less is known about the cause of negative outcomes in psychotherapy, although the deterioration of some clients has been consistently documented, even in controlled studies of outcome (Lambert & Ogles, 2004). Although therapy hurts a portion of clients, no particular modality seems to be responsible for these effects. Negative outcomes have been associated with individual therapy, group therapy, and marriage and family therapy and have been associated with all of the major schools of psychotherapy, as have positive outcomes.

Case studies and surveys on sexual involvement with therapists, as well as other gross therapeutic errors, have been related to client deterioration. For example, Pope and Tabachnick (1994) surveyed psychologists who had been in therapy. Of those, 22% found therapy harmful. They identified sexual acts or attempted sexual acts, therapist's incompetence, therapist's emotional abuse, therapist's failure to understand them, and boundary violations most frequently as the causes of the harm. These kinds of reports, as well as the data reviewed by Lambert and Ogles, speak to the need to continue to study this area since it helps to define incompetent therapeutic practice. For example, it will be important to identify whether or not evidence-based therapy leads to fewer negative outcomes. Data on negative outcomes and therapeutic effectiveness also speak to the importance of ethical psychologists and counselors remaining knowledgeable about the psychotherapy outcome and process literature. It would be hard to defend a practice as competent—and therefore ethical—if it has been consistently related to negative psychotherapy outcomes.

Competence in Assessment

Some of the most egregious errors of competence have involved assessments. Practitioners have failed to take into consideration the cultural background of the individual being assessed, have made recommendations in child abuse cases based on measures that have poor reliability and no validity for such predictions, have failed to provide adequate feedback to clients regarding assessment results, have based important decisions on outdated testing material, and have overstated the strength of their conclusions. In many cases, the consequences for the people involved were serious. Case 8-1 was one example, the following case is another.

Case 8-4

A woman complained to an ethics committee about a psychologist who assessed her for a position as a police officer in her hometown. She indicated that she first applied after high school. She was tested by a psychologist and turned down for the position without an explanation. She then entered the military and served for several years as a member of the military police. After being honorably discharged from the military, she returned home and reapplied for a job as a police officer. She was referred to the same psychologist who reviewed her file and asked her a few questions about her military service. She was again turned down for the position. The psychologist indicated that he had recommended that she not be employed on the basis of the scores from the tests she had taken almost 10 years earlier. He said that the experience with the military had not changed his mind that she was not the type of woman who could be successful as a civilian police officer. When asked, he was unable to substantiate, using any scientific literature, what "type" of woman would or would not be successful in police work nor for his use of outdated test scores (APA, 1987a).

The failure of the psychologist to gather recent testing data, his decision to draw conclusions on the basis of obsolete test scores, and the lack of scientific validity for his predictions of which women would and would not make suitable police officers illustrate the ethical dangers in incompetent assessment.

Assessment touches the public's life in a variety of arenas. It is used to place children in special programs in schools. It is used in psychotherapy to evaluate progress and as an aid in diagnosis. It has been used and maligned as an asset in making social policy decisions, and it has been used in the workplace to make decisions about hiring, firing, promotions, and placement. In addition, the courts use it to help make decisions about issues from child custody to the death penalty. Although research suggests that psychological tests, when used appropriately, improve the quality of both clinical and selection decisions involving people (Murphy & Davidshofer, 2004), they can also be used inappropriately to label, segregate, institutionalize, and deny some people access to desired goals (DeMers, 1986). In other words although assessments are designed to benefit clients and important decision-making about clients, sometimes they are used to harm them.

Because of the use of psychological tests for educational placements, as well as for the hiring and firing of employees, this area of practice has come under intense legal scrutiny (Bersoff, 1981). In particular, questions about test bias and whether tests are being used fairly have been debated because of gender-based, racially based, and ethnically based differences in test scores (Gottfredson, 1988; Lerner, 1989; Murphy & Davidshofer, 2004; Scarr, 1989). For example, it was documented that using the standard Scholastic Achievement Test (SAT), particularly the mathematics section, to award college scholarships resulted in fewer scholarships for women despite the fact that women received higher grades in college (Murphy & Davidshofer, 2004). (Issues of justice in assessment are addressed in Chapter 13.)

Considering the arenas in which assessment has been considered relevant, as well as its legal and social justice implications, competent practice becomes a critical ethical issue. Although it is possible to be competent and unethical when doing psychological assessments, it is not possible to be ethical and incompetent (Weiner, 1989). Similarly, a psychological assessment cannot be incompetent and fair. Competence is so important that some ethics texts (Koocher & Keith-Spiegel, 2008; Pope & Vasquez, 2007) review basic information about psychological tests and test administration, perhaps because of errors made in psychological assessments sometimes seem so elementary.

Professional associations have spent a great deal of time and effort in trying to define competence in assessment. Because psychologists have played a critical and historical role in the science and practice of assessment and psychologists continue to be major providers of psychological testing and assessment services (Krishnamurthy et al., 2004), APA has been particularly concerned about the qualifications and misuse of psychological tests. However, ACA has also developed specific sets of guidelines for the use and qualifications of those who do testing, for example, Responsibilities of Users of Standardized Tests (American Association for Counseling and Development, 1998). APA has also worked with other organizations (American Educational Research Association [AERA], 1999; APA, 2000; National Council on Measurement in Education [NCME], 1999) in formulating standards on the use of psychological and educational tests namely, *The Standards for Educational and Psychological Testing.*

Because of a concern about test misuse, APA established a task force on test user qualifications to develop guidelines that are for both test users and the general public so that they are informed of the qualifications that APA considered important for the competent and responsible use of psychological tests (Turner, DeMers, Fox, & Reed, 2001). Both the APA task force and the members of the committee from the Competency Conference as well as standard texts on psychological assessment emphasize the importance of distinguishing testing from psychological assessment. One involves giving and scoring the test, the other involves doing a comprehensive assessment, including a psychosocial history to integrate with test scores, using tests properly, which involves exercising appropriate quality control; having appropriate psychometric knowledge, including basic principles of measurement; maintaining the integrity of test results by correctly applying psychometric principles when interpreting results; accurately scoring tests; appropriately using test norms; and providing correct interpretations of test results to consumers. The APA Task Force (Turner et al., 2001) defines psychological assessment as a complex task "requiring the interplay of knowledge of psychometric concepts with expertise in the area of professional practice or application. Assessment is a conceptual, problem solving process of gathering dependable, relevant information about an individual, group, or institution to make informed decisions" (p. 1100). They differentiated between generic knowledge and skills necessary for anyone to do assessments and those necessary within a particular context like employment, education, career counseling, forensics and so on.

The Competency Conference (Krishnamurthy et al., 2004, p. 732) identified eight general core competencies, which include:

1. Knowledge of the basics of psychometric theory including descriptive statistics.
2. The knowledge, skill, and techniques needed to assess the cognitive, affective, behavioral, and personality dimensions of individuals and systems.
3. Knowledge about the scientific, theoretical, empirical, and contextual basis of psychological assessment.
4. The ability to assess the outcome of treatments or interventions.
5. The ability to evaluate their roles and relationships within which practitioners function and the impact of these on assessment functions.
6. The ability to establish, maintain, and understand that assessment is a collaborative professional relationship.

7. In understanding of the relationship between assessment and intervention, assessment as an intervention, and intervention planning. It is becoming increasingly obvious that assessment has an impact on the client or group being assessed and this must be taken into consideration to ethically benefit the group or individual being assessed.

8. Several technical assessment skills, for example, identification of the goal or problem, and understanding of the appropriate assessment methods including both test and observational data, the ability to integrate information, draw inferences, and provide analysis of the results, and the ability to communicate the findings in a way that benefits the client whether it is a group, family, or individual. In order to identify goals, the practitioner would need to be aware of the literature about the object of assessment, for example, depression.

Based on the work of the Task Force, we would add the importance of understanding and considering ethnic, racial, cultural, gender, age, and linguistic variables. As Carter and Forsyth (2007) have pointed out, the mental health profession does not have a particularly strong record on including race or ethnicity as variables in research studies which would include studies of tests and assessment techniques. Furthermore, there are legal and regulatory limits as how test information can be used to assess individuals from particular subgroups such as race or ethnicity, culture, language, gender, age, and people with disabilities.

The Task Force also emphasized the importance of knowing about the legal and ethical issues surrounding test administration and interpretation procedures. These would include confidentiality, the legal rights of the test takers, issues related to the release of test materials, as well as safeguards for protecting test material against copyright infringement. Furthermore, particular settings lead to particular kinds of ethical problems about which the practitioner should be aware. For example, in hospital and school settings a common problem that psychological reports are sometimes kept in the patient or student's records. Often nonmaleficence needs to be balanced with beneficence in careful ways to protect the person's autonomy. Sometimes there is a need for the data to be available quickly. On the other hand, the person or person's guardian has a right to know who has seen the data and how it will be used (Brabender & Bricklin, 2001).

The importance of supervised training for students in both testing and assessment cannot be underemphasized because competence depends on more than knowledge of the tests but actual administration and interpretation of the tests with supervised feedback. This, however, can lead to a plethora of ethical dilemmas (Yalof & Brabender, 2001). Who should be the participants of students' initial assessments? Should they provide feedback to the person or persons being assessed? Who should supervise the students? Should these initial experiences take place in the doctoral program or in practicum or internships? Take the following case an example.

Case 8-5

Mary needed to complete the requirements for her personality assessment class. Jim, another student in the class, was trying to help her complete her requirements and so referred a client to her. He had merely told his patient that the assessment would obtain information that would help therapy. When Mary interviewed the patient, she discussed many necessary elements of informed consent: her own student status and the fact of being supervised, the parameters of confidentiality, the provisions for feedback and so on. But she never clearly acknowledged that the assessment was being done largely to accommodate her training needs and not to gather essential clinical information (based on cases from Yalof and Brabender, 2001).

As Yalof and Brabender point out, the assessment was not made because of the genuine clinical need of the client but by the training needs of Mary. Respect for autonomy requires that the client had a right to know the real purpose of the assessment and to make a choice about whether or not to participate. Furthermore, the client should know that refusing to participate would not affect Jim's treatment of him or her and that the testing could be stopped at any time without influencing the therapeutic relationship. Furthermore, oftentimes students present a case in class and it is critical that they understand their ethical responsibility to protect the identity of the person being assessed and that this requirement goes beyond merely withholding the participant's name. There are multiple opportunities in such classes for students to explore the real life meaning of confidentiality, informed consent and other ethical issues.

Finally, Krishnamurthy et al. (2004) emphasized the importance of better collaboration between training programs, internships and work settings, and training new practitioners for ethical and competent assessment. Part of what they emphasize, which will be discussed in a later section, is the importance of training students in the supervision of psychological assessment. As they point out "there is a dearth of information, and a general absence of empirically tested guidelines, for supervision and training in assessment skills, which is in sharp contrast to the literature available on psychotherapy supervision" (p. 735). They recommended that specific models of supervision of psychological assessment be developed.

More than any other area of practice, standards of competence for assessments have been defined, and there are resources available that provide clarification of those standards. Yet, errors of competence continue to occur. Why they continue to occur is a matter of some speculation. There is some evidence that often errors occur because of inadequate training or outdated information about tests and their uses which would suggest deficits in both knowledge and skills. Additionally, it is tempting to see psychological tests, as well as diagnoses, as answers to difficult human problems. Consequently, psychologists and counselors and those who use the information provided by them may be tempted to overstate their usefulness and their implications. As Anastasi (1992) argued "test scores tell us how well individuals perform at the time of testing not why they perform the way they do" (p. 612). It is up to the psychologist or counselor to provide a useful and accurate interpretation.

The question often arises regarding what kind of feedback should be provided to clients. In therapy, arguments have been made that providing clients with information from assessments can be used as an adjunct to treatment and that withholding information is parentalistic and disrespectful of client autonomy (Bersoff, 1995; Duckworth, 1990). Yet Berndt (1983) found that many clinicians were ambivalent about how much information, particularly about projective tests, should be shared with clients. Clinicians indicated that although they did not refuse clients' requests for feedback, they only provided information that they believed the client could use on the basis of their clinical judgment. They cited limited time commitments and the fragility of patients as reasons for their ambivalence regarding full disclosure. By contrast, Duckworth argued that feedback should be provided about clients' strengths and weaknesses in a nonpejorative manner to help clients get a total picture of themselves. In doing so, issues of beneficence need to be balanced with those of harming clients.

Pope (1992) emphasized that feedback ought to be a "dynamic, interactive process" (p. 268) during which a thoughtful discussion of the results, their meaning, and their implications can take place. He noted, however, that there are a variety of professional forces that mitigate against viewing feedback in this manner, including the clinician's own discomfort in discussing the results, lack of time, and a fear that negative results will be aversive for the client. Whatever the reasons for the ambivalence about providing test takers with feedback, unless it is mandated for a particular purpose, for example, if it is court ordered, generally the ACA and APA ethics codes (2005, 2002, respectively) have required practitioners to provide clients feedback.

Psychologists and counselors need to consider how to provide feedback from assessment results and seek supervision if they have difficulty doing so, because there is some data that doing so is therapeutically beneficial. In a review of test interpretation research, Goodyear (1990) concluded that therapy and counseling clients who receive feedback from testing improve more than do those in control conditions. For example, Finn and Tonsager (1992) found that college students who received feedback on their MMPI scores experienced a significant decrease in their distress symptoms and experienced no negative effects. Others have argued feedback improves rapport, the therapeutic relationship, and attitudes toward testing (Finn & Butcher, 1991; Fischer, 1986).

Matarazzo (1986a) pointed out that psychological assessments involve a certain invasion of the individual's privacy. In essence, tests or other assessments are used to get people to provide information about themselves that they either cannot or are unwilling to provide. In a very real sense, psychologists and counselors are asking them to give up their right to make autonomous decisions about to whom they reveal fundamental and, perhaps, embarrassing information about themselves. This information can have a variety of dire consequences, including prolonged, restrictive hospitalization. In one case, testing data from a Thematic Apperception Test suggested severe sexual aggression and dangerousness. It led a hospital staff to extend the hospitalization of a 17-year-old Haitian African-American man (Pam & Rivera, 1995) despite questions about the appropriateness of the test for such populations. He eventually committed suicide because he had lost hope of being released. If the prediction of dangerousness was a false positive, it contributed unfairly to the events that led to the young man's suicide. If, however, assessment of no dangerousness was a false negative, it could have led to dire consequences for the young man's victims (Pam & Rivera, 1995). In either case, it is unlikely that the young man would have revealed the information about himself if he fully understood the implications of the information he was providing. Furthermore, it is an example of how professionals ignorant of multicultural differences make dire ethical errors.

This example emphasizes psychologists' and counselors' responsibilities to the individual who is being assessed as well as to society to provide useful and reliable information. For the individual, the issue is one of fidelity. People assume that those who test them are trustworthy and honest and are, at minimum, knowledgeable and skilled both in administration and interpretation. In some cases, their lives, jobs, school placements, or futures are riding on it. The social responsibility is daunting because the information the professional provides may have far-reaching consequences for the individuals assessed and those their life touches.

Competence in Supervision

Supervision is critical to the training of both psychologists and counselors. Despite the fact that supervision is so important, the majority of psychologists have not received formal training in supervision (Scott, Ingram, Vitanza, & Smith, 2000). It has often been the case that because someone is a good therapist or researcher, it has been assumed that they could also supervise with competence. Barnett (2007a) presents a typical scenario which he calls the recent graduate (p. 269).

Case 8-6

A recently licensed psychologist accepts a salaried position at a local community mental health center. The position involves providing assessment and treatment services as well as providing clinical supervision to two externs and one intern. Although she has received extensive supervision during her own graduate training, the psychologist has never provided supervision before. The graduate school did offer a course in supervision as an elective, but it did not fit her schedule, and she was unable to participate in it. Yet, she's very excited about supervising trainees and very much looking forward to the experience. She approaches this new experience with eagerness and enthusiasm.

Yet, the skills of supervision, practice, and even teaching are quite different (Bernard & Goodyear, 2004). In supervision learning occurs through instructor learner dialogue. There is some uncertainty involved because the specific outcome of the interaction is typically unclear as they begin a teaching episode much like it is in psychotherapy. Unlike therapy, however, the instructor uses modeling and other techniques so that the learner begins to "think like" a practitioner or researcher. One of the book authors was in a similar position when she was asked to supervise a psychology practicum student with only a master's degree in counseling.

ACA and its associated organization the Association for Counselor Education and Supervision (ACES) have taken a leadership role in defining competencies in supervision. ACES (1990) wrote The Standards for Counseling Supervisors and the Ethical Guidelines for Counseling Supervisors (1993). Getz (1999) argued that there was a need to assess and evaluate the competence of supervisors according to the ACES guidelines. He wrote that competency-based supervision implies that supervisors are taught to obtain the specific abilities to function in a supervisory role. The competencies that he expected of the supervisors he trained were are an understanding of the models of supervision, counselor development, supervision and techniques, the supervisory relationship, ethical, legal, and professional regulatory issues, evaluation and administrators skills.

These competencies are remarkably similar to those that were defined by the members of the APA competency conference who identified competencies in psychological supervision (Falender et al., 2004). They suggested that several overarching factors affect all aspects of professional development and are central to the practice and learning of supervision. First, there needs to be recognition that acquiring supervision competency is a lifelong, cumulative, developmental process. In addition, diversity of all kinds relates to every aspect of the supervision process and requires a special kind of competence including attention to the supervision–supervisee pairings as well as the supervisee's relationship with the client. Furthermore, training is influenced by both professional and personal factors which include the individuals' values, beliefs, and their personal biases and conflicts. Although they did not identify it as such, it involves how the individual has acculturated to the profession (Anderson & Handelsman, 2010). Last, both self and peer assessment should occur regularly at all levels of supervisory development.

In addition to identifying the overarching issues, they applied them to the specific knowledge, skills, and values that defined supervision competencies for the *entry-level* psychologist. Supervisors should have knowledge of the area being supervised whether it's psychotherapy, research, assessments or other aspects of the professional's development. In addition they should have knowledge of models, theories, and research on supervision as well as professional/supervisee development and how competencies in supervision should be are evaluated.

Knowledge of the ethics and legal issues specific to supervision was also emphasized. Unfortunately, Ladany (2002) found more than 50% of trainees who were surveyed reported that they believe their supervisors had engaged in at least one unethical practice during the course of supervision. Cornish (2007) uses as an example Barnett's novice supervisor (See Case 8-6). She points out that because the supervisor had neither taken a graduate course in supervision nor supervised anyone previously under supervision, it would be unethical for her supervise the trainees.

Importantly, they need relationship skills or the ability to build the supervisory alliance. As Barnett (2007a) has elaborated the supervisee must feel like the supervisor has an emotional investment in the relationship which should be trusting and collaborative. In addition, they need to be able to provide clear feedback. As one trainee suggested the supervisors she identified as good were ones that could provide feedback about what the trainee does well. She said "words of encouragement ... go a long way" (Barnett, Youngstrom, & Smook, 2001, p. 223), especially for the supervisee who is anxious and for whom this may be the first supervisory experience. Other skills that were emphasized included the ability to assess the learning needs and developmental level of the supervisee, teaching and didactic skills, and the ability to set boundaries. Furthermore, the supervisor needs to be flexible, model scientific thinking, and translate scientific findings to the practice of supervision as well as to the area (e.g., assessment) that they are supervising.

Values identified included understanding that the responsibility for the client and the supervisee rests with the supervisor. The supervisor should be respectful, find a balance between support and challenge, help empower the supervisee, as have a commitment to lifelong learning and professional growth, find a balance between clinical and training needs, value ethical principles and make a commitment both to know the scientific knowledge related to supervision as well as one's own limitations.

Barnett, Youngstrom, and Smook (2001) asked a supervisee to identify the competencies that are necessary for good supervision. These included taking supervision seriously. For example, supervisors should set regular meeting times, not allow interruptions, and seldom cancel supervision. They should provide trainees with ways to reach them in an emergency. This information helps their anxiety and provides relief when they need advice. Good supervisors should also provide a safe environment for open discussion. The student emphasized the importance of building rapport before discussing cases which is critical to the trainee's comfort and willingness to ask questions. She also suggested that supervisors use a variety of teaching techniques including like cotherapy and videotaping. Last, she points out that of truly fortunate trainees are ones whose supervisors go beyond specifics of supervision and become a mentor who invests additional time to discuss the trainees' professional goals and help them develop a professional identity.

Several perspectives have been brought to bear on the competencies necessary for supervision; however there seems to be consensus about several issues. Foremost is the fact the supervision requires a unique set of skills. It is neither psychotherapy nor teaching but borrows components of each into its own specific pedagogy. Furthermore, in supervision both the supervisee and supervisor are developing. In order to understand the needs of one's supervisee the supervisor must understand where the supervisee is in that development. In addition, multicultural issues need to be taken into consideration in supervision pairings and supervisors must also be aware of the multicultural issues between supervisees and their clients. Last, the supervisory alliance is critical for the supervisee to trust the supervisor. From the student's perspective, this seems to be the most critical issue. It is necessary for students to feel respected in order to open themselves to the feedback without fearing that they will be harmed. Those or not trained in supervision skills may not only fail to benefit the supervisee, but they may end up harming them fulfilling the student's fears. It is not uncommon for trainees to carry *supervision wounds* for months and even years beyond the termination of toxic supervision.

Competence in Forensic Settings

Although forensics is not considered a core competency, psychologists and counselors are being increasingly drawn into the legal system as forensic specialists or expert witnesses. A forensic psychologist is one who specializes in working with the legal system in applying psychological information from research or assessments to legal questions (Grisso, 1987). They often spend a large portion of their time working with lawyers or testifying in a courtroom. However, "every psychologist—whether clinician, scientist, or academician—is a potential expert witness, and each must be prepared to interact with the legal system" (Bersoff, 1995, p. 416). Furthermore, it is becoming increasingly true for counselors as they are drawn into child custody and divorce proceedings. Often psychologists and counselors end up making serious ethical blunders because they are uninformed about this area of practice since they often have had little or no training. Take the following case as an example.

Case 8-7

A therapist had been seeing a father for several weeks to deal with his feelings regarding his impending divorce. At one meeting, the father asked if he could bring his children with him since their relationship had become strained. After the therapist agreed the children met with them several times and he frequently heard them complain that their mother, the primary child care provider, was very demanding and strict. When the therapist suggested including a mother in their meetings, the father refused saying he thought it would just confound the issue of his relationship with the children. When the father's lawyer suggested calling the therapist as an expert witness, the father agreed although the therapist informed him that he might lose his privileged communication. When the therapist was on the stand, the father's lawyer asked him who would be the better parent. Based on the fact that the father had spent time in therapy working on his relationship with the children and the children's comments about their mother, the therapist told the court that he thought the father would probably be the better parent. However, under cross examination the mother's lawyer asked him if he knew of any behavior that might make him question his assessment of the father and his parenting skills, he did note that the father had a sexual liaison with a woman before the divorce proceedings began and that he had come to a couple of sessions with alcohol in his breath. The father appeared shocked if the therapist had betrayed his confidence.

Cases such as this are common fodder for ethics committees. The therapist not only failed to assess the mother prior to drawing his conclusions, he had apparently not explained in enough detail what it meant to lose privileged communication. (See Chapter 10 for further information on privileged communication.)

As Knapp and VandeCreek (2001) point out few masters or doctoral programs train students to work in forensic settings. Consequently, they are not familiar with the usual roles, legal standards and rules, as well as the ethical dilemmas that forensic practice presents.

In addition to custody issues, psychologists and sometimes counselors may be involved with criminal courts testifying on the competence of defendants to stand trial, with civil courts testifying about the civil commitment of an individual prone to violent acts, with the juvenile system evaluating youthful offenders charged of serious crimes, and so on (Bersoff, 1995; Clark, 1993). They may testify as experts on a variety of issues, such as divorce, child abuse, the affects of sexual harassment, or other traumatic events, or the scientific evidence on repressed memory syndrome. Thus, they can play a variety of roles and are required to be competent in those roles just as they are in any other professional role that they accept.

As mental health professionals have been drawn into the legal arena, professional associations like APA and ACA and have begun to develop ethical guidelines to clarify ethical professional behavior. For example, the 1992 APA ethics code published its first set of ethical standards on forensic work and the 2005 ACA code of ethics had standards regarding forensic work. In addition, in 1994 APA published "Guidelines for Child Custody Evaluations in Divorce Proceedings" and the Committee on Ethical Guidelines for Forensic Psychologists (1991) wrote specialty guidelines, which were adopted by the Forensic Division of APA. In other words professional organizations are increasingly aware of the pitfalls involved in forensic practice.

Like supervision, one of the biggest threats to competent work in forensic settings is a lack of training and a consequent failure to understand the differences between scientific standards of truth and legal ones (Anderten et al., 1980). The legal system is adversarial. The assumption is that truth will be obtained when opposing sides support their own position with the strongest evidence and powers of persuasion that they can muster. Although lawyers cannot knowingly provide misinformation, they have no obligation to provide contradictory evidence. Tolerance for indecision is low because the law insists on a decision about the truth based on the evidence available. Consequently, lawyers may seek out the most persuasive expert whose interpretations of the data most closely suit their cause rather than the best psychologist or scientist (Sales & Shuman, 1993). By contrast, the method of science involves weighing the evidence on both sides of an issue as dispassionately as possible, considering the ambiguity of the evidence, and only drawing tentative conclusions when the evidence is incomplete or ambiguous (Anderten et al., 1980; Sales & Shuman, 1993).

When professionals enter the legal field without understanding the rules, they can blunder into making ethical errors because they are operating in unfamiliar territory. Attorneys may pressure them into drawing firm conclusions on the basis of weak data, or they may be seduced into testifying outside the boundaries of their own expertise (Sales & Shuman, 1993). The demand characteristics of the courtroom setting are such that even well-trained professionals can be induced to make more absolute conclusions than they can support or justify scientifically (Haas, 1993). Although attorneys cannot tell experts what to say, they can and do coach their witnesses (Sales & Shuman, 1993). Furthermore, evidence suggests that experts are susceptible to being coached (Champagne, Shuman, & Whitaker, 1991). However, even when they are operating within the legal arena, psychologists and counselors are bound by their own ethical standards and can be held accountable for incompetent testimony or assessment in this domain just as they can in others. Mental health ethics codes acknowledge that work based on the standards of psychology or counseling can sometimes conflict with those in the legal arena. When this occurs, the codes obligate professionals to point out their commitment to their own ethical standards and to attempt to resolve the conflict responsibly.

Furthermore, mental health professionals may be involved in a forensic setting in a variety of roles. They may be involved in forensic evaluations either as court appointed evaluators or they may be employed by the client's attorney. When hired by the attorney, their work may be covered by attorney–client privilege. Some courts have ruled that after reviewing the reports the attorney may actually choose not to use them (Knapp, VandeCreek, & Fulero, 1993). The court may also point of therapist as a treating expert, particularly in child custody cases. In these cases, the therapist's focus is narrow and longitudinal and consequently he or she may be qualified to give an opinion on the child's diagnosis, behavior patterns, coping skills, parental relationships and other aspects of the child's needs. They may also help the parent and the children to achieve developmental tasks. This role is inconsistent with the more distant, neutral, fact finding goal of a custody evaluator. It is critical, however for the therapist, to report factual information or opinions that are scientifically based and not be seduced into offering opinions about parents they have not seen which may be biased because of the children's perspective or that of the other parent. In the end treating therapists can cause a great deal of harm to everyone involved as was true in Case 8-7.

Haas (1993) identified several additional threats to competent practice in a forensic setting. He pointed out that many professionals do not grasp that acting as an expert witness entitles them to testify about matters of opinion (Swenson, 1997). Any lay person can testify about issues of fact or be a fact witness. However, if testifying as an expert witness, professionals should base their opinions on adequate preparation so that the content of the information provided to the court is accurate and up-to-date. Haas argued that some professionals are arrogant and are seduced by the power of the courtroom, which can lead them to rely on memory, ignore record-keeping standards, misuse assessment information, or diagnose in absentia. As he noted, diagnosing in absentia is a frequent source of ethics complaints. When in-person interviews are not possible, counselors or psychologists should clarify the tentative nature of their conclusions. Furthermore, Haas argued that some professionals allow the legal system to sway their testimony away from what can be scientifically supported to advocate a particular position. In such cases, the witness often fails to adequately evaluate the social consequences of testimony and abandons standards of competence based on the assumption that the adversarial process will lead to a reasonable outcome. Although there are differences of opinion regarding the appropriateness of assuming this role (Loftus, 1986), when psychologists or counselors do so, they are in essence abandoning their own ethical standards for those of the legal system. Fidelity requires that that psychologists or counselors testify truthfully, acknowledge their biases, and indicate the limits of their conclusions. Finally, Haas pointed out that greed can threaten adequate practice. Forensic practice is very lucrative and can tempt professionals to pad their bills, provide unnecessary assessments, and inflate the time involved in their work. Doing so, however, is not only unethical, it is fraudulent.

Multicultural competence is particularly important in forensic settings since members of racial and ethnic minority groups are overrepresented in populations served by forensic psychologists and counselors (Carter & Forsyth, 2007). Carter and Forsyth investigated the extent to which forensic journals addressed issues of race and culture between 1998 and 2003. They found that nearly half (47.5%) of the empirical articles failed to even report the race or ethnicity of the sample. In addition, their content analysis found that validity tests of the measures used in forensic evaluations had not been done for populations of color or had not been reported. Weinstein (2005) claims that the lack of validity of these tests for racial and ethnic minorities leave forensics open to concerns about their evaluations and particularly to biases in their interpretation. Carter and Forsyth point out that several recent studies provide evidence for the existence of racial disparities and possible biases in forensic evaluations (Pinals, Packer, Fisher, & Roy-Bujnowski, 2004; Warren, Murrie, Chauhan, Dietz, & Morris, 2004). For example, Warren et al. (2004) found a significant negative relationship between opinions of insanity and racial/ethnic minority status with favorable opinions of insanity reached more frequently for white defendants.

Since some of the tests are used to assess sanity for execution the moral implications are appalling. Carter and Forsyth (2007) say the services provided "within the forensic field have the potential to permanently impact the course of clients lives in a matter that is unparalleled in any other psychology specialty areas" (p. 140). Nothing is more permanent than death. Clearly, forensic practitioners should not use measures that have not been validated samples that include people of color.

Haas (1993) suggested that issues of character are particularly important in moving beyond merely competent practice to providing forensic services that are characterized by integrity and excellence. In addition to the virtues discussed earlier in this book, he argued for the importance of "objectivity, loyalty to the facts, recognition of the limits of psychological knowledge and intent to benefit human welfare" (Haas, 1993, p. 264). Carter and Forsyth would add that the principles of justice and respect for persons are also critical if not more so.

Competence in Teaching

The responsibility to be competent in academic settings and in teaching arises from the principles of beneficence and nonmaleficence, as it does in other areas of practice and research. Generally, the relationship between faculty and students should be guided by the duty to promote students' welfare (Kitchener, 1992b), which requires, at minimum, that faculty are competent at what they do. Prior to the 1980s silence best characterize the discussion of ethical responsibilities of faculty members toward students in higher education in general and psychology in particular (Dill, 1982; Kitchener, 1992). As Scriven (1982, p. 308) argued, academics have done a better job of "telling others how they should behave" than they do at identifying their own obligations. It is well known that modeling has a profound impact on behavior. In fact, Rest (1983) argued that one reason people may choose to act morally is because others have modeled acting that way. If that is the case and faculty act immorally, their actions may have the opposite effect.

The responsibility to benefit students is probably the least controversial and most apparent of the ethical responsibilities of faculty members. The concept has its roots in the Socratic claim that those who are in professions should not seek their own advantage which should benefit those whom they serve (Plato, 1930). In other words, the relationship between faculty and students should be guided primarily by the need to promote student welfare. How to promote student welfare is another issue about which there are little data. For example, as the few studies that will be reported suggest faculty need to balance compassion, respect and support for students with honest relationships and intellectual rigor. However, the data are minimal and there are few data on what may harm students.

In a study of psychology educators, Tabachnick et al. (1991) found that few respondents reported teaching material they had not mastered, teaching a class without adequate preparation, failing to update lecture notes when reteaching a course, or teaching in a nonobjective or incomplete matter is "fairly or very often." On the other hand, over 90% of faculty indicated that they had taught without mastering content or without adequate preparation "on rare occasions." These data would suggest that by in large the majority of faculty members take preparation for courses seriously and try to remain objective about the material they teach. However, as Tabachnick et al. (1991) noted,

> it is likely that life's vicissitudes will prevent a less-than-superhuman psychologist showing up for every class adequately prepared. Teaching material not completely mastered may in some cases be attributable to a department's less than ideal allocation of introductory and required courses among its faculty, or to the difficulties in keeping up with the information explosion, even in one's own specialty. (p. 509)

Although competence in teaching has not received the same attention as has competence and practice, there is a new awareness of the importance of the scholarship of teaching. Still, clear statements regarding what it means to be competent in teaching are rare. Canada's Society for Teaching and Learning in Higher Education developed a set of ethical standards for college and university teaching. They identified competent instruction as having two parts: content competence and pedagogical competence (Murray, Gillese, Lennon, Mercer, & Robinson, 1996). Content competence presumes that the instructor has a high degree of subject matter knowledge and that course content is both accurate and current. Murray et al. argued that instructors should also ensure that course content is appropriate for the stated objectives and purposes and provides students with adequate background for courses for which it is a prerequisite.

Pedagogical competence assumes instructors not only have appropriate knowledge but can also communicate it to students in a way that meets the course objectives. In other words, they have the skills and ability to communicate the course content. By implication, to remain pedagogically competent, instructors need to remain current about teaching strategies and how to adapt these to the needs of different student groups (Murray et al., 1996).

Competence in an instructional setting involves more than just attending to content and pedagogical issues, however. It also involves dealing with sensitive topics in honest and respectful ways, including distinguishing between fact and personal opinions (Brown & Krager, 1985; Murray et al., 1996). Similarly, it means knowing the relative merits of different ways to assess students' performance and using assessment techniques that are both consistent with course goals and as reliable and valid as possible (Murray, 1996). It also means fulfilling other faculty roles, from adviser to curriculum planner, with equal attention to competence.

During the past three decades, however, teaching researchers have used a variety of evidence to examine the usefulness of different teaching activities. More commonly referred to as the scholarship of teaching and learning (SoTL) (Gurung, Ansburg, Alexander, Lawrence, &

Johnson, 2008), this form of scholarship pays attention to pedagogical research processes and the basis of good teaching and learning. According to Gurung et al. (2008), in the 1980s colleges and universities began to take a closer look at faculty priorities. In one study, Gray, Froh, and Diamond (1992) studied 23,000 faculty, chairs, and administrators and found that they believed that in a relationship to research too little attention was given to teaching. This led major institutions to take a closer look at the faculty reward structure and what constitutes scholarship in higher education. Consequently, SoTL emerged as a more important area of study. In APA, it has been championed by Division 2, the Society for the Teaching of Psychology (STP).

One way to identify the characteristics of competent instructors is to identify effective teaching techniques from the perspectives of participants identified by their peers as outstanding teachers. Buskist (2002) surveyed the STP teaching award winners from two-year and four-year colleges and universities to discover the attributes and characteristics that made them effective teachers. Although there were great differences between the award winners, many stated that they lecture less now than they did earlier in their careers and they have become more student oriented. In general, the awardees stressed on the eight following themes:

1. Encourage students to become active participants in their education.
2. Care for learning and helping others to learn.
3. Make learning fun and focus on changing attitudes about learning.
4. Help students reach their intellectual potential.
5. Be enthusiastic about both the students and the subject matter.
6. Consider the developmental level of the audience.
7. Strive to be a positive role model.
8. Set high but obtainable standards.

Buskist concludes that there is no single way to become a competent teacher; however, according to Buskist, it is clear that a couple of themes appear necessary. All these participants shared a love of their subject matter and their students and emphasized the interaction between the students and themselves.

A series of studies based on the work of Buskist, Sikorski, Buckley, and Saville (2002) studied student and faculty perceptions of effective teaching. Buskist et al. (2002) recruited undergraduate and faculty participants at doctoral research universities asking them to identify the top 10 qualities and behaviors most important to a master teacher among 28 qualities and behaviors. This study was followed by a replication at a community college (Schaeffer, Epting, Zinn, & Buskist, 2003) and with two independent samples of Canadian undergraduate students (Vulcano, 2007). After completing his study Vulcano compared the ratings of the qualities and behaviors across all three studies. He found considerable consistency particularly among the top 15 categories of qualities and behaviors of effective teachers. In fact 86% of the students' responses were in those categories. In many ways the qualities and behaviors identified are quite similar to the ones found by Buskist (2002). All three samples rated six behaviors among the top 10. These included the faculty person or instructor being knowledgeable, providing interesting and creative lectures, being approachable, be enthusiastic about teaching, having fair and realistic expectations, and being happy humorous or positive. Encouraging student participation and encouraging or caring for students were also rated highly.

Tomcho and Foels (2008) did a meta-analytic study of published teaching activities in *Teaching of Psychology* between 1974 and 2006. Each study had to contain a description of the teaching activities and methods as well as data on at least one type of learning outcome. They concluded teaching activities and methods were moderately effective in producing changes in student learning. In general, teaching activities produce greater changes in knowledge and behavior than in attitudes, however, they pointed out that attitudes are more stable characteristics of the individual and may require longer exposure to produce change. They pointed out that with the available data they were unable to evaluate whether the results might be better accounted for by the teaching relationship rather than the method or activity. They point out, however, that other researchers have shown that the student teacher relationship (Cornelius-White, 2007) and teacher immediacy behaviors that demonstrate psychological availability in the classroom (Witt, Wheeless, & Alan, 2004) also have moderate effect sizes in relationship to learning outcomes. It is interesting that like psychotherapy and supervision, the relationship variable seems important in all human interactions especially ones that involve vulnerability and learning.

As in psychotherapy, there is a call for education activities to be evidence-based (Marsh, 2005). Tomcho and Foels (2008) recommend that if researchers begin to look at EBP in teaching, they should examine the role of the student-teacher relationship in any tested activity and compare effective teaching activities and methods. If they do so they may be able to identify whether there exists activities, methods, and processes that constitute best educational practices. Doing so, it would go a long way in identifying what it meant to be a competent instructor. However, to end for this chapter as it began, "if faculty model unethical behavior is very possible that the most influential ethical attitudes that students learn will not come from explicit ethics education but from the experiences they have in other areas of the curriculum" (Kitchener, 1992, p. 190). Take the following case as a potential example.

Case 8-8

A newspaper article recently revealed that a local university, it was well known that students in one particular department commonly socialized with the faculty. This included 18-year-olds and faculty of all ages and marital commitments. Faculty often provided marijuana and alcoholic beverages for the students, who in the state were under age. Often the relationships between faculty and students were sexualized. Although several students complained over the years, nothing was done until a new president was appointed who was personally appalled by the behavior of the faculty. On the other hand, one or two students defended the faculty saying they felt like they were a big happy family.

The faculty were not only modeling unethical relationships behaviors between students and faculty, they were also modeling illegal behaviors. One wonders, if these were psychology or counseling students in an ethics class, whether what they learned in their reading, discussions, and other teaching activities could compensate for the modeling provided by the faculty.

Competence in Research

It should be clear that throughout the discussion of the prior issues, the competent practice of alternative treatments, supervision techniques, assessments, forensic practices, and teaching are all based on the scientific evidence behind them. Although increased attention has been focused on the ethics of research with human participants since the mid-1970s (McGaha & Korn, 1995), most attention has focused on issues of consent, confidentiality, and potential harm to participants. Comparatively little attention has focused on issues of competence. However, as Rosenthal (1994) argued bad science is tantamount to bad ethics. As he pointed out, if the research design is poor, no positive benefits of the study can accrue, thus, there is no way to rationalize the use of assets, including money, the time of the participants or the investigators, and the space required. Particularly in periods of scarce resources, incompetent research cannot be justified because it uses time that money and other assets needed elsewhere. Those resources could be invested in educational experiences that may be more beneficial or in research that has a greater potential for yielding meaningful results. Poor research can lead to inaccurate conclusions that may harm individuals, social groups, or society as a whole. It is for these reasons that ethics codes emphasize the importance of competence in planning research. As Smith (2000) argues competence is assumed to be essential for the design and conduct of responsible research. He uses the example that risks and benefits of a research project are best informed by expertise in the area to be studied. Competence of the researcher implies expertise in the area.

The principles of beneficence and nonmaleficence require competence in order to maximize positive outcomes for science, the participants, and humanity while minimizing the potential of unnecessary harm or risks (National Commission, 1978a; Sieber, 1992) as well as of the wasting of scarce resources and the drawing of false conclusions. Typically, when cost-utility evaluations are done by IRBs or human participants committees, they consider the costs and risks in terms of possible negative effects on participants, the institution, the community, and the funding agency in relationship to the potential benefits of the research. They seldom consider research design, yet clearly it is important to do so. Poorly conceived research could never justify risks of any kind, whether they are to humans or animals. Smith (2000) points out that the cost to participants cannot be balanced against the benefits to science, thus, the researcher cannot avoid moral responsibility for the decision.

Competence is also required when selecting participants, conducting the research, analyzing data, and reporting the results. Clearly, the participants selected must be appropriate for answering the research questions, representative of the population studied, and numerous enough to draw valid conclusions. However, competence also includes understanding the populations from which the participants will be drawn well enough to assess their potential vulnerabilities and, therefore, the potential risks (Stanley & Sieber, 1991). If, for example, a study is being done of attitudes toward HIV testing in the Latino community, the researcher needs to understand the values of the group toward family, the medical community, homosexuality, and drug use. Similarly, if research is being done with children, the researcher needs to understand how the risks vary with the child's age. Understanding the group being studied is critical if the researcher is going to be able to assess whether, at minimum, the participants will emerge from the research unharmed. Sieber (2000) points out that many difficulties can be avoided if ethical considerations are integrated with practical and scientific considerations at the outset of the research.

Competence in conducting research is as important as competence in planning it (National Commission, 1978b). In fact, APA (1993a) has developed rather detailed guidelines for the competent care of animal subjects prior to, during, and after a research project. Not only can incompetent practices invalidate research based on good designs, they can potentially harm both people and animals and violate the respect due to human participants.

Ethical errors in data analysis and reporting psychological research can range from mistakes due to failure to understand statistical analyses to more serious transgressions that involve actual fabrication of data or dropping data that do not fit the hypotheses (Rosenthal, 1994). Although, there may be legitimate scientific reasons to drop outliers or subsets of the data, dropping them because they do not fit the researcher's theory exemplifies academic dishonesty. Furthermore, competence involves considering alternative hypotheses. Sieber (2000) uses an example in the early 20th century study of immigrants for whom English was a second language. The immigrants were given IQ tests in English on which they performed poorly. Criminals were also tested and found to have low IQs. The researcher concluded that allowing immigrants into the country would introduce a criminal element, never considering the alternative hypothesis that proficiency in English rather than immigrant status produced the correlations. Misrepresenting findings because of incompetent data interpretation impedes the progress of science, is disrespectful of the time and energy participants gave to the project, and wastes the resources devoted to the project.

Deliberately misinterpreting findings involves scientific fraud and seriously violates the public trust. The U.S. Public Health Service (1989) defined scientific misconduct as involving two elements: (a) falsification, fabrication or plagiarism in proposing, conducting or reporting research; or (b) other practices that seriously deviate from those commonly accepted by the scientific community for honestly proposing, reporting or carrying out research (p. 2). Rosenthal (1994) argued that such behavior, if detected, ought to end the scientific career of the researcher. Scientific fraud damages everyone involved. It can lead to the public perception that psychological research is not to be trusted and undermines federal support for scientific psychology (Grisso et al., 1991).

Sieber also points out that competence is essential in planning and disseminating research findings. This is particularly true if the research involves socially sensitive issues that can offend or upset people not connected directly with the study. Researchers need to give careful consideration how their research findings could be interpreted, yet, she points out that even the most thoughtful presentations of the research can backfire. She uses a study by Shedler and Block (1990, p. 612) as an example. The following is a summary of that case.

Case 8-9

The investigators studied the psychological characteristics and drug use longitudinally on children from preschool through 18 years of age. Adolescents who engaged in some drug experimentation (primarily with marijuana) were the best adjusted in the sample. Adolescents who used drugs frequently were the most maladjusted, showing a distinct personality syndrome marked by interpersonal alienation, poor impulse control and manifest emotional distress. Those who by 18 years had never experimented with any drug were relatively anxious, emotionally constricted and lacking in social skills. The differences between frequent drug users, the experimenters and abstainers could be traced to the earliest periods of childhood and were related to the quality of parenting received. They concluded that drug use is a symptom, not a cause of personal and social maladjustment and the meaning of drug use can only be understood in the context of the individual's personality structure and developmental history. The researchers knew their article would be highly controversial and were extremely careful in reporting the results to indicate that the media might misrepresent their findings as indicating that drug use might somehow improve and adolescents' psychological health. They stated categorically that their findings did not support such a view nor should anything they said remotely encourage such a misrepresentation.

Despite the care that they used in spelling out the dangers of misrepresenting their findings, a furor was raised in newspapers and among drug counselors. They were even told it harmed society by broadcasting their distractive views.

They thought that they had taken reasonable steps to avoid misrepresentation of their results by clearly stating how they might be misrepresented. However, thinking retrospectively, other steps might have been taken. They might have met with members of the community, particularly drug counselors, to explain their results prior to publication and/or with members of the media to explain their study. Unfortunately, sometimes members of such groups are unwilling to spend the time talking with researchers until the results are published. As psychology and counseling continued to investigate controversial issues, they need to take particular responsibility in avoiding harm that there studies might cause to the public, to their participants, to the researchers, to their institutions and to society. At the same time it would be ethically irresponsible to avoid studying such important issues. When studying and reporting on controversial issues, Sieber (2000) recommends consulting with others including the IRB, members of the community, research participants themselves and others to clarify the risks and benefits involved in doing and reporting such research.

Although it is critical that the researchers are competent about the topic studied, the methodology involved, the statistical analyses, and how the research is reported, it is just as important that they educate their students and research staff to perform similarly (Fisher, Wertz, & Goodman, 2009; Tangney, 2000). Researchers have an ethical responsibility not only to train their staff adequately but also to supervise them to assure that their training is being applied competently. They point out that is particularly important to train and supervise the research staff to be sensitive to individual differences including age, cultural background, heterosexuality or other differences they may encounter when administering consent procedures, explaining confidentiality, or conducting the research. They pointed out that sometimes when the research staff conducts interviews on personally relevant topics like episodes of stress or trauma, they may be tempted to overstep the bounds of their role as researchers and offer advice or guidance. They suggest that the training of students and staff is most effective when it is considered an ongoing process. Although initial training is critical, it is important that the researcher-supervisor acknowledge that their staff may encounter situations, like listening to participants talk about trauma, that they do not have the resources to handle. Furthermore, the staff should understand they should not try to handle these kinds of issues without consultation and doing so does not reflect negatively on them. Researchers themselves should not supervise outside the bounds of their own competence. For example, when supervising dissertations researchers need to recognize that they do not have expertise in all areas and they may have to turn to knowledgeable colleagues for consultation and assistance in supervision.

Ultimately, incompetent or dishonest practice in research is a failure of scientific integrity because it fails to uphold the core values of science. These includes the commitment to seek new knowledge, the valuing of truth and honesty in reporting results, a concern about asking unpopular questions, and the refusal to endorse unrealistic expectations about answers that science can provide (Baumrind, 1990; Kitchener, 1996b). Just as in therapy, good character is important to the practice of good science. Having integrity as well as being trustworthy are critical to the long-term health of scientific psychology and counseling. The failure of either can lead to public cynicism about science in general as well as the aims and benefits of particular studies.

Conclusion

The topic of competence can sometimes be overwhelming. Unlike many of the other ethical issues discussed in this book, there is an aspect of relativity that makes competence difficult to pin down. Questions such as the following frequently arise:

a. Competent in comparison with whom?
b. Competent by what standards?
c. What exactly is a reasonable person standard?
d. With the reality of how quickly new information becomes accessible, how up-to-date should a professional's knowledge be?

The standards are always stretching because the knowledge base is always growing. As already noted, sometimes even competent professionals with deep personal integrity and high standards of responsibility, cannot remain on top of the rapid expansion of knowledge even in their own areas of expertise. Furthermore, the vicissitudes of everyday life often push professionals to the limits of their expertise. The excellent faculty member may get tapped for an administrative position with little support or training, or the excellent clinician may be asked to testify as a fact witness in a custody hearing with little or no prior experience in courtroom work and no legal way to defer the responsibility.

Issues of responsibility are some of the most difficult with which to deal in professions like counseling and psychology because our work affects the lives of other humans. At the same time, we cannot be held to superhuman standards that never allow for an error in judgment. The reasonable person standard is the standard that a reasonable professional dealing with a particular issue or case would be expected to meet. It is not a standard of perfection. At the same time, we must aspire to provide the most effective services and do the most skilled science of which we are capable. In addition, when we do make errors, we need to examine why they occurred, whether they are a sign of impairment, and how we can avoid making similar mistakes in the future.

Questions for Discussion or Consideration

1. Are there areas in which you are currently working that you question your competence? If so, what might you do to improve your competence?
2. Have you ever worked when you were too tired or sick to be effective? If so, what compelled you to continue working?
3. Do you know of colleagues (or other students) who are incompetent or impaired? If so, have you confronted them? If not, what keeps you from confronting them or at least discussing the issue with them? What is your ethical obligation according to your code of ethics when you know of such a situation?
4. If you want to change areas of practice or add new ones like supervision, how do you do so without being unethical?
5. Why do you think the scientific basis of competence has been emphasized? Has it been over emphasized? If you think it has been over emphasized, what are alternatives?

9
Respecting Others with Informed Consent

You walk up to the receptionist in a doctors or therapists office and the receptionist hands you to two single spaced pages and says "sign at the bottom" and then stands there impatiently. The writing is dense so you sign it being assured by the receptionist that it is just a formality. This scenario fits with a cynical view of informed consent that involves an initial hurdle for therapeutic and research activities (Johnson-Green, 2007). Hochhauser (1999) would call this dealing with informed consent as a "rite" not a "right" (p. 1).

Considering how often such a practice is played out, it is surprising that in a review of the cases opened by the APA Ethics Committee during the past few years (APA, 2007, 2008) issues of informed consent are not ones that the public find troublesome. Furthermore, with few exceptions there been a few articles written on informed consent as a construct in the last 10 years. Similarly, in their survey of ethical dilemmas encountered by APA members, Pope and Vetter (1992) did not highlight informed consent as an area that psychologists identified as troublesome. This is despite the fact that both the 2002 APA Code of Ethics and 2005 ACA Code of Ethics contained between 15 and 20 references to consent in the standards of practice. However, problems related to consent are often implicit in the problems professionals face and in cases adjudicated by the ethics committees. In addition, questions relating to informed consent regarding the therapeutic contract underlie most cases involving professional liability (Bennett, Bryant, VandenBos, & Greenwood, 1990). Take the following three cases as examples.

Case 9-1

A psychologist was asked by a court to act as a mediator in a custody case. Prior to beginning the mediation, the psychologist explained the nature of mediation and how they would be meeting together to find a satisfactory custody arrangement for the couple's daughter. After five sessions, however, the conflict between the couple was so great that they discontinued the mediation. The psychologist referred the case back to the court and voluntarily submitted a custody evaluation to the court on both parents recommending that custody be awarded to the mother because she had been more willing to compromise during the mediation. On learning that the psychologist had submitted the evaluation reports, both parents were upset because they had not been informed ahead of time that their behavior was being evaluated during the mediation process (APA, 1987a, p. 78).

Case 9-2

A group of researchers (Campbell, Sanderson, & Laverty, 1964) wanted to study the effects of traumatic conditioning. Hospitalized alcoholic patients were approached about volunteering for the study. They were told that the study was connected to a "possible therapy for alcoholism." In fact, the study had nothing to do with a treatment for alcoholism; rather, Campbell et al. (1964) were studying a classical conditioning paradigm that paired a neutral tone with intense fear. The "volunteers" heard a tone and were injected with Scoline, a drug that produces motor paralysis. The paralysis includes the diaphragm and muscles, so the participants could not move or breathe for almost 2 min. It also produced such intense fear that some participants reported that they thought they were dying. Although no permanent physical harm resulted, the procedure produced a long-lasting fear response to the sound. In some patients, the response could not be extinguished even after several attempts (Diener & Crandell, 1978).

Case 9-3

After entering a doctoral program involving training to be a therapist, students are told that they will be required to participate in psychotherapy for a year prior to beginning their internships. Students are given a list of practitioners who will provide the therapy at a reduced cost. Nevertheless, several students complained that there was nothing in the program materials that they received that indicated that participating in therapy was a requirement and that even though it was being provided at a reduced cost, it was an expense for which they had not planned.

In each case, the clients, research participants, and students felt that they had been misinformed or poorly informed about actions that affected their lives and as a consequence felt mistreated or treated unjustly. In Case 9-2, the researchers actually lied to the participants. Consequently, their consent to participate was ethically invalid. Although requiring students to engage in therapy without including the requirement in program materials was explicitly forbidden in the 2002 APA Ethics Code, it was not explicitly covered in the 2005 ACA Ethics Code. In addition to cases like these, there are other particularly troublesome issues involving consent in psychology and counseling such as those involving mental patients or children, consent for treatment or research of the mentally impaired, and deceptive research. Further, issues that is more troublesome because of the use of the Internet in therapy, supervision, and research.

Informed Consent Defined

The nature of informed consent is sometimes confusing because it has come to have many meanings, including legal, ethical, and process ones. In fact, Appelbaum, Lidz, and Meisel (1987) included all of these components in their definition of consent:

> Informed consent refers to legal rules that prescribe behaviors for physicians in their interactions with patients and provide for penalties, under given circumstances, if physicians deviate from those expectations; to an ethical doctrine rooted in our society's cherished value of autonomy, that insures to patients their right of self-determination when medical decisions need to be made; and to an interpersonal process whereby physicians interact with patients to select an appropriate course of medical care (p. 3).

Although Appelbaum et al. (1987) referred to physicians, their definition applies equally well to psychologists or counselors. Informed consent pertains to the legal requirements or administrative regulations that specify how and what mental health professionals should tell clients or research participants about their participation in treatment or a scientific study. It also refers to the ethical responsibility to help individuals make responsible, informed, and autonomous decisions about treatment or research, and it sometimes refers to the interpersonal process through which both of those goals are fulfilled. The core meaning of consent is that decisions about participation in medical or mental health care or research should be made in a collaborative manner with both the mental health professional and consumer taking part (Appelbaum et al., 1987). Although the term *informed consent* originated in the law, both ethics and the law have contributed to the evolution of the meaning (Appelbaum et al., 1987).

In fact, Barnett (2007a) points out that up until the early twentieth century physicians did not obtain consent from their patients for treatment, but went by what has been referred to as the "doctor knows best" system (Welfel, 2006). According to Barnett's the foundation for informed consent began with the legal case Schloendorf versus Society of New York Hospital (1914). The case established the precedent that competent adults have the right to decide what should be done to their bodies. Spurred by the atrocities done by Nazi physicians, Barnett pointed out that in the late 1940s and 1950s there was an increase in legal rulings that contributed to the legal meaning of informed consent. In Salgo versus Stanford (1957), the California Court of Appeals added that the person must both comprehend the information and the risks and benefits associated with it. Going beyond this decision in Canterbury versus Spence (1972), the courts decided it was insufficient to merrily answer patient's questions that all information should be shared so the patient can make an intelligent, informed decision about participating.

The Purpose of Informed Consent

Conceptually, informed consent is fundamentally tied to the idea that respect for autonomy requires that people must have the information necessary to make reasonable choices. To deny people adequate information is to deny them their rights as autonomous agents and to the respect that is due to them as people. Providing informed consent allows people to make decisions about events that may affect them and to weigh the risks and benefits for themselves or their loved ones.

In Western societies, there is a strong emphasis on freedom of choice. Reflecting this emphasis, most if not all professional codes identify informed consent as a central tenant. For example, the first ethical principle for research with human participants in the Nuremberg Code (1949/1964) stated that "the voluntary consent of the human subject is absolutely essential" (p. 553). Without a commitment to consent, psychologists could coerce or manipulate others into participating in activities that might not be in their best interests as occurred in Nazi Germany. Smith (1983) provided a vivid image of coercive participation:

> To appreciate the need for informed consent one has only to imagine a totalitarian society in which individuals are selected arbitrarily to serve as subjects for research. Unwilling and uninformed they would be victims rather than collaborators, and like the victims of a crime, such an experience would undermine two fundamental beliefs; a sense of trust and a sense of control over their lives. (p. 303)

One commonsense justification for informed consent is "the idea that people's rights and welfare are usually best protected when they themselves made decisions about things that directly affect them" (Diener & Crandall, 1978, p. 36). Consent allows research participants, clients, or students to decide what is in their best interests and to avoid situations that they judge to be hazardous. It also helps researchers, therapists, and instructors to avoid harming individuals when they have a responsibility to help, or at least, to leave them unharmed (nonmaleficence). Had the alcoholic patients in Case 9-1 been told that they were being asked to participate in a fear-inducing study and about Scoline's terrifying effects, they could have made the decision about whether it might be harmful for them. In fact, Diener and Crandell pointed out that physicians did volunteer for the study, despite knowing the effects of Scoline and they too developed the conditioned fear. The deception did not serve any methodological purpose other than to get the alcoholic patients to participate. It should be noted that this study would probably not be allowed under current IRB regulations regarding consent.

In a similar manner, the principle of fidelity is made explicit in the consent agreement because it identifies the nature of the relationship between the psychologist or counselor and the consumer. If the agreement is inadequate or not truthful, it undermines the professional relationship and may ultimately destroy the consumer's faith in the possibility of trustworthy relationships. By contrast, if the agreement is thorough and clear and a good-faith effort is made to uphold it, it can enhance the those that who relationship between the consumer and the mental health professional in therapy (Everstine et al., 1980; Handelsman, 1990; Hare-Mustin, Marecek, Kaplan, & Liss-Levinson 1979), research (Diener & Crandall, 1978), and academic settings (Handelsman, Rosen, & Arguello, 1987). In fact, Sullivan, Martin, and Handelsman (1993) found that psychotherapists who used an informed-consent procedure were rated as more expert and trustworthy than those that who had not and that participants were more willing to recommend those who used consent to a friend and to go to those mental health professionals themselves.

Understanding informed consent as a process further upholds the principles of autonomy and fidelity. It appears to be for these reasons that Barnett (2007a) defined consent as "a shared decision-making process in which the professional communicates sufficient information to the other individual so that he or she can make an informed decision about participating in the professional relationship" (p. 179). This process allows clients, research participants, supervisees, and others to trust the professional relationship. It allows them to assume that they are aware of the possible risks and harms and are entering the relationship freely with that knowledge. As Wise (2007) pointed out such a process emphasizes an active engagement in generating an agreement on the part of the participant.

Several authors (Appelbaum et al., 1987; Diener & Crandall, 1978; Kovacs, 1984) have argued that using informed consent can help professionals limit legal liability. By specifying the nature and limits of the relationship and by upholding those limits, the psychologist has some protection in malpractice suits (Bennett et al., 1990). No procedure guarantees whether a client or research participant will sue, however, practicing wisely and in a way that is consistent with a generally recognized standard of care can help protect both the professional and the consumer (Bennett et al., 1990).

In summary, the use of informed consent is based on the principle of autonomy and helps the professional uphold the principles of beneficence, nonmaleficence, and fidelity (Diener & Crandall, 1978; Handelsman et al., 1995). Informed consent:

1. Allows individuals to make critical decisions about their own lives and ensures that participation is voluntary.
2. Helps to protect consumers from harm by allowing them to evaluate the potential for a treatment, research procedure, or educational experience to affect them in negative ways, thus helping mental health professionals avoid situations in which they might harm the consumer.
3. Can help build trust and respect between the consumer and the professional.
4. May help the professional avoid malpractice suits or ethical charges.

What Is Adequate Informed Consent?

What counts as adequate informed consent depends on whether one means meeting the social or institutional rules that mandate what is legally or institutionally required or whether one means meeting the ethical spirit of consent. It is possible to meet the requirements of the first without meeting the requirements of the second. For example, a researcher who is criticized for inadequately informing participants about the nature of a study might defend herself by saying, "It was approved by the institutional review board." Although she has met the institutional requirements for consent, it is unclear whether she has fulfilled the ethical spirit of consent.

A similar problem exists with legally mandated consent forms for therapy. For example, Colorado requires that all psychotherapists in the state disclose certain legally mandated information to all clients. Despite this requirement, Handelsman et al. (1995) found that although the majority (96.4%) of the forms they reviewed fulfilled the legal mandate by indicating that there were limits to confidentiality, relatively few forms indicated what those limits might be. Indicating that there were limits of confidentiality but not specifying the nature of those limits met the legal requirements for consent but not the ethical responsibility to help clients make reasonable decisions. In fact, Handelsman et al. (1995) argued that "informing clients that information is confidential—without telling them all of the limits of that confidentiality—may be more misleading for clients than telling them nothing at all" (p. 125). This is particularly true if information is going to be transmitted via the Internet because even if a warning statement is included in the message, it does not protect the privacy the person receiving the message from nosy partners, roommates, or children (Keller & Lee, 2003; Pittenger, 2002).

What does it mean to fulfill the spirit of consent? Several components that are necessary for having true consent have been identified (APA, 1992; Appelbaum et al., 1987; Barnett, 2007a; Beauchamp & Childress, 2001), including competence, disclosure, understanding, voluntariness, and consent (or authorization).

Competence

Beauchamp and Childress (2001) called competence a threshold element for consent to occur. In other words, before initiating a consent procedure, the individual must be competent to give consent. The rationale is based on the relationship between competence and autonomy as discussed in Chapter 3. They argue that competent judgments serve a "gatekeeping role in healthcare by distinguishing persons whose decisions should be solicited or accepted from persons whose decisions should not be" (p. 69). If people are not competent to understand what is being disclosed, then they cannot make a reasonable choice about whether or not to give consent. Under those circumstances, their decisions need to be evaluated and could be overridden by a surrogate or court appointed guardian (Beauchamp & Childress, 2001).

For legal purposes, a decision must be made about whether individuals are competent or not to give consent, that is, competence, for legal purposes, is dichotomous. They are competent or they are not. Patients or that the in a competent research participants must be able to meet certain minimal requirements in order to participate legally in the process. Individuals are competent to give consent if they have the capacity to understand and process the information, to consider the consequences of their actions, including the risks and benefits involved, and to make a decision based on the information that is provided and their consideration of it (Beauchamp & Childress, 1994). Because most of these criteria involve cognitive processes, the ability to assess and understand mental status and knowledge of cognitive development is highly valuable. Take the following case as an example.

Case 9-4

Alice, a 25-year-old woman with schizophrenia, hates the side effects of the medication that is successfully controlling her thought disorder. She consents to enroll in a medical research study designed to test how long persons with schizophrenia can remain free of psychiatric problems after stopping medication. Two weeks into the study, her parents begin to worry that some of Alice's "bizarre" behavior may be returning. When they ask Alice to withdraw from the study, she refuses. Her parents approach the hospital conducting the study to challenge the legitimacy of Alice's consent to remain in the study that places her mental health at risk (Fisher, 2002, p. 279).

As Fisher (200) points out the special cognitive status of people with mental deficits does not change the responsibility of researchers or therapists to communicate with them honestly and respect their autonomy, however, to do so may require special procedures to ensure that these claims are fairly met and are not treated irresponsibly. As she asks "How do we balance our moral obligation to respect the dignity and autonomy of persons with mental disorders to make their own decisions with the obligation to ensure that ill formed or incompetent choices should not jeopardize their welfare or leave them open to exploitation?" (p. 281). This is especially true in cases like Alice who has fluctuating decisional capacity.

As Wise (2007) points out some clients or research participants may have little interest or ability to understand the long complex consent documents. Further, clients from different cultural backgrounds may believe it to be disrespectful to ask questions about the meaning of what is written. It is for this reason that Barnett (2007a) recommends both a verbal and written consent process.

Although the law recognizes that some people are not competent to give consent, there is no well-established legal standard that defines incompetency (Appelbaum et al., 1987). In general, decisions involving competency ought to balance respect for the individual's autonomous decision making with beneficence or concern for the person's well-being. This involves the person's ability to understand the treatment, research, or other procedures and to calculate the risks and benefits involved. Holding people to this standard has often justified substitute decision making for those with mental impairments, especially if a disabled person disagrees with a risk–benefit assessment of his/her own family or physician (Fisher, 2002). If individuals are not competent because of a temporary condition, such as drug or alcohol consumption, a psychologist should ideally wait until their competence is restored rather than proceed with the consent process or turn to a surrogate decision maker. In reality, however, some decisions about treatment initially take place in a crisis. In those situations, a family member may have to take over and act for the person until his or her competency is restored.

Unfortunately, it is often the case that the kinds of mental conditions that affect people's competence to make rational decisions are the same ones that bring people in for mental health treatment. For example, in order to receive treatment, individuals may be required to sign consent forms when suffering from major depressive symptoms, although they may be literally unable to process the information in a meaningful way. For similar reasons, Widiger and Rorer (1984) argued that participation in the consent process is beyond the capacity of many psychotherapy clients or mental patients.

This may indeed be true if consent is conceptualized as an event that occurs at a particular point in time, usually at the beginning of a psychotherapeutic relationship. Appelbaum et al. (1987) contrasted the *event model* of consent with what they call the *process model*. In fact, Barnett (2007a) asserts that "informed consent should be viewed as a process, not a singular event that occurs at the outset of treatment (or supervision, research, or any other professional relationship)" (p. 180). The process model is based on the assumption that decision making, particularly in mental health situations, should be a continuous exchange of information that takes place throughout the relationship as the circumstances change. For example, there may be changes in the type of treatment recommended as a client reveals more information about him or herself or improves (Barnett, 2007a). Additionally, clients' ability to understand the nature of therapy, as well as the nature of consent, may change as their symptoms lift (Pope & Vasquez, 2007). Although the law or institutional regulations may require getting signed consent prior to beginning treatment, ethical psychologists or counselors have an obligation to continue to ensure that patients understand the process in which they are engaged. In addition, professionals who are trustworthy, compassionate, and respectful should, as a person's capacity for understanding improves, increasingly involve the client in making decisions about his or her treatment.

Disclosure

Beauchamp and Childress (2001) referred to disclosure as one of the information elements of consent. Disclosure may be the most immediately apparent component of consent because in order to be informed, relevant information must be made available to the consumer. However, what constitutes adequate disclosure is more difficult to define.

Many consumers are not knowledgeable about types of treatment, their consequences, their strengths and weaknesses, their potential for causing harm as well as good, and so on. Consumers, unless they are seasoned therapy participants, often have misconceptions about the nature of therapy, its cost, and its length. Similarly, research participants may have little understanding about the array of possible scenarios in which they may be placed. It is often difficult for an outsider to determine whether an experience will be harmful or stressful for a particular person. Providing basic information about the nature of the experience allows individuals the opportunity to judge whether or not participation is in their best interests. The amount and type of information that needs to be disclosed may depend on the person involved.

The courts (Appelbaum et al., 1987) have identified two standards for disclosure: (a) the professional practice standard, and (b) the reasonable person standard. In the professional practice standard, the professional community determines adequate disclosure; the adequacy of disclosure is measured against customary practice among other similar professionals regarding similar procedures. This standard assumes that the professional community has the best interests of the consumer in mind and can determine what the consumer needs to know. However several problems affect this standard. Initially is uncertain whether a customary standard exists in many situations and if custom did not have the best interests of the consumer in mind, negligence could be perpetuated without consequences (Beauchamp & Childress, 2001). By contrast, the reasonable person standard measures adequate consent against what a reasonable person would want to know in a similar situation. Of course, deciding what a "reasonable" person would want to know is not always an easy task. Furthermore, it is difficult to apply in practice because the professional would have to project a reasonable client would need to know. Diener and Crandall (1978) have suggested that in research, a pilot study could be run that asks participants to comment on the adequacy of the information provided in the consent.

Beauchamp and Childress (2001) argued that what they call the subjective standard of consent is the most ethically justifiable one because the "specific informational needs of the individual person" (p. 149) are taken into consideration. In other words, what is disclosed depends on the needs of the particular person. This standard may be the preferable moral one because it alone acknowledges the individuals' particular informational needs. Wise (2007) suggests that mental health professionals should ask themselves what they would want to know if either they or a loved one were contemplating the proposed treatment (and we would add research or other psychological intervention). This would allow them to more meaningfully take the perspective of a client, research participant or other consumer. Although this approach alone is insufficient because people often do not know what information would be relevant and mental health professionals could not possibly do an exhaustive background check to determine what information would be relevant. It's probably for these reasons that the reasonable person standard has gained acceptance in over half of the legal jurisdictions in the United States (Beauchamp & Childress, 2001). On the other hand, as Wise suggests it does suggest the importance of taking extra time with clients or others who are acutely distressed or whose cultural background might make it difficult for them to question a professional.

In thinking about what information to disclose, it is important to remember that more information does not necessarily lead to more adequate understanding. In fact, studies of the relationship between length of consent forms and comprehension of critical information found that consumers remembered less after reading longer consent forms (Epstein & Lasagna, 1969; Mann, 1994). Additionally, after signing consent forms some research participants believed that they lost the right to sue the researcher, even for negligence (Mann, 1994). It is for reasons like these, as well as the difficulty with deciding what and how much needs to be disclosed, that some

(Handelsman & Galvin, 1988; Mann, 1994) have recommended moving to a question and answer format for consent.

In particular, Handelsman and Galvin (1988) suggested that therapy patients should be provided with a series of questions such as "How does your therapy work?" "What are the possible risks (divorce, feeling worse, etc.) involved?" "How are appointments scheduled?" and "Under what conditions are you allowed to tell others about the things we discuss?" More recently Pomerantz and Handelsman (2004) updated questions from Handelsman and Galvin's original form because of developments in the field of psychotherapy in the last 15 years. Now included are questions on insurance and managed care as well as opportunities to talk about alternative forms of treatment like evidence-based and manualized therapy. Patients could then decide what information they wanted from their potential therapists. Handelsman and Galvin (1988) argued that such a format preserves patients' rights to refuse some information because they would not have to ask the question if they were not interested. It also fosters communication between the therapist and the client, which allows the therapist to be sensitive to a particular client's need for information. Such a format might help fulfill the psychologist's responsibility to promote informed decision making and would exemplify informed consent as a process rather than an event. Further, conversations based on these questions could facilitate open and honest discussions about important issues in psychotherapy and improve the therapeutic alliance. Both Handelsman and Galvin (1988) and Pomerantz and Handelsman (2004) point out that the discussions based on these questions are not meant to replace written informed consent but rather to complement it. In addition, in research federal regulations mandate that certain information be disclosed to participants, so omitting information would not be an option (U.S. Department of Health and Human Services [HHS], 1991–1994). This is also true of the Health Insurance Portability and Accountability Act (HIPAA, 1996) which, as already noted, protects an individual's physical and mental health data.

Understanding

Although disclosure is necessary, understanding is equally essential for valid consent. In fact, Beauchamp and Childress (2001) referred to it as the second informational element of consent. If consumers do not understand what is disclosed to them, the consent process is a sham. It is for this reason that overly legalistic consent forms, which are too technical for the consumer to comprehend, undermine the spirit of consent.

Research on cognitive processes suggests that the way that information is disclosed may influence understanding. For example, Tversky and Kahneman (1981, 1984) found that choice is influenced by whether information regarding risk is presented as providing an opportunity or a loss for a person. Similarly, work on formal operational thinking may be important in evaluating a person's ability to understand the information disclosed because it affects an individual's ability to consider abstract consequences, to think ahead, and to process hypothetical possibilities and impossibilities (King, 1986; Neimark, 1982).

There are other, more general concerns that influence understanding of consent. Pope and Vasquez (2007) noted that illiteracy is a serious problem in the United States. Many consumers or research participants may be unable to read, unable to read in English, or able to read at only a minimal level. In addition, researchers have consistently documented that written consent forms in medicine (Grunder, 1980), research (National Commission for the Protection of Human Subjects of Biomedical and Behavioral Research [National Commission], 1978b), and therapy (Handelsman, Kemper, Kesson-Craig, McLain, & Johnsrud, 1986; Handelsman et al., 1995) are written substantially beyond the reading ability of most of the public. For example, Handelsman et al. (1986) found that when he tested the consent forms of psychologists in private practice, the readability was in the difficult range and equivalent to an academically oriented magazine.

Hochhauser (1999) points out that virtually all researchers have concluded that consent forms are too complicated if the readability is above an eighth-grade level. After summarizing the data, Hochhauser points out that although on the average Americans have 12.5 years of education, they probably read three or four grades below that. Since most consent forms are written at the college reading level they may be five or six grades higher than the reading level of the average client. In addition, some clients and research participants may be more at a risk for reading problems than others. For example, one study of drug users found client reading level between the sixth and eighth grade (Johnson, Fisher, & Davis, 1996) and in a study of active or passive consent from children's parents, Dent, Galaif, and Sussman (1993) found the passive consent group contained a greater percentage of African-Americans, Hispanics and other ethnicities and had parents who were less educated. It is probably the case that less education equates with a lower reading level. If this is true than consent form readability for ethnic minorities with less education may be a critical factor in their ability to understand what they are consenting to.

Hochhauser points out that although there has been a great deal of research on the readability of consent forms, less is known about the consent process itself. He points to a study by Titus and Keane (1996) who found that about one-third of the researchers in their study had no indication about how to talk to research participants about the consent process. Unlike the open-ended questions recommended by Handelsman and Galvin (1988) and Pomerantz and Handelsman (2004), the researchers used close-ended questions like "Do you understand that?" Since many people may be embarrassed to admit that they do not understand the consent form, close-ended questions do not help the process and in fact, in therapy may hinder developing the therapeutic alliance.

When psychologists serve consumers who are nonnative English speakers and those with minimal reading skills, the readability of consent forms is a critical issue. The 2005 ACA Ethics Code required providing an interpreter if the person was a nonnative speaker and did not comprehend consent in English. Conceiving of consent as a process in which consumers are engaged in a dialogue may be the best way of improving understanding and in fact, the 2005 ACA Ethics Code also required that informed consent therapy involve an ongoing process. Although this may be more practical in therapy or supervision than in research, researchers still have an ethical responsibility to write consent forms in a language that participants can understand. Communication with those whose reading level is limited may be supplemented by a variety of nonwritten material like videotapes and computer-based multimedia programs (Hochhauser, 1999).

Understanding is also an issue with clients who, because of their current mental status, have comprehension difficulties. This is particularly true when consent is legally mandated. Despite this, Pope and Vasquez (2007) concluded that the mental health professional is the one who is responsible for ensuring that the client actually understands the information. Again, engaging clients in a dialogue regarding their rights and responsibilities and following up with readable material that they can refer to at a later date may help understanding. Understanding consent as a process also allows psychologists to engage consumers in discussions and decisions regarding treatment at points when their mental processes are less clouded.

Voluntariness

According to *Webster's Ninth New Collegiate Dictionary* (1988), an act is voluntary if it proceeds from the person's will or own choice, is unconstrained by interference, and/or involves the power of free choice. All of these definitions are central to the voluntariness of consent. In essence, consent is not voluntary if it is coerced or results from others' manipulations rather than from a person's autonomous choice.

Coercion uses the threat of harm to control or influence participation and to displace a person's self-directedness (Beauchamp & Childress, 2001). Cases of coercion that involve the threat of physical harm seldom arise in psychology or counseling, although reports have been made of researchers using grades to coerce students to participate in research projects.

Voluntariness can also be limited by manipulation, an example of what legally could be considered undue influence. Manipulation means to control another by artful, unfair or insidious means, particularly to one's own advantage (*Webster's Ninth New Collegiate Dictionary,* 1988). Manipulation may involve swaying people to do what you want them to do by presenting information in unfair ways. Sometimes it involves deliberately deceiving people about the nature of the situation or it may involve misleading exaggerations about aspects of the situation, or the alternatives involved. It may also involve providing such high incentives for participation in research that people who have limited resources feel like that they have no option except to participate, a topic that is discussed later in this chapter.

The following case, adapted from *Ethical Principles in the Conduct of Research with Human Participants* (APA, 1973, p. 67), illustrates both coercion and manipulation.

Case 9-5

A researcher studying pain used an apparatus that included numerous screws that could be tightened to press against the participant's head. According to the published report, some students agreed to participate because they thought it was a requirement for a course in which they were enrolled. They thought that if they refused it would affect their medical school grades and alienate the researcher who also taught the class. The participants were told to endure the pain inflicted by the head apparatus as long as possible. After one of the participants reported that he could no longer endure the pain, the experimenter mentioned that others had braved it much longer and, in other ways, threatened the participant's self-image and masculinity, thus inducing him to continue to wear the head gear for a longer time period.

In this case, students were coerced by the threat of a lower grade in a highly competitive medical school environment. Clearly, the threat was effective in inducing participation, but there is little doubt that by using it the researcher violated the students' autonomy. Furthermore, at least one participant was also manipulated to continue in the study long after he believed it was in his best interest to stop. By exaggerating others' ability to tolerate pain, the researcher also violated the principle of nonmaleficence.

Although explicit manipulation in therapy may occur less often, it is not unheard of. Take, for example, Case 9-6.

Case 9-6

Mr and Mrs Mean's son, Mark aged 3 years, was diagnosed with severe autism. Consequently, they placed him an inpatient facility for treatment. Mark's symptoms included head banging and other self-injurious behavior. Although several treatments were tried after admission, none were successful. After about 6 months, Dr. Smith, the chief psychologist, approached the parents. She informed them that all of the conventional treatments had failed but that the staff would like to try an experimental, electroshock therapy. She indicated that they would have to sign a special form giving them consent to use the treatment. She indicated this was the only alternative that had any possibility of helping Mark. In addition, she told them that if they did not give permission, they would have to move Mark out of the facility because he was becoming too difficult to control. Mr and Mrs Mean felt confused and concerned about the use of a painful treatment with their child who was still a toddler. They also felt on the spot because the only alternative treatment facility was over 100 miles away. Reluctantly, they signed the agreement. On returning home, however, they called Dr. Samuels, the psychologist who initially diagnosed Mark. He indicated that although he had not seen Mark's treatment history, there were several new treatments that had been successful with children like Mark. He also recommended another hospital where these treatments were being used. On the basis of this information, the Means decided to move Mark to the new facility, even though it was further from their home.

Because the transfer was going to take several days to arrange, the Means called Dr. Smith and told her to stop using the shock treatment. Dr. Smith indicated that because they had already signed a consent form, the facility would continue to use the treatment on him unless the Mean family wanted to remove him from the facility the next day. After making arrangements for Mark to move, the Means consulted a lawyer and filed an ethics complaint with the state psychological association.

Obviously, the Means were both coerced and manipulated. By framing information about the shock therapy in a positive manner and by withholding information about possible alternatives, Dr. Smith manipulated the Means for her own advantage, namely, to test an experimental treatment. Furthermore, she coerced the Means by threatening to have Mark removed from the facility if they did not agree. Thus, the consent that the parents gave under these conditions was not ethically valid and could probably be legally challenged.

Voluntariness can also be limited by internal constraints (Appelbaum et al., 1987). Individuals may feel intimidated by the power and prestige that are associated with being a professional or with the title, "Doctor." For example, the Means may have been initially intimidated by Dr. Smith's title and position as the "chief psychologist." Faced with a similar situation, a person with a poor self-concept or who has a problem with authority figures may lack the emotional strength to act autonomously. Again, understanding consent as a process rather than as an event may help build self-esteem as people are invited into the decision-making process and their views are respected.

Authorization or Consent

The last element in the process is the actual consent that authorizes treatment or participation in research. Authorization may be either verbal or written. In research, funding agencies and IRBs may require written consent forms and both the 2002 APA and 2005 ACA ethics codes required some kind of documentation of consent. If an individual is not competent to give full consent, they should be asked for their assent. (See section on consent with adolescents and children.) Although there is some appeal to using consent forms that clients can sign, Appelbaum et al. (1987) claimed that there is no legal requirement that written consent forms be used in practice settings. In fact, "a number of courts have specifically stated that they are not necessary, and a number of opinions in informed consent have largely discounted their value" (Appelbaum et al., 1987, p. 180). This is particularly true if the information contained in them is overly complex or obscure or if the consumer was manipulated into signing them. Thus, written consent forms can lull professionals into a false sense of security in the belief that a signed form constitutes consent (Appelbaum et al., 1987).

Consent in Therapy and Psychological Testing

Even if consent is conceptualized as a process, when clients begin therapy or enter into psychological testing, the psychologist must confront the questions of what initial information to provide and how to provide it. It is easy to err on either side of the problem: telling clients too little or overwhelming them with so much information that they do not absorb it. Haas (1991) provided examples of each extreme. At one extreme, he pointed to a

> very experienced psychotherapist in a small town [who] is telephoned by a prospective client. The caller asks, "What do you typically do with people who have my kind of problem?" The therapist replies, "Come in to see me and I'll show you." The caller responds, "But I want to know what you do before I come in." The therapist responds, "If you want to know what I have to offer you'll have to try it out." (Haas, 1991, p. 176)

At the other extreme, Haas (1991) pointed to a graduate student therapist who works in a training clinic and is telephoned by a prospective client.

> The client asks, "What do you typically do with people who have my kind of problem?" The therapist responds, "Well, these problems are not very fixed, as I am still a student in training and I'm learning quite a lot about what to do with clients. But I expect that I will begin with some attentive listening to your problem and show an interest in helping you identify alternatives. Then, I will probably consult with my supervisor (who listens to tape recordings of all of my sessions), and my supervisor will advise me how to proceed. Then, I will try out some suggestions on you and perhaps some interpretations suggesting ways in which your problems may be symbolizing deeper conflicts. Finally, I will attempt to see if these procedures lead you to some new understanding of your situation. If you seem puzzled by my interpretations, I will try to determine whether your confusion is a result of my approach or your defensiveness. I will also discuss your case thoroughly with my supervisor, who is a more experienced therapist than I am. I should inform you that I am in my second year of training; if you would prefer a more experienced therapist, I will try to find one of the more senior graduate students in the clinic." (p. 177)

As Haas (1991) observed, it is not likely that the prospective client would enter therapy with either therapist. In the first example, the caller is left with no more information regarding entering therapy than when he or she picked up the phone. In the second example, the neophyte therapist may have responded to his or her own needs and insecurities more than to the needs of the prospective client. If hope and faith (Frank, 1982) are critical aspects of the therapeutic process, the trainee may have undermined the potential effectiveness of any therapeutic relationship with the prospective client.

Although the graduate student therapist provided the prospective client with detailed information about the therapy process, too much information can be overwhelming, leaving the recipient less enlightened than he or she would have been with less information. As already noted, more information does not necessarily mean better understanding (Epstein & Lasagna, 1969; Mann, 1994).

Several authors (Bennett et al., 1990; Haas, 1991; Hare-Mustin et al., 1979) have provided lists of the information that should be disclosed to clients. These include:

a. The kind of treatment or testing provided and the risks and benefits of the treatment or testing.
b. The logistics.
c. Information on the therapist's credentials and qualifications.
d. Risks and benefits of alternative kinds of treatment approaches or of foregoing testing.
e. The meaning of confidentiality and its limits.
f. Emergency procedures.

However, individuals should consult the code of ethics for their profession because they often provide clear criteria for what is expected of consent for therapy. This was true, for example, of both the 2002 APA Code of Ethics and the 2005 ACA Code of Ethics. Despite the attention that informed consent received in the codes of ethics and its underlying importance in many ethics cases as Johnson-Green (2007) points out "there is an appalling lack of empirical investigations of informed consent for clinical services. Thus, recommendations about informed consent are a matter of ethical statements made by professional guilds or based on legal advice, personal beliefs and morals, clinical lore and educated guesses" (p. 183–184). In other words, what clients need to know or want to know is basically unknown.

Clients are generally naive about the differences in therapeutic approaches as well as about psychological tests. Although some of the subtle differences between therapies may not be necessary to disclose to clients, typical practices, such as involving family members or using homework assignments, and unusual practices, that have little or no scientific evidence to support their efficacy, such as "therapeutic canoe trips," should be disclosed. When there is an empirically based treatment available for the particular problem the client is presenting, it should be mentioned and the reasons for or against using it discussed. Similarly, the potential risks and benefits of treatment should be discussed. For example, often couples enter marital therapy with the assumption that the therapist will save their marriage. Although this may be a goal in some cases, no therapist can guarantee that outcome will be achieved.

In terms of psychological testing, the purposes of the tests should be disclosed, as well as any risks associated with taking them. Take Case 9-7 as an example.

Case 9-7

A psychologist was asked to conduct a presentencing psychological evaluation of a man who had been convicted of murdering two children. The evaluation would be used to aid the court in deciding whether or not to sentence him to death. The psychologist met with the convicted killer and told him the purpose of the evaluation: to gather information that would be used to decide whether he would get the death penalty. She went on to explain that "the courts could consider certain psychological problems or histories as mitigating factors, lessening the likelihood of the death penalty, whereas other problems or histories could be considered aggravating factors, and so increase the likelihood of the death penalty." She also indicated that she would not use projective tests because clients are not always aware of what they are revealing when they respond to such tests (APA, 1987a, p. 77).

As it turned out, the district attorney who referred the case to the psychologist complained to the APA Ethics Committee that the psychologist had provided the client with too much information. The committee, however, did not find the psychologist guilty of breaking the code. Rather, the committee cited the psychologist as exemplary in protecting the welfare of the client, noting that in court-ordered evaluations, psychologists bear a heavy social responsibility and have special obligations to inform clients about their role and the evaluation process.

In terms of the logistics of treatment and testing, clients may be unclear about how often they will be expected to meet with the psychologist or about the length of sessions. Some clients are so naive about therapy, they might not even know that it involves multiple sessions. Many psychologists who do not inform clients about the length of therapy fail to do so because length of therapy cannot be easily predicted (Somberg, Stone, & Claiborn, 1993). Nevertheless, most therapists can tell clients about the typical length of therapy for people with similar problems and whether they use a brief therapy model or a long-term one. Furthermore, clients' resources are often limited either by third-party payers or their own finances, so knowing the kind of financial commitment they are making may be important in their decision to enter therapy. Policies regarding fees, cancellations, and any limits therapists place on their practice also need to be clarified.

The client should also have access to information on the therapist's credentials and qualifications. This includes the psychologist's training and experience regarding the problem for which the client is requesting treatment or testing or with particular groups, such as ethnic minorities or gay men or lesbians.

The risks and benefits of alternative kinds of treatment approaches, such as self-help groups, should be identified. Ideally, the potential consequences of not seeking treatment should be discussed. With many studies supporting the effectiveness and the efficacy of psychotherapy, therapists should not shy away from these questions (Hollon, 1996; Lambert & Ogles, 2004; Seligman, 1995). In terms of psychological testing, information about alternative kinds of assessments should be disclosed as well as the risks of foregoing evaluation (see Case 5-7).

Discussing the meaning of confidentiality and its limits may be one of the most important aspects of consent. This is particularly true because the majority of clients believe that everything in a therapy relationship is confidential (Miller & Thelen, 1986). But although some psychologists continue to believe that confidentiality should be absolute, in reality there are a variety of conditions in which it may be violated. Fisher (2008) argues that what mental-health professionals can really offer their clients is what she calls "conditional confidentiality" (p. 3). As she points out the initial informed consent interview is the first opportunity and sometimes the only one available to protect the confidentiality rights of clients especially because some confidences may later be unprotectable due to legal requirements. For example, laws often require breaching confidentiality when there is potential harm to self or others (including cases of child abuse). (See Chapter 10 for a further discussion.) Honest conversations about the limits to confidentiality protects clients' autonomy by allowing them to decide whether to consent and confide or to exercise their right to "informed refusal" of services, thus, it is particularly important that mental health professionals not make or imply confidentiality promises that will not and cannot be kept. Failing to do so according to Fisher (2008) deprives the client to the right to be informed about the risk that confidential information might be disclosed as well as the right to give or refuse consent to accept the risk.

Some therapists believe that disclosing the limits of confidentiality makes establishing a therapeutic relationship more difficult (Somberg et al., 1993). However, as Haas (1991) noted, "including this information reduces the chance that the client will accuse the therapist of entrapment after the client has revealed information that signals dangerousness" (p. 184) and they have been promised confidentiality. Further, evidence exists that informed consent when it is done well can actually enhance client perceptions of therapist trustworthiness and expertise (Sullivan et al., 1993).

Clients should also be informed about other limits of confidentiality including the use of insurance or HMOs and collection agencies. Clients give up some privacy rights when they use their insurance benefits because often insurance companies and HMOs do not observe the same level of confidentiality as do mental health professionals (Bennett et al., 1990; Haas, 1991). Although we agree with Haas and Malouf (1989) that collection agencies should be avoided, if they are used, clients should be informed of that fact early in treatment. At minimum, clients must be informed if the mental health professional decides to use them and clients must be given the opportunity to pay before the agency is contacted.

In testing situations, other confidentiality concerns are important to clarify, such as who will have access to the data. This is particularly important when the evaluation is a part of a forensic procedure or when it occurs in an employment setting. Although addressed by both the APA and ACA Codes of Ethics, according to Bucky (2007) informed consent as it relates to assessment seems to be less clear and more variable. As he points out the lack of clear informed consent, particularly in custody evaluations, is too common (e.g., they are the most common source of complaints against psychologists in the state of California) and according to Gold (2007) often leads to disciplinary action and serious degrees of stress for the professional that often lasts for years. He emphasizes the importance of sensitivity to language and culture and the importance of being cautious about using the most recently published tests with well-established reliability and validity for the group that is being tested.

Finally, emergency procedures should be described. The client needs to know how the psychologist handles after-hour calls. For example, is there someone else who takes calls on a periodic basis? Does the psychologist have admitting privileges at a hospital?

Anyone looking at this list may feel overwhelmed by the difficulty in providing clients with adequate information and understanding without it getting in the way of the therapeutic or evaluation process. Others have struggled with this issue and have developed some interesting and unique ways to deal with it. For example, some psychologists have developed a consumer information pamphlet for their own practice that they either send to clients prior to the first session or provide to clients during the first session. The pamphlet gives clients information about training, experience and credentials, professional practice policies, such as the services offered, length of treatment, information on appointments, fees and cancellations, and the nature of confidentiality and its limits, and so on (Nagy, 1987). Including in such a pamphlet a list of questions that clients may wish to ask their therapists may help engage clients in an ongoing consent process. Questions might include "What kind of therapy do you do and how does it work?" "How long does therapy for my problem typically take?" and "Are there any risks associated with this kind of therapy?" (For a list of possible questions that clients may want to ask their therapists, see Handelsman & Galvin, 1988 and Pomerantz & Handelsman, 2004.) In this age of technology, therapists might also want to explore the idea of using a video or an interactive computer program to involve clients in the consent process. A computer could also be used to check on comprehension of the information provided.

Even with these kind of educational efforts, a prudent professional is may still want clients to sign a written form that indicates they have read the material and/or have been given an opportunity to ask questions regarding therapy or evaluation. A signed consent form can be a support for a verbal discussion in which the important information about treatment and its limits is documented. If such a consent form is not used, at minimum practitioners should carefully document in the client's file what has been disclosed to the client and how it was done. Even if a signed consent form is used, subsequent discussions with the client about treatment and its limits can be described in case notes to verify the ongoing validity of the consent process. Bennett et al. (1990) also recommended describing the level of the client's emotional turmoil or other aspects of relationship that may affect the client's comprehension of the information provided and giving the client a signed copy of the consent document as a way to reduce liability risks. Although it may or may not reduce liability, it can serve as an educational tool because clients would have a variety of information regarding services at their fingertips; thus, it may enhance the ethicality of the consent process.

The Use of Deception in Therapy

The use of informed consent has conflicted with therapeutic interventions, such as paradoxical ones, because they sometimes mislead clients regarding the nature and purpose of the treatment involved. The use of paradox refers to a wide variety of interventions that have one thing in common: "They are designed to eliminate the client's symptoms by encouraging it, either directly or indirectly" (Betts & Remer, 1993, p. 164). For example, a psychologist might tell an argumentative family that arguing is a way for them to express caring and that they should do it every day, thereby "tricking" them into arguing less. Although more typical of the family systems approaches, these methods have also been advocated by Gestalt therapists, Adlerians, existentialists, and others (Seltzer, 1986).

Because therapists who use these techniques appear to endorse the symptomatic behavior that they are trying to change, they deceive clients about the nature of the change process. The question thus arises as to whether informed consent is possible. Basically, the ethical issue comes down to whether the end justifies the means (Brown & Slee, 1986; Johnson, 1986; Schmidt, 1986). Those who argue for paradoxical interventions suggest the beneficent outcome justifies the sacrifice of autonomy, fidelity, and honesty.

The issue is not whether paradoxical interventions work because several reviews and meta-analyses suggest that they are effective for both individuals and families (DeBord, 1989; Dowd & Milne, 1986; Hill, 1987). The issue is whether interventions based on deception should be used. This question is particularly important because some data (Ascher & Turner, 1980) substantiate the view that paradoxical interventions work even when clients are informed about their nature. On the basis of findings like these, there appears to be little ethical justification for not informing the client that certain procedures may be used that appear counterintuitive and even contrary to the client's well-being but that they are used with the intention of helping the client (Haas, 1991).

Consent for Research Participation

In terms of therapy, Barnett (2007a) asked whether there was too much informed consent or not enough. At this point in time, this same question seems particularly critical in terms of informed consent for research. Unlike therapy, because of the public funding provided for research, the federal government has taken a strong interest in identifying the components necessary for consent. For example, *The Belmont Report* (National Commission, for the Projection of Human Subjects of Biomedical and Behavioral Research, 1978a) strongly advocated the importance of informed consent based on the principle of respect for persons, beneficence (which included both maximizing benefits while minimizing risk, harm or wrong), and justice. Ostensibly based on these principles, the DHHS (1991/1994) provided guidelines for adequate consent in federally funded research and set up Institutional Review Boards (IRBs) to ensure that they were carried out. Sieber (2004b) argues that as IRB's began to take hold informed consent was taken to mean a signature on the consent form rather than a process that involves communication between the researcher and the participant. Often behavioral scientists find the forms to be "inappropriate, incomprehensible, coercive, or insulting to otherwise willing research participants" (p. 298). In addition, if the research had to do with healthcare (including mental health care), the federal Health Insurance Portability and Accountability Act (HIPAA, 1996) required another form that was often presented as a dogmatic "rite."

Certainly, basic ethical issues regarding competence, disclosure, understanding, voluntariness, and authorization remain central for consent in research and follow from the principles articulated in the Belmont Report and those discussed earlier in this book. The principles of beneficence and nonmaleficence because there is reason to believe that in some cases participants need protection. Unlike therapists behavioral scientists do not engaged in research for the benefit of consumers, and in "pure" research there is no assumption that participants will benefit directly from taking part. Optimistically, in pure research, participants are there to generate new knowledge or for other altruistic reasons. From a more cynical perspective, participants are there to benefit investigators' careers because tenure or career advancement may depend on the ability to induce people to participate. In the case of therapy, risks or deceptions, should they occur, are intended to benefit the consumer. Such is not the case in research.

Even when studies involve evaluation of therapeutic procedures, the potential for conflicts of interest remain high. The primary goal of science is to produce generalizable knowledge rather than to benefit individual participants. Consequently, although investigators might believe that one treatment is better for a particular individual than another, randomization may demand a different treatment; thus, some participants may lose the benefit of therapists' "informed speculation" (Appelbaum et al., 1987, p. 239). Further, when a researcher's career is being built on the outcome of the investigation, a participant's well-being may be intentionally ignored or inadvertently slighted. Under these conditions, the role of consent is critical. This is particularly true of therapeutic research, given that some evidence suggests that participants may ignore cautions stated in consent forms because they believe that the "principle of personal care" will take precedence. That is, they believe that their well-being will take priority over the study's design and methodology. Some have argued that investigators need to dispel the misconception that therapeutic benefits will be more important than the research design through discussions of the difference between therapy and research and how the procedure might differ from the ordinary care a patient would receive (Appelbaum et al., 1987).

On the other hand, much behavioral research does not involve therapeutic procedures or pose a threat to the participant and in fact Federal Policy for the Protection of Human Subjects (2001) allows exemptions from the use of consent forms relying on the good ethical judgment of the researcher and the IRB to decide when it should be waived. For example it permits waiver or alteration of informed consent requirements particularly in cases where the risk is relative to the risks and activities of everyday life and it allows waiver of parental permission for minors' participation in research in some cases (Sieber, 2004b).

As already noted, one aspect of consent involves promising confidentiality to respect the privacy of the persons involved. However, the issue of privacy is particularly problematic in transcultural research. Monshi and Zieglmayer (2004) found this when trying to apply Western codes of ethics in Sri Lanka where participants were very uncomfortable when researchers tried to impose the idea that health information needed to be kept confidential. In Sri Lanka therapeutic interventions take place as public acts and whole families participate. Therefore, people who had been eager to participate in the research were visibly uncomfortable when the researcher led them into a private room by themselves to inquire about health issues; a typical requirement of IRB's to maintain confidentiality. They end by asking how can strict compliance with research regulations be ethically justifiable when following them is contrary to cultural values and causes unease for participants?

Similarly, research regulations can seriously impede research with adolescents when they are engaging in activities, like smoking, drug abuse or sexual activity, unknown to their parents (Diviak, Curry, Emery, & Mermelstein, 2004). Many of these activities are important to study, yet, if participants had to get parental consent they would refuse to participate. As already noted Federal Policy (2001) allows IRBs to waive this requirement if the research involves no more than minimal risk, the waiver would not adversely affect the welfare of the adolescent, and the research could not be carried out without the waiver. Diviak et al. (2004) studied 13 researchers relationship with their IRBs who requested a waiver of consent. Of those, only four were given permission to get adolescent assent only. Whether this conservative reaction was ethically justifiable out of a concern to protect and respect participants or whether it was a consequence of just focusing on documenting consent to avoid possible legal hassles is not clear. It appears that some IRB's may be requiring a more strict interpretation of federal guidelines than the Federal Policy for the Protection of Human Subjects (2001) would require. Further, it does not seem that it is being done for the correct reasons, to protect research participants from harm or injustice.

De Vries, DeBruin, and Goodgame (2004) point out that ethics' committees face it exceedingly difficult tasks when faced with social science research. They point out that behavioral health problems including mental illness, alcohol, and drug abuse are the leading causes of disability in Western industrialized societies. If Alzheimer's and dementia are also included, then the numbers are even more striking. Consequently, the need for research to alleviate these harms is enormous. They go on to say, "at the same time we must not allow this research to proceed without the proper safeguards for vulnerable participants. We must, as a society, strike a balance between promoting valuable research and protecting research participants" (p. 365). IRBs play an important role in maintaining this balance but they need social scientists represented in the membership of the committees in order to understand real risks and benefits of social science research. Since many guidelines were written for medical and biological research, they may need to be rewritten for social science research so that they are clear and appropriate for the studies to be considered. Unfortunately, this is not always the case and IRB's have come under criticism from social scientists for at least 40 years for their failure to be applicable to social science research (De Vries et al., 2004). Issues that are of particular concern in social science research are definitions of risks and benefits, the lack of fit between regulations and some social science methods, and definitions of research with human participants. Somewhere in the process the ethics of informed consent and its basic purpose which is to appropriately protect individuals' privacy and ensure a just process gets lost.

Despite the problems, the DHHS (1991/1994) have provided the following guidelines for adequate consent in federally funded research. It is the role of the IRB's to interpret and apply them to ensure they are carried out.

1. Consent is only initiated in situations where the investigator attempts to minimize undue influence or coercion and after the participant is given the opportunity to consider whether or not to participate.
2. Consent must use language that is reasonably understandable to the person giving consent.
3. No person can be asked to waive any of his or her legal rights or release the investigator or the sponsoring institution or agency from liability negligence.
4. Participants must be provided with:
   a. A statement that the study involves research and its purposes, duration, and the procedures involved.
   b. A description of reasonably foreseeable risks of participation.
   c. A description of any benefits of the research.
   d. A disclosure of alternative treatments that might be of benefit to the participant if treatment is involved.
   e. A statement describing the way confidentiality will be maintained, along with a disclosure of the limits of confidentiality.
   f. A disclosure about potential compensation or treatment and whom to contact should something go awry.
   g. The name, address, and phone number of whom to contact for questions or concerns.
   h. A statement that participation is voluntary and that the participant has a right to withdraw at any time.

These guidelines were consistent with the requirements in the 2002 APA and 2005 ACA ethics codes. The codes added that participants should be informed of the consequences of withdrawing or not participating and emphasized that participants would not be penalized for declining participation. Further, when children or others who cannot give legal consent are included in research, they should be provided with an explanation of the research in a vocabulary that they can understand and they should be given the opportunity to assent or dissent to participation. In addition, when research is done with students as part of a course requirement or for extra credit equitable alternatives to research participation should be offered. Unfortunately, all too often students feel coerced into participation as Case 9-8 illustrates.

Case 9-8

A psychology department instituted a 2-hour research participation requirement for all students enrolled in introductory psychology classes. Students who did not wish to participate in the research had set up a meeting to explain their objections to the instructor and to write a 15-page paper on a research topic approved by the professor. In anonymous course evaluations, many students said they participated in the required research because they were afraid they would get a bad grade in the course if the professor knew they did not want to participate in the subject pool or they believed it would take more than 2 h to complete a 15-page paper (Fisher, 2003a, p. 156).

Under the circumstances, the students' concerns were probably quite justifiable.

Interestingly, the 2002 APA ethics code added a new standard that tried to address the "therapeutic misconception" in intervention research that the experimental treatment must be the better treatment and that the person conducting the intervention would have the best interests of the participant in mind. Consequently, it required that the researcher explain the experimental nature of the treatment, the way that assignment to control and treatment groups would be made, what services would be available if the person did not want to participate in the research or wanted to withdraw once the study began. It also addressed compensation and whether or not services would be available to the control group or groups. A summary of a positive example of researchers fulfilling these responsibilities was offered by Fisher (2003a, p. 152) in the following case.

Case 9-9

A team including psychologists received IRB approval to assess side effects of medication recently approved by the Food and Drug Administration (FDA) as an alternative to Ritalin for the treatment of hyperactive children. Using a Latin square design each child would be given two weeks of five experimental conditions (placebo, three different dose levels of the new medication and one dose of Ritalin). Although there had been no long-lasting negative side effects observed in adults, there was some controversy in the literature about whether animal studies demonstrating some negative side effects of the new drug were applicable to humans. The researchers include a paragraph in a parental permission forms describing the animal results in stating there was some unknown risk that the drug could cause permanent neurological damage to children. Many of the parents had children who had not been helped by Ritalin. To avoid inadvertently implying that the animal data suggested that the medication was a better drug, the investigators were also careful to clarify in the permission information that the reason the study was being conducted is because as yet there was no empirical evidence indicating the agent would be more effective than Ritalin. On entry to the study, parents were also informed that at the end of the child's participation, investigators would prepare a summary letter for the parent and with signed parental permission the child's primary physician would also receive a letter and any recommendations for treatment than emerge from the study.

Despite the attempts of the federal government to regulate consent and despite the fact that concerns about consent in research dates back at least five decades to the trials of the Nazi physicians at Nuremberg, unlike the researchers in the above case it often happens that researchers approach consent as if it were a nuisance rather than out of respect for their participants.* In fact, in a study of how U.S. psychology departments complied with the APA ethics code that

---

* These remarks are based, to some extent on, the paper, "The Science of Psychology With and Without Virtue," by K. S. Kitchener, presented at a symposium titled *Considering Character: Science, Practice, and Policies* at the University of Notre Dame, December 5, 1996.

existed at the time, Sieber and Saks (1989) found that only 12% of the departments complied fully with the code and about half did not use participant pools ethically. Thus, many of the psychology departments failed to provide participants with equitable alternatives to participation, used undue influence to coerce participation, and so on.

As Appelbaum et al. (1987) noted after reviewing the legal and ethical history of consent,

> although some changes have occurred ..., we believe in the long run attempts to force people to respect others are doomed to failure. One can create a framework in which respect can develop. One can even compel behavior similar to what would occur were respect to exist. But respect is so personal a characteristic that it either flows from a genuine source, or not at all. In essence, this is the paradox in which the law of informed consent has been caught. The legal requirements have gone as far as they can. The framework for respect has been created and codes of behavior have been prescribed. And that is not enough (p. 264).

In addition to the problems with IRB's, the failure to successfully legislate the morality of consent may reflect an inadequate attention in social science training programs and in science in general, to questions of character. As Appelbaum et al. (1987) observed, we cannot make scientists respect and care for their research participants by creating more rules. We need to attend more explicitly to issues of character, as was suggested in Chapter 5.

DuBois (2004) points to the virtues identified by the National Academy of Science (1995) that identified honesty, skepticism, openness, fairness, and collegiality as foundational virtues for the character of researchers. DuBois asks whether compliance with federal regulations regarding consent should be added to the list. Currently, despite the problems, most who have served on IRB's would be hard-pressed to deny that they offer some protection for participants by identifying key components missing from consent forms, inadequate protection of confidentiality or worse (Getz, 2002). On the other hand, over half the researchers studied by De Vries, DeBruin, and Goodgame (2004) believed IRB demands discouraged good research and were unjust. To the extent that that is the case they may ignore the demands and find ways of bypassing them despite potential financial and regulatory sanctions. Should they comply with rules they believe are unjust? Du Bois basically answers "yes." He points out that the interests of researchers to a great extent are not those of participants and since there is a history of human participant abuses society needs to provide oversight of the research enterprise (Getz, 2002).

He suggests a sensible answer requires balance. He points out that there may be times when a researcher should not comply if, for example, compliance might hurt a participant or violate professional covenants. On the other hand, he suggests it is imprudent to encourage researchers to deliberately consider in every case whether they should comply with the regulation. He also points out, however, that some change needs to come from regulators. The National Science Foundation has developed guidelines that show how behavioral and social science researchers can conduct ethical and scientifically sound research within the confines of our current system of regulations (National Science Foundation, 2002). IRB's have considerable leeway to exempt studies, to waive informed consent to allow adolescent percent in lieu of parental permission and so on, but they must be willing to take the risk to use the discretion that they are allowed and they must do so in a way that respects the foundational principles of respect for persons, beneficence, and justice.

Deception in Research

Probably no area of social science research has caused so much ethical debate or has been so consistently vilified than has the use of deceptive research practices (Baumrind, 1985, 1990; Diener & Crandall, 1978; Fisher & Fryberg, 1994; Hertwig & Ortman, 2008; Kelman, 1972;

Koocher & Keith-Spiegel, 1998; Sieber, Lannuzzo, & Rodriguez, 1995). Although the incidence of its use in social psychology dropped in the mid-1980s, it rose again in the 1990s (Sieber et al., 1995) and has remained stable since then (Hertwig & Ortman, 2008). Adair, Dushenko, and Lindsey (1985) noted that deception was a normative practice in social psychology in the 1980s despite its drop in incidence. Hertwig and Ortman (2008) reviewed the prevalence of the use of deception in major social psychology journals concluding that regardless of the decline between one-third and one-half of all the studies published in the 1990s still employed deception. Kimmel (2001) reported similar findings. In other words it is not unlikely that even today many students who participate in subject pools will experience deception personally. Furthermore, typically ethics codes (ACA, 2005; APA, 1992, 2002) typically forbid deceptive practices unless alternative procedures are not possible and the research is of great importance; however, the high incidence of deceptive practices reported journals hardly suggest that it is a method of last resort (Hertwig & Ortman, 2008). Hertwig and Ortman point out that experimental economic studies that address similar questions, as to those reported in psychology journals, do so without using deception.

Anecdotally, one of the authors was invited to be the outside chairperson of a social psychology dissertation. It involved deception. In the discussion after the student presented an overview of the study, the author ask the student what alternative methods he had considered. The student appeared dumbfounded. His advisor came to his rescue and said "yes" there was an alternative method that could have used. Clearly, the student had not considered it; but, in addition, he was unfamiliar with the ethical standard. There was a clear failure on the part of the advisor teach the student about the rule and help consider alternative methods. Without such leadership, it is no wonder that deception remains a popular methodology.

Deception can be either intentional or unintentional (Baumrind, 1985). Intentional deception has been defined as "withholding information in order to obtain participation that the participant might otherwise decline, using deceptive instructions and confederate manipulations in laboratory research, and employing concealment and staged manipulations in field settings" (Baumrind, 1985, p. 165). In contrast, unintentional deception includes those instances in which there is a discrepancy between full disclosure of all the information regarding a psychological study and the information necessary for a person to make a reasonably informed decision about participating. Generally, the reasonable person standard has not been seen as ethically problematic (Baumrind, 1985; Beauchamp & Childress, 1994; Diener & Crandall, 1978), especially because shorter, less detailed consent forms have led to greater participant comprehension than have longer, more detailed ones (Mann, 1994).

By contrast, with the publication of *Ethical Principles in the Conduct of Research with Human Participants* (APA, 1973), APA has singled out intentionally deceptive research as an ethical problem. In that publication, the recommendation was made to waive informed consent only when the research was of great importance and research participants were allowed to withdraw from the study. These recommendations were echoed in *The Belmont Report* (National Commission for the Protection of Human Subjects of Biomedical and Behavioral Research, 1979a), which acknowledged that sometimes adequately informing participants might decrease the validity of the results. However, it also argued that participants should still be informed that some aspects of the research may not be identified until after the study ended and that participants should never be deceived about the risks, for example, physical pain or severe emotional distress, involved in participation. The later point was included in the 2002 APA ethics code; however, the 2005 ACA ethics code went further and forbid any deceptive research practices which might cause emotional or physical harm despite the respective value of the potential research. Hertwig and Ortman (2008) point out that the discipline of experimental economics has basically prohibited the use of deception in their studies altogether even though they study many of the same things that social psychology does.

The ethical arguments against the use of intentional deceptive methods are quite clear. First, deception interferes with a person's ability to make an autonomous decision because the researcher actively lies to participants or "tricks" them by engaging confederates to convince them that a real-life event is occurring. Consequently, the disclosure component of consent is compromised.

Second, deception involves actively lying to participants, deceiving them, or distorting the truth, thus, it undermines conventional norms about the importance of honesty and can lead to the further erosion of trust in science. Baumrind (1985) argued that if it becomes known that research, participants are often deceived in psychological research then research participants may feel no obligation to be honest in their responses. A great deal of debate has surrounded her claim. Kimmel (1998), based on his review of the literature, concluded that "the effects of suspiciousness on research performance, although somewhat inconsistent, appear to be negligible" (p. 804). There are no major differences between the data of suspicious and naïve participants. However, Hartwig and Ortman (2008) point out that several studies suggest that this may not be so. They analyzed three sets of studies one compared the conformity behavior of participants who were identified posted experimentally as being either suspicious or unsuspicious of deception. The second were studies that intentionally provoked expectation of deception at the outset and then examined behavior as a function of it and the third set included people who had previously been in deception studies. They concluded that in the first group that the behavior of participants who were suspicious and those of naïve participants are different. In the second group if participants were explicitly told they would be deceived or had knowledge before hand of experimental manipulation, suspicion altered their experimental performance. In the third group the results suggested that first-hand experience with deception or manipulation affected the performance of participants. On the other hand, just disclosure of the possibility of deception did not have the same effect. They concluded that if the effects of suspicion are not always strong, they can be substantial.

Referring to personal experience again, when teaching ethics, one of us asks students to reflect on any psychological research in which they participated as undergraduates. At least one or two students would talk with disgust about being a part of a study that involved deception. Often students pointed out that they were skeptical of the honesty of the researcher from the beginning. In his description about being a confederate in deceptive research, Oliansky (1991) revealed that some participants were suspicious from the start, and acknowledged their suspicions at the end of the study, thus undermining the so-called control that the deceptive design was supposed to create. Other participants were successfully deceived. Some took the news that they had been deceived without much apparent discomfort. Others left angry or with negative feelings about the research process. Participants who revealed private information about themselves on the basis of what they had assumed was an environment of mutual trust were particularly upset, even though they were informed ahead of time that the study might involve some deception.

As already noted, Baumrind (1985) and Kelman (1967) predicted that if social scientists continued to use deception, potential participants would become increasingly distrustful and research results would become increasingly biased. Although a great deal of direct empirical evidence on this issue is lacking, Hertwig and Ortman (2004) and Pittenger (2002) claim that these dire threats have not materialized. Hertwig and Ortman (2004) suggest that the use of introductory psychology participant pools may to some extent mitigate the possibility of this happening since they are more likely to be naïve about the possibility of deceptive practices. Pittenger also points out that there is no evidence that former participants have sought sanctions against psychologists who use deception and that several research teams found that perspective participants did not find many commonly used deceptive practices to be objectionable. However, just because these negative consequences have not occurred does not make the procedure any more or less ethically objectionable. In fact, Pittenger points out that studies using deception rarely, if ever report participants reactions to being informed that they were deceived so that if deception were having negative consequences the research community would not have access to that information.

When children are involved, the issue of deliberately lying is particularly ethically troublesome. Take Case 9-10 as an example.

Case 9-10

A counselor wanted to study the effects of peer pressure on children. To study the issue, she identified elementary school samples and asked parents' permission to include their child in a study of peer pressure. The students answered questions about their preferences for several toys and then joined a discussion group. Without telling the participants, she trained a group of confederates to endorse preferences that were different from the ones chosen by the research participants. When participants were asked about their preferences in the group, they were faced with indicating an unpopular choice. In the debriefing, participants were told that the confederates were instructed not to say what they really liked but to choose what the participant did not. Although many students thought the study was fun, a few look perplexed. One asked the researcher why she told the group members to "lie." Several parents objected to the study and argued that it unintentionally endorsed lying, a behavior they tried to discourage in their children.

Although the researcher did not lie to the parents, she did omit a critical piece of information. In fact, the parents' permission to allow their child to participate in the study might have been influenced by the fact that the child was going to be deceived. When the investigator withheld that information, the parents could not consider it.

The third problem with deceptive research is related to the principle of beneficence. The goal of the researcher in Case 9-10 was to "do good" by helping people understand peer pressure. Although a variety of "goods" can arise from psychological research, beneficence implies that research participants should not be harmed. With deception research, the concern is that some participants will actually be harmed, whereas others will be only annoyed or embarrassed when informed about the deception (Baumrind, 1985; Fisher & Fryberg, 1994; Wilson & Donnerstein, 1976). Even if only a few participants are harmed, harming research participants is difficult to justify, especially because the results of most studies are seldom earthshaking. Even one research participant who is extremely upset may be ethically troublesome and could cause the researcher substantial legal and professional problems (Wilson & Donnerstein, 1976).

Sieber et al. (1995) argued that there are some approaches to deception that are more respectful than others. For example, individuals may give consent to participate in one of several conditions without knowing in which one they will actually participate, they may consent to participate in deceptive research if they are debriefed, or they may waive their right to be informed. Sieber et al. (1995) also suggested that there may be some critical topics, such as violent behavior, teen pregnancy, or the spread of HIV, that may not be validly studied without using some form of deception. They argued that on the basis of a cost–benefit ratio, research that compromises full consent on these topics may be justified. However, a strong case would need to be made for the validity of the design, the importance of the topic, and the inability to gather data in any other way.

Participants should always be informed about aspects of the research that might negatively influence their decision to consent. For example, researchers should never trick people into participating in research that involves behaviors they would find unacceptable, such as violating their own moral norms (Sieber et al., 1995). In settings where deceptive research is common, participants should routinely be told that deception might be a part of any research in which they participate. Given research participants' relative powerlessness and the position of power and prestige that is associated with being a "scientist" (Kelman, 1972), such admonitions will work if only researchers take the process of consent seriously and emphasize that participants can decline to participate without fear of retribution.

Additionally, if deceptive practices are used, appropriate and thorough debriefings are essential. As Sales and Folkman (1998) noted, people often maintain initial impressions even after learning that the data on which the impressions are based are false. They pointed as an example to a study (Misra, 1992) in which consumers were told that red worm meat was added to ground beef by a fast food chain. Participants maintained a negative attitude toward the chain even after a debriefing.

Based on the work of Rawls (1955), Pittenger (2002) argues psychologists need to examine the policies that govern the use of deception in research. If they do so, they will be in a better position to determine the utility of permitting the use of deception using a framework of rules that continue to be scrutinized. He then makes three recommendations which he believes will lead to clearer guiding principles for researchers and research boards as well is protect the people who participate in behavioral and social science research. First, he suggests that psychologists include discussions of ethically sensitive topics in their research reports, including the rationale for the use of the particular technique and the steps taken to minimize risks. This would ensure both a concern for the welfare of research participants as well as the ability to assess permissibility of the rules that governed the research. Second, he recommended that professional organizations offer more specific guidelines for the appropriate use of deception. Last he recommended that as a part of consent participants should be informed that they cannot be informed of all the details of the study and that deception will be used in this study. Obviously, this does not solve the problem of confounding the research because participants might attempt to figure out how they are being deceived, however, the question remains whether this distraction is greater than the natural suspiciousness of the typical research participant.

Consent with Adolescents and Children

Difficult problems regarding consent to treatment or research arise when working with adolescents and children. This is particularly true with adolescents. Perhaps because adolescents are developmentally between adults and children, the law has been ambivalent about whether they should be treated as one or the other. Furthermore, parents and guardians are the ones responsible for teaching minors their values, so it is reasonable for them to have an interest in the mental health treatment of their children as well as in any research in which they participate (Gaylin, 1982). Generally, the legal system presumes that parents act in the best interests of their children and thus should have a say in their care, however, as Masty and Fisher (2008) point out for some parents, like those who abuse or neglect their children, this may not be the case. For the past 30 years, many have argued that older minors have some rights regarding consent or dissent to treatment (Grisso & Vierling, 1978; Kaser-Boyd, Adelman, & Taylor, 1985; Masty and Fisher, 2008; Sobocinski, 1990). Further, it is increasingly accepted that children need to assent to participation in research (Abramovitch, Freedman, Henry, & Van Brunschot, 1995). This is especially true in pure research where children are not expected to benefit directly from it (Weithorn & Scherer, 1994). In fact, DHHS requires that minors under the age of 18 years assent to participation (Sieber, 1992). Further, the DHHS indicates that children should not be asked to participate in research unless the risks involved do not exceed those of everyday life or the child may directly benefit from participation. Although some exceptions to these rules exist (Sieber, 1992), they are few and require a strong rationale.

Every state has set a legal age of majority. Beyond this age, adult competence is assumed. Below it, competence is questioned and parental or guardian approval is needed for many activities. In most states, the legal age is 18 years, although in some states it is 19 years and in the others it is 21 years (Hempelman, 1994). In addition, most states also have laws regarding the age at which an individual can legally consent to mental health treatment that may or may not coincide with the age of majority. However, even if children below the age of majority can legally consent to treatment, many states still require notifying the parent and it may also be necessary for reimbursement reasons. Lawrence and Kurpius (2000) claim that if informed parental consent is not used, mental health professionals risk being sued for battery, failure to obtain consent, and/or child enticement. It should be remembered that when obtaining parental consent if parents are divorced the consent needs to be provided by the custodial parent. Lawsuits and ethical complaints have been brought against professionals who get the noncustodial parent's consent but failed to obtain it from the custodial parent. However, although something is legal, it may not be the best ethical choice which is why working with adolescents is so ethically challenging.

Because consent is an agreement that a competent person makes to participate in an activity, it cannot be delegated to others. In other words, a parent cannot consent for a child (Koocher & Keith-Spiegel, 1990). If a minor cannot legally consent to treatment, then the parents must give *permission* for children to participate. Permission indicates that they allow their child to take part in the agreed-upon activity. Parental involvement can, however, lead to confusing claims regarding what information should be disclosed and to whom (Koocher & Keith-Spiegel, 1990; Plotkin, 1981; Sobocinski, 1990). Take Case 9-11 as an example.

Case 9-11

Mary started seeing Dr. Sinski at a mental health center. She admitted lying about her age on the intake forms so that she could get treatment without her mother's knowledge. She was only 17 years old, but the legal age for consent in that state was 18 years. She told the therapist that she was worried about her sexuality and it was making her so anxious and upset, it was interfering with her sleep. Dr. Sinski told Mary he had to inform her mother that she was seeking treatment, but that the only time he would break confidentiality and talk with her mother was if he thought she was a danger to herself or to others or if he discovered she was being abused. They agreed that Mary would tell her mother that she needed help because she was having difficulty sleeping. Mary agreed to treatment under those circumstances, and her mother gave legal permission for Mary's treatment with the same limitations.

As Mary got into treatment, she confided being attracted to some girls at her school and being fearful that she was a lesbian. Dr. Sinski worked with Mary for several weeks to establish a noncoercive environment in which she could explore her sexuality. At one point, however, Mary's mother called and accused Dr. Sinski of breaking his promise. She had found out that Mary was talking to him about "sexual deviance," which was a "danger" to Mary's soul. She demanded that Dr. Sinski either stop seeing Mary or stop talking about that "homosexuality stuff" with her (Sobocinski, 1990).

Unfortunately, there has been a gap between what has been documented in research about children's competence and recommendations regarding policies about children's ability to be involved in the consent process. Yet, scientific data regarding children's abilities should provide a cornerstone for the development of policies and standards regarding children's consent or assent to both research and treatment (Miller, Drotar, & Kodish, 2004; Sieber, 2008). In a review of the studies on children's competence to assent or consent to treatment or research, Miller et al. (2004) found that more studies have investigated children's competence to consent to research than treatment and only half of the studies of the 10 involving treatment evaluated children's competence to consent to psychological treatment (the others were medical). In addition, differences in methodology made it difficult to compare the results of different studies. They use the studies of Halpern-Felsher and Cauffman (2001) and Weithorn and Campbell (1982) as examples. In the Weithorn and Campbell's (1982) study, participants were asked what they would do in a hypothetical situation and then detailed questions and probes were used to assess competence. In contrast, while Halpern-Felsher and Cauffman (2001) also used the same hypothetical situation, they evaluated their spontaneous answers with open-ended questions. Not surprisingly the study by Weithorn and Campbell (1082) concluded that 14-year-olds were similar to adults in terms of competence while the other study found that adults have superior competence compared to children and adolescents up through 12th grade.

More recently Masty and Fisher (2008) concluded that based on many empirical studies on comprehension of research consent that minors approximately 15 years old and older have the competence to both understand the nature of research and their rights. In fact, Fisher (2002) reported that both parents and adolescents agreed that 14-year-old teenagers could be responsible for making independent decisions. On some characteristics, the decision-making abilities of 14- to 15-year-olds cannot be distinguished from young adults who are considered legally to be above the age of majority (aged 18–21 years). On the other hand, this may say more about the poor decision-making ability of 18- to 21-year-olds than the effectiveness of the decisions of those between 15- and 18-year-olds.* It must be recalled that these studies were carried out on consent for research. As was obvious in Case 9-11, parents' feelings regarding consent for therapy and the content of that therapy may lead them to feel quite differently.

In terms of younger children, there is evidence that children aged between 5 and 12 years can comprehend the procedures associated with research, although they may have difficulty in inferring potential risks (Abramovitch et al., 1995). Attending to how information is disclosed may enhance understanding. For example, "repetition, concrete examples, and response to quizzical expressions during disclosure can facilitate children's understanding" (Whitehorn & Shearer, 1994, p. 144). Although prior parental permission does not seem to influence children's freedom to decline to participate, researchers need to be very explicit with children about their freedom to withdraw from a study once it has begun (Abramovitch et al., 1995; Weithorn & Scherer, 1994). Although this may be inconvenient for researchers (because it may lead some children to discontinue participating), it is a necessary precaution, given that children are easily manipulated. Ensuring assent in pure research is especially critical because there is little ethical or legal basis for allowing anyone to coerce a child into participating.

It should be noted in the review of 29 studies on children's comprehension to assent by Miller et al. (2004), the race of the participants was not reported in 15 studies. In the 14 studies that did report race, majority White samples were used in 11 studies. In addition, within 14 studies SES was not reported. They point out that the lack of ethnically diverse samples limits the generalizability of the findings. Further, prior research has shown that minority status and low SES are strong predictors of parental understanding of informed consent (Miller, Drotar, Burant, & Kodish, 2005) further suggesting the findings in this area must be generalized with caution. Sieber (2008) and Masty and Fisher (2008) echo the same caution four years later.

Children as young as 9 years of age have been found to exhibit some characteristics associated with competence and understanding. However, although some argue that individuals in this age group are capable of meaningful involvement in personal health-care decision making (Weithorn & Campbell, 1982, p. 1596), Masty and Fisher (2008) point out that assent content tailored only to the age of the child may not take into consideration current cognitive or emotional deficiencies. In other words, there is probably no absolute measure of "true" competence (Gaylin, 1982); age is only a rough marker and does not provide a complete picture of minors' competence.

The existing data on minors' competence imply that older children and adolescents are competent to assent treatment or to research, even if they cannot give legal consent. Assent is the child's agreement to participate with certain stipulated conditions (Sieber, 1992). The concept of

---

* I thank David G. Scherer, PhD, for this observation.

assent developed as a way to distinguish children's "agreement" from legally valid authorization (Miller et al., 2004). Basically assent requires basic comprehension of procedures and purpose and the ability to indicate a preference. Mary's agreement to participate in therapy after Dr. Sinski described the limitations of confidentiality and how he would relate to her mother is an example of obtaining an adolescent's assent. Involving adolescents or children in the consent process by seeking their assent respects the limited autonomy of the minor, promotes fidelity, and is beneficent because it may facilitate development of the therapeutic alliance. In particular, the failure to involve adolescents in decision making can lead to negative reactions and lack of cooperation in treatment (Adelman et al., 1985).

Although determining the ability of minors to competently engage in the assent or consent process is a critical issue, clarifying the degree of risk involved is also important. Contrast the autonomy issues when dealing with an older, adolescent client, like Mary, who enters therapy with sexual identity concerns and a younger client who is engaging in unprotected anal intercourse with older, adolescent boys. In the second example, the competence of the client has to be considered in relationship to the information about the AIDS epidemic and the possible life-threatening consequences of her sexual behavior (Sobocinski, 1990). The added risk may ethically justify acting in a more parentalistic manner than might be the case if the risk were minor or nonexistent.

In light of the problems with which Mary entered therapy, Dr. Sinski was justified in developing a contract with her that limited disclosures to actions that involved dangerousness. After Mary's mother's accusations, however, he would need to get Mary to reconsider their contract so that he could possibly involve her mother in joint sessions to facilitate communication regarding Mary's anxiety about her emerging sexuality.

Another issue regarding minors' participation in the consent process relates to the voluntariness of their decision making. Can minors provide consent that is more than acquiescence to authority or conformity to peers? Generally, the data suggest that deference to authority and peer group pressure peaks in the preadolescent years and diminishes in individuals aged between 15 and 17 years (Grisso & Vierling, 1978; Mann et al., 1989). On the other hand, a strong tendency to acquiesce to authority has been found in both children and adults (Brehm, 1977; Milgram, 1974). Scherer (1991) found that children, adolescents, and young adults (aged 21–25 years) were all deferent to parental wishes regarding most medical decisions. In fact, in many instances, participation in counseling or therapy may not be a voluntary act for minors. When it is, however, the child's right to dissent should be considered.

Masty and Fisher (2008) have suggested using what they call a goodness of fit approach to obtaining assent or consent in research participation; however, it could also be adapted to therapy. They suggest involving the child, his or her parents and the investigator or therapist in a consent conference. They made four recommendations regarding the nature of that conference. First, the child's cognitive and emotional maturity, the nature of the problem and possible reactions to the assent information need to be considered. Second, the conference also needs to fit with parental knowledge and characteristics. This would allow multicultural issues to be taken into consideration. Third, the investigator or therapist needs to consider each family's decision-making history. For example, do they usually involve their children to be involved in decision making. Fourth, they need to respect the family's profile of child autonomy. In other words do they shield their children from serious questions and decisions or do they encourage increasing autonomy as the children grow older. Masty and Fisher (2008) point out that this can be an opportunity to help parents find the right balance of encouraging children's autonomy and protecting them by asking for a child's opinion and then encouraging parents to take it into account in making their decision. This can also ensure that a child's participation in a research study is not coerced. The following is the case based on the one used in their article.

Case 9-12

Ned is the 8-year-old son of the Passaic family. He is being interviewed for participation in the psychosocial study to treat emotional outbursts. Initially, the investigators asked the parents to describe Ned's current functioning try to understand whether he has the capacity to understand the study information. She also involves him in a brief conversation, however, he acts out, describes the study is a silly waste of time and does not appear to understand what a research study is. Consequently, she suggests it might be more comfortable for Ned to temporarily play in the outer room while the adults continue their conversation. She explains the study to the parents and then asks them to explain back to her what they see as the key aspects of this study and their rights. She then asks the parents how they usually make family decisions and finds that they seldom invite Ned to help make important decisions because he usually chooses the opposite of what they think is best for him out of spite. As a result, they decide the parents will make the ultimate decision about his participation; however, he will still be consulted. At that point, Ned is invited back into the room, but the investigator encourages his developing autonomy be by saying something like, "Before your parents make the final decision, I'd like to tell you more about the study so you can ask any questions and help your parents understand what you would like them to take into consideration." Ned says he does not want to miss school, so the researcher assures him their time together will take place after school and although she reminds him that his parents will be making a final decision, she tells him he will be able to make several decisions along the way. For example, she says if it is okay with his parents he can decide what day he wants to start study.

This approach allowed the investigator to get a good sense of each member of the family and their level of understanding as well as the family's decision-making culture. She tried to respect Ned's level of understanding and attempts to become more autonomous allowing him to assent to some decisions regarding participation. She also assured that the parents understood what they were consenting to. This approach to informed consent is a process that can actually be educational for both the parents and the child.

In summary, current data on minors' decision making lead to conclusions similar to those of Grisso and Vierling (1978) and Powell (1984). Fifteen-year-olds and older adolescents who are of average intelligence can engage in the consent process as competently as 18- to 21-year-olds, assuming the material is written at a level that they can comprehend. With individuals aged between 11 and 14 years, caution should be exercised regarding their abilities to understand the complexities and consequences of treatment, confidentiality, and so on. This is particularly true with high-risk decisions because adolescents have the greater part of their lives ahead of them and their decisions may have long-term consequences (Gaylin, 1982; Powell, 1984). Finally, children under the age of 11 years may be able to participate in making treatment decisions, but their reliance on authority and difficulties in understanding suggest that burdening them with ultimate responsibility for making the decisions may be more harmful than beneficial. Even they, however, can assent to treatment, assuming the process, limits to confidentiality, and so on are explained in a vocabulary that they can comprehend. Last, multicultural differences both in family structure and potential for understanding consent material depending on the level of education need to be taken into consideration (Miller et al., 2004; Masty & Fisher, 2008; Sieber, 2008).

Consent with Other Vulnerable Populations

In both research and therapy informed consent with "vulnerable" populations is troublesome. Sieber (1992) identified seven following ways in which individuals may be vulnerable:

a. They are rich or famous and have resources that make them liable for lawsuits.
b. They lack resources or autonomy (e.g., minors, mentally ill patients, and students).

c. They are in a weakened position or subject to undue influence because of their status in an institution (e.g., a prison or the military).

d. They cannot talk for themselves (e.g., nonEnglish speakers).

e. They have committed illegal acts that could become known to law enforcement agencies because of the research.

f. They are stigmatized by others' attitudes (e.g., gay men, lesbians, rape victims, or those infected with AIDS).

g. They are vulnerable because of their association with research participants (e.g., parents of children who reveal information about child abuse).

Obtaining adequate consent from potentially vulnerable populations involves paying particular attention to risks. Conducting focus groups or consulting with others in the community before developing a consent procedure may sensitize the researcher to the concerns of the population, particularly to the kinds of risks that potential participants anticipate (Sieber, 1992). Such occasions can also help establish the trust of the individuals who may later be research participants.

It should be noted that voluntariness is of particular importance with vulnerable populations, including students, those in poverty, and those in need of psychological services, because they can be manipulated by excessive inducements. The inducements could be so high (e.g., improved grades, money, and opportunities for free services) that vulnerable individuals could not afford to refuse, even if it was against their better judgment. On the other hand, Sieber (1992) argued that members of many marginal groups will not participate unless they receive substantial financial rewards. Further, she suggested that when balancing the potential benefits and risks, inducements may bring about more good than harm to the participants. Consequently, investigators need to carefully consider the consequences of the inducements they are using. Conversations with community members may help investigators make a reasonable assessment of the risks (e.g., threats to autonomous decision making) and benefits of participation.

Sieber (1992) used Case 5-12 to illustrate the use of a simple meal to develop a collaborative research or intervention plan with a vulnerable population. She noted the importance of identifying formal or informal community gatekeepers, leaders who can evaluate whether an outsider has the potential to help or harm the community. The gatekeeper can help the researcher understand the community culture and establish trust with community members. In the following case was no visible community gatekeeper so the researchers had to be creative.

Case 9-13

A researcher-intervener wanted to establish a needle exchange program among street people and needed to know about her clientele and their concerns: Are they diverse populations, or are they homogeneous? How will she identify individuals for repeated measures? How can she best arrange to meet with them and avoid police arrest for exchanging needles? What are their needs and concerns? There was no established gatekeeper except some street people who were respected by their peers. After some conversations with individuals in the area where she considered establishing the needle exchange program, she issued a word-of-mouth invitation to dinner. She rented a hotel room in a flophouse and cooked hot dogs, sauerkraut, and soup; she also served cake, donuts, and soda pop in abundance. Her hot dog ethnography, as it has been called, was a great success. Most street people are quite hungry. About 40 people attended, which is surprising, given that they are a stigmatized population and police entrapment was a possibility. The researcher was known to them from her previous outreach efforts, which helped engender trust (Case, 1990).

Informed Consent and the Internet

The use of the Internet for a variety of purposes has exploded particularly in the last 10 years. The Internet has been used as an alternative to face-to-face therapy, as an adjunct to therapy, as a supplement to supervision and particularly as a research tool. It allows researchers to sample from larger and more heterogeneous groups than those typically found on college or university campuses. It has brought with it a variety of ethical problems particularly those involving privacy and informed consent. The issue of privacy will be dealt with in Chapter 10; however, privacy and informed consent are closely tied.

Whether using the Internet or traditional methods of therapy, supervision, or research the issues of informed consent remain the same. Participants need to acknowledge that they understand the nature of the interaction, their role in it and the responsibilities of the psychologist. In other words, the standards governing consent in therapy, research, or supervision remain the same. Particular problems arise, however, when using the Internet for research purposes, so the remainder of this section will focus on research.

Because the Internet provides almost complete anonymity, the identity of the person giving consent cannot be verified (Keller & Lee, 2003). Consequently, there is no way to know whether the person is a minor or an individual of limited cognitive or psychological capacity. Since minors cannot legally consent to participate in research, but only assent, the researcher needs to take particular precautions regarding the person who was completing the study. Although the researcher may ask for the age or birth date of the person completing the research, the problem is there is no completely trustworthy way to verify whether they have done so truthfully (Keller & Lee, 2003; Pittenger, 2003). As noted previously regulations that govern research in humans excuse the researcher from getting parental consent if the research poses little or no risk to the participants. Pittenger points out that much of the current Internet research is quite benign. He gives examples of experiments in sensation and perception, general opinion surveys that measure personality, so for much of the research the issues of minors offering informed consent appears to be minimal.

The problem with verifying the age of the person giving consent becomes critical when the researcher wants to investigate problems of a controversial nature like ones involving sexual activity. Other studies may involve some risks to the participants like those involving deception. Children can easily use their parent's Internet service and pretend to act as their parent when it comes to offering consent to participate in the research. Whether the participant is an adult or child there is an additional problem that arises when the research involves deception since participants can break the link with the web page prior to the end of the study and the dehoaxing section.

Pittenger offers several suggestions about how to avoid these ethical pitfalls. Researchers could ask participants submit their e-mail address so that the researchers can send debriefing information even if the person breaks the link. Although this compromises anonymity, it may be necessary to protect the participant from harmful consequences. If the research involves controversial issues or ones that may be harmful, the researcher could use the Internet to solicit participants and use other means to collect data ensuring the age of the participant. Further, once researchers have solicited participants using the Internet, they may need to identify trusted colleagues or other gatekeepers who can verify the age and/or the cognitive ability of the volunteers.

Just as forensics raised new ethical problems for psychologists and counselors, the use of the Internet provides new ethical challenges. It is probably the case that we are just beginning to understand what those problems may be. For example, using the Internet for therapy and supervision raises all kinds of privacy issues. Whether these can be overcome remains to be seen.

Consent in Academia*

Consent with Students

Generally, neither educational institutions nor faculty have conceptualized their obligations to students in terms of informed consent (Handelsman, 1987; Kitchener, 1992b). Certainly, students are seldom asked explicitly whether they understand their obligations as members of an educational community or whether they are clear about the obligations of the faculty. In some ways, their consent is implied when they enter the institution. At the same time, if informed consent is understood as a way to guard students' ability to make autonomous decisions, then, as with a formal consent situation, students need adequate information on which to make reasonable choices. This is why the accuracy of both programmatic material and course outlines is of particular importance (see Case 9-3).

Chambers (1981) conceptualized the relationship between students and their educational institution as a contract. Students, at least those at the college or university level, make the decision to enter a college or a graduate program on the basis of the information they receive from that institution or department. Thus, the institution incurs the responsibility to ensure that the information is accurate and written in a manner that potential students can understand. If the educational institution fails to live up to its promises, then students have a right to complain, as they did in Case 9-3. Reciprocally, student handbooks spell out responsibilities of students or their part of the contract. If students fail to comply with their part of the contract, they can be asked to leave the institution or program.

Handelsman (1987) argued that there is a similar relationship between faculty members and students. Faculty members are obliged to provide students with adequate information that is not misleading in course syllabi and other written materials. Activities that place unusual demands on students, such as self-disclosure of personal information, participation in deceptive research, or some work with laboratory animals, may be particularly important to disclose because some students may not be emotionally prepared for the consequences of participation (Handelsman, 1987). The principle of nonmaleficence suggests that students should be informed about unusual or risky aspects of a course before their choices have negative consequences for them. When instructors change requirements at midterm, they break their implicit contract with students. Such actions may erode students' respect for the faculty and the profession (Handelsman, 1987).

Students implicitly agree to abide by the rules when they enter an institution or class. They do so based on the assumption that the institution, department, or faculty members will fulfill the promises made in written materials or in oral agreements. Because students are in a less powerful position than are faculty members or administrators, they are in a position of vulnerability. Although most contracts assume that the parties are equally mature and powerful (Chambers, 1981), this is not the case in educational settings. As a consequence, faculty members have a strong ethical obligation to ensure that the information they provide is clear, especially about requirements that are in some respects unusual.

Consent in Supervision

Even though supervision does not always take place in academia, individuals' first experience with supervision in a mental health professional typically takes place in beginning practicum and continues through advanced practicum and internship. In other words it takes place as part of an educational program. Like other educational experiences students are in a less powerful position and consequently are vulnerable to the evaluations of faculty or other practicum supervisors. In addition, until recently like in other educational settings, the contract between

---

* This section is based in part on the study by Kitchener (1992b).

supervisor and supervisee has often been an implicit one. Students if they have been supervised in other settings like on a construction job or in a department store may find themselves confused and frightened of the expectations in supervision. Rather than being rewarded for sharing their successes oftentimes they are rewarded for discussing errors or at least difficulties they are having with clients. Nonmaleficence and fidelity requires that instructors or supervisors clearly clarify expectations and requirements.

It should be noted that psychologists are increasingly called upon to supervise unlicensed or master's licensed professionals as a part of their job description (Sutter, McPherson, & Greesman, 2002). These supervisees most often enter supervision with prior knowledge of some of the expectations of mental health supervision. However, contracts between supervisors and supervisees have often been minimal, spelling out fees for services, length of supervision and limits of supervision. Particular expectations of the supervisor involved may or may not be articulated. Like students supervisees are in a less powerful position and vulnerable to the requirements and evaluation of the supervisor.

Although informed consent has been a critical and widely accepted component of therapy and research, as already noted the same cannot be said of supervision. For example, even though the 2005 ACA Ethics Code had specific sections both ensuring that supervisees were using informed consent with their clients and supervisors were using informed consent with their supervisees, the 2002 APA ethics code did not mention the use of informed consent in supervision. Although implications for supervision could be drawn from sections regarding consultation services, the attention was minimal.

There been many calls for the need to incorporate informed consent in supervision as well as describing the format of doing so (Barnett, 2005; Bernard & Goodyear, 2004; Borders & Brown, 2005; Falander & Shafranske, 2004; Sutter et al., 2002). See Thomas (2007) for a more complete list. Problems exist, however, in the application of informed consent provisions to supervision that do not exist in its application to therapy or research. As discussed earlier five components namely competence, disclosure, understanding, voluntariness, and authorization are necessary for true informed consent. As Thomas (2007) notes the issue of voluntariness is only partially applicable in supervision. Except in extreme cases we can generally assume that supervisees are competent to make informed choices. Clearly, disclosure and understanding are also critical. Many difficulties in beginning practicum could be avoided if supervisors disclosed the competencies they expected supervisees to develop at the beginning of supervision and the parameters of their relationship so that students knew their expectations and how they differed from other supervision they had experienced. Thomas (2007) offers an example of what can happen when disclosure and understanding are not included in the initial meetings with the supervisee. The following is a summary of the case (p. 224).

Case 9-14

Dan was a doctoral practicum student who was receiving supervision from Dr. Lopez. Dan reported in supervision that he was irritated by the behavior of one of his clients, who, like Dan's father, was an alcoholic and estranged from his family. They processed the counter transference during supervision, and it did not seem problematic in subsequent work. When Dr. Lopez completed Dan's evaluation at the end of the quarter, he mentioned that being a child of an alcoholic had created some difficulties early in supervision, but they had overcome them appropriately. He gave Dan a very positive evaluation and sent Dan's faculty supervisor a copy of the evaluation.

After reviewing the evaluation, Dan was shocked that Dr. Lopez would disclose such personal information to one of his professors. He felt betrayed because he believed that what they shared would be kept private. Dr. Lopez explained that he routinely consulted with faculty. Furthermore he pointed out that the anecdote provided a useful illustration supporting the favorable evaluation.

This case illustrates problems that might be avoided if the supervisor attended to issues of disclosure and understanding at the beginning of supervision. Although supervisees may understand the complex ethical issues surrounding confidentiality and privacy with clients, they may assume the same ethical standards apply in supervision. Obviously, supervisors cannot foresee all potential misunderstandings that may occur; however, there are some, like privacy and confidentiality, which are common and should be included in every new supervisee's orientation to supervision. We will return to this issue later in this section.

The component that differs most drastically from true informed consent is voluntariness. Supervisees enter supervision as a part of the requirement for practicum, for internship, for licensure or for reeducation after being found guilty of an ethical or legal violation. Supervisees may have some choice of the supervisor with whom they will work and the setting they will work in; however, they do not have a choice about forgoing supervision since it is a critical component of their educational experience, a requirement of their job, or a stipulation of a court or licensing board.

Cobia and Boes (2000) suggested two strategies for meeting the disclosure and understanding requirements of informed consent to the best degree possible. Although they do not eradicate the problem of voluntariness, they may help supervisee choose between supervisors. The first is a professional disclosure statement the intention of which is to inform the prospective supervisee of the rights and responsibilities of both the supervisor and supervisee, the parameters of supervision, the methods of evaluation, the desired outcomes or competencies, and the potential risks and benefits of participation in supervision. They point out this document can facilitate the establishment of a professional relationship and rapport between the supervisor and supervisee. Further, it provides the supervisee with the opportunity to better understand the supervisor and make a voluntary choice between supervisors and the circumstances with which supervision is conducted when this is possible.

The second document they recommended is a formal plan for supervision. It can best be conceptualized as an individualized learner contract. It would include mutually agreed-upon goals for supervision, for example, competencies to be learned, how these competencies will be evaluated and responsibilities of both the supervisor and supervisee if the competencies are not achieved. Thomas points out that the formal plan is very similar to a treatment plan used in psychotherapy (Barnett, 2005).

Thomas (2002) provides a comprehensive list of potential components to include in their professional disclosure statement or formal plan. She notes that not all would be applicable to every supervisee in all situations; however, this list provides a supervisor with the issues to consider. They include:

1. *The supervisor's background:* this provides supervisees with information to choose a supervisor by providing them information about the supervisors' academic degrees, certifications and clinical specialties. In order to be licensed, supervisees may be required to be supervised by an individual with particular credentials and this would provide them the opportunity to evaluate whether the supervisor had the required background. In addition, they may want to be supervised by someone with a particular theoretical orientation.

2. *Supervisory methods:* particularly beginning supervisees may be unfamiliar with the kinds of techniques that are used in supervision, for example, audio or videotaping, in vivo supervision, cotherapy, and so on. Knowing this ahead of time helps the supervisee to know what to expect as well as to use that information in his or her selection process.

3. *Supervisor's responsibilities and requirements*: sometimes supervisors are responsible for overseeing particular aspects of the supervisee's practice like testing or couples therapy. If this is the case, not only should the supervisor be competent to practice in that area but the contract should clarify the areas of practice for which the supervisor is responsible. Supervisors are also accountable for being available in case of emergencies. The personal disclosure statement should clarify how the supervisee should contact the supervisor in such situations and who is responsible if the supervisor is unavailable.

4. *Supervisee's responsibilities*: just as students have responsibilities in educational settings supervisees also have responsibilities. Supervisors should review and perhaps provide written documentation about what these responsibilities are. This is particularly important since supervisors are legally liable for the supervisees' errors. Supervisors may want to provide their supervisees guidelines regarding types of situations and problems about which they want to be informed. For example, these might include potential situations that involve child abuse or danger to self or others, other high risk situations, allegations of unethical or illegal behavior, counter transference issues including possible clinical or ethical errors, and any contact with clients outside of the supervisee's professional role. Both Thomas (2007) and Sutter et al. (2002) provide examples of statements that could be signed by the supervisee agreeing to these requirements.

5. *Other potential requirements*: Thomas points that like therapy just as supervision progresses problems that were not evident at the beginning of supervision may develop or become apparent. These might include impairment, substance abuse, skill deficits or ethical incompetence each of which might require something remedial treatment or education. Supervisees should be aware that if such events might occur, the original supervision contract might need to change.

6. *Confidentiality versus privacy*: one of the most commonly misunderstood issues in supervision is the difference between privacy and confidentiality and although this issue will be taken up in more detail in Chapter 10, it is important to note here that although supervisors may promise their supervisees privacy they cannot offer them confidentiality. Privacy means respecting the individual enough not to share information about the supervisee with everyone or anyone who asks. Confidentiality is a promise to keep information private unless there is a legal or ethical requirement that the supervisor must divulge the information. Supervisees are entitled to privacy. Most professional ethical codes require that professionals discuss the limits of confidentiality and the circumstances under which are require to breach the supervisees' privacy. Supervision is unique in that in addition to reporting obligations others may and probably will have access to information about the supervisee. Just as in Case 9-14 Dr. Lopez shared information about Dan with his educational institution, this is true with most supervision situations. Information about students is typically shared with the educational institution from which they are receiving their degree and information derived from supervision that is required for a professional who is on probation would also be communicated to the appropriate agency.

7. *Documentation of supervision*: just as psychotherapy sessions are documented by notes regarding the day and content of the session, many have recommended similar documentation take place regarding supervision. Falvey, Caldwell, and Cohen (2002) have written extensively on the kinds of documentation recommended for supervision and published examples of forms that could be used. Included are narrative descriptions of supervision sessions, a log of hours and meeting dates, evaluation forms, and so on. Thomas points out that part of the informed consent process should familiarize the

supervisee with the kinds of documentation that will be kept and who will have access to the records other than the supervisor and the supervisee.

8. *Financial policies*: although students who are in their doctoral program typically do not pay for supervision, this is not the case in the postdoctoral phase. Clearly, potential supervisees need to know the cost supervision prior to agreeing to see a particular supervisor.

9. *Risks and benefits*: Thomas suggests the supervisees can make a better informed decision about their participation in supervision if they are aware of the risks and benefits. She uses the emotional discomfort of having one's work scrutinized as an example of risks. On the other hand supervision has the ability to increase supervisees' understanding of themselves and their background and how this might both positively and negatively affect their work.

10. *Evaluation*: as already noted under documentation, supervisees should know how they are being evaluated in advance. Like other aspects of the informed consent process this may change over time and if so the supervisee needs to be apprised of it.

11. *Complaint procedures and due process*: even though due process procedures are usually described in the student handbook it may be worthwhile to repeat that information in what Cobia and Boes called the professional disclosure statement. As Thomas points out such a statement acknowledges the possibility of dissatisfaction or problems with supervision and instructs supervisees about how to ameliorate their dissatisfaction. This might prevent a misunderstanding from turning into an impasse or formal complaint.

12. *Professional development goals*: each supervisee comes into supervision with certain goals which may have been predetermined by their program or other agency or they can be negotiated with the supervisor. These would be a part of the formal plan as defined by Cobia and Boes. These would be specific competencies that the supervisee either needs or wants to learn. It would be important to address particular deficits that the supervisee wants or needs to ameliorate. The negotiation of these goals may be an important part of building a relationship between supervisee and the supervisor.

13. *Endorsement*: in many ways supervisors are the gatekeepers of the profession they are expected to endorse the supervisee for particular events like completion of internship or licensure. It is important to acknowledge that the 2005 ACA Code of Ethics specifically required supervisors not to endorse supervisees who they believed to be deficient in any way that could interfere with their performance as professionals. As Thomas points out these issues should be brought to the attention of supervisees substantially sooner than the end of their contract. In fact when identified they may become one of the goals or the most important goal in the professional development contract. Sometimes even with concentrated work, however, supervisees may be unable to overcome their deficiencies. This possibility should also be spelled out in their professional development contract. The supervisor is not obligated to pass the supervisee despite progress that the supervisee may have made. If substantial deficiencies still exist at the end of supervision, the supervisor has an ethical obligation based on nonmaleficence not to pass the supervisee. Consequently, supervisees need to be informed of the supervisor's gatekeeping function.

14. *Duration and termination of the supervision contract*: normally the date of termination would be set ahead of time by the student's program, the licensure requirements, or other external criteria. However, there may be extraordinary circumstances in which the supervisors or supervisee feels necessary to terminate early or to extend beyond the originally agreed-upon date. For example, the supervisor may feel ethically obligated to terminate if the supervisee violates ethical standards or the law, refuses to follow the supervisor's directives, or cannot practice with reasonable skill and safety. On the

other hand the supervisee may also feel obligated to terminate their contract if the supervisor consistently fails to keep appointments or gives the supervisee directives that he or she feels are unethical.

As Thomas (2002) says "obtaining informed consent at the outset of supervision means securing the supervisee's agreement to participate in light of all relevant factors" (p. 229). All of the issues just articulated may not be relevant for every supervisee and there may be others that have not been included. Although it is not required that a formal contract be written that includes the policies and information relevant a particular supervision, it is highly recommended and there are many examples in the literature (Falander & Shafranske, 2002; Sutter et al., 2002). This is an area standards of practice are evolving rapidly and the incorporation of informed consent in supervision of research or practice is becoming more common and expected.

Conclusion

The use of informed consent in research, practice, teaching and supervision is certainly no panacea for the ethical problems psychologists face. On the other hand, informing consumers or participants ahead of time about the aspects of the experience that may cause them discomfort or clarifying misconceptions could go a long way to helping psychologists and counselors avoid ethical mistakes. For example, many of the ethical dilemmas that therapists face in the realm of confidentiality may be avoided if they discussed the limits of confidentiality with clients. The last case provided an example of how it can be avoided in supervision. Similarly, in the forensic area, misconceptions regarding who has access to the data from assessments and how it will be used can be avoided with forethought about how clients can be informed about the process and its products.

Whether in practice or in research attending to the competence of the participant to give consent, the clear disclosure of necessary information, the participant's understanding of the information, the voluntariness of the decision, and the right of the person to authorize consent helps fulfill the spirit of consent. It may be necessary to experiment with different methods of providing consent depending on the group or area involved. What works with adolescents, for example, may not work as well with either children or adults. Additionally, with children and adolescents, professionals should remember that even if they cannot legally or ethically consent to participate, their assent should be solicited, as well as parental permission. Although the situation in educational settings has some differences, there are also parallels and it would behoove faculty members to consider what they are promising students and whether their requirements take advantage of students' vulnerability.

At its core the mental health profession is dependent on the belief of clients, research participants, students, and other consumers in the fidelity of psychologists or counselors. To the extent that the consent process helps uphold our contract with them, it will help maintain the respect for the profession that is necessary for it to remain viable.

Questions for Discussion and Consideration

1. From your perspective, why is informed consent so important in supervision?
2. Is there any way that informed consent can be made more explicit in educational settings?
3. Explain your own words the components of the consent process and why they are important.
4. From your perspective, is deceptive research ethical? Explain your point of view.
5. When working with adolescents who are mandated for therapy, what components of the consent process are missing and under those circumstances what components are important for you to emphasize and how would you do it?

10
Confidentiality
Doing Good, Avoiding Harm, and Maintaining Trust

with RANDI SMITH

Confidentiality has long been thought of as the cornerstone of the therapeutic relationship. Its centrality to therapy was even affirmed by the U.S. Supreme Court, which in 1996 affirmed that "(e)ffective psychotherapy ... depends upon an atmosphere of confidence and trust in which the patient is willing to make a frank and complete disclosure of facts, emotions, memories, and fears. Because of the sensitive nature of the problems for which individuals consult psychotherapists, disclosure of confidential communication made during counseling sessions may cause embarrassment or disgrace. For this reason, the mere possibility of disclosure may impede development of the confidential relationship necessary for successful treatment" (*Jaffee v. Redmond*, 1996).

At its core, confidentiality seems to be a simple concept: Psychologists and counselors respect the privacy of their clients or research participants and do not share divulged information with other people. In practice, however, confidentiality is neither simple nor absolute. If it is the metaphorical cornerstone of psychotherapy, it is a cornerstone with cracks and chips, and one that may even shift its position over time. Likewise in research, academia, and other settings, mental health professionals may be certain about the importance of confidentiality, but less-than-certain about how to assure its preservation.

Confidentiality can be thought of as professional secret-keeping. It is recognized not only as an aid to building trust and, consequently, achieving good outcomes in therapy and obtaining good data in research, but also as a duty or obligation that the therapist upholds for his or her clients and research participants, and ultimately for his or her profession. Each of the professional therapy organizations (e.g., the American Psychological Association, the American Counseling Association) mandates confidentiality in its ethics code. In addition, many states have legislation that further defines the therapist's responsibility to maintain confidences.

Confidentiality and Privacy

Upholding the confidentiality of the therapeutic relationship, means protecting the privacy of those who seek therapy or participate in research. But while confidentiality and privacy are closely related terms, they are certainly not interchangeable. Privacy belongs, at least in theory, to the individual. Each of us decides when and how much to reveal of ourselves to others, with some people guarding their privacy closely while others voluntarily share vast amounts of personal information, even with total strangers. How much people value and protect their privacy varies drastically by culture, as well. Within twenty-first century American society, social scientists have noted an erosion of privacy, such that its very concept is changing (Dyson, 2008). Social networking tools like Facebook, MySpace, and Twitter—where people post not just their photos and demographic information, but information about their sex lives, what they ate for dinner, and how many pounds they have shed since last Tuesday—create a possibly unprecedented transparency into the "private" details of individuals.

This changing concept of personal privacy may challenge traditional and professional views of psychotherapy as a uniquely private undertaking. Consider the following scenario: A psychotherapist is at a dinner party when an acquaintance tells him that she has been hearing great things about his therapy. Uncertain to what she is referring, the therapist asks for clarification. The woman says, "Oh, you know, Joycie. She always posts little pieces on Facebook about how much progress she's making in therapy with you." The therapist, who does in fact treat Joycie, is surprised to learn about her Facebook postings of their therapy and is unsure how to respond to the remarks of this acquaintance.

While it has always been possible for clients to tell others that they are in therapy and even to reveal the contents of their sessions, there are several factors that have increased the likelihood of extra-therapy disclosures by clients in today's world. First, therapy is no longer as stigmatized as it once was (Corrigan, 2004); consequently many people no longer feel the need to keep their mental health treatment a secret. Second, blogs and other internet communications are sometimes expressly designed for the revelation of intimate details to the world, and there is ample modeling by people, both famous and uncelebrated, who share their journeys through addiction, mental disorders, marital counseling, etc. in public forums.

The publicizing of what once would likely have been a closely guarded secret—the fact of one's undergoing mental health treatment—can be confusing to people both within and outside of the counseling professions. That very confusion magnifies the importance of distinguishing privacy from confidentiality. Even though personal information is in many ways becoming increasingly public, this changing concept of privacy does not equate to changing the meaning of confidentiality, which is a specific professional obligation. So regardless how much a client may choose to share about his or her experiences in therapy, and even if those disclosures are made in very public forums like internet blogs or social networking sites, the therapist's duty to uphold the confidentiality of the therapeutic relationship remains intact.

Confidentiality can also be distinguished from the legal concept of privacy, which protects individuals and their homes from unwarranted intrusion by the government or other official entity. Though privacy *per se* is not a right granted by the U.S. Constitution, it has been recognized as a constitutional right by the Supreme Court (Bersoff, 2008). Typically, though, the right to privacy has a fairly narrow scope, such as protecting individuals from unwarranted search and seizure and preserving individuals' freedom to exercise choices over personal associations and values (Smith-Bell & Winslade, 1994). Legal rights to privacy have been further elucidated by the Privacy Rule of the Health Insurance Portability and Accountability Act of 1996 (HIPAA), which established, for the first time, a set of national standards for the protection of individually identifiable health information, including information about mental health conditions and treatment. Because the Privacy Rule is "designed to be flexible and comprehensive to cover the variety of uses and disclosures that need to be addressed" (U.S. Department of Health and Human Services, 2003, p.1) and because it is limited largely to electronic transmission of health information, it is neither a replacement for nor an alternative to the ethical obligation of mental health providers to maintain confidentiality.

Privacy, then, is an ambiguous term—one that has ethical, social, and legal connotations. On its own, the right to privacy does little to protect access to information shared in a professional relationship, which is why confidentiality rules and laws were enacted. Confidentiality is a more specific term than privacy. In general, confidentiality means that all information provided to psychologists or counselors in the course of their professional work is to be kept private, including details which could result in the mere identification of a patient, client, or research participant (Donner, 2008). In other words, without explicit consent or special legal authorization, the psychologist or counselor can disclose neither the content of treatment nor the identity of those treated. So whereas privacy is an individual right, confidentiality involves private information that is divulged in a professional relationship between two or more people (Smith-Bell & Winslade, 1994). As the U.S. Supreme Court confirmed, it is central to the work of psychotherapists and researchers. Take the following cases as examples.

Case 10-1

A therapist working within a managed care facility files a request for additional individual sessions for one of her clients. One of the managed care company's conditions for reauthorization involves a review of the client's file, including session notes. Although the therapist informed the client of the legal limits of confidentiality at the start of therapy (harm to self, others, or child abuse), she has not reviewed the issue since the first session. Several weeks into therapy, the client revealed his struggles with a sexual fetish and exhibitionism. The client is extremely fearful that his employer, family, or others will learn about his "problem." After the managed care company authorizes additional visits for the client, and the client is informed of this, he asks the therapist whether the managed care company was informed as to the reason he is in therapy. When the therapist acknowledges that the managed care company had access to client data, the client becomes enraged and accuses the therapist of failing to inform him of all the limits to confidentiality.

Case 10-2

A counselor has been providing individual therapy to a 15-year-old girl whose parents are concerned about her recently declining school performance and her withdrawal from many social activities. At the outset of the treatment, the parents agreed to the counselor's recommendation that their daughter's treatment be kept confidential unless she was a danger to herself or to others. This meant that, even though the parents legally have a right to access information regarding their minor child's treatment, they wished to respect the therapeutic relationship and not request information. Several weeks into therapy, the daughter has disclosed that she is involved in a sexual relationship with a 20-year-old male, who has also introduced her to cocaine. Although the adolescent client is not threatening to harm herself or anyone else, her behaviors are not only risky, but have potentially life-altering consequences. The counselor wonders at what point confidentiality must be sacrificed so that the child's parents can take steps to protect her.

Case 10-3

A psychologist is conducting research on the health habits of men diagnosed with HIV/AIDS. The psychologist's consent form assures participants of confidentiality, with the exceptions of harm to self, harm to others, or reported child abuse. Although the psychologist, who designed the study, is responsible for conducting the data analysis, research assistants conduct the face-to-face interviews with the HIV/AIDS participants. While reviewing the files, the psychologist discovers that one of the participants is her sister's husband. The psychologist does not believe that her sister is aware of her husband's HIV-positive status and is concerned that the lack of information could jeopardize (or prove lethal to) her sister's health. The psychologist considers breaking confidentiality and informing her sister of her husband's HIV status.

Each of these cases pits the responsibility to maintain confidentiality against other ethical responsibilities. In Case 10-1, the benefit from providing additional therapy sessions must be balanced against the harm that might occur if the managed care company reveals the client's sexual fetish. In Cases 10-2 and 10-3, the benefits and harms associated with maintaining confidentiality have to be evaluated against the potential harms that could occur if the psychologist or counselor maintains silence. Resolving these concerns requires mental health professionals to be knowledgeable of the ethical principles involved, relevant professional ethical codes, limits to confidentiality, and pertinent legal statutes.

Foundational Ethical Principles

From an ethical perspective, maintaining confidentiality is grounded in the principles of autonomy, fidelity, beneficence, and nonmaleficence. Upholding the autonomy of clients, patients, research participants, and students means respecting and even encouraging their own decision making (Beauchamp & Childress, 2001). In therapy, for example, clients have the right to make decisions about those with whom they wish to share private information and those from whom they wish to withhold it. Without control over who has access to records about themselves, individuals could not protect private information or guard against dangerous disclosures (Bok, 1988). Likewise, without clear knowledge of what those records include, clients may be ill-equipped to make autonomous decisions about information sharing. According to VandeCreek (2008), "principles of confidentiality and client autonomy suggest that providers need to fully inform their clients about the nature and content of the records that will be released" (p. 373). To do so in the most complete way would entail sharing the record with the client before sending it on.

The duty of confidentiality is also influenced by the ethical principle of fidelity, which is at the core of all trusting human relationships. Unlike ordinary relationships, though, the professional relationship is undergirded by a fiduciary contract, so that a professional promise of confidentiality goes well beyond the loyalty and discretion that one can only hope for in friendships and other nonprofessional associations. When a psychologist or counselor extends a promise of confidentiality, the principle of fidelity demands that the promise is extended truthfully, with sufficient information about the purposes of, and limits to, confidentiality. And when consumers or research participants share private information about themselves they can expect that the professional will faithfully protect their disclosures.

Finally, allowing the professional to keep information confidential fulfills a useful purpose, both for the individual and society (Bok, 1988). Individuals benefit (beneficence) by getting help for problems that might be embarrassing or might put them at risk of harm. When therapists uphold the ethical obligation of confidentiality, they help ensure that harm will not befall their clients (nonmaleficence). For example, the client in Case 10-1 might be harmed if information about his sexual fetish were disclosed to his wife or business associates. Additionally, there are many cases in which society benefits from the confidentiality afforded to clients or research participants. It is unlikely that individuals would reveal potentially helpful information to researchers if they could not be assured confidentiality around such areas as antisocial behavior, underage drug and alcohol use patterns, the psychology of the spread of contagious diseases, and so on. Similarly, individuals who are suffering from psychological problems that might cause them to harm others or keep them from living fulfilling, socially productive lives might not enter therapy if they did not believe that their secrets would be kept confidential.

Because there are such strong ethical reasons for keeping confidentiality, it is not surprising that professional organizations place such a high value on maintaining it. The professional ethics codes of all of the major mental health professions (i.e., American Association for Marriage and Family Therapy [AAMFT], 2001; American Counseling Association [ACA], 2005; American Psychiatric Association, 2009; American Psychological Association [APA], 2002; and National Association of Social Workers [NASW], 2008) define and delineate confidentiality protections for clients and research participants. Similarly, confidentiality has been written into law in most states' mental health statutes. Clearly, a high priority is placed on maintaining client confidentiality in the mental health field, regardless of the professional's specific discipline.

The emphasis on confidentiality in mental health codes does not mean, however, that keeping confidentiality is an absolute obligation. It is a prima facie duty, that is, respecting the confidentiality of individuals is considered ethically binding unless it is in conflict with equally strong ethical duties. In the absence of competing ethical obligations, the weight is on keeping material private; however, there are good ethical reasons for breaking confidentiality in some instances. For example, in Case 10-2, the weight of protecting the client from the potential danger of cocaine use, which could not only be life altering but could lead to death, may outweigh keeping material confidential. This is especially true because it is probably the case that the adolescent client's judgment has not fully developed (King & Kitchener, 1994; Kitchener, King, & DeLuca, 2006).

Professional Ethics Codes

In the early years of mental health care, the obligation to maintain patients' confidentiality was unambiguous, with professionals virtually guaranteeing the secrecy of all communications (Fisher, 2008). Today, mental health ethics codes have whole sections devoted to confidentiality, because this bedrock of the helping relationship is now fraught with caveats and conditions. Each professional code, though slightly different the codes of its sister professions, contains two types of standards. The first type of standard provides directives to safeguard the confidential information obtained by clients or research participants, and to disclose such information only with their consent. The second type of standard defines and delimits the first type by addressing the exceptions to confidentiality. For example, the 2002 APA Ethics Code indicated that psychologist had a primary obligation to protect confidential information but also recognized that psychologists might need to disclose confidential information without the consent of the individual for several reasons, including obtaining appropriate professional consultations and protecting the client/patient, psychologist, or others from harm. Similarly, the 2005 ACA Code of Ethics instructed counselors not to share confidential information without client consent; yet like other professional codes it allowed breaking confidentiality in some specific circumstances. In other words, codes of ethics recognize that confidentiality is only prima facie binding.

Because confidentiality is no longer absolute, ethical practice involves informing clients, research participants, and others of its limits. "If confidentiality will be conditional, clients have a right to be informed about the 'conditions' before they consent to confide, regardless of the clinical consequences of that conversation" (Fisher, 2008, p. 3). Professional ethics codes agree that providers of mental health services and conductors of research should explain the exceptions to confidentiality at the outset of the relationship and throughout the professional involvement as warranted by changing circumstances or foreseeable situations in which the confidentiality may be jeopardized. The professional codes do not necessarily agree on just what those circumstances or situations are. For instance, the 2005 ACA Code of Ethics stated that counselors might be justified in disclosing information if a third party is known to be at a high risk as a result of contact with a client who has a contagious, life-threatening disease; the 2002 APA Code contained no such provision. Conversely, the APA allowed for disclosure of information without client consent when necessary to obtain payment for services, while the 2005 ACA Code did not. In general, mental health professionals need to be careful about disclosing confidential information and should always consult their current professional code for guidance. If some disclosure of confidential information is necessary, psychologists and counselors must be diligent about disclosing only relevant and necessary information in all situations, whether to insurance companies, to other health care providers, to police officers, etc. (Fisher, 2003).

Regardless which ethics code is being consulted, the circumstances listed as exceptions to confidentiality are not considered exhaustive. Further, deciding if and when to breach confidentiality may be complicated by legal guidelines, since state and federal laws and court orders are not always consistent with the ethical values of the mental health professions (Knapp, Gottlieb, Berman, & Handelsman, 2007). As outlined in Chapter 4, professionals need to identify legal as well as ethical concerns, which may mean consulting state laws and federal regulations, and then considering if and how the law confirms, or competes with, the professional ethical obligation.

The Law and Confidentiality

Fortunately, laws that regulate the practice of psychotherapy are generally consistent with ethical values, as in the prohibitions against insurance fraud and therapist/client sexual relationships (Knapp et al., 2007). Some laws that impact confidentiality, for example, privilege laws, are also in step with ethical values. However, the gradual erosion of confidentiality as an absolute obligation has occurred largely because of legal demands, many of which may conflict with professional ethical duties. All states place some limits on the confidential relationship; thus, when psychologist or counselors begin to consider ethical issues, decisions will often be influenced by legal requirements. At first blush, a practitioner may assume that the law always trumps ethical standards. Yet where the law and ethics codes collide, there is an opportunity, and even an obligation, to continue deliberate and thoughtful decision making, since being an ethical professional does not necessarily demand unmitigated conformity to the law (Knapp et al., 2007).

The relationship between ethical obligations and legal requirements can be quite complex when confidentiality is considered. For example, a state law may require the divulging of specific confidential information without the client's consent, as in the case of child abuse reporting. In some instances there may be good ethical reasons for not following the law (e.g., when reporting the child abuse would expose the child to greater harm than not doing so). Consider a scenario in which the abuse took place in the past, the perpetrator is not in the home and does not have access to the child, and the client vehemently opposes the disclosure because it is likely to cause some harm to his or her family. There is no imminent danger or even potential for danger. The therapist may face the dilemma of either upholding confidentiality (and thereby violating the state law) or making the report as required by statute (and thereby breaching the client's confidentiality). Laws related to mandatory child abuse reporting—and the similar "duty to protect laws"—will be considered ahead in more detail, under "Difficult Confidentiality Questions in Therapy."

Privileged Communications

Because of their conceptual overlap, the concepts of privilege and confidentiality can easily be confused, but privilege applies only in a legal setting. Psychotherapist–client privilege offers legal protection to the confidential therapeutic relationship by granting mental health professionals a release from revealing information that might be useful in a judicial arena. Whereas generally all available information is fair game in the legal system, such that businesses can be compelled to turn over their accounting records and parents can be ordered to testify against their own children, clients of psychotherapy have a special exception to the truth-seeking task of the court (Donner, 2008). Privilege may be invoked by the mental health professional, but generally it is a protection held by the client, who determines whether to exercise the privilege or waive his or her privilege rights (Smith-Bell & Winslade, 1994). Privilege only extends to information disclosed in a therapeutic relationship; it cannot be evoked to protect research participants or students.

It should be noted that in most circumstances privilege cannot be waived in part. In other words, if a client waives his or her privilege rights, thereby granting the therapist permission to testify in a court of law, all information revealed in the therapeutic relationship is open to discovery. If asked, the therapist cannot hold back information about a specific aspect of the client's life. Furthermore, privilege can be lost if the professional does not raise it as an issue. Consequently, if a therapist is called to testify and is asked questions on the stand regarding confidential information and does not indicate that the information is privileged, clients can lose their privilege rights.

All 50 states and the District of Columbia have statutes recognizing some form of psychotherapist–client privilege, though the scope and details of the privilege protection vary widely (Younggren & Harris, 2008). The majority of states guarantee privilege to professional relationships involving a physician or psychologist and their respective clients; however, fewer states have granted privilege status to relationships involving other psychotherapists (e.g., counselors and social workers) and their clients (Smith-Bell & Winslade, 1994). In most states, privilege can be invoked both in criminal and in civil proceedings, but some states limit the right to civil trials only (Younggren & Harris, 2008). State laws differ somewhat on the requirements for information to be considered privileged, but generally there needs to be a professional relationship between a licensed therapist and the client, the information exchanged must be relevant to diagnosis and treatment, and it must be kept confidential (Smith-Bell & Winslade, 1994; Younggren & Harris, 2008).

Privilege is not an absolute right. In fact, there are seven general legal exceptions to it: (a) when a client's mental condition is raised in a court proceeding, (b) when a legal dispute arises between the therapist and client (e.g., if a client filed a lawsuit against a therapist), (c) when a psychological evaluation is court ordered, (d) when the client presents a danger to self or others, (e) when the client is involuntarily hospitalized, (f) when there is suspected child abuse or neglect, and (g) when a client's competency is at issue (Glosoff, Herlihy, Herlihy, & Spence, 1997). Glossoff et al. (1997) advise therapists to check the statutes and legal exceptions to privilege in the state in which they practice.

Privilege is a significant legal protection for the clients of psychologists and, in some states, counselors and is viewed by many in the mental health field as "an important restraint on litigant and governmental intrusion on the therapeutic process" (Smith-Bell & Winslade, 1994, p. 185). The difficulty is that each case of privilege has often been decided on its own merit; consequently, therapists have never been quite sure whether communication with clients would be protected or not. However, the magnitude of privilege was recognized by U.S. Supreme Court in *Jaffee v. Redmond* (1996), which acknowledged for the first time the importance that trust and confidentiality play in the psychotherapeutic relationship and that privacy is a cornerstone of psychotherapy's effectiveness. At issue in Jaffee was whether conversations between a police officer and her therapist, a social worker, were privileged communications and hence protected from disclosure in a civil proceeding. On the line of duty, the police officer had killed a man. The administrator of the deceased's estate, Carrie Jaffee, alleged that the officer had used excessive force and violated the constitutional rights of her client. Jaffee sought the officer's therapy records, but her therapist refused to disclose information, citing the privilege rule (Lens, 2000). In deciding in favor of the police officer and her therapist, the Supreme Court not only affirmed the importance of confidentiality as a prerequisite to effective therapy, it also acknowledged that privacy in psychotherapy served the good of society (DeBell & Jones, 1997). Additionally, it extended the concept of privilege to confidential information between licensed psychotherapists and their patients, not just to psychologists and psychiatrists (DeBell & Jones, 1997).

Despite the Supreme Court's strong and definitive support of confidentiality evidenced in the Jaffee case, federal courts have since found exceptions to privilege rights, and state statutes have not necessarily fallen in step (Younggren & Harris, 2008). The mere fact is that privilege exists neither assure that courts and their representatives are aware of the right, nor do they accept the limits it imposes. It is, therefore, incumbent on the professional to be versed in the protections that privilege grants, and to exercise the rights to privilege by being informed and informing others. The APA Committee on Legal Issues (2006) proposed at least five strategies for mental health providers who receive subpoenas:

a. Determine whether the request for information is a valid subpoena that carries the force of law, since sometimes demands for information, even from attorneys, are not legally enforceable.

    b. Contact the client and discuss the implications of divulging confidential information, remembering that the client may choose to consent to the release of information.

    c. Negotiate with the requester, asserting psychotherapist–patient privilege if the client does not consent to disclosure of confidential material.

    d. Seek guidance from the court, perhaps writing a letter requesting that the court consider the ethical obligation—and legal protection—to maintain confidentiality.

    e. File a motion to quash the subpoena or a motion for a protective order to prevent or limit disclosure of sensitive information.

Because privilege blocks the introduction of information that might be valuable in a trial, courts are "typically loathe to recognize privileges and quick to find exceptions" (Simon & Shuman, 2007, p. 45). The consequence is that therapists need to remain vigilant about informing their clients of the limits of confidentiality in legal settings and helping them understand how this might affect therapy. The case of rape counselor Jennifer Bier illustrates how a therapist can bring the virtues of integrity, compassion, and responsibility to the issue.

Case 10-4

Bier, a private civilian therapist, provided counseling for Jessica Brakey, an Air Force Academy cadet who had accused a fellow cadet, Joseph Harding, of sexual assault. Preparing for Harding's court-martial, his attorneys subpoenaed the treatment records of his accuser's therapy with Bier, stating that their client's right to a fair trial superseded any right to privacy on the part of Ms Brakey. Bier, upholding her client's privilege, refused to turn over any records, even when she faced a contempt of court warrant, potential arrest, and possible time in jail. "There's really no other ethical or moral way for me to act' Bier said. 'It's really a difficult position. I'm not a disobedient American. I don't take refusal of a subpoena lightly" (Kohler, 2005). Eventually a federal appeals court blocked the military from arresting Bier, but her willingness to stand firm and faithful to the promise of confidentiality in the face of imminent arrest was a remarkable demonstration of ethical virtue.

Difficult Confidentiality Questions in Therapy

On one hand, confidentiality has been described as "a hallmark of the therapeutic relationship, a sine qua non for successful therapy, and the cornerstone of therapeutic trust" (Corcoran & Winslade, 1994, p. 354) because it enables clients to seek help for problems that might incur a stigma if disclosed to others, such as sexual orientation or alcohol or drug abuse problems. The freedom from fear of the consequences of disclosure allows information that is germane to the client's problem to be discussed, and a relationship of trust can form between the client and the therapist. The development of a trusting relationship between client and therapist has been recognized as "the very means by which treatment is effected" (*Tarasoff v. Regents of the University of California*, 1976, minority opinion, p. 359). As already noted, this position has been acknowledged by the Supreme Court in *Jaffee v. Redmond* (1996). Obviously, maintaining confidentiality is extremely for the continuing viability of the mental health profession.

On the other hand, maintaining confidentiality is not an absolute obligation, but one affected by various nuances in mental health codes and laws. As already noted, it is a prima facie duty, that is, it is ethically binding unless it is in conflict with equal or stronger ethical duties (Beauchamp & Childress, 2001). Other things being equal, the weight is on keeping material private. But because there are sometimes good ethical reasons for, and/or laws that mandate, breaking confidentiality, this obligation can come into conflict with other duties or laws. Perhaps these complexities, as well as the all-too-human challenge of keeping secrets, contribute to the problems professionals have in maintaining confidentiality. For despite its status as a primary responsibility, confidentiality is one of the most commonly violated of the ethical obligations. As

Bersoff (2008) stated, "there is probably no ethical duty more misunderstood or honored by its breach rather than by its fulfillment" (p. 159).

Concerns about confidentiality (and/or privileged communication) were rated as both the most frequently encountered and the most problematic ethical dilemmas in one study (Haas, Malouf, & Mayerson, 1986) and were most frequently described when psychologists were asked to identify ethically troubling incidents in another study (Pope & Vetter, 1992). These surveys reveal that practicing mental health professionals often face agonizing moral conflicts regarding when and whether to break confidentiality in service of the client or society. Take, for example, the psychologist who reported he was providing therapy for a woman who had been sexually assaulted but whose story had not been believed by the police. He later discovered he was also treating the man who assaulted her (Pope & Vetter, 1992).

In fact, therapists' anxiety regarding the limits of confidentiality is well placed. The realities of practicing in the modern world, where notes are created and stored electronically, where managed care companies make decisions about the necessity of continued treatment, where clients set appointments and ask questions over their BlackBerrys and iPhones, mean that therapists face multiple decisions weekly about how and whether to protect clients' privacy. For example, therapists who use cell phones to make and receive calls from clients may consider warning clients explicitly that mobile phone conversations and messages can be intercepted. In addition to the growing complexities created by electronic advances, the legally demanded and professionally condoned exceptions to confidentiality are increasing (Gonsiorek, 2008). As a consequence, Bok (1988) suggested that "the prohibition against breaking confidentiality must be especially strong in order to combat the pressures on insiders to do so, especially in view of the ease and frequency with which it is done" (p. 233).

Clients also have difficulty understanding the parameters surrounding confidentiality. Generally, what they want and expect from psychotherapy is a safe, secure, and private relationship where they can talk freely "without fear of repercussion" (Cullari, 2001, p. 104). Most people believe that the information divulged to the therapist will remain confidential and are unaware of many of the real limits (Hillerbrand & Claiborn, 1988; Rubanowitz, 1987). In fact, research on the public's level of knowledge surrounding confidentiality in a therapeutic relationship (Miller & Thelen, 1986) confirmed that the majority of the respondents (69%) expected all information divulged to a mental health professional to be kept confidential. In addition, approximately 74% of the respondents believed there should be no limitations or exceptions for protecting confidentiality and only 20% believed that confidentiality should be broken when there is a danger to self or others. In other words, there is a substantial difference in clients' expectations about the limits of confidentiality and real-world exceptions. These discrepancies confirm how crucial it is for psychologists to carefully explain to clients any and all limits to confidentiality. In fact, Fisher (2008) cautioned that failing to explain the exceptions to confidentiality deprives clients not just of important information, but of the right to consent (or refuse) to therapy within the actual parameters and risks of imposed by confidentiality limitations, and that such failure constitutes "blatant disregard for the client's informed consent rights" (p. 3). As noted in the previous chapter, limits to confidentiality should be included in the therapist's consent form. In addition, conversations about confidentiality should take into account timing (i.e., before clients unwittingly disclose information that may not be protected by confidentiality), honesty, clarity, and repetition (Fisher, 2008).

The Dangerous Client: Tarasoff and Beyond

The best known challenges to therapist–client confidentiality involve the "duty to protect" a third party from a client's threatened violent acts, which arose from *Tarasoff v. Regents of the University of California* (1974, 1976). The case began when Prosenjit Poddar killed a young woman, Tatiana Tarasoff, on October 27, 1969, in Berkeley, California. Two months earlier, Poddar was a voluntary outpatient at a hospital in Berkeley. While hospitalized, Poddar confided to a psychologist, Dr. Lawrence Moore, his intention to kill a young woman when she returned from a summer vacation. Poddar did not identify the intended victim by name, but it was later established that her identity could have been discerned. Dr. Moore both telephoned the campus police and wrote a letter to the chief of the campus police, requesting that they observe Poddar and assess him for possible dangerousness. The campus police detained Poddar and questioned him but later released him as he appeared to be rational and he promised to stay away from Tarasoff. At no time were Tarasoff or her parents warned of Poddar's threats. During this time, Dr. Moore's supervisor asked the campus police to refrain from taking any further action against Poddar, asked that the note written by Dr. Moore be returned, and ordered the note and therapy notes for the case be destroyed (Beauchamp & Childress, 1989; Everstine et al., 1980).

Shortly after Tarasoff returned from her vacation, Poddar killed her. Following her death, Tarasoff's parents filed a lawsuit against the Board of Regents of the University of California, the campus chief of police and four officers, and employees of the hospital. A lower court initially dismissed the suit. This decision was affirmed by the court of appeals. Tarasoff's parents appealed to the California Supreme Court, which rendered two decisions on the case. In *Tarasoff I* (*Tarasoff v. Regents of the University of California*, 1974), the California Supreme Court reversed the decision of the lower courts and ruled that the psychotherapists in the case had a duty to warn Tarasoff of Poddar's threat to kill her. The court held that the duty was justified because of the special relationship that exists between psychotherapists and their patients (Rosenhan, Teitelbaum, Teitelbaum, & Davidson, 1993).

The *Tarasoff I* decision provoked a spirited debate within both the legal and mental health literatures, and the court was petitioned to reconsider it. The California Supreme Court agreed and heard new arguments, which led to the *Tarasoff II* decision (*Tarasoff v. Regents of the University of California*, 1976). In the court's second decision, psychotherapists' duty to warn was upheld but was now defined more broadly in terms of a duty to protect. The Tarasoff family settled the suit out of court, so the case was not pursued to the U.S. Supreme Court. Because this was a California court opinion, states other than California were not legally bound to adjudicate similar cases in the same way, but the *Tarasoff* model has spread across the country. Currently, about half of the states require mental health professionals to warn potential victims against whom clients make credible threats of violence (Starr, 2007).

The 1976 majority ruling of the *Tarasoff* case requires therapists to break their prima facie ethical obligation of upholding confidentiality when the safety of an identifiable victim is involved or to take other reasonable precautions to protect the third party. The majority opinion, written by Justice Tobriner, held that

> When a therapist determines, or pursuant to the standards of his profession should determine, that his patient presents a serious danger of violence to another, he incurs an obligation to use reasonable care to protect the intended victim against such danger. The discharge of this duty may require the therapist to take one or more of various steps, depending upon the nature of the case. Thus it may call for him to warn the intended victim or others likely to apprise the victim of the danger, to notify the police, or to take whatever steps are reasonably necessary under the circumstances. (*Tarasoff v. Regents of the University of California*, 1976, p. 340.)

Thus, the court ruled that the therapist's ethical obligation of confidentiality could be superseded by a competing obligation to a third party when safety concerns were involved. The majority opinion acknowledged the importance of confidentiality in maintaining the therapist–client relationship but concluded that the "protective privilege ends where the public peril begins"

(*Tarasoff v. Regents of the University of California,* 1976, p. 347). Although the professional responsibility implied by this decision is often referred to as the duty to warn, it is better understood as the duty to protect a potential victim, because in *Tarasoff II* the court offered alternatives to warning the victim, such as notifying the police or initiating hospitalization to insure the safety of the third party (Younggren & Harris, 2008).

The dissenting minority court opinion, written by Justice Clark, discussed the potential liabilities of the ruling for the mental health field. Justice Clark wrote that imposing a duty-to-warn obligation on therapists would (a) deter clients from seeking treatment; (b) limit clients' disclosures in session; (c) risk confining clients and restricting their liberty on the basis of threats made by the client; and (d) erode client trust in the therapist (*Tarasoff v. Regents of the University of California,* 1976, p. 359). Justice Clark's perspective has been echoed by others (Donner, 2008; Starr, 2007) who share concerns that the *Tarasoff* decision negatively impacts the therapist–client relationship, and that the confidentiality that animates the relationship is besieged (Gonsiorek, 2008). There is some evidence that these fears have been realized, because some therapists have reported being less willing to probe for dangerousness (Wise, 1978) and because clients' understanding of the limits of confidentiality may influence their willingness to self-disclose serious or extreme behaviors (Mangalmurti, 1994; Nowell & Spruill, 1993).

The majority opinion in the *Tarasoff* case made clear, for the first time, that mental health professionals may have a professional duty to someone other than the client. Although confidentiality is a prima facie obligation, there are some circumstances when there are other ethical responsibilities that supersede it. The court argued that such a condition was "where the public peril begins" (*Tarasoff v. Regents of the University of California,* 1976, p. 347). In other words, people's choices can be limited when they put others at a risk of being harmed. Autonomy cannot be a shield when someone plans violent acts against another innocent person. Furthermore, Bok (1988) argued that no one should expect professionals to keep their promise to guard confidentiality in such circumstances because it would make them partially complicit in the commission of violent acts.

The difficulty with applying the *Tarasoff* ruling is that in many cases deciding whether a client or patient is dangerous is not easy. Angry clients sometimes make implicitly threatening statements about "getting even" or "making others sorry" with no intention of really causing anyone physical harm. The *Tarasoff* model rests on the assumption that mental health professionals can reliably assess risk in the present, and that such assessment can be a valid and reliable predictor of future risk. Some would argue that that assumption is not only imprecise, but "mere fantasy" (Gonsiorek, 2008, p. 374). How, then, might a professional decide when a breach of confidentiality is warranted? Beauchamp and Childress (1994, p. 297) proposed careful consideration of both the probability of harm and the magnitude of harm, such that as each increases, so does the responsibility of the professional to take action.

For example, in the case of a teenage client who has a history of violent acts and who is threatening someone's life, the probability and magnitude of harm are both high; thus, the ethical obligation to breach confidentiality is also high in order to prevent a potentially harmful act from occurring. Conversely, when probability and magnitude are low—as in the case of a client with no history of aggression who says she is having a fantasy of locking her emotionally abusive husband out of house naked in a snowstorm—the therapist's obligation to maintain confidentiality overrides the risk to a third party. This probability and magnitude model takes into account that the prediction of harm cannot be made with absolute accuracy.

Using the risk assessment model, along with accurate information on the risk factors involved with dangerousness, may help ensure that therapists' actions do not fall below the expected standard of care, thereby protecting them from malpractice suits and protecting clients from the over-prediction of dangerousness (Lane & Spruill, 1980). The consensus suggests seeking consultation from a colleague, mentor, or supervisor to help ensure that the therapist is not overlooking important information that might clarify the degree of dangerousness (Lane & Spruill, 1980; Starr, 2007; Younggren & Harris, 2008). In addition to carefully assessing dangerousness and consulting with colleagues, therapists should (a) educate themselves on pertinent state laws, regulations, and standards of practice; (b) carefully document the client's threats and steps taken in response to the threats; and (c) consider alternative interventions, including placing the client in a safe environment, like a locked ward in a hospital (Lane & Spruill, 1980; Younggren & Harris, 2008).

If possible, it is always better to identify interventions that both maintain confidentiality and protect the public from harm. For example, therapists might consider helping the client change environmental stimuli (e.g., turning in weapons to the police or removing themselves from the situation), engaging a social support system (e.g., involving family members in the therapy, especially if they are possible victims), referring the client for medication or a reevaluation of his or her medication, or obtaining permission from the client to contact possible victims (Bersoff, 1995; Starr, 2007). If these do not seem feasible or useful, therapists may need to contact both the police and the potential victim.

What the *Tarasoff* ruling did was raise a compelling ethical issue: whether mental health professionals owe complete loyalty to their clients or whether the competing welfare of society supersedes responsibilities to clients in some cases. Once the *Tarasoff* ruling opened the floodgates, the concept of inviolate confidentiality has been bombarded with a series of related problems, including maintaining confidentiality with suicidal clients, in child abuse cases, and with clients who have life-threatening contagious diseases.

The Suicidal Client

Worldwide, more people die from suicide than from homicide or war (World Health Organization, 2002). About 30,000 people commit suicide each year in the United States (Barlow & Durand, 2009). Most practitioners, at some point during their careers, will have to deal with clients who threaten, attempt, or complete suicide. In fact, a study of psychologists found that the most widespread fear, expressed by over 97% of the practicing therapists sampled, was that a client would commit suicide. About a quarter of all therapists experience at least one client suicide (McAdams & Foster, 2000; Pope & Tabachnick, 1993). Both professionals and trainees find dealing with suicidal clients deeply stressful and completed suicides often cause therapists profound feelings of grief, loss, and depression as well as guilt, inadequacy, self-doubt, and self-blame (Chemtob, Bauer, Hamada, Pelowski, & Muraoka, 1988; Kleespies, Smith, & Becker, 1990).

Despite the identification of important risk factors, predicting suicide is difficult and imprecise (Barlow & Durand, 2009). As a result, practitioners are faced with thorny ethical problems, the most common of which is when and whether to break confidentiality in order to protect clients from taking their own lives. There are several reasons why the ethical concerns about suicide are both more difficult and different from other ethical concerns in therapy. First, in most treatments both the therapist and the client have a common goal—the improvement of the client's life or circumstances. However, the suicidal client and his or her therapist hold opposing goals. The therapist may wish to save the client's life, whereas the client is expressing the wish to eliminate psychological or physical pain via suicidal behavior. Instead of working collaboratively toward the client's desired outcomes for treatment, clinicians may find themselves in an almost adversarial position, needing to actively persuade suicidal clients to change their plans, often through attempting to get the client to sign a no-suicide contract (Rudd, Cukrowicz, & Bryan, 2008).

Second, there may be a fundamental conflict between therapists' values regarding the sanctity of life and the client's view that life is not worth living (Heyd & Bloch, 1981). Because the decision to commit suicide expresses a value that is contrary to the value that most mental health care professionals hold, the decision to commit suicide is value laden. Inexperienced therapists can find themselves entrapped by existential conversations regarding whether life is worth living.

Third, to keep a client from following through on suicidal ideation, therapists may have to take actions that breach the confidentiality of the therapist–client contract and in doing so may damage one of the few relationships that sustains the client's will to live. Taking parental action, and thereby depriving clients of their autonomy can irreparably harm the therapeutic relationship; in other cases when therapists set limits on clients' suicidal gestures, clients sometimes perceive an act of caring that allows them hope for the future. Regardless, the decisions involved are deeply difficult to make.

Fourth, suicidal clients can arouse "like me" issues for therapists by stimulating feelings about the unfairness of life and questions regarding whether they themselves would want to live in similar circumstances (Snipe, 1988). When the therapist is so enmeshed in the client's perspective, the "ability to perceive and evaluate the autonomy of the other is, at best at risk" (Snipe, 1988, p. 133).

Intervening with clients who express suicidal ideation is based on the assumption that suicide is an irrational action and that those who are suicidal are not making a competent autonomous decision. Thus, parentalism in the form of some kind of intervention, such as breaking confidentiality, can be justified on the basis of beneficence. Although there are arguments to the contrary (Szasz, 1971/1990), this assumption is based on the close association between suicide and other mental disorders, especially depression, alcohol abuse, and clinical syndromes that are characterized by impulsivity, such as borderline personality disorder (Barlow & Durand, 2009).

The act of suicide, if it is successful, is an irreversible decision. As Heyd and Bloch (1981) suggested, ethically "it is better to err on the side of preserving life than on the side of letting it be lost" (p. 201). Therefore, it is better to intervene in some way, even if it means breaking confidentiality, so that the client can live to reevaluate the decision at a later point. As one therapist put it when describing her response to a client's suicidal ideology, "My position was that life was a necessary condition to allow her to find new meaning in it" (Snipe, 1988, p. 129).

Competence in working with suicidal clients is critical so that the therapist can effectively screen for suicidal ideation as well as take the steps necessary to prevent ideation from becoming action. Knowing the methods for obtaining and documenting risk assessment information, the warning signs and risk factors of suicide, and the decision rules for safety plans and treatment is essential (Rudd et al., 2008). In addition to interviewing the patient, this may involve checking records of past and current treatment, particularly if the person has been hospitalized, as well as interviewing significant others. Therapists are also encouraged to ask about current protective factors, such as the client's social support system, which can provide clues for managing the suicidality.

Before taking the drastic step of breaking confidentiality to protect the client, it may be possible for the clinician to obtain consent to communicate with the client's family members, friends, partners, or significant others about the crisis and plans to promote safety and treatment adherence (Bryan, Corso, Neal-Walden, & Rudd, 2009). And with a caring and collaborative approach by the therapist, suicidal clients who cannot commit to a safety plan or whose intentions pose too great of a risk may be convinced to admit themselves into a hospital voluntarily, thus preserving both their autonomy and their outpatient treatment information. Good resources are available on this topic, and practitioners should be aware of them (see the appendix of Rudd et al.'s 2008 article for a reading list on assessment and management of suicide risk).

Reporting Suspected Child Abuse and/or Neglect

In 2007, an estimated 3.2 million child abuse reports, involving the alleged maltreatment of approximately 5.8 million children, were made to child protective service agencies. More than half of these reports were made by professionals (U.S. Department of Health & Human Services, 2009). In the 25 years since reporting laws have been in effect across the country, referrals to child protective services have continued to rise (Renninger, Veach, & Bagdade, 2002). As disturbing as these statistics are, incidence studies estimate that reported cases represent only 40% of all abuse and neglect cases (Kalichman, 1993).

Every state has legislation requiring that certain professionals, such as doctors, teachers, and mental health professionals, report cases of suspected child abuse to authorities for investigation (Koocher & Keith-Spiegel, 1990). State mandatory reporting laws differ, but they all incorporate elements that specify who must report, reportable circumstances, age limits of reportable children, the level of certainty for mandated reporters, sanctions for not reporting, and immunity from prosecution for reporting (U.S. Department of Health & Human Services, 2009; Small, Lyons, & Guy, 2002). The state laws show more variability in definitions of abuse and the circumstances in which reporting abuse is required (Kalichman, 1993). Typically, most states will include physical abuse, sexual abuse, neglect, and emotional maltreatment as circumstances professionals are required to report (Kalichman, 1993). Most child abuse laws require a quick response from the mental health professional—within a day or two of learning about the abuse—and professionals who fail to file reports may be subject to criminal prosecution (Swenson, 1997).

These laws reflect a governmental philosophy that essentially places protecting the welfare of children who have been or are at risk above protecting the confidentiality of clients (Younggren & Harris, 2008). While most rational individuals would agree that keeping children safe from abuse is a vital task that often requires public intervention, the obligation to report is not a simple one. Kalichman (1993) viewed reporting child abuse as a "special case of duty to warn" (p. 47) as it involves the prevention of harm, constrains the boundaries of confidentiality, and operates within the legal constraints that govern professional duties. Research on compliance rates of clinicians in breaking client confidentiality and reporting suspected child abuse have consistently found, however, that approximately one third of professionals fail to report a case of suspected abuse—even though they were aware of mandatory reporting laws (Kalichman, 1993; Nicolai & Scott, 1994). Studies have found that some mental health providers fear that reporting suspected abuse will negatively impact the progress of therapy, destabilize the family, necessitate unwanted engagement with an overwhelmed child welfare system, and lead to other disruptive outcomes (Koocher, 2008). Some clinicians choose not to report due to a belief that child protective service agencies are ineffective and nonresponsive (Crenshaw, Lichtenberg, & Bartell, 1993). Despite these reasons for failing to report individual cases, a majority of mental health providers believe that mandatory reporting laws are both adequate and necessary (Crenshaw et al., 1993; Renninger et al., 2002).

Still, it could be argued that in some cases mandated reporting does more harm than good. Undoubtedly many children have been spared ongoing abuse and neglect as a result of mandatory child abuse reporting, but might mandatory reporting laws also exact a cost, not just to the individual therapist who wrestles with the conflict, but to society as a whole? According to Gonsiorek (2008), the costs of mandatory reporting include "depleting resources in health care, compromising informed consent, demoralizing professionals, and weakening that core patient–professional relationship" (p. 375). Further, because state laws often require reports not just of current danger but of past child abuse, mental health professionals may find themselves sacrificing confidentiality in service of investigations into events long since over.

Ignoring for the moment the legal mandate to report and considering just the ethical perspective, reporting or not reporting suspected child abuse would involve a careful weighing of the ethical principles involved: autonomy, nonmaleficence, and beneficence. Does the client's right to not have his or her actions controlled by others (autonomy) outweigh the ethical obligation to either remove harm (nonmaleficence) or benefit another (beneficence)? Child abuse is often identified as a relatively clear example of when confidentiality can be breached because of competing moral and legal obligations. Children are not in a position to choose or not to choose to be abused because they are often physically weaker than their abuser. Additionally, abuse often puts them at grave physical and/or emotional risk, including the risk of death. The assumption is that reporting will protect the child from harm.

Kalichman (1993) discussed the need for therapists to formulate a minimum "reporting threshold" (p. 64) because the indicators of child abuse are not always clear. For example, if a child is bruised, it would suggest a higher probability of abuse than if he or she vaguely reported being hurt. The reporting threshold combines physical indicators of possible abuse, such as bruises, with verbal reports of suspected abuse. Mental health providers consider both the probability of harm and the magnitude of harm in their decision making. In addition, deliberating on whether or not to report child abuse includes weighing the risks (e.g., erosion of trust in therapy, dissolution of the therapeutic relationship altogether) of reporting a suspected abuse case that turns out to be false versus the risks (e.g., continued harm to the child) of failing to report a case when abuse has actually occurred. As the level of suspicion increases and as the potential costs of inaction increase, so does the obligation to report.

While there may be some child abuse-related disclosures that fail to reach the reporting threshold, this does not mean that clinicians are ethically or legally excused from reporting if they have good reason to believe child abuse has occurred. To fail to report could have dire consequences for the child, not to mention legal risks for the mental health professional. On the other hand, the clearly beneficent intentions of child abuse laws do not always have entirely positive outcomes. Take Case 10-5 as an example.

Case 10-5

Mr and Mrs Ben brought their daughter Kerry, aged 13 years, and son Tom, aged 16 years, in for family counseling because they had been "playing doctor" and their daughter was upset about it. Kerry had told her mother that Tom came into her bedroom at night and sometimes touched her "down there." He told her he was just "checking her out like a doctor to make sure she was growing right." Although Kerry did not initially resist, when Tom put his finger in her vagina she got scared and told him to stop. After that incident, she told her mother that she did not want Tom to come into her bedroom again. Tom, who was embarrassed by the incident, said he had not meant to hurt his sister but that he was just "fooling around."

After hearing the family's report, the therapist reminded the Ben family of the consent form they had signed and indicated he was obligated to report the incident to child protective services. At that point the entire family begged him not to do so. They pointed out that they were living in a small town and were known by everyone. Mr Ben was in a position of power and authority, which might be undermined if this information came out. Furthermore, because they were one of the few African-American families in town, he was afraid that disclosure of the incident would exacerbate stereotypes of African Americans and prejudice against his family. They said that the local department of social services was known to leak information into the community and one of Mrs Ben's best friends worked there. They argued that they were taking action to make sure that nothing like this happened again and that if the information got out the whole family would be ruined.

Incidents like those in Case 10-5 makes clear that reporting may have both positive and negative effects. On one hand, the Bens' rights to privacy may be violated in order to protect

Kerry from further sexual abuse, and this may lead to negative consequences for the whole family. On the other hand, although no one denied that sexual contact occurred, the family was minimizing it by calling it "playing doctor." Kerry needed further protection, particularly until it became clear whether she was safe from Tom, and Mr and Mrs Ben could and would adequately protect her. Furthermore, if the counselor did not report, he could be seen as colluding with the family to minimize the importance of the sexual contact.

Psychotherapists could feel comfortable that they met their legal responsibility and the moral minimum if they filed an abuse report. But therapists who are respectful and caring would attempt to minimize the harm that might occur if the Bens' privacy was violated. For example, they might first contact social services anonymously to verify that the agency would consider this a reportable case. Because Tom was a minor, depending on state law, his actions might not be considered child abuse. Because the parents had failed to adequately protect Kerry, however, their failure might be seen as child neglect. Second, if it was considered abuse or neglect, the counselor might contact the director of the agency to emphasize the importance of privacy in this case and the need to avoid allowing Mrs Ben's close friend access to the file. If not satisfied with these options or with the agency's responsiveness, they could go to a family court judge and ask for a special order, backed by legal sanctions, that required privacy in the treatment of the case or ask for the appointment of a special child advocate to oversee the case (Shoeman, 1983).

If a therapy or assessment client has been informed of the limits to confidentiality and still divulges information that leads the therapist to suspect child abuse, what steps should the therapist take? Stadler (1989) proposed a decision tree that offers four possible options to consider in these situations. First, the clinician should again inform the client of the mandatory reporting obligation and then integrate this with Option 1: the client makes the report him or herself from the clinician's office, with the clinician verifying the information to the service agency. This option is most respectful of the client's autonomy. The remaining three options decrease the amount of control the client has over how the information is divulged and increase the therapist's control. Although clients may not initially choose Option 1, once they hear the remaining options, it becomes the option many prefer. If the client declines to call, he or she is offered Option 2, which involves the clinician reporting the abuse while the client listens. If the client is not comfortable with this option, Option 3 is described, which is the clinician offers to report the abuse from another room while the client waits. If the client refuses any of the first three options, the clinician is forced to initiate Option 4, which involves the clinician reporting the abuse after the session without any involvement from the client and possibly without the client's permission. This last option clearly overrides the client's autonomy and places the ethical obligation of removing harm (nonmaleficence) as prima facie (Stadler, 1989). Engaging in Options 1 through 3 allows for the resumption of the therapy or testing session once the report has been made and the opportunity to "explore issues that have arisen in the reporting process" (Stadler, 1989, p. 108). If therapists anticipate that clients may become violent during the session if abuse is reported, Option 4—in which the clinician reports without warning the client in advance—should be strongly considered. The protection of the clinician's safety supersedes the autonomy of the client, and notification of the report to the client can take place at a future session when the safety of the therapist has been secured (Stadler, 1989). Regardless which of these options is selected, there are times, as Case 10-5 illustrates, when therapists should play a more active role in the reporting process to help avoid some of the negative consequences that reporting might cause.

Confidentiality with Children and Adolescents

Even when abuse and neglect do not present reporting issues, there are special ethical considerations that emerge when working with children and adolescents. When treating adult clients, the promise of confidentiality and disclosure of its limits, are closely linked to the informed consent process. Yet children and adolescents are typically not consenting to treatment in the same autonomous way that adults do. In addition, children and adolescents are generally not independent consumers of services; even if they receive individual counseling, it is often at the insistence—or at least the agreement—of adults who may transport them to sessions, pay for services, and have involvement and interest in the outcome.

Chapter 9 outlined the importance of the therapist assessing minor clients for their cognitive capacity to consent to therapy. If the client is an adolescent and the therapist determines he or she is capable, legally and cognitively, of giving consent for treatment, then the therapist needs to carefully consider the confidentiality implications. Law, rules, and practices for confidentiality with consenting adolescents vary widely by state, and even by institutional policy. Under the Health Insurance Portability and Accountability Act of 1996 (HIPAA), however, parents have the legal authority to access their child's records (Koocher, 2008). In some cases parents will agree to waive their legal right to the information that emerges in treatment, so that their son or daughter can establish a trusting and productive relationship with the therapist (Bennett et al., 2006). Even in these situations, therapists and parents of adolescent clients need to discuss in advance what type of treatment information will and will not be shared.

Naturally, the ordinary limits of confidentiality (e.g., imminent danger to others) apply to adolescent clients, but for many and perhaps most therapists, those exceptions alone do not cover a wide enough array of circumstances to assure that the clinician can provide beneficent and nonmaleficent care. At a developmental stage characterized by risk-taking behavior, adolescents may reveal, in therapy, experiences with drugs and alcohol, sexual encounters, internet "hook-ups," criminal involvement, self-mutilation, peer conflicts, and a host of other activities that can jeopardize their well-being (consider Case 10-2 at the start of this chapter). At what point does the therapist decide that such information can no longer be kept confidential because the risks are too great?

Although there is no precise answer to that question, researchers like Sullivan, Ramirez, Rae, Razo, and George (2002) have found that as the frequency, intensity, and severity of risk-taking behavior increases, the likelihood that therapists will find it ethical to break confidentiality likewise increases. So while there is variability in the extent to which therapists will tolerate risky and dangerous behaviors from their adolescent clients, as those behaviors increase or become more profoundly unsafe, therapists may place the safety of the client above the maintenance of his or her privacy (Sullivan et al., 2002). As with any potential breach of confidentiality, it is extremely helpful for therapists to be aware of their own risky-behavior thresholds at the outset, so that they can clearly delineate with the client and the client's parents what sorts of situations would warrant disclosure. Giving examples (e.g., "If Jack told me that he was smoking cigarettes, I would not feel the need to violate his confidentiality. However, if Jack were to tell me that he was shooting up heroin that is something I could no longer keep secret.") can help clarify for the client and the family what the parameters of the therapeutic relationship are.

If the threshold of risk is crossed and the therapist determines that the adolescent's behavior cannot be kept confidential, there are alternatives to breaching confidentiality to notify the parents. As with mandated reporting of child abuse, allowing the client to retain as much of his or her autonomy as possible is often the most ethical of actions. This means that adolescents themselves can be encouraged to inform their parents, in the presence of the therapist, of the dangerous behavior, or the therapist can inform the parents in the presence of the adolescent (Sullivan et al., 2002). Because these options are more transparent than the after-session private disclosure to the parents, taking such steps may help to preserve the therapeutic relationship and prevent feelings of betrayal and mistrust by the adolescent.

This process can be referred to as "informed, forced consent," and can apply to treatment with both adolescents and smaller children (Glenn, 1980; Ross, 1958). When the therapist determines that information must be shared, the minor client is told what specific information will be disclosed to parents and is allowed to voice objections, though not to overrule the disclosure. Hence, the child is being informed, but is not providing consent. Although this may seem inconsistent with principles of fidelity and autonomy, it may be the most ethical position to take (Hendrix, 1991). Therapists should not make a promise of confidentiality that they may not be able to keep (fidelity) and should disclose information only if it will advance the client's therapy (beneficence). The minor client should always be told what will be disclosed and should be given a chance to state any objections (autonomy), and the therapist should take the client's reactions into account, revise the disclosure plan if necessary, and try to minimize any unforeseen difficulties (nonmaleficence). The informed, forced consent policy also recognizes the different decision-making abilities of minors and adults and that they are not treated as equals (justice). In addition, because this approach allows for a dialogue, the therapist may be able to help the child talk directly with his or her parents about the issue, thus respecting the child's limited autonomy as well as maintaining confidentiality.

Regardless the age of minor clients, pretreatment family meetings can be invaluable (Gustafson & McNamara, 1987; Koocher, 2008; Sullivan et al., 2002). At the meeting, the therapist should inform both the minor client and the client's parents of confidentiality limits, the rationale for those limits, and the implications for all parties. Including the limits of confidentiality on the consent form or other written agreement, to be signed by both the client and his or her parents, can also prevent misunderstandings further down the road (Gustafson & McNamara, 1987; Sullivan et al., 2002). It is also critical that therapists consider any relevant statutes concerning confidentiality with minors to ensure that their adopted policy is consistent with legal requirements. Balancing legal constraints and ethical obligations toward minor client and their parents is complex and requires forethought, but, with intentionality and frank discussion, therapists can achieve not only ethical, but virtuous confidentiality practices.

Confidentiality in Family Therapy

Although confidentiality issues are generally complex, they are particularly so when a therapist is working with multiple clients, such as in family therapy, where each client brings his or her own secrets and fears into therapy. One could even think of family and couples work as "forced multiple relationships" (Koocher, 2008, p. 606; see also Chapter 11). In addition, the legal parameters in family and couple therapy are often different. For example, in some states, privileged communication may not extend to information disclosed in a family session (Margolin, 1982). Furthermore, problems arise when one family member enters into court proceedings and wants to release information from family therapy without the consent of other family members. Finally, multiple clients have no duty of confidentiality to each other, and therapists can do little to prevent them from bringing up sensitive issues with each other or with uninvolved parties outside of the treatment (Knapp & VandeCreek, 2006).

Probably the most important question that therapists working with families and couples must ask is to what extent should information shared by different family members remain confidential from other members who are also in therapy? Most therapists do not engage in couples therapy for long before one member of the pair reveals information to the therapist regarding an extramarital affair or other incident that he or she fears sharing with his or her partner. The therapist is then in a position of having to decide what to do with the information.

Generally, the literature on confidentiality in couples and family counseling allows for different approaches, and therapists disagree about which approach is best (Fisher, 2009). One approach maintains that therapists treat information from each family member with the same commitment to confidentiality that the person would be afforded in individual treatment. From this perspective, the therapist would not reveal any information to the partner or other family members, but might work with the client to help him or her disclose important information in the conjoint sessions. A second position argues that the therapist should keep no secrets that might jeopardize the familial relationships, and that anything confided to the therapist individually should be shared with other family members, at least when those members are adults (Stratton & Smith, 2006). In either case, all participants need to understand the parameters of confidentiality prior to beginning treatment so that they can make decisions about what information to share and what not to disclose.

Karpel (1980) advocated a third position that is intermediate between keeping all confidences and not keeping any secrets, thereby placing the responsibility on the therapist for deciding what information is to be shared with other family members and what is not. Karpel distinguished between private information and secret information on the basis of how relevant the information is to the current issue with which the couple or family is dealing. For an example of private information, Huber (1994) described a traumatic episode that occurred during childhood that is now reasonably resolved and that is not affecting the problem on which the family is currently working. The therapist would not be compelled to reveal this kind of information. On the other hand, information about a current extramarital affair would be considered a secret because it violates current trust and is dishonest. Consequently, Karpel advocated a kind of confidentiality with discretion, meaning that some secrets are shared but that the therapist remains respectful of private information and does not insist on it being shared it if it is not relevant to the problems on which the couple or family are working.

However, there are potential ethical problems with each of these positions, some more than others. The position of keeping all secrets and working with family members to reveal them clearly respects the individual autonomy of each family member. On one hand, therapists taking this position might get information that would allow a better understanding of the family as a whole. As Margolin (1982) pointed out, however, therapists are limited in their options about what to do with the information unless the family member is willing to reveal it, thus, it may or may not benefit the family. In addition, should the information come out unexpectedly and other family members discover that the therapist has had knowledge of it, the trustworthiness of the therapist can be undermined and the inadvertent disclosures may exacerbate trust problems that already existed in the family (Margolin, 1982). Further, this position places a burden on the therapist of remembering what is secret and what is not. Revealing information that was disclosed in confidence by mistake because the therapist forgot that it had not been jointly shared would violate the autonomy and trust of the individual who shared the information and could harm the family. Consequently, in most cases the risks would outweigh the ethical benefits of this stance.

The policy of keeping no secrets also has some risks and benefits. On the risk side, the therapist may not become privy to important information that is keeping the couple or family at an impasse. Extramarital affairs, financial crises, secret adoptions, bisexuality, and so on could be very difficult for individuals to reveal but could also be the problems that are keeping the relationship dysfunctional. On the other hand, if clients know that no secrets will be kept, they are able to make the decision from the beginning about what they will share with the therapist and what they will keep private. If the information is disclosed, even if it is done so individually with the therapist, they know that it will be jointly discussed. Although this position does risk leading to relationship crises, it also is honest and provides the foundation and modeling for trustworthy relationships. Further, the therapist need not worry about unwittingly revealing information that was given with an understanding that it would remain confidential. In addition, some of the risks can be minimized if the therapist discusses, in an initial session, the problems with not sharing critical information openly. The therapist can offer, up front, to help the various parties identify ways to disclose information that may be contributing to intrafamilial conflict or distress. Ethically, the position of keeping no secrets has the clearest boundaries and is probably the safest, particularly for the beginning therapist.

The third position, using clinical discretion about sharing secrets but not necessarily private information, requires that therapists be clinically astute and very clear with their clients ahead of time. They would have to indicate that any information that is provided individually may be shared with the rest of the family and will be shared if the therapist believes that it is relevant to the problems on which the family or couple is working. Further, therapists need to be clear with clients ahead of time that they should never give the therapist information with the expectation that it will be kept private. This position respects the autonomy of all members, and it allows the therapist to make decisions not to use information that could harm an individual client, or at least cause him or her pain, if the relationship or family unit will not benefit from it in any way. Additionally, it does not trap therapists into promising secrecy about information that they then may inadvertently reveal. Figure 10.1 provides an example of a consent form for couples that clarify confidentiality with multiple clients. This consent form is used in conjunction with a disclosure statement that spells out other aspects necessary for full consent.

Agreement & Policies for Therapy with Couples

When working with the two of you as a couple, I view each of you *and your relationship* as my clients. In order to maintain fidelity to both of you and to the relationship you have together, I ask you to agree to the following policies:

1) *Any information conveyed to me by either of you may be shared by me with the other member of the couple.* At times, there arise instances where one partner in a couple wants to tell me something without the other knowing about it. Please do not expect me to keep secrets where doing so jeopardizes the therapeutic work or my relationships with either of you individually or with you as a couple. Be aware that information you choose to share with me that is pertinent to both of you may come out in therapy. This pertains to all verbal, written, and telephone communications.

2) If I meet with one or both of you in individual sessions, we will likely share the contents of that meeting with your partner in the next couples session.

3) *All information revealed to me by each of you shall be considered strictly confidential and I will not reveal it to any other person without the mutual consent of both of you,* except in the case of legal exceptions to confidentiality (threat of serious harm to self or others, as in the case of child abuse, suicide, or grave disability). Furthermore, each of you waives the right to subpoena me or my records for testimony. This further supports my fidelity to both of you and to your relationship, and discourages my taking either side in a legal dispute.

4) *Continued participation in therapy by each person is voluntary.* Either participant may suspend or terminate the therapy at her or his individual request.

I have read the above statement and agree to abide by the policies.

Client signatures   Date

_____   _____

_____   _____

Figure 10.1 Agreement and policies for couple's therapy. (Thanks to Timothy Patrick Dea, PhD, for the basic format of this consent form.)

The third position is particularly defensible when working with a family unit. There may be concerns that the parents need to work on that would strengthen their relationship, but knowledge of these concerns would not benefit and might harm their children (Koocher, 1995; Margolin, 1982). Parents need to establish their own boundaries as well as to have some privacy. Further, some information may be developmentally inappropriate for children to understand or too frightening or provocative for them to handle (Koocher, 1995; Margolin, 1980). Similarly, children may need to have some boundaries from their parents. It needs to be stressed, however, that if a therapist takes this position, the boundaries of confidentiality need to be worked out with all members of the family present and the therapist needs to be clear that he or she is the final arbiter. Taking this position and doing it well would probably require that the therapist exhibit some of the virtues (e.g., integrity, responsibility, respect, and caring) that were discussed in Chapter 5.

The most indefensible position for a therapist is to not have clarified with couples or family members the parameters of confidentiality ahead of time, including what would happen if one person wants information about treatment released and the other does not. Such a position is disrespectful of autonomy, undermines fidelity, and can damage both the individuals and the family system. We've provided a sample Consent form for Couples (Figure 10.1).

A related concern involves confidentiality questions related to caregivers of adult family members who have mental illness, who suffer from dementia, or who are otherwise impaired in some way. In these cases, families may assume that they have the right to information about their relative's mental health treatment, even without that person's permission (O'Leary & Barry, 2005). On the other hand, although clients with limited competence have the right to a confidential relationship, it is often not in the best interests of the client and certainly difficult for family members if they have no knowledge of or involvement in the treatment process (Marsh, 1995). An impermeable barrier of confidentiality is seldom helpful for the client or the family (Zipple, Langle, Spaniol, & Fisher, 1990). The question in these situations becomes how to respect the clients' already limited autonomy without putting an undue burden on the family that is caring for them.

Careful forethought by therapists can avoid some of these problems if the client, when lucid, is asked for a release of information so that the therapist can contact family members and the client is helped to understand that this will be done to enhance treatment outcome (Marsh, 1995). Thus, clients can be engaged in a dialogue upon entering treatment about what information will be shared with family members and how it will be shared. Furthermore, as Marsh suggested confidentiality does not, in most cases, preclude practitioners from listening to the concerns of family members or giving family members general information about the mental illness involved in the case, the typical course of treatment, and usual outcomes.

Reporting Past Crimes

Sometimes mental health professionals assume that because there may be a legal and ethical responsibility to protect potential victims of violent acts there is also a responsibility to report past crimes. Take the following case as an example:

Case 10-6

A practicum student called her campus practicum instructor asking for advice. A current client reported robbing a gas station at gunpoint 2 years earlier. He had never been caught for his crime and felt guilty. He said that no one was hurt in the robbery and at that point in his life he was desperate for cash. He had not committed a crime since then and believed he had turned his life around. When the student talked with her on-site supervisor, the supervisor said she had to report the client because he had committed a felony.

The on-site supervisor was wrong in the state where the case took place, and would have been wrong in most other states. If counselors had to report all crimes about which they had knowledge, the idea of confidentiality would be lost, and psychotherapists could end up as little more than police informants. Most courts have respected the importance of therapist–client confidentiality and restricted the responsibility resulting from the *Tarasoff* decision to serious threats of violence. Those threats must be imminent. Ethically, because of the fiduciary relationships, therapists' primary responsibility is to the client, and for the reasons discussed earlier, both the probability of harm and the magnitude of harm have to be high to violate the relationship. Unless there is reason to believe that breaking confidentiality might protect others in the future, there would be little reason to report the client in Case 10-6 except to have him punished.

Although Case 10-6 is fairly clear-cut, sometimes ethical and legal responsibilities are more difficult to decipher. Take Case 10-7 as an example.

Case 10-7

A therapist had been working on anger management with Mary for two months. Mary reported that she had been more successful recently in controlling her verbal outbursts when she was upset and that she felt less angry. In the process of discussing her success, she also indicated she did not feel like setting fires any more. As the therapist explored the last statement, Mary admitted setting a fire in the ladies room at work as recently as two weeks after therapy started. She said she set the fire in a trash container hoping her boss would find it and have to clean up the mess. She indicated she did not believe the fire was dangerous, nor had she done anything like that previously. She did admit, however, that she liked playing with matches as a child and that once while playing with matches, she had set a bush on fire in her parents' yard.

In Case 10-7, the issue is not that Mary may have committed a crime in the past but whether her behavior suggests that she poses a threat of serious physical violence to those at her workplace in the future. Courts have held psychotherapists to a higher standard of accuracy in predicting dangerousness than the layperson (Gonsiorek, 2008). Consequently, a therapist working with a client like Mary would have a responsibility to assess, as accurately as possible, the probability that Mary would commit a violent act in the future and the probability that Mary intended to physically harm her boss or others. An explicit threat would have to be taken very seriously under these circumstances. In addition, on the basis of the principle of beneficence, Mary's use of fire as an outlet for her anger would need to be explored and her failure to acknowledge the physical danger in which she placed her coworkers confronted.

Is There a Duty to Protect Partners of Clients with HIV?

The HIV/AIDS epidemic has raised for therapists a series of new ethical dilemmas, some of which are related to the duty to protect. Because HIV/AIDS is a communicable disease with potentially deadly consequences and known means of transmission, clinicians treating clients with HIV/AIDS may face difficult decisions about whether to breach confidentiality to protect third parties from exposure. Clients with HIV who engage in unsafe sexual practices (as in the case of Jerry in Chapter 4) or IV drug use may be considered, on some level, "dangerous," hence creating potential ethical dilemmas for clinicians who are knowledgeable about their clients' sexual or drug use behavior (Chenneville, 2000). Yet divulging information about clients' HIV status can have immensely damaging consequences, since people with HIV/AIDS risk discrimination and social rejection, lifestyle exposure (e.g., sexual orientation and drug use), and disruption of existing relationships if their health status becomes known (Chenneville, 2000). Data suggest that AIDS patients are stigmatized by a broad cross-section of the public, including health professionals (Katz et al., 1987), and that these attitudes are generally related to homophobia (Crawford, Humfleet, Ribordy, Ho, & Vickers, 1991; Royse & Birge, 1987).

Consequently, maintaining confidentiality, particularly about clients' HIV status, is of utmost importance. But because *Tarasoff*-like concerns have been raised regarding whether therapists have a duty to protect the sexual or needle partners of clients by disclosing clients' HIV status, there is no other AIDS-related ethical or legal issue that has raised as much concern or has generated as much dialogue among mental health providers (Stevenson & Kitchener, 2001). Considerable debate has surrounded the question of whether a duty to protect applies in AIDS-related cases (Appelbaum & Appelbaum, 1990; Appelbaum, 1988; Grey & Harding, 1988; Knapp & VandeCreek, 1990; Kozlowski, Rupert, & Crawford, 1998; Melton, 1988; Reamer, 1991; Totten, Lamb, & Reeder, 1990). Authors have come to different conclusions regarding whether the courts would decide that the circumstances are similar enough that the criteria established in the *Tarasoff* case would apply. In fact, because there has been no legal opinion regarding the issue, what exists is pure speculation (Stevenson & Kitchener, 2001). State statutes differ in their interpretations of *Tarasoff*-type cases, even when the assessment of potential danger may be clearer than it is with AIDS clients (Greenberg, 1992; Lake, 1995). California therapists are bound by the *Tarasoff* decision to consider breaking confidentiality when there is an identifiable victim; however, California has also passed legislation that makes it illegal to disclose HIV test results without written consent (except for very specific exceptions involving health care employees; California Health and Safety Code [Section 121010], 1996; Morrison, 1989). Even though the application of the *Tarasoff* decision to HIV-related cases is speculative, the discussions surrounding its applicability ought to alert therapists to some of the relevant ethical and legal concerns involved. These concerns are briefly outlined in the following paragraphs.

Several criteria that the courts used in the *Tarasoff* case have been considered in relation to generalizing the duty to protect to HIV-related cases: the existence of a special relationship, the foreseeability of harm, and the identifiability of the victim (Chenneville, 2000). The criterion that seems most clear-cut is the existence of a special relationship. As with the *Tarasoff* case, a special relationship exists between a therapist and a client that extends the therapist's responsibility beyond the client to those who could foreseeably be harmed by the client. By this line of reasoning, a duty of care to third parties exists (*Tarasoff v. Regents of the University of California*, 1976).

The second criterion, foreseeability of harm, which was also considered critical in the *Tarasoff* case, is the most controversial aspect of the duty to protect in HIV cases. In these cases, dangerousness is related to several factors, including whether the client engages in high-risk behaviors like anal intercourse, shares needles with other intravenous drug users, or uses safer sex practices. The client's medical diagnosis is also relevant (Stevenson & Kitchener, 2001). Melton (1988) concluded that the foreseeability of harm is substantially greater with an armed client than when an HIV-infected person has unprotected sex. He noted that the latter "often results in no harm to the partner because of the biological variability involved in becoming infected by the AIDS virus, but the harm from being the target of a gunshot is virtually certain" (p. 942). Anal or vaginal intercourse without condom protection increases the probability of harm to a third party and may reach a level that warrants breaking confidentiality (Melton, 1988). On the other hand, other sexual practices like mutual masturbation may not. To determine the specifics of the client's sexual behavior may mean violating the client's privacy; even in the context of the therapeutic relationship, counselors must show respect for personal privacy and "solicit private information from clients only when it is beneficial to the counseling process" (American Counseling Association, 2005, p. 7).

The role of mental health professionals in predicting harm is complicated by the fact that AIDS is a medical disease, not a psychological one, which may explain why what limited HIV-notification laws that do exist apply almost exclusively to physicians (Burris, 2001). Because diagnosis and treatment are dependent on medical expertise, therapists' competence to predict harm is limited (Kain, 1988; Lamb, Clark, Drumheller, Frizzell, & Surrey, 1989). If the client's health status has been diagnosed by a physician and is known by the mental health professional, then assessing danger to third parties would need to focus on the specific behaviors in which the client is engaging and their potential for harming a third party. Again, this task may extend beyond the boundaries of the client's privacy and beyond the boundaries of the therapist's competence.

This issue is made more complex by the finding that homophobia has emerged as a significant predictor of counselors' willingness to break confidentiality (McGuire, Nieri, Abbot, Sheridan, & Fisher, 1995). Mental health providers are more likely to break confidentiality when they perceive dangerousness with some groups (homosexuals and prostitutes with HIV) than with others (bisexuals and intravenous drug users with HIV). These findings suggest that attitudes toward gay, lesbian, or bisexual clients may bias some clinicians' predictions of harm. By implication, therapists working with HIV-infected clients have a strong ethical obligation to closely examine their attitudes toward gay, lesbian, and bisexual individuals to avoid over-predicting harm. A therapist who keeps up on the latest available information regarding transmission of the AIDS virus and high-risk behaviors would exemplify a professional who goes beyond complying with ethical codes and actually engages in virtuous behavior.

The third criterion that some have suggested that needs to be considered is the identifiability of the victim. Here, both sexual and needle partners would need to be considered. Some authors (Appelbaum & Appelbaum, 1990; Lamb et al., 1989) suggest that notification, if necessary, should be limited to individuals who are at risk because of current behavior. On the other hand, some (Kain, 1988) have argued that victims in HIV-related cases are substantially different than victims of violence. Both adult sexual and needle partners are, for the most part, willing and often knowledgeable participants. They may not know that their particular partner is infected, but if they are engaging in high-risk behavior, they probably know that those behaviors bring a high risk of contracting HIV. In these cases, it can be argued that they are making an autonomous decision to participate. On the other hand, if the partner is not an adult, is mentally incompetent or under the influence of drugs, or has no reason to suspect that his or her partner engages in risky behavior (as in a long-term relationship), this may not be the case (Appelbaum & Appelbaum, 1990).

Melton (1988) argued that therapists should also weigh the cost to society when considering breaches of confidentiality with clients who have AIDS/HIV. Potential negative consequences for the client if disclosure is made can range from social stigma to criminal penalties. In addition, breaches of confidentiality strain the already tenuous relationships between mental health professionals and those groups most impacted by AIDS. The strained relationships can lead to increased distrust of the profession and could deter potential clients from seeking much-needed mental health services.

As discussed earlier, when considering whether to breach confidentiality with clients who are dangerous, therapists should consider both the magnitude and probability of harm. Similar criteria can be applied with HIV/AIDS cases. For example, although the magnitude of harm from contracting HIV is high, assessing the probability of harm requires prudent judgment. As noted earlier, the best alternative is often somewhere between breaching confidentiality and remaining silent. Appropriate therapeutic interventions with clients should be tried first (Chenneville, 2000; Stevenson & Kitchener, 2001). The interventions can be educative about the nature of the disease and supportive as the client faces fear of abandonment. Treatment can be directed at improving problem-solving skills as the client considers the consequences of not informing partners. Educative efforts in the community can also help protect anonymous partners. On the other hand, if a therapist decides that confidentiality must be broken without the client's permission, respect requires that the client be informed of the decision prior to the disclosure (Cohen, 1990; Erikson, 1993). Further, disclosures should be made only to the parties directly endangered and be as limited as possible. In other words, it should only include information regarding the person's diagnosis. A caring therapist would also want to provide the partner with information regarding where he or she could get support to deal with the information.

When providing services to HIV/AIDS clients, it is important to understand pertinent state laws governing sexually transmitted diseases. While there is some variation, in most states there are no laws that would require breaching confidentiality to report a client's HIV/AIDS status (Burris, 2001). If state laws do necessitate disclosure in certain situations, therapists need to be aware if these potential infringements to confidentiality at the start of treatment so that clients understand the parameters of their privacy. Although some circumstances cannot be predicted, therapists who anticipate potential difficult dilemmas have opportunities to (a) establish clear policies up front, and (b) explain the implications of those policies to clients in advance (Fisher, 2008). Additionally, identifying alternatives that do the least amount of avoidable harm to both the client and others involved is both caring and prudent. As Donner (2008) noted, "the overriding consideration should be to maintain confidentiality and address the issue clinically" (p. 371).

Confidentiality after Death

Although it might seem that the compact to maintain a client's confidentiality would be void upon the death of either the client or the therapist, this assumption is untrue. The death of famous poet Anne Sexton and the subsequent authorization by her daughter to release hundreds of hours of therapy tapes and notes for Sexton's biography brought into stark relief issues related to postmortem confidentiality. Sexton, who committed suicide in 1974, had been treated by a psychiatrist for eight years, and her sessions had been recorded. Although Sexton had never provided any written instruction or consent to use the tapes after her death, her right to confidentiality was posthumously waived by her daughter. This prompted outrage among mental health professionals. Commentaries in the *New York Times* described the release of Sexton's records as a betrayal, and noted that the client's right to confidentiality survives death, regardless what the family wants (Burke, 1995).

Disposition of clients' records following their deaths is not uniformly articulated in ethics codes. For example, the 2002 APA Code of Ethics did not explicitly address client death (Bersoff, 2008), while the 2005 ACA Code specifically instructed counselors to "protect the confidentiality of deceased clients, consistent with legal requirements and agency or setting policies" (American Counseling Association, 2005, p. 8). Either way, most professionals agree that "the duty to maintain confidentiality that existed in life follows the patient in death" (Younggren & Harris, 2008, p. 597). Unless the informed consent process included discussion of, and permission for, divulging information after death, there is usually no justification for a therapist to break the promise of confidentiality. Postdeath disclosures can undermine trust in the mental health professions, foster reservations and doubt in current and prospective clients, and create confusion among practicing and future clinicians (Burke, 1995).

Still, there may be cases where confidentiality is not upheld postdeath. Courts have found, in some jurisdictions that privilege does not survive once the holder of that privilege is deceased. In the 1997 *United States v. Hansen* case, the defendant in a murder trial claimed that her actions were justified to defend herself against the aggressions of the deceased. Since the mental and emotional condition of the deceased patient was central to her position, records of his treatment were sought. But although the therapist maintained that the treatment information was protected by psychotherapist–patient privilege, the court ruled that the defendant's need for the information was greater than the interest in protecting the privacy of a patient now dead (Younggren & Harris, 2008).

Just as the laws and practices are a bit vague with respect to deceased patients, there is limited direction with regard to confidentiality and deceased therapists. Though therapists might imagine taking all their clients' secrets to the grave, in the event of the untimely death or disability of a therapist, there are likely to be treatment records and psychotherapy notes that have not been properly disposed of or accounted for. Planning thoughtfully for the unexpected means considering who will have access to the records, who will safeguard the records, and who will eventually destroy the records (Bennett et al., 2006). In larger treatment centers and organizations, there may be an existing protocol for maintenance and subsequent destruction of records, but clinicians in independent practice may need to arrange for a colleague or executor to handle protected client information to avoid postdeath betrayals of confidentiality (Purves, 2005).

Confidentiality and Managed Care/Third Party Payers

In Case 10-1, the psychologist adhered to ethical obligations (and possible legal requirements) by discussing the general limits to confidentiality with the client prior to therapy. However, one specific confidentiality limit that pertained to managed care was not addressed. Psychologists working within a managed care/third party payer system may encounter ethical dilemmas that are unique to that type of mental health delivery system, and they need to foresee the possibility of the dilemmas arising.

Use of the term *managed care* has become commonplace since the health care reforms of the 1970s and 1980s, when the primary vehicle for reimbursement of medical and mental health care costs shifted from a fee-for-service system to a health-maintenance-organization (HMO) system, under which care is typically "managed" in order to keep costs in line. Care management is conducted through utilization reviews, during which staff of the managed care company examine client information from the therapist to authorize treatment and payment for services (Sanchez & Turner, 2003). All managed care approaches retain the power to deny payment for services proposed or rendered, contingent on the managed care company's in-house utilization review. Because of their pervasiveness, managed care plans—and their attendant utilization reviews—have influenced the limits of confidentiality.

Managed care reviewers, whose job it is to determine the appropriateness and effectiveness of the treatment plan, contact psychotherapy providers by phone, mail, computers, and fax machines to procure client treatment information so that future treatment can be authorized (or denied). The reviewer's objective is to "minimize costs to the organization by ensuring that only medically necessary cases are seen" by the therapist (Macklin, 1995, p. 63). Managed care programs shift treatment authorizations from agreements established between therapists and clients to a triad arrangement of therapist, client, and reviewer (Herron & Adlerstein, 1994; Parsi, Winslade, & Corcoran, 1995). Problems with maintaining client confidentiality while operating within the confines of a managed care setting have been noted by physicians (Geraty, Hendren, & Flaa, 1992; LaPuma, Schiedermayer, & Seigler, 1995), mental health administrators (Fox, 1995), and researchers (Karon, 1995; Parsi et al., 1995; Rimler & Morrison, 1993). The issue is particularly difficult because managed care reviewers may not have the same professional ethical obligation to protect confidentiality as do psychotherapists, nor are they covered by privileged communication laws.

Codes of ethics and mental health statutes instruct therapists to discuss with clients the limits to confidentiality, usually at the outset of therapy. Consequently, when treating a client covered by a managed care company, the therapist or counselor should inform the client of the type of information the managed care company will require to make an authorization decision regarding the client's treatment. Providing the client this information requires that the therapist is knowledgeable and current on the requirements of the managed care company's review procedure. Assuming that the therapist discloses to the client the types of information the managed care company will likely request, and that the client gives consent to the release of confidential information, a question still remains as to whether the consent was truly "informed." Because clients may not be fully aware of the problems that they will address in future sessions (as was true in Case 10-1) both they and their therapists need to be alert when potentially sensitive topics arise. Additionally, the client needs to be aware that if the therapist refuses to divulge requested information to the managed care company, the client's claim for payment may be denied and other payment arrangements will need to be made. Providing the client with this information prior to therapy respects the autonomy of the client and allows the client to give a consent that is truly informed.

At the same time, research suggests that providing clients full information about the limits of confidentiality significantly decreases the amount of information they are willing to disclose in therapy (Kremer & Gesten, 1998; Nowell & Spruill, 1993). In fact, the differences between the willingness to disclose under the limits described in a typical consent situation and under one that explained the limits in a managed care review were substantial. In light of Miller and Thelen's (1986) findings that clients expect everything in therapy to be confidential, knowing the realities of the limits of confidentiality in a managed care setting may undermine the therapeutic relationship and ultimately, therapeutic effectiveness.

In addition, when requests for information from insurance providers or managed care companies arrive, it can be deceptively easy to reply without considering the consequences for confidentiality, especially if the client has already signed a HIPAA Privacy Notice at the start of therapy. (HIPAA regulations require that, when possible, therapists provide clients with the Privacy Notice by the end of the first session and obtain client signatures by the second session; Bennett et al., 2006.) Privacy Notice and informed consent forms notwithstanding, therapists should not release to third party payers confidential information without the written consent of the client. Furthermore, in keeping with the general policy of minimizing disclosures when confidential information must be shared outside of the treatment relationship, it may be best for clinicians to limit the clinical record to the treatment plan, the dates of subsequent treatment, brief session notes, changes in the treatment plan, and "sufficient information to justify medical necessity and to survive a retroactive utilization review" (Bennett et al., 2006, p. 116).

Difficult Confidentiality Issues in Research

Whereas in years past the work of researchers and the work of clinicians may have been entirely unconnected and independent, the lines between research and practice are increasingly blurred. Managed care companies are constantly seeking data about treatment outcomes, schools and community agencies face heightened pressures to demonstrate efficacy of mental health programs, and the evidence-based practice movement promotes the collection of data and the monitoring of progress to produce effective outcomes (Welfel, 2006). To some extent, the ethical concerns with confidentiality in research overlap with those in therapy. However, the fact that research data, sometimes sensitive data, are gathered and stored on large groups of people, that they are made public, that courts have different expectations of researchers than they do of therapists, and that confidentiality in research does not enjoy the same legal protection that "privileged" client–therapist interactions do makes some of the confidentiality issues unique. Additionally, the risks of privacy violations are seldom balanced out by the benefits of participation, since, unlike therapy, research is not always aimed at the removal or reduction of suffering, and in many cases the participants may not benefit at all from the role they play in research

(Bersoff, 2008). Following examples are some of the scenarios described by Sieber (1992) that illustrate confidentiality problems in research:

1. A researcher working in industry on workers' attitudes toward automation locks data in a desk on the premises of the company. An executive uses a skeleton key to access the data and subsequently fires complaining employees.
2. A conservative sheriff looking for drug-trafficking information raids a researcher's office. Longitudinal AIDS data that have been kept in a locked file cabinet are seized.
3. A researcher studying moral behavior stores data on a mainframe. The link between the data, coded by number only, and the participants is kept in a separate file on the computer. A hacker accesses both files and blackmails some of the participants.
4. Data from a study are subpoenaed by a drug company for a trial to prove some of the plaintiffs were aware of the risks involved with taking the drug.

As Sieber pointed out, in each of these cases, the participants were harmed and the responsibility for the harm lay with the researcher.

Generally, codes of ethics take the position that researchers have obligations to maintain research records in a secure manner and to let participants know of any limits of confidentiality that can reasonably be expected (American Counseling Association, 2005; APA Code of Ethics, 2002). Whether the researchers in examples 1–4 took "reasonable precautions" could be debated; however, a post hoc perspective makes it clear that the precautions were not sufficient. Emphasis in ethics codes is also placed on fully informing participants about any limits to confidentiality before the outset of data collection. If confidentiality is assured, researchers incur a fiduciary obligation to protect the anonymity of their data by using codes, storing identifying information separate from the collected data, and/or destroying identifying information as soon as it is no longer needed for the research project. If data will be made available to third parties, the participant should be informed of this before data collection; hence, the disposition of confidential information needs to be an integral part of the signed consent form.

Certain types of research, such as studies about drug use, sexual behavior, illegal conduct, and AIDS/HIV status, are particularly sensitive with regard to safeguarding confidentiality. Consequently, even the title of the project may need to be chosen in such a way as to shield the privacy of participants. For example, Sieber (1994) suggested calling a project a health study rather than an AIDS or syphilis study because privacy could be threatened even by receiving an invitation to participate in an explicitly labeled study. Information about the specific topic studied could be relayed by a follow-up phone call if the person indicated an interest in volunteering. Research participants should be fully informed of the security measures the researcher will follow to ensure that third parties (particularly law enforcement officials) will not be privy to the confidential information. In addition, a researcher can further safeguard data by applying for a confidentiality certificate through the U.S. Department of Health and Human Services, whose task it is to assure that research minimizes risk and demonstrates a favorable balance of benefits over harms (Margolin et al., 2005).

These Certificates of Confidentiality, authorized by Congress, are intended to promote research on sensitive topics. They permit the researcher to withhold identifying information on participants from any local, state, or federal authorities that may request the information (NIH, 2003). Some researchers have suggested, though, that the use of certificates to avoid state reporting requirement may be ethically and morally indefensible (Margolin et al., 2005). (For further information, contact the DHHS Office for Human Research Protections, http://www.hhs.gov/ohrp/.)

Sometimes problems regarding confidentiality in research can be avoided simply by gathering data anonymously (i.e., without identifiers that could trace the response back to a specific participant). On the other hand, because data are stored and the researcher may need to access participants' identities in the future, for example in longitudinal studies, researchers may need to keep a record of participants' identities. In these cases, there is a particularly strong obligation to keep the identities of the participants stored and locked in a separate place, especially if the data could be used to harm the participants. In addition, because of the harm that could occur, researchers should take care when they aggregate data that no individual can be identified through deductive disclosure. In other words, it should not be aggregated in a way that the single African American in a study, for example, can be linked to his or her opinions. (For some practical suggestions about avoiding these problems, see Sieber, 1992.)

Do Researchers Have a Duty to Protect?

Arguably, some of the most serious and important topics for psychologists to study involve the causes of violent or suicidal behavior, drug and alcohol abuse, and the spread of HIV or other infectious diseases. Yet each of these topics means that researchers are working with high-risk as well as socially vulnerable populations. On one hand, keeping participants' confidences about sometimes dangerous or illegal behavior allows psychologists to gather essential, but socially sensitive, data. On the other hand, the question arises, "Do researchers have obligations similar to therapists when the behavior of research participants may be harmful to themselves or others?"

Legally, the duty to protect has not been applied in a research setting. Some have argued that applying *Tarasoff*-like duties on researchers would negatively impact research on sensitive topics (Appelbaum & Rosenbaum, 1989; Lakeman & FitzGerald, 2009). However, if a researcher's duty to protect were considered in court, the focus would likely be on whether there was a special relationship that would allow the researcher to predict or prevent harm (Appelbaum & Rosenbaum, 1989). The training of the researcher and the nature of the research may be key considerations. For example, the training of social, experimental, and developmental psychologists is quite different from that of counselors, marriage and family therapists, and clinical psychologists. In the latter specialties, a court might hold a reasonable expectation that the researchers' training would cover risk factors of violent or suicidal behavior, whereas that would not be true of the former specialties. On the other hand, researchers untrained as clinicians but conducting research on therapy during which a client receives treatment might be subject to similar requirements as are therapists.

Even when researchers have obtained certificates of confidentiality which guard against forced disclosure of sensitive information, the obligations are not entirely clear when the researcher uncovers information that reveals potential serious harm to either a participant or an identifiable third party, as was true in Case 10-3. There may be no legal duty to protect, but the researcher is caught between competing ethical obligations to uphold the participants' confidentiality and to protect identifiable third parties. As with psychotherapy, researchers have a prima facie duty to guard confidentiality, but in some cases the protection of life may take precedence over privacy. Also as with psychotherapy, researchers should discuss these potential limits to confidentiality beforehand as a part of the consent process. In socially sensitive research, when researchers can anticipate conflicts between protecting the individual and social responsibility, it may be necessary to indicate what information would warrant confidentiality being broken and to whom the confidential information might be divulged.

Take Case 10-3 as an example. The psychologist provided each participant with a consent form that indicated that confidentiality might be limited when there was a risk of harm to others. Under these circumstances, a prudent psychologist would need to balance the ethical "pluses" and "minuses" when deciding whether to break confidentiality. These would include:

(a) the impact on future research in the area of HIV/AIDS if confidentiality is broken; (b) the impact on the researcher's sister if she is not warned about her husband's HIV status; (c) the implications for other participants (e.g., Is the researcher willing to break confidentiality and warn all known partners of HIV-positive participants?); and (d) the legal consequences of breaking confidentiality or maintaining it. In addition, using the rule of thumb mentioned earlier that when possible it is better to both maintain confidentiality and protect others from harm, the researcher ought to consider how both may be respected in this case. For example, presuming the researcher's name was on the consent form, the participant must have been aware that his sister-in-law would have access to the data. The researcher might contact the brother-in-law, taking care that the contact was private, and ask him whether he has informed his wife of his HIV status. If he has not, the researcher might encourage him to do so by pointing out the possible consequences of remaining silent, offer to help him reveal the information, and/or refer him to counseling for help in revealing the information.

Should Researchers Report Child Abuse?

A related question for researchers is how mandatory child abuse reporting laws apply to psychologists engaged in research in which knowledge of child abuse may arise. Case law has not yet set a precedent to guide researchers in determining their legal obligation to report or the consequences of breaching confidentiality (Liss, 1994). Individual state mandatory reporting statutes differ in whom they classify as a *mandated reporter* (no choice in whether to report once abuse is suspected) versus a *discretionary reporter* (has the option of whether or not to report suspected abuse) (Liss, 1994; Richards, 2003). In examining state mandatory reporting laws, Liss concluded that there was no answer that was simple or that applied to all researchers. Each researcher, therefore, must determine what his or her responsibilities are in terms of the state-mandated reporting of child abuse and neglect (Richards, 2003). The investigator's decision to report should depend on the individual state's laws, the definition of the scope of practice of the investigator's discipline, the particular research protocol, and the type of disclosure made by the subject participant. Institutional Review Boards (IRBs) and institutions themselves may also set policies that require disclosure in these cases. All these considerations should then be balanced with the ethical duties to protect participant confidentiality, as well as to protect and safeguard participants from harm.

As with the duty-to-protect dilemma, even researchers who have received certificate of confidentiality from the DHHS are not clearly exempt from mandatory state reporting laws regarding child abuse discovered during the research process (Hoagwood, 1994). The DHHS legal council determined that the certificate of confidentiality preempts mandatory state reporting laws; however, in the DHHS National Child Abuse and Neglect Office legal council's opinion, the certificate does not allow such an exemption (Sieber, 1994). Thus, even the experts disagree about this issue.

To complicate matters, a researcher who obtains a certificate of confidentiality and then violates confidentiality is not subject to a legal penalty. But if a researcher fails to adhere to a state reporting law by keeping suspected child abuse information confidential, he or she could face a criminal penalty (Sieber, 1994). In the absence of case law to test which takes precedence (state law or the federal exemption), researchers are faced with potentially conflicting research objectives: (a) to advance science and humanity with research that is valid and has utility; and (b) to help individuals, particularly research participants (Sieber, 1994). Hoagwood (1994) asserted that research investigators have a "moral obligation" (p. 126) to conform to mandatory state reporting laws when the suspected child abuse involves a current situation because the "safety of children supersedes promises of confidentiality" (p. 127). However, when past abuse is divulged to the researcher, Hoagwood maintained that a certificate of confidentiality would allow a researcher to keep the information confidential.

As noted in the section on the duty to protect, it is essential that researchers inform participants in advance of any possible limits to confidentiality. Thus, the development of the researcher's consent form requires a great deal of forethought to ensure that legal and ethical considerations are adequately addressed. Researchers who anticipate and plan for potential ethical conflicts occurring during their data collection can then evaluate options for resolving the conflicts and address the implications in their consent form (Hoagwood, 1994).

Sieber (1992) advocated that researchers include a statement in their informed consent agreement that addresses the specific limits to confidentiality such as "reasonable suspicion that a child, elder, or dependent adult has been abused" (p. 53). The consent form warns the participant of the foreseeable consequences if he or she reveals certain types of information to the researcher (Sieber, 1992). This respects the participant's autonomy and allows the participant to make informed choices about what specific information he or she will divulge to the researcher. In addition to respect for autonomy, Sieber argued that beneficence would require maximizing the benefits to science, society, and individual participants while minimizing the potential risk or harm. She also suggested that justice required an equitable distribution of the risks and benefits so that "those who bear the risks of research are those who benefit from it (distributive justice)" (Sieber, 1994, p. 15).

Nevertheless, from a scientific perspective, complying with mandatory reporting laws and informing participants ahead of time that confidentiality may be broken to protect abused children may lead to skewed samples and invalid responses of research participants if they know that the personal data they provide the researcher may be passed on to state authorities for prosecution (Sieber, 1994). Therefore, the benefit society might derive from valid data could be sacrificed for the benefit of individual children. However, this does not justify 'doing away with informed consent.' Rather, it means thinking very carefully ahead of time about how to protect the confidentiality of participants.

For example, Sieber (1994) reported that after obtaining a certificate of confidentiality, some researchers visited the local agency to which they would be required to report suspected abuse, explained their research plans, and requested a letter stating their exemption from the mandatory reporting laws. The combination of the certificate of confidentiality and exemption letter increased the probability that the researcher could produce research results that were valid but did not address the "moral obligation" (p. 126) to protect children's safety, an issue that Hoagwood (1994) addressed. As Bok (1988) argued,

> The premises supporting confidentiality are strong but they cannot support practices of secrecy—whether by individual clients, institutions, or professionals themselves—that undermine and contradict the very respect for persons and for human bonds that confidentiality was meant to protect (p. 238).

There are at least three competing stances a researcher can take when faced with the decision of how best to handle confidentiality and potential child abuse revelations:

1. Provide the research participant with information regarding the specific limits to confidentiality if child abuse is divulged so that an informed consent is obtained, and then break confidentiality if child abuse is suspected.
2. Same as Position 1, except that the researcher would not report suspected child abuse, even if it is divulged, but would instead maintain confidentiality.
3. The researcher obtains a certificate of confidentiality as well as a letter of exemption from compliance with state reporting laws and does not report any suspected child abuse.

Legally and ethically, Position 2 is not a defensible stance, since it violates state mandatory reporting laws and is dishonest. Further, it does not fulfill the principle of beneficence because any research gains that might be made—if confidentiality were promised—are lost by the risks of the child being unprotected. Positions 1 and 3 exemplify the competing obligations of researchers—whether to focus on the social utility of their prospective research findings or whether to focus on protecting the individual child whom they suspect is being abused. Both positions are ethically and legally defensible but have potential differing outcomes. Position 1 (informed consent to report abuse) respects the participant's autonomy to decide what information to divulge to the researcher and to know the consequences in advance for divulging information concerning child abuse. This position also allows researchers to take measures to protect any child they suspect of being abused (beneficence) and to adhere to their reporting obligations. The downside to Position 1, however, is that the focus on protection of the child may serve to diminish the potential utility of the research findings. Research participants may be understandably loath to divulge any information that they suspect will be reported to the legal authorities; hence, data may either be falsified or withheld from the researcher. This is particularly problematic if the researcher is studying child abuse and the study cannot be done anonymously. The million-dollar question is whether the immediate protection of the child should always take precedence over the potential social utility of a well-conducted child abuse research study.

Position 3 (obtaining a certificate of confidentiality and not reporting abuse) protects the researcher from any adverse consequences should child abuse information be divulged. The researcher informs the participants ahead of time that confidentiality will not be violated, even if child abuse is suspected, which respects the participants' autonomy, as well as the fiduciary relationship between researcher and participant. Theoretically, research participants who are immune from legal consequences would be more likely to provide researchers with accurate data than participants who fear legal prosecution. The higher probability of obtaining accurate data increases the prospects for research findings that will prove beneficial to society as a whole. Valid research findings on sensitive topics such as child abuse could elicit potentially beneficial information such as (a) the circumstances under which children are at higher risk for being abused, or (b) the types of intervention programs that are more likely to succeed with abusive parents. Obviously, the major drawback to this position is that the safety and well-being of the individual child is sacrificed for the good of society.

Indeed, this is a conundrum for researchers in this sensitive area. There are ethical and legal justifications for both positions. From our perspective, however, Position 1 (informed consent regarding confidentiality limits and reporting suspected abuse) has an edge because it protects the autonomy of the research participant and the welfare of the child. Thus, it is the position we would wish for our children and ourselves, although it may sacrifice some of the social benefits of the research. For us, the social utility of the study, including the research design, would have to be very strong in terms of its potential for protecting many children in the future to sacrifice the protection of an individual child. Still, complying with mandatory reporting laws is not without its own risks, such as the possibility of incorrectly assessing the situation and, as a result of the abuse report, actually increasing the risk to the child (Koocher & Keith-Spiegel, 1990).

Perhaps the most prudent course for researchers is to (a) carefully assess the goals and potential utility of their particular research project; (b) explore their options regarding local mandatory reporting laws and pertinent ethical standards; (c) consult with others when deciding on an ethically and legally justifiable course of action; and (d) ensure that the research participants receive specific information on how confidentiality with child abuse information will be handled so that an informed decision on participation can be made. In addition, a caring researcher who takes Position 1 and reports suspected child abuse to the legal authorities could remain in contact with the child and family, working to see that as many available resources as possible are being used to support the family system. Researchers with integrity who choose Position 1 would also ensure that their data are interpreted cautiously because of the limitations in how forthright participants could be in providing information given the limits of confidentiality. Although research psychologists who choose Position 3 and obtain a certificate of confidentiality would be exempt from reporting suspected child abuse to the legal authorities, this does not mean that they need abandon all attempts to intervene and try to protect the child. The researcher could (a) provide the family with psychoeducational materials regarding child abuse and intervention options available to them; (b) refer the family to counseling, low cost if necessary, with the caveat that therapists are legally and ethically required to report suspected child abuse; or (c) refer the parents to community-based parenting classes to teach appropriate methods for disciplining children. These interventions may or may not be as effective in protecting the child as alerting the legal authorities could be, however, taking these steps while attempting to collect relevant valid data on a sensitive research topic would be reflective of the stance a virtuous psychologist would take. As the field currently stands, there is not a clear position to endorse emphatically—both positions are ethically defensible, yet both positions have significant limitations. The integration of moral virtues within the two positions addresses some, but certainly not all, of the concerns raised earlier regarding the researcher's conflict between focusing on the safety of the individual child versus focusing on the potential benefits to society of the research findings.

Difficult Confidentiality Questions in Academia and Supervision

When counselors and psychologists hold academic and/or supervisory roles, issues of privacy and confidentiality are no longer as explicitly defined as in therapy and research. In addition, competing (and often conflicting) professional obligations may strongly impact the limits of confidentiality for students or supervisees. Consider the following, in which the professor in possession of the "private" information has competing obligations—to the student, to colleagues, and to the profession.

Case 10-8

A student in a graduate counseling program discloses to her professor that she was recently the victim of rape, and that the trauma has made it difficult to concentrate or complete her work. She asks him to keep the information confidential. At a subsequent department meeting, other faculty members note that the student has not been attending classes, and they share their concerns that her erratic behavior suggests a lack of responsibility and a disregard for the program.

Educational and supervisory relationships are both similar to and different from therapy relationships and research relationships. Like all human relationships, respect for autonomy would suggest a need to value agreements made with students or supervisees to keep information confidential. Similarly, the principle of fidelity would suggest that, to remain trustworthy, confidences should be respected. Research shows that professors are considered more ethical when they show respect for their students by maintaining confidences (Birch, Elliott, & Trankel, 1999). And when students or supervisees disclose private information to professors or supervisors, they may assume that, like a therapeutic relationship, similar parameters regarding confidentiality will extend to the current relationship. Because of the power differential inherent in the relationship and the potential damage that misuse of private information can do, there is considerable potential for students to be harmed in these situations (see Chapter 11 for a further discussion of these topics).

On the other hand, unlike therapy and research, there is typically no professional promise of confidentiality presumed or automatically extended in the teacher–student or supervisor-supervisee relationships. There is no contract offering confidentiality as a consent form does in therapy and research, and there is no legal protection for it. Students or supervisees may request such a promise, but it is not automatically offered, nor necessarily expected by the professionals involved, although (as discussed in Chapter 9) there is an increasing emphasis on including a consent form in supervision.

Furthermore, in academia and in supervision, there is an obligation to evaluate students, and this obligation may conflict with any promises made to students to keep information confidential. Faculty members are ethically obligated to attempt to benefit students; however, sometimes helping a student may involve sharing private information about the student with the rest of the faculty so that an academic program can be adjusted or remediation plans developed. Additionally, both faculty members and supervisors have to balance what is in the best interests of students and supervisees with what is in the best interests of the public, which the student may serve at a later date (Kitchener, 1992b).

Consequently, it is critical for professors and supervisors in these situations to be clear for themselves and to be explicit with those with whom they work regarding whether or not they can promise confidentiality and within what limits the promise would be extended. In particular, they need to be clear to indicate under what circumstances they might need to divulge private information. When that need arises, a professor or supervisor who is both respectful and caring would ask the permission of the student to provide others with the information, or would at least inform the student or supervisee that it will be done.

The aforementioned example does not specify whether the professor agreed to honor the graduate student's request for confidentiality. If an agreement was made to keep information confidential, then the psychologist should have informed the student about circumstances under which that promise would no longer be honored. If the professor promised confidentiality and then decided to breach it, several ethical errors may have occurred. These errors include failure to provide the student with appropriate information on whether the information could be kept confidential and the limits of confidentiality within academia. Caught without clarifying the nature of confidentiality in the first place, the professor in Case 10-8 would need to carefully weigh the competing ethical obligations of respecting autonomy, confidentiality, and the fiduciary relationship in the advisor role versus truthfulness, beneficence, and nonmaleficence in the evaluator role. Maintaining confidentiality in this case may result in the student being placed on academic probation, whereas violating confidentiality may irreparably mar the advisor–advisee relationship. Avoiding of this type of ethical dilemma by clearly defining the role of an advisor and articulating limits to confidentiality at the outset of the relationship is the preferred option. The professor should have told the student that her privacy would be respected to the extent possible but that information might have to be shared with the rest of the faculty under some circumstances. It is in situations like these that the virtues of respectfulness, caring, and prudence are particularly important.

Confidentiality in Supervision

Case 10-9

In a supervision group at the college counseling center where she is interning, Jackie shares her growing frustration with a client whom she sees in individual therapy. She mentions that he came to his last session smelling of alcohol, even though he maintains that he is in recovery. Though she doesn't mention him by name, Jackie reveals enough information about this client that Sheri, who is a practicum student at the counseling center, recognizes the client as a fellow student in one of her classes. Sheri blurts out, "Oh my goodness, I know him. I think he was drunk in class last week, too." The group supervisor aborts the conversation, aware that this client's confidentiality has been compromised, that the "clinical" discussion has devolved into something bordering on gossip, and that both Jackie and Sheri have revealed, through their disclosures, information about *themselves* that is potentially important to their evaluations as developing clinicians.

For counselors and psychologists who supervise trainees, confidentiality agreements and obligations are multifaceted, in that they affect both the clients in treatment and the supervisees providing the treatment. Typically the only explicit promise of confidentiality in supervision is to protect the confidentiality of the client. Because the supervisors of unlicensed trainees bear responsibility if ethical or legal lapses occur in the therapy (Bennett et al., 2006), supervisors have a right to, and a need for, essential information about the clients being treated by their supervisees, including identifying information. Supervisors assume the same legal and ethical responsibilities to maintain confidentiality as do psychotherapists themselves, which is described more completely in Chapter 9.

Clients, for their part, have a right to know that their confidentiality is already limited when they see trainees. Clients should be informed, at the outset of treatment, of the supervised status of their therapist, and they should provide written consent signifying their understanding that their personal information will be discussed within the confines of individual and group supervision. In addition, clients should be given the supervisor's contact information, in case they wish to communicate with the supervisor directly (Bennett et al., 2006). Even given these written reminders of the limits of confidentiality, clients may not understand that someone they know in a more casual manner could be working at the same center, school, or agency from which they are receiving treatment, so that, as in Case 10-9, they are unwittingly disclosing personal information not just to "professionals," but to classmates, neighbors, or others they may know from nontherapeutic relationships (Ruby, Grimmett, & Brown, 2008).

For more advanced clinicians, supervision is generally not required to meet licensure criteria or agency policy and is instead conducted for purposes of ongoing competence and professional awareness. When advisor/advisee relationships involve two or more licensed clinicians who are meeting for professional consultation, it is best for client information to be discussed in a way that maintains anonymity (Morrissey, 2005). In other words, every effort should be made to protect the client's identity (American Counseling Association, 2005). This may mean disguising key features of the client (such as sex or ethnicity) or the client's personal information (such as place of employment).

Although the legal and ethical emphasis in supervision is on maintaining client confidentiality, supervisees sometimes believe the information they reveal about themselves has similar protections. Consequently, supervisees, like clients, need information up front about the parameters of confidentiality, which is why the use of consent forms in supervision was emphasized in Chapter 9. For example, supervisors can discuss, at the outset of supervision, what types of information will be passed along to the training director or the supervisor's supervisor. It is important to discuss with the supervisee the difference between keeping information private and protecting confidentiality, because supervisees may assume that the same kind of confidentiality exists in supervision that exists in therapy. This can become particularly confusing for the supervisee when personal information is shared in supervision that is similar to what is shared in psychotherapy. But although the supervisory relationship may bear some resemblance to the therapeutic relationship, there is no promise of confidentiality in supervision. When faced with dilemmas related to the private information of trainees and their clients, supervisors must place the client's welfare above the relationship with the supervisee (Morrissey, 2005). In addition, they may need to place the training needs of the supervisee above the confidentiality of the supervisory relationship.

Conclusion

Mental health professionals need to be aware of their ethical and legal obligations regarding confidentiality—whether working in academia, in clinical practice, in research, or in assessment. Respecting confidentiality is considered to be a prima facie duty in many aspects of mental health work. Accordingly, therapists, counselors, and researchers need to be vigilant so that unnecessary breaches do not occur. On the other hand, sometimes there are good ethical and legal reasons for breaking confidentiality; to accommodate those situations, psychologists and counselors have an ethical obligation to inform consumers upfront of exceptions to the rule of confidentiality so that consumers can make informed decisions about what to divulge. Work with vulnerable individuals, particularly those who experience themselves as powerless or who are susceptible to public scorn if private information about them is revealed, takes particular care. Similarly, work with children and adolescents requires sensitivity to developmental limits (and how these limits affect their understanding of the parameters of confidentiality), as well as thoughtful consideration about how to address them.

Although knowledge of professional ethics codes and state and federal statutes is a necessary prerequisite for ethical decision making, knowledge alone is not sufficient to ensure ethical behavior. Because there are myriad situations that can occur that are not explicitly addressed in laws and ethical standards, therapists need to develop sound ethical reasoning regarding confidentiality and its limits, and a refined ability to communicate the various confidentiality nuances with consumers. The increasing intrusions into confidentiality from technology (e.g., faxes, email, and text messages) and managed care companies underscore the salience of thinking well about how to protect clients', research participants', and others' privacy and confidentiality. As the world in which mental health professionals operate becomes more and more complex, it becomes correspondingly vital that professionals equip themselves with as much ethical training and knowledge as possible. Thus, when confronted with an ethical dilemma, they will be able to make a decision that is ethically sound, is legally defensible, and demonstrates the care and respect for others that the profession embodies.

Questions for Discussion or Consideration

1. Describe how the process of informed consent is inextricably connected to issues of confidentiality in therapy, research, and other professional settings.
2. Although the concepts of confidentiality and privilege overlap, they are not synonymous. Describe the differences between these two terms.
3. Despite the public perception that any information divulged to a psychotherapist will remain confidential, there are actually many exceptions to the promise of confidentiality. Name five situations or concerns that might limit the therapist's ability to maintain client confidentiality.
4. Sometimes beginner therapists think that if a client expresses suicidal ideation, confidentiality must be breached in order to protect that client. Describe the other interventions that can and should be explored before deciding to break the contract of confidentiality.
5. Some beginner therapists believe that the therapist in the famous *Tarasoff* case was remiss in not recognizing that Podar was potentially dangerous/homicidal. In fact, the therapist did identify Podar's potential lethality and broke confidentiality to report his concerns to the police. What, then, did the California courts find that the therapist had failed to do?
6. What is the difference in saying something is confidential in research and in therapy? What can be done to protect the confidentiality of research participants?

11
Professional Boundaries and Conflicts of Interest
Providing Benefit and Avoiding Harm

Multiple relationships and the possibilities of conflicts of interest are among the most interesting and at times the troublesome issues faced by psychologists and counselors. Professionals identify multiple relationships as one of their major ethical concerns. (Pope & Vetter, 1992). The reasons for this are many. First, the relationship itself between the professional and client is a key factor in successful outcomes in counseling and psychotherapy (Gelso & Hayes, 1998). Second, our personal and professional lives are "complex, interconnected, and fluid" (Sommers-Flanagan & Sommers-Flanagan, 2007, p. 160). Professionals identify multiple relationships as one of their major ethical concerns (Pope & Vetter, 1992). Psychologists and counselors cannot nor should not be expected to live in a vacuum. At the same time, these same professionals are expected to honor their roles with clients, students, research participants, and colleagues in an ethical manner. Third, the humanness of psychologists and counselors makes them vulnerable to the "slippery slope" phenomena (Anderson & Handelsman, 2010; Sonne, 1994).

Multiple relationships continue to be a source of ethics complaints opened against psychologists and counselors (APA, 2007, 2008, 2009; ACA, 2006). The since 1981 APA and ACA codes explicitly prohibited psychologists and counselors from entering sexual relationships with clients, students, and others who are consumers of services by psychologists and counselors but are less clear and helpful when it comes to facing nonsexual multiple relationships between professionals and those with whom they work. General issues regarding nonsexual multiple relationships are discussed in this chapter while the specific problems that arise when relationships are sexualized are covered in Chapter 12.

Defining Multiple Relationships and the Issue of Boundaries

Generally, multiple relationships arise when an individual participates simultaneously or sequentially in two or more relationships with another person. Harmful multiple relationships typically arise when there are substantial differences or conflicts between the two roles. As this definition suggests, multiple relationships do not necessarily or only involve a professional person and a client, student, or research participant. They can and do happen in everyday professional and personal life. For example, the authors of this book have been in multiple roles with each other. Our first interaction/relationship was as faculty member and student at the doctoral program orientation meeting. During the four years of Sharon's doctoral work, the roles expanded to include coteachers for a master's ethics course and doctoral advisor/advisee. Since then our professional roles have included copresenters at conferences and workshops, cowriters on professional works including the one you are currently reading. On the personal side, we have been part of the support system for each other during times of family and personal hardships.

It is, however, when multiple relationships occur in professional relationships that they can become ethically troublesome for psychologists and counselors. Sonne (1994) wrote that multiple relationships in psychology include those in which the psychologist is playing two or more professional roles as well as those in which the psychologist is involved in another nonprofessional "definitive and intended role" (p. 336). Herlihy and Corey (1997) share, "Multiple relationship issues exist throughout our profession and affect virtually all counselors, regardless of their work setting. … No professional remains untouched by the potential difficulties inherent in dual or multiple relationships" (p. 1). The multiplicity of roles can be sequential as well as concurrent (Kitchener, 1988; Pope & Vasquez, 1991; Sonne, 1994). For example, the APA (2002) and ACA (2005) ethics codes point to sequential sexual relationships as ethically problematic, including those that involve taking a former sexual partner as a client as well as making a former client a current sexual partner. Because our professional and personal lives are so interconnected, it is important to address the issues of social role and professional boundaries (Gutheil & Gabbard, 1993).

The word *boundary* suggests a separation or division between two things or in this discussion a separation, space or division between two people. A boundary can be a healthy way to describe or delineate where one person and their emotional needs end and where another person and their emotional needs begin. Boundaries or rules about boundaries provide all types of information for appropriate and proper interactions such as personal space, dress and touch between individuals, and even communication styles depending on age and gender (Sommers-Flanagan & Sommers-Flanagan, 2007).

Although the term boundary can suggest a definite and inflexible demarcation—a line in the sand so to speak—in real life, the line cannot be applied with inflexibility (Austin, Bergum, Nuttgens, & Peternelj-Taylor, 2006). By their very nature, boundaries between humans are or can be permeable. Professionals need to identify key factors within the relationship that suggest the decision to temporarily change or modify the boundary will most likely benefit rather than harm the consumer. To temporarily change or modify the boundary could be referred to as a boundary crossing or boundary extension.

The terms boundary crossing or boundary extension refer to a temporary change in the relationship from common practice, by the professional, for the benefit of the other party (Sommers-Flanagan, Elliott, & Sommers-Flanagan, 1998; Remley & Herlihy, 2007). The following are some examples of boundary crossings or boundary extensions. A therapist accepts the invitation from a client to attend the client's wedding, believing her attendance at the ceremony will enhance the therapeutic relationship. A faculty person offers his frequent flyer miles to a graduate student so the student can fly home to see an ailing parent. Recognizing that a doctoral intern might be struggling with the adjustment to the new living location as well as practice site, a supervisor and his wife invite the intern to join them for dinner at a local restaurant. As psychologists and counselors consider these types of modifications in boundaries, guidelines and considerations that promote clear thinking will help to ensure professional objectivity and promote the benefit for the consumer rather than bring on the harm. Later in the chapter we highlight such guidelines for professionals to consider.

The term boundary violation also suggests a change in the relationship by the professional from what is seen as common practice; however, this change results in harm to the other party. Boundary violations can result in harmful multiple relationships because there are substantial differences or conflicts between the two roles. Probably the most obvious of boundary violations is the sexual interaction between a therapist and client.

Difficulties with Multiple Relationships

The troublesome nature of multiple relationships can involve entanglements on a broad continuum, from those that are intentional, which include both boundary crossings and boundary violations, to those that are circumstantial. Time-limited encounters growing out of a chance meeting, such as a client and therapist seeing each other their children's school function or a student and faculty member working out at the same gym are not typically considered examples of multiple relationships. Unfortunately, the potential for harm or negative disruption in the professional relationship does not necessarily coincide with the intentionality of the occurrence. For example, an unintentional encounter between a client and therapist can bring with it negative consequences and develop into a full-blown multiple relationship if the therapist and the client extend the relationship into one that is more than circumstantial.

It is undoubtedly for these reasons that the ethics codes of all of the major mental health organizations discuss the need to assess the potential for harm with different kinds of multiple relationships in which mental health professionals can participate (ACA, 2005; APA, 2002; NASW, 2008). The last several versions of the APA and ACA ethics codes have encouraged professionals to avoid multiple relationships with clients if possible when harm is foreseeable. The APA ethics code acknowledged that some multiple relationships may be unavoidable and warned psychologists against entering into a new or secondary relationship with a consumer if it might impair objectivity or interfere in other ways with a psychologist's effectiveness and harm the consumer. For both psychologists and counselors, the codes admonish them to remediate problems that grow out of harmful multiple relationships. The remediation process is meant to address the best interests of the consumer. Over the years, the prohibition against harmful multiple relationships in both codes has been extended to research participants, supervisees, students and other consumers of mental services. Additionally, the codes address bartering, exploitative relationships, sexual harassment, sexual intimacies with current and former clients, and taking a former partner as a client as examples of problematic multiple relationships.

There is a continuum of perspective about avoiding multiple-role relationships with clients which we address later. Although some therapists recognize that avoiding multiple relationships is the ideal, the ideal is often impossible to achieve on a daily basis (Gottlieb, 1993; Haas & Malouf, 1989; Koocher & Keith-Spiegel, 1998; Kitchener, 1988). Three questions that need to be answered are:

> Under what conditions should multiple relationships with clients be absolutely avoided?
> How should those that cannot be avoided be managed?
> What criteria should be used to make these decisions?

The remainder of this chapter focuses on the general issues and problems that multiple relationships raise therapy and assessment, teaching and supervision, and research. Chapter 12 addresses the unique concerns and issues when professional relationships become sexualized.

Problematic Relationships in Clinical Practice

Although multiple relationships are always difficult to handle, they involve particularly difficult choices in clinical and counseling practice. Often these choices do not involve true ethical dilemmas but rather involve being clear that the consumer's welfare should be the primary consideration and then considering how to ensure that it remains so. Take the following cases as examples.

Case 11-1

A psychologist works in a rural community where he is a member and the deacon of a local church. There are very few mental health resources in the community as well as in a 100-mile radius. People from the church he attends often seek out his services, both because they know him already and because he understands their spiritual perspective. Sometimes they come to him after they have tried other mental health resources in the community and are dissatisfied with the quality of the help they have received elsewhere (Borys & Pope, 1989).

Case 11-2

A new therapist in a mental health center works for 6 months with Becky, a client who has problems in inter-personal relationships. As they near termination, the therapist discovers that Becky is dating John, one of her husband's best friends. One night after she and her husband have gone to a movie, they stop at a local coffee shop and bump into Becky who is with John. John asks the therapist and her husband to join them at a table. When the therapist resists, her husband asks her why she does not want to be sociable. She feels caught because she cannot break Becky's confidentiality to let her husband know why the situation is awkward. Because her husband insists, they join the other couple and John introduces them to his date, who does not acknowledge that she and the therapist have a prior relationship. At the end of the evening, John suggests they get together the next weekend. The therapist thanks him for the offer but indicates that she is busy. When they leave the coffee shop, her husband gets angry because they don't have other plans and accuses her of not liking his best friend.

Case 11-3

A psychologist provided intermittent couple and family therapy to Mr and Mrs Gonzales over several years. During this period, the psychologist was approached by Mr Gonzales to work as a consultant for the human resources department in the company where Mr Gonzales was a regional vice president. Two years later, Mr Gonzales was fired for mismanagement. The psychologist, who was a consultant for the human resources department, was brought in to facilitate the termination meeting. After Mr Gonzales was fired, he and his wife experienced deepened marital distress and they again sought the psychologist's help. Eventually, Mrs Gonzales brought ethics charges against the psychologist for participating in a multiple-role relationship that might have led to a loss of objectivity and for failing to resolve a multiple relationship once it had arisen (APA, 1996, p. 904).

As these cases illustrate, multiple relationships in clinical settings can vary substantially. As already noted, some might involve accidental or incidental contacts. Others may involve two or more full-fledged relationships between the therapist and the client, as illustrated by Case 11-3. Some relationships are circumstantial and difficult to avoid, as in Case 11-2, while the others are intentional (Anderson & Kitchener, 1998).

Further, practicing in some communities makes even intentional relationships difficult to avoid. Rural communities are an example of such a community, but even large cities have numerous small communities (e.g., African American, Chicano/Latino, or gay–lesbian–bisexual–transgendered) where multiple relationships may be difficult to avoid. A lesbian friend once remarked that she sometimes felt like she could not have a social life and see clients in the same city. Most of her referrals came from the lesbian community, and consequently she would run into clients at social gatherings, which was often difficult for both her and her client.

Problematic Relationships in Academic Settings

Just as multiple relationships confuse therapeutic relationships, they can also confuse academic, supervisory, and research relationships. Multiple relationships are endemic in academic settings (Blevins-Knabe, 1992; Kitchener, 1992b; Sommers-Flanagan & Sommers-Flanagan, 2007; Welfel, 2010). Faculty serves as advisers for students, whom they also teach and evaluate or grade in their classes. At the graduate level, they hire students as research or teaching assistants while evaluating them in classes. Further, they may be coauthoring publications with these same students. Although each of these instances involves the opportunity for mentoring, they also can lead to exploitation. Take Case 11-4 as an example.

Case 11-4

A graduate student felt very lucky to be asked to be a teaching assistant for a respected faculty member's course in psychopathology. In addition to getting a stipend and a tuition waiver, the student got to know the faculty member on a more personal basis and eventually the faculty member asked the student to work on an article with him. The student, excited about the prospects, worked long hours with the faculty member on the potential publication. One afternoon while they were engaged in a discussion, the faculty member looked at his date book and realized that he had double-scheduled the next hour. He was supposed to pick up his children at the day care center and be a guest speaker in an ill colleague's class. The student volunteered to pick up his children and bring them back to the faculty member's office. Over the next few weeks, the faculty member's requests for "little favors" increased. Although the student resented these intrusions into his own tight schedule, he was afraid to turn the faculty member down because he was dependent on him for his job as well as the publication.

Cases like this one illustrate the fine line between mentoring for benefit and exploitation for harm and the difficulty that the power differential between faculty and students sometimes imposes on the relationship. Confusion about role obligations and expectation can also be difficult to handle, as is discussed in the next section.

Problematic Relationships in Supervision

Many of the role conflict problems that are inherent in an academic setting have parallels in supervisory relationships. Supervision in and of itself involves multiple obligations that can be confusing to both the supervisor and the supervisee (Sherry, 1991; Sherry, Teschendorf, Anderson, & Guzman, 1991). For example, supervisors have the responsibility to enhance supervisees' development, to evaluate them as a protection for the public, and to ensure clients of a reasonable standard of care (Kitchener, 1994). In addition, a supervisor may work with a supervisee in several nonsupervisory capacities, such as participating in off-site consultations where they operate more like peers. Furthermore, supervisors and supervisees may present a case together at a staff meeting, coauthor papers together, and, frequently, interact in informal settings. Take Case 11-5 as an example.

Case 11-5

A student entered into an advanced practicum at a university counseling center where she is assigned a supervisor. After working together for a semester, the supervisor evaluates the student "at the expected level" for her amount of training. During this same period, the supervisor and the student conduct a short research project together and submit it for presentation at a regional convention. When the paper is accepted, both are elated and agree to travel to the convention together. During the convention, the student discovers that the supervisor is engaged in an illegal activity and confronts her about it. At this point, their relationship deteriorates. At the end of spring semester, the supervisor again evaluates the student, this time "below the expected level" in her capacity to accept supervisory input and in her defensiveness. She suggests that the student needs remedial work. On being questioned by the training director, the student reports that she never felt safe in supervision after the encounter at the convention and did not know how to handle her supervisor's hostility.

Supervisory relationships can be confusing enough for trainees or new professionals without adding a personal component. Supervisors are in positions of power and their personal feelings may interfere with their ability to be objective when evaluating supervisees.

Problematic Relationships in Research

Because relationships are often more prescribed in research settings, multiple relationships may be less problematic. However, because of the inherent imbalance of power between the research participant and the researcher, the potential for harmful boundary violations still exists. Take, for example, the research assistant who took the opportunity when testing participants in a study to write down the telephone numbers and information about women that he found attractive. Because the study involved disclosing some relatively intimate information, he used the information to "blackmail" participants into dating him until one participant became angry and informed his supervisor. There are other, less Machiavellian role conflicts that can arise in research settings as Case 11-6 illustrates.

Case 11-6

A well-known psychology professor is interested in studying differences in problem-solving skills between college and graduate students as a result of different environmental variables. Because he works in a setting where there is a large graduate program, he solicits volunteers from his classes. Although the project is entirely voluntary, some students report that they felt like they could not afford to refuse to participate because they were not only students in his class but also because he was also the department chairman. Further, they worried that he would have access to their problem-solving data and that if they performed poorly on the test, he might be biased against them.

When Are Multiple Relationships Problematic and Can They Be Beneficial?

It would be comforting if a formula existed that established exactly when multiple relationships and boundary crossings become problematic and unethical, however, this is not the case. The professions have decided that some types of relationships, such as sexual relationships between therapists and clients, former clients, and faculty with current students, are so potentially harmful that they are unethical (ACA, 2005; APA, 2002). Ethicists (Borys, 1994; Brown, 1994a; Gottlieb, 1993; Kitchener, 1988, 2000; Pope & Vasquez, 2007; Remley & Herlihy, 2010; Sommers-Flanagan & Sommers-Flanagan, 2007) have emphasized the need to train professionals to understand the reasoning behind maintaining conventional boundaries and the potential problems that can arise when boundaries are altered in nonprofessional ways. In some ways, it may be that avoiding harmful relationships is more an issue of character or a mismatch between personal values and motivations and the standards of the profession than it is of decision making. Prudence, integrity, and caring or compassion and how they are expressed may be critical in discerning how to avoid harmful multiple relationships and how to handle them and when they occur. The case below highlights the character of care and prudence with which a therapist handles a potentially harmful multiple relationship/interaction.

Case 11-7

Dr. Kaye and Christine had worked together as therapist and client for 1 year. They had developed a good relationship over the 12 months and Christine felt like her goals had been obtained. In a final session the two agreed to meet again should Christine see the need. Two months later Dr. Kaye was contacted by his former program chair and asked to meet with the program faculty and a few doctoral students to discuss possible changes to the curriculum. To Dr. Kaye's surprise Christine was at the meeting. He was very uncomfortable. To his knowledge the faculty did not know that they had worked together as therapist and client. Several options came to mind; he could think of an excuse for leaving the meeting as soon as possible, pretend to know-not know Christine when introduced, or try to find way to chat with her in confidence assessing her comfort with him being there? Just as he was getting ready to excuse himself with an "emergency" Christine came up to him and quietly said, "I hope you can stay. Because of our good work together I encouraged the faculty to ask you to join us." Dr. Kaye felt less ethically awkward about the situation and stayed for the meeting, fully participating with ideas about changes for the training program based on current practice issues. At the same time he was careful to honor the therapeutic relationship with Christine by not referring to his work with her or any other work he had been part of with students from the program. Although Christine had shared the information with the faculty about her therapy relationship with faculty, the ethical issue still remained that Dr. Kaye needed to keep his role clear in the context. He was there at the meeting to share his current understanding of the profession which would help in program planning.

Several decision-making models, guidelines and rules (Brown, 1994a; Gottlieb, 1993; Gutheil & Gabbard, 1993; Youngren & Gottlieb, 2004; Welfel, 2010) have been conceived to help mental health professionals think through the potential consequence of crossing boundaries. Although most of these were formulated for the therapeutic relationship, some have implications more broadly for other kinds of multiple-role relationships. For example, Gottlieb (1993) suggested that three elements must be considered when evaluating the potential harmfulness of both therapeutic and nontherapeutic multiple relationships. These include the amount of power that the psychologist has in relationship to the consumer, the duration of the relationship, and the clarity of ending the professional relationship. Brown (1994a) pointed to objectifying the consumer for the use of the professional, acting on impulse rather than from careful consideration of the consequences, and placing the needs of the more powerful person (the professional) over those of the client or consumer as key elements in role violations. Each needs to be considered in order to avoid harmful boundary violations. In a more recent work, Youngren and Gottlieb (2004) suggested practitioners consider a series of five questions, one of which investigates the probability of benefit; Welfel (2010) proposed a series of thoughtful questions for the professional to consider in assessing whether the multiple relationship would be ethical.

Before moving on to guidelines for identifying probable harm in multiple relationships, it is important to note some unique wording in the 2005 ACA code. The ACA ethics code introduces the idea of "potentially beneficial interactions" with clients or other consumers of the counselor's expertise. This standard comes with a challenge (Welfel, 2010; Sommers-Flanagan & Sommers-Flanagan, 2007). The code does not provide a definition for the term "potentially beneficial" leaving the assessment or determination of beneficial up to the practitioner. One type of boundary crossing or extension may be considered potentially beneficial for one client where for another client, the boundary crossing would be potentially harmful (Sommers-Flanagan & Sommers-Flanagan, 2007; Welfel, 2010). Of course a code of ethics can never completely address all the complexities and nuances of multiple relationships or nonprofessional interactions. Being asked to attend a personal event such as wedding or graduation ceremony may very well be beneficial for the client and the therapeutic relationship. The ethical counselor and psychologist will need to draw upon objective reasoning, assess their motivations and intentions, and seek consultation and involve the client or consumer of services in good discussion about the potential benefits as well as the possible harms.

Guidelines for Assessing Potential for Benefit and the Probability for Harm

As noted, counselors and psychologists are called upon to assess the potential for benefit as well as the probability for harm when entering a secondary relationship with clients and other consumers. In an earlier work, Kitchener (1988) proposed the utility of role theory from social psychology (Kitchener, 1988, 2000). Social role theory (Deutsch & Krauss, 1965; Getzels & Guba, 1954; Secord & Backman, 1974) suggests that roles carry with them certain expectations about behavior. These include rights and privileges as well as duties, expectations, and obligations. For example, students expect faculty to be competent in their instruction of different theories related to psychotherapy and skills related to those theories. Students also expect them to be fair in their assessment of their work and provide helpful feedback. When this does not happen, faculty fail to meet the expectations associated with the role students feel angry, surprised, frustrated, and/ or disgusted. In addition to role expectations, there are also role obligations. Staying with the previous example, faculty has role obligations to instruct or teach students about psychotherapy or counseling while simultaneously protecting the consumer of this psychotherapy from harmful practice. Students also have a role obligation. One of their obligations is to be honest with their supervisors during supervision.

It is difficult to operate as an adult in our society or in our professional world without occupying several roles at the same time. However, when the behavior or obligations associated with one role are incompatible with the behavior expected in another role, role conflict occurs. Role competition occurs when the person does not have the time to completely honor the expectations and obligations associated with the two or more roles. When the expectations of the different roles compete or conflict with each other, people sometimes have difficulty in deciding which behavior is appropriate. In the prior example, faculty are obligated to their role of trainer and supervisor to further the student's professional growth as well as act as gatekeepers to the profession and protect the client from harmful psychotherapy or counseling. If faculty are not clear with students from the start of the potential conflict of these two role obligations (See Chapter 9 on informed consent process.), there is greater potential for students interacting with the faculty person to be confused, angry, and frustrated because they are also unclear about the role they are expected to play and what can be expected from the instructor. Another example is the expectations of therapy clients are remarkably different from those of lovers. In therapy, one would reasonably expect that the therapist's primary role is to help the client benefit from treatment; however, as a lover, that same therapist would have some expectations that his or her own needs would be met in the relationship. This may be one reason why sexual relationships between therapists and clients are so damaging. The client may enter into the sexual relationship fantasizing that it will be an extension of the therapeutic one where the therapist qua lover is focused on being with the client qua sexual partner. When the psychologist's own needs intrude into this fantasy, the client feels disappointed, angry, and betrayed.

When role conflict and role competition occur, the potential for conflicts of interest increases. Conflicts of interest arise when the obligations of a counselor's or psychologist's professional position, such as attending to the welfare of the client or consumer, conflict with the professional's own personal, financial, social, or political interests. Thus, if a teacher becomes involved in a real estate sale with a student, a conflict of interest may arise. The faculty person may be reluctant to give the student a negative evaluation fearing that the student could retaliate and in some way damage the faculty member's financial position. There was a conflict of interest when the professor in Case 11-4 asked the student to do "little favors" for him, when the research assistant used information from a study to coerce women into dating him, and in when Case 11-5, the supervisor's personal feeling appear to have conflicted with her professional responsibilities to evaluate the student fairly. In each of these cases, the loyalty and objectivity that the psychologist was obligated to give the consumer was compromised by a personal role. There are times when psychologists and counselors may be faced with conflicts of interest when they are not strictly in multiple relationships. For example, psychologists and counselors are faced with upholding the integrity of science and reporting research results accurately or modifying results to please funding agencies. (This issue is discussed further under the topic of multiple relationships and conflicts of interest in research.)

Because the roles of a psychologist and counselor carry with them expectations of knowledge, wisdom, and trustworthiness, substantial amounts of power and prestige become associated with the professional (Brown, 1994a; Gottlieb, 1993; Haug, 1999; Remely & Herlihy, 2010). Consequently, relationships with consumers are often asymmetrical because psychologists and counselors are in potentially influential positions. Clients, students, supervisees, research participants, and others may not be in positions to objectively evaluate the advice, requests, and recommendations that a professional makes and may be unable to reject them even when it is in their best interest to do so. As Brown and other feminists have observed, there is a real political and social context within which professional relationships operate. Abuses of power are facilitated by hierarchies that grant some people privileged positions. As the cases in this chapter illustrate, some professionals exploit their powerful position to the detriment of her consumers, who often feel too powerless to object to or question the professional's opinions or motives.

Based on role theory, the following guidelines can be used to assess the potential harmful consequences as well as benefits of entering into a new role with a consumer when there is a prior professional one or into a professional relationship when there is a prior personal one (Kitchener, 1988).

1. As the differences in expectations and obligations between the roles increase, so does the probability for misunderstanding, confusion, frustration, and anger. For example, there is a substantial difference in expectations between the role of a supervisor and a therapist, even though they may use some of the same skills. A supervisor is obligated to evaluate the supervisee and protect the public from potentially ill-trained or personally disturbed supervisees, as well as to enhance the development of the supervisee. By contrast, a therapist is obligated to make the well-being of the client a primary concern. If a supervisor provides therapy for a supervisee, there is a conflict in the expectations and obligations associated with the two roles.

2. As the potential for conflicts of interest between the roles the psychologist is playing increases, so does the potential for loss of objectivity about the consumer's best interests and the potential for the professional's needs to become primary. When this occurs, Brown (1994a) suggested that clients, students, research participants, and other consumers are objectified and can become a source of personal gratification for the professional. A lack of respect and a lack of appropriate professional caring is clearly demonstrated when the professional's need for personal gratification supersedes the needs of the consumer.

3. As the power and prestige between the professional's position and the position of the consumer diverge, the potential for exploitation and harm also increases. As already noted, the role of psychologist or counselor with the concomitant title of "doctor" carries with it inherent power. This power can be exacerbated by certain roles like "therapist" or "professor" that the professional plays, as well as by what some call transference and others refer to as stimulus generalizations. It is not unusual for clients, students, and even research participants to view therapists, professors, or researchers in excessively positive ways that exacerbates their vulnerability. Furthermore, power, when it is misused, is always potentially harmful, which is why multiple relationships always have the capability of creating harm.

4. As the professional and the consumer can clarify and agree on the expectations and obligations of the secondary roles and the use of power by the professional is used for good, the probability of benefit increases. Some multiple relationships or interactions are unavoidable and in fact may be beneficial. In addition, the power associated with a role is not automatically a source for harm. It can be used for good.

When role expectations are incompatible, when the power differential is great, and when conflicts of interest are involved, multiple relationships are particularly dangerous because of the harm that can befall the consumer through exploitation as well as through confusion and misunderstanding. It is these kinds of multiple relationships that should be considered a priori unethical. For example, Glaser and Thorpe (1986) suggested that because of the disparity in expectations and the potential for misuse of power, sexual relationships between faculty members and current students are ethically troublesome. There is also a conflict of interest because the faculty member's own sexual needs may conflict with what might be considered best for the student in other circumstances. In both the APA (2002) and ACA (2005) codes, these kinds of relationships were identified as unethical.

By contrast when the power differential is small, when conflicts of interest are minimal, and when role expectations are clear or compatible, there is little danger of harm (Kitchener, 1988). For example, friendships and joint authorship projects between professors and former graduate students involve few conflicts of interest and little power differential. If role expectations can be realigned, the potential for harm is low. In Case 11-7, the therapist and client were clear about the therapist's role at the meeting as well as his obligation to maintain confidentiality. There would be little justification to see these relationships or interactions as a priori unethical.

At the same time, if the role expectations and obligations are somewhat compatible, even though the power differential is great, the potential for benefit exists. As an example is the faculty member who collaborates with graduate students on a research project and uses his power to help make the project successful, get presented at a regional conference and later published. Another example is Case 11-7. In this case Dr. Kaye was able to honor both roles: that of former therapist to Christine and as program consultant to the clinical program. From the case we might assume that he provided direct benefit to the program and program faculty through consultation, and in addition provided some benefit to Christine's personal and professional development in that she saw firsthand her own therapist handle the multiple roles with integrity and prudence.

The four guidelines just explicated and the general decision-making model discussed in Chapter 2 can be used to develop a course of action for potential multiple relationship conflicts. Take Case 11-2 as an example. The facts of the case suggest the meeting at the restaurant is accidental or circumstantial, but it could develop into a full-fledged dual role if the psychologist's client, Becky, continues to date John and the couples socialize together. The second relevant fact involves confidentiality: the therapist has promised it, and the client has not waived it. Moreover, the psychologist feels caught between breaching confidentiality and explaining the situation to her husband or agreeing to meet with the couple the next weekend, which would lead to a multiple relationship.

Moving to the critical-evaluative level of ethical decision making, the APA and ACA ethics codes should remind the psychologist and counselor that confidentiality is a priority. Furthermore, the codes require that professionals refrain from entering new roles with clients when the relationship may interfere with the professional's objectivity, may negatively affect the therapeutic relationship, or may harm the client.

Social role theory can help identify questions of beneficence and nonmaleficence when considering the new relationship. It, for example, would suggest that the expectations and obligations of being a therapist differ substantially from those associated with being friends. The confidentiality issue is one example, but friends also share secrets, do things together, and provide mutual support. These are not typically true of therapy, thus, entering the new role may confuse the client and impair the therapist's ability to be therapeutic. Furthermore, the therapist may become enmeshed in a conflict of interest between her loyalty to her husband and her loyalty to Becky. Finally, the therapist is the more powerful person in the relationship. Although it does not seem likely that the therapist will use her power to exploit the client, it is likely that the power imbalance may leave both Becky and the therapist feeling uncomfortable and never really equals in the quasi-friendship.

Thus, the differences between the expectations and obligations of the new role and the therapeutic one are large, the possibility of a conflict of interest is high, and the power differential is also high. Taken together, the guidelines suggest that the probability of harm occurring as an outgrowth of developing a social relationship is high and, therefore, the new relationship should be avoided. The analysis suggests that the therapist's original impulse to turn the invitation down for another social event was appropriate.

Both the ethics codes and respect for Becky's autonomy suggest that the therapist should not inform her husband that Becky is her client without Becky's consent. On the other hand, this same respect may lead her to process the social meeting with Becky during their next session as well as develop a plan that they can mutually agree on for handling similar situations in the future. This may include helping Becky decide whether to disclose her relationship with the therapist to John and whether she wants to give the therapist permission to disclose their relationship to her husband. It may also include some discussion of the impact on the therapeutic relationship and their posttherapy relationship if the client's relationship with John becomes a long-term one. (See the section on nonerotic posttherapy relationships for some questions the therapist may need to discuss with the client.)

When psychologists' and counselors' professional responsibilities negatively influence their personal lives, making ethical decisions that are in the client's best interests are particularly burdensome. Experienced therapists who are both prudent and caring about their own loved ones as well as their clients foresee these kinds of problems and take precautionary measures. For example, one therapist indicated that she warned her spouse that they might encounter social situations in which she could not disclose how she knew someone and/or she might have to bow out of social situations if a conflict of interest occurred. She had to ask him to trust her not to use her professional role as an excuse unless the situation really warranted it.

Although understanding role expectations, conflicts of interest, and the power differential can provide general concerns to consider when evaluating the potential for harm to occur in multiple relationships, specifics regarding these kinds of relationships in clinical settings, academia, and research are discussed in the following sections. Because all multiple relationships involve some degree of risk, the potential for harm should always be evaluated (Gottlieb, 1993). Careful thought and consultation can help avoid impulsive blunders (Borys, 1994; Brown, 1994a) that traumatize consumers and risk collegial sanctions.

Blurred Roles and Boundaries in Therapy

According to Pope and Keith-Spiegel (2008), the issue of professional boundaries has been the main focus of over 1,500 scholarly works including journal articles, books, and other types of scholarship since the early 1980's. Over the last fifteen to twenty years, professionals have debated the benefit and harm of multiple nonsexual/nonromantic relationships between therapists and their clients. The result of this debate has been a continuum of perspectives. On one end of the continuum are those that see multiple roles with clients as beneficial and serving the public in a positive manner. On the other end are those that view multiple role relationships with caution. Across the continuum, there is a concerted effort to understand and make a distinction between boundary crossings or extensions and boundary violations. In the following sections we'll highlight the key issues of the debate behind the continuum and provide an overview of the related research.

Continuum of Perspective on Multiple Relationships

Historically, the issue of having another relationship with a client in addition to the therapeutic relationship was seen as risky business. Law suits involving sexual activity between therapist and client or former client prompted a response by ethicists and the professional associations such as APA and ACA to encourage members to be very careful in their interactions with clients outside of therapy. Barnett (2007a) suggests this response was from a "risk management" perspective. The belief was that practitioners who ultimately end up in a sexual relationship with clients did so by making a series of progressively more inappropriate behaviors with clients ultimately ending up in harmful and exploitive behaviors (Gabbard, 1989, 1994; Gutheil, 1989). To prevent the "slippery slope" phenomena from happening most of those who contributed to the literature encouraged practitioners to be wary of any outside contact which might lead to ethical missteps (Gutheil & Gabbard, 1993; Simon, 1989).

Currently ethicists recorded in the literature voice a continuum of perspective. On one end of the continuum are ethicists and practitioners who see the restriction by ethical codes as impractical and unproductive and even embrace the notion that multiple relationships with clients can be and many times are beneficial (Cottone, 2005; Ebert, 1997; Herlihy & Corey, 2006; Lazarus & Zur, 2002; Moleski & Kiselica, 2005). The conversations on this side of the continuum suggest that psychology and counseling are professions where overlapping boundaries should be expected and could in fact, be a good thing (Schank & Skovholt, 2006). In addition, some would suggest that the profession is too concerned with boundaries and the setting up of rigid rules which actually harms the therapeutic bond (Fay, 2002; Lazarus & Zur, 2002). Ethicists and practitioners with this view would suggest that there are benefits to having connections and relationships with clients beyond the therapy setting. Schank and Skovholt (1997) suggest that out of therapy contact can facilitate the use of psychological services by people who live in rural areas. Other researchers and writers have suggested that people in other small communities also benefit from secondary relationships with their therapist. These small communities include religious communities (Case, McMinn, & Meek, 1997), college campuses (Schank & Skovholt, 2006), and communities of color (Pedersen, 1997).

On the other end of the continuum is research and discussion in the literature to suggest that multiple relationships can bring unnecessary complications to the professional relationship and should be avoided whenever possible. Multiple relationships are problematic and capable of being harmful in therapy even when they do not involve sexual encounters (Borys, 1994; Gabbard, 1994; Pope, 1991; Pope & Vasquez, 1991; Sonne, 1994). Kitchener (1988) and Sonne (1994) present the view that professional counselors and psychologists may not be able to predict in an accurate way the level of or amount of harm that might come from entering into another relationship with a client. Anderson and Handelsman (2010) describe the professional relationship between a therapist and a client as a "delicate flower" and suggest that taking the relationship out of the "greenhouse" (therapeutic relationship) will result in harm. Others (Borys, 1992; Herlihy & Corey, 1992; Pope, 1991) support this notion of maintaining firm professional boundaries as well suggesting that the role expectations become confusing when psychotherapists enter a multiple relationship with clients and role confusion can result in psychological harm to the client and the therapeutic relationship. Pope and Vasquez (2007), question the justifications made by psychotherapist who enter into secondary relationships with clients. Sonne (1994) discusses the idea of a "slippery slope" and Smith and Fitzpatrick (1995) propose a similar notion with the term "role slippage." As therapists feel comfortable to extend the boundary in one context they become more comfortable to extend the boundary in another context. Ultimately, the erosion of boundaries can lead to more serious violations (Gabbard, 1994; Gutheil & Gabbard, 1993; Strasburger, Jorgenson, & Sutherland, 1992). For example, playing tennis with a client after hours may lead to a confusion of therapeutic boundaries and more intimate contact at a later date. In fact, Borys (1988) found a positive relationship between some nonsexual nontherapeutic relationships with clients and sexual involvement with clients. A study by Lamb and Catanzaro (1998) found that therapists, supervisors and instructors in a training or academic settings— who admitted to sexual relationships with clients, supervisees, and students—were more likely to cross boundaries with clients by disclosing personal issues or attending a special event of the client's. In addition, these same participants evaluated the nonsexual relationships between themselves and the client, supervisee or students less negatively than those participants who had not crossed the professional boundary.

Of course there is an increasing awareness that cultural differences and the complex web of personal and professional roles that characterize small communities make clear fixed rules difficult to formulate (Barnett, 2007a; Schank & Skovholt, 1997; Vasquez, 2007). Further, even different therapeutic schools can see the same event through distinct lenses, interpreting it as a potentially unethical boundary violation or an appropriate therapeutic intervention (Pope, Sonne, & Holroyd, 1993). A walk outside with a client may be an appropriate part of an *in vivo* desensitization for a cognitive-behavioral therapist but may represent a clear boundary violation to someone who is more psychodynamically oriented. How, then, do we make decisions about relationships with clients in these circumstances? The guidelines formulated in the last section offer a place to begin.

Sonne (1994) clarified the kinds of expectations that therapists and clients typically hold when they enter into a therapeutic relationship. The first and foremost expectation is that the relationship is a fiduciary one, meaning that the therapist identifies the best interests of the client as primary. Both expect that the purpose of the relationship is to help the client deal with the difficulty that brings him or her into therapy. This may include both assessment and treatment. If a walk outside is identified by the therapist as an appropriate therapeutic intervention that will help the client accomplish a therapeutic goal, and it is consistent with the treatment plan, it probably does not constitute a boundary violation, as long as the client understands the intervention in the same light. The therapist is not playing two roles but rather is using a different venue to accomplish the therapeutic task. On the other hand, if a therapist becomes an ongoing tennis partner of a client, he or she has entered into a social role as well as a therapeutic one with the client. Although some may argue that such a role might provide additional therapeutic information (Lazarus, 1994), others might suggest that clients' responses to such events are complicated and often unpredictable (Borys, 1994; Sommers-Flanagan & Sommers-Flanagan, 2007). As Gabbard (1994) pointed out, difficulties arise for both the therapist and the client in knowing when and whether to disregard boundaries or when and whether to honor them.

Sonne (1994) noted that clients may have other expectations about therapeutic roles:

> [Clients are] expected to come to scheduled sessions to discuss concerns often of an intimate nature, and to pay an agreed-on fee, among other expectations. The individual in the therapist role is expected to use abilities gained through education and training to assess and treat the problems brought in by the client, to exercise sound professional judgment, to recognize and respond appropriately to transference or counter transference, to maintain confidentiality, to keep records, to present testimony if subpoenaed, and so on. (p. 338)

Multiple-role relationships often upend these expectations and, thus, violate the fiduciary nature of the relationship.

The nature and importance of the therapeutic alliance makes taking on any kind of new role with a client particularly complex (Sonne, 1994). What is sometimes called the therapeutic bond, therapeutic alliance, or just the relationship between the client and the therapist is recognized across theoretical perspectives as a critical factor in positive psychotherapy outcome (Lambert & Ogles, 2004). Current research continues to support the key finding that the relationship between the therapist and the client is critical to therapeutic treatment (Hubble, Duncan, & Miller, 1999; Lambert & Ogles, 2004; Wampold, 2001). The therapeutic bond appears to provide the leverage that allows therapists to influence clients to make changes. Consequently, when this bond is destroyed or betrayed by conflicts of interest in which therapists' needs predominate, the effects on the client can be devastating.

Moreover, clients enter into therapy in a vulnerable emotional position. Because of intra or interpersonal discomfort, they seek the help of a professional person who offers them hope of relief from their pain. To get that relief, they must reveal information that they might find embarrassing, dangerous, or emotionally traumatic. Such revelations make them even more vulnerable, thus, the therapeutic alliance is central to their recovery and exacerbates the power differential in the relationship, making clients particularly susceptible to exploitation. Anderson and Handelsman (2010) have referred to the therapeutic relationship as a fragile flower that needs special care and nurturance. If cared for in the right conditions the flower will blossom into a beautiful flower. If exposed to harmful elements the flower will shrivel and die on the stem.

Multiple relationships can cause conflicts of interest in therapy (Pope, 1991). As noted earlier, the therapist by definition is in a fiduciary relationship with the client and therefore has implicitly or explicitly promised to put the client's needs foremost. If the therapist's own social, financial, or sexual needs conflict with that obligation, it can compromise sound professional judgment. Consequently, management of clients' feelings and beliefs about their therapist and their relationship become particularly troublesome. From a psychodynamic perspective, transference and counter-transference complicate this because residues of past relationships are unconsciously projected on the other person.

Few predictors of therapists' involvement in multiple relationships have been identified, with the exception of gender. In early studies of therapist–patient sexual intimacy, the general trend was for older male therapists to become sexually involved with younger female clients, although relationships between male therapists and male clients, between female therapists and male clients, and between female therapists and female clients have also occurred (Pope & Bouhoutsos, 1986). More current data based on cases adjudicated by the APA Ethics Committee in 2006 and 2007 suggest that this trend continues. In 2006 (APA, 2007), 100% all of the cases involving sexual relationships were between male therapists and adult female clients. In 2007 (APA, 2007), this trend continued with 64% of the cases involving male therapists committing sexual misconduct with a client.

These data have some parallels in nationals' surveys of therapists' attitudes toward multiple relationships. In a study of psychologists, psychiatrists, and social workers, Borys and Pope (1989) found that male therapists evaluated nonerotic, extratherapy involvements with clients as more ethical than did female therapists. Further, they found male therapists evaluated these involvements more ethical with female clients than with male clients. Similarly, Baer and Murdock (1995) found that male psychologists were more likely to rate nonerotic dual relationships as more ethical than were female psychologists.

When it comes to attitudes toward multiple relationships, therapists' theoretical orientation appears to be a factor. Several studies (Baer & Murdock, 1995; Borys & Pope, 1989; Holroyd & Brodsky, 1977; Pope, Tabachnick, & Keith-Spiegel, 1987) have found that therapists with a psychodynamic orientation rate nonerotic, nontherapeutic contact with clients as more unethical than do humanistic or cognitive–behavioral therapists. Because psychodynamic theory emphasizes unconscious processes, it may be that these therapists have a greater awareness of the implications of stretching role boundaries and the importance of maintaining a clear differentiation of what is therapy and what is not. This is not to say that appropriate cognitive behavioral interventions are unethical. It does mean however, that cognitive behavioral therapists need to be particularly careful of defining boundaries if they use in vivo interventions.

The degree to which therapists can maintain clear interpersonal boundaries between themselves and others has most recently been identified as a possible predictor of the ability to decipher potentially troublesome multiple relationships (Baer & Murdock, 1995). Baer and Murdock hypothesized that therapists' management of interpersonal boundaries would affect their ethical judgments about nonerotic dual relationships. They operationalized management of interpersonal boundaries as the degree of differentiation participants had from others. In fact, they found that respondents who were not well differentiated and under high levels of stress endorsed nonerotic contact with clients as more ethical than did respondents who were not under high levels of stress. Their data suggest that those who had more difficulty maintaining personal boundaries were less likely to see nonerotic, nontherapeutic contact as unethical.

The importance of maintaining clear boundaries with clients has been emphasized by several authors (Anderson & Handelsman, 2010; Borys, 1994; Gabbard, 1994; Sommers-Flanagan & Sommers-Flanagan, 2007; Sonne, 1994) who suggest that clear boundaries provide a sense of safety and structure within which the therapeutic alliance can be created. Further, they have argued that clients' responses to a shift in boundaries are difficult to anticipate ahead of time. Additionally, for some clients, particularly those who have been abused or victimized as children, a change in boundaries may reinforce the idea that care will only be provided when caretakers own needs are gratified (Borys, 1994). Additionally, the importance of maintaining boundaries in the presence of severe psychopathology (e.g., with clients who manifest borderline personality features or with victims of trauma or assault) goes without saying. Finally, clear boundaries help ensure that therapists will not use clients for their own gratification (Gabbard, 1994).

What Kinds of Nonerotic Multiple Relationships Are Potentially Harmful?

Although there are no explicit guidelines for deciding when particular multiple relationships are unethical, several studies have explored practitioners and clients perspectives. There is a range of perspective. Baer and Murdock (1995) and Borys and Pope (1989) found four interactions or relationships that therapists consider to be most problematic and rated as never ethical: selling a product or gift to a client, providing therapy to a current employee, engaging in sex with a client after therapy, and inviting a client to a personal party or social event. Additionally, respondents in the Borys and Pope's (1989) study rated sexual activity with a current client as never ethical. (The mean for this item was not reported in the Baer and Murdock study.) The majority of respondents in both studies also rated employing a client as always unethical or ethical only under rare conditions. Only two behaviors—accepting a gift worth less than $10 and accepting a client's invitation to a special occasion—were rated as ethical under some conditions by a majority of the respondents. Providing therapy to a friend, relative, or lover of an ongoing client was also endorsed as an activity that was ethical under some conditions. In a factor analysis of their research data (which surveyed psychologist, psychiatrists, and social workers) Borys and Pope found three significant factors: (a) incidental involvements that usually involved one-time events where therapeutic boundaries were altered at the client's request; (b) social or financial involvements such as becoming friends with a client after therapy; and (c) dual professional roles, such as providing therapy to a current student or supervisee. In a recent study of Canadian counselors, 23% suggested that it was ethical to invite a client to a social activity while 77% considered such a behavior as never ethical (Nigro, 2004). In other studies the perspective of professionals may show greater tolerance for developing multiple relationships (e.g., friendships) with clients and former clients. For example, 70% of therapists (Salisbury & Kinnier, 1996) and 83% of counselors (Nigro, 2004) saw developing a friendship with a former client as ethical at least some of the time. Sharkin and Birky (1992) investigated the beliefs and feelings of college and university counseling center therapists ($N = 573$) when it came to interactions or possible interactions with clients outside of the counseling session. A majority of participants expressed concern about nontherapy interactions with clients. They indicated that these interactions could lead to boundary violations and compromised confidentiality. When Pulakos (1994) asked clients about the same scenario—seeing their therapist outside of therapy—the response was opposite. Most clients indicated they were comfortable with the nontherapeutic interaction but for those that shared a negative response it had to do with wanting the therapist to interact more with them when these occasions occurred. On the other hand, when clients and former clients were interviewed about their experience of multiple relationships with their therapists, many reported awkward to negative results indicating they felt confused or devastated from the relationship Gibb, 2005).

In practice, multiple relationships are a reality for at least some practitioners. For example, Lamb, Catanzaro and Moorman (2004) surveyed 298 psychologists and found that many of them had confronted the issue of multiple relationships with current and former clients. More specifically, over half (60%) of their participants had negotiated a social relationship with a former client and 4% had negotiated a social relationships with current clients. Collegial and religious affiliation relationships with current and former client also occurred for these participants but less frequently. In rural settings, research has shown that out of therapy contact is a typical occurrence for mental health professionals (Horst, 1989; Schank & Skovholt, 1997; Younggren, 2002). In a qualitative study of lesbian and bisexual psychotherapists, Graham and Liddle (2009) found that almost half of their 52 respondents described social contact with clients or former clients. Most of these social interactions were incidental occurring at LGBT community functions or dances, sporting events or parties. Thirteen of the participants mentioned overlapping boundaries with clients in professional or work related context.

Social Relationships

Social relationships and interactions with clients can run the gamut from those that appear to be benign to those that are more clearly manipulative. Those that are manipulative are clearly unethical on the part of the professional and come from a place of conflict of interest as well an abusive use of power. However, even those that appear benign can have an adverse effect on therapy, as one of the authors learned the hard way. Early in Karen's career she had been working as a therapist in a university counseling center. In this context she had contact with several women who worked in student services. These were not deep interpersonal friendships but rather collegial in nature. Later, when Karen opened a private practice in town, one of the women sought her out for therapy and although the collegial relationship seemed to facilitate the establishment of the initial therapeutic bond little to none progress was made. After consultation with another psychologist Karen realized she had hoped this client would become a friend and these feelings hindered Karen from confronting the client about issues that needed addressing. As Karen remembers, she and client were not able to realign the relationship and the client left therapy without taking a referral.

The APA Ethics Committee has adjudicated similar cases. Take Case 11-8 as an example.

Case 11-8

Mr Sand had once participated in business-related workshops with a psychologist, after which they met for drinks a few times. Two years later, the psychologist called Mr Sand to say that he had recently opened a private psychotherapy practice and was taking referrals. Mr Sand confided that he and his wife were experiencing marital difficulties. The psychologist indicated his willingness to see them. Mr Sand was unsure whether his wife would agree, considering their earlier socializing. The psychologist said he saw no problem because it had been more than 2 years and suggested that it might be easier to talk with an acquaintance than a stranger. Mr Sand agreed, and an appointment was arranged. In the first sessions, Mrs Sand stated that she doubted the psychologist's ability to be fair and unbiased, given his previous friendship with her husband. Both the psychologist and Mr Sand assured her that no such relationship currently existed. Therapy proceeded, and

Mrs Sand repeatedly challenged the psychologist's impartiality, stating that she felt his interpretations were biased toward her husband (APA, 1987a, pp. 83–84).

In this case, as well as the one from Karen's own experience, prior social contacts interfered with the therapy process in ways that the therapist did not anticipate. In Case 11-8, the wife eventually filed an ethics complaint against the psychologist and the Ethics Committee found that the psychologist had engaged in a dual relationship with a client and had failed to terminate when it was clear that the therapy was not in the clients' best interests. The psychologist was censured. The ethics code for both psychologists and counselors encourages professionals to consider the possible negative outcomes of entering another professional role with a client. The APA code addresses the issue more specifically and encourages psychologists to refrain "from taking on professional or scientific obligations when preexisting relationships would create a risk of such harm."

Current social contacts with clients can be equally troublesome and confusing for clients (Anderson & Govan, 2001; Gibb, 2005). Meeting a busy client over lunch rather than in the office can be interpreted by the client as a sexual overture even if the client initiates it. Attending a special social event, such as a college graduation at a client's request, can also be misinterpreted, even though 35% of the therapists in the Borys and Pope (1989) study admitted to attending special occasions with at least some clients. If therapists choose to attend such events, and occasionally it may be therapeutic for the client for the therapist to do so, the therapist should be prepared to process the event with the client before attending the event and after returning. Most therapists with whom we have discussed these kinds of events admit that when they participate in them, they are always somewhat uncomfortable and on guard, aware that what they are saying and doing may have a therapeutic impact, either positive or negative. Thus, because therapists must be careful about their behavior to avoid damaging the therapeutic relationship, these events may not be very enjoyable and even feel ethically awkward for them.

Financial Relationships: Bartering and Beyond

Financial relationships between therapists and clients can be equally tricky. As one therapist noted, "The issue of money is quite complicated. There are many cases where the people need help and they obviously can't afford it. At least, they can't afford the kinds of help they need." (Lakin, 1988, p. 19). Consequently, therapists have to make difficult decisions about referring the client to resources they can afford or reducing their own fee. Some therapists have turned to bartering as a way to respond to clients' needs for services when clients have limited resources.

Bartering, whether it is for services or goods, continues to be a controversial issue. Several pitfalls await the therapist who decides to barter or exchange services for therapy (Remley & Herlihy, 2010). For example, exchanging services such as house cleaning, gardening or bookkeeping for the services of therapy puts the therapist in a multiple relationship with a client because the therapist becomes both the client's employer and therapist. Such a relationship can lead to exploitation of clients, as occurred in the following case.

Case 11-9

A therapist had been seen a client for several sessions, however, her insurance refused to pay for any more sessions. The client had very good computer skills and offered to trade her computer skills for additional therapy sessions. Because the therapist charged more for his sessions then was the going rate for "secretarial services," the client eventually fell further and further behind in her payments. Eventually, for all intents and purposes, the client became an indentured servant for the therapist (based on a case from APA, 1987a).

Above is the vivid description of the first pitfall. One hour of the client's services in computer skills was not equal to one hour of therapy. Although the therapist may have entered the arrangement with the best intentions, the outcome in the case above could be a resentful client and a frustrated therapist. A second potential pitfall with bartering for services is the quality of exchanged services. In the case above, the computer work could have been far below the expected level by the therapist. This could then become a therapeutic issue. The therapist may feel angry and betrayed, whereas the client may act out her own ambivalence about therapy in their work.

Although the issue of bartering for goods is also controversial, some have argued that if a fair market price can be put on the goods (e.g., a painting), then accepting goods was not an automatic ethics violation (APA, 1986; Hall & Hare-Mustin, 1983). At least, bartering for goods does not place the professional in the role of an employer of the client. On the other hand, if the product is not of good quality or in some other way is a disappointment to the therapist, it can also become a therapeutic issue. Koocher and Keith-Spiegel (2008) suggest that if in fact the "goods" to be used for bartering are of value, there is little need to have the therapist as the buyer. Other individuals would likely be just as interested in purchasing the object of value.

On the other hand, Welfel (2010) and others have suggested that there exist some valid reasons to not totally prohibit the practice of bartering. First, bartering does provide a way for making therapy and other professional services within the mental health field available to those who do not have the monetary resources available. Second, some communities such as rural communities and well as cultural groups see bartering as social norm. To resist this type of financial arrangement would run counter to the norms of the community (Helbok, 2003) and be seen as overlooking an essential practice within the culture (Sommers-Flanagan & Sommers-Flanagan, 2007).

The issues just stated, as well as others, build a rationale for the 2002 APA and 2005 ACA ethics codes not prohibiting bartering for goods or services. For the APA code, the issue really comes down to the use of such tactics if they are not contraindicated clinically or exploitative. In addition, to the tactic not being exploitative or harmful, the ACA code provides more guidance for the practitioner. First, the client must initiate the request. Second, bartering for the service needs to be seen as a common practice among professionals within the community. And third, the counselor is expected to consider and discuss the implications of bartering with the client and document the agreement in a clear written contract. This last issue or step is one that Woody (1998) recommended.

Because of the problems noted earlier, the conditions of no harm or exploitation are very difficult to meet. In fact, Woody (1998) argued that "bartering seems so fraught with risks for both parties that it seems illogical even to consider it as an option" (p. 176). Clearly, the therapist ought to consider other alternatives before agreeing to such a relationship, such as offering services at a very low or no cost or referring the client to another therapist or agency. Furthermore, a therapist would need to balance the good that might come from bartering against the potential harms that might occur. We believe that if bartering is considered, bartering for goods is ethically less problematic than bartering for services because the probability for harm is less likely.

Other financial relationships with clients, such as participating in a business venture, are equally problematic. Pope (1991) has noted that because of the power differential, the therapist and client cannot enter into a business relationship with a client on equal footing. Because of confidentiality, clients would face difficult obstacles in legally redressing a problem if they felt wronged in the financial situation. Further, therapists could discredit clients by using false diagnostic labels. Additionally, if it were common practice for therapists to use therapy as a way to engage in new business ventures, then screening for clients might become dependent on whether the client might improve the therapist's business opportunities. Clearly this is problematic. The therapist is already in a conflict of interest position. His or her interests in working with clients who offer the potential for business ventures are competing with the ethics of accurately assessing the client's needs for therapy and their (the therapist's) ability to meet those needs.

Multiple Relationships and Nonprofession Interactions in Small-Community Settings

At times multiple relationships are unavoidable. For example, many professionals are part of small communities. Practicing in some communities makes even unintentional relationships difficult to avoid. Rural communities are an example of such a community (Campbell & Gordon, 2003; Schank & Skovholt, 1997). Practitioners in rural settings are frequently faced with secondary relationships with clients outside the therapy setting. One only has to read the examples of professionals such as Welfel (2010) as being the only psychologist in a community of 8,000 to feel the unique challenges of small communities. Of course, professionals working and living in large cities might be part of a "shared community" with those who would seek their professional's services (Adelman & Barrett, 1990). For example, LGBT psychotherapists and their clients who also identify as LGBT are very likely to see each other at LGBT community events or in social settings (Brown, 1989; Dworkin, 1992; Kessler & Waehler, 2005). After reviewing multiple studies, Morrow (2000) suggested vast majority of LGBT therapists (up to 95%) see clients in settings outside the psychotherapy office. As a corroborating story, a lesbian friend of one of the authors once remarked that she sometimes felt like she could not have a social life and see clients in the same city. Most of her referrals came from the lesbian community, and consequently she would run into clients at social gatherings, which was often difficult for both her and her client. Other small or shared communities include the military bases, religious or spiritual communities, cultural or ethnic enclaves, and deaf communities. Living and working in these small communities means that multiple relationships are a given.

Several characteristics of small-community settings, make limiting multiple relationships or nonprofessional interactions between professionals and clients particularly difficult. First, living and working in smaller communities leads to complex formal and informal social and political relationships that are often intense and interrelated. In this setting, there are often multiple levels of personal and professional relationships (Flax, Wagenfeld, Ivens, & Weiss, 1979; Hargrove, 1986). Clients who are part of a ethnic cultural community (e.g., Latino) may expect their psychotherapists who are also be of the same ethnic or cultural background to be involved community members (Kertesz, 2002). Second, although people in larger communities might expect and even prefer professionals to be personally unknown to them, research suggests that people in small communities or share communities prefer the familiar face because they trust the person they know in social contexts (Helbok, 2003; Guthman & Sandberg, 2002). For example, because of the unique cultural experience of individuals who live in and are part of the Deaf community, people needing psychotherapy specifically seek out psychotherapist who are known and trusted (Guthman & Sandberg, 2002). Third, because of the long distances between communities of large and small populations, it may be impossible to avoid a variety of relationships with clients. Take Case 11-10 for an example.

Case 11-10

A therapist signed his son up for Little League baseball. After he had done so, he found out that the former coach was no longer available and that one of his current clients had stepped into the position. They saw each other frequently at games and when the therapist took his son to practice. The therapist was particularly vocal about how the team should be run and expressed his feelings during the game. The therapeutic alliance was irreparably damaged because the client felt the therapist no longer approved of her.

Facing the complexities of small community settings and unavoidable multiple relationships with clients calls for therapists to consider several issues. Morrow (2000) suggested that LGBT therapists working with LGBT clients not automatically build rigid boundaries around nonprofessional relationships because this approach might actually do more harm than good to the therapy relationship. Psychotherapists who might be tempted to steer clear of or successfully avoid multiple relationships with clients from some ethnic cultures could be seen as unapproachable and emotional distant (Kertesz, 2002) or in actuality be doing more harm by denying clients who are deaf their only means of culturally sensitive therapeutic treatment (Guthman & Sandberg, 2002). With this said, words of caution still apply. For example, therapists who pride themselves in and practice from a feminist perspective need to stay aware of the inherent power differential within the relationship and issues of confidentiality that extend beyond the therapy hour (Brown, 1989; Keeler & Waehler, 2005). We believe the following three important questions can be asked:

> Under what conditions should multiple relationships and nonprofessional interactions with clients be absolutely avoided?
> How should relationships and interaction that cannot be avoided be managed?
> What criteria should be used to make these decisions?

Ethicists have offered different models or ways to address questions such as above. Templeman (1989) offers one such model. He suggested that in small-community settings, therapists need to assess the potential intensity and intimacy of the second or third relationship with clients. He argued that as the intensity of the relationship increases, so does the potential for harm. This may be because the differences in expectations and potential conflicts of interest are greater. Templeman differentiated between what he called low-impact transactions, such as passing contacts and common outside affiliations, and high-impact transactions, which have high bonding and expectations for sharing intimate information. Ordering a prescription from a pharmacist or participating in a Rotary club might fit in the first category, whereas participating in a Bible study, support group, or friendship might fit into the second category (Templeman, 1989). He suggested that therapists need to learn to manage high-impact contacts with the best interests of the consumer in mind which is what the therapist in Case 11-9 did not do. This includes clarifying with a client prior to beginning a therapeutic relationship the nature of any prior relationships and how they might influence therapy, the likelihood of future contacts once therapy has begun, the potential harm that prior contacts might have on treatment, the potential harm that might occur from future outside contacts, and the cost to clients of being referred elsewhere or not receiving treatment. The nature and limits of confidentiality need also to be discussed. Some agreement needs to be reached with the client about whether the therapist will acknowledge that the client is in therapy and how other confidential information will be handled in these alternative settings. Further, time needs to be spent during the therapeutic hour processing these alternative contacts and how they are affecting therapeutic progress.

A relatively new issue that impacts professional boundaries and creates a different type of "small community" for psychologists and counselors is cyberspace (Zur, 2008). According to Internet World Stats, 28.7% of the world's population and 77.3% of the United States population are Internet users (Internet World Stats, 2010). Lehavot, Barnett, and Powers (2010) suggest the use of internet sets the stage for numerous ethical dilemmas or ethical complexity in professional relationships. For example, should the psychologist or counselor post personal information on a social network site, clients are only a few clicks away from discovering personal information about their therapist or requesting the therapist "friend" them via the social network. Of course, some personal disclosure on Facebook or Twitter by the psychologist or counselor may be harmless to the professional relationship with the clients. However, should professionals post information of a more intimate nature that is easily accessible to clients, the distinct line between professional and personal entities can quickly vanish (Lehavot et al., 2010) and unintentional harm to the therapeutic relationship could occur.

In addition to the ethical issue of careful self-disclosure via the internet, psychologists and counselors can sometimes find or seek out personal information of clients (Lehavot et al., 2010). This is also an ethical issue. The second author recalls an incident where a practicum student used the internet to "check on a client" via a social networking site to learn if the client was talking of harm to self or to others. On the one hand, the act of seeking out additional information because of concern is admirable and suggests that the student was acting beneficently. However, on the other, the practicum student's actions could have resulted in damaging the therapeutic alliance. The client did not invite the practicum student to visit their personal site and could have felt that a trust was violated. Most clients enter a therapy relationship expecting the right to share information with the therapist at the level and pace they choose, basically the right to autonomy. When psychologists or counselors seek out information about the client from the internet without the client's permission or awareness, it suggests a violation of the principle of fidelity which is vitally important for a trusting therapeutic relationship.

Professionals and students in training are in need of guidance to negotiate the complexities that the internet, and more specifically social networking, promotes for the professional and his or her clients. Organizations such as ACA (1999) and the Canadian Psychological Association (2008) have developed standards for online services. Barnett (2008) and Lehavot (2007) have offered recommendations and questions for psychologists and counselors to consider before they hit the post or submit button on their social networking site. The ethics of using the internet for good and not for harm will need to be addressed in future APA and ACA codes.

In summary, some practitioners are faced with the issue of multiple relationships and nonprofessional interactions because of where they live and practice or the overlap between their expertise as a therapist and who they are as a person. As Jennings suggested (1992), practitioners in these setting need to make a solid commitment to the ethical principles and values of the profession and be flexible enough to work through the fluid nature of overlapping personal and professional boundaries. Generally, ethics codes are clear on encouraging mental health professionals to consider the context as they decide whether or not to enter into a multiple relationship with a client (Knapp & VandeCreek, 2003) beyond this there is little guidance. For example, the 2005 ACA code mentioned the possibility of beneficial nontherapy relationships, but it offered no guidance about how to assess whether the added relationship would be beneficial or exploitive.

Posttherapy Relationships with Clients

Discussions of ethical obligations with former clients have been relatively scarce until recent years. There has been a general understanding that confidentiality promises remain in force in perpetuity, that psychologists need to maintain records, and that they may be called to testify regarding former clients. Still, it was not until the late 1980s and early 1990s that discussions began regarding whether psychologists and counselors should enter into sexual relationships with former clients (Akamatsu, 1988; Borys & Pope, 1989; Kitchener, 1992a; Pope & Vetter, 1992; Sell, Gottlieb, & Schoenfeld, 1986; Vasquez, 1991). Other ethical obligations of therapists to former clients had been generally ignored until recently (Anderson & Kitchener, 1996, 1998; Bleiberg & Baron, 2004; Lamb et al., 1994; Pipes, 1997; Remley & Herlihy, 2007; Sommers-Flanagan & Sommers-Flanagan, 2007; Welfel, 2010); however, studies (Anderson & Kitchener, 1996; Bouhoutsos, Holroyd, Lerman, Forer, & Greenberg, 1983; Borys & Pope, 1989; Conte, Plutchik, Picard, & Karasu, 1989; Lamb et al., 2003, 2004; Nigor, 2004; Pope et al., 1987) have suggested that therapists have had to struggle with whether to enter a full range of nonsexual, nonromantic relationships with former clients. Research would suggest that practitioners are currently feeling freer to enter posttherapy relationships with clients than they have in the past. For example, in 1989, Borys and Pope found that approximately 46% of their respondents believed becoming friends with former clients was ethical under some conditions. In 1996, Salisbury and Kinnier found 70% of their respondents held this belief. And in 2004, Nigro found 83% of respondents believed becoming friends with former clients was ethical at least some of the time.

In an exploratory study, Anderson and Kitchener (1996) identified the following eight kinds of posttherapy relationships in which psychologists described participating:

1. Brief and/or unplanned social interactions in which the two parties had participated in joint events.
2. Personal or friendship relationships in which therapists and former clients were both personally invested and were more than social acquaintances.
3. Business or financial relationships in which money was paid for the former client's expertise or the therapist and former client entered a joint business venture.
4. Supervisory relationships where the former therapist supervised or evaluated the former client.
5. Relationships centered on celebrations or work in a religious setting.
6. Collegial relationships in which the therapist and former client held positions generally equal in power.
7. A combination of social and collegial relationships in which they participated in a variety of activities.
8. Coincidental collegial relationships where the former client was hired as an employee of the same business.

In almost all categories, some of the relationships occurred because of changing circumstances, such as when a therapist became a neighbor of a former client or a former client registered for the former therapist's class. Others involved conscious choices on the part of either the therapist or the client. There was little consensus among the psychologists participating in these roles about the ethicality of these relationships. Some believed that "once a client, always a client" and that the proscriptions about dual-role relationships ought to apply to former clients. Others did not perceive an ethical problem with the relationships they had entered.

Given the range of potential relationships with former clients, thinking carefully about the ethical issues involved when either circumstantial or intentional opportunities arise to enter into relationships with former clients becomes critical. Defining who classifies as a former client is not as easy as it might appear. Pipes (1997) defined former clients as those "for whom there has been a responsible and appropriately documented termination process, who do not anticipate returning for therapy, and who have in no way been led to believe that they are free to return to therapy" (p. 28). He noted, however, that sometimes it is difficult to specify whether a client is really a former client. For example, the APA Ethics Committee took the position that a termination for the purpose of entering into a sexual relationship with a client is not a legitimate termination (*Sex with Ex-clients*, 1987). Pipes also argued that those who are told by their therapists to drop by in a couple of months are not truly former clients and that some clients consider returning to therapy long after termination has occurred.

Anderson and Kitchener (1998) suggested that therapists consider four concerns when evaluating the ethical risks involved in entering a posttherapy relationship and when considering how to handle interactions that are unintentional or involve limited contacts.

Component 1—Involves the Therapeutic Contract   The contract includes the limits of confidentiality, the duration of the relationship, and the respective roles of therapist and client. When considering a relationship with a former client, the therapist needs to consider each aspect of the contract and how it will be handled in the new relationship. Anderson and Kitchener (1998) suggested asking the following questions:

Did you and the client come to a clear closure?

Did you process the termination?

Has enough time passed for you and your client to engage in new role behaviors?

How will confidentiality be handled?

Were the presenting problems resolved?

Does the client understand that entering a new relationship will mean that a return to therapy with you will be unfeasible?

Component 2—Involves the Therapeutic Bond   The bond can remain a potent influence even after therapy ends because transference or strong feelings about the former therapist may be unresolved (Pipes, 1997) and the power differential may not have changed substantially. Former clients, because of their psychological history, remain vulnerable to exploitation after therapy terminates. Anderson and Kitchener (1998) suggested considering the following questions:

What was the strength of the therapeutic bond, and did you and the client process changes in it?

In light of the power differential, to what extent is the former client's decision to enter into a new relationship an autonomous one?

Did therapy encourage self-reliance and responsibility or dependence?

Ignoring the nature of the therapeutic bond can lead to relationships that are at minimum uncomfortable for therapists, even if they may not be harmful for former clients. As one therapist said,

Can you be friends with patients? It is something I've always been taught was an absolute no-no, but I resisted the idea. It happened that one young woman I treated, well, we were on the same wavelength. She asked me to have lunch with her. I did lots of soul-searching and said that I would. Over the years I've done the same thing with two others. The truth is that it did set up some kind of dependency thing that continues to this day. It's never really been an equal friendship, and it can't possibly be. (Lakin, 1988, p. 26)

Component 3—Involves Social Role Issues   These issues were discussed earlier in this chapter and include confusion about role expectations between the former role and new role. Questions that the therapist might ask include the following:

Have the former client and I clarified how our roles will change, and are our expectations realistic?

How might our perceptions of each other gained in therapy influence our perceptions in our new roles?

To what extent can we be equals in the new relationship?

Component 4—Involves the Therapist's Motivation   Therapists can have competing values and motivations for entering into a posttherapy relationship. As a result, therapists should consider the following questions:

Will the former client will be exploited by the new relationship?

If the new relationship is avoidable, why do I want to enter into it?

What personal benefits might I derive from entering the relationship?

When evaluating the answers to these questions, therapists need to balance the principles of autonomy with those of fidelity, nonmaleficence, justice, and beneficence. On one hand, therapists do not want to undermine clients' trust in themselves and suggest that they can never freely decide to interact with their former therapists. To do so would be grossly parentalistic and truly violate the principle of autonomy. On the other hand, at least some posttherapy relationships with clients, even nonsexual ones, can be problematic and harmful. Therapists always should avoid entering into relationships with clients that are potentially harmful and that undo the gains clients have made and for which they have paid (Anderson & Kitchener, 1998; Kitchener, 1992a).

Anderson and Kitchener (1998) suggested processing these concerns first with a trusted colleague and then with the former client. Working with a trusted colleague can help therapists examine their own reasoning and motivation. Particularly, they need to evaluate why they might want to become involved in the relationship and how it might affect the therapeutic gains clients have made. Processing the issues with former clients can help clients make a more informed decision about entering into the new relationship by better understanding the consequences of doing so, including the fact that the new relationship probably precludes returning to therapy with their former therapist.

Managed Care and Conflicts of Interest

In the early 1970's with the HMO Act, managed care became a mechanism to control the costs of health care including mental health (DeLeon, VandenBos, & Balatao, 1991). Since the 1980's, a large percentage of mental health care costs have been provided for by "behavior health care-out plans" (Sanchez & Turner, 2003, p. 116) sometimes referred to as "managed care." In 2003, it was estimate that 88% of the insured managed care population was served or enrolled in a managed mental health care program (Sanchez & Turner, 2003). Although there may be some good or benefit that has evolved out of managed care such as increased access to mental health services (Cooper & Gottlieb, 2000), a large scale study surveying almost 16,000 psychologists found four out of every five participants reporting negative consequences and impact on their professional activities because of managed care (Phelps, Eisman, & Kohout, 1998). Of the negative impacts, ethical dilemmas were one their top five issues.

Several authors have addressed the ethical issues that come with managed care organizations (MCO) involvement (Cooper & Gottlieb, 2000; Daniels, 2001; Danzinger & Welfel, 2001; La Roche & Turner, 2002; Tjeltveit, 2000). One of the key ethical issues is an inherent conflict of interest. Koocher and Keith-Spiegel (1998) argued that the paramount ethical dilemma for psychologists when working with managed care involved "conflicting loyalties" (p. 251). Psychologists and counselors have a primary responsibility to the consumer to provide good therapy while at the same time support the managed care's goal of cost containment (Cooper & Gottlieb, 2000). Many managed care companies use a variety of hidden incentives (Miller, 1996a). For example, participation in panels or preferred provider lists requires the therapist to maintain a cooperative working relationship as determined by the managed care organization or the therapist might be dropped from the list. This cooperative working relationship is translated into brief therapy even for clients who have severe mental health needs (Cooper & Gottlieb, 2000). In essence, therapists are expected to complete client care with certain time limits and given report cards, so to speak, based on this criteria. Poor performance by the practitioner could result in dismissal from panels or preferred provider lists (Miller, 1996a). Furthermore, sometimes participation on panels is accompanied by gag rules that forbid the professional from providing consumers with information about the incentives that they receive for limiting services.

These policies can lead to serious conflicts of interest for providers. Take Case 11-11 as an example.

Case 11-11

Mr Rand contacts a psychologist for treatment of depression. After a thorough assessment, the psychologist diagnoses him with a major depression and formulates a treatment plan. When the psychologist contacts Mr Rand's MCO, the case manager tells him that he is cleared to provide up to six psychotherapy sessions and that he should also refer Mr Rand to a psychiatrist for antidepressant medication. When the psychologist reminds the case manager that Mr Rand's policy allows up to 20 sessions of psychotherapy, the case manager points out that the psychologist is already over his quota for long-term patients (those that continue beyond six sessions) and that if he cannot treat Mr Rand in six sessions, there are others on the provider panel who can. She argues that most depressed clients get better within this period of time when psychotherapy is combined with medication.

Subtle or not-so-subtle coercion from case managers or others in managed care organizations creates clear conflicts of interest for mental health professionals. The numbers of therapists on provider panels for managed care organizations is often limited, and dismissal from these panels may seriously threaten a professional's livelihood.

In addition, appropriate treatment for some clients involves longer term psychotherapy. Failing to provide follow-up treatment to clients who clearly need it could be construed as abandoning a client which is an ethical issue for both psychologists and counselors. The codes (ACA, 2005; APA, 2002) required therapists to discuss with clients as early as feasible any anticipated limitations on services because of financing. This implies that agreeing to a gag order would probably also be viewed as unethical. The principles of autonomy, beneficence, and nonmaleficence would support his position. Failing to provide adequate information to clients would prohibit them from understanding the true parameters of treatment and to make choices accordingly. It may also ultimately lead to inadequate treatment and harmful outcomes.

Miller (1996a) argued that agreeing to a gag order and not referring clients for further treatment could also lead to legal liability. He pointed to a case in which a severely depressed man committed suicide after having been told that six sessions of psychotherapy and medication was all that was "medically necessary" (Miller, 1996a, p. 585). The man's wife sued the HMO and the therapist claiming her husband's decision to kill himself was based on the belief that he had received all of the treatment that was medically appropriate, but he was still depressed. He was not told that long-term therapy was even an option.

Multiple Relationships in Forensics

A variety of problematic multiple professional role relationships have been documented, such as providing therapy to a current employee or providing therapy to a current student or supervisee. Some of the most far-reaching in terms of their implications involve forensics, as was illustrated by Case 9-1. In that case, a psychologist was asked by the court to act as a mediator. After the mediation failed, the psychologist voluntarily submitted an evaluation on the parents and recommended that custody be given to the mother.

By taking on both the roles of mediator and evaluator, the psychologist entered into a dual professional role with the couple. Further, she failed to inform the couple that she was engaged in both of these roles and did not get the couple's consent to release confidential information from the mediation to the court. The mother filed a complaint with the APA Ethics Committee, and the psychologist was censured for entering into a multiple-role relationship about which she did not inform the couple and for breaking confidentiality without permission or a court order.

The economic changes in clinical practice and the non presence of managed care in forensic services, tempts psychologists and counselors to enter into forensic roles as expert witnesses for their clients (Woody, 2009). Greenberg and Shuman (1997) suggested that although therapists may want to assist their clients and their pocket books through expert testimony, these types of multiple relationships "often leads to bad results for patients, courts, and clinicians" (p. 50). They pointed out that there are irreconcilable conflicts between a therapeutic role and a forensic role and their recommendation is that therapist should not serve a consumer in both roles (Greenberg & Shuman, 2007). To clarify the issue, it is important to differentiate *fact witnesses* and *expert witnesses* in a legal proceeding. A fact witness can provide factual evidence in a legal proceeding. Acting as a fact witness is a duty of all citizens unless privileged communication or other confidentiality laws preclude it. When called to testify as a fact witness, therapists can and must testify about what a client said about a particular issue, assuming that they have a waiver of confidentiality. No special knowledge is required to be a fact witness because one is testifying about what is known firsthand (Greenberg & Shuman, 1997).

Acting as an expert witness puts a psychologist or counselor in a different role. An expert witness is a person who, because of his or her education or specialized experience, has superior knowledge regarding a subject about which others who have no particular training are incapable of forming an accurate opinion (Black, 1979). An expert is permitted to offer his or her opinion about psycho-legal issues on the basis of his or her specialized knowledge. It is when therapists enter into expert witness roles that role conflicts can occur. Sometimes therapists blunder into dual roles with their clients because they do not understand the difference between acting as a fact witness and acting as an expert witness for their client.

Greenberg and Shuman (1997) pointed out that the nature of the therapeutic role and the nature of the expert witness role create an inherent conflict for several reasons. They identified several aspects of the forensic role that particularly conflict with a therapeutic one. First, in a therapeutic setting, the person involved in the litigation (client-litigant) is the client of the therapist for purposes of treatment. However, the client-litigant is also the client of an attorney for legal purposes. If the attorney hires the therapist as an expert witness, the therapist now works for both the client and the attorney. Second, the rules regarding privileged communication are substantially different between therapy and forensic evaluations. Third, the relationship between a therapist and a client is typically supportive, accepting, and empathic, whereas the forensic evaluator role is neutral, objective, and detached. When a therapist acts as an expert witness, he or she is actually a "part of the fabric of the case ... evaluating the impact of his or her own participation" (Greenberg & Shuman, 2007, p. 130) in the client's mental health or condition. Due to the likelihood of conflicting interests, the professional's judgment will be compromised and lack objectivity. Fourth, a therapist's role is a helping one, whereas a forensic evaluator often plays an adversarial role, seeking information that may both support and refute the client's claims. Additionally, the focus of a therapeutic relationship is to benefit the client, whereas the evaluator is really working for the benefit of the court. In a forensic evaluation, the psychologist or counselor is taking an evaluative, judgmental stance, whereas a therapist typically avoids being judgmental; in fact, taking such a stance may negatively affect the therapeutic alliance.

Psychologists and counselors must be clear about the nature of their relationship with clients when they step into a legal setting. Acting as an expert witness for a therapy client can lead to a series of conflicts of interest that can eventually damage the therapeutic alliance and lead to confusion, frustration, and pain for the client. In a forensic role, the psychologist or counselor can be seen as operating in "double-agentry" (VandenBos, 2007) where the therapist's loyalty to the client is competing with the demands of the judicial system. Even when a therapist acts as a fact witness, clients can be confused about the nature of confidentiality and information that might be revealed. It is always best when moving from a therapeutic role to one that involves the courts to discuss the potential problems with clients ahead of time.

Multiple Relationships in Academe through Teaching and Mentoring

As faculty members in a psychology or counseling programs, multiple relationships with students are undoubtedly part of everyday experience. A faculty member will in one day move in and out of several roles with a student or students which have different responsibilities (Brown & Krager, 1985; Kitchener, 1992b; Rupert & Holmes, 1997; Welfel, 2010). For example, in the morning the faculty member teaches a course on therapy theories, at noon meets with her advisee about the student's dissertation, and later that afternoon works with two other students on a manuscript for publication. Her last meeting of the day is with her protégé about an upcoming conference where the two of them will copresent a research project. To complicate matters further, department heads that typically engage in most of the same roles as other faculty members also make decisions about terminating students from graduate programs (Kitchener, 2000).

Faculty and students are sometimes encouraged to spend time together in informal settings because of the belief that such involvement helps to motivate students, socialize them into academic settings, and bolsters the profession (Astin, 1993; Hardy, 1994; Johnson & Nelson, 1999; O'Neil, 1981; Tabachnick, Keith-Spiegel, & Pope, 1991). When a faculty member takes a personal interest in a student, it may enhance the student's esteem as a learner as well as provide the opportunity for intellectual dialogue about academic questions. In fact, informal out-of-class contacts between faculty and students have been empirically related to the development of general cognitive skills and academic performance in college; intrinsic occupational values; acculturation to the profession and professional identity development; professional networking; assistance in career choice; and mental health or psychological wellbeing (Allen, Eby, Poteet, Lentz, & Lima, 2004; Astin, 1993; Atkinson, Neville, & Casas, 1991; Johnson, 2002; Pascarella & Terenzini, 1991; Schlosser & Gelso, 2001; Wilson & Johnson, 2001). Students who report the greatest cognitive growth during college also report having a close, influential relationship with one or more faculty members.

Some authors refer to these relationships as "mentor-protégé" relationships (Johnson & Nelson, 1999), and see them as having great value (Bowman, Hatley, & Bowman, 1995; Schweibert, 2000; Welfel, 2010). The benefits include informal guidance, role modeling, and support for professional development that is beyond the typical advisor/advisee relationship. Clark, Harden, and Johnson (2000) completed a study of 1,000 recent graduates from clinical psychology programs regarding their experience of mentoring during the doctoral program. Around 80 % responded to the survey. Women and men were equally likely to have received mentoring and those that received mentoring were more satisfied with their doctoral program experience.

As previously mentioned, the protégé receives some benefits but so too does the mentor (Barnett, 2007a). The mentor reaps the possible benefit of intellectual and professional collaboration and stimulation, the encouragement to stay aware and current of the field, personal/professional friendship and connection, and networking opportunities (Johnson, 2003; Johnson, Koch, Fallow, & Hume, 2000; Russell & Adams, 1997).

On the other hand, mentor or protégé relationships have the potential for ethical concerns (Johnson & Nelson, 1999; Clark et al., 2000). For example, in Clark et al.'s (2000) study a little over 10% (almost equally men and women) of the respondents (almost equally men and women) identified 79 specific ethical concerns about the mentor or the mentoring relationship. Four of more frequently identified concerns were relationship issues: sexualized relationships between the mentor and the protégé, or sexualized relationships between the mentor and another student in the program; and the mentor having inappropriate boundaries by being too emotionally involved with students.

Mentoring relationships can also carry with them the opportunity for confusion regarding role expectations and obligations because clear boundaries between faculty and students are somewhat blurred and difficult to define (Rupert & Holmes, 1997). The consequence is that sometimes students and faculty may become confused about appropriate expectations and obligations. Moving in and out of these interactions and role responsibilities with students and protégés, calls for clarity in role obligations by the faculty person. Without this in place, ethical missteps by the faculty person are most likely to occur.

This confusion about appropriate expectations and obligations might be especially true for the recent graduate/new faculty member. Most graduate programs don't train those headed for a career in academe for the change of "cultures" they soon to experience. Moving from one role in the culture (doctoral student in-training) to another (new faculty member and the expectations, obligations, and power that comes with the role) could be considered an acculturation process. The psychology and counseling faculty culture are subsets of the larger professional cultures. In many ways, the new faculty member might still feel like and identify with students enrolled in his or her courses. The new faculty member might send (unintentionally) mixed messages to the students about friendship outside the classroom (Johnson & Nelson, 1999). Note the case below.

Case 11-12

Dr. Cheryl's first semester as a faculty person was rather difficult. She had moved across the country for this new position and a support system within the department was slow in coming. Several of her doctoral students seemed to gather at her office on Friday afternoon to discuss upcoming weekend events (both personal and academic). One particular doctoral student in particular, LaVonna, seemed to find many reasons and opportunities to connect with Dr. Cheryl outside the classroom. In fact, right before the semester break, LaVonna invited Dr. Cheryl over to her home for dinner with her and her family. When Dr. Cheryl accepted the invitation the student responded, "Oh good! I have other friends coming too. I really want you to meet them. They are just like you. They've been really supportive friends for me this semester." Dr. Cheryl was a little surprised and taken aback. Friend? Is that how LaVonna saw her? She started to rethink her decision to attend the dinner and wondered how she would address the possible miscommunication about their relationship.

A similar scenario occurred for Karen and her husband. Early in the professorate career of Karen's husband they were invited to a student's house for dinner. As soon as they sat down, they realized they had made a mistake. They felt very uncomfortable and left as soon as possible. Her husband had to call the student into his office and clarify his role as a faculty member. Although they have both subsequently invited students to their home, they have been very clear that they are doing so in roles as faculty members. The situation just described and Case 11-12 highlight an interesting, critical issue of student perception. Although on one level new faculty members and teachers may be cognizant of their role obligations and expectations, students may have a different take on the interaction and relationship (Kobert, Morgan, & Brendel, 2002). Misperceptions and misunderstanding of professional roles and boundaries need to addressed and clarified by the faculty as soon as they become aware of the miscommunication.

Faculty members may also be faced with making decisions regarding other, more explicit multiple relationships. For example, they might have to work with a friend or client who enrolls in a class they are teaching. The faculty person they might consider entering a business venture with a student, they might be members of the same social or religious organization as are their students, or they might have the opportunity to engage in a social or sexual relationship with a student (Blevins-Knabe, 1992). Some might consider hiring students as child or house sitters. Take for example the following case.

Case 11-13

Dr. Sanders was trying to figure out what to do. He and his wife had been planning a trip for over six months and now the child care person they had hired to watch their two young children was in the hospital and would not be able to work for them. As parents, Dr. Sanders and his wife were cautious about who they hired as sitters. They had two bad experiences and weren't willing to trust just anyone. One person, a student in the program came to mind. Dr. Sanders knew he could trust Tiffany. She was a very good student and loved kids. In a month she would graduate from the program. She would be a graduate, a former student three days before Dr. Sanders and his wife would leave for their trip. Dr. Sanders decided to ask Tiffany if she would watch his children.

Nonsexual forms of multiple relationships between faculty members and students are not uncommon. In a study of faculty members in a cross-section of disciplines, Fitzgerald, Gold, Ormerod, and Weitzman (1988) found that 80% of the respondents indicated they had friendships with students, 76% admitted giving advice to students, and 21% said they loaned money to students. Similarly, in a study of academic psychologists, Tabachnick et al. (1991) found that at least on some occasion 76% of the respondents asked students for small favors (e.g., a ride home), 66% lent money to students, 86% accepted a student's invitation to a party, and 87% accepted an inexpensive gift from a student. Additionally, 49% bartered course credit instead of salary for student research assistants.

On the other hand, because the mentor–protégé relationship can be "complex and emotionally intense" (Hardy, 1994, p. 198) relationships between faculty and student can turn to sexual encounters or interactions. In the study by Clark et al. (2000) of recent psychology doctoral graduates, 4% felt their mentor's actions were sexually seductive, and 2% reported that the mentor acted on these behaviors and sexualized the relationship.

In some ways, different role responsibilities are inherent in the multiple obligations of academic faculty because they are accountable both for enhancing the welfare of their students and for protecting the public from incompetent psychologists or counselors. As a result, faculty have to navigate through promoting the principles of nonmaleficence (keeping harm from happening to unsuspecting clients) and fidelity, which is the promise to train students who might become part of the profession, and work with clients. In many ways, faculty are the gatekeepers to the profession (Vacha-Haase, Davenport, & Kerewsky, 2004). Because of the multiple expectations associated with the roles that faculty members play, role theory suggests that students may experience confusion and distress as they try to figure out what role they should play in response to shifting relationships with faculty. This becomes particularly problematic when faculty tries to combine their evaluative role with friendships. Take Case 11-14 as an example.

Case 11-14

A new faculty member at a comprehensive university sometimes played tennis at a local health club where one of his older undergraduate students was also a member. At one point, the student challenged the faculty member to a game of tennis and the faculty member accepted. After that, they played almost weekly. When the student did poorly on the midsemester examination, the faculty member took him aside and offered to help him with the material if he needed it. The student did not take him up on the offer. They continued to play tennis. Later in the semester, the student invited the faculty member and his wife over to his home for dinner. The faculty member naively accepted. Sometime during the evening, the student dropped the hint that because he and the faculty member were such good friends, he would certainly do well in the class. The faculty member indicated, however, that their personal relationship would not affect how he graded. When the student got a D grade, he was frustrated and angry. When the faculty member asked him why he did not take him up on the offer for extra help, the student indicated he wanted to be friends with the faculty member and did not want to appear stupid.

The role of a faculty member like the role of a therapist carries with it unrealistic expectations about being all knowing and constantly wise. Thus, students may be unable to adequately or objectively evaluate the feedback or recommendations that a faculty member makes and may reject suggestions when it is in their best interests to follow them (Kitchener, 1992b). The relationships between faculty and students are inherently asymmetrical in the sense that faculty have the responsibility to make decisions about the success or failure of students who are enrolled in educational programs, thus, faculty wield very real power over the outcomes of students' lives and careers. As a result of the power differential and role expectations associated with being a faculty member, students may be unable to make reasonable decisions about the risks and benefits of entering into multiple relationships with them or they may feel subtle coercion. This was probably true in Case 11-4, in which the faculty member asked the graduate student for a series of "little" favors. In Case 11-13, the student who was asked to take care of Dr. Sanders children might have a difficult time saying "no" even if she wanted to. Even though she would officially be a "former student," the power differential may still feel present and similar to the therapist–client relationship and the graduate may still feel like a student of Dr. Sanders.

The power differential also leaves open the potential for faculty to exploit students, and students, because of their relative powerlessness, have little opportunity for retribution. Take as an example a faculty member who publishes a student's idea or paper under the faculty member's name. The student may both be afraid of complaining and be unclear to whom to take the complaint. In fact, Goodyear, Crego, and Johnston (1992) offered numerous examples of faculty supervising research assistants who used their positions of power to exploit students by coercing them to fraudulently tamper with data, by failing to give them credit for their participation on research projects, or by plagiarizing student work directly. Such activities violate faculty members' fiduciary responsibilities to students and undermine their responsibility to benefit students. Students are vulnerable to further harm if they "blow the whistle" on the faculty member and try to report the inappropriate behavior or even if they resist the faculty member's requests.

The difficulty students have in acting as their own advocates may be an outgrowth of the implicit contract between students who enter into a college or university and the faculty who teach in it (Chambers, 1981; Kitchener, 1992b). Students make decisions about entering into undergraduate or graduate programs on the basis of promises made in bulletins and descriptive materials about the nature of the educational experience (Johnson & Nelson, 1999). Those materials imply that in return for attending, paying money, abiding by the rules of the institution, and studying, students, if they have sufficient talent and do the required work, will benefit from the educational experience. As a result, when they enter into relationships with faculty, students do so with the assumption that they will not be harmed by those relationships, that faculty will act with their educational best interests in mind, and that faculty will be fair when evaluating them. Thus, students are hampered in protecting themselves by their real vulnerability in light of the power differential with faculty. In addition, they are also hampered by their expectation that faculty will act with their welfare in mind.

The point should not be lost, however, that there is opportunity for substantial benefits in some of the multiple relationships in which academics engage with students. As already noted, some out-of-class experiences play powerful roles in the intellectual and personal growth of undergraduates (Astin, 1993; Pascarella & Terenzini, 1991). Furthermore, mentoring relationships provide opportunities for enriching learning experiences and professional development that might not otherwise be open to students. The support and modeling they offer female students or students of color may be particularly powerful in enhancing their self-concepts as professionals (Kitchener, 1999). At the same time mentoring relationship provides support and modeling, they also involve inherent ethical tensions. Johnson and Nelson (1999) highlight several of these tensions which include faculty competence to be an ethical mentor; students having equal access to faculty mentoring; faculty exploitation of a protégé; and multiple demands on the faculty during a mentoring relationship.

What guidelines ought to direct faculty when they consider their multiple relationships with students? First, as already noted, they should remember that as the difference between expectations and obligations, the power differential, and conflicts of interest increase, so does the potential for harm. Faculty members need to be clear with students—and themselves—that different roles require different sets of expectations and obligations. Being clear may help students avoid the frustrations associated with just being confused. In addition, faculty need to be honest with themselves and students that evaluation is a part of every relationship with every student. The responsibility to evaluate does not disappear even with very good students. Diluting the appearance of this responsibility, for example, by treating students as if they were friends may unjustly obscure the real nature of the relationship. Faculty need to remember that the relationship between themselves and students is a fiduciary one albeit not a confidential relationship. Other things being equal, faculty are responsible for benefiting, not harming, students as well as treating them fairly.

Ethicists have offered some clear guidance for faculty to use as they approach the possibility of mentoring relationships. For example, Welfel (2010) presents nine criteria for honoring boundaries in the faculty–student relationship (pp. 413–414). Some of these criteria include: steering clear of using students as confidants for personal and professional concerns; time spent with students should mostly be about professional growth for the student; clarification of the roles is important from the very beginning; ensure a student can step out of the mentoring relationship in a way demonstrates respect for the student with no retribution to come; and use consultation with colleagues regarding mentoring issues. In addition to Welfel's suggestions, Blevins-Knabe (1992, pp. 154–155) suggested asking several questions to help evaluate whether faculty members' role responsibilities are being compromised when they enter into multiple-roles with students. (a) What is the student in the relationship learning? Is he or she learning to be competent or dependent? (b) What are other students learning? Are they learning that special relationships lead to special favors or are they learning about fair treatment on the basis of merit? (c) Do students have a choice about participating in the relationship, or are they fearful of refusing requests because of the power differential? (d) Do all students have equal opportunities for the professor's attention? (e) Is there an actual or perceived loss of objectivity now, or will there be one in the future? (Sometimes other students' perceptions of a conflict of interest and loss of objectivity may be as damaging as a real loss of objectivity). (f) What are the consequences for other faculty? Is this relationship compromising other faculty members' relationships with students? (g) Is the faculty member's professorial role compromised? and (h) Is the student being exploited?

Faculty also needs to consider their motivations for participating in multiple relationships with students (Blevins-Knabe, 1992). On the positive side, motivation could include a desire to enhance students' professional and intellectual development, to improve their bond to the university or college, or to strengthen the possibility that the student will remain in school rather than dropping out. On the negative side, motivations could range from greed to self-aggrandizement. As psychology and counseling faculty members should be aware that modeling is a powerful source of learning. The nature of their relationships with students—whether respectful or disrespectful, caring or exploitative, enhancing a student's development or destroying it—may be sources of learning for other students, and this learning may be as influential as what they gain in the classroom.

Ultimately, faculty members are responsible for anticipating possible complications from the relationships they enter with students. In addition, faculty needs to be aware that multiple relationships may cause confusion and frustration even if the faculty member does not purposefully exploit the student.

Multiple Relationships in Supervision

The multiple relationship concerns that arise in teaching and mentoring have a variety of parallels in supervision (Kitchener, 1994). Similar to teaching and mentoring, supervision implicitly involves multiple obligations, some to the supervisee and others to the clients of the supervisee. To the supervisee is the responsibility to help him or her develop knowledge and skills as well as to evaluate the supervisee on their ability to deliver their knowledge and skill in an effective way. The supervisor also has role obligations protect the public from incompetent or inept therapists, and to assure the client a decent standard of care. As noted earlier, the supervisee may be involved with the supervisor in a variety of other roles, including consulting, coauthoring papers or presentations, and attending social functions together. In fact, some have commented on the inevitability of multiple relationships in supervision (Bernard & Goodyear, 2004, 1998; Goodyear & Sinnett, 1984). Using the list of seven identified multiple relationships from a prior study (Anderson & Kitchener, 1996), Lamb et al. (2004) asked 1,000 psychologists to report which of these eight relationships they found themselves needing to address with current and former clients, students, and supervisees. Of the 1,000 surveys sent, 298 returned surveys were usable for data analysis. Within the seven relationship types, four of the relationship types (collegial or professional, collegial or professional with social, evaluative, and workplace) were the ones most frequently necessary to discuss with supervisees.

As in teaching, the supervisor's role may carry with it unrealistic expectations about being knowledgeable and wise. And also like the teacher–student relationship, the supervisor–supervisee relationship is asymmetrical. Supervisors have the responsibility and power to make decisions, such as whether the supervisee will succeed or fail, will receive good recommendations or poor ones, or will be referred for new job opportunities or not. The inequality of status, power, and expertise between supervisors and supervisees have been identified as the key sources of supervisees' vulnerability with supervisors (Bernard & Goodyear, 2004; Kitchener, 1994; Newman, 1981; Sherry, 1991; Tromski-Klingshirn & Davis, 2007).

Multiple relationships with supervisees also have some parallels with therapy. Many authors have commented on the therapy like nature of supervision. Parallels include the frequency of sessions, feelings of transference and counter-transference, and issues of parallel process (Doehrman, 1976; Sherry, 1991). The supervisee–supervisor bond has similarities to the therapeutic bond. Some have argued that it is a critical ingredient of successful supervision (Bernard & Goodyear, 2004; Bordin, 1983; Loganbill, Hardy, & Delworth, 1983) because it may help the supervisee endure painful change processes. Unlike therapy relationships, however, supervisors and supervisees work together in the same setting and will often join in other activities together, thus, the multiplicity of roles cannot always be avoided (Bernard & Goodyear, 1998). On the other hand, because supervision may involve the revelation of personal secrets that may be blocking work with clients, supervisees may be much more personally vulnerable than those who are in a teacher–student relationship.

As with other multiple relationships, the multiple roles in supervision have the potential for leaving the supervisee confused because of the ambiguity inherent in role conflicts. These role conflicts have two sources in supervision: those that are inherent in the role itself, such as helping the student develop as a therapist and evaluating the supervisee, and those that involve extra supervisory roles, such as being a supervisor and a therapist for the same trainee or being the clinical and administrative supervisor of therapist. Because the supervisory role includes both therapy like components and evaluative components, sometimes the line between using the therapy like nature of supervision to help a supervisee explore personal blocks with a particular client and therapy itself is difficult to draw (Kitchener, 1994).

It is because of the evaluative component of supervision and its inherent conflict with a true therapy relationship that acting as a therapist for one's own supervisee is generally considered unethical even though practiced by professionals. For example, Sherry et al. (1991) found that at least 48% of mental health professionals in university and college counseling centers reported being in the role of "therapist" at least on a rare occasion for their supervisee. Of this group of respondents, 3% reported being in the role of therapist with supervisees fairly often. As noted earlier, therapy assumes that material will be kept confidential. In supervision, because of the evaluative component and the responsibility of the supervisor to ensure the welfare of the client, confidentiality does not have the same status. Similarly, in therapy, the client's welfare is primary in most situations; however, when a supervisor tries to play therapist in addition to being a supervisor, loyalties are split between the supervisee qua client, the supervisees' clients, and the public. Consequently, the potential of either harming the supervisee or allowing harm to occur to the supervisee's client is high. Because of the potential for students to become confused about the line between therapy and supervision, it is important that the supervisor is clear that personal exploration in supervision is done to help the supervisee work with a particular client or particular kinds of clients. Any work that moves beyond that line should be referred to a therapist unconnected to the supervisor or the training program so that the supervisee's confidentiality and welfare as a client can be the primary concern (Bernard & Goodyear, 2004; Kitchener, 1988; Patrick, 1989). Whiston and Emerson (1989) offer some important guidelines to distinguish supervision from counseling or therapy. More recently the issue of "informed consent" has become an additional issue to address supervisor and supervisee which would clarify the parameters around role expectations.

Furthermore, supervisors can be alert to other confusion that supervisees may have regarding the inherent conflicts in a supervisory role. As Bernard and Goodyear (2004) suggested, they can attenuate the potential for confusion to some extent by informing the supervisee at the beginning of the relationship that such conflicts may occur and that they need to discuss them if they do. In particular, supervisors need to be clear about the evaluative component of supervision. Such information can help supervisees make more autonomous decisions about what they want to reveal, and it may help supervisors avoid harming them unintentionally.

Extra supervisory roles to some extent can be avoided, but as suggested earlier they can never be entirely eliminated. For one thing, they contain the potential for powerful learning. Writing an article with a supervisor may help supervisees' self-concepts as well as provide additional benefits when they search for a job. Consulting off-site about an issue of common interest may help the supervisee begin to see him or herself as a professional with real expertise. In this respect, it is important to differentiate between those multiple relationships that abuse power and exploit the supervisee and those that are a part of the mentoring relationship that helps the supervisee develop as a mature professional (Aponte, 1994).

On the other hand, just as in teaching, the responsibility to evaluate the supervisee never disappears. Even if the supervisor and supervisee have relatively equal roles in a joint consultation experience, the supervisor will still have an evaluative function. As one of us has said elsewhere, "diluting the appearance of the responsibility to evaluate by being pals with the supervisee may unjustly obscure the real nature of the relationship. Typically, friends do not evaluate each other. Supervisors do evaluate trainees," (Kitchener, 1994, p. 7). The "slippery slope" elsewhere described also pertains to supervisors who begin to compromise the professional boundaries between themselves and those they supervise (Gottlieb, Robinson, & Younggren, 2007). Role confusion in such situations can leave the supervisee with a negative feeling about supervision, and it can obscure the supervisor's judgment. In fact, research suggests that boundary issue which result in role confusion happen with some frequency. According to Navin, Beamish, and Johnson (1995) 25% of field supervisors reported social interactions and relationships between supervisees and supervisors that believed were in conflict with supervisory responsibilities. It is for the same reasons that it is probably unwise to enter into a friendship with a current supervisee.

In addition, supervisors have the responsibility to ensure that they are not exploiting their supervisees. Because supervisors have real power over supervisees, even simple requests may be difficult to turn down because the supervisee may want to please the supervisor (Sherry, 1991).

It should be noted that graduate teaching assistants who are sometimes asked to play supervisory roles have a particularly difficult time defining their roles and avoiding multiple-role relationships (Montgomery, 1997). They may be supervising other students in their graduate program who are at a less advanced level. On the other hand, they may take classes with these same students or interact with them in social settings. Faculty have a particularly strong responsibility in these circumstances to help the teaching assistants understand the limits and dangers of their role and to help them structure their nonteaching relationships with the students they are supervising.

We end this section with highlighting two key issues related to the relationship between the supervisor and supervisee. First, Bernard and Goodyear (2004) have defined supervision as:

An intervention provided by a more senior member of a profession. This relationship is evaluative; extends over time, and has the simultaneous purposes of enhancing the professional functions of the more junior person(s), monitoring the quality of professional services offered to the clients that she/he, or they see, and serving as a gatekeeper for those who are to enter the particular profession. (p. 8)

We appreciate the depth and comprehensiveness of this definition and yet would suggest that there is an important piece missing from the definition explicitly stating the role of supervisor as holder and promoter of the ethical relationship between the supervisor and supervisee. As we have already addressed, there is a power differential in the relationship and the supervisor (similar to the therapist) is the responsible part to ensure the supervisory relationship is one that exemplifies ethical and professional boundaries and is beneficial to the supervisee and all those he or she services.

The second issue is the due diligence supervisors can implement, through a type of assessment, as they consider the potential of a secondary relationship with a supervisee. The following questions were created by Gottlieb et al. (2007) and they offer the professional some good opportunities for reflection entering into a secondary relationship with a supervisee:

Is the secondary relationship necessary?
Can this secondary relationship bring harm to the supervisee?
If harm is not likely would benefit be an outcome?
Could the secondary relationship compromise the supervisory relationship?
Can the supervisor remain objective to evaluate the supervisee fairly?

In asking these questions the supervisor is working toward honoring beneficence and fidelity in the supervisory relationship.

Multiple Relationships and Conflicts of Interest in Research

Until recently the literature discussing research ethics have generally been silent on the issue of multiple relationships in a research setting (Koocher & Keith-Spiegel, 1998; Levine, 1988; Sieber,

1992; Welfel, 2009); however, that is beginning to change (Sales & Folkman, 1998). The research setting is not invulnerable to role conflicts exacerbated by a power differential. These issues include conflicts of interest between different aspects of the researcher's roles, participants' vulnerability to the undue influences of researchers to coerce participation, and role confusion when working with students.

Needless to say, researchers can be swayed by the same kinds of conflicts their academic colleagues have when working with research assistants with whom they play both an evaluative and developmental role such as mentor for budding protégé. Researchers can down play the power differential between themselves and their research assistants and subtlety coerce them into doing tasks that are not associated with the researcher role or they can engage in social relationships that blur evaluative responsibilities. For example, in the study by Clark et al. (2000) the second most identified ethical concern from the protégé's perspective was the mentor's behavior related to research. Respondents mentioned such behaviors as mentor's altering findings to support the hypotheses, suggesting to the protégé that they alter the results and if they do they would receive some type of financial reward, or the mentor claiming credit for work actually completed by the protégé.

Although relationships in research do not tend to be as intense as those in therapy or supervision, there is still potential for role conflict leading to confusion, frustration, and anger. As with other roles that psychologists and counselors play, those working in a research setting need to be cautious about entering into multiple relationships with supervisees or research participants and assess the potential of those roles to create harm or create a conflict of interest that would impair scientific judgment and objectivity. Because students are in a less powerful position, they may find it difficult to turn requests down for participation in research projects that faculty members are sponsoring. Consequently, recent APA (2002) and ACA (2005) ethics codes encourage researchers to consider the necessary steps to protect students/research assistants and participants from harm or negative consequences should they decide not to participate for course credit but are given other alternatives that facilitate learning.

There are other role conflicts, however, that are unique to the research setting. Take the conflict between the role of researcher and clinician that can arise when doing psychotherapy research. The professional's responsibility to provide the best care for their clients can conflict with their responsibility to create new knowledge. This is exacerbated by the research participant/clients' belief that the principle of personal care will take precedence and that their well-being will receive higher priority than the research design (Appelbaum et al., 1987).

Researchers can also find themselves in multiple-role conflicts with employers, funding agencies, or organizations they are evaluating. Although these concerns seldom have received pubic attention in psychology or counseling, sometimes a researcher's responsibility to accurately and honestly report findings may conflict with an employer's desire to keep adverse findings quiet (Korenman, 1993; Sales & Folkman, 1998). Similarly, research may be funded by an organization that might have an investment in the results. In cases like these, it may be deceptively easy to sacrifice scientific integrity in accurately reporting results to the goal of getting additional funding. Program evaluators can face similar role conflicts with the organizations that are paying them for their evaluations or with the social consequences of their conclusions (Newman & Brown, 1996). Take, for example, the following case.

Case 11-15

Dr. Jenkins works with an evaluation team within a large nonprofit organization. At a staff meeting, one team member suggests watering down the negative aspects of an evaluation of a federally funded project because it was doing good work. The team member points out that in the competitive grant-funding world, any negative comment may lead to the funding being terminated. Dr. Jenkins feels caught between his responsibility to accurately report the findings and a responsibility to provide support for what he believes is a worthwhile project (Newman & Brown, 1996, p. 154).

As already noted, psychologists and counselors can feel pulled in multiple directions by the many roles they play, including their role as a member of society. Here, again, the virtues of integrity and prudence may be critical in finding the right balance of ethical responsibilities. However, sacrificing scientific integrity by misrepresenting conclusions can seldom be justified.

Conclusion

Multiple relationships, whether they occur within or outside of a professional relationship, have the potential for becoming problematic because of the confusion and frustration that arise from the conflicting obligations and expectations associated with the roles. When one of the parties is a psychologist or counselor, conflicts of interest and the power differential can exacerbate the role confusion and open up the possibility of exploitation and harm. Therapeutic, educational, and research relationships with consumers have particular potential to be problematic in this regard because the professionals in these relationships carry with them the expectation of being knowledgeable, wise, and trustworthy. Consequently, consumers may not be in a position to objectively evaluate and reject the advice of the professional even when it may not be in their best interests to follow it. Ending the relationship per se does not automatically change the nature of these concerns, thus, posttherapy relationships carry with them their own risks. Postgraduate relationships between educators and students may be less risky than those that follow therapy, however, psychology faculty and counselor educators need to acknowledge that even these relationships carry additional baggage and, at minimum, new role expectations will have to be negotiated. In regards to this "additional baggage," Remely and Herlihy (2010) pose an interesting observation: "professors always have a degree of power over former students. Professors are asked throughout the careers of former students for recommendations for jobs, certifications, and licenses" (p. 328).

When gender socialization issues are added to this mix, women, in particular, often end up victimized by a person who is supposed to be in a professional role and who is supposed to be benefiting them in some way (Gilbert & Scher, 1989). In fact, data from a variety of sources (APA, 1997a; Baer & Murdock, 1995; Borys & Pope, 1989; Holroyd & Brodsky, 1977; Pope, 1993; Pope, Levenson, & Schover, 1979) suggest that male therapists more often become involved in multiple relationships and see such relationships as more ethical than do female. It may be that female psychologists and counselors' views of multiple relationships are colored by the knowledge that it is often other women who are hurt by these relationships.

Research in psychology and counseling is not immune from its own role conflicts. Although some of these occur between the researcher and research participants or employees, others occur between the researcher's responsibility to report findings accurately and the implications of the findings for funding sources, employers, and society at large. Clearly, researchers need to consider the kinds of conflicts that may arise and evaluate the ethical implications of different choices. Doing so should help avoid negative outcomes as well as uphold the integrity of science.

Whenever psychologists and counselors consider participating in a multiple relationship or whenever they find themselves a part of one because of unforeseen circumstances, it is their responsibility to evaluate the potential for the new relationship to interfere with their professional obligations and to place the welfare of consumers ahead of their own. Ultimately, they must evaluate the potential for the new relationship to harm the consumer, and if the probability of harm is high, they should avoid the relationship. Even if the probability of harm is low, the psychologist or counselor should at least talk about the implications of the new role with the consumer and point out how it might change the nature of the professional relationship. These are fundamental ethical obligations and ones that often become clouded when counselors and psychologists add new roles to existing professional ones.

Multiple relationships and the complexities that come with them are will be with professionals throughout their careers (Herlihy & Corey, 1997) and more ethical rule and guidelines will not guarantee ethical choices by professionals. As previously stated, psychologists and counselors will need to work toward clear reasoning and honorable motivations as they maneuver through multiple relationships and nonprofessional interaction.

Before leaving this chapter we want to address two more issues, namely the importance of self-care in light of multiple relationships and "gatekeeping" of the profession. Self-care by the professional is critical for him or her to be effective in their world of work (Sommers-Flanagan & Sommers-Flanagan, 2007; Nickel, 2004). According to Gilroy, Carrol, and Murra (2002), "the key to [burnout] prevention lies in establishing a professional ethos in which self-care is viewed as a moral imperative" (p. 406). Without good self-care, professionals lose their ability to sustain good boundaries with consumers of their services and are more vulnerable to ethical lapses. One of us remembers a guest presenter in an ethics class who shared her ethical lapse, which resulted in an ethics complaint and disciplinary action by the licensing board. The practitioner recounted how her lack of self care directly affected her ability to think through a series of decisions which ultimately resulted in boundary crossings and a client feeling harmed. We finish this chapter with a quote from Larzarus (2005):

> There are therapists who display poor social judgment, disordered thinking, and impaired reality test. Some are sociopathic or have narcissistic or borderline personalities. But in my opinion, many other these unscrupulous practitioners will not be cowed or deterred by facing longer and more stringent rules and regulations. What we need are far more careful selection criteria so that we weed out these people before they enter into our graduate schools and training programs. (p. 26)

Questions for Discussion or Consideration

1. What is your experience thus far with multiple relationships in your training as a psychologist or counselor?
2. What have you found to be most surprising about multiple relationships? What still seems counterintuitive to you when it comes to multiple relationships?
3. What have you found to be the most difficult part of handling multiple relationships?
4. What have you found to be easiest part of handling multiple relationships?

12
Sexualized Professional Relationships
Clearly Causing Harm

In the previous chapter we discussed the complexity and problems that arise when professionals choose to enter into a secondary or multiple relationships with a client, student, or others. We also indicated there is a continuum of perspectives about the ethics of entering into multiple relationships with clients. We discussed the potential for causing harm when nonsexual multiple relationships occur but the reality of harm occurring from sexualized or romantic relationships is even more likely to ensue. Problems and conflicts that exist in any nonsexual multiple relationship are exacerbated when the multiple relationship introduces sexual intimacy. The power differential remains great, the differences in expectations between a therapist, supervisor, or professor and a lover or romantic partner are enormous, and the conflict of interest between roles the professional tries to fulfill are profound. It is just not possible for the professional to work for the best interests of the consumer and also try to meet his or her own sexual or romantic needs. Consequently, the potential for harm is great, almost inevitable.

Prohibition against Sexualized Therapeutic Relationships

Because the potential for harm is so high, all of the major mental health professional associations have identified sexual relationships between current clients and therapists as unethical. The APA (2002) standard on sexualized relationships with clients was one of the clearest and most concise in the APA ethics code. The language was adamant—psychologists do not engage in sexual intimacy with current clients. Furthermore, the APA code stated that psychologists should not accept as clients those with whom they have been sexually intimate. This prohibition against sexualized relationships was even extended to "close relatives, guardians, and significant others" of current clients. The ACA (2005) ethics code was also clear and concise—counselors are prohibited from engaging in sexual or romantic interactions or relationship with current clients and their family members.

The prohibition against sexual relationships between health care providers and their clients is not new and, in fact, can be traced back to such documents such as the Hippocratic Oath for physicians. The oath states that "in whatever house where I visit, I will come for the benefit of the sick, remaining free of all intentional injustice, of all mischief, and in particular of sexual relations with both female and male persons, be they free or slaves" (Edelstein, 1967, p. 6). Brodsky (1989) reports that this philosophy of forbidding sexual intimacy between a healer and "patient," mentioned in the ancient code of Nigerian medicine men. A third document, "The Physician," written sometime between the ancient code of Nigerian medicine men and the Hippocratic Oath encouraged physicians to have self-control. "The intimacy also between physician and patient is close. Patients in fact put themselves into the hands of their physician, and at every moment he meets women, maidens and possessions very precious indeed. So toward all these self-control must be sued. Such then should the physician [be], both in body and soul" (Campbell, 1989, p. 303).

Although the Hippocratic Oath and the other two documents were written for physicians, Freud set similar prohibitions in the early years of psychoanalysis, noting that entering into a sexual relationship with a patient would end the curative aspects of analyses (Freud, 1915/1963).

In fact, he believed, the consequences of sexual involvement to be so devastating that he warned his colleagues against kissing and other kinds of quasi-sexual overtures (Jones, 1961).

In comparison to the Hippocratic Oath and other documents denouncing sex between the physician and patient, the prohibition against sexual or romantic relationships with clients has a relatively short history. In fact at one time, psychologists and other mental health practitioners pronounced and even wrote about what they believed to be the possible benefits of sexual intimacy with clients (McCarthy, 1967; Shepard, 1971). Finally, in 1981, the American Psychological Association created a standard in the code explicitly forbidding psychologists from having sex with clients. The American Counseling Association, once known as the American Personnel and Guidance Association, developed a standard in 1981 suggesting that counselors avoid "dual relationships" with clients that might compromise the counselor's objectivity and professional judgment. The dual relationships listed in the code included "sexual intimacies" with clients (personal communication with Howard Smith, December 2009). In 1988, a separate standard was created stating that counselors should avoid any type of sexual intimacy with clients and declaring sexual relationships with clients as unethical.

According to Pope and Bouhoutsos (1986), there are several reasons for this prohibition in addition to the potential for harm to the client (which we discuss in the next section). First, the psychologist or counselor is a professional who receives money for services. In return for the status and other benefits derived from this status, the therapist agrees to make the welfare of the consumer a primary concern. This does not occur when the professional relationship is sexualized. For example, the role expectations in a therapy relationship are remarkably different from those in a romantic or sexual relationship. In therapy, one would reasonably expect that the therapist's primary role is to help the client benefit from treatment; however, as a lover, that same therapist would have some expectations that his or her own needs were met in the romantic/sexual relationship. The client may enter into the sexual relationship fantasizing that the care and concern of the therapist is really just an extension of that which occurs in therapy where the client's needs are of upmost importance. But in reality when the psychologist's or counselor's own needs intrude into this fantasy, the client feels disappointed, angry, and betrayed. This may be one reason why sexual relationships between therapists and clients are so damaging. Second, psychotherapy clients sometimes reveal uncomfortable and private information about themselves and their life situations and as a result become vulnerable to therapist exploitation. In addition, because of the special meaning the therapist has in the client's life, the therapist can become a symbol of parental caring and wisdom.

In addition to being unethical, sexual relationships between clients (and sometimes former clients) and therapists are illegal in many states (Haspel, Jorgenson, Wineze, & Parsons, 1997; Jorgenson, 1994; Kane, 1995). At least 17 states have enacted criminal charges penalties for sexual misconduct. These states include: Arizona, California, Colorado, Connecticut, Florida, Georgia, Iowa, Maine, Michigan, Minnesota, New Hampshire, New Mexico, North Dakota, Ohio, South Dakota, Texas, and Wisconsin. Each state has its own wording for the statute but most of these states include the titles of psychologist and counselor as those who can be prosecuted for sexual misconduct if found guilty. Some of the states have enacted additional statutes asking or requiring subsequent psychotherapists to disclosure sexual involvement between a client and previous therapist (Welfel, 2010). At least one state, Minnesota, actually requires therapists to report sexual misconduct by another therapist with or without client permission (Haspel et al., 1997). In addition to criminal charges, psychologists and counselors who become engaged in sexual liaisons with clients or former clients can face (a) civil charges, (b) disciplinary sanctions, including the revocation of licenses to practice by licensing boards, and (c) other penalties, including loss of membership from professional associations. These judgments are often followed by a loss of professional insurance because insurance carriers are often unwilling to cover psychotherapists who have harmed their clients and been found guilty of unethical or illegal activities.

Before we move to the discussion of research findings on the harm experienced by clients and prevelance of sexualized therapeutic relationships with clients, we feel it is important to address an interesting observation. One can't help but wonder what took professional associations, such as the American Psychological Association and the American Counseling Association so long to address the unethical behavior of sex with clients. As you might recall Freud came out strongly against any hint of sexual activity with patients because he believed this type of interaction or relationship between patient and psychoanalysis would end the curative aspects of analyses (Freud, 1915/1963). Davidson (1977) suggested that therapist–client sexual intimacy was the "problem with no name" because the mental health professions were unwilling to stand up to the issue. Pope (1988) referred to the professions' reluctance to confront the issue as "massive denial" (p. 222). It was not until 70 years later that both APA and ACA along with other helping organizations decided to formally address the issue.

In addition to massive denial it is possible the professions or those in leadership of the professions, APA and ACA, had not stopped to consider the organization's ethical acculturation journey and as a result behaved or implemented a separation strategy related to this specific issue. Both APA and ACA were founded on the very principle of beneficence and nonmaleficence—to do good and not do harm to the consumer of their service and expertise. However, at the same time of valuing these principles, the associations choose to overlook, ignore, or even deny the harm done to clients by some of its own membership. As Davidson (1977) suggests, on one hand the professions knew this harmful behavior existed making null and void any good accomplished in therapy, but on the other hand chose to value the relationship with and reputation of colleagues over the welfare of the clients being violated. The professions struggled and actually failed to secure a coherent ethical identity as an organization (Anderson, Lujan, & Hageman, 2010) by ignoring the contradiction, and colluding with some of its members who were involved with clients. We could say that on some level APA and ACA were choosing to value the professions' image and their relationships with colleagues who were sexually involved with clients over the professional value of client welfare resulting in a separation strategy, or, even worse, a marginalization strategy.

Research on Sexualized Therapeutic Relationships with Current Clients

Masters and Johnson (1966, 1970, 1975) were possibly the first to conduct research on the emotional aftermath of therapist and client sexualized relationships. They suggested that such relationships were comparable with criminal rape and led to tragic consequences for the clients. The Masters and Johnson's findings have been supported by subsequent findings. For example, books share firsthand accounts of the difficulties faced by individuals who were victims of therapists' intimacies (Bates & Brodsky, 1989; Noel & Watterson, 1992). As already described, Melissa Roberts Henry, in her self-reported story in the *Frontline* special, "My Doctor, My Lover" (Storring, 1991), shared her emotional confusion and psychological deterioration due to the sexual relationship with her therapist. Landmark studies by Pope (1986, 1988) addressed the sexual activity between professionals in psychology and counseling with their clients; and Gartrell, Herman, Olarte, Felstein, and Localio (1987) reported on psychiatrists' sexual involvement with clients. Reports in refereed journals including surveys of victims, reports of subsequent therapists, and evaluations by independent clinicians, identify substantial client deterioration after sexual involvement with a therapist (Pope, 1990). According to one study, at least 90% of clients who were sexually involved with their therapist were harmed by the experience as reported by subsequent therapists (Bouhoutsos, Holroyd, Lerman, Forer & Greenberg, 1983). Although the research has been criticized for having the biases that are often associated with retrospective, self-report studies, data from these and other sources emphasize the harmful nature of these entanglements. Pope (1988) summarized these into 10 general categories:

1. Ambivalence about the treating therapist, including rage and fear and other negative feelings on one hand and fear of losing the therapist on the other.
2. Guilt for somehow being responsible for what occurred.
3. Emptiness and isolation, including feeling estranged from others and unworthy of other relationships.
4. Confusion regarding sexuality that may lead to additional traumatic sexual encounters or to a series of self-destructive sexual relationships.
5. Impaired ability to trust because the therapist has violated the fiduciary nature of the relationship at a time when the client was particularly vulnerable.
6. Boundary disturbances and diffusion of identity because the therapist violated the boundaries of the relationship. Clients loose clarity about their own needs, boundaries, and identity. For example, are they the client or the helper? Are they the client or the lover?
7. Feeling emotionally labile, especially depressed, because they may be confused and overwhelmed by their response to the situation.
8. Suppressed rage at being victimized.
9. Increased suicidal risk when rage turns inward and becomes self-loathing.
10. Cognitive dysfunction, such as intrusive thoughts, unbidden images, flashbacks, and nightmares.

Even though sex with clients has been explicitly forbidden since 1982 by APA and 1981 by ACA, research suggests that the "forbidden" was still occurring into the late 1990's. Studies conducted during the 1980's and early 1990's reported between 1% and 9% of male psychologists and 0.04% and 2.5% of female psychologists sexually involved with clients. Studies that looked a sexual activity between mental health professionals including psychologists, reported approximately 7% of male therapists and 1.6% of female therapists admitted to sexual involvement with current and former clients (Akamatsu, 1988; Borys, 1988; Pope & Bouhoutsos, 1986; Salisbury & Kinnier, 1996). Earlier studies conducted in the 1970's reported percentages as high as 12% for male psychologists and 3% for female psychologists (Holroyd & Brodsky, 1977; Pope, 1993; Pope et al., 1979). Studies completed in the late 1980's and 1990's have suggested a possible decrease in psychologists sexually violating client boundaries. These studies reported 4%–6% of practicing psychologists admitted to sexual involvement with clients (Lamb & Catanzar, 1998; Lamb et al., 1994; Pope, 1990; Rodolfa, Kitzrow, Vohra, & Wilson, 1990). In the 1990's, two studies specifically looked at counselor sexual misconduct with clients (Thoreson, Shaughnessy, Heppner, & Cook, 1993; Thoreson, Shaughnessy, & Frazier, 1995). These studies reported rates ranging from 0.7% (female) to 1.7% (male) of the participants reporting sexual involvement with clients. In a study completed within the last decade, 2% of practicing psychologists self reported having a sexual relationship with clients (Lamb, Catanzaro, & Moorman, 2003).

Some patterns in sexualized relationships seem to remain consistent across the years of research and appear to be similar to patterns for nonsexual multiple relationships: male psychotherapists, with much greater frequency than female psychotherapists, engage in sexual intimacies with their clients, and most often female clients are the ones victimized (Bisbang et al., 1995; Borys & Pope, 1989; Garrett, 1998; Pope, 1990, 1994, 2000; Somer & Saadon, 1999, 2005; Wincze et al., 1996). These figures hold even when the overall rates of male and female therapists and clients are considered (Sonne & Pope, 1991). Another pattern is the aspect of "repeat offender." According to Holroyd and Brodsky (1977), 80% of psychologists who admitted to sexual misconduct with clients reported being sexually involved with more than one client over the course of their professional practice.

Typically, when these figures are reported to students, they presume that therapists are having sex with single, relatively attractive, adult clients. Although physical attractiveness has been linked to male therapists' sexual attraction to clients (Pope, Keith-Spiegel, & Tabachnick, 1986), a variety of incidents have been described. These include engaging in group sex with clients, seducing a client participating in marital therapy while her husband was in the waiting room, engaging in sex with children, abusing developmentally disabled teenagers, using vibrators and other sexual paraphernalia on female clients who were incest victims, forcibly raping a client, drugging and then sexually assaulting a client, whipping the buttocks and extremities of a naked adolescent, and engaging in mutual masturbation with numerous patients, including a 65 year-old nun (Noel & Watterson, 1992; Pope et al., 1993; Sonne & Pope, 1991). Research suggests that children and adolescents are among those victimized with reports of girls as young as 3 years old and boys as young as 7 years old being sexually violated by therapists (Bajt & Pope, 1989; Welfel, 2010). We are also personally familiar with cases where institutionalized boys were repeatedly sodomized by their therapist and teenage girls were taken periodically from a group home to have an "affair" with their therapist.

As reported incidents suggest, the types of sexual behavior in which therapists engage with their clients involves more than sexual intercourse and in states such as Colorado, the law addressing sex between client and therapist involves more than sexual intercourse. The Colorado Mental Health Licensing Statute (CRS 12-43-704) includes sexual contact, sexual intrusion, or sexual penetration among the activities in which therapists are prohibited from engaging with a current client. Although this definition of sexual behavior may not hold in other legal arenas, it should remind therapists of the array of activities that may be included in what are considered illegal and unethical sexual contact.

Possibly one of the more positive trends in the research on sexual contact between therapists and clients has been the recent decrease in the self-reported incidence (Lamb et al., 2003). The decreases may be real and reflect a change in behavior that has resulted from the attention that the press, the profession, and the law have paid to this issue in the past few years. In addition, therapists may be less likely to risk sexual contact with clients because of an increased awareness of the risks for clients, themselves, and the profession (Pope et al., 1987). On the other hand, a decrease in self reported incidents may also reflect a reluctance on the part of the professional to reflect back on his or her actions, when even from the start they recognized their choice as unethical (Lamb et al., 2003) or to admit guilt for an illegal and unethical act even on an anonymous questionnaire (Stake & Oliver, 1991). Welfel (2010) suggests that the actual number of psychotherapists who become sexually intimate with clients is much greater than the number of filed complaints would suggest. In s study completed by Noel (2008) looking at the percentage of clinical psychologists who knew about sexual misconduct by other professionals, 84% of the respondents surveyed knew of such activity. Of the 84% only 35% encouraged the client to file a formal grievance and only 10% assisted the client with the grievance process. Other research studies suggest that a small percentage of clients who have been sexually violated by therapists (around 5%) should actually file a formal complaint (Bouhoutsos, 1984; Pope & Bouhoutsos, 1986).

Why Does Sexual Intimacy between Therapists and Current Client Continue?

Since the late 1980's, the prohibition in the ethical codes has been absolutely clear and research has offered conclusive evidence of the harm done to clients when psychologists and counselors sexualize the therapeutic relationship. The responsibility for steering clear of this boundary violation rests clearly with the professional. As Vasquez (1993) has said,

> Under no circumstances should a therapist ever have sex with a client, and under no circumstances should a therapist ever communicate, either explicitly or implicitly, that

sexual intimacies with a client are a possibility. It is solely the therapist's responsibility to ensure that no sexual intimacies occur with a patient. (p. xi)

Yet, sexual intimacy still occurs. Why? We answer this question discussing several issues or clues that have been highlighted in the literature including therapist factors, client factors, and societal factors. We also use the lens of ethical acculturation to explore some of the case studies.

Therapist Factors

One demographic variable, therapist gender, seems to be somewhat consistent. Research indicates that male therapists become sexually involved with their clients more often than female therapists; 1.5–9 times more frequently (Pope, 1994, 2000). This is not to say that female therapists are immune to sexual misconduct with clients. The following case was reported in a Denver newspaper.

Case 12-1

A 17-year-old adolescent male entered a 30-day drug and alcohol treatment program. Within 2 weeks of his arrival, a female therapist began making sexual advances toward him. She bribed him with alcohol and drove him to a motel where they had sex. When discovered, the therapist was sued by the boy's parents and charged with a felony (Newcomer, 1990).

In addition to therapist gender being somewhat of a constant variable or pattern, age difference between therapist and client is also a clue. Therapists who commit sexual misconduct are typically older than the client. Research does suggest that the therapists are typically in their early 40s and that clients are typically in their early 30s (Bouhoutsos et al., 1983; Gartrell, Herman, Olarte, Feldstein, & Localio, 1986; Pope, 1990). In an international study (Somer & Saadon, 1999), therapist age ranged from 30 to 70 years old and client age from 19 to 46 years. Pope and Vetter (1991) reported in one study where 5% of the victims of therapist sexual abuse were minors.

There are some therapist variables that appear not to predict a relationship with sexual misconduct. For example, type of profession is not an indicator or predictor of sexual misconduct. In a study that surveyed psychiatrists, psychologists, and social workers with the same measure during the same time period, no significant differences in the rates were found in which members of these three professions became sexually involved with their clients (Borys & Pope, 1989; Pope, 1990). In addition, the amount of formal education, professional recognition, and personal therapy do not seem to reduce the incidence of sexual misconduct. In fact, there have been numerous cases of well-known psychologists, even members of ethics committees, who have engaged in sexual behavior with their clients and at least one study of psychiatrists found that those who had psychotherapy or analysis were *more* likely to become sexually involved with patients (Gartrell et al., 1986; Pope, 1990). Finally, there has been no significant relationship between a therapist's theoretical orientation and sexual misconduct (Pope, 1990).

Although therapist demographic variables, other than gender, appear to present an ambiguous picture, patterns of behavior provide some clues. For instance, one contributing factor to sexual misconduct is the slow fading of professional boundaries by the psychologist or counselor. What has been called the "slippery slope of boundary violations" has been the focus of several discussions (Gutheil & Gabbard, 1993; Simon, 1989; Strasburger et al., 1992). Speculation suggests that therapists begin to blur boundaries with seemingly inconsequential changes in the therapeutic routine such as scheduling longer time for a particular client, meeting him or her after other staff members have gone home, talking with the client frequently by phone, and using excessive self-disclosure. The therapist may then begin to waive fees or suggest therapy over lunch. The blurring of the therapeutic relationship happens so gradually that neither therapist nor client seems to notice until the boundaries that provide the structure for therapy have eroded along with rules about abstaining from sexual relationships (Strasburger et al., 1992).

Self report by both therapists, who have violated the client's boundary, as well as the client who has been sexually violated, seem to support the slippery slope phenomena. Pogrebin, Poole, and Martinez (1991) completed a content analysis of the written responses of 24 therapists who admitted sexual involvement with clients. The following case incorporates one therapist's explanation demonstrating the erosion of boundaries.

Case 12-2

I had been seeing Ann for almost a year regarding self-esteem issues surrounding her feelings about being an attractive woman. She had been making good progress until we seemed to hit an impasse in therapy. I adjusted the treatment to overcome resistance. I employed several tactics, one of which was to share more of my personal life with her; another was to see her outside the usual office setting. Eventually, I disclosed that I found her attractive and we ended up having sex.

A qualitative analysis of clients' retrospective reports of sexual activity with a therapist (Somer & Saadon, 1999) suggests a similar erosion of boundaries. These participants described how their therapist disclosed more about themselves and their personal life, such emotional or marital problems; began to initiate physical contact like touching, hugging or kissing; and at times, would share the conflict they felt because of their attraction toward the client. The fading of boundaries resulted in a sexual interaction or relationship.

As suggested above, touching can become a gateway for sexual misconduct. In fact, Kertay and Reviere (1993) suggested that professional steer clear from even nonerotic touch if there is any sexual attraction toward the client. There is some evidence that those who nonerotically touch opposite-gender patients, but not same-gender patients, are more likely to become sexually involved (Holroyd & Brodsky, 1980). In other words, it is not touching per se but the differential touching of opposite-gender patients that seems to be related. Furthermore, Baer and Murdock's (1995) finding that therapists who had difficulty managing personal boundaries were less likely to see nonerotic relationships as unethical may be related.

Some researchers have proposed a type of profile for offending counselors and psychologists. One profile suggests an isolated, male therapist who is dealing with a personal crisis or distress, feels burnout on the job, and looks to female clients to meet his emotional needs (Simon, 1987; Smith & Fitzpatrick, 1995). Another type of profile paints a spectrum of professionals who become sexually involved with clients (Golden, 1990; Schoener & Gonsiorek, 1988). The range spans from the naïve therapist uniformed about ethical guidelines, to the other end where psychotherapists who are narcissictic and borderline personalities, or sociopathic see the client as there to meet the therapist's need. They have little to no appreciation of the harm their behavior will cause.

Research suggests that therapists who get involved with clients have different ways of explaining their ethical lapse. In their content analysis of the written responses of 24 therapists who admitted sexual involvement with clients, Pogrebin, Poole, and Martinez (1991) found that most had some kind of justification or excuse for their behavior. Some rationalized their actions by pointing out they did not intend to hurt their client, as in Case 12-2. Others blamed the victim.

Case 12-3

That I became involved in a sexual relationship with her is true. While my actions were reprehensible, both morally and professionally, I did not mislead or seduce her or intend to take advantage of her. My fault, instead, was
failing to adequately safeguard myself from her seductiveness, covert and overt (Pogrebin et al., 1991, p. 8).

Still others justified their actions by providing a sad tale of their own life problems or by
denying that the client was injured. Finally, some apologized, acknowledging the ethical error.
They sometimes suggested that a past self was responsible and that they had subsequently
changed, usually by entering therapy themselves.

Case 12-4

I truly had no prior awareness of my vulnerability to a homosexual relationship before she became a client. In
fact, it was such an ego dystonic experience for me that I soon ended up in the hospital myself and had two
years of psychotherapy. From this therapy, as well as some follow-up therapy, I have come to understand the
needs, which led to such behavior. I regret the negative impact it has had on both of our lives (Pogrebin et al.,
1991, p. 14).

Ethical Acculturation Lens

In reviewing some of the explanations above we can understand them in relationship to one of the
four ethical acculturation strategies the therapist was using. As a quick review, each of the ethical
strategies indicates the level of keeping one's ethics and values of origin as well as connecting and
participating with the profession's ethical perspective. The integration strategy is when the therapist has drawn upon both his or her personal ethics and values and the ethics and values of the
profession to make the ethical decision. Of course, to be able to use both, there must be good align-
ment between the two: the personal ethics and values and those of the profession. Typically, consistently right or ethical choices are made when this strategy is employed. The assimilation strategy
is where the therapist has decided to draw solely or mostly upon the ethics of the profession to
make the ethical decision. As reminder, this strategy is one employed with the therapist has likely
embraced ethical practice as a "must" to stay out of trouble, but has not really explored how the
ethical principles and guidelines align with his or her ethics and values of origin. At times of personal stress or professional burnout a therapist who usually or typically just follows the rules to
stay out of ethical trouble is vulnerable to ethical missteps or errors (Anderson & Handelsman,
2010). When therapists see little to no value in the professional ethics and choose to draw solely
from their values and personal ethics, they are choosing to use a separation strategy. Therapists
who draw upon this strategy tend to see the ethical guidelines as bothersome and feel comfortable
using their own ethics to guide their practice. These practitioners too are vulnerable to ethical
errors. They may very well desire to do good in their professional practice but actually end up cas-
cading down a path of choices that may end up hurting the client or undoing the good done in
therapy and damaging themselves professionally. The last ethical acculturation strategy is marginalization. Here therapists are choosing to disregard professional ethics and for various reasons are
also choosing to ignore guidance they might get from their personal ethics and values, or, in all
actuality, the therapist came into the profession with little to no personal ethics.

If we look at the cases previously mentioned we can hypothesize the therapist's ethical acculturation strategy. With Case 12-1 we could hypothesize that the therapist's actions were really
those that evolved out of the marginalization strategy. From the brief information given, the

therapist clearly violated the ethical principles of beneficence and nonmaleficence, along with ethical guidelines to uphold professional boundaries. To take advantage of a client by using the client's addiction as a bribe for sexual favors seems professionally as well as personally unthinkable. We might suggest that this therapist came into the profession without a personal foundation of ethics and has been upholding the ethical code to stay out of trouble, but when personal needs and desires (sexual in this case) came into play, she had neither the true commitment to the ethics code nor personal ethics, which allowed her to do the unthinkable. In Case 12-3, we might hypothesize that the therapist was justifying his behavior based on the assimilation strategy. The therapist's explanation of the boundary violation includes a statement of admission—recognizing the lack of upholding professional behavior—yet blaming the client's seductive behavior as the reason for his sexual misconduct. Maybe the therapist's usual way of handling ethical choices was just to follow the rules (assimilation). But in this particular scenario, the rules were not enough to keep the therapist from violating the client's boundaries, and a personal foundation of ethics was not in place to help the therapist resist temptation.

Client Factors

It should be remembered that clients enter therapy because they need help, and in a therapeutic relationship emphasis is placed on setting aside customary defenses (Pope & Bouhoutsos, 1986). Consequently, clients are particularly emotionally vulnerable, and their judgment may be diminished. Additionally, the therapist knows the client's defenses and vulnerabilities and can use them as a source of additional power over the client. As a result, therapists can never assume that clients can give autonomous consent to participate in a sexual relationship. Take Case 12-5 as an example.

Case 12-5

Joan's therapist declared his love for her early in their relationship, announced that the therapy was over, invited her to dinner that evening, and eventually married her. Two and a half years after they wed, he cast her off for another woman. Joan ended up taking antipsychotic medication. "What happens is, you've given away your secrets," Joan said. "He knew what was wrong with me. He knew how to push my buttons" (Winokur, 1991, p. A1).

Clients begin therapy with the expectation that their therapists are engaging in the relationship to help them and are knowledgeable about doing so. Because the relationship is asymmetrical in terms of power and prestige, clients may be unable to objectively evaluate the professionals' advice and reject it when it is not in their best interests to follow it (Kitchener, 1988), as the following case illustrates.

Case 12-6

Kim saw her psychotherapist twice a week for 2 years. It was always the same. She said there was 10 minutes of talk, and then she serviced him sexually. "He told me it would be unethical for him to reciprocate," Kim remembered. "But I thought, 'He loves me.'" After each session, Kim paid her $50 hourly fee because, she explained, she didn't want her therapist to think she was taking advantage of him. "It's hard for me to talk about this now without feeling stupid" (Winokur, 1991, p. A1).

As in Case 12-6, some therapists deliberately use their power to manipulate a client's dependency on them (Pope & Bouhoutsos, 1986).

Clients may presume and even be told by the therapist that when the relationship becomes sexualized, the therapist is doing it for the client's benefit. Melissa Roberts Henry, in her poignant description of her relationship with psychiatrist Jason Richter said, "I thought a sexual relationship would be good because he was already my doctor and helping me. And if he became my lover he would help me that much more. Then he would really care about me, really help me. He would be my doctor and my lover" (Zaritsky, 1991). In many cases, as in this one, clients are unaware that when sexual relationships begin, the objectivity necessary for a therapeutic relationship also ends.

From a psychodynamic perspective, clients' role confusion and vulnerability are exacerbated by transference issues (Pope & Bouhoutsos, 1986). Either consciously or unconsciously, clients project feelings and beliefs from childhood on to the therapist and thus regard the therapist as they might view a parent. The relationship is more like a parent–child relationship than it is one between two adults. If the client is a child or adolescent, these feelings are heightened even more. Although therapists should, through their own training, understand their counter transference toward the client, clients have no one to turn for help in understanding except their therapist. Thus, transference makes clients even more vulnerable to therapists' power than they were when they entered therapy. Although not all therapists recognize transference as a therapeutic phenomenon, they should be aware that the courts recognize it (Joregeson, Randles, & Strasburger, 1991) and have used it to lay culpability for a sexual encounter clearly on the therapist (*Simmons v. United States*, 1986). Furthermore, other schools of psychotherapy recognize similar phenomena.

Societal Factors

Finally, both the therapist's seductiveness and the client's susceptibility to seduction need to be understood in terms of gender roles and socialization. This is particularly true in light of the data that suggest that the majority of cases of sexual involvement take place between a male therapist and a female client (Pope, 1993). Gilbert and Scher (1989) pointed out that no one, including the women and men who enter psychology as a profession or their clients, escapes the gender belief systems that remain pervasive in our society. These beliefs include the view that women need to attract men to be healthy and that to do so they need to please and understand them. The situation in Case 12-6 is an example. Kim believed she should meet her therapist's sexual needs as well as pay him for his time.

On the other side, society sends a message to men that they need to affirm their dominance, superiority, and independence and are entitled to have their needs take precedence over those of women. As Gilbert and Scher (1989) pointed out, these feelings stand in marked contrast to the ideal of a more egalitarian relationship between men and women that many therapists espouse. Women are conditioned to focus their lives on pleasing men, and men are conditioned to use women to meet their needs. In therapy, male therapists may use their female clients to validate themselves as men. In these circumstances, "holding a female client responsible for a therapist's sexual acting out or excusing such behavior on the part of the therapist essentially ignores the fundamental nature of the sexism inherent in such behavior" (Gilbert & Scher, 1989, p. 103).

Few men who enter the helping fields think of themselves as sexists, yet it is also probably the case that few grew up believing or seeing women as equals. Gender socialization and stereotypic beliefs run deep. Both men and women who enter psychology and counseling need to examine how such beliefs unconsciously affect their work with clients and each other.

Clearly, there are many contributing factors to why psychologists and counselors continue to act out sexually with their clients. A lack of healthy ethical acculturation to the profession (Anderson & Handelsman, 2010), naiveté and lack of knowledge, psychological vulnerability, mild to severe emotional problems including but not limited to poor impulse control, character disorders, and impaired reality testing probably all play a part (Schoener & Gonsiorek, 1988).

However, the bottom line remains that there are no good excuses or justifications for entering a sexual relationship with clients. No matter what the circumstances, no matter how seductive the client, no matter if the client disrobes in the therapist's office, no matter if the therapist is "in love with" the client, it is always the therapist's responsibility to say "no." Practicing therapists, as well as those training them, need to be aware of the variety of paths and potential avenues that lead to becoming sexually entangled with clients.

Are Sexual Relationships Ever Permissible after Therapy Is Terminated?

Prevalence of Posttherapy Sexual Activity

The prevalence of posttherapy sexual relationships between therapists and former clients appears similar to the rate between therapists and current clients. In studies reported between the late 1970's and late 1990's, the rate of therapist sexual activity with former clients ranged from 3.9% to 11% (Akamatsu, 1988; Borys & Pope 1989; Holroyd & Brodsky, 1997; Lamb & Catanzaro, 1998; Salisbruy & Kinnier, 1996; Thoreson et al., 1993, 1995). Recent studies do not reflect a decline in these activities. This may be because some psychologists and counselors remain ambivalent about prohibiting sexual activity after therapy has terminated. Several studies have examined the professional's view of sexual involvement with former clients. Lamb et al. (1994) found that when the interval between termination and the sexual activity was less than a month, most psychologists condemned the activity; however, when the interval increased, fewer respondents believed the behavior to be unethical. In Akamatsu's 1998 study, 23% of the participants saw the activity as "neither ethical nor unethical" (p. 455). In a study of counselors, Salisbury and Kinnier (1996) found that a third of their participants saw sexual intimacy with former clients, under certain situations, as appropriate, and Gibson and Pope (1993) found that 23% of the counselors believed sexual intimacy with former clients to be ethical.

The ACA and APA Codes and a Continuum of Perspectives

Little attention was focused on posttherapy sexual relationships until the late 1980s when Sell et al. (1986) discovered that psychologists who admitted that a sexual liaison with a client had occurred after termination of therapy were more likely to be found guilty of a violation by state and provincial ethics committees and by state licensing boards than those not making this claim. In other words, state ethics committees and licensing boards were considering posttherapy sexual relationships as serious as those that occurred prior to termination, even though there was no formal standard that identified such actions as unethical. In response to several cases where it was apparent that psychotherapists had terminated a client's therapy for the purpose of starting a sexual liaison, the APA Ethics Committee (*Sex with Ex-Clients,* 1987) developed a rule to cover such situations. Essentially, the rule said that if duplicity occurred in the termination in order to begin a sexual relationship, psychologists could be found in violation of engaging in sexual relationships, even though there was no explicit rule about posttherapy sexual encounters at that time.

Since the early 1990's, the ACA and APA codes addressed the issue but called upon the practitioner to judge whether the relationship was ethical since the last therapy contact. For counselors, sexual or romantic interactions or relationships with former clients was prohibited for a period of 2 years after the last professional contact (ACA, 1995). After that period, the counselor was called upon to "demonstrate forethought and document" whether the sexual or romantic relationship/interactions might be exploitative or potentially harm the former client. If exploitation or harm was possible, the counselor was to "avoid" the relationship/interaction. The 2005 ACA Code of Ethics and Standards of Practice increased the waiting period to 5 years following the last professional contact.

The APA code (1992, 2002) mandated a 2-year period of time after "cessation or termination of therapy." After 2 years, psychologists were expected to "bear the burden" of proof by addressing several factors including: the intensity and nature of therapy as well as duration, reasons for and amount of time since termination, the former client's personal history and current mental health, the potential of adverse impact on the former client, and any type of communication the psychologist might have made during therapy to suggest the possibility of a posttherapy sexual relationship. Canter et al. (1994) suggested that this rule was best understood as an "almost never" rule and that psychologists who engage in sexual relationships after the 2-year period needed to seriously consider the phrase "all relevant factors" when evaluating whether exploitation would be involved. The standard articulates many, but not necessarily all, of the factors that might be considered relevant by ethics committees, licensing boards, or courts. Welfel (2010) reports that the first 15 drafts of the 1992 APA Ethics Code actually "banned all sexual intimacies with former clients" (p. 11), but the final version which permitted sexual contact two years after termination was the one approved by the governing body. It is interesting to note that at the writing of this second edition, the American Psychiatric Association (2009) is the only code that draws a clear line in the sand: "Sexual activity with a current or former patient is unethical" (p. 4).

According to some, the APA (2002) tried to balance the ethical principles of beneficence and nonmaleficence with the ethical principle of respect and to draw upon clinical and research perspectives (Behnke, 2004). The discourse that highlights this balance is somewhat similar to the continuum of perspectives on the ethics of nonsexual multiple relationships with current clients. There are those who suggest sexual relationships with former clients are never a good idea (Flanagan & Flanagan, 2007). These authors cite the research that suggests "once a client, always a client." They offer several arguments the power differential continues (Lamb, Catanzaro, & Moorman, 2004). The former client may want to return to therapy (Vasquez, 1991), and the good work obtained in therapy can be compromised by a posttherapy relationship gone awry (Kitchener, 2000).

Gabbard (1994, 2002) gives some five additional arguments for always considering posttherapy relationships to be unethical. First, he points out there is no empirical support for the 2-year designation as being a sufficient time period to resolve any transference issues in the therapeutic relationship. In fact, a study completed by Geller, Cooley, and Hartley (1981–1982) in the early 1980's suggests that transference and thoughts of returning to therapy with the former therapist linger for years after the termination. Symbolic representations of the therapist continue after therapy has ended (Geller et al., 1981–1982) and may be linked to the continued benefits of therapy. This finding would speak to Gottlieb's (1993) claim that only the former client can determine if the therapeutic relationship has really ended. Second, it seems somewhat suspecting to think that a therapist who is considering a sexual relationship with a former client is a reliable source for determining the successful resolution of any residual transference (Hartlaub, Martin, & Rhine, 1986). Third, the notion that the therapist responsibilities to the client ends after two years is contradictory when compared to other professional standards such as client confidentiality, which is to be maintained in perpetuity. In addition, responsibilities for keeping records and testifying in court proceedings do not end. Fourth, research does not support the claim that a posttherapy sexual relationship is risk free. On the contrary, some studies have suggested that posttherapy sexual relationships can result in harm to former clients (Brown, 1988; Pope & Vetter, 1991). Finally, developing a sexual posttherapy relationship eliminates the possibility of a future therapeutic relationship, and it puts the therapist's current needs above the former client's future ones.

On the other side of the argument are those who see the ethical standard as too parentalistic. This perspective was reflected in the response to the publication of the 1992 APA Ethics Code, with some psychologists arguing that even a 2-year prohibition on sexual relationships with former clients had gone too far. In an interesting study that explored the time lapse between the last therapy contact and the beginning of a sexual activity, the mean interval was 15.6 months (Akamatsu, 1988). Bersoff (1994) argued that although the new standard upheld the principles of beneficence and nonmaleficence, it violated the principle of autonomy. He argued that psychology should be committed to respecting individual's values and their right to make choices about their own lives. This respect included honoring clients' choices about their sexual partners, even if the partner was a former therapist. In essence, he argued that concern about post-termination sexual relationships was based on the belief that there would always be power imbalance between the former therapist, who was usually male, and the former client, who was usually female. This claim, he suggested, assumes that women who enter therapy will never be autonomous or able to make reasonably informed decisions about their sexual partners, and disregards their moral maturity. Some have claimed that this position is inherently sexist (Coleman, 1988; Slovenko, 1992). Furthermore, others have pointed out that the fiduciary responsibilities between therapists and former clients are not as strong after therapy as they are during therapy. Former clients should be respected as emotionally stable individuals who can make an autonomous decision when it comes to posttherapy relationships.

From the legal perspective, states have taken a diverse stand regarding laws governing sexual contact between therapist and former client. For example, in Colorado, the statute draws the line at two years posttherapy, meaning that it is "legal" for a psychotherapist to become sexually involved with a former client two years after termination. However, in Florida it is a crime for a therapist become sexually involved with a former client no matter how long ago therapy ended. It is interesting to note that although a state's legal waiting period may be months or years, former clients have filed malpractice suits claiming psychological damage developing due to a sexual relationship even four years post therapy (Gottlieb, Sell, & Schoenfeld, 1988).

Honoring the Ethical Principles

Therapists need to remember that although their perceptions of clients may change, clients' perceptions may not. This latter point was illustrated vividly for a former colleague of ours by the following incident.

Case 12-7

I was walking through a mall one day and noticed a very tall, good-looking man walking toward me. He was the kind of man I was often attracted to, and I had a brief fantasy about dating him. Suddenly, I realized he was a former client. He approached me and indicated he was happy to see me because he had been thinking about contacting me for a few more sessions of therapy. When he walked away, I realized that although my perceptions of him might have changed, his perceptions of me had not. He saw me as his therapist, not as a potential dating partner.

The concern about client autonomy is an important one. Therapists want to encourage the self-reliance and decision-making capacity of their clients and should not treat them parentalistically once therapy has ended. However, assuming gender socialization remains a major influence in posttermination relationships, former female clients may not have abandoned their view that men are entitled to their favors and that they should serve them. If this is the case, the former client's decision to enter into a sexual relationship with a former therapist is not an autonomous one.

Additionally, the choice to enter into a posttherapy relationship with a client has two participants. Just because one of the participants, the client, wishes to enter into the relationship does not mean that the other participant, the therapist, should agree. Therapists, too, need to make a decision based on full knowledge of the consequences of such relationships for themselves, the former client, and for the profession (Kitchener, 1988). This includes knowledge of all the problems associated with multiple-role relationships, especially sexual ones, as well as knowledge of the role obligations associated with being a psychotherapist. Clearly, this includes making the welfare of the consumer a primary consideration.

Gender socialization concerns aside, some power imbalance undoubtedly remain in the posttherapy setting. The therapist knows the hopes, fears, fantasies, and vulnerabilities of the former client, whereas the client knows very little about the former therapist. The potential for exploiting that power differential remains large and may further undermine the ability of the client to make an autonomous decision.

Bermant (1988) argued that therapists cannot enter therapy with a "fingers crossed" (p. 1) attitude, that is, they cannot enter therapy with the attitude that someday their client may be a sexual partner. Such an attitude would threaten the trust that is essential for the therapeutic alliance and could ultimately undermine the nature of therapy. If this were the case, therapists could turn their practice into a kind of dating service, where they could scan clients for their potential as future sexual partners (Gabbard, 1994), undermining the safety of the therapeutic process. Rather than having a "fingers crossed" attitude, Bermant (1988) suggested:

> The profession should be able to state its position unequivocally, and mean it, and the public should be able to have complete confidence in the integrity of practitioners to forgo fulfillment of personal gratification based on a relationship that began on a fee-for-service basis. Psychotherapists occupy a unique and privileged position vis-à-vis their clients. They are paid to hear and respond to secrets, to advise, counsel, and cure. They are not paid to create future possibilities for themselves, to widen their social spheres of influence or gratification. (p. 2)

All arguments considered, we believe the risks of allowing posttherapy sexual relationships are much greater than potential benefits that might accrue from allowing them. The role of psychotherapist is a privileged one in our society. Therapists are licensed, allowed to charge fees for their services, and valued for their expertise. Sometimes taking the professional role means giving up certain rights. The professions have decided that for dating former clients it is one of these norms: for psychologists at least 2 years after therapy has ended, and for counselors 5 years after therapy has ended. As Gabbard (1994) pointed out, however, when one considers that there are billions of people on the planet from whom to choose as a dating partner, that sacrifice should not be too heavy of a burden, particularly when one considers the costs involved.

Attraction and Sexual Feelings in Therapy

Probably one of the more courageous and important studies about sexual intimacies in therapy explored psychotherapists' sexual attraction to their clients, how they deal with such feelings, and the extent to which they believed their training in this area was adequate (Pope et al., 1986). Pope et al. noted that sexual feelings between therapists and clients were traditionally viewed as countertransference. The assumption was that they occurred rarely and when they did, the therapist was engaged in some kind of an unconscious distortion. Additionally, the traditional view argued that having such feelings was tantamount to committing a therapeutic error. Consequently, the view held that therapists who were sexually attracted to clients should feel ashamed and embarrassed. Under these conditions, sexual feelings were often kept hidden from supervisors, professors, and colleagues. By contrast, Pope et al. took the position that having sexual feelings about clients was not necessarily unethical; it really came down to what the therapist does with the feelings.

According to some authors (Pope et al., 1986; Pope, Sonne, & Holroyd, 1993), if therapy is other than short term and narrowly focused on nonsexual issues, some level of sexual feeling, attraction, or arousal is bound to be experienced. In fact, they (Pope et al., 1986) found that the vast majority of therapists (87%) had been sexually attracted to at least one if not more of their clients. In general, more male therapists were attracted to their clients (96%) than were female therapists (76%). Younger therapists were more often attracted to clients than were older therapists. On the other hand, the vast majority of respondents (82%) indicated that they had never seriously considered acting on their feelings. At the same time, many (63%) reported feeling guilty, anxious, or confused about their feelings. A follow-up study (Pope & Tabachnick, 1993) reported data that were remarkably consistent with the initial figures. Thus, for most therapists, the question is not whether such feelings will occur, but rather what they should do about them when they do occur. Across various studies, almost half the respondents indicated they had received little to no formal training in how to manage sexual attraction to clients (Bernsen, Tabachnick, & Pope, 1994; Blanchard & Lichtenberg, 1998; Nickell, Hecker, Ray, Bercik, 1995; Pope et al., 1986; Rodolfa et al., 1994).

In general, the profession has resisted addressing the question of how therapists should respond when sexual feelings occur (Fisher, 2004; Pope et al., 1993, 2006), perhaps because acknowledging that therapists have such feelings about clients may not fit the image of therapists that professional organizations try to promote. In addition, the feelings may be discordant with therapists' self-image, clients may find the information threatening, and, like suicide, some may believe that if the issues are discussed openly, people may be more likely to act on them (Pope et al., 1993, 2006). Consequently, there has been no consensus about how to handle such sexual feelings except for reiterating the prohibition against sexual contact. In the single study on the issue, Goodyear and Shumate (1996) found in an analogue study that psychotherapists rated a therapist who disclosed his or her feelings of mutual attraction to a client as less therapeutic and less expert than one who did not. This, of course, was not live therapy, and therapists were rating other therapists; therefore, the findings may not reflect real clients' reactions.

One question that has been raised in the literature is whether therapists should disclose their sexual feelings toward the client. Some authors suggest that disclosing sexual attraction to a client is likely to be harmful and possibly received as sexual harassment (Bridges, 2001; Gabbard, 1997; Smith & Fitzpatrick, 1995). Pope et al. (1993, 2006), however, argued that in a safe, supportive, respectful atmosphere that is sensitive, encourages openness, provides appropriate privacy and acceptance, and allows frank discussions, therapists can begin to identify ways to handle their feelings. They also pointed out that failing to address these concerns can lead to serious negative consequences for the therapeutic alliance because they engender a variety of negative feelings in the therapist, such as anger, fear of losing control, frustration, and confusion about the therapeutic task, as well as boundaries. When therapists are confused about boundaries, they may be more apt to slide down the "slippery slope" toward acting on their sexual feelings.

There is probably not a single right formula that therapists can use to identify an appropriate course of action when they become aware that they are sexually attracted to a client. Sometimes introspection can be helpful. At other times, entering or reentering personal therapy may be important. At minimum, therapists need to identify a group of respected colleagues or a supervisor with whom they can consult when faced with discordant feelings about clients. One red flag to the possibility that a therapist's feelings and actions may be lead toward a boundary violation is the desire to keep the feelings a secret. If therapists are afraid to discuss their relationship with other respected professionals, they need to ask why they are afraid to do so. On the other hand, it should be noted that when therapists are tempted to act out sexually, they may seek "subversive, phony, or pro forma consultation" (Pope et al., 1993, p. 189) as a way to rid themselves of doubt or obtain permission for acting out. This is again an argument for the need to develop professional integrity and a true sense of compassion for clients. Pope et al.'s book (2006) offers some additional suggestions about how to become more aware of unacknowledged sexual feelings, as well as some exercises for dealing with them.

Preparing Future Psychologists and Counselors to Deal with Attraction and Sexual Feelings

It takes courage for therapists to admit they have sexual feelings about clients. This is particularly true for therapists in training because they fear that sharing their feelings with supervisors may lead supervisors to reprimand them or become overly suspicious of their behavior. In some cases, their fears may be accurate. Yet, it is important for therapists and therapists in training to find safe places where they can discuss these concerns and identify ways to handle them so that they do not damage clients or lead to a therapeutic impasse. In many ways, graduate training programs are perfect places for budding professionals to explore themselves as sexual beings since they are entering a profession where conversations with clients will stir feelings of intimacy for both the client and the therapist (Flanagan & Flanagan, 2007). In the exploration of personal ethics, values and needs, psychotherapists in training can come to know themselves better and be better prepared to recognize the "red flags" of a slippery slope ahead (Anderson & Handelsman, 2010). Research suggests that training programs are not adequately preparing future psychotherapists to effectively handle sexual attraction (Paxton, Lovett, & Riggs, 2001; Pope, 2000; Pope, Sonne, & Greene, 2006). Programs need to move beyond a discussion of the prohibition and rules and on to a more positive ethics approach by exploring the trainees' ethical acculturation journey related to this topic and others (Anderson & Handelsman, 2010; Bashe, Anderson, Handelsman, & Klevansky, 2007).

A helpful place to start this training is to normalize the experience by helping students understand that sexual attraction to clients is a common occurrence for most therapists. According to research, up to 90% of psychologists reported sexual attraction to at least one client (Blanchard & Lichtenberg, 1998; Giovazolias & Davis, 2001; Pope et al., 2001; Pope et al., 1986; Stake & Oliver, 1991). The following is a personal example:

> When I (Karen) was aware of being attracted to a client for the first time, I felt both terrified of my feelings and guilty for having them. In addition, I realized I had reached an impasse with the client. Luckily, my supervisor was available. After processing the issue, I was able to understand where my feelings originated and how they were a response to the client's problems. Once I became clear, I was able to use my feelings as a source of information, break the impasse, and help the client move on.

It is also helpful for students to understand that the sexual attraction alone, or not acted upon, is not unethical. If training programs can bring the "taboo topic" into the curriculum, this will better prepare future therapists to address the issue in supervision or consultation and benefit clients in therapy. Unfortunately, such an ideal supervisory situation may not always be accessible.

Research is beginning to explore what training programs are providing students to prepare them to ethically deal with sexual attraction to clients. One study asked psychologists to recall their training experience related to this topic (Paxton et al., 2001). A majority of the respondents, 78%, remembered feeling of sexual attraction toward a client during their training. Related to training in how to deal with sexual feelings toward clients, 14% of the respondents stated there was no training, while 66% responded that their training had prepared them "somewhat" or "moderately well," and 20% believed the program had prepared them "very well." It is important to note a majority of the sample did not recall their training experience as providing opportunities to develop ways to ethically and therapeutically deal with sexual attraction, nor did they have opportunities to explore personal beliefs and attitudes as a sexual beings in the profession.

On a positive note, Paxton et al. (2001) believe their data suggested an improvement from earlier studies (Bernsen et al., 1994; Pope et al., 1986, 1993; Rodolfa et al., 1994). Pope et al. (2006) provided steps in student training and professional development that could enhance therapist understanding in this area. Other authors have developed resources and activities to prepare psychotherapists and helping field professionals explore personal ethics and values related to this topic and others (Anderson & Handelsman, 2010; Bashe et al., 2007; Flanagan & Flanagan, 2007; Corey, Corey, & Callahan, 2010).

The Specter of Harm: Nonerotic Touch in Therapy

Because there may be a relationship between differential, nonerotic touch based on the client's gender and a greater incidence of sexual relationships between therapists and clients (Holroyd & Brodsky, 1980), the question of whether therapists ought to use nonerotic touch in psychotherapy has become increasingly controversial. Nonerotic touch can include several types of physical contact that ranges from a handshake at the end of therapy, to a reassuring pat on an arm or back, to a hug. Bacorn and Dixon (1984) defined nonerotic touch as "physical contact between the hands of the counselor and the hands, arms, shoulders, legs or upper back of the client" (p. 491). The following discussion uses Bacorn and Dixon's definition, with the assumption that touch to the client's legs occurs to the lower three fourths of the leg (Bley, 1991). Generally, therapists see kissing as more closely related to overt sexual behavior than to nonerotic touching and hugging as an ambiguous behavior (Stake & Oliver, 1991).

On one hand, there are data that suggest that touching is necessary for normal development in both animals and humans. Note that Harlow in his work with the mother–infant bond in rhesus monkeys and Spitz (1945) in studies of hospitalized children support the basic developmental benefit of touching. Although there are not a lot of data that evaluate the use of touch in therapy, research has suggested that therapists who touch are seen as more expert (Hubble, Noble, & Robinson, 1981); that touch increases self-disclosure in clients (Jourard & Friedman, 1970); and that it can enhance the therapeutic alliance (Beutler, Machado, & Neufeldt, 1994). Some have argued that it is essential to use in working with children who have experienced a delay in the attachment process (Hopkins, 1987; Mitchum, 1987). Similarly, others have argued that touch is important in working with elderly clients (Baldwin, 1986; Weisberg & Haberman, 1989). From this perspective, when used appropriately with some clients and in some contexts, touch may enhance the therapeutic process by modeling appropriate caring and appropriate physical contact in a way that does not end in abuse or seduction (Bley, 1991). Research suggests that most psychotherapists use some type of nonerotic touch with their clients, such as a handshake, and see this behavior as ethical and therapeutic (Nigro, 2004; Stenzel & Rupert, 2004).

On the other hand, the line between erotic and nonerotic touch is not always clear, neither for therapists (Stake & Oliver, 1991) nor for clients. This is particularly true when there are gender or cultural differences between the patient and the therapist. Little is known about cultural differences in relationship to the use of touch in psychotherapy. Considering, however, that there are different standards of intimacy between cultural groups (Sue & Sue, 1990), as well as different ways intimacy is communicated (Russell, 1988), it would not be surprising if there were differences in the amount and kind of therapeutic touch that is considered socially acceptable. Even when a therapist does not consider contact to be erotic or when a typical Euro-American client might not consider it erotic, an Asian Indian or Chinese client might consider it to be so. For example, in India, physical contact is limited to family and very close friends. Such contact with members of the opposite gender, unless they are family members, is not condoned (Behari, 1991). If physical contact were to occur with a therapist of the opposite gender, an Asian Indian client could be offended, question the motives of the therapist, and lose confidence in therapy and the therapist. Additionally, clients may feel guilt about their own role in initiating the therapist's actions.

Furthermore, touch can be particularly dangerous between male therapists and female clients. According to Alyn (1988),

> it may very well reinforce the already unequal power relationship between therapist and client. It may blur boundary definitions in the treatment relationship, reproducing the routine violation of women's boundaries that occurs in sexualizing experiences. (p. 133)

Because the erosion of boundaries may be a precipitant of sexual relationships in therapy, touch has to be considered a potentially risky therapeutic technique, both for the therapist and client. Additionally, even if touch does not lead to explicit sexual contact, if it occurs between a male therapist and an adult female client, which is the most common pattern (Borys & Pope, 1989; Holroyd & Brodsky, 1980), it may reinforce the patriarchal ideal of womanhood where a woman gains her self-esteem when she is valued or reassured by a man (Gilbert & Scher, 1989). In addition, because of the myth of "male entitlement," when touch occurs between a male therapist and a female client, the effect on a woman's self-concept may occur without the male therapist even being aware that it has transpired (Gilbert & Scher, 1989). If this reinforces a woman's belief that male needs should take precedence over her own or that men are the source of women's well-being, then harm has occurred even from nonerotic touch.

In addition to gender and culture, there may be other contextual variables that affect the client's perception of nonerotic touch. Diagnosis is a critical one. Clients who have experienced victimization and trauma and clients who are borderline, paranoid, particularly manipulative, or psychotic may misinterpret even nonerotic touch, view it as a boundary violation, and become demoralized (Borys, 1994). For some clients, particularly women who have been victims of sexual assault or incest, touch may be perceived as another assault (Vasquez, 1991).

Religion has also been linked to beliefs about sexuality and physical contact. Some religious beliefs discourage touching as potentially sexually stimulating (Borenzweig, 1983). Finally, sexual orientation factors may also lead to the misinterpretation of certain behaviors. The therapist may intend a pat on the knee to be merely supportive, whereas the client sees it as a sexual overture. As Brown (1992, personal communication) and Pope et al. (1993) has suggested, the therapist's own sexual orientation may lead him or her to discount the sexual meaning of particular actions.

Theoretical orientation plays a central role in evaluating the use and importance of nonerotic touch in a clinical setting (Holub & Lee, 1990; Pope et al., 1993). There is a strong taboo in the psychoanalytic community that suggests even nonerotic touch should be avoided, although some have argued otherwise (Goodman & Teicher, 1988). At the other end of the spectrum, some more experiential therapies take the perspective that one goal of therapy is to increase bodily awareness and unblock energy that has been trapped in the body. Some therapies direct therapists to use physical contact to unleash the energy (Leland, 1976; Rappaport, 1975). In fact, Holroyd and Brodsky (1977) found that 30% of humanistic therapists but only 6% of dynamic therapists thought that nonerotic touch might be helpful to clients frequently or always. Sixty-eight percent of psychodynamic therapists and less than 20% of humanistic therapists thought it would rarely or never benefit clients. Most dynamic therapists thought it would be frequently or always misunderstood, whereas the majority of humanistic therapists thought it would be rarely or never misunderstood. Although these data are 30 years old and the perspective of both groups may have changed, they do emphasize the role that theory plays in assessing the potential usefulness of nonerotic touch.

In this era, when sensitivity to the potential for sexualizing therapeutic relationships has been heightened, if therapists are going to use touch in psychotherapy, they must consider whether more benefit than harm will occur as a result of the touch, whether the client's autonomy is being respected, and whether the touch will support or damage the fiduciary nature of the relationship. The following series of questions should serve as a guide when therapists are balancing the potential for the intervention to be harmful or helpful and issues of client autonomous choice.

1. What therapeutic goal will touching the client achieve? Is it consistent with the rest of the treatment plan, and can it be theoretically defended to be in the best interests of the client?

2. How will the client receive the touch? How will the particular client with his or her cultural, religious, psychosexual background understand the meaning of the touch? Will it indeed fulfill the therapist's goal, assuming that the goal is to benefit the client, or will it cause unintentional harm? (See Case 2-5 as an example of how touch was misinterpreted because of cultural differences.) As Brown (1994a) has said, "When a hug is given to a client, a therapist has the burden of understanding and accounting for the symbolic meanings of that action and taking it (the action) with deliberation and conscious attention" (p. 279). She suggested that it is not the use of nonerotic touch per se that is the problem, but rather its impulsive use without considering its implications for the client that is problematic. Using perspective taking, therapists can purposely place themselves in the "shoes" of their clients and try to anticipate how the touch will be received and understood.

3. Are there other therapeutic techniques that could be considered to achieve the same gains that are less risky? If so, then the use of even nonerotic touch may not be justifiable.

4. Whose needs are being met by the touching? When touch is used to lessen therapists' anxiety or meet their intimacy needs or when the client is treated as an object, it is exploitation.

5. Will the use of nonerotic touch lead to or increase the risk for sexual intimacies with the client (Pope et al., 1993)? Is it the first step that blurs boundaries and confuses both the client and therapist about their appropriate roles?

6. Can the client assert his or her right to refuse the touch? Pope et al. (1993) pointed out there are many instances in which clients are asked to participate in activities to which they never gave voluntary consent. Not to allow clients to refuse a touch would be disrespectful of their autonomy.

7. Is the therapist competent to use the nonerotic touch in a therapeutic way (Pope et al., 1993)? Whether the intervention is conceptualized in a behavioral framework, a humanistic framework, or a psychodynamic framework, therapists must assess whether they have the training and skill to use it to benefit the client's welfare and to assess its potential for harm. Therapists must understand "touch as a powerful form of communication with comfort and erotic potential" (Flanagan & Flanagan, 2007, p. 179). This awareness is a key piece of competence to use nonerotic touch in a therapeutic way.

In no way and under no conditions should the therapist suggest that touching means the relationship is a sexual one or has the potential to become a sexual one. Whatever action the therapist chooses should be consistent with this communication (Pope et al., 1993). It must be clear to the client that the nonerotic touch does not mean that this basic communication can or will change. If touching involves more than a handshake, clients should be asked if they would feel comfortable with the touch and how they would interpret its meaning. After the hug or pat or other touch is given, the therapist should again talk about the meaning of the experience for the client.

When the Teaching or Supervisory Relationship Is Sexualized

What Is the Prevalence?

Both the APA and the ACA ethics codes have addressed sexual relationships between professionals and students and supervisees. Similar to the prohibition of sex with clients, educators and supervisors are prohibited from engaging in sexual and romantic relationships with students and supervisees. As with psychotherapy, when teaching or supervisory relationships are sexualized, harm can occur. Several studies have investigated the incidence of sexual intimacy between psychology educators and their students and have found remarkably similar results. In the first study (Pope et al., 1979), members of APA's psychotherapy division were surveyed about the sexual contacts they experienced as students with educators. Although less than 10% reported such contact, when the results were divided by gender, differences were substantial. Over 16% of female respondents reported such contact, but only 3% of male respondents reported similar experiences. Subsequent studies found remarkably similar results (Glaser & Thorpe, 1986; Hammel, Olkin, & Taube, 1996; Robinson & Reid, 1985). Between 14% and 18% of female psychologists reported sexual contact with psychology educators and the numbers were about the same whether applied or scientific divisions of APA were surveyed. The only other study (Hammel et al., 1996) that questioned male respondents found that 2% reported such contact.

In a related study, Tabachnick et al. (1991) surveyed male and female APA members who were in academic departments and/or were members of the division on the teaching of psychology. They did not find a gender difference between male and female psychology educators who indicated they had become sexually involved with a student for whom they had current evaluative responsibility, nor between those who had dated students. They did, however, find that male educators were more likely to engage in sexual fantasies about students, were more likely to be sexually attracted to students, and were more likely to become sexually involved with former students.

A study completed on the incidence of sexual relationships in supervision by Rudolfa, Rowen, Steier, Nicassio, and Gordon (1994) reported 3% of psychology interns indicated that they had a sexual relationship with their clinical supervisors and 7% reported being sexually harassed by them. Rudolfa et al. (1994) also reported that 25% of interns reported feeling sexually attracted to their supervisors. Several authors have identified sexual attraction and intimacy as common supervisory concerns (Bartell & Rubin, 1990; Ellis & Douce, 1994).

More recent studies cautiously suggest a possible decrease of sexual involvement between psychology educators and supervisors with their students and supervisees. For example, Lamb and Catanzaro (1998) reported teacher–student sexual involvement at 1.7%. Supervisor–supervisee sexual relationships were reported as 1%–4% (Lamb & Catanzaro, 1998; Robinson & Reid, 1985). Lamb, Catanaro, and Moorman (2003) found a similar rate reported by their sample: 1% of their sample reported a sexual boundary violation with a supervisee and 3% reported sexual boundary violations with students (50% of these claiming the relationship occurred after the teaching role was done).

To a lesser extent, sexual involvement between counselor educators and students and supervisees has been studied. Of the studies reported, the incident rate of counselor educator and student sexual relationships is 6%–7%, with the predominant pattern being male faculty and female graduate student (Miller & Larrabee, 1995; Thoreson, Morrow, Frazier, & Kerstner, 1990).

Some studies have asked professionals to reflect back on their experience as graduate students and any unwanted sexual advances, that is, sexual harassment, by faculty and/or supervisors. In two early studies of psychology educators (Robinson & Reid, 1985) and practicing psychologists (Glaser & Thorpe, 1986), participants reported 48% and 33% of unwanted sexual advances by faculty and supervisors, respectively. In a study looking at unwanted sexual advances experienced by counselor educators, 18.7% of a sample reported having such an experience during graduate training (Miller & Larrabee, 1995). In a more recent study, 17.8% of psychologists reported sexual harassment as graduate student (Ahlstrand, Crumlins, Korinek, Lasky, & Kitchener, 2003). Studies in this arena in both psychology and counseling reflect a similar pattern in sexual misconduct with clients. In other words, it was a male professor becoming involved with a female student (Remley & Herlihy, 2010; Welfel, 2010).

Why It's an Ethical Issue?

Sexual relationships with either students or supervisees for whom the educator has an evaluative responsibility increase the risk of impairing the educator's judgment and the potential for exploitation. As discussed in the previous chapter, the psychology and counselor educator's obligation is to promote the welfare of the student and the supervisor's obligation is to enhance the development of the supervisee and protect the welfare of the client. It is difficult, if not impossible, to put the needs of a student or supervisee first if one is also invested in meeting one's own sexual needs. It is a clear conflict of interest. Professional responsibilities require self-sacrifice, including putting the needs of the consumer above one's own (Bobbitt, 1952; Creegan, 1958; Holtzman, 1960).

It should be noted that some students do not perceive sexual contacts with educators to be ethically problematic or harmful (Glaser & Thorpe, 1986; Hammel et al., 1996). At the time the sexual relationships occurred, the majority of those who responded to the surveys did not perceive them to be so; however, in retrospect, the majority of respondents identified aspects that were ethically troublesome. There are more recent studies that support this change in perspective. More than just a few studies show that professionals at the time of being a student didn't see their sexual relationship with faculty or supervisors as harmful, and even saw it as consensual. Reflecting back, however, they saw the romantic or sexual relationship in a different and more negative light (Ahlstrand et al., 2003; Lamb & Catanzaro, 1998; Lamb et al., 2003; Miller & Larrabee, 1995). In fact, students may experience a variety of negative consequences, including feeling coerced, harmful effects on the working relationship, feeling awkward around other members of the faculty and students, peer jealousy, confusion and emotional distress, failed marriages, and expulsion from or coercion to leave graduate programs. Some of these may not be immediately apparent, or students may focus on the positive aspects of the relationship until it is over.

As with sexual liaisons in therapy, the counselor and psychology educator are responsible for being clear about the ethical issues involved in such relationships. Although there has been some legal debate about the consensual nature of adult students who are sexually involved with faculty members (Chamallas, 1988), most ethicists see the problematic nature of sex between faculty and students. First, there is the issue of a power differential (Flanagan & Flanagan, 2007). Counseling and psychology educators and supervisors are unequal to students, both in terms of power and knowledge. Having this difference in power and knowledge means that faculty and supervisors have a special ethical obligation to be fair and to protect the welfare of the more vulnerable party (Robinson & Reid, 1985), in this case, the student. Even if the student does not see the relationship as problematic, it may become so. If the psychologist removes him or herself from the role of educator or supervisor in order to avoid the multiple roles, the student is denied the opportunity to have that person as a mentor or instructor. As one student commented, "Sex is easily available elsewhere; training isn't. It's the responsibility of the faculty (and the students) to stick to the job they're there for." Additionally, because sexual relationships in educational settings are so overwhelmingly between male educators and female students, it perpetuates the myth that women can be treated as sex objects, despite professional obligations toward them, as well as the myth of male entitlement. Thus, it perpetuates, rather than confronts, the stereotype (Gilbert & Scher, 1989).

Finally, sexual involvement with one student skews objectivity and fairness to other students (Caldwell, 2003). Sexual and romantic relationships are often common knowledge but are treated like "dirty secrets," and therefore they affect the atmosphere of the training program. Rather than valuing integrity, respectfulness, and truthfulness, which underlie trustful human relationships, secrecy and deceit become the more common values; thus, all students are affected. Even more insidious are the jealousies and mistrust engendered when it is common knowledge that some students are receiving favors because of special relationships. Such attitudes and modeling lead to a devaluing of the ethical (Kitchener, 1992b).

As noted earlier, most therapists have experienced sexual feelings toward their clients. Therapists in training are no different than licensed professionals in this respect. Pope et al. (1987) suggested therapists in training need a safe environment where they can discuss their sexual feelings about clients without fearing that these discussions will be taken as seductive or provocative or as inviting sexual advances. When an atmosphere of distrust and subtle or not-so-subtle sexual harassment exists in a training program, such discussions are not likely to occur.

Bernard and Goodyear (1998) pointed out that when adults work together intensely, as they do in supervision, it is not surprising that feelings of sexual and personal attraction might develop. They suggested that if intimate, romantic feelings arise, supervisors should deal with them in a way that poses no ethical compromise for the trainee and no negative consequences for the trainee's client or other students. The position taken here is that supervisors are ethically obligated not to act on those feelings until the supervisory relationship with its evaluative component is terminated. To do otherwise would be a clear conflict of interest and would compromise supervisors' evaluative roles.

In a study by Huebert, Keenan, Kitchener, and Moorman (1998) of stresses encountered by interns, one respondent commented that a supervisor had revealed that he felt sexually attracted to her. Although he processed his feelings with her and did not suggest they act on them, she indicated that she never felt safe in the relationship after his self-disclosure. Thus, she failed to benefit from the supervision to the extent that she might have. Romantic feelings on either side may not be reciprocated and may feel threatening, particularly to the less powerful person in the relationship. Trying to turn romantic feelings into a romantic involvement while maintaining supervisory responsibilities is ethically unacceptable.

On the other hand, as in therapy, it is a difficult call on the part of supervisors to decide whether to try to process such feelings with the supervisee, especially if an impasse has occurred in supervision. If the supervisor decides to do so, supervisees may feel unsafe or even sexually harassed. If the supervisor does not do so, the supervisory relationship may remain blocked. In these circumstances, supervisors should consult with a trusted, objective colleague when deciding how to deal with their feelings and proceed with caution if they decide to process them. Similarly, there should be safe places where supervisees can discuss their own feelings of sexual attraction toward their supervisors. They need to understand that their feelings are not wrong and that they need help in assessing the extent to which their feelings are impeding supervision. They may also need help to verify that if supervisors attempt to act on their feelings of sexual attraction, they would be acting unethically. As Rudolfa et al. (1994) pointed out, staff training about dealing with sexual feelings can provide a training climate in which supervisees feel safe in exploring their understanding of themselves and their relationships with others. Several unsolicited comments by participants in the Lamb et al. (2003) study stated that, as students they wished there would have been more overt and explicit conversation and required trainings related to professional boundaries and ways that graduate students are vulnerable to inappropriate behavior by faculty and supervisors.

If the issue is sexual harassment, whether in teaching or in supervision, clear policies and supports need to be in place. Someone needs to act as an advocate for the student or supervisee, who is in a vulnerable position, and due process must be followed.

Are Romantic/Sexual Relationships Acceptable after Graduation?

Sometimes questions arise regarding whether romantic or sexual relationships are acceptable between faculty or supervisors and former students or supervisees. As already noted, the APA and ACA ethics codes are quite explicit that the prohibition of sexual intimacy extends to faculty or supervisors who have has some type of evaluative authority over the supervisee or student. However, the APA code (1992, 2002) did not address former students and the ACA code (2005) encouraged faculty and supervisors to remain aware of the possible power differential and the need for honest communication before entering a sexual relationship with a former student. On one hand, the evaluative role may be over and those obligations ended. On the other hand, evaluative authority can take many forms. For students who are not in class with a faculty member, these can range from participating in departmental-wide student reviews, to reading comprehensive examinations, to evaluating students' credentials for graduation. Thus, faculty should not delude themselves into thinking that just because students are not enrolled in their classes they can necessarily become dating partners.

Autonomy concerns need to be raised when considering whether to enter into relationships with former students or supervisees. On one hand are issues regarding the importance of accepting the choices that mature, consenting adults make, even if we believe them to be mistaken. On the other hand, issues also need to be raised regarding the extent to which the former student or supervisee's decisions are truly free because of the psychological power conferred by the status differential (Fitzgerald, Weitzman, Gold, & Ormerod, 1988). It is very difficult to clearly separate fully consenting relationships from those that are exploitative. Fitzgerald et al. (1988) found this to be true both empirically and philosophically.

Certainly, there are difficulties that arise as role expectations change from mentor and student to a more egalitarian set of roles. A variety of factors may affect the success of such efforts. Perhaps the best conclusion is the one Fitzgerald et al. (1988) drew is that relationships that are built on a prior power differential may not be explicitly unethical; however, they are "almost always unwise" (p. 339) and are risky for both parties.

Conclusions

When professional roles become sexualized, issues of role confusion, conflicts of interest, and the asymmetrical power differential become profoundly exacerbated. This is particularly true in therapy because of the client's vulnerability. Clients enter therapy with emotional distress and often desperately need a safe haven where they can explore sometimes intense and frightening feelings and behavior. Sharing these feelings and behavior adds to their existing vulnerability. Therapists can and have used this vulnerability to exploit clients by using their power to convince them that sexualizing the relationship is in the client's best interests. However, the harm that results from sexualized therapeutic relationships has been well documented (Pope et al., 1993) and represents a denigration of the therapeutic ideal. As a result, although having sexual feelings about clients is common, mental health associations have universally condemned acting on those feelings.

Sexualizing teaching and supervisory relationships has also been identified as unethical for psychologists and counselors (ACA, 2005; APA, 2002). Although the harm does not seems as profound for most victims as that which occurs when therapy relationships are sexualized, some educational careers have been ruined and a variety of other negative effects have been identified.

As with all multiple relationships, psychologists and counselors are responsible for being aware of the consequences of becoming involved sexually with clients, students or other consumers of their services or participants in their research. In the case of therapeutic relationships, the ethical standards are absolutely clear: in no circumstances are sexual encounters with clients acceptable, nor are therapeutic relationships with former sexual partners. With students and supervisees, both APA (2002) and ACA (2005) have set a similarly clear standard: when psychologists and counselors have evaluative responsibility for the student or supervisee, sexual relationships are unacceptable. Even when such responsibility is not apparent, psychologists and counselors must consider how such a relationship will affect their ability to fulfill their professional responsibility, how it will affect the environment and other people with whom they work, and whether it will harm the student or supervisee.

Questions for Discussion or Consideration

1. What part or parts of this chapter surprised you and why?

2. If you were called upon to help ACA or APA to rewrite the portion or portions of the code that dealt with sexual intimacy, what type of changes would you make to the code? Why?

3. When you think about sexual attraction and feelings toward a client, what types of feelings do you experience? What do you now know about sexual attraction toward clients that you did not know before?

4. If your client asked you out for a date, how would you respond and why? If a former client asked you out for a date, how would you respond and why? If your professor asked to explain you response to each of these questions using the ethical principles as a foundation of your answer, how would you respond?

5. Have you ever felt sexually attracted to a client? How did you handle your feelings?

13

Social Justice

Beyond Being Fair, to Advocacy

As noted in Chapter 3, issues of justice have to do with deciding how to treat others in a fair, impartial, or equitable manner. In modern times, theories of justice have been tied to conceptions of human rights, which include assumptions about peoples' basic needs, such as education, medical attention and a decent standard of living (Benn, 1967b; Rawls, 1971). Mental health professionals have struggled with whether people have a right to a basic level of services and whether it is unjust or unfair when they do not receive it. The question of whether mental health professional services are luxuries to be enjoyed by the wealthy or necessities that all people should be able to use is one of social justice. In psychology and counseling, however, the concept of social justice has come to mean much more.

Questions of human rights are tied to the respect due to all people. Thus, people, regardless of their ethnicity, gender, social class, their gender orientation, or whether they are differently abled, are owed fair treatment. It is unjust or unfair to treat them otherwise. In other words, issues of justice go beyond beneficence to questions of what people are due or owed (Beauchamp & Childress, 2004).

Although the formal principle of justice states that equals should be treated equally and unequals treated unequally according to their relevant differences (Benn, 1967a), justifying the relevant or irrelevant differences is an extremely complex task. For example, what differences might be relevant or irrelevant in making a decision about whether someone deserved treatment for a mental health problem? Would age or race or gender be relevant or irrelevant characteristics? Obviously, they could not be totally irrelevant because they are an intrinsic part of the person. The characteristics that are relevant or irrelevant depend to some extent on one's theory of justice as well as the issue under discussion.

Both ACA and APA have taken strong stands that their members should not engage in unfair discrimination based on age, gender, race, ethnicity, national origin, religion, sexual orientation, disability, or socioeconomic status. They do not, however, define unfair discrimination. In fact, the line between what is unfairly discriminatory and what is not is sometimes slim. For example, is it unfair discrimination to assign someone with lower intelligence to a behavioral treatment and another person with higher intelligence to psychodynamic treatment or is that a reasonable discrimination based on treatment efficacy? There are other cases, however, that such assignment has clearly been shown to be discriminatory. For example, African Americans are assigned to inpatient and drug therapy at a much higher proportion than their representation in the population (Garfield, 1994; Snowden & Chung, 1990).

Issues of justice often arise when resources are limited and there is a greater demand for goods or services than there are available resources. Deciding how the benefits and burdens associated with living in a community should be distributed in a fair or equitable manner involves issues of distributive justice. Distributive justice asks on what basis should the goods or services be proportioned, especially when there are competing demands, and on what basis should the burdens associated with society be distributed. A variety of issues in psychology and counseling, both in research and practice, involve these kinds of questions of justice. For example, although the principle of justice was highlighted in the 2002 APA ethics code, questions about what it means to distribute psychological or counseling services fairly are seldom raised. Similarly, discussions are infrequent regarding who should bear the burden of participation in research, which often falls on populations who have little power to protest (Sieber, 1992). The courts in the *Hopwood* decision (*Hopwood v. State of Texas*, 1994, 1996) have challenged disciplines like psychology and counseling to consider what it means to fairly distribute the benefits associated with a graduate education. Is racial background a relevant or irrelevant variable? Issues of social justice enter at this point since it raises the issue of what criteria are being used to make the decision and whether or not psychologists and counselors have a responsibility to advocate for a system that considers racial background an important variable since racial and ethnic minorities are still underrepresented and needed in our professions.

As Thompson, Alfred, Edwards, and Garcia (2006) point out, despite improvement in educational access for nonwhites in the United States, irrespective of school setting, African-American, Latino/Latina and Native American students achieve less academically and are chronically underrepresented among students who perform very high academically. This is reflected at the college level in that only 13% of bachelor's degrees are awarded to students of color despite their making up 30% of the population. Qualitative studies done by the College Board (1999) have shown underlying racism in predominantly white schools (Tatum, 1997) and those students of color experience a variety of subtle cues that they are not wanted or that they are intimidating. These kinds of cues affect the performance of students and ultimately leave them less able to compete for positions in graduate programs in traditional ways. Social justice asks how counselors and psychologists can intervene to change the atmosphere that undermines success for students of color at a very early age. It also requires challenging decisions like Hopwood and/or developing admissions criteria that values the diversity of perspectives that people of color bring to graduate programs.

Until recently, discussions of social responsibility were scarce outside of the feminist and the multicultural literatures, with a few exceptions. Clark (1993), for example, argued that although social responsibility involves furthering human welfare, it is a "duty owed to society at large" (p. 307) and one that sometimes involves not only questioning community standard, but also opposing them. Furthermore, he maintained that professional activity that is motivated simply by self-interest, including the maximization of personal wealth, is not ethical because it is not socially responsible. Based on a review of several ethics codes, Toporek and Williams (2006) also emphasized the importance of responsibility in social justice work. They argued that psychologists and counselors had a duty to assure equal access to mental health services, minimize the effects of bias and discrimination and serve oppressed communities. Although for some psychologists or counselors this may seem like a controversial position, it suggests psychologists should develop virtues like charity along with integrity and respectfulness. Feminist ethics goes further and argues that the advancement of social justice was a basic ethical responsibility (Brown, 1997a).

Concepts of Justice

Social Justice: A Definition

The concept of social justice has seen a renaissance in the last 10 years. Called Advocacy Counseling by the American Counseling Association, in 2003 the ACA governing Council endorsed 18 advocacy counseling domains that represent skills counselors need to develop in order to become social change agents. Subsequently, school counseling accepted these skills as essential for school counselors as they advocate for their students (Ratts, DeKruyf, & Chen-Hayes, 2007).

Although APA has endorsed guidelines for the competent practice, research, and teaching of racial and ethnic minorities (Appendix A), for gay, lesbian and bisexual individuals (Appendix B), for the elderly (Appendix C), and girls and women (Appendix D), they suggest few initiatives for changing the system in which individuals live and in which psychology operates. ACA led the way with the formation of the Association of Multicultural Counseling and Development (AMCD). Thomas Parham, the president of AMCD, charged its professional standards committee to develop a set of recommendations that could be used as a template for culturally competent counseling (Arredondo, Tovar-Blank, & Parham, 2008). This important document developed by Sue, Arredondo, & McDavis (1992) proposed 31 competencies in three areas: (a) awareness of biases and assumptions, (b) awareness of the client world view, and (c) intervention strategies that were culturally appropriate. Although later criticized by Vera and Speight (2003) for not being grounded strongly enough in social justice theory, they paved the way for APA's multicultural guidelines (Appendix A).

In the last 10 years, coming primarily from community and counseling psychology and counseling literature, multiple publications have been written describing the need for social justice programs and the description of programs that have been successful. For example, *The Handbook for Social Justice in Counseling Psychology* (Toporek et al., 2006), not only defines social justice, but also provides numerous examples of social justice programs that have been effective. It clarifies the implications for training and supervision, intervening at the policy and legislative levels as well as addresses multiple other topics. In addition, whole issues of ACA as well as Counseling Psychology journals have been devoted to issues of advocacy counseling or social justice. Although there is a rich history both in counseling and psychology of attempts to initiate social justice programs, the breakthrough in the last few years seems to be a commitment of organizations and not just individuals to social justice interventions.

Although Advocacy Counseling is the preferred term in ACA, we will use the term social justice or social justice advocacy because it appears to have broader implications for interventions that involve research, supervision, and teaching as well as practice. Several authors both in counseling and psychology have put forth definitions of social justice. Vera and Speight (2003) suggest that "a social justice perspective emphasizes societal concerns, including issues of equity, self-determination, interdependence, and social responsibility" (p. 254). It includes how advantages and disadvantages are distributed in society and that a commitment to social justice means expanding professional roles beyond individual counseling. As they point out these ideas are not new, feminist scholars, particularly those writing in the last 10 years have strongly advocated for a more political analysis of oppressed groups. In fact, Brabeck and Ting (2000) write that feminist ethics requires action directed at achieving social justice. Goodman et al. (2004) argue that "the target of social justice work is the social context" (p. 797). They argue that social justice work must extend from therapy, to advocacy and intervention at the community or political level.

At a conference to clarify the specialty of counseling psychology, one of the more thorough definitions of social justice was created: "A concept that advocates engaging individuals as co-participants in decisions that directly affect their lives, it involves taking some action and educating individuals in order to open possibilities, and to act with value and respect for individuals and their group identities, considering power differentials in all aspects of counseling practice and research" (Fouad, 2004, p. 43). Speight and Vera (2004) argue that the goal of social advocacy is attainment of justice for exploited, dominated, and marginalized people and communities. They contend that mental health professionals must explore ways to change inequitable systems that contribute to psychological distress and refocus counseling and psychology on the environment. Promoting a good life which allows people to develop and express their own capacities and to determine their own actions and the conditions of their actions, social justice involves promoting the values of self development and self-determination for everyone (Young, 1990).

Toporek and Liu (2001) distinguished between advocacy, empowerment, social action, and social justice. They argue that advocacy is an "action a mental health professional, counselor, or psychologist takes in assisting clients and groups to achieve therapy goals through participating in their clients' environments" (p. 387). They describe a model with advocacy as the unifying construct with empowerment on one end of the continuum and social action on the other. Empowerment is an action taken with clients to help them act in the face of oppression. By contrast they describe social action as an act taken by the mental health professional, external to the client attempting to confront oppression on behalf of the client.

Why social responsibility is linked to justice may not be readily apparent. However, acting in a socially responsible way would include an ethical duty to challenge injustice when it exists. In fact, opposing community standards is probably most defensible when an issue clearly involves injustice. Furthermore, if some people do not receive a fair share of life's benefits through no fault of their own but because of their social environment, the social system is an unjust one and individuals who are committed to contributing to others' welfare have a social responsibility to change it. In fact, if a basic minimum of mental health services are a right and it is unjust for people to go without them, then psychologists and counselors have a duty to provide them. As Prilleltensky (1999) argued:

> Psychological problems do not exist on their own, nor do they come out of thin air, they are connected to people's social support, employment status, housing conditions, history of discrimination, and overall personal and political power. … promoting complete health means promoting social justice for there cannot be health in the absence of justice. (p. 99)

From this perspective, the target of interventions in social justice work or advocacy counseling is a social context. Thus, the target of interventions in social justice work is the social context. From this perspective psychologists or counselors need to locate the source of individuals suffering in the social conditions and then attempt to change them (Goodman et al., 2004). This is a much stronger position than a claim based on charity and would need to be balanced with a professional's right to make a decent living.

Taking action to overcome oppression is a key construct that runs through all of these definitions. Oppression is not just a few people mistreating others but is woven into the fabric of major economic, political, and cultural institutions. This is felt in the mundane activities of everyday life (like with the African-American, Latino/Latina, and Native American schoolchildren) as well as in the explicit violence of discrimination. According to Speight and Vera (2004), oppression is pervasive, restricting, hierarchical and internalized. They claim for every oppressed group there is a group that is privileged in relationship to them. According to Young (1990), oppression includes exploitation, marginalization, powerlessness, cultural imperialism, and violence.

Social justice raises the obligations associated with creating a just society from passive to active. It requires mental health professionals be concerned about the welfare of others. It takes an expansive view of ethics. It is not enough to "do no harm" but rather to remove the harm that has already been done. It is not enough to benefit others but to refuse to accept human suffering and exploitation. It requires working for the liberation of oppressed people through our various professional roles. Speight and Vera argue that as long as counseling and psychology persist in defining all problems interpsychically and individually, they helped perpetuate social injustice. Rather, individuals' problems need to be considered in relationship to context.

Case 13-1

An academically promising Latina teenager asks for an appointment with a school counselor. She explains that she's pregnant and depressed. She admits being gang raped by a group of primarily white members of the football team. She didn't want to make a big fuss and was afraid to do so because of the power and prestige that football players have in typical high schools. From an intrapsychic perspective the counselor could use traditional cognitive behavioral therapy to help her deal with her depression and family counseling to help her tell her family about her pregnancy. On the other hand, the girl had been raped. From a social justice perspective he had to do much more. He needed to make an intervention with the football coach, the players, and the principal.

It is not that cognitive behavioral therapy and family counseling might not be needed. It is that from a social justice perspective, the school counselor had an obligation to intervene in the context in which the events occurred, so they did not occur again (Dohir & Stone, 2009). He would be acting as an advocate both for the client and the social costs, for example, the reduction of racism. His actions would probably not be popular with parents and the school administration; however, to do less would be reinforcing the idea that the incident was the young woman's fault and not the consequence of the context in which it occurred. Ivey and Collins (2003) described this psychotherapy as liberation (Ivey, 1995) which has as its goal individual problem solving, a resolution of concerns, and an awareness of the social context in which they were generated. As Watts (2004) points out although the psychology of liberation or social justice requires developing new skills and tools, it would be a mistake to ignore some of the concepts and interventions of traditional psychology and counseling that might be rehabilitated and employed in social justice work.

Although individual professionals are seldom involved in discussions of these issues, the Public Interest Directorate of APA is committed to raising social justice issues and using psychological knowledge in a way that is socially responsible. In fact, the objectives of the Public Interest Directorate (1998) include promoting

> the fundamental problems of human justice and equitable and fair treatment of all segments of society; to encourage the utilization and dissemination of psychological knowledge to advance equal opportunity and to foster empowerment of those who do not share equitably in society's resources. (p. 1)

Additionally, APA, along with other mental health associations, frequently files amicus curiae briefs when court cases raise social justice issues that research can address. For example, APA has filed briefs in several court cases that involved discrimination against lesbians and gay men, pointing to psychological knowledge regarding the effects of prejudice and discrimination due to ignorance and stereotypes.

This section on social justice raises many questions regarding the meaning of justice and social responsibility. It challenges the goals with which many budding psychologists and counselors enter the field. Hopefully, it provokes the reader to consider his or her own responsibility for addressing issues of justice and responding appropriately when injustice is being done.

Distributive Justice: Its Foundation and Implications

Although social justice is one issue that impacts the role psychologists and counselors play, the mental health field is also faced with serious moral questions regarding the distribution of mental health resources. Data suggest that characteristics such as race, gender, intelligence, and level of mental health have been used sometimes to make decisions about access to and type of mental health treatment that clients are assigned. For example, social class has been positively related to acceptance for clinical treatment, with higher social class clients being accepted more frequently than lower class clients (Lubin, Hornstra, Lewis, & Bechtel, 1973). Additionally, educational level, occupation, age, race, and diagnosis have all been linked to the type of treatment offered to potential clients. Those with less education are assigned disproportionately to inpatient treatment. This is also true of being African American or over the age of 39 years (Snowden & Cheung, 1990). Low socioeconomic class has also been associated with receiving medication rather than psychotherapy (Shader, 1970). Both being female and being from a middle to upper middle socioeconomic class have been associated with acceptance for long-term psychoanalytic treatment (Kadushin, 1969; Ryan, 1969; Weber, Solomon, & Bachrach, 1985). Although these characteristics have been used to make treatment decisions, the question is whether they should be.

One justification for differential treatment would be that research supported the use of a treatment because it led to better outcomes for a specific group. However, to our knowledge, there are no data that support, for example, the disproportionate assignment of African Americans to inpatient treatment. By contrast, some have argued that a higher educational level is important for psychoanalytic treatment. Others might argue that if inpatient or drug therapy is cheaper but effective, it would be justified to use it more frequently with those who have fewer resources to pay for services because it would be less of a financial burden on society. These latter arguments run contrary to many fundamental values in psychology or counseling that would argue for using the most effective treatment for each person.

As was apparent in the congressional debate regarding universal health coverage, the reality is that there are huge gaps in mental and physical services available to the general population. For example, the mental health report of the Surgeon General (Satcher, 2010) found that in the U.S. population, 84% had mental health coverage through either private insurance or government programs, but 16% had no coverage at all. The report estimated that 28% of the population had a diagnosable mental health problem, but less than one-third of them received treatment. Worry about costs was listed as the highest reason for not receiving care. However research also documents that many members of minority groups fear, or feel ill at ease with the mental health system (Lin et al., 1982; Scheffler & Miller, 1991; Susman et al., 1987). According to the Surgeon General's report these groups experience the mental health system as the product of white, European culture and shaped by research primarily on white, European populations. In addition, because there are few mental health providers of color, they may only find clinicians who represent a white middle-class orientation. They worry about their cultural values as well as biases, misconceptions and stereotypes of other cultures. As the Surgeon General reported, the mental health system in the United States is not well organized to meet the needs of racial and ethnic minority groups.

One of the problems is that competing values and goals characterize the whole health delivery system. Beauchamp and Childress (2004) articulated the problem in the following way. People in many countries, including the United States and Canada,

> seek to provide the best possible health care for all citizens, while promoting the public interest through cost-containment programs. They promote the ideal of equal access to health care for everyone, including care for indigents, while maintaining a free-market competitive environment. These laudable goals of superior care, equality of access, freedom of choice, and social efficiency are extremely difficult to render coherent in a social system. (p. 231)

Because these problems are still all encompassing, psychologists and counselors must ask how the needs of competing groups should be balanced in response to the need for mental health care. What are and are not legitimate decision rules that should be used when distributing services? How can we decide which characteristics are important when deciding who should get services and who should not?

Furthermore, these are not just problems for providing services, but also for research, supervision, and training. Who should bear the burden of research and what kinds of research should be done to promote social justice? What kind of training is necessary to facilitate the ability to develop social justice interventions and how can these be accommodated by the ACA and APA accreditation standards as well as licensure? These are some of the many distributive and social justice issues that face academicians and supervisors.

Justice Issues in Practice

Case 13-2

A school psychologist was asked to assess an 8-year-old boy who had been acting out in class. In the past, he had been withdrawn and the other children considered him to be strange. For the past several months, however, he had been disrupting the class with bizarre statements and sometimes had destroyed other students' property. At one point, his teacher caught him starting a fire in the restroom. She was very stressed and told the psychologist that she desperately needed help. After assessing the boy, there was no question in the school psychologist's mind that he would fit the criteria for being seriously emotionally disturbed under the Individuals with Disabilities Act (1997). She was also aware that the Individuals with Disabilities Act required that such children be provided with a free education that met their unique needs. She agreed with the teacher that the boy was not able to get a proper education in the classroom. In addition, he was depriving other students of their education and might be a danger to them. However, the special education class available for such children was already overflowing. There was a private school where he could be referred, but the facility was very expensive. Furthermore, if the school referred him, they would have to provide the funds for his placement. Consequently, other students with special needs would suffer because the budget was tight and there would be less in the budget to support their education. The psychologist wondered if she ought to word her report in such a way to minimize the boy's problems so that he didn't fit the criteria for seriously emotionally disturbed and work with the teacher to help her control his behavior in the classroom.

Putting aside the ethical issue of distorting a report, the school psychologist was faced with a problem of distributive justice. Resources were scarce, and providing services for this particular child would mean that fewer resources were available for other children.

Case 13-3

Dr. Land was employed by a community mental health agency in a remote section of a Western state. The agency was located in a prosperous town, but clients were drawn from as far as 100 miles away because Dr. Land was the only licensed psychologist within that area. Consequently, his caseload was quite full. The area included a community of Native Americans who had access to no other mental health professionals. However, when approached by individuals who were Native American, Dr. Land simply refused to see them, saying only that he did not want to work with people from that community. A nurse who worked with patients in the Native American community heard about one such episode and talked to him. She was especially confused because she knew that he had served his internship in a Native American community. He indicated that his internship had nothing to do with it; he simply preferred not to work with Native Americans. He noted that because he already had a full caseload and a waiting list, he could use whatever criteria he wished in deciding whom to see (APA, 1987a).

Here, issues of both distributive and social justice arise. Clearly, resources were scarce and Dr. Land's services were overtaxed; however, racial bias is never a criterion that should be used to fairly refuse to meet the needs of a population. According to Bell (1997), social justice implies a version of distributive justice in which resource distribution is equitable. It allows full and equal access by all groups to the services they need and reduces the barriers that keep them from receiving it. Dr. Land's supervisor needed to be advised of the situation and had an ethical responsibility to intervene. Whatever barriers were keeping the Native American population from receiving services needed to be addressed with Dr. Land through retraining, confrontation, and poor evaluations. It was probably the case that Dr. Land had been hired because of his internship in a Native American community and although it may not have been explicit, the expectation was probably that they would be a substantial part of his caseload.

Theories of Justice and Balancing Diverse Needs

Different theories of justice have been proposed to help develop a systematic way to balance diverse needs. Libertarian theory argues that justice consists of setting up fair procedures rather than being concerned about outcomes like meeting the mental health needs of indigents. The argument is that if everyone is allowed the same opportunities, then the system is a fair one. The opportunities that libertarians advocate are those of a free marketplace. In this system, all people have the right to use their skill, take responsibility for their lives, and in turn be rewarded for their merit. If they choose to do so, they have the right to purchase insurance that would cover mental health benefits. Although libertarians might regret the fact that this procedure leaves some people without services, they do not believe that society has a responsibility to provide these services. Thus, merit and money are the relevant characteristics. On the other hand, libertarians would encourage people to be charitable, although they would see no role for government in ensuring that mental health care was available for everyone (Beauchamp & Childress, 2004).

Although it would seem that many psychologists would refrain from advocating a libertarian system, public mental health policy in the United States has strongly been influenced by it and much of psychotherapy is distributed on the basis of it. Those who can pay out of pocket or through their insurance are the ones who get the greatest mental health benefits.

By contrast, Rawls (1971) pointed out that the natural distribution of abilities and talents is somewhat arbitrary and that a justice system based purely on merit gives undue weight to abilities that people have arbitrarily received through what he called the natural lottery. Because people are subjected to social conditions that are not of their choosing, he acknowledged that people can neither be faulted nor credited with their ability to use their talents. He proposed instead, that justice be served only when basic inequalities are minimized. From this egalitarian perspective, everyone should have a fair opportunity to obtain services based on their needs rather than on characteristics, such as race, intelligence, or gender, that are distributed through the natural lottery or even on merit, given that merit is achieved based on characteristics that are derived from the lottery. From this viewpoint, need is the most relevant characteristic when it comes to the distribution of mental health resources. Evaluated from Rawls's perspective, the psychologist in Case 13-3 was being unjust in refusing to provide services to the Native Americans in his area because race is a characteristic distributed by the natural lottery and is irrelevant when it comes to evaluating need for services.

On the basis of Rawls's (1971) work, Daniels (1985, 1996) has argued that society needs to provide the services that allow individuals a fair opportunity to pursue a life plan commensurate with their skills and talents. He has argued that a decent minimum of health care is necessary for individuals to do so. The *fair opportunity* rule implies that services should be offered to compensate people for disadvantages for which they are not responsible, especially if they interfere with the person getting a fair chance in life. Based on such reasoning, the Individuals with Disabilities Act (1997; see also Case 13-2) requires that states provide students with learning disabilities an education that suits their needs.

If the fair opportunity rule was applied to the mental health arena, a large share of mental health resources would be distributed to those who were disadvantaged by their mental condition. Distribution based on wealth, merit, and effort would cease, and justice would depend on diminishing critical disadvantages associated with the natural lottery. Although it is unlikely that such a major overhaul will take place, it is clear that the fair opportunity rule would not permit policies that deprive individuals of the most appropriate mental health care available on the basis of characteristics such as gender, race, or disabilities.

The outcome in Case 13-2, for example, depends on the interpretation of the fair opportunity rule, especially because meeting the needs of one disadvantaged child would be at the cost of several others. Although there are many interpretations of the fair opportunity rule, as Beauchamp and Childress (2004) suggest, justice demands a fair share, not one that is unfairly large. Additionally, Daniels (1996) argued that needs should be distinguished from preferences and that needs should be limited to things people require in order to "maintain, restore, or provide functional equivalents (where possible) to normal species functioning" (p. 187). From this perspective, it is doubtful that justice would be served either by falsifying the report about the boy or by recommending that he be placed in the private school. Although not ideal, it may be best to refer him to the special education class for emotionally disturbed children and lobby for additional resources for all of those students. In other words, the psychologist would need to move beyond how to fairly distribute services to advocating for more resources.

Vera and Speight (2003) criticized the traditional theories of justice because of their emphasis on outcome (e.g., distribution of resources), rather than a process related to social equality that guides decisions. Liberationist and communitarian theories extend Rawls's and Daniels' emphasis to social reform and social justice. Communitarian theories emphasize the responsibility of the community to the individual and the individual to the community (Beauchamp & Childress, 2004). Justice is fulfilled when there are guarantees that socially valued services that are consistent with community goals are available. Social organization and processes are evaluated to identify domination, privilege, and oppression. Vera and Speight argue that "the processes that facilitated unequal outcomes to begin with must be scrutinized and transcended" (p. 260).

Mental health professionals should be concerned about the role of society in oppression and their responsibility toward people who are disadvantaged (Prillenltensky, 1997). From this perspective, psychology and counseling should redirect some of its efforts from investigating individual causes of mental illness to examining their social origins (Albee, 1986; Prillenltensky, 1997). Prillenltensky argued that mental health professionals perpetuate social injustice by focusing on individual factors to explain social behavior. Justice would involve providing resources to prevent the social ills that exacerbate mental problems in the first place.

According to a liberationist perspective, professionals need to avoid an ethic that just serves the social system that currently exists (dos Anjos, 1994). Rather, justice must be perceived from the perspective of the poor and those who are marginalized by society. Watts (2004) argues that it should go further and that liberation psychology should be developing population specific psychologies. In fact recently, Gone (2010) has described a therapeutic integration between American Indian traditional healing practices and contemporary psychotherapy.

According to the Surgeon General's report (Satcher, 2010), it is widely assumed, but difficult to prove that traditional forms of psychotherapy lead to outcomes that are inferior for minority groups. In one of the few well-designed pre–post treatment outcomes studies, Sue et al. (1992) found that African-Americans fared more poorly than other minority groups who were treated as outpatients suggesting the need for treatments carefully geared toward particular groups, especially those that have been oppressed. This would include persons of color but others like gay, lesbian and bisexual clients as well. It is clear that ethnic and cultural influences can alter an individual's responses to medications (pharmacotherapies) (Satcher, 2010). Again, this would argue for Watts's point that psychology and counseling need to be considering population specific treatments.

Ivey and Collins (2003) argued that psychotherapy as liberation has as its goal individual problem solving, resolution of concerns and helping clients understand the social context in which the concerns were generated. This method helps to bring a better awareness of oppression and social justice issues. Multicultural counseling and therapy (MCT), broadly conceived, focuses on the liberation of consciousness. Whereas traditional psychotherapy focuses on self-actualization, discovery of the role of the past and the present, or behavior change, "MCT emphasizes the importance of expanding personal, family, group and organizational consciousness of the place of self-in-relation, family-in-relation, and organization-in-relation. This results in therapy that is not only alternately contextual and orientation, but also draws on traditional methods of healing from many cultures." (Sue et al., 1996, p. 22). They claim that despite the efforts to bring multicultural and social justice issues to the foreground, there are many who feel that psychology has been too hesitant to promote change. They point out that when Vera and Speight (2003) talk about changing the status quo, it means that psychology and counseling must pay more attention to psychoeducational, preventative and community psychology. This means that psychology and counseling must restructure their training programs and state licensing requirements.

Social health policies that give preference to remedial services rather than preventative ones perpetuate the status quo, whereas prevention efforts often require a redistribution of power as well as social change (Albee, 1986). dos Anjos (1994) argued that strong economic forces oppose such change and concluded that "sickness must exist so profit can be made from it" (p. 137). From this perspective, health care professionals need to be concerned with the economic realities behind mental health care options.

Although none of these theories completely answer the question of how needs for services should be balanced, each offers an important perspective to consider. Mental health providers should be aware that at a national level different perspectives on these issues can and will affect their day-to-day practice through legislation. Social justice and liberation perspectives argue that mental health providers have a responsibility to affect that legislation.

Skills Necessary for Social Justice Counseling

As discussed in Chapter 8, APA has a made a commitment to evidence-based practice as a key strategy for promoting effective psychological services (Hunsley, 2007). Unfortunately, evidence-based practice has focused almost completely on therapeutic interventions that are focused on treating mental health problems that already exist and most often the populations studied are White. In addition, the APA practice directorate in the last 20 years has focused almost entirely on seeking parity with health care providers to cover the costs of treating mental illness. In fact in January of 2010 practice directorate issued a statement that one of its primary focuses was on seeking appropriate Medicare reimbursements for psychotherapy services. Humphreys (1996) argued that monetary values have lured clinical and counseling psychologists away from an emphasis on preventative interventions. He suggests that psychologists and counselors could be more effective by making commitments to changing institutions like schools and social policy than by focusing entirely on psychotherapy. Even though this may be true, because of the emphasis on evidence-based practice as well as the policies of managed care that reimburse for mental health problems, little research is done on preventative interventions.

On the other hand, ACA, Counseling Psychology and Community Psychology have begun to focus on the skills necessary for social justice or advocacy counseling. Advocacy counseling is another term for the social justice approach. The focus is that counselors should work as advocates when they plead on behalf of their clients or social causes (Lee, 1998). As Goodman et al. (2004) point out "the target of social justice work is the social context" (p. 797).

The advocacy counseling domains developed by Lewis, Arnold, House, and Toporek for ACA in 2003 can be best envisioned as having two dimensions. One side represents action (acting on behalf of versus acting with). The second side describes the level of intervention from the micro level to the macro level, in other words, the arena in which the intervention is made from the client or student to the community or school to the public arena. An advocacy orientation involves not only systems change interventions but also implementing empowerment strategies in direct counseling.

Mental health professionals using the empowerment strategy recognize the impact of social, political, economic and cultural factors on human development and they help their clients understand their own lives in context. In order to use these competencies the professional must be able to identify the strengths and resources of their clients, identify the contextual factors that affect the client, recognize signs indicating that a person's behaviors reflect responses to internalized oppression, help clients identify external barriers that affect their development, and develop action plans. Sometimes empowerment also includes assisting students or clients to carry out their action plans.

Case 13-4

Based on a true story, the film *Stand and Deliver* (Musca & Menendez, 1988) illustrated well the impact this strategy can have on the lives of oppressed adolescents. In East Los Angeles in 1982, a new math teacher, Jaime Escalante, is hired to teach basic math skills to poor, primarily Latino students in underfunded, inner-city high school. Recognizing that his students had more ability than they were given credit for, he inspires them, first, to enjoy math and then, to recognize their own skills. Over a 2-year period, he helps them develop not only basic math skills, but algebra, trigonometry and calculus. Sacrificing his own summers and time after school, he is determined to change the system and challenge the students. By the end of their senior year, he teaches them AP calculus, which would give them credit toward college, a goal none of them envisioned, and initially even their parents did not believe they could achieve. Meeting with parents helped them understand the importance of their sons' and daughters' potential achievement and began to nurture them as additional support systems. Eventually, all the students in his class took and passed the Educational Testing Service's (ETS) exam that would give them credit toward college. However, because of inherent racism and belief that poor students could not achieve at that level, the ETS accused the entire class of cheating. Escalante intervened and encourage ETS to give the students a second exam with their own examiners as proctors. Again, all students passed. Escalante had not only provided students with the first step toward college, but also a new belief and confidence in themselves.

Although the person making the intervention was not a psychologist or counselor, he exhibited the skills necessary to empower students to develop in new and unimagined ways. As Ratts, DeKruyf, and Chen-Hayes (2007) point out, school counselors and psychologists can help lead efforts to challenge educational inequities stemming from racism and oppression.

Client advocacy strategies are needed when counselors or psychologists become aware of external factors that act as barriers to individual development. In some ways Escalante acted as an advocate when he insisted that ETS retest his students. These skills are particularly important when individuals or groups lack access to needed services. This means professionals must be able to help their clients gain access to the needed resources, identify barriers, develop action plans and identify allies for confronting the barriers.

Community collaboration strategies involve becoming aware of the specific difficulties in the environment and responding to such challenges by alerting existing organizations that might have an interest in helping. Often the professional's primary role is an ally to help other organizations using their particular interpersonal, communication, training and research skills. Clearly these depend on the ability of the counselor or psychologist to identify environmental factors that impinge on their client's development. They must alert community school groups with common concerns and develop alliances all working for change. They need to use effective listening skills to understand goals and identify the strengths and resources different group members bring to the process of change. They need to communicate recognition and respect for the strengths and resources and office skills they have that may help the collaboration.

Systems advocacy interventions are needed when professionals identify systemic factors that act as barriers to their client's development. Change in the system requires vision, persistence, leadership, collaboration, systems analysis, and strong data. The competencies needed include the ability to identify environmental factors impinging on the person's development, to provide the data to show the need for change, to collaborate with other stakeholders to develop a vision to guide change, and to analyze sources of political power and social influence within the system. As with the other strategies, it is critical that the professional develop a plan to implement the change process and know how to respond to resistance or other negative responses. Last, as with the other strategies, it is essential to assess the effect of the advocacy efforts on the system and its constituents.

Public information strategies are applied across different settings and specialties as well as theoretical perspectives. This domain depends on the recognition of the impact of oppression and other barriers to healthy development as well as identifying the environmental factors that are protective of healthy development. The mental health professional would need to be able to compare materials that provide explanations of the role of explicit factors in human development and communicate this information in ways that are ethical and appropriate for the population. This would include disseminating information and collaborating with other professionals who are also involved in disseminating public information, assessing the effects.

Social/political advocacy strategies involve being able to distinguish problems that can best be resolved at the social/political level and in identifying mechanisms to address the problems. Again, learning to seek out and join potential allies in order to gain support for change is a critical skill. These strategies involve lobbying legislators and other policymakers and providing feedback to the communities and clients to make sure that the social/political advocacy is consistent with the goals of the community.

Although the ACA Advocacy Competency Domains (Lewis, Arnold, House, & Toporek, 2003) are the most thorough descriptions of the domains and competencies necessary for social justice interventions, Goodman et al. (2004) also argue for the importance of moving from therapy to advocacy and intervention at the community level and identify principles on which that change depends. They draw six principles from both feminist and multicultural theories of counseling and apply it to social justice work.

First, there must be ongoing self-examination. Mental health professionals must engage in the process of evaluating their own biases and stereotypes about people and groups from which they differ. As Goodman et al. point out that sometimes these biases are deep and may unintentionally shape the counselors' feelings and behaviors toward culturally diverse populations. Thus, mental health researchers and practitioners need to reflect on and make explicit the values and biases that they bring into their practice or the assumptions on which their research questions are based.

Crethar, Rivera, and Nash (2008) argue that part of the process must be an awareness of the social cultural privileges that are connected to being the dominant group in society. They define the term privilege as "the systematic and unearned benefits select groups of persons in society are bestowed based on specific variables" (p. 269). They suggest these could include one's racial/ethnic/cultural background, gender, socioeconomic class, age, sexual orientation, and physical/mental ability. In particular, they point out that in United States, there are a broad range of unearned privileges and benefits that White, middle-and upper-class, heterosexual, English-speaking, males, especially those that are able-bodied, possess that disempower individuals who do not have these characteristics. Privilege also comes from being highly educated or having special credentials. If professionals are truly concerned with social justice they must examine the way their privilege affects persons in devalued groups.

Second, they must be willing to share power. In feminist theory, the therapeutic relationship is based on consensual decision making. The therapist's expertise is one source of information rather than just the best or most objective of such sources (Brabeck & Brown, 1997). Similarly multicultural counseling theories also carry an underlying assumption that clinicians should always be aware of the inherent power differentials that exist when they work with individuals from oppressed minority groups (Helms & Cook, 1999). In both cases professional therapists must not abuse the power they hold within these relationships and use their power to advocate for and learn from their clients.

Goodman et al. (2004) called the third principle "giving voice" (p. 802). Derived from feminist theorizing, there is recognition that the voices or views of oppressed or marginalized groups have been silenced or suppressed. Multicultural theorists have also argued that a therapist's credibility with individuals from oppressed groups is often dependent on ability to move away from abstract theorizing to conceptualize the problem in a way that fits with the client's belief system. Goodman et al. suggest two main values follow from this idea. The first is that psychologists or counselors should approach communities with the belief that the communities know what questions or problems they want addressed. The second is that mental health professionals need to find ways to intensify the views of community members so that others can learn about their needs, strengths, and wishes.

The fourth principle is consciousness-raising, which means helping clients understand that their individual and private difficulties are rooted in larger historical, social and political forces (Helms & Cook, 1999; Ivey et al., 2002). Although this principle means listening to the stories of community members and helping them identify barriers, it also means helping them become aware of the socioeconomic and cultural circumstances that have affected their lives and their ability to change the patterns of oppression created by social institutions or norms.

Focusing on strengths is the fifth principle that Goodman et al. (2004) identify as central to social justice work. One tool used in feminist therapy is cognitive reframing, which is used to help clients see their apparently problematic behavior really as adaptive responses in the face of oppression. Similarly, multicultural counselors help their clients gain an understanding of how social oppression contributes to their emotional difficulties and helps them identify internal sources of strength.

The last principle that Goodman et al. (2004) identified is leaving clients with tools of self-determination that they can use when future problems arise. This may include teaching them about available support systems. As a result counselors and psychologists need to know the kinds of support systems that are available in the indigenous culture like the extended family and religious support groups as well as in the larger social/political society. What resources are available to community members if they have legal problems or problems with the welfare system? The idea is to leave the members with systems they can use to support themselves rather than to develop a hierarchical dependency on the therapist or counselor. This means ongoing consultation with community members about what tools are available and knowledge of how to use them.

These principles, whether from ACA's Advocacy Counseling Guidelines or from sources like Goodman et al. (2004), leave mental health professionals with new kinds of ethical problems. As Goodman et al. point out we must recognize that our own personal values and the values of the organizations and systems in which we work affect the way we relate to individuals, families and communities. Second, both "the processes and outcomes of our work should entail empowerment and collaboration rather than exploitation and objectification" (p. 819). Toporek and Williams (2006) add several others. As they point out, professional boundaries may be understood differently in different communities and become blurred because they require psychologists or counselors to move into nontraditional roles. Doing so, however, as pointed out in Chapter 11, carries with it the potential for overstepping boundaries and doing more harm than good. Informed consent may also have different meanings because the mental health professional would be intervening on several levels. Pope (1990) suggested collaborative development of general agreements regarding methods used in community interventions. Still this requires answering the question, whose consent is necessary? A third issue that may appear different from a social justice perspective is the principle of doing no harm since its meaning may depend upon the population and the context. The intervention may affect not just an individual but also the social ecology of the system in which the individual lives and the question must be raised whether the individual as well as the community is harmed or helped.

Toporek and Williams (2006) present an excellent case in which the principles discussed above are applied ethically to help a couple and their nephew who are having difficulties with the justice system. (For a full description of the case, see Toporek and Williams, 2006, pp. 28–30.) A summary of the case follows.

Case 13-5

An African-American male therapist met with a middle-aged, heterosexual African-American couple. Because the husband was on a conditional release from the state mental health agency, he had to maintain regular contact with a designated mental health agency. During his regular meeting with a therapist, the couple indicated they were depressed because their nephew was being prosecuted for murder that he did not commit. The therapist, believing that he had the competent training to address social political forces, decided to take a social justice approach to some aspects of the case. Initially he emphasized with the couple's feelings of hopelessness pertaining to helping their nephew. In other words, he validated their feelings without agreeing that the situation was hopeless. After establishing rapport, he shifted his questions to ask them what they would like to do in order to help their nephew. They indicated they wanted him to have "justice," but had no ideas about how to help him receive it. Although the therapist initially assumed the couple had already attempted to develop solutions to the problem, he found they had not tried any. The therapist then shifted toward collaborating with them on developing solutions, rather than paternalistically imposing them. Since he knew the family's history and worldview, it allowed him to make informed choices about how to empower them and what roles to take in the process. Basically he operated from the principle of "only do for a family and what it cannot do for itself" (Toporek & Williams, 2006, p. 29). The couple indicated they would like to support their nephew during his court appearances but they did not have any other ideas on how they could help him. At that point, the therapist shifted from the role of a collaborator to that of an expert and explained to them the role of the attorney general and how the attorney general's responsibility was to look into cases that might involve some improprieties. The move from collaborator to expert was done because in the therapist's assessment, the couple was uninformed about the legal system and their options. On the other hand, he was also aware that he needed to maintain appropriate boundaries and limit his role as an advocate. Realizing the case might be public issue, he used informed consent to help the couple understand the possible consequences they might face if indeed he received public attention. Throughout the session the therapist refrained from imposing his social justice agenda and used informed consent at each step in the process. This is important because mental health professionals who are involved in social justice may forget sometimes their clients may not understand self advocacy or feel entitled to it. Consistent with this principle of not doing more for families than they can do for themselves, the therapist collaborated with the couple toward initiating action beyond just supporting their nephew in court. He helped them learn how to identify and contact appropriate government officials and then role-played with them how they might talk to the attorney general or district attorney. He offered them the option of making the call from his office, but they chose to do it on their own. Eventually, the couple was able to facilitate a second trial for their nephew.

Although the therapist was privileged in relationship to his clients, he was able to reflect on himself and his role to achieve a social justice agenda while respecting the needs and self-respect of his clients. Because he was aware of his own beliefs and intentions, he was able to collaborate with rather than patronize the family and help them develop new skills that they could use throughout their lives. As Toporek and Williams point out, it is also important to prepare individuals for failure because not all social interventions work. The vignette shows how traditional psychotherapy works with social justice. It is not an either–or choice. It takes learning new skills, but not at the expense of giving up old ones.

Mental Health Services: Who Should Pay and for What Kind of Services?

The issue of who should pay for mental health services and who should receive them is both a problem of distributive and social justice. As much as members of the mental health profession believe that anyone who has mental disorders or substance abuse problems should have access to needed mental health services, questions of how much treatment is reasonable and who should provide the funding for it are incredibly complex. Furthermore, answers often depend on one's theory of justice. Interestingly, in a report to the U.S. Senate Committee on Appropriations, the National Advisory Mental Health Council (1993) advocated for a system that responded to need for services:

> As we rethink the structure and costs of health care in the United States, one essential goal must be to create a system that enables Americans with severe mental illnesses to obtain the care they need to function at their best. These individuals continue to suffer from misunderstanding, stigmatization, and inadequate societal resources—a cruel and unnecessary addition to the burden of illness. (p. 1448)

The council argued that both humane and economic benefits would derive from improving the financial accessibility of mental health coverage. In addition to the financial savings, the humane benefits would be immense, including a reduction in the number of suicides, the number of people living in poverty, and the number of people incarcerated for crimes.

In the late 1980s, patients paid 45% of outpatient mental health services for themselves, whereas private insurance covered just over 26%, and government sources covered almost 27% (Olfson & Pincus, 1994). Pro bono services represented less than 1% of mental health outpatient coverage. As already noted, the system was based on a justice of merit, reflecting to some extent the libertarian perspective. Thus, those who could afford services had the most access to them, either through private insurance or through their own resources. Charitable acts on the part of mental health professionals contributed very little.

Two events have changed this picture, though their full impact on the fairness of the financing, quality, and coverage of mental health services is still unknown. The first was the Mental Health Parity Act of 1996 and the second was the explosion of managed care (National Advisory Mental Health Council, 1998).

Partly in response to public concern about mental health benefits, the Mental Health Parity Act (P.L. 104–204) was signed into U.S. law in September, 1996 (Frank et al., 1997), and has recently been renewed. (Parity refers to the idea that insurance coverage for mental health services should have the same benefits and restrictions as does insurance for other kinds of health problems.) The bill was an attempt to legislate a more just distribution of insurance benefits between mental health problems and other health problems. In the past, lifetime mental health limits were lower and it was very easy for those with chronic mental illnesses to reach these limits. But under the Mental Health Parity Act, this changed because individuals with chronic mental illnesses had access to more coverage. In their final report to Congress, the National Advisory Mental Health Council (Kirschstein, 2000) reported that 31 of the 50 states had also passed some form of parity legislation. Furthermore, in 2001, President Clinton announced that a parity level benefit would be implemented for all of the beneficiaries of the Federal Employees Health Benefit Program.

There were two major consequences of parity legislation. In every state where parity was established, managed mental health care increased. In addition, there was reduction in total mental health costs (National Advisory Mental Health Council, 1998). Generally, the implementation of the federal law has increased the speed of the move to managed care.

The unanswered question is whether the new system is more just or unjust. The answer revolves around the impact of managed care on mental health services and depends not just on financial issues, but also on issues of who is getting access to treatment, and the quality of that treatment (Miller, 1996c; National Advisory Mental Health Council, 1998). Furthermore, the whole parity movement has basically ignored social justice issues in the sense that it is about the treatment of people who are mentally ill and ignores the social causes of the problems and interventions that could have avoided the problems in the first place.

Managed Care, Advocacy and Justice

Managed care is not something psychologists and counselors can afford to ignore, either financially or ethically. Between 1992 and 1997, fee-for-service plans dropped from being the most prevalent medical plan (62%) in 1992 to the least prevalent (20%) in 1997 (National Advisory Mental Health Council, 1998). The consequences of these changes for both providers and participants are still emerging. As discussed earlier, there are serious ethical issues with these plans that involve both confidentiality and informed consent. The question raised here is whether they are more or less just than the prior system.

Ideally, both access and quality of care would increase with managed care. Thus, more people who have need for mental health services would be served, and the quality of that care would be high enough to make a difference in their lives. Often this is how managed care is sold to both employers and clients—that managed care can help potential clients to access services and resources they might not otherwise be aware of. In fact, data generally support the claim that under managed care plans, more people who have needs for services are receiving services (National Advisory Mental Health Council, 2000). Specific managed care policies, however, lead to a variety of financial incentives that are sometimes used to limit access to care by those who need it the most. For example, in some preferred provider networks, the provider's offices may be located in areas of a city where the neediest clients do not live. This may be especially problematic for clients who need therapists with specialty expertise in, for example, alcohol or drug abuse or eating disorders, or whose financial resources are already limited and thus have transportation difficulties. The consequence is that those who have the greatest need for services may have the most difficulty in accessing them. Furthermore, according to Barlow (2004, 2010), some of the earlier guidelines established by managed care companies lacked even the basic rudiments of the evidence on which their guidelines were based.

Even more ethically troublesome are rationing systems that provide financial incentives to providers and organizations to limit the number of specialty referrals or length of treatment (Miller, 1996c; National Advisory Mental Health Council, 1998) or to disallow therapy for problems that are particularly difficult to treat (Brown, 1997a). Besides disregarding people's autonomy, organizations that forbid providers to tell consumers about time limits or to recommend longer treatment when it is advisable are unethical because they require that therapists sacrifice their integrity for financial gain.

Although the ultra-brief therapy models that most managed care companies embrace may provide the most benefit to those who have problems that are the easiest to treat, those with the most serious conditions and most in need of long-term treatment may receive the least benefit (Lambert, Bergin, & Garfield, 2004; Lambert & Ogles, 2004). Some (Brown, 1997; Miller 1996a) have asked questions about what split loyalties will do to psychologists' and counselors' abilities to act as their client's advocate. When therapists are pressured to get people out of therapy as quickly as possible and are provided incentives to do so, how can they remain loyal to their clients' best interests?

This latter issue relates to quality of care. Since the 1960s, there has been a movement in psychology and other mental health fields toward briefer psychotherapy (Lambert, Bergin, & Garfield, 2004). This has been supported by claims that, on average, briefer therapies can be as effective as longer term therapies (Bloom, 1992; Koss & Shiang, 1994). Managed care companies have embraced these claims not just to support brief therapy (up to 25 sessions) but also to support ultra-brief therapy, averaging 2.5–6.6 sessions (Miller, 1996b). Unfortunately, the view that brief therapy can be as effective as long-term therapy does not adequately reflect the psychotherapy literature, nor does it lead to the conclusion that everyone can be adequately treated in brief therapy. Even brief therapy advocates point out that it is not as effective with patients with more severe problems, such as psychosis, substance abuse, or a personality disorder (Koss & Shiang, 1994; Lambert & Ogles, 2004). Furthermore, dose–effect research suggests that although about 53% of patients improve in 8 sessions, almost an equal number take more sessions, with some needing as many as 102 sessions (Howard, Kopta, Krause, & Orlinsky, 1986). In fact, in their review of psychotherapy process and outcome literature, Lambert, and Ogles (2004) concluded that although the relationship between outcome and time in treatment is not linear, in general, the longer patients stay in treatment, the more they improve.

We know that therapy can make people better, but we also know there are potential negative effects (Barlow, 2010; Dimidjian & Holon, 2010). For example, the use of conversion therapy for gays and lesbians is not only harmful to the client, but also reinforces social stereotypes, prejudice, and stigma (Dimidjian & Holon, 2010). As Dimidjian and Holon argue, there are need for checks on the fidelity and quality of treatment because their data suggest that the same psychological service (delivered slightly differently) can produce very different results. Based on a study of African-American students (Cohen, Garcia, Apfel, & Master, 2006; Cohen, Purdie-Vaugn's, Apfel, & Brzustoski, 2009), researchers found that writing affirmation statements significantly improved academic performance over the course of middle school years. However, these interventions are not universally beneficial in terms of counteracting negative effects of prejudice. That depends on who is leading the interventions and the nature of the affirmations. In other words, the "one size fits all" style of some managed care companies may actually produce more harm than benefit.

There are few direct data that report on the effects of managed care on outcome or other measures of treatment quality, although several studies are underway (National Advisory Mental Health Council, 1998). One study reported by the National Advisory Mental Health Council found that 87% of psychotherapy patients were rated as improved by their therapists (although this is a highly prejudicial outcome measure). Compared with the control group that was receiving therapy in an outpatient setting, those in the managed care system were less likely to terminate therapy prematurely and formed more stable alliances with their therapists. Other data, however, suggest those treated in prepaid arrangements have worse outcomes than those who do not, and that fewer depressed patients are accurately diagnosed in managed care settings (Miller & Luft, 1994; Seligman, 1995). As already noted, sometimes managed mental health plans have resulted in limited mental health access. Limited mental health access has been related to decreased work performance, increased absenteeism, and a greater use of medical care. It is possible that cost savings are more than consumed by new problems.

Although the limits of managed care and the question of who will pay for mental health services may seem abstract, for individual psychologists and counselors, these are very difficult justice and social responsibility questions that must be tackled. Take the following case as an example.

Case 13-6

A client contacts a psychologist who is a provider for her managed care insurance. She is allowed only eight sessions. When the psychologist requests an extension of services, the administrators of the managed care insurance agree to do so only in the case of a major mental disorder or if the patient is a danger to self or others. The client's diagnosis, dysthymia, does not qualify. The client's financial status is restricted, so the psychologist agrees to provide services on an as-needed basis for the client on a sliding-fee scale. A month later, the psychologist is dropped as a provider by the managed care company. Two months later, the client contacts the psychologist through the emergency answering service and indicates that she has overdosed (Vasquez, 1994, p. 323).

Most mental health ethics codes (ACA, 2005; APA 2002) forbid therapists from abandoning their clients. Even though it is unclear who will cover the costs of services or whether they will be covered at all, the therapist must, at least, ensure that the client is stabilized. After doing so, future alternatives for treatment and treatment payment can be considered (Vasquez, 1994). Thus, the therapist must consider what constitutes fair treatment for the client, and what constitutes fair compensation for him or herself.

Focusing on the fairness of insurance coverage, however, may obscure the larger issue of how mental health services are paid for. As Brown (1997a) pointed out, avoiding managed care and insisting on a fee-for-service practice may work well if psychologists

> see only upper- and middle-class clients, but what about the needs of working women and men and their children who have more insurance than money and are still hurting and in pain or very poor individuals who have no insurance or no money? (p. 456)

Questions of who should pay for mental health care and how much they should pay are difficult ones. Whether the system is one of fee-for-service or managed care, often employers are paying the bill, which leads to the question of how much mental health service should they provide when their biggest concern is employee productivity.

Daniels and Sabin (1996) suggested there are three models that are often used (and confused) in considering how much therapy should be covered by benefits. The first argues that people ought to have an equal opportunity for normal functioning. Here, the target would be to restore people to the capability they would have had without a mental disorder. This model is based on a mental illness model of mental health and disavows help for mental problems that were a result of an unjust social system or social environmental stressors. The second argues that health care ought to give priority to those with diminished capabilities, such as problems with self-confidence or sociability. It does not require that mental illness cause the diminished capacity; rather, the goal would be to improve people's capabilities, whatever the cause of their disadvantage. The third model, called the welfare model, focuses on repairing any unchosen constraints on the potential for happiness as long as the person involved is willing and able to change attitudes and behavior that cause suffering.

Although not articulated by Daniels and Sabin, a fourth, social justice-based model could be defended. In this model, resources should be spent on reducing the contextual influences that lead to mental health problems. Insurance pays for preventative healthcare services like yearly physicals or mammograms, but to our knowledge, few similar programs have been established in the mental health arena. It should be noted, however, that at one time, university counseling centers provided a model of what a system might look like, since a major part of their mission was to provide outreach and consultation services for the campus, for example, going to dormitories for suicide and sexual assault prevention, consulting with faculty on how to use group process in classroom discussions, and so on.

The question is not which model should be accepted, because a justification could be made for each of them. The question is whether health insurance should pay for the treatment of all potential problems. Unfortunately, these questions are seldom addressed in mental health literature, though the issue of what constitutes a decent minimum of services is based to some extent on which model is accepted.

As Beauchamp and Childress (2004) argued, many aspects of the system as it now exists are unfair because it is so dependent on employers to finance the system or on personal wealth. Many people remain uncovered, including both divorced women and men who were formerly covered by their spouse's employer, part-time workers, people who work for small firms that do not provide insurance, and, of course, the unemployed. Beauchamp and Childress also pointed out that government-based services vary dramatically across all states and, as already noted, not everyone who is below the poverty line is covered. At the time this was written it was unclear whether Congress would pass a health care insurance act; however, in the long run it is probably the case that only some kind of national health insurance that covers mental health problems will address the issue. Even then, the question of how needs should be defined will remain.

Vera and Speight (2003) point to Humphreys (1996), who argued that monetary values lured clinical psychology away from the emphasis on preventative interactions. Counseling psychology and counseling followed suit and were similarly lured from their traditional missions in order to compete for the money that managed care and insurance companies were willing to pay for primary care services. Vera and Speight argued that psychology could be more effective by making a commitment to change institutions like school and social policy than by focusing on psychotherapy.

Fouad (2004) drawing on Patton (1992) pointed out that in the 1980s and 1990s, a sizable amount of APA's resources and its Practice Division were being used to persuade Association members as well as insurance companies that an important mission of organized psychology was to gain parity with medicine in the provision of health services. Even as this is being written, the first author received an e-mail from the APA Practice Directorate (January 8, 2010) indicating they were fighting for "appropriate" Medicare reimbursement for psychology and the healthcare reform bill. By the end of the 90s social advocacy was becoming an important issue in ACA and APA. The dormant emphasis on social advocacy was beginning to change, especially in some divisions. This change led to increasing advocacy for women, social and ethnic minorities, people with disabilities, and the elderly, which led to the writing of the guidelines summarized in Appendices A through D.

In fact, the *Handbook for Social Justice in Counseling Psychology* (Toporek et al., 2006) provides numerous examples of how psychologists have entered the field in social advocacy roles. For example Thompson, Alfred, Edwards, and Garcia (2006) use Helms' racial identity theory in a school-based project. They help students understand how African–Americans, Whites and other people of color develop increasingly complex perspectives on racism in relationship to their own role in life and how they see themselves. The project was targeted at correcting manifestations of racism at the local school level. As with other ethical social justice interventions this one was driven primarily by community residents who were trained by the authors. They provided 2-hr sessions from kindergarten through eighth grade during the school year on Saturdays and then during the summers to provide a high quality learning environment as well as a focus on racial identity development. As they point out, the project involved careful assessment of the community's needs using the community members as consultants, maintaining a caring attitude and confronting issues like racism.

At this point, psychologists and counselors are at a unique point in defining their discipline and themselves within their discipline. Mental health professionals have a responsibility to at least enter the dialogue on payment for mental health services as well as to help define adequate outcomes. In addition, they need to conduct scientific investigations that show that preventative interventions are cost-effective. It is unlikely that the concerns about managed care will go away soon, but if quality is being sacrificed or professionals are required to be unethical to participate in certain programs, then governmental agencies may begin to listen and set limits on managed care practices.

A Pragmatic View of Social Justice

The title of this section was borrowed from Helms (2003, p. 305) who pointed out that there are two opposing forces operating in the marketplace. The first is the social justice catalyst that encourages psychologists to change roles, become more inclusive and attentive to the needs of disempowered groups and the individuals in the group. It is essentially an appeal to the morality of justice. The second, she points out, is ensuring the employability of graduates and the survival needs of psychologists and counselors who often end their graduate programs deeply in debt and in need to support themselves. Areas like counseling and counseling psychology have been known for their exceptional focus on multiculturalism. With focus on the strengths and positive mental health of clients rather than deficits and pathology, on prevention, and on the use of psychosocial interventions to help people avoid life crises and other mental health problems, remediation of mental "illness" has traditionally taken the backseat. However, as Kiselica (2004) points out "right now the bucks compensate traditional psychotherapy" (p. 842). Consequently, social justice work requires sacrifice. It is often time-consuming and affords little compensation. Kiselica goes on to say that the "current managed care requires many of us who are dedicated to social justice initiatives to do much of our advocacy work out of our hides" (p. 842). The problem is that the more time a practitioner spends on the social justice issues that often underlie mental health problems, the less time he or she has for more highly compensated work. The consequence is not surprising: many practitioners avoid social justice work. He argues that it is critical that major mental health professions combine their resources to convince legislatures to compensate practitioners for expanded efforts to cover services that prevent mental health problems in the first place. As he says:

> We must convince Congress that preventing schoolwide bullying, school dropout, or teenage parenthood is important as preventing the flu and that our nation has responsibility for

promoting the holistic well-being of its people through an expansion of compensated mental health services, including preventative mental health services. (p. 843)

What is missing from this perspective is the fact that the systems which would be required to change if social justice ideals were implemented may not be receptive to the interventions, particularly ones that threaten the status quo of the high stakes holders (Helms, 2003).

Ivey and Collins (2003) provide an example. Ivey was working as a consultant to the Veterans Administration using microskills training with long-term hospitalized veterans. The project was proving highly successful; however, the hospital administration canceled the project when it was halfway through data collection. One part of the treatment was encouraging patients to consider the systemic and environmental contingencies that brought them to the hospital. The hospital was unhappy with the idea of patients becoming aware of environmental issues; particularly with training patients as change agents in the family and in the community.

Helms points out that administrators and policy makers do not usually support social justice services either ideologically or economically. Like Kiselica, she argues that in the current political and economic climate, social justice interventions will often have to be provided pro bono. She reasons that even graduate students who are trained in communitarian social justice activities may leave these activities behind as they move in the professional world because there are no systems to support these new roles. As she says "failure to take on this new social justice role will not be caused by a lack of moral fiber … but rather by the need to sustain themselves in human service delivery systems that are not necessarily responsive to social justice interventions" (p. 311).

It is difficult to argue with a social justice perspective that encourages psychologists and counselors to work toward a culture that is more inclusive, fairer, and distributes goods and services in a way that improves the mental and physical health of all citizens. On the other hand, mental health professionals should not enter into these activities idealistically thinking they are going to be easy or that they are not going to hit social and political barriers. Each person must consider the kinds of sacrifices they are willing to make in order to make the world a more just community.

Psychological Assessment: Fair Outcomes and Processes

One of the biggest concerns regarding psychological tests involves whether they are fair. In this case, the fairness of the process needs to be differentiated from the fairness of the outcomes (Greenberg, 1987). The process of testing can be affected by a variety of administration factors that may or may not consider appropriate implementation or take into account critical characteristics of the person being tested. These can range from cultural differences between the test examiner and the examinee to response formats that may be more familiar to some examinees than others (Berk, 1982).

There is no question that tests discriminate; that is their purpose (Arvey & Faley, 1988). For example, the purpose of an employment test is to discriminate between applicants who would be good candidates for a position and those who would not. The ethical question is whether tests discriminate fairly. Do they take into account relevant or irrelevant characteristics of the person or groups being tested for the purpose for which they are being assessed? Issues range from whether tests have validity for the discriminations they are making, such as between candidates for a job, to the consequences of the decisions for society at large. Additionally, validity judgments involve issues of values, and well-meaning and reasonable people sometimes disagree on the relevant values involved (Anastasi & Urbina, 1997; Messick, 1995).

The fairness of either the outcome or the process needs to be distinguished from the issue of test bias. In the vernacular, the concepts of bias and fairness seem to be interrelated. People might talk about a bias as being unfair. In testing, bias is a statistical characteristic of the scores (Murphy & Davidshofer, 2005). As Murphy and Davidshofer (2005) put it, "Bias is said to exist when a test makes systematic errors in measurement or prediction" (p. 317). As an example, they point to a college admissions test that consistently overpredicts the performance of men and underpredicts how women will do. In this case, the test is said to be a biased predictor. Depending on admissions goals, it also may be unfair.

Whereas evaluating the bias of tests involves a scientific judgment, deciding whether a test is fair or not involves a question of values (Murphy & Davidshofer, 2005). Evaluating whether a test is fair depends to some extent on the definition of justice being used and the situation to which it is being applied. Furthermore, because the decisions involved often affect access to needed services like education or to sources of sustenance like employment, the federal government has stipulated the models of fairness that must be used. Mental ability and employment testing and their consequences for educational and employment decisions, respectively, provide the most salient examples.

Justice in Ability Testing

Although the full scope of concerns surrounding bias and fairness in ability testing are too complex to discuss in detail here, it is important to recognize that there are two issues involved: First, whether a particular ability test is biased and second, what the implications are for social justice decisions. Again, whether a particular test is biased or not involves a scientific judgment; however, even these judgments can be controversial. Kiselica and Robinson (2001) point out that the controversy has had a long life; noting that it was in the 1930s that the validity of using tests standardized on Whites with African-Americans and Latinos/Latinas was first challenged. Probably the issue that has raised the most controversy is the different perspectives on issues of IQ, social class, and race (Eckberg, 1979; Flynn, 1980; Jensen, 1980; Joseph, 1977; Kamin, 1974; Scarr, 1989). Because social policy decisions are based on conclusions drawn from ability tests, the principles of beneficence, nonmaleficence, and fidelity require that they be drawn carefully after consideration of alternative hypotheses.

When conclusions based on ability tests affect individuals, using multiple methods that include an evaluation of adaptive behavior can help compensate for the weakness in any single measure (Murphy & Davidshofer, 2005). It is noteworthy that the manuals for both The Scholastic Assessment Test (SAT) and the Graduate Record Examination (GRE), designed to help in admissions decisions to undergraduate and graduate schools, respectively, discuss the limitations of test scores and indicate they should not be the only basis for admission decisions (Murphy & Davidschofer, 2004). Additionally, as the "Guidelines on Multicultural Education, Training, Research, Practice, and Organizational Change for Psychologists" (APA, 2003; Appendix A) points out, when members of nonmajority groups are being evaluated, the cultural and linguistic characteristics of the person being assessed need to be considered. In addition, standardized measures whose validity and reliability have been assessed using culturally diverse samples should be used (Council of the National Association for the Advancement of Ethnic Minority Interests, 2000). Researchers should also use pilot tests and interviews to determine the cultural validity of the measures (Samantha, 1998; Sue, Kurasaki, & Srinivasan, 1999). In other words, they need to evaluate whether the constructs assessed by the measure have the same meaning across cultures (Rogler, 1999).

Social justice issues particularly come into play when consideration is given to the implications of test scores for access to education and employment or for the placement of children in remedial or advanced classes. This is especially true because both federal and state courts have concluded that tests sometimes discriminate unfairly, thus violating the Fourteenth Amendment to the Constitution. Essentially, the Fourteenth Amendment requires that people who are in similar situations be treated similarly unless there is a justifiable reason to do otherwise (DeMers, 1986). The question becomes whether psychological assessments constitute a justifiable reason for treating some students differently if the consequence is placement in special education programs or denial of access to certain benefits, such as a college education.

Several court cases have addressed the question of whether individual intelligence tests can be used to place minority group children in remedial education classes. Probably the best known is *Larry P. v. Wilson Riles* (1972). The crux of this case was whether the use of intelligence tests unfairly led to a disproportionate share of African American students being classified as educationally mentally retarded (EMR) and placed in special education classes, thus denying their rights to have equal access to educational benefits. The courts ultimately decided in favor of the plaintiffs, arguing that the original versions of the tests did not include African Americans in their standardization samples. Even though at the time of the litigation students would have been assessed by a test that had an adequate representation of minority students in the sample, the court argued that recent attempts to update standardization did not ensure differential validity for minority groups. Furthermore, the court pointed out that IQ tests were often the sole or most important criterion used in placement and that such decisions ignored the adaptive behavior of the child (Bersoff, 1983; DeMers, 1986). The court was concerned that using tests led to a larger number of African American children being placed in EMR classes than would have been predicted on the basis of the proportion of African Americans in the population.

Ironically, less than a year later, a federal court in Illinois heard a similar case, *PACE v. Hannon* (1980), and made almost an opposite decision. Again, the plaintiffs argued that African Americans were overrepresented in EMR classes. The defendants argued that their decisions were not based solely on test scores. Additionally, they pointed out that if they did not use psychological tests they would have to use more subjective criteria. The judge generally agreed with the defendants and concluded that even if the IQ tests were biased, it did not mean that the whole process was biased because multiple measures and multidisciplinary teams were used (Bersoff, 1983; DeMers, 1986). It may have been that the ability of the Chicago schools to show that multiple measures and multiple perspectives were used to make the decision influenced the court to believe the process and outcome were fair (DeMers & Bersoff, 1985).

Justice in Employment Selection

The courts also intervened in employment decisions when claims were made that psychological assessments led to unfair discrimination against racial minorities, women, elderly individuals, and individuals with disabilities (Arvey & Faley, 1988). Initially, discriminatory employment practices were seen as unfair on the basis of both merit and need. These practices were blamed for the economic deprivation of minorities and identified as a symptom of civil rights abuses (Murphy & Davidshofer, 2005). Title VII of the Civil Rights Act of 1964 was passed as a response to this perception, forbidding unfair discrimination on the basis of race, color, religion, gender, or national origin in employment. The act did not, however, address the use of selection procedures or tests that validly identify good and poor job applicants.

Again, several court cases have addressed these issues. One of the most important was *Griggs v. Duke Power Co.* (1971). Prior to the Civil Rights Act of 1964, African–American employees of Duke Power had been limited to the lowest level jobs. After the passage of the Civil Rights Act, Duke Power used standardized ability tests to establish criteria for movement into higher paying and more responsible positions using a cutoff point on tests to indicate appropriate preparation for a job. A suit was filed claiming the new procedures also discriminated unfairly. The Supreme Court found for the African American plaintiffs, arguing that employers must demonstrate the "job-relatedness" of any assessment; that is, an assessment must have a rational and meaningful connection to job performance and success (DeMers, 1986). Furthermore, both the consequences and intent of an employment practice needed to be considered in evaluating whether a selection practice discriminated unfairly (Arvey & Faley, 1988).

Although *Griggs v. Duke Power Co.* (1971) was one of the most important and earliest cases to consider questions of unfair discrimination and selection, it is only one of many. Hundreds of cases have been adjudicated in this area, and the legal swings between liberal and conservative positions are difficult to follow (Arvey & Faley, 1988). Additionally, after Title VII of the Civil Rights Act of 1964 was passed, the Equal Employment Opportunity Commission (EEOC) was established to enforce it. Thus, the federal government has been deeply involved in defining fair employment practices and consequently the fair use of psychological assessments.

It should be noted that doing away with tests does not solve the problem of unfair selection bias. For example, some might argue that a qualitative interview that evaluates the individual's preparation for a job might be fairer. However, even introductory assessment texts point out that such interviews have questionable reliability and validity (Murphy & Davidshofer, 2005). In addition, there is evidence that interviews are biased against older job applicants and in some situations may be biased against women and African Americans (Arvey & Faley, 1988).

The courts have determined that psychological assessments can and have been used to unfairly discriminate against certain groups. The question mental health professionals must ask is how to use them fairly. Incompetent assessment cannot be fair. Competence includes understanding information about test bias as well as validity. It also means considering the implications of recommendations made on the basis of tests, particularly when results can be used to deny people access to needed services or employment. In some ways, psychologists or counselors might consider that the courts have done them a favor by allowing them to lobby for multifaceted assessments that have been evaluated for the purpose they are being used, rather than being forced to use quick and cheap single-measure assessments with tests of questionable validity (DeMers, 1986).

Social Justice and Individual Assessments

Up to now we have been talking about assessments in the formal sense of testing, but assessments also take place every day in the office of individual psychologists and counselors and issues of social justice can and do enter into these assessments. Some have argued that to advocate for social justice can threaten role integrity because it may involve deception (Clark, 1993). Clark (1993) argued that sometimes mental health professionals pretend to be objective when they are actually engaged in a subjective activity. He provided the following case as an example of such (self-)deceptive behavior.

Case 13-7

A psychologist who has been treating the 8-year-old child of separated parents learns that the mother and father are contesting custody of the child in the pending divorce proceedings. The focus of the treatment has been the child's fears and anxieties before and after visits with her father and the mother's concerns that the child may have been sexually abused. The psychologist strongly believes that children, especially girls, are most often better raised by their mothers, whom she believes have better nurturing skills. The psychologist is soon asked by the mother's attorney to offer an opinion on the custody question ... and what sorts of visitation arrangements with the father would be most appropriate. Without conducting further evaluation of the child, the mother, or the father, whom the therapist has never met, the psychologist offers the opinion that custody should be awarded to the mother and that, in light of the child's anxieties and the uncertainty of what may have occurred during past visits, visitation with the father should be halted until he had been evaluated (Clark, 1993, p. 304).

Clark argued that the objectivity of this psychologist was compromised because her explicit social agenda was to see that girls remain with their mother. This agenda led to poor forensic practices. For example, the psychologist offered an opinion on custody without evaluating all of the parties involved, without observing the mother and the child together and without assessing the father. Additionally, the psychologist's opinion was given as if it were an objective evaluation, rather than being affected by her relationship with the child, the mother and her own beliefs.

By contrast, feminists (Brown, 1994b, 1997a; Feminist Therapy Institute, 1990) take the position that every aspect of feminist practice is and ought to be framed to work for social change. From this perspective, working for social change with individual clients is an ethical imperative. They would argue, however, that deception is not a reasonable alternative. Rather, social activism and change ought to be an explicit agenda (Brown, 1997a). For example, when Brown (1997a) does forensic work, she lets the attorneys know that she is a feminist and will be working from that perspective. She gives the following example as an illustration of how a feminist should conduct a forensic evaluation.

Case 13-8

You respond to a request from the court to conduct an evaluation in a situation of contested custody. You carefully study each parent in relationship to their two small children, observing their capacities to be empathic, set limits, and resonate to the developmental needs of each child. The mother, although genuinely and desperately trying to do well, continues in situation after situation to appear less capable in the parental role than the father, who seems at ease, tuned in to both son and daughter, and able to be present with them rather than anxious about pleasing you, the evaluator (Brown, 1994b, p. 201).

Brown (1994b) pointed out that, like others who do custody evaluations, her commitment is to the best interests of the children. The issue from a feminist perspective is how she interprets the data. That is, how does she take into consideration the information that the father is, like the evaluator, a professional who is verbally fluent and comfortable with evaluations, whereas the mother is fearful of evaluation and deferential to authority because of her experience in her marriage? Brown suggested that to ignore these issues in the evaluation process would be a failure to understand how the social political context affects the ecological validity of the assessment methods. Thus, she would ask additional questions, like whether there are strategies for observing the mother that might strengthen the chance that the her best skills as a parent might be observed. She might also question the competitive framework of the evaluation and whether it is necessary to indicate that one parent is better than the other. Although she may draw the same conclusion as the more traditional evaluator, her objective is to raise questions about the underlying fairness of the process to ensure that the benefits and burdens associated with living in a patriarchal society are distributed fairly.

At what point, however, do social justice issues simply become questions of values and to what extent should mental health professionals act on their own values with clients? Clearly, they need to be aware of their own value assumptions and how these assumptions affect the work they do. These are not questions that just affect individual assessments. Therapists have a variety of social values that they could rationalize advocating. These can range from religious values to ones involving abortion or divorce or gay-lesbian issues or interracial marriages.

Certainly, dishonesty with oneself and others about any kind of value when it plays a central role in one's work is unethical. Honesty with clients about one's values is critical. To do less would be disrespectful of clients' rights to make reasonable decisions about with whom they want to work. For example, a therapist might tell couples that he cannot work with them if they enter counseling with the goal of separating from each other. Because he values maintaining families, his first goal is to help them evaluate whether their marriage can be saved. If they do not want to initially consider that goal, he refers them to another therapist. If individuals regularly work toward social justice issues in their practice, they, like the therapist just mentioned, need to be clear about them prior to beginning treatment, assessments, or evaluations.

Furthermore, directly lying or distorting information to enhance one's political agenda is difficult to justify ethically in almost every case (Bok, 1989). In the end, distorting truth, no matter what the cause, often ends up reflecting badly on both the profession and the professional and undermines the confidence that others have in the ability of mental health professionals to provide information and services that others can trust.

Issues of Distributive and Social Justice in Academia

As in therapy, assessments, and forensic work, academic psychologists cannot escape issues of justice. Traditional models of evaluation that involve assigning grades immediately raise issues of justice when instructors have to make decisions about how to assign them in a fair, impartial, and equitable manner. Typically, some model of merit is used in which students are rewarded for different degrees of praiseworthy efforts. Faculty members decide which differences are relevant ones; thus, students are evaluated against a model of competence. Irrelevant characteristics such as race, sexual preference, or gender should not be considered.

Academic psychologists and counselors also need to make decisions about whom to hire as research or teaching assistants or to offer mentoring support. Because their personal resources are limited, faculty members have to weigh whether special opportunities should be awarded to students on basis of merit or need and whether special characteristics like a multicultural background or gender should be considered.

The area in academia that raises most questions regarding issues of distributive justice involves college and graduate school admissions. Positions in most institutions of higher education are restricted because resources are limited. More applicants want admission than the institution can serve. Here, as in other areas, the question surfaces regarding fair criteria on which to base admissions. Consider the following case as an example. If a faculty had to choose between the candidates, what criteria would be fair?

Case 13-9

Juan Pena applied for admission to a doctoral program in Counseling Psychology. He is the son of Mexican immigrant farm workers but was born in the United States. His verbal Graduate Record Examination (GRE) score was 420, and his math score was 620. His combined score was just under the 1,050 cutoff for the program. Jack Higgens, who was in the same applicant pool, grew up in an upper-middle-class family in Iowa. His verbal and math GRE scores were 620 and 610, respectively. Both prospective students had good recommendations, undergraduate grades and equivalent writing samples. Mr Pena explicitly stated his commitment to work with Mexican Americans. His research interests involved self-efficacy issues in the same population. Mr Higgens' research interests were very similar to a faculty member's, and he explicitly indicated a desire to work with that faculty member on research.

Part of the difficulty in evaluating candidates like these has been confusion with regard to which models of justice to use. For years, most institutions have avowed a model of merit, awarding admissions to those with the highest tested aptitude, prior evidence of academic excellence, or a combination of both. Choosing these criteria along with others was based on the assumption that they would be the best predictors of success and that graduates would reflect well on the institution. To some extent this remains true, despite warnings in the SAT and GRE manuals that they should not be the only criteria used in admissions. Although talent for advanced educational work seems like a relevant property, problems arose both on an institutional and on a federal level when consideration was given to whether everyone had a fair opportunity to develop their talents so that they could meet admissions criteria.

Data suggest that test scores are not a fixed attribute of a person. Rather, they are a sample of present behavior. Although there may be some genetic limitations on an individual's ability to learn, many of the skills required for success in an educational setting can be mastered given a normal range of ability and an appropriate environment. In fact, it has been our experience that students who enter with the highest test scores are not necessarily the most successful in school nor after graduation. Thus, educational institutions must ask; how much basic ability is enough? Furthermore, both individual institutions and the federal government have had to consider to what extent institutions of higher education should take responsibility for remediating prior deficits and compensating some groups, such as racial and ethnic minorities, for past injustice (e.g., institutional racism) in elementary and secondary schools (May, 1990). These latter two issues have provided the rationale for many affirmative action programs.

In addition to compensating some groups for past injustice and correcting current inequities, affirmative action has been touted as promoting intellectual diversity and fostering the development of racial and ethnic minority role models (Amirkham, Betancourt, Graham, Lopez, & Weiner, 1995). These issues have been seen as particularly relevant to psychology and counseling because they claim to avow promoting human welfare (Powers & Richardson, 1996). Doing so without attending to the cultural components of human behavior has often led to overgeneralizations about the universality of psychological theories and principles (Betancourt & Lopez, 1993; Sue & Sue, 1990). Some have argued that attempts at color blindness have perpetuated racism because they deny the existence of discrimination as daily experiences for members of minority groups and undermine the legitimacy of alternative values and views of the good life (Fowers & Richardson, 1996; Jahoda, 1988; Sue & Sue, 1990). Denial of experiences like discrimination can lead to harmful consequences for marginalized individuals because central components of their identity are disavowed.

Consequently, psychology and counseling have taken the position that affirmative action programs are intellectually and morally essential because they repudiate the monocultural bias in the field. As Fowers and Richardson (1996) argued, "the core of the multicultural program is a principled moral argument that a monocultural perspective is not simply less accurate or generalizable, but positively distortive and oppressive" (p. 611). Arguments like these have led the accrediting bodies for ACA and APA to mandate that training programs increase diversity in the field by actively recruiting minority students.

These issues provide the backdrop for several court cases and university policy decisions that affect how departments can meet accreditation requirements. For example, in 1996, the University of California Board of Regents voted to eliminate race as a special factor in university admissions (Inouye, 1997). The Board of Regents' decision used a merit-based model of justice. Affirmative action was eliminated so that the "desire for diversity" did not overshadow the "need for the best qualified students" (Inouye, 1997, p. 415).

Policy decisions like the one made in California have been supported by several court cases. In *Regents of the University of California v. Bakke* (1978), the court ruled that although having separate admissions criteria for minorities and race-based quotas were not legal, race could be used as one criterion among others (Kier & Davenport, 1997). However, even these criteria have been challenged.

In *Hopwood v. State of Texas* (1996), White students who applied for but who were not admitted to the University of Texas Law School filed suit under the Equal Protection Clause of the Fourteenth Amendment, claiming that they had experienced unconstitutional racial discrimination. Two different courts have ruled against the law school in favor of the White students. The District Court essentially agreed with the *Bakke* decision. Race could be used as a "plus factor," as long as other factors were used that allowed each applicant to be compared with other applicants on a case-by-case basis (*Hopwood v. State of Texas*, 1994). Following the ruling, the University of Texas amended its application procedures to meet the District Court's criteria, but the plaintiffs appealed the ruling (Kier & Davenport, 1997). The Fifth Circuit Court of Appeals also ruled against the law school. This court argued that racial categorizations encouraged stigmatization and stereotypes of minorities and that the "use of ethnic diversity simply to achieve racial heterogeneity, even as a part of the consideration of a number of factors, is unconstitutional" (*Hopwood v. State of Texas*, 1996, pp. 945–946). The court agreed that the White students' constitutional rights were violated because, for example, the law school used lower cutoff points on test scores for minority students than for White students (Kier & Davenport, 1997; Wiener, 1996). On the other hand, as late as 2001 the state of Texas was still seeking a legal review of the Hopwood decision (State of Texas et al. v Cheryl Hopwood et al., June 10, 2001).

Although the decision only applies to the Fifth Circuit, both sides recognized its national significance. Kier and Davenport (1997) argued that, if the *Hopwood* decision stands, programs will be legally prohibited from using race in any way in admissions criteria. They pointed out that under these circumstances it may be very difficult for some training programs in psychology and counseling to meet accreditation criteria. They also argued that discontinuing fellowships and scholarships that are based on ethnicity will leave many programs with few ways to fund their minority students. According to Kier and Davenport (1997), fewer minority students will enter mental health training programs and fewer students will mean fewer minority mental health professionals, which will, in turn, lead to fewer minority mentors to spark future minority students to become interested in the field. "This effect may also decrease research into minority concerns and reduce the effectiveness of mental health services to minorities" (p. 489).

Assuming that psychology and counseling have a moral imperative to increase diversity in the field, one way to do so is by increasing the numbers of students of color as well as gay, lesbian and bisexual students, or older adults in graduate training programs. Given the court decisions, mental health programs may have to rethink their criteria for admissions, particularly their reliance on test scores and grade point averages. Alternative criteria already in use include essays, letters of recommendation, and interviews, although, as already noted, interviews are not without their own sources of bias. Adding additional criteria, such as increasing the diversity of the program, may be legitimate if they are applied evenhandedly to include White men and women, students with disabilities, and older students, as well as racial and ethnic minorities, depending on the current mix of the student body.

Other means will also need to be used to attract qualified minority students to apply to and remain in programs, including policies and statements that make it clear that programs have a commitment to recruiting and graduating a diverse group of students. These suggestions, however, will not work unless the admissions problem is faced. Professional organizations like APA and ACA need to take an active role in helping programs rethink admissions policies. They may have to support affirmative action policies in the courts if admissions policies are challenged; arguing that based on research, there is a compelling reason for race to be considered in admissions.

Justice Issues in Research

Distributive and Social Justice Issues

The importance of justice concerns in research was formally recognized in 1978 by the National Commission for the Protection of Human Subjects in Biomedical Behavioral Research in *The*

Belmont Report. Although they did not label it as such, the commission's concerns were with issues of both distributive and social justice; namely, who should obtain the benefits and bear the burdens of research? The commission argued that an injustice occurs when a person is denied benefits to which he or she would have otherwise been entitled or when a burden is imposed unfairly as a result of research participation. The most extreme example of the latter would be imposing some kind of harmful experimental treatment on research participants and then withholding curative treatment, as was done in the Tuskegee syphilis study. In this study, 400 African American men with syphilis were recruited in the 1930s without informed consent to study the effects of treatment (using drugs like arsenic) for syphilis. They were told that they were receiving special, free treatment. The study was continued even though the death rate was twice as high among those treated than among the controls. Even when it became clear in the 1940s that penicillin was an effective treatment for syphilis, the study was not discontinued, neither were the men informed of the availability of an effective treatment (Levine, 1988).

When faced with studies like the Tuskegee experiment, the National Commission struggled with how to define a fair distribution of burdens. Some members of the commission argued for a utilitarian definition (Levine, 1988), in which the fairest distribution would be one that creates the most benefits for society. The commission rejected this formulation, however, because it conflicted with the basic equality of people and the belief that justice requires special protection for those who are powerless, less advantaged, or vulnerable. Selection, the commission argued,

> needs to be scrutinized in order to determine whether some classes (e.g., welfare patients, particular racial and ethnic minorities, or persons confined to institutions) are being systematically selected because of their easy availability, their compromised position, or their manipulability, rather than for reasons directly related to the problem being studied. (National Commission, 1978a, p. 9)

The commission maintained that social justice requires that investigators evaluate whether undue burdens are being placed on members of a group who are already burdened in unfair ways (e.g., institutionalized mental patients or prisoners). Particularly if risks are involved, other groups of people should be used first, unless there are clear benefits to the group being solicited. Furthermore, if public funds are used to develop new therapeutic insights, the benefits that arise from the research should be available to everyone, not just the wealthy. If certain groups of people will not benefit from the applications of the research, they should not be subject to the burdens of participating in the research.

The 2005 ACA ethics code went further and suggested that counselors had a responsibility to do research that led to a healthier and more just society. Concerns about social justice, particularly whether there is a fair distribution of the benefits and burdens of research have also been recognized as central in psychology (Fisher & Tryon, 1990; Meara & Schmidt, 1991, Sieber, 1992). In fact, the APA Board of Scientific Affairs (Sales & Folkman, 1998) identified justice as a key ethical issue. The board argued that threats to justice arise particularly because of the power differential between experimenters and research participants, making members of racial and ethnic minority groups and women particularly vulnerable to exploitation (Sales & Folkman, 1998).

Vulnerable groups (e.g., racial and ethnic minorities or institutionalized patients) should not be targeted as participants just because of their easy availability and their vulnerability. As noted earlier, coercion is often very subtle. Because of the history of racism in the United States, some members of minority groups may not believe that participation is really voluntary or that they can refuse to participate. On the other hand, the powerlessness of some groups has led to their underinclusion in samples. Thus, conclusions based on participants who were White men may be unfairly generalized to groups who were not included in the original design. When generalizations are inaccurate, they may actually cause harm (Sales & Folkman, 1998).

Others have pointed to the failure of mainstream researchers to study the strengths of under-represented groups (Scarr, 1988). Furthermore, because there are relatively few minority investigators, important questions remain unanswered. The result is that the benefits of research have not been fairly distributed. Obviously, these issues merge with those of social responsibility. Often, research questions about racial and ethnic minorities, people with disabilities, and women are conceptualized in terms of deficits (i.e., what is wrong with or how these groups are different from White men?). When differences are found, they are sometimes cast in a negative light. As Scarr (1988) noted:

> If, on the other hand, one asks how women actually solve mathematical problems, how Black males learn to read, or how children of lower socioeconomic status (SES) get jobs, one may actually learn how to help others to use socially and culturally available means to succeed in the society. (p. 57)

Increasingly, federal grants are requiring investigators to provide evidence of the inclusion of minorities and women in samples and to provide a rationale if they are excluded (Sales & Folkman, 1998). Although there may be an appropriate justification for the inclusion or exclusion of particular groups in a specific study, the problem is an overall imbalance of information. Investigators can work for a more just distribution of the benefits and burdens of research through their own work, as reviewers of proposed research, and in the editorial process (Sales & Folkman, 1998).

Sometimes, though, mainstream researchers blunder in their attempts to do research on underrepresented groups, as in the following case.

Case 13-10

The director of a community health center in a Black Haitian community charged a psychologist with violating the APA ethics code. The psychologist was investigating the presence of voodoo beliefs and spiritual healing among Haitians. The director charged the psychologist with using an interview methodology that was insensitive and ignorant of the community's cultural traditions. He stated further that the students used to do the interviewing insulted members of the community. The psychologist indicated that she believed she understood the culture and felt qualified to conduct the research because she had spent several years in Haiti and had done her doctoral dissertation on spiritual healing. She also spoke French and patois. In addition, she had trained her graduate students both in interviewing and about the culture. In hindsight, she indicated that she may not have trained them thoroughly. She suggested that the real problem was a political one because she began the investigation without consulting the director of the community center, which was the locus of the neighborhood council (APA, 1987a).

Although the investigator may have been knowledgeable about some aspects of the Haitian culture, she and her students were insensitive to the power structure and, perhaps, to some of the cultural standards of the community in which they were working. In addition, she failed to adequately train her research assistants to be sensitive to cultural norms. Such problems reflect the delicate balance between doing harm, being competent, and trying to remediate the imbalance in research on underrepresented groups. When members of one culture are doing research on members of another, at minimum individuals from the community, other investigators, and even surrogate research participants should be asked to evaluate the research procedure for cultural sensitivity and potential for harm. Even better is involving members of the community to help design the research and design it in such a way that the community benefits from the results. Had the investigator in Case 13-10 consulted with community leaders she may have designed a more socially valid study as well as one that avoided an ethics charge. Consulting with community members does not absolve the investigator from the responsibility for doing ethically sound research, but it can help ensure a more culturally sensitive process and avoid an unjust exploitation of research participants.

Prilleltensky (1997) argued that research should produce knowledge that is a tool for social action. From a communitarian perspective, research should be collaborative, action oriented, and socially relevant to the community being investigated. These criteria may take the scientists outside of the traditional realm of research design to issues like needs assessment and evaluating the impact of public policy. For example, La-Framboise and Howard-Pitney's (1995) study of preventing suicide among Sunni adolescents evaluated the impact of suicide prevention procedures. Prilleltensky also pointed out that reducing the distance between the researchers and the participants may lead to more meaningful research questions and improve their usefulness in changing public policy. He argued that the purpose of social justice research should be empowerment and it should be addressed in the design as well is than issues like the ownership and use of the data.

Similarly, research dissemination would need to be expanded from the typical articles written for other scholars (Vera & Speight, 2003). Respect for persons and social justice would argue for the participants themselves being informed of the results through community newsletters, pamphlets distributed at schools or health centers, or other means that the researcher might have at his/her disposal. If this is done, research can be used by the community with or without the support of the researchers to advocate for change in public policy.

Just as there are challenges to implementing social justice approaches in therapy, Ivey and Collins (2003) pointed out that research is usually done in an academic setting, which is an environment focused primarily on research that provides money through public or private grants. These grants usually focus on large theoretical issues rather than, for example, a needs assessment of an individual community. Consequently, the ideas and ideals of social justice advocacy research are at variance with the University and other large systems. A colleague of Ivey's pointed out that even the developmental and outreach functions of college counseling centers have decreased over the years, so that the focus is increasingly on individual psychotherapy. He pointed out that society does not want to change but rather expects individuals to adapt to the existing systems.

Justice also extends to the interpretation of research results. This is particularly critical when researchers are studying sensitive topics that may be misinterpreted by the media as well as other professionals. This does not mean that socially sensitive research should not be conducted, but rather that investigators need to consider how to enhance the validity of their findings and to communicate the results in a socially sensitive way to a variety of constituencies, including the research participants, the community in which they live, the media, and Congress (Sales & Folkman, 1998).

Issues of Procedural Justice

Investigators need ensure that research procedures are fair at all stages of the research process. In addition to being concerned about fairly soliciting research participants, considering the community in which the research is conducted, and considering whether and what social justice issues need to be investigated, researchers need to establish fair procedures for assigning authorship credit and for acknowledging material drawn from other sources. Although it seems straightforward that investigators ought to benefit from the fruits of their own labors, the issues are not always clear. Take Case 13-11 as an example.

Case 13-11

Dr. Yaro was a developmental psychologist with a large multiyear grant working on predictors of suicide among low-income youth. He recently accepted some additional responsibilities in the department as the section head, which involved him in fund-raising and other administrative obligations. Consequently, he allowed a postdoctoral research associate, Dr. Zapata, to take the primary responsibility for organizing data collection and analysis on the grant. In addition, with his consent, she began to investigate some variables that had not been a part of Dr. Yaro's original conceptualization of the relevant issues. In fact, Dr. Zapata's hypotheses paid off and the study produced some very interesting findings. Because Dr. Yaro was so busy with his new responsibilities, Dr. Zapata wrote the article for publication, putting her name first on the draft of the manuscript. She then gave it to Dr. Yaro for comments and suggestions. When he returned the manuscript, the first thing she noticed was that he had switched the order of their names. When she complained that she had done most of the work and, in fact, contributed the ideas that led to the interesting results, he pointed out that it was his grant and he initially conceptualized the study.

If authorship is used to indicate to the public and other scholars the person who is primarily responsible for the work and the ideas on which it is based (Sales & Folkman, 1998), which investigator should receive first authorship credit in this case?

Although to an outsider order of authorship might not seem like a large issue, job offers and promotions in academia often hinge on order of authorship. It also indicates who is primarily responsible for the conclusions drawn in the study. Thus, the first author may also have to bear the burden of justifying inferences and responding to critical comments. To be considered as the first author, an author must first meet several minimal criteria for authorship; that is, he or she should have contributed significantly to the conceptualization, design, execution, interpretation, and manuscript that reports the research (Sales & Folkman, 1998). In addition, principal authorship should accurately reflect the relative scientific or professional contributions of the individuals involved, regardless of their relative status. In other words, it should not matter whether the principal investigator has a PhD or other symbol of status. Fine and Kurdick (1993) recommended balancing the principles of justice and beneficence in making these decisions.

Who made the greater scientific or professional contribution in Case 13-11? Both researchers appear to meet the minimal criteria for authorship. In many cases, first authorship goes to the person who provided the primary conceptual leadership for the project (Murray, 1998). Sometimes a senior researcher will give the junior investigator first authorship when their contributions are not substantially different based on the principle of beneficence. Both of these conventions would support giving Dr. Zapata first authorship. Although the specifics of the research program may lead to a different conclusion, because the project pursued variables that Dr. Zapata conceptualized which were not in the original research plan and which were the basis for important results, one can argue that Dr. Zapata provided the more substantial intellectual contribution to the project. However, her perceptions of her contribution may not be accurate, since Dr. Yaro had conceptualized the variables in the grant. From a different perspective, there may be a gender bias involved, with the senior researcher, Dr. Yaro, trying to take advantage of his more powerful position.

Authorship issues like the one in Case 13-11 are often sticky at best. In fact, Goodyear et al. (1992) found that authorship issues were among the most difficult ethical issues identified by experienced researchers. The issues are further complicated when psychologists or counselors author publications with researchers from other disciplines that have different authorship rules (Murray, 1998) or when they work with students. When authorship questions involve students, the same issues that are of a concern in other situations should be considered such as who made the primary conceptual contribution to the work. Because of the power differences involved, however, students may be easily exploited or they may perceive themselves to be exploited. Under these circumstances, faculty members need to take particular care to clarify authorship issues early and to safeguard students' contributions.

Because dissertation research assumes that the student formulated the major research question and conducted the study relatively independently, both the 2005 ACA and the 2002 APA ethics codes stipulated that except in unusual circumstances the student should be listed as principal author on any multiple-authored article that is substantially based on the student's dissertation, thesis, or course paper. On the other hand, some students piggyback their thesis or dissertation on their adviser's research projects or have little experience when beginning their own work. In these instances, advisers often contribute a great deal to the conceptualization and design of the project. Thus, it may be justifiable for the adviser to be included as an author on publications that result from the dissertation (Fine & Kurdick, 1993; Sales & Folkman, 1998). If the article is based primarily on research by the adviser, but includes data from the dissertation as one aspect, it may be appropriate for the adviser to be the first author. However, faculty members should not presume that just because they advise a dissertation, their contribution will always reach the level that it deserves any authorship recognition.

Virtues like integrity and respectfulness may be more important in solving such difficult authorship issues than specific decision rules. In addition, it is helpful if authorship credit can be decided by consensus among the people involved (Sales & Folkman, 1998). Discussions regarding authorship are often most helpful if they are conducted at the beginning of a research project, although admittedly, the contributions of particular people may shift during the project and agreements may need to be renegotiated. Additionally, if students are involved, senior researchers may need to provide them with information about the difference between a professional or scientific contribution and nonprofessional contributions like data entry. They may also need information on the importance of authorship order and credit. For example, students may not be aware that the profession values an intellectual contribution more highly than just time and effort (Fine & Kurdick, 1993). To participate as fully as possible in decisions about authorship credit, new professionals need to have adequate information on which to make those decisions. Again, the virtue of trustworthiness may be important. If team members perceive the senior researcher as trustworthy and having integrity, they may be more willing to raise authorship issues. If disagreements about authorship arise, senior researchers should consult with other trusted colleagues about how to evaluate relative contributions and reach a fair solution (Fine & Kurdick, 1993).

Just as an honest attribution of authorship credit is essential on new publications, acknowledging contributions of earlier sources to current work is not only honest, it is also just because it gives people the credit that they are due for their work. In fact, one of the few clear consistent prohibitions in both the ACA and the APA ethics codes has involved this issue under the rubric of plagiarism. Basically, it means that researchers do not claim substantial portions or elements of another's work or data as their own. Clearly, appropriately citing others' work is an essential requirement to being an ethical professional.

Although this section appears to move the discussion away from issues of social justice, that is not entirely the case. Throughout the process of deciding authorship credit, issues of power, sexism, and racism can arise, as they may have in Case 13-11. There are clear power differentials between professors and students and using that power to claim authorship credit is not just unfair. It is a social injustice.

Implications of Social Justice Advocacy for Training in Psychology and Counseling

The definition of social justice by Fouad (2006) included educating professionals in a way that will allow them to treat both individuals and group members with value and respect. However, considering the power differential in all aspects of their professional career may make education professionals in social justice a difficult task. As Toporek and McNally (2006) point out, since social justice issues have waxed and waned in both psychology and counseling, framing entire training programs around the issue is controversial. Generally, teaching about social justice has been implemented primarily through multicultural and women's studies classes. Although more recently, some schools have integrated it through an annual event like a social justice conference and others have instilled it throughout the curriculum. As with other social justice issues, there are challenges facing schools that want to make these kinds of curricular changes including the prominence of the scientist–practitioner model, the demands of licensing and managed care and traditional training requirements (Toporek & McNally, 2006). Furthermore, substantial changes can be hampered by the rigid accreditation criteria of ACA or APA that require substantial coursework and programs must consider the cost–benefit ratio for trainees as they vie for competitive internships, postdoctoral placements and licensure.

Steele (2008) developed a model that can be used to infuse social justice advocacy into regular coursework like theories of counseling or ethics. The model was based on Freire's (1993) philosophy of education which encourages reflection and action upon the world in order to transform it. The model has four phases. First, it calls for an investigation and examination of society in the United States to identify the underlying cultural and political ideology. Using dialogue, lectures, journaling, and media, she encourages students to examine the underlying power structure and methods of oppression. The second phase involves examining the profession's purpose and underlying ideology. One purpose is to remove the feelings of privilege that become associated with having dominant knowledge in counseling, as well as the underlying assumptions of the counseling theories themselves. Again using a variety of methods, she helps students evaluate the use of language and its influences on shaping social practices and assumptions. The third phase involves an interdisciplinary study of an issue or problem identified in steps one and two. Generally, she encourages students to focus on broad issues like education, wealth, technology, religion and so forth, and then define specific problems within the broad areas, such as the effects of poverty on educational opportunities. She encourages students to read literature from related fields as well as from psychology and counseling and do interviews with those affected. She has students work in small groups and do a written report that integrates their findings. Last, she asks the students to develop a plan of action which involves identifying the stakeholders and how they would go about altering the conditions that negatively affect the people involved and present their plan to the class.

As with other aspects of social justice advocacy, there are potential problems. Students may dislike giving up the instructor as the only or primary source of knowledge and/or think social justice issues are outside the realm a responsibility of counselors or psychologists. The content may also raise negative emotions as they do when issues of racial discrimination are discussed. Consequently, the instructor must create a safe environment and allow time for students to process their feelings.

Although Steele's model can be adapted by individual instructors, some programs have changed total curriculums. One example is the counseling psychology program at Boston College (Goodman et al., 2004). In order to train students to think about themselves and their roles extending beyond traditional, individually focused work of counseling and psychotherapy, they initiated what they called the "first-year experience" (FYE). The purpose is for students to gain an awareness of the systemic factors that affect issues like mental health and career development, to learn to work in conjunction with other professions, to do real advocacy work with underserved populations, and to learn how to design and evaluate such interventions. The FYE involves first-year doctoral students working in community sites like public schools, courts, or community organizing agencies. Rather than playing traditional roles of psychotherapists or counselors, "students develop skills in prevention, interprofessional collaboration, and advocacy" (Goodman et al., 2004, p. 808). All students working on the sites have a main on-site supervisor and in addition take part in an FYE seminar that meets monthly on campus. In this seminar, students have the opportunity to discuss their experiences with each other and explore the ways in which their own gender, race and class affect those experiences. As in Steele's model, at the end of the experience, students do an oral presentation to the students and faculty of the program.

Although the FYE does not extend formally into the rest of the students' program, sometimes students continue to work on the sites where they were originally assigned or take on other aspects of social justice work. In addition, other coursework continues to engage students in issues of social justice including research courses, counseling theory, assessment and so on. In other words, the curriculum change meant that the primary faculty members were all committed to the project.

Another student project described by Goodman et al. (2004) is with the Juvenile Rights Advocacy Project, which is connected to the college's law school. In this project, students work at three levels. At the micro level, they conduct in-depth interviews with girls in the justice system to understand their circumstances and needs. At the meso level, they work with law students to help them to understand the context in which their clients live. Last, at the macro level, they work to change the legal system by educating new lawyers and other justice system agents about the social and contextual dimensions of clients' lives. For example, many lawyers come from middle or upper-class families where they have many privileges and opportunities. By contrast, it is often the case that their clients are poor and struggling just to keep food on the table. They may not always be clean or have sophisticated vocabularies, but it does not mean they are stupid or don't aspire to higher goals. They may not believe, however, that those goals are within their reach or that they even deserve them. Changing lawyers' perceptions of their clients may change how they represent them and ultimately, how the justice system treats them.

As with other aspects of social justice advocacy work, there is a cost involved. It takes a substantial amount of time from faculty members, which may be unappreciated by those who are evaluating them, to arrange the placements in the community by collaborating with community members. Although the authors do not discuss it, undoubtedly, it involves building trust with community leaders that they are making a true commitment to the individuals involved and to the community. In addition, not all projects are successful, students may be disappointed in outcomes, and likely there are occasions when faculty must intervene with the community to mend fences.

Conclusions

Questions of justice should lead psychologists and counselors to consider issues that go beyond their treatment of individual students or clients or the design of their particular research study. They should lead to larger questions regarding the distribution of benefits and burdens associated with the discipline and in society.

The reality is that psychology and counseling are practiced in societies in which there are large disparities of wealth, power, and prestige. In the United States, those who are poor and earn $10,000 a year or less die prematurely at three times the rate of those who earn more. Lack of medical care, pollution, and street violence are only part of the cause. Research has found that variables such as racism, classism, and the lack of social relationships and social supports may add to the volatile mix (Lantz et al., 1998). Furthermore, of the world's richest industrial nations, American children have the highest poverty rates. More than one in five children lives below the poverty line (Wright, 1996). Children in poor families have fewer resources and fewer opportunities to get mental health help, although they probably need it the most.

A profession committed to enhancing human welfare needs to address these kinds of disparities. Individual psychologists and counselors need to identify how their own work contributes to or challenges these disparities. They need to consider what model of justice they should endorse, and they should encourage the profession to clarify its own values regarding the distribution of psychological services as well as the benefits and burdens of research.

At the same time, individual psychologists and counselors need to decide how to apportion their time and use their own resources fairly. Practitioners must consider whether they will contribute a portion of their time at low or no cost and how they will respond when clients who need ongoing treatment lose their insurance benefits or personal resources. On a daily basis, academic psychologists and counselors need to evaluate how they will distribute their time and energy. How much should go to students who are paying for their services, and how much should go to research and administration, which are also part of their job requirements? Similarly, researchers must balance their own contributions to projects with those of colleagues and students in deciding how recognition for the project should be distributed. These are very personal justice concerns.

Acting fairly often involves aspirational action. No one can compel psychologists or counselors to address social justice issues or to act as advocates. The ethics committees can censure individuals when they discriminate unfairly and harm others by their lack of sensitivity to individual differences or when they fail to assign authorship credit fairly. Federal funding agencies can refuse to support research studies that exclude women and minorities without a reasonable justification. Professional organizations can and do encourage the use of knowledge to foster equal opportunity and empower those who do not share reasonably in society's benefits. Individual responsibility, however, derives from a character that is compassionate and caring, prudent with how compassion is exhibited, and respectful of others' legitimate concerns and differences.

Questions for Discussion or Consideration

1. What was your initial reaction to including social justice advocacy as a part of the responsibilities of psychologists and counselors?
2. Would you have entered your master's or doctoral program if you knew that social justice would be emphasized in the curriculum?
3. Would emphasizing social justice affect your acculturation to the profession?
4. Make a case on who should get the first authorship credit in Case 13-11.
5. What do you see as the major barriers to including social justice as a major part of the curriculum?

Appendices

The following resources are available online as PDF downloads on the publisher's Web site:
http://www.routledgementalhealth.com/foundations-of-ethical-practice-research-and-teaching-in-psychology-9780415965415

Appendix A: American Psychological Association Guidelines on Multicultural Education, Training, Research, Practice, and Organizational Change for Psychologists

Appendix B: American Psychological Association Guidelines for Psychotherapy with Lesbian, Gay, and Bisexual Clients

Appendix C: American Psychological Association Guidelines for Psychological Practice with Older Adults

Appendix D: Guidelines for Psychological Practice with Girls and Women

Appendix E: Ethics Cases

References

Abelson, R., & Nielsen, K. (1967). History of ethics. In P. Edwards (Ed.), *The encyclopedia of philosophy* (Vol. 3, pp. 81–117). New York: Macmillan.

Abramovitch, R., Freedman, J. L., Henry, K., & Van Brunschot, M. (1995). Children's capacity to agree to psychological research: Knowledge of risks and benefits and voluntariness. *Ethics and Behavior, 5*, 25–48.

Abramovitch, R., Freedman, J. L., Thoden, K., & Nikolich, C. (1991). Children's capacity to consent to participation in psychological research: Empirical findings. *Child Development, 62*, 1000–1109.

Adair, J. G., Dushenko, T. W., & Lindsey, R. C. L. (1985). Ethical regulations and their effect on research practice. *American Psychologist, 40*, 59–72.

Adelman, H. S., Lusk, R., Alvarez, V., & Acosta, N. K. (1985). Competence of minors to understand, evaluate, and communicate about their psycho-educational problems. *Professional Psychology: Research and Practice, 16*, 426–434.

Adelman, J., & Barrett, S. E. (1990). Overlapping relationships: Importance of the feminist ethical perspective. In H. Lerman & N. Porter (Eds.), *Feminist ethics in psychotherapy* (pp. 87–91). New York: Springer.

Ad Hoc Committee on Women of Division 17. (1979). Principles concerning the counseling and therapy of women. *The Counseling Psychologist, 8*, 21.

Ahlstrand, K. R., Crumlin, J., Korinek, L. L., Lasky, G. B., & Kitchener, K. S. (2003, August). *Sexual contact between students and educators: Issues and ethics.* Paper presented at the annual meeting of the American Psychological Association, Toronto, Canada.

Akamatsu, T. J. (1988). Intimate relationships with former clients: National survey of attitudes and behavior among practitioners. *Professional Psychology: Research and Practice, 19*, 454–458.

Albee, G. W. (1986). Toward a just society: Lessons from observations on the primary prevention of psychopathology. *American Psychologist, 41*, 891–898.

Allen, J. (2007). A multicultural assessment supervision model to guide research and practice. *Professional Psychology: Research and Practice, 38*(3), 248–258.

Allen, T. D., Eby, L. T., Poteet, M. L., Lentz, E., & Lima, L. (2004). Career benefits associated with mentoring for protégés: A meta-analysis. *Journal of Applied Psychology, 89*, 127–136.

Almason, A. L. (1997). Personal liability implications of the duty to warn are hard pills to swallow: From *Thrasoff* to *Hutchinson v. Patel* and beyond. *Journal of Contemporary Health Law and Policy, 13*, 471–496.

Altman, L. K. (1997, June 22). Is the longer life the healthier life? *New York Times*, p. WH 158.

Alyn, J. H. (1988). The politics of touch in therapy: A response to Willison and Masson. *Journal of Counseling and Development, 66*, 432–433.

American Association for Marriage and Family Therapy. (2001). *AAMFT Code of Ethics*. Washington, DC: Author.

American Counseling Association. (2005). *Code of ethics and standards of practice*. Annapolis Junction, MD: Author.

American Educational Research Association, American Psychological Association, & National Council on Measurement in Education. (1999). *Standards for educational and psychological testing*. Washington, DC: American Educational Research Association.

American Psychiatric Association. (2000). *Diagnostic and statistical manual of mental disorders* (4th ed., text revision). Washington, DC: Author.

American Psychological Association. (1953). *Ethical standards of psychologists*. Washington, DC: Author.

American Psychological Association. (1959). Ethical standards of psychologists. *American Psychologist, 14*, 279–282.

American Psychological Association. (1973). *Ethical principles in the conduct of research with human participants*. Washington, DC: Author.

American Psychological Association. (1975). Report of the task force on sex bias and sex-role stereotyping in psychotherapeutic practice. *American Psychologist, 30*, 1169–1175.

American Psychological Association. (1977). *Ethical standards of psychologists*. Washington, DC: Author.

American Psychological Association. (1981a). Ethical principles of psychologists. *American Psychologist, 36,* 635–638.

American Psychological Association. (1981b). *Specialty guidelines for the delivery of services.* Washington, DC: Author.

American Psychological Association. (1982). *Ethical principles in the conduct of research with human participants.* Washington, DC: Author.

American Psychological Association. (1987a). *Casebook on ethical principles of psychologists.* Washington, DC: Author.

American Psychological Association. (1987b). *General guidelines for providers of psychological services.* Washington, DC: Author.

American Psychological Association. (1992). Ethical principles of psychologists and code of conduct. *American Psychologist, 47,* 1597–1611.

American Psychological Association. (1993a). *Guidelines for ethical conduct in the care and use of animals.* Washington, DC: Author.

American Psychological Association. (1993b). Guidelines for providers of psychological services to ethnic, linguistic, and culturally diverse populations. *American Psychologist, 48,* 45–48.

American Psychological Association. (1994). Guidelines for child custody evaluations in divorce proceedings. *American Psychologist, 49,* 677–680.

American Psychological Association. (1997). *Visions and transformations. The final report: Commission on Ethnic Minority Recruitment, Retention, and Training in Psychology.* Washington, DC: Author.

American Psychological Association. (1997). Commission on Ethnic Minority Recruitment, Retention and Training in Psychology (CEMRATT). Washington, DC: Author.

American Psychological Association. (2000). Guidelines for psychotherapy with lesbian, gay, and bisexual clients. *American Psychologist, 55,* 1440–1451.

American Psychological Association. (2002). Ethical principles of psychologists and code of conduct. Retrieved September 6, 2010, from the World Wide Web: http://www.apa.org/ethics/code/index.aspx

American Psychological Association. (2004). Guidelines for psychological practice with older adults. *American Psychologist, 59,* 236–260.

American Psychological Association. (2007). Guidelines for psychological practice with girls and women. *American Psychologist, 62*(9), 949–979.

American Psychological Association. (2007). Report of the Ethics Committee, 2006. *American Psychologist, 62,* 504–511.

American Psychological Association. (2008). Report of the Ethics Committee, 2007. *American Psychologist 63*(5), 452–459.

American Psychological Association. (2009). Report of the Ethics Committee, 2008. *American Psychologist, 64,* 464–473.

American Psychological Association Committee on Legal Issues. (2006). Strategies for private practitioners coping with subpoenas or compelled testimony for client records or test data. *Professional Psychology: Research and Practice, 37,* 215–222.

American Psychological Association, Office of Program Consultation and Accreditation and Education Directorate. (1996). *Guidelines and principles for accreditation of programs in professional psychology.* Washington, DC: Author.

American Psychological Association Presidential Task Force on Evidence-Based Practice. (2006). Evidence-based practice in psychology. *American Psychologist, 61,* 271–285.

American Psychological Association, Public Interest Directorate. (1998). *About the public interest directorate.* Retrieved September 6, 2010, from World Wide Web: http://www.apa. org/pi/about/index.aspx

Americans with Disabilities Act of 1990, 42 U.S.C.A. 12101 *et seq.* (West 1993).

Amirkham, J., Betancourt, H., Graham, S., Lopez, S. R., & Weiner, B. (1995). Reflections on affirmative action goals in psychology admissions. *American Psychological Society, 6,* 140–148.

Anastasi, A. (1992). What counselors should know about the use and interpretation of psychological tests. *Journal of Counseling and Development, 70,* 610–615.

Anastasi, A., & Urbina, S. (1997). *Psychological Testing* (7th ed.). Englewood Cliffs, NJ: Prentice-Hall.

Anderson, D., & Freeman, L. T. (2006). Report of the ACA ethics committee. *Journal of Counseling and Development, 84,* 225–227.

Anderson, J., & Barret, R. L. (Eds.). (2001). *Ethics and AIDS: A mental health practitioner's guide.* Washington, DC: American Psychological Association.

Anderson, M. S., Louis, K. S., & Earle, J. (1994). Disciplinary and departmental effects on observations of faculty and graduate student misconduct. *Journal of Higher Education, 65,* 331–350.

Anderson, S. K., Govan, D., & Middleton, V. A. (2001). Nonromantic/nonsexual post-therapy relationships between former clients and psychotherapists: The former client's perspective. Unpublished manuscript.

Anderson, S. K., & Handelsman, M. M. (2010). *Ethics for psychotherapists and counselors: A proactive approach.* Malden, MA: Wiley-Blackwell.

Anderson, S. K., Lujan, L., & Hegeman, D. (2009). Prepared for challenges: The importance of professional and institutional ethical identity. In P. Farrell & C. Harbour (Eds.), *New directions for community colleges-institutional ethics* (pp. 17–29). San Francisco: Wiley Periodicals.

Anderson, S. K., & Kitchener, K. S. (1996). Nonromantic nonsexual posttherapy relationships between psychologists and former clients: An exploratory study of critical incidents. *Professional Psychology: Research and Practice, 27,* 59–66.

Anderson, S. K., & Kitchener, K. S. (1998). Nonsexual posttherapy relationships: A conceptual framework to assess ethical risks. *Professional Psychology: Research and Practice, 29,* 91–99.

Anderson, S. K., & Middleton, V. A. (2011). An awakening to privilege, oppression, and discrimination. In S. K. Anderson & V. A. Middleton (Eds.), *Explorations in diversity: Examining privilege and oppression in a multicultural society* (2nd ed.), (pp. 5–10). Belmont, CA: Thomson Brooks/Cole Cengage Learning.

Anderson, S. K., Wagoner, H., & Moore, G. K. (2006). Ethical choice: An outcome of being, blending, and doing. In P. Williams & S. K. Anderson (Eds.), *Law and ethics in coaching: How to solve and avoid difficult problems in your practice* (pp. 39–61). Hoboken, NJ: John Wiley and Sons.

Anderten, P., Staulcup, V., & Grisso, T. (1980). On being ethical in legal places. *Professional Psychology, 11,* 764–773.

Annas, J. (1993). *The morality of happiness.* Oxford, England: Oxford University Press.

Aponte, H. J. (1994). How personal can training get? *Journal of Marital and Family Therapy, 20,* 3–15.

Appelbaum, K., & Appelbaum, P. S. (1990). The *HIV antibody patient.* In J. C. Beck (Ed.), *Confidentiality versus the duty to protect: Foreseeable harm in the practice of psychiatry* (pp. 121–140). Washington, DC: American Psychiatric Press.

Appelbaum, P. S. (1988). AIDS, psychiatry, and the law. *Hospital and Community Psychiatry, 39,* 13–14.

Appelbaum, P. S. (1993). Legal liability and managed care. *American Psychologist, 48,* 251–257.

Appelbaum, P. S., Lidz, C. W., & Meisel, A. (1987) *Informed consent: Legal theory and clinical practice.* New York: Oxford University Press.

Appelbaum, P. S., & Rosenbaum, A. (1989). *Tarasoff* and the researcher: Does the duty to protect apply in the research setting? *American Psychologist, 44,* 885–894.

Arvey, R. D., & Faley, R. H. (1988). *Fairness in selecting employees* (2nd ed.). Reading, MA: Addison-Wesley.

Ascher, L. M., & Tuner, R. M. (1980). A comparison of two methods for the administration of paradoxical intention. *Behavior Research and Treatment, 18,* 121–126.

Association for Counselor Education and Supervision. (1990). Standards for counseling supervisors. *Journal of Counseling & Development, 69,* 30–32.

Association for Counselor Education and Supervision. (1993, Summer). ACES ethical guidelines for counseling supervisors. *ACES Spectrum, 53*(4), 5–8.

Association for Lesbian, Gay, Bisexual, and Transgender Issues in Counseling. (2009). Competencies for Counseling with Transgender Clients. Retrieved March 9, 2010 from http://www.algbtic.org/ALGBTIC_Counseling_Transgender_Clients_Competencies.pdf

Astin, A. W. (1993). *What matters in college?* San Francisco: Jossey-Bass.

Atkinson, D. R., Casas, A., & Abreu, J. (1992). Mexican-American acculturation, counselor ethnicity and cultural sensitivity, and perceived counselor competence. *Journal of Counseling Psychology, 39,* 515–520.

Atkinson, D. R., & Israel, T. (2003). The future of multicultural counseling competence. In D. B. Pope-Davis, H. L. K. Coleman, W. M. Liu, & R. L. Toporek (Eds.), *Handbook of multicultural competencies in counseling and psychology* (pp. 591–606). Thousand Oaks, CA: Sage.

Atkinson, D. R., & Lowe, S. M. (1995). The role of ethnicity, cultural knowledge, and conventional techniques in counseling and psychotherapy. In J. G. Ponerotto, J. M. Casea, L. A. Suzuki, & C. M. Alexander (Eds.), *Handbook of multicultural counseling* (pp. 387–414). Thousand Oaks, CA: Sage.

Atkinson, D. R., Neville, H., & Casas, A. (1991). The mentorship of ethnic minorities in professional psychology. *Professional Psychology: Research and Practice, 22,* 336–338.

Austin, W., Bergum, V., Nuttgens, S., & Peternelj-Taylor, C. (2006). A re-visioning of boundaries in professional helping relationships: Exploring other metaphors. *Ethics and Behavior, 16,* 77–94.

Bacorn, C., & Dixon, D. (1984). The effects of touch on depressed and vocationally undecided clients. *Journal of Counseling Psychology, 31*, 488–496.

Baer, B. E., & Murdock, N. L. (1995). Nonerotic dual relationships between therapist and clients: The effects of sex, theoretical orientation, and interpersonal boundaries. *Ethics and Behavior, 5*, 131–145.

Baker, E. K. (2007). Therapist self-care: Challenges within ourselves and within the profession. *Professional Psychology: Research and Practice, 38*(6), 607–608.

Baier, A. (1993). What do women want in a moral theory? In M. J. Larrabee (Ed.), *An ethic of care* (pp. 19–32). New York: Routledge. (Reprinted from *Nous, 19*, 53–63, 1985).

Baier, K. (1958). *The moral point of view*. Ithaca, NY: Cornell University Press.

Bajt, T. R., & Pope, K. S. (1989). Therapist–patient sexual intimacy involving children and adolescents. *American Psychologist, 44*, 455.

Baldwin, L. C. (1986). The therapeutic use of touch with the elderly. *Physical and Occupational Therapy in Geriatrics, 4*, 45–50.

Barber, B. (1982). Professions and emerging professions. In J. C. Callahan (Ed.), *Ethical issues in professional life* (pp. 35–39). Oxford, England: Oxford University Press.

Barlow, D. H. (2004). Psychological treatment. *American Psychologist, 59*, 869–878.

Barlow, D. H. (2010). Negative effects from psychological treatments. *American Psychologist, 65*(1), 13–20.

Barlow, D. H., & Durand, V. M. (2009). *Abnormal psychology: An integrated approach* (5th ed.). Belmont, CA: Wadsworth.

Barnett, J. E. (2005). Important ethical, legal issues surround supervision roles. *National Psychologist, 14*, 9.

Barnett, J. E. (2007a). In search of the effective supervisor. *Professional Psychology: Research and Practice, 38*(3), 268–271.

Barnett, J. E. (2007b). Commentaries on the ethical and effective practice of clinical supervision. *Professional Psychology: Research and Practice, 38*, 268–275.

Barnett, J. E., Baker, E. K., Elman, N. S., & Schoener, G. R. (2007). In pursuit of wellness: The self-care imperative. *Professional Psychology: Research and Practice, 38*(6), 603–612.

Barnett, J. E., Cornish, J. A. E., Goodyear, R. K., & Lichtenberg, J. W. (2007). Commentaries on the ethical and effective practice of clinical supervision. *Professional Psychology: Research and Practice, 38*(3), 268–275.

Barnett, J., Cornish, J. A. E., & Kitchener, K. S. (2008, August). Ethical incidents in supervision: Implications for the profession. Paper presented at the annual meeting of the American Psychological Association, Boston, MA.

Barnett, J. E., & Hillard, D. (2001). Psychologist distress and impairment: The availability, nature, and use of colleague assistance programs for psychology. *Professional Psychology: Research and Practice, 32*(2), 205–211.

Barnett, J. E., Johnston, L. C., & Hilliard, D. (2006). Psychotherapist wellness as an ethical imperative. In L. VandeCreek & J. B. Allen (Eds.), *Innovations in clinical practice: Focus on health and wellness* (pp. 257–271). Sarasota, FL: Professional Resources Press.

Barnett, J. E., Lazars, A. A., Vasquez, M. J. T., & Moorehead-Slaughter, O. (2007). Boundary issues and multiple relationships: Fantasy and reality. *Professional Psychology: Research and Practice, 38*(4), 401–410.

Barnett, J. E., Wise, E. H., Johnson-Greene, D., & Bucky, S. F. (2007). Informed consent: Too much of a good thing or not enough? *Professional Psychology: Research and Practice, 38*(2), 179–186.

Barnett, J. E., Youngstrom, J. K., & Smook, R. G. (2001). Super-vision insights: Brief commentaries on super-vision. *The Clinical Supervisor, 20*(2), 217–230.

Barret, B., Kitchener, K. S., & Burris, S. (2001). A decision model for ethical dilemmas in HIV-related psychotherapy and its application to the case of Jerry. In J. Anderson & R. L. Barret (Eds.), *Ethics and AIDS: A mental health practitioner's guide*. Washington, DC: American Psychological Association.

Bartell, P. A., & Rubin, L. J. (1990). Dangerous liaisons: Sexual intimacies in supervision. *Professional Psychology: Research and Practice, 21*, 442–450.

Bashe, A., Anderson, S. K., Handelsman, M. M., & Klevansky, R. (2007). An acculturation model for ethics training: The ethics autobiography and beyond. *Professional Psychology: Research and Practice, 38*, 60–67.

Bates, C. M., & Brodsky, A. M. (1989). *Sex in the therapy hour: A case of professional incest*. New York: Guilford.

Baumrind, D. (1985). Research using intentional deception: Ethical issues revisited. *American Psychologist, 40*, 165–174.

Bayles, M. D. (1981). *Professional ethics*. Belmont, CA: Wadsworth.

Beauchamp, T. L., & Childress, J. P. (1979). *Principles of biomedical ethics.* Oxford, England: Oxford University Press.

Beauchamp, T. L., & Childress, J. F. (1989). *Principles of biomedical ethics* (3rd ed.). Oxford, England: Oxford University Press.

Beauchamp, T. L., & Childress, J. F. (1994). *Principles of biomedical ethics* (4th ed.). Oxford, England: Oxford University Press.

Beauchamp, T. L., & Childress, J. F. (2004). *Principles of biomedical ethics* (5th ed.). Oxford, England: Oxford University Press.

Behari, R. (1991). *Use of non-erotic physical contact in cross-cultural counseling.* Unpublished manuscript, University of Denver.

Behnke, S. (2004). Multiple relationships and APA's new ethics code: Values and applications. *Monitor on Psychology, 35,* 66–67.

Behnke, S. (2004). Sexual involvements with former clients: A delicate balance of core values. *Monitor on Psychology, 35*(11), 76–78.

Benn, S. I. (1967a). Justice. In P. Edwards (Ed.), *The encyclopedia of philosophy* (Vol. 4, pp. 298–301). New York: Macmillan.

Benn, S. I. (1967b). Rights. In P. Edwards (Ed.), *The encyclopedia of philosophy* (Vol. 7, pp. 195–199). New York: Macmillan.

Bennett, B. E., Bricklin, P. M., Harris, E., Knapp, S., VandeCreek, L., & Younggren, J. N. (2006). *Assessing and managing risk in psychological practice: An individualized approach.* Rockville, MD: The Trust.

Bennett, B. E., Bryant, B. K., VandenBos, G. R., & Greenwood, A. (1990). *Professional liability and risk management.* Washington, DC: American Psychological Association.

Berk, R. A. (1982). *Handbook for detecting test bias.* Baltimore: Johns Hopkins University Press.

Bermant, G. (1988). *Why psychologists should forgo the development of intimate relationships with former clients.* Washington, DC: Federal Judicial Center.

Bernard, J. M., & Goodyear, R. K. (2004). *Fundamentals of clinical supervision* (3rd ed.). Boston: Pearson Education.

Berndt, D. J. (1983). Ethical and professional considerations in psychological assessment. *Professional Psychology: Research and Practice, 14,* 580–587.

Berry, J. W. (1980). Acculturation as varieties of adaptation. In A. M. Padilla (Ed.), *Acculturation: Theory, models, and some new findings* (pp. 9–25). Boulder, CO: Westview Press.

Berry, J. W. (2003). Conceptual approaches to acculturation. In K. M. Chun, P. B. Organista, & G. Marin (Eds.), *Acculturation: Advances in theory, measurement, and applied research* (pp. 17–37). Washington, DC: American Psychological Association.

Bersoff, D. N. (1976). Therapists as protectors and policemen: New roles as a result of *Tarasoff. Professional Psychology: Research and Practice, 7,* 267–273.

Bersoff, D. N. (1981). Testing and the law. *American Psychologist, 36,* 1047–1056.

Bersoff, D. N. (1983). Regarding psychologists testily: The legal regulation of psychological assessment. In C. J. Scheirer & B. L. Hammonds (Eds.), *The master lecture series: Psychology and the law* (Vol. 2, pp. 41–88). Washington, DC: American Psychological Association.

Bersoff, D. N. (1994). Explicit ambiguity: The 1992 ethics code as an Oxymoron. *Professional Psychology: Research and Practice, 25,* 382–387.

Bersoff, D. N. (1996). The virtue of principle ethics. *The Counseling Psychologist, 24,* 86–91.

Bersoff, D. N. (Ed.). (2003). *Ethical conflicts in psychology* (3rd ed.). Washington, DC: American Psychological Association.

Bersoff, D. N. (2008). *Ethical conflicts in psychology* (4th ed.). Washington, DC: American Psychological Association.

Betancourt, H., & Lopez, S. R. (1993). The study of culture, ethnicity and race in American psychology. *American Psychologist, 48,* 629–637.

Betts, G. R., & Remer, R. (1993). The impact of paradoxical interventions on perceptions of the therapist and ratings of treatment acceptability. *Professional Psychology: Research and Practice, 24,* 164–170.

Birch, M., Elliott, D., & Trankel, M. A. (1999). Black and white and shades of gray: A portrait of the ethical professor. *Ethics and Behavior, 9,* 243–261.

Bissell, L. (1983). Alcoholism in physicians: Tactics to improve the salvage rate. *Postgraduate Medicine, 74,* 177–230.

Black, H. C. (1979). *Black's law dictionary* (5th ed.). St. Paul, MN: West.

Bleiberg, J. R., & Baron, J. (2004). Entanglement in dual relationships in a university counseling center. *Journal of College Student Psychotherapy, 19,* 21–34.

Blevins-Knabe, B. (1992). The ethics of dual relationships in higher education. *Ethics and Behavior, 2,* 151–163.

Bley, G. (1991). *Nonsexual touch in therapy.* Unpublished manuscript, University of Denver.

Bloom, B. L. (1992). *Planned short-term psychotherapy: A clinical handbook.* Boston: Allyn & Bacon.

Board of Registration in Medicine. (1994, March/April). Maintenance of boundaries in the practice of psychotherapy by physicians (adult patients). *Massachusetts Psychiatric Society Perspectives, 28*(2), 6–7.

Bobbitt, J. M. (1952). Some arguments for a code of ethics. *American Psychologist, 7,* 428–429.

Bok, S. (1988). The limits of confidentiality. In J. C. Callahan (Ed.), *Ethical issues in professional life* (pp. 230–239). Oxford, England: Oxford University Press. (Reprinted from Bok, S. (1982). *Secrets: The ethics of concealment and revelation* (pp. 116–135). New York: Random House.)

Bok, S. (1989). *Lying: Moral choice in public and private life.* New York: Vintage Books.

Bordin, E. (1983). A working alliance based model of supervision. *The Counseling Psychologist, 11,* 35–42.

Borenzweig, H. (1983). Touching in clinical social work. *Social Casework, 64,* 238–242.

Borys, D. S. (1988). *Dual relationships between therapist and client: A national survey of clinicians' attitudes and practices.* Unpublished doctoral dissertation, University of California, Los Angeles.

Borys, D. S. (1994). Maintaining therapeutic boundaries: The motive is therapeutic effectiveness, not defensive practice. *Ethics and Behavior, 4,* 267–273.

Borys, D. S., & Pope, K. S. (1989). Dual relationships between therapist and client: A national study of psychologists, psychiatrists, and social workers. *Professional Psychology: Research and Practice, 20,* 283–293.

Bouhoutsos, J., Holroyd, J., Lerman, H., Forer, B. R., & Greenberg, M. (1983). Sexual intimacies between therapists and their former clients. *Psychotherapy, 25,* 249–257.

Bowman, V. E., Hatley, L. D., & Bowman, R. L. (1995). Faculty-student relationships: The dual role controversy. *Counselor Education and Supervision, 34,* 232–242.

Brabeck, M. M. (Ed.). (1989). *Who cares? Theory, research, and educational implications of the ethic of care.* New York: Praeger.

Brabeck, M., & Brown, L. (1997). Feminist theory and psychological practice. In J. Worrell & N. G. Johnson (Eds.), *Shaping the future of feminist psychology: Education, research, and practice* (pp. 15–35). Washington, DC: American Psychological Association Press.

Brabeck, M. M., & Ting, K. (2000). Feminist ethics: Lenses for examining ethical psychological practice. In M. M. Brabeck (Ed.), *Practicing feminist ethics in psychology* (pp. 17–35). Washington, DC: American Psychological Association.

Brabender, V., & Bricklin, P. (2001). Ethical issues in psychological assessment in different settings. *Journal of Personality Assessment, 77*(2), 192–194.

Bradley, F. H. (1951). *Ethical studies: Selected essays.* New York: The Liberal Press.

Brandt, R. B. (1967). Ethical relativism. In P. Edwards (Ed.), *The encyclopedia of philosophy* (Vol. 3, pp. 75–78). New York: Macmillan.

Brandt, R. B. (1979). *A theory of the good and the right.* Oxford, England: Clarendon.

Brehm, S. S. (1977). The effect of adult influence on children's preferences: Compliance versus opposition. *Journal of Abnormal Child Psychology, 5,* 31–41.

Bridges, N. A. (2001). Therapist's self-disclosure: Expanding the comfort zone. *Psychotherapy, 38,* 21–30.

Brodsky, A. M. (1980). A decade of feminist influence on psychotherapy. *Psychology of Women Quarterly, 4,* 331–344.

Brodsky, A. M. (1989). Sex between patient and therapist: Psychology's data and response. In G. Gabbard (Ed.), *Sexual exploitation in professional relationships* (pp. 153–177). Washington, DC: American Psychiatric Press, Inc.

Brodsky, A. M., & Hare-Mustin, R. T. (1980). Psychotherapy and women: Priorities for research. In A. M. Brodsky & R. T. Hare-Mustin (Eds.), *Women and psychotherapy: An assessment of research and practice* (pp. 385–409). New York: Guilford.

Brofenbrenner, U. (1995). Developmental ecology through space and time: A future perspective. In P. Moen, G. H. Elder, & K. Luscher (Eds.)., *Examining lives in context: Perspectives on the ecology of human development* (pp. 619–647). Washington, DC: American Psychological Association.

Brown, J. E., & Slee, P. T. (1986). Paradoxical strategies. The ethics of intervention. *Professional Psychology: Research and Practice, 17,* 519–523.

Brown, L. S. (1989). Beyond thou shalt not: Thinking about ethics in the lesbian therapy community. *Women and Therapy, 8,* 13–25.

Brown, L. S. (1994a). Concrete boundaries and the problem of literal-mindedness: A response to Lazarus. *Ethics and Behavior, 4*, 275–281.

Brown, L. S. (1994b). *Subversive dialogues: Theory in feminist therapy.* New York: Basic Books.

Brown, L. S. (1997a). The private practice of subversion: Psychology as *tikkun olam. American Psychologist, 52*, 449–462.

Brown, L. S. (1997b). Remediation, amends, or denial? *Professional Psychology: Research and Practice, 28*, 297–299.

Brown, R. D., & Krager, L. A. (1985). Ethical issues in graduate education. *Journal of Higher Education, 56*, 403–418.

Bryan, C. J., Corso, K. A., Neal-Walden, T. A., & Rudd, M. D. (2009). Managing suicide risk in primary care: Practice recommendations for behavioral health consultants. *Professional Psychology: Research and Practice, 40*, 148–155.

Bucher, R., & Stelling, J. G. (1977). *Becoming professional.* Beverly Hills: Sage.

Bucky, S. F. (2007). Informed consent: A brief attempt to clarify some of the ambiguities. *Professional Psychology: Research and Practice 38*(2), 184–186.

Burian, B. K., & Slimp, A. (2000). Social dual-role relationships during internship: A decision making model. *Professional Psychology: Research and Practice, 31*(3), 332–338.

Burke, C. A. (1995). Until death do us part: An exploration into confidentiality following the death of a client. *Professional Psychology: Research and Practice, 26*, 278–280.

Burn, D. (1992). Ethical implications in cross-cultural counseling and training. *Journal of Counseling and Development, 70*, 578–583.

Burris, S. (2001). Clinical decision making in the shadow of the law. In J. Anderson & R. L. Barret (Eds.), *Ethics and AIDS: A mental health practitioner's guide.* Washington, DC: American Psychological Association.

Buskist, W. (2002). Effective teaching: Perspectives and insights from division two's 2- and 4-year awardees. *Teaching of Psychology, 29*(3), 188–193.

Buskist, W., Sikorski, J., Buckley, T., & Saville, B. K. (2002). Elements of master teaching. In S. F. Davis & W. Buskist (eds.), *The teaching of psychology: Essays in honor of Wilbert J. McKeachie and Charles L. Brewer* (pp. 27–39). Mahwah, NJ: Lawrence Erlbaum Associates, Inc.

Buss, D. M. (1995). Psychological sex differences: Origins through sexual selection. *American Psychologist, 50*, 164–168.

Caldwell, L. W. (2003). Sexual relationships between supervisors and supervisees during psychology graduate training. *Dissertation Abstracts International, 63B*, 4879.

California Health and Safety Code. (1996). Section 121010. In *Mandated blood testing and confidentiality to protect public health.* St. Paul, MN: West.

Callahan, J. C. (1988). Basics and background. In J. C. Callahan (Ed.), *Ethical issues in professional practice* (pp. 3–25). Oxford, England: Oxford University Press.

Campbell, C. D., & Gordon, M. C. (2003). Acknowledging the inevitable: Understanding multiple relationships in rural practice. *Professional Psychology: Research and Practice, 34*(4), 430–434.

Campbell, D., Sanderson, R. E., & Laverty, S. G. (1964). Characteristics of a conditioned response in human subjects during extinction trials following a single traumatic conditioning trail. *Journal of Abnormal and Social Psychology, 68*, 627–639.

Campbell, M. L. (1989). The oath: An investigation of the injunction prohibiting physician-patient sexual relations. *Perspectives in Biology and Medicine, 32*(2), 300–308.

Canter, M. B., Bennett, B. E., Jones, S. E., & Nagy, T. E. (1994). *Ethics for psychologists: A commentary on the APA Ethics Code.* Washington, DC: American Psychological Association.

Canterbury v. Spence, 464 F.2d 772 (D.C. Cir. 1972).

Cardea, C. (1985). The lesbian revolution and the 50-minute hour: A working-class look at the therapy and the movement. *Lesbian Ethics, 2*, 5–22.

Carter, R. T. (1991). Cultural values: A review of empirical research and implications for counseling. *Journal of Counseling and Development, 70*, 164–173.

Carter, R. T., & Forsyth, J. M. (2007). Examining race and culture in psychology journals: The case of forensic psychology. *Professional Psychology: Research and Practice, 38*(2), 133–142.

Cartwright, B. Y., Daniels, J., & Zhang, S. (2008). Assessing multicultural competence: Perceived versus demonstrated performance. *Journal of Counseling & Development, 86*, 318–322.

Case, P. (1990). The prevention point needle exchange program. In J. E. Sieber, Y. Song-Kim, & P. Kelzer (Eds.), *Vulnerable populations and AIDS: Ethical and procedural requirements for social and behavioral research and intervention.* Hayward, CA: Pioneer Bookstore.

Case, P. W., McMinn, M. R., & Meek, K. R. (1997). Sexual attraction and religious therapists: Survey findings and implications. *Counseling and Values, 41,* 141–154.

Cashwell, A. L. (2011). Increasing awareness of heterosexism and homophobia: A personal and professional exploration. In S. K. Anderson & V. A. Middleton (Eds.), *Explorations in diversity: Examining privilege and oppression in a multicultural society* (2nd ed.), (pp. 59–63). Belmont, CA: Thomson Brooks/Cole Cengage Learning.

Cavanaugh, J. C. (1997). *Adult development and aging* (3rd ed.). Pacific Grove, CA: Brooks/Cole.

Cayleff, S. E. (1986). Ethical issues in counseling gender, race, and culturally distinct groups. *Journal of Counseling and Development, 64,* 345–347.

Chamallas, M. (1988). Consent, equality and the legal control of sexual conduct. *Southern California Law Review, 61,* 777–862.

Chambers, C. M. (1981). Foundations of ethical responsibility in higher education. In R. H. Stein & M. C. Baca (Eds.), *Professional ethics in university administration* (pp. 1–12). San Francisco: Jossey-Bass.

Champagne, A., Shuman, D. W., & Whitaker, E. (1991). The use of expert witnesses in American courts. *Judicature, 31,* 375–392.

Chemtob, C. M., Bauer, G. B., Hamada, R. S., Pelowski, S. R., & Muraoka, M. Y. (1988). Patient suicide: Occupational hazards for psychologists and psychiatrists. *Professional Psychology: Research and Practice, 20,* 294–300.

Chenneville, T. (2000). HIV, confidentiality, and duty to protect: A decision-making model. *Professional Psychology: Research and Practice, 31,* 661–670.

Chesler, P. (1972). *Women and madness.* New York: Doubleday.

Childress, J. F., Meslin, E. M., & Shapiro, H. T. (Eds.) (2005). *Belmont revisited: Ethical principles for research with human subjects.* Washington, DC: Georgetown University Press.

Churchill, L. R. (1994). Rejecting principlism, affirming principles: A philosopher reflects on the ferment in U.S. bioethics. In E. R. DuBose, R. P. Hamel, & L. J. O'Connell (Eds.), *A matter of principles? Ferment in U.S. bioethics* (pp. 321–331). Valley Forge, PA: Trinity Press International.

Churchman, C. W. (1971). *The design of inquiring systems: Basic concepts of systems and organizations.* New York: Basic Books.

Clark, C. R. (1993). Social responsibility ethics: Doing right, doing good, doing well. *Ethics and Behavior, 3,* 303–328.

Clark, R. A., Harden, S. L., & Johnson, W. B. (2000). Mentor relationships in clinical psychology doctoral training: Results of a national survey. *Teaching of Psychology, 27*(4), 262–268.

Cobia, D. C., & Boes, S. R. (2000). Professional disclosure statements and formal plans for supervision: Two strategies for minimizing the risk of ethical conflicts in post-master's supervision. *Journal of Counseling and Development, 78,* 293–296.

Cohen, E. D. (1990). Confidentiality, counseling and clients who have AIDS: Ethical foundations of a model rule. *Journal of Counseling and Development, 68,* 282–286.

Cohen, G. L., Garcia, J., Apfel, N., & Master, A. (2006, September 1). Reducing the racial achievement gap: A social-psychological intervention. *Science, 313,* 1307–1310.

Cohen, G. L., Garcia, J., Purdie-Vaugns, V., Apfel, N., & Brzustoski, P. (2009, April 17). Recursive processes in self-affirmation: Intervening to close the minority achievement gap. *Science, 324,* 400–403.

Coleman, R. (1988). Sex between psychiatrist and former patient: A proposal for a "no harm, no fault" rule. *Oklahoma Law Review, 41,* 1–52.

Collins, K. S., Hughes, D. L., Doty, M. M., Ives, B. I., Edwards, J. N., & Tenney, K. (2002). *Diverse communities, common concerns: Assessing health care quality for minority Americans.* Finding from the Commonwealth Fund 2001 health care quality survey. Washington, DC: Commonwealth Fund.

Colorado Revised Statute. (1991 & Supp. 1994). *5b,* 12-43-214.

Committee on Ethical Guidelines for Forensic Psychologists. (1991). Specialty guidelines for forensic psychologists. *Law & Human Behavior, 15,* 655–665.

Committee on Ethical Standards of Psychologists. (1958). Standards of ethical behavior for psychologists: Report of the Committee on Ethical Standards of Psychologists. *American Psychologist, 13,* 266–267.

Constantine, M. G. (2001). Predictors of observer ratings of multicultural counseling competence in Black, Latino, and White American trainees. *Journal of Counseling Psychology, 48,* 456–462.

Conte, H. R., Plutchik, R., Picard, M., & Karasu, R. (1989). Ethics in the practice of psychotherapy: A survey. *American Journal of Psychotherapy, 43,* 32–42.

Cooper, C. C., & Gottlieb, M. C. (2000). Ethical issues with managed care: Challenges facing counseling psychology. *The Counseling Psychologist, 28,* 179–236.

Corcoran, K., & Winslade, J. (1994). Eavesdropping on the 50-minute hour: Managed mental health care and confidentiality. *Behavioral Sciences and the Law, 12*, 351–365.

Corey, G., Corey, M. S., & Callanan, P. (2010). *Issues and ethics in the helping professions* (8th ed.). Pacific Grove, CA: Brooks/Cole.

Cornelius-White, J. (2007). Learner-centered teacher-student relationships are effective: A meta-analysis. *Review of Educational Research, 77*, 113–143.

Corning, A., & Myers, D. (2002). Individual orientation toward engagement in social action. *Political Psychology, 23*(4), 703–729.

Corrigan, P. (2004). How stigma interferes with mental health care. *American Psychologist, 59*, 614–625.

Coster, J. S., & Schwebel, M. (1997). Well-functioning in professional psychologists. *Professional Psychology: Research and Practice, 28*, 5–13.

Cottone, R. R. (2005). Detrimental therapist-client relationships beyond thinking of dual or multiple roles: Reflections on the 2001 AAMFT Code of Ethics. *The American Journal of Family Therapy, 33*, 1–17.

Crawford, I., Humfleet, G., Ribordy, S. C., Ho, F. C., & Vickers, V. L. (1991). Stigmatization of AIDS patients by mental health professionals. *Professional Psychology: Research and Practice, 2*, 357–361.

Creegan, R. F. (1958). Concerning professional ethics. *American Psychologist, 13*, 272–275.

Crenshaw, W., Lichtenberg, J., & Bartell, P. (1993). Mental health providers and child sexual abuse: A multivariate analysis of the decision to report. *Journal of Child Sexual Abuse, 2*(4), 19–42.

Crethar, H. C., Rivera, E. T., & Nash, S. (2008). In search of common threads: Linking multicultural, feminist, and social justice counseling paradigms. *Journal of Counseling and Development, 86*, 269–273.

Cullari, S. (2001). The client's perspective of psychotherapy. In S. Cullari (Ed.), *Counseling and psychotherapy* (pp. 92–116). Boston: Allyn & Bacon.

Curd, M., & May, L. (1984). *Professional responsibility for harmful actions.* Dubuque, IA: Kendall/Hunt.

Dahir, C. A., & Stone, C. B. (2009). School counselor accountability: The path to social justice and systemic change. *Journal of Counseling and Development, 87*, 12–20.

Daniel, J. H., Roysircar, G., Abeles, N., & Boyd, C. (2004). Individual and cultural-diversity competency: Focus on the therapist. *Journal of Clinical Psychology, 60*(7), 755–770.

Daniels, J. A. (2001). Managed care, ethics, and counseling. *Journal of Counseling and Development, 79*(1), 119–122.

Daniels, N. (1985). *Just health care.* New York: Cambridge University Press.

Daniels, N. (1996). *Justice and justification: Reflective equilibrium in theory and practice.* Cambridge, England: Cambridge University Press.

Daniels, N., & Sabin, J. E. (1996). Determining "medical necessity" in mental health practice. In N. Daniels (Ed.), *Justice and justification: Reflective equilibrium in theory and practice* (pp. 232–251). Cambridge, England: Cambridge University Press.

Danziger, P. R., & Welfel, E. R. (2001). The impact of managed care on mental health counselors: A survey of perceptions, practices, and compliance with ethical standards. *Journal of Mental Health Counseling, 23*(2), 137–150.

Darou, W. G., Hum, A., & Kurtness, J. (1993). An investigation of the impact of psychosocial research on a native population. *Professional Psychology: Research and Practice, 24*, 325–329.

Darwell, S. L. (1992). Two kinds of respect. In J. Deigh (Ed.), *Ethics and personality: Essays in moral psychology* (pp. 65–78). Chicago: University of Chicago Press.

Davidson, V. (1977). Psychiatry's problem with no name: Therapist-patient sex. *American Journal of Psychoanalysis, 37*, 43–50.

Dawes, R. M. (1988). *Rational choice in an uncertain world.* New York: Harcourt Brace Jovanovich.

D'Andrea, M., & Heckman, E. F. (2008). Contributing to the ongoing evolution of the multicultural counseling movement: An introduction to the special issue. *Journal of Counseling & Development, 86*, 259–260.

Dean, J. (1976). *Blind Ambition.* New York: Simon & Schuster.

DeBell, C., & Jones, R. D. (1997). Privileged communication at last? An overview of *Jaffey v. Redmond. Professional Psychology: Research and Practice, 28*, 559–566.

DeBord, J. B. (1989). Paradoxical interventions. A review of the recent literature. *Journal of Counseling and Development, 67*, 394–398.

DeLeon, P. H., VandenBos, G. R., & Bulatao, E. Q. (1991). Managed mental health care: A history of the federal policy initiative. *Professional Psychology: Research and Practice, 22*, 15–25.

DeMers, S. T. (1986). Legal and ethical issues in child and adolescent personality assessment. In H. M. Knoff (Ed.), *The assessment of child and adolescent personality* (pp. 35–55). New York: Guilford.

DeMers, S. T., & Bersoff, D. N. (1985). Legal issues in school psychological practice. In J. Bergan (Ed.), *School psychology in contemporary society: An introduction.* Columbus, OH: Merrill.

Deutsch, C. J. (1985). A survey of therapists' personal problems and treatment. *Professional Psychology: Research and Practice, 16*, 305–315.

Deutsch, M., & Krauss, R. M. (1965). *Theories in social psychology*. New York: Basic Books.

DeVries, R., DeBruin, D. A., & Goodgame, A. (2004). Ethics review of social, behavioral, and economic research: Where should we go from here? *Ethics & Behavior, 14*(4), 351–368.

Diener, E., & Crandall, R. (1978). *Ethics in social and behavioral research*. Chicago: University of Chicago Press.

Dill, D. D. (1982). Introduction. *Journal of Higher Education, 53*, 243–254.

Dimidjian, S., & Hollon, S. D. (2010). How would we know if psychotherapy were harmful? *American Psychologist, 65*(1), 21–33.

Diviak, K. R., Curry, S. J., Emery, S. L., & Mermelstein, R. J. (2004). Human participants challenges in youth tobacco cessation research: Researchers' perspectives. *Ethics & Behavior, 14*(3), 321–334.

Division 441 Committee on Lesbian, Gay, and Bisexual Concerns Joint Task Force on Guidelines for Psychotherapy with Lesbian, Gay and Bisexual Clients. (2000). Guidelines for psychotherapy with lesbian, gay and bisexual clients. *American Psychologist, 55*, 1440–1451.

Doehrman, M. G. (1976). Parallel process in supervision and psychotherapy. *Bulletin of the Menniger Clinic, 40*, 9–104.

Donner, M. B. (2008). Unbalancing confidentiality. *Professional Psychology: Research and Practice, 39*, 369–372.

dos Anjos, M. F. (1994). Bioethics in a liber-ationist key. In E. R. DuBose, R. P. Hamel, & L. J. O'Connell (Eds.), *A matter of principles? Ferment in U.S. bioethics* (pp. 130–147). Valley Forge, PA: Trinity Press International.

Dowd, E. T., & Milne, C. R. (1986). Paradoxical interventions in counseling psychology. *The Counseling Psychologist, 14*, 237–282.

Drane, J. F. (1982). Ethics and psychotherapy: A philosophical perspective. In M. Rosenbaum (Ed.). *Ethics and values in psychotherapy* (pp. 15–50). New York: The Free Press.

Drane, J. F. (1994). Character and the moral life: A virtue approach to biomedical ethics. In E. R. DuBose, R. P., Hamel, & L. J. O'Connell (Eds.), *A matter of principles? Ferment in U.S. bioethics* (pp. 284–309). Valley Forge, PA: Trinity Press International.

Dube, S. R., Anda, R. F., Whitfield, C. L., Brown, D. W., Felitti, V. J., Dong, M., et al. (2005). *American Journal of Preventive Medicine, 28*(5), 430–438.

Dubin, S. S. (1972). Obsolescence or lifelong education: A choice for the professional. *American Psychologist, 27*, 486–498.

Dubois, J. M. (2004). Universal ethical principles in a diverse universe: A commentary on Monshi and Zieglmayer's case study. *Ethics & Behavior 14*(4), 313–319.

Duckworth, J. (1990). The counseling approach to the use of testing. *The Counseling Psychologist 18*, 198–204.

Durkin, S. J., & Paxton, S. J. (2002). Predictors of vulnerability to reduced body image satisfaction and psychological well being in response to exposure to idealized female media images in adolescent girls. *Journal of Psychosomatic Research, 53*, 995–1005.

Dworkin, S. H. (1992). Some ethical considerations when counseling gay, lesbian, and bisexual clients. In S. H. Dworkin & F. J. Gutierrez (Eds.), *Counseling gay men and lesbians: Journey to the end of the rainbow* (pp. 325–334). Alexandria, VA: American Association for Counseling and Development.

Dyer, L. A. (1992). If only resistance counted as forbearance on student loans. *Sinister Wisdom, 17*(48), 74–78.

Dyson, E. (2008). Reflections on privacy 2.0. *Scientific American, 299*, 50–55.

Ebert, B. W. (1997). Dual-role relationships prohibitions: A concept whose time never should have come. *Applied Preventive Psychology, 6*, 137–156.

Eckberg, D. L. (1979). *Intelligence and race: The origins and dimensions of the IQ controversy*. New York: Praeger.

Edelstein, L. (1967). The Hippocratic Oath: Text, translation and interpretation. In O. Temkin & C. L. Temkin (Eds.), *Ancient medicine: Selected works of Ludwig Edelstein* (pp. 3–63). Baltimore: Johns Hopkins University Press.

Elliott, D. M., & Guy, J. D. (1993). Mental health professionals versus non-mental health professionals: Childhood trauma and adult functioning. *Professional Psychology: Research and Practice, 24*, 83–90.

Ellis, M. V., & Douce, L. A. (1994). Group supervision of novice clinical supervisors: Eight recurring issues. *Journal of Counseling and Development, 72*, 520–525.

Elman, N. S., & Forrest, L. (2007). From trainee impairment to professional competence problems: Seeking new terminology that facilitates effective action. *Professional Psychology: Research and Practice, 38*(5), 501–509.

Epstein, L. C., & Lasagna, L. (1969). Obtaining informed consent—Form or substance? *Archives of Internal Medicine, 123*, 682–688.

Epstein, R. M., & Hundert, E. M. (2002). Defining and assessing professional competence. *Journal of the American Medical Association, 287*, 226–235.

Erikson, S. H. (1993). Counseling the irresponsible AIDS client: Guidelines for decision making. *Journal of Counseling and Development, 68*, 454–455.

Everstine, L., Everstine, D. S., Heymann, G. M., True, R. H., Frey, D. H., Johnson, H. G. et al. (1980). Privacy and confidentiality in psychotherapy. *American Psychologist, 35*, 828–840.

Eyde, L. D., Robertson, G. J., Kruf, S. E., Moreland, K. L., Robertson, A. G., Shewan, C. M., et al. (1993). *Responsible test use: Case studies for assessing human behavior*. Washington, DC: American Psychological Association.

Falender, C. A., Collins, C., & Shafranske, E. P. (2005). Use of the term "impairment" in psychology supervision. *The California Psychologist*, Nov/Dec, 21–22.

Falender, C. A., Erickson-Cornish, J. A., Goodyear, R., Hatcher, R., Kaslow, N. J., Levelthal, G., et al. (2004). Defining competencies in psychology supervision: A consensus statement. *Journal of Clinical Psychology, 60*(7), 771–785.

Falender, C. A., & Shafranske, E. P. (2004). *Clinical supervision: A competency-based approach*. Washington, DC: American Psychological Association.

Falender, C. A., & Shafranske, E. P. (2007). Competence in competency-based supervision practice: Construct and application. *Professional Psychology: Research and Practice, 38*(3), 232–240.

Fay, A. I. (2002). The case against boundaries in psychotherapy. In A. A. Lazarus & O. Zur (Eds.), *Dual relationships and psychotherapy* (pp. 146–168). New York: Springer.

Federal Policy for the Protection of Human Subjects, 45 C.F.R. 46. (2001). Retrieved November 9, 2004, from http://www.hhs.gov/ohrp/humansubjects/guidance/45cfr46.htm

Feminist Therapy Institute. (1990). Feminist Therapy Institute Code of Ethics. In H. Lerman & N. Porter (Eds.), *Feminist ethics in psychotherapy* (pp. 38–40). New York: Springer.

Fine, M. A., & Kurdick, L. A. (1993). Reflections on determining authorship credit on faculty-student collaborations. *American Psychologist 48*, 1141–1147.

Finn, S. E., & Butcher, J. N. (1991). Clinical objective personality assessment. In M. Hersen, A. E. Kazdin, & A. S. Bellack (Eds.), *The clinical psychology hand-book* (2nd ed., pp. 362–373). New York: Pergamon.

Finn, S. E., & Tonsager, M. E. (1992). Therapeutic effects of providing MMPI-2 test feedback to college students awaiting therapy. *Psychological Assessment, 4*, 278–287.

Fischer, C. T. (1986). *Individualizing psychological assessment*. Pacific Grove, CA: Brooks/Cole.

Fisher, C. B. (2000). Relational ethics in psychological research: One feminist's journey. In M. M. Brabeck (Ed.), *Practicing feminist ethics in psychology* (pp. 125–142). Washington, DC: American Psychological Association.

Fisher, C. B. (2002). Respecting and protecting mentally impaired persons in medical research. *Ethics and Behavior, 12*(3), 280–283.

Fisher, C. B. (2003). *Decoding the ethics code: A practical guide for psychologists*. Thousand Oaks, CA: Sage.

Fisher, C. B. (2003). A goodness-of-fit ethic for child assent to nonbeneficial research. *American Journal of Bioethics, 3*(4), 27–28.

Fisher, C. B., & Fryberg, D. (1994). Participant partners: College students weigh the costs and benefits of deceptive research. *American Psychologist, 59*, 417–427.

Fisher, C. B., & Tryon, W. W. (1990). Emerging ethical issues in an emerging field. In C. B. Fisher & W. W. Tryon (Eds.), *Ethics in applied developmental psychology: Emerging issues in an emerging field* (pp. 1–14). Norwood, NJ: Ablex.

Fisher, C. B., Wertz, F. J., & Goodman, S. J. (2009). Graduate training in responsible conduct of social science research: The role of mentors and departmental climate. In D. M. Mertens & P. E. Ginsberg (Eds.), *The handbook of social research ethics* (pp. 550–564). Thousand Oaks, CA: Sage.

Fisher, C. B., & Younggren, J. N. (1997). The value and utility of the 1992 Ethics Code. *Professional Psychology: Research and Practice, 28*, 582–592.

Fisher, C. D. (2004). Ethical issues in therapy: Therapist self-disclosure of sexual feelings. *Ethics & Behavior, 14*(2), 105–121.

Fisher, M. A. (2008). Protecting confidentiality rights: The need for an ethical practice model. *American Psychologist, 63*, 1–13.

Fisher, M. A. (2009). Replacing "Who is the client?" with a different ethical question. *Professional Psychology: Research and Practice, 40*, 1–7.

Fitting, M. D. (1986). Ethical dilemmas in counseling elderly adults. *Journal of Counseling and Development, 64*, 325–327.

Fitzgerald, L. F., Weitzman, L., Gold, Y., & Ormerod, A. J. (1988). Academic harassment: Sex and denial in scholarly garb. *Psychology of Women Quarterly, 12*, 329–340.

Flax, J. W., Wagenfeld, M. O., Ivens, R. E., & Weiss, R. J. (1979). *Mental health and rural America: An overview and annotated bibliography*. Washington, DC: U.S. Government Printing Office.

Flynn, J. R. (1980). *Race, IQ and Jensen*. London: Routledge & Kegan Paul.

Foot, P. (1978). *Virtues and vices and other essays in moral philosophy*. London: Oxford University Press.

Forrest, L., Elman, N., & Gizara, S. (1997, August). *Professional standards for identifying, remediating and terminating impaired or incompetent trainees in psychology: A review of the literature*. Paper presented at the 105th Annual Convention of the American Psychological Association, Chicago, IL.

Forrest, L., Elman, N., Gizara, S., & Vacha-Hasse, T. (1999). Trainee impairment: Identifying, remediating, and terminating impaired trainees in psychology. *The Counseling Psychologist, 27*, 627–686.

Forrest, L., Shen Miller, D. S., & Elman, N. S. (2008). Psychology trainees with competence problems: From individual to ecological conceptualizations. *Training and Education in Professional Psychology, 2*(4), 183–192.

Fouad, N. A., Gerstein, L. H., & Toporek, R. L. (2006). Social justice and counseling psychology in context. In R. L. Toporek, L. H. Gerstein, N. A. Fouad, G. Roysircar, & T. Israel (Eds.), *Handbook for Social Justice in Counseling Psychology: Leadership, Vision, and Action*. Thousand Oaks, CA: Sage.

Fouad, N. A., McPherson, R. H., Gerstein, L., Blustein, D. L., Elman, N., Helledy, K. I. et al. (2004). Houston, 2001: Context and Legacy. *The Counseling Psychologist, 32*, 15–77.

Fowers, B. J. (2005). Virtue and psychology: Pursuing excellence in ordinary practices. Washington, DC: American Psychological Association.

Fowers, B. J., & Richardson, F. C. (1996). Why is multiculturalism good? *American Psychologist, 51*, 609–621.

Fox, R. E. (1995). The rape of psychotherapy. *Professional Psychology: Research and Practice, 26*, 147–155.

Frank, J. D. (1982). In J. H. Harvey & M. M. Parks (Eds.), *Therapeutic components shared by all psychotherapies. Psychotherapy research and behavior change*. Washington, DC: American Psychological Association.

Frank, R. G., Koyanagi, C., & McGuire, T. G. (1997). The politics and economics of mental health "parity" laws. *Health Affairs, 16*, 108–119.

Frankena, W. K. (1963). *Ethics*. Englewood Cliffs, NY: Prentice-Hall.

Freire, P. (1998). Cultural action and conscientization. *Harvard Education Review, 68*(4), 499–522.

Freud, S. (1963). Observations on transference-love. In P. Reiff & J. Strachey (Eds.), (Trans.), *Sigmund Freud: Therapy and technique* (pp. 167–179). New York: Collier books. (Original work published 1915.)

Friedman, M. (1992). Feminism and modern friendship: Dislocating the community. In S. Avineri & de-Shalit (Eds.), *Communitarianism and individualism* (pp. 101–119). New York: Oxford University Press. (Reprinted from *Ethics, 99*, 275–290, 1989.)

Fuertes, J. N., Mueller, L. N., Chauhan, R. V., Walker, J. A., & Ladany, N. (2002). An investigation of Euro-American therapists' approach to counseling African–American clients. *The Counseling Psychologist, 30*(5), 763–788.

Gabbard, G. O. (1994). Reconsidering the American Psychological Association's policy on sex with former patients: Is it justifiable? *Professional Psychology: Research and Practice, 25*, 329–335.

Gabbard, G. O. (2002). Post-termination sexual boundary violations. *Psychiatric Clinics of North America, 25*, 593–603.

Gartrell, N., Herman, J., Olarte, S., Feldstein, M., & Localio, R. (1986). Psychiatrist-patient sexual contact: Results of a national survey. *American Journal of Psychiatry, 143*, 112–131.

Gawthrop, J. C., & Uhlemann, M. R. (1992). Effects of the problem-solving approach to ethics training. *Professional Psychology: Research and Practice, 23*, 38–42.

Gaylin, W. (1982). The "competence" of children: No longer all or none. *Journal of the American Academy of Child Psychiatry, 21*, 153–162.

Geller, J. D., Cooley, R. S., & Hartley, D. (1981–1982). Images of the psychotherapist: A theoretical and methodological perspective. *Imagination, Cognition & Personality, 1*, 125–146.

Geraty, R. D., Hendren, R. L., & Flaa, C. J. (1992). Ethical perspectives on managed care as it relates to child and adolescent psychiatry. *Journal of the American Academy of Child and Adolescent Psychiatry, 31*, 398–401.

Gert, B. (1988). *Morality: A new justification of the moral rules*. New York: Oxford University Press.

Getz, H. G. (1999). Assessment of clinical supervisor competencies. *Journal of Counseling and Development, 77*, 491–497.

Getz, K. (2002). *Informed consent: A guide to the risks and benefits of volunteering for clinical trials.* Boston: CenterWatch.

Getzels, J. W., & Guba, E. G. (1954). Role, role conflict, effectiveness. *American Sociological Review, 19*, 164–175.

Gewirth, A. (1978). *Reason and morality.* Chicago: University of Chicago Press.

Gibb, J. J. (2005). Patients' experience of friendship with their therapist: A phenomenological study of nonsexual dual relationships. *Dissertation Abstracts International, 65B*, 3707.

Gibson, N. T., & Pope, K. S. (1993). The ethics of counseling: A national survey of certified counselors. *Journal of Counseling and Development, 71*, 330–336.

Gidyez, C. A., & Koss, M. P. (1990). A comparison of group and individual sexual assault victims. *Psychology of Women Quarterly, 14*, 325–342.

Gifford, N. L. (1983). *When in Rome: An introduction to relativism and knowledge.* Albany: State University of New York Press.

Gilroy, P. J., Carroll, L., & Murra, J. (2002). A preliminary survey of counseling psychologists' personal experiences with depression and treatment. *Professional Psychology: Research and Practice, 33*, 402–407.

Gilley, J. W., Anderson, S. K., & Gilley, A. (2008). Ethics in human resources. In S. Quatro (Ed.), *Executive ethics: Ethical dilemmas and challenges for the c-suite* (pp. 191–212). Charlotte, NC: Information Age Publishing.

Gilligan, C. (1982). *In a different voice: Psychological theory and women's development.* Cambridge, MA: Harvard University Press.

Gilligan, C. (1993). A reply to critics. In M. J. Larrabee (Ed.), *An ethic of care* (pp. 207–214). New York: Routledge. (Reprinted from *Signs: Journal of Women in Culture and Society, 11*, 324–333, 1986.)

Ginn, R. H., Atkinson, D. R., & Kim, S. J. (1991). Asian–American acculturation, counselor ethnicity and cultural sensitivity, and ratings of counselors. *Journal of Counseling Psychology, 38*, 57–62.

Giovazolias, T., & Davis, P. (2001). How common is sexual attraction to clients? The experiences of sexual attraction of counseling psychologists toward their clients and the impact on the therapeutic process. *Counseling Psychology Quarterly, 14*, 281–286.

Gizara, S. S., & Forrest, L. (2004). Supervisors' experiences of trainee impairment and incompetence at APA-accredited internship sites. *Professional Psychology: Research and Practice, 35*, 131–140.

Glaser, R. D., & Thorpe, J. S. (1986). Unethical intimacy: A survey of sexual contact and advances between psychology educators and female graduate students. *American Psychologist, 41*, 43–51.

Glenn, C. M. (1980). Ethical issues in the practice of child psychotherapy. *Professional Psychology: Research and Practice, 11*, 613–619.

Glosoff, H. L., Corey, G., & Herlihy, B. (2006). Avoiding detrimental multiple relationships. In B. Herlihy & G. Corey (Eds.), *ACA ethical standards casebook* (6th ed., pp. 209–215). Alexandria, VA: American Counseling Association.

Glosoff, H. L., Herlihy, S. B., Herlihy, B., & Spence, E. B. (1997). Privileged communication in the psychologist–client relationship. *Professional Psychology: Research and Practice, 28*, 573–581.

Golann, S. E. (1970). Ethical standards for psychology: Development and revision, 1938–1968. *Annals of the New York Academy of Sciences, 169*, 398–405.

Gold, R. (2007). Evaluating child custody cases: Techniques and maintaining objectivity. In S. Bucky, J. Callan, & G. Stricker (Eds.), *Ethical and legal issues for mental health professionals: In forensic settings.* New York: Haworth Press.

Goldstein, R. L., & Calderone, J. M. (1992). The *Tarasoff* raid: A new extension of the duty to protect. *Bulletin of American Academy of Psychiatry and Law, 20*, 335–342.

Gone, J. P. (2010). Psychotherapy and traditional healing for American Indians: Exploring the prospects for therapeutic integration. *The Counseling Psychologist, 38*(2), 166–235.

Gonsiorek, J. C. (1997). Suggested remediation to "Remediation." *Professional Psychology: Research and Practice, 28*, 300–303.

Gonsiorek, J. C. (2008). Informed consent can solve some confidentiality dilemmas, but others remain. *Professional Psychology: Research and Practice, 39*, 374–375.

Goodman, L. A., Liang, B., Helms, J. E., Latta, R. E., Sparks, E., & Weintraub, S. R. (2004). Training counseling psychologists as social justice agents: Feminist and multicultural principles in action. *The Counseling Psychologist, 32*, 793–837.

Goodman, M., & Teicher, A. (1988). To touch or not to touch. *Psychotherapy, 25*, 492–500.

Goodyear, R. K. (1990). Research on the effects of test interpretation: A review. *The Counseling Psychologist, 18*, 240–257.

Goodyear, R. K. (2007). Toward an effective signature pedagogy for psychology: Comments supporting the case for competent supervisors. *Professional Psychology: Research and Practice, 38*(3), 273–274.

Goodyear, R. K., Crego, C. A., & Johnston, M. W. (1992). Ethical issues in the supervision of student research: A study of critical incidents. *Professional Psychology: Research and Practice, 23*, 203–210.

Goodyear, R. K., & Shumate, J. L. (1996). Perceived effects of therapist self-disclosure of attraction to clients. *Professional Psychology: Research and Practice, 27*, 613–616.

Goodyear, R. K., & Sinnett, E. D. (1984). Current and emerging issues for counseling psychologists. *The Counseling Psychologist, 12*, 87–98.

Gottfredson, L. S. (1988). Reconsidering fairness: A matter of social and ethical priorities. *Journal of Vocational Behavior, 33*, 295–319.

Gottlieb, M. C., Robinson, K., & Younggren, J. N. (2007). Multiple relations in supervision: Guidance for administrators, supervisors, and students. *Professional Psychology, 38*(3), 241–247.

Gottlieb, M. C. (1993). Avoiding exploitative dual relationships: A decision-making model. *Psychotherapy, 30*, 41–47.

Gottlieb, M. D., Handelsman, M. M., & Knapp, S. (2002). *Training ethical psychologists: An acculturation model.* Paper presented at the Annual Meeting of the American Psychological Association (110th), Chicago, IL, August 22–25.

Graham, S. R., & Liddle, B. J. (2009). Multiple relationships encountered by lesbian bisexual psychotherapists: How close is too close? *Professional Psychology: Research and Practice, 40*(1), 15–21.

Gray, P., Froh, R., & Diamond, R. (1992). *A national study of research universities: On the balance between research and undergraduate teaching.* Syracuse, NY: Syracuse University Center for Instructional Development.

Greenberg, A. C. (1992). Florida rejects a *Tarasoff* duty to protect. *Stetson Law Review, 22*, 239–282.

Greenberg, J. (1987). A taxonomy of organizational justice theories. *Academy of Management Review, 12*, 9–22.

Greenberg, S. A., & Shuman, D. W. (1997). Irreconcilable conflict between therapeutic and forensic roles. *Professional Psychology: Research and Practice, 28*, 50–57.

Greenberg, S. A., & Shuman, D. W. (2007). When worlds collide: Therapeutic and forensic roles. *Professional Psychology: Research and Practice, 38*(2), 129–132.

Greenspan, M. (2002). Out of bounds. In A. A. Lazarus & O. Zur (Eds.), *Dual relationships and psychotherapy* (pp. 425–431). New York: Springer.

Grey, L. A., & Harding, A. K. (1988). Confidentiality limits with clients who have the AIDS virus. *Journal of Counseling and Development, 66*, 219–223.

Griggs v. Duke Power Co., 401 U.S. 424 (1971).

Grisso, T. (1987). The economic and scientific future of forensic psychological assessment. *American Psychologist, 42*, 831–839.

Grisso, T., Baldwin, E., Blanck, P. D., Rotheram-Borus, M. J., Schooler, N. R., & Thompson, T. (1991). Standards in research: APA's mechanism for monitoring the challenges. *American Psychologist, 46*, 758–766.

Grisso, T., & Vierling, L. (1978). Minors' consent to treatment: A developmental perspective. *Professional Psychology: Research and Practice, 9*, 412–427.

Grunder, T. M. (1980). On the readability of surgical consent forms. *New England Journal of Medicine, 302*, 900–902.

Gurung, R. A. R., Ansburg, P. I., Alexander, P. A., Lawrence, N. K., & Johnson, D. E. (2008). The state of the scholarship of teaching and learning in psychology. *Teaching of Psychology, 35*, 249–261.

Gustafson, K. E., & McNamara, J. R. (1987). Confidentiality with minor clients: Issues and guidelines for therapists. *Professional Psychology: Research and Practice, 18*, 503–508.

Gutek, B. A. (1989, March). *Sexual harassment: A source of stress for employed women.* Paper presented at the Radcliffe Conference on Women in the 21st century, Cambridge, MA.

Gutheil, T. G., & Gabbard, G. O. (1993). The concept of boundaries in clinical practice: Theoretical and risk-management dimensions. *American Journal of Psychiatry, 150*, 188–196.

Guthman, D., & Sandberg, K. A. (2002). Dual relationships in the Deaf community: When dual relationships are unavoidable and essential. In A. A. Lazarus & O. Zur (Eds.), *Dual relationships and psychotherapy* (pp. 287–297). New York: Springer.

Guy, J. D., Poelstra, P. L., & Stark, M. J. (1989). Personal distress and therapeutic effectiveness: National survey of psychologist practicing psychotherapy. *Professional Psychology: Research and Practice, 20*, 48–50.

Haas, L. J. (1991). Hide-and-seek or show-and-tell? Emerging issues of informed consent. *Ethics and Behavior, 1*, 175–189.

Haas, L. J. (1993). Competence and quality in the performance of forensic psychologists. *Ethics and Behavior, 3*, 251–266.

Haas, L. J., & Malouf, J. L. (1989). *Keeping up the good work: A practitioner's guide to mental health ethics.* Sarasota, FL: Professional Resource Exchange.

Haas, L. J., Malouf, J. L., & Mayerson, N. H. (1986). Ethical dilemmas in psychological practice: Results of a national survey. *Professional Psychology: Research and Practice, 17*, 316–321.

Halfon, M. S. (1989). *Integrity: A philosophical inquiry.* Philadelphia: Temple University Press.

Hall, J. E., & Hare-Mustin, R. T. (1983). Sanctions and the diversity of complaints against psychologists. *American Psychologist, 38*, 714–729.

Hammel, G. A., Olkin, R., & Taube, D. O. (1996). Student-educator sex in clinical and counseling psychology doctoral training. *Professional Psychology: Research and Practice, 27*, 93–97.

Handelsman, M. M. (1987). Informed consent of students: How much information is enough? *Teaching of Psychology, 14*, 107–109.

Handelsman, M. M. (1990). Do written consent forms influence clients' first impressions of therapists? *Professional Psychology: Research and Practice, 21*, 451–454.

Handelsman, M. M., & Galvin, M. D. (1988). Facilitating informed consent for outpatient psychotherapy: A suggested written format. *Professional Psychology: Research and Practice, 19*, 223–225.

Handelsman, M. M., Gottlieb, M. C., & Knapp, S. (2005). Training ethical psychologists: An acculturation model. *Professional Psychology: Research and Practice, 36*(1), 59–65.

Handelsman, M. M., Kemper, M. B., Kesson-Craig, P., McLain, J., & Johnsrud, C. (1986). Use, content, and readability of written informed consent forms for treatment. *Professional Psychology: Research and Practice, 17*, 514–518.

Handelsman, M. M., Martinez, A., Geisendorfer, S., Jordan, L., Wagner, L., Daniel, P. et al. (1995). Does legally mandated consent to psychotherapy ensure ethical appropriateness? The Colorado experience. *Ethics and Behavior, 5*, 119–129.

Handelsman, M. M., Rosen, J., & Arguello, A. (1987). Informed consent of students: How much information is enough? *Teaching of Psychology, 14*, 107–109.

Hansen, J. T. (2008). Neopragmatic thought and counseling values: Reconsidering the role of values in counseling from an alternative perspective. *Counseling and Values, 52*, 100–112.

Hanson, N. D., & Goldberg, S. G. (1999). Navigating the nuances: A matrix of considerations for ethical-legal dilemmas. *Professional Psychology: Research and Practice, 30*, 495–503.

Hardy, C. J. (1994). Nurturing our future through effective mentoring: Developing roots as well as wings. *Journal of Applied Sport Psychology, 6*, 196–204.

Hare, R. (1981). The philosophical basis of psychiatric ethics. In S. Block & P. Chodoff (Eds.), *Psychiatric Ethics* (pp. 31–45). Oxford, England: Oxford University Press.

Hare-Mustin, R. T. (1985). An appraisal of the relationship between women and psychotherapy. *American Psychologist, 38*, 593–601.

Hare-Mustin, R. T., Marecek, J., Kaplan, A. G., & Liss-Levinson, N. (1979). Rights of clients, responsibilities of therapists. *American Psychologist, 34*, 3–16.

Hargrove, D. S. (1986). Ethical issues in rural mental health practice. *Professional Psychology: Research and Practice, 17*, 20–23.

Haspel, K. C., Jorgenson, L. M., Wincze, J. P., & Parsons, J. P. (1997). Legislative intervention regarding therapist sexual misconduct: An overview. *Professional Psychology: Research and Practice, 28*, 63–72.

Haug, I. E. (1999). Boundaries and the use and misuse of power and authority: Ethical complexities for clergy psychotherapists. *Journal of Counseling and Development, 77*, 411–417.

Health Omnibus Program Extension Act of 1988, 242a, 42 U.S.C 301 (d) (1988).

Helbok, C. M. (2003). The practice of psychology in rural communities: Potential ethical dilemmas. *Ethics and Behavior, 13*, 367–384.

Helbok, C. M., Marinelli, R. P., & Walls, R. T. (2006). National survey of ethical practices across rural and urban communities. *Professional Psychology: Research and Practice, 37*(1), 36–44.

Helms, J. E. (1990). *Black and white racial identity: Theory, research, and practice.* New York: Greenwood.

Helms, J. E., & Cook, D. A. (1999). *Using race and culture in counseling and psychotherapy: Theory and process.* Boston: Allyn & Bacon.

Halpern-Felsher, B. L., & Cauffman, E. (2001). Costs and benefits of a decision: Decision-making competence in adolescents and adults. *Applied Developmental Psychology, 22,* 257–273.

Hempelman, K. A. (1994). *Teen legal rights: A guide for the 90's.* Westport, CT: Green-wood.

Hendrix, D. H. (1991). Ethics and intrafamily confidentiality in counseling with children. *Mental Health Counseling, 13,* 323–333.

Herlihy, B., & Corey, G. (2006). *ACA ethical standards casebook* (6th ed.). Alexandria, VA: American Counseling Association.

Herman, D. H. J., & Burris, S. (1993). Torts: Private lawsuits about HIV. In S. Burris, H. L. Dalton, & J. L. Miller (Eds.), *AIDS law today.* New Haven, CT: Yale University Press.

Herron, W. G., & Adlerstein, L. K. (1994). *Psychological Reports, 75,* 723–741.

Hertwig, R., & Ortmann, A. (2008). Deception in experiments: Revising the arguments in its defense. *Ethics & Behavior, 18*(1), 59–92.

Heyd, D., & Bloch, S. (1981). The ethics of suicide. In S. Bloch & P. Chodoff (Eds.), *Psychiatric ethics* (pp. 185–202). Oxford, England: Oxford University Press.

Hill, K. A. (1987). Meta-analysis of paradoxical interventions. *Psychotherapy, 24,* 266–270.

Hillenbrand, E. T., & Claiborn, C. D. (1988). Ethical knowledge exhibited by clients and non-clients. *Professional Psychology: Research and Practice, 19,* 527–531.

Hoagwood, K. (1994). The Certificate of Confidentiality at the National Institute of Mental Health: Discretionary considerations in its applicability in research on child and adolescent mental disorders. *Ethics and Behavior, 4,* 123–131.

Hochhauser, M. (1999). Informed consent and patient's rights documents: A right, a rite, or a Rewrite? *Ethics & Behavior, 9*(1), 1–20.

Hollon, S. D. (1996). The efficacy and effectiveness of psychotherapy relative to medications. *American Psychologist, 51,* 1025–1030.

Holroyd, J. C., & Brodsky, A. M. (1977). Psychologists attitudes and practices regarding erotic and nonerotic physical contact with clients. *American Psychologist, 32,* 843–849.

Holroyd, J. C., & Brodsky, A. M. (1980). Does touching patients lead to sexual intercourse? *Professional Psychology, 11,* 807–811.

Holtzman, W. H. (1960). Some problems defining ethical behavior. *American Psychologist, 15,* 247–250.

Holub, E. A., & Lee, S. S. (1990). Therapists' use of nonerotic physical contact: Ethical concerns. *Professional Psychology: Research and Practice, 21,* 115–117.

Hopkins, J. (1987). Failure of the holding relationship: Some effects of physical rejection on the child's attachment and on his inner experience. *Journal of Child Psychotherapy, 13,* 5–17.

Hopwood v. State of Texas, 861 F. Supp. 551 (W.D. Tex. 1994).

Hopwood v. State of Texas, 78 F.3d 932, 945–948 (5th Cir. 1996).

Hospers, J. (1961). *Human conduct: An introduction to the problems of ethics.* New York: Harcourt, Brace & World.

Housman, L. M., & Stake, J. E. (1999). The current state of sexual ethics training in clinical psychology: Issues of quantity, quality, and effectiveness. *Professional Psychology: Research and Practice, 30*(3), 302–311.

Howard, K. I., Kopta, S. M., Krause, M. S., & Orlinsky, D. E. (1986). The dose effect relationship in psychotherapy. *American Psychologist, 41,* 24–28.

Hubble, M. A., Duncan, B. L., & Miller, S. D. (1999). *The heart and soul of change: What works in therapy.* Washington, DC: American Psychological Association.

Hubble, M. A., Noble, F. C., & Robinson, E. E. (1981). The effects of counselor touch in an initial counseling session. *Journal of Counseling Psychology, 28,* 533–535.

Huber, C. H. (1994). *Ethical, legal, and professional issues in the practice of marriage and family therapy.* New York: Macmillan.

Hunsley, J. (2007). Addressing key challenges in evidence-based practice in psychology. *Professional Psychology: Research and Practice, 38*(2), 113–128.

Hunsley, J., & Lee, C. M. (2006). *Introduction to clinical psychology: An evidence-based approach.* Toronto: Wiley.

Huprich, S. K., & Rudd, M. D. (2004). National survey of trainee impairment in counseling, clinical, and school psychology programs and internship. *Journal of Clinical Psychology, 60,* 43–52.

Individuals with Disabilities Act of 1997, 20 U.S.C. ch. 33, Pub. L. No. 105–117.

Inouye, M. (1997). The diversity justification for affirmative action in higher education: Is *Hopwood v. Texas* right? *Notre Dame Journal of Law, Ethics & Public Policy, 11,* 385–417.

Ivey, A. (1995). Psychotherapy as liberation: Toward specific skills and strategies in multicultural counseling and therapy. In J. Ponterotto, J. Casas, L. Suzuki, & C. Alexander (Eds.), *Handbook of multicultural counseling* (pp. 53–72). Thousand Oaks, CA: Sage.

Ivey, A. E., & Collins, N. M. (2003). Social justice: A long-term challenge for counseling psychology. *The Counseling Psychologist, 31,* 290–298.

Ivey, A. E., D'Andrea, M., Bradford Ivey, M., & Simek-Morgan, L. (2002). *Theories of counseling and psychotherapy: A multicultural perspective* (5th ed.). Boston: Allyn & Bacon.

Jaffee v. Redmond, 51f.3d 1346. (7th Cir. 1995).

Jaffee v. Redmond, 518 U.S. 1 (1996).

Jacob, S., & Hartshorne, T. (1991). *Ethics and law for school psychologists.* Brandon, VT: Clinical Psychology Publishing.

Jahoda, G. (1988). J'accuse. In M. H. Bond (Ed.), *The cross-cultural challenge to social psychology* (pp. 86–95). Newbury Park, CA: Sage.

Jennings, F. L. (1992). Ethics of rural practice. *Psychotherapy in Private Practice, 10,* 85–104.

Jensen, A. R. (1980). *Bias in mental testing.* New York: The Free Press.

Jensen, G. A., Morrisey, M. A., Gaffney, S., & Liston, D. (1997). The new dominance of managed care: Insurance trends in the 1990s. *Health Affairs, 16,* 125–136.

Jensen, R. E. (1979). Competent professional service in psychology: The real issue behind continuing education. *Professional Psychology, 10,* 381–388.

Jerrel, J. M. (1995). The effects of client-counselor match on service use and costs. *Administration and Policy in Mental Health, 23,* 119–126.

Jimenez, J. (2002). The history of grandmothers in the African American community. *Social Service Review, 76,* 523–551.

Johnson, M. (1986). Paradoxical interventions. From repugnance to cautious curiosity. *The Counseling Psychologist, 14,* 297–302.

Johnson, W. B. (2002). The intentional mentor: Strategies and guidelines for the practice of mentoring. *Professional Psychology: Research and Practice, 33,* 88–96.

Johnson, W. B. (2003). A framework for conceptualizing competence to mentor. *Ethics and Behavior, 13,* 127–151.

Johnson, W. B. (2008). Can psychologists find a way to stop the hot potato game? *Professional Psychology: Research and Practice, 39*(6), 589–599.

Johnson, W. B., Koch, C., Fallow, G. O., & Huwe, J. M. (2000). Prevalence of mentoring in clinical versus experimental doctoral programs: Survey findings, implications and recommendations. *Psychotherapy, 37,* 325–334.

Johnson, W. B., & Nelson, N. (1999). Mentor-protégé relationships in graduate training: Some ethical concerns. *Ethics and Behavior, 9*(3), 189–210.

Johnson, M. E., Fisher, D. G., & Davis, D. C. (1996). Assessing reading level of drug users for HIV and AIDS prevention purposes. *AIDS Education and Prevention, 8,* 323–334.

Johnson-Greene, D. (2007). Evolving standards for informed consent: Is it time for an individualized and flexible approach? *Professional Psychology: Research and Practice, 38*(2), 183–184.

Jones, E. (1961). *The life and work of Sigmund Freud.* New York: Basic Books.

Jorden, A. E., & Meara, N. M. (1990). Ethics and the professional practice of psychologists. *Professional Psychology: Research and Practice, 21,* 107–114.

Jorgenson, L. M. (1994, August). *Legal liability, licensing, and malpractice insurance considerations.* Paper presented at the 102nd Annual Convention of the American Psychological Association, Los Angeles, CA.

Jorgenson, L. M., Randles, R., & Strasburger, L. H. (1991). The furor over psychotherapist-patient sexual contact: New solutions to old problems. *William & Mary Law Review, 32,* 645–733.

Joseph, A. (1977). *Intelligence, IQ, and race—When, how, and why they became associated.* San Francisco: R & E Research Associates.

Jourard, S., & Friedman, R. (1970). Experimenter-subject distance and self-disclosure. *Journal of Personality and Social Psychology, 4,* 278–281.

Kadushin, C. (1969). *Why people go to psychiatrists.* New York: Atherton.

Kahneman, D., & Tversky, A. (1984). Choices, values and frames. *American Psychologist, 39,* 341–350.

Kain, C. D. (1988). To breach or not to breach: Is that the question? A response to Gray and Harding. *Journal of Counseling and Development, 66,* 224–225.

Kalichman, S. C. (1993). *Mandated reporting of suspected child abuse: Ethics, law, & policy.* Washington, DC: American Psychological Association.

Kamin, L. (1974). *The science and politics of IQ.* Hillsdale, NJ: Lawrence Erlbaum Associates.

Karon, B. P. (1995). Provision of psychotherapy under managed health care: A growing crisis and national nightmare. *Professional Psychology: Research and Practice, 26,* 5–9.

Karpel, M. A. (1980). Family secrets: I. Conceptual and ethical issues in the relational context. II: Ethical and practical considerations in therapeutic management. *Family Process, 19,* 295–306.

Kaser-Boyd, N., Adelman, H. S., & Taylor, L. (1985). *Professional Psychology: Research and Practice, 16,* 411–417.

Kaslow, N. J., Rubin, N. J., Bebeau, M. J., Leigh, I. W., Lichtenberg, J. W., Nelson, P. D., et al. (2007a). Guiding principles and recommendations for the assessment of competence. *Professional Psychology: Research and Practice, 38*(5), 441–451.

Kaslow, N. J., Rubin, N. J., Forrest, L., Elman, N. S., Van Horne, B. A., Jacobs, S. C., et al. (2007b). Recognizing, assessing, and intervening with problems of professional competence. *Professional Psychology: Research and Practice, 38*(5), 479–492.

Katz, I., Mass, R. G., Parisi, N., Astone, J., McEvaddy, D., & Lucido, D. J. (1987). Lay peoples and health care personnel's perceptions of cancer, AIDS, cardiac, and diabetic patients. *Psychological Reports, 60,* 615–629.

Katz, J. H. (1985). The sociopolitical nature of counseling. *The Counseling Psychologist, 13,* 615–624.

Keith-Spiegel, P. (1994). Teaching psychologists and the new APA Ethics Code: Do we fit in? *Professional Psychology: Research and Practice, 25,* 362–368.

Keller, H. B., & Lee, S. (2003). Ethical issues surrounding human participants research using the Internet. *Ethics and Behavior, 13*(3), 211–220.

Kelman, H. C. (1972). The rights of the subject in social research: An analysis in terms of relative power and legitimacy. *American Psychologist, 27,* 989–1016.

Kertesz, R. (2002). Dual relationships in psychotherapy in Latin America. In A. A. Lazarus & O. Zur (Eds.), *Dual relationships and psychotherapy* (pp. 329–334). New York: Springer.

Kessler, L. E., & Waehler, C. A. (2005). Addressing multiple relationships between clients and therapists in lesbian, gay, bisexual and transgender communities. *Professional Psychology: Research and Practice, 36*(1), 66–72.

Kier, F. J., & Davenport, D. S. (1997). Ramifications of *Hopwood v. Texas* on the process of applicant selection in APA-accredited professional psychology programs. *Professional Psychology: Research and Practice, 28,* 486–491.

Kilburg, R. R. (1986). The distressed professional: The nature of the problem. In R. R. Kilburg, P. E. Nathan, & R. W. Thoreson (Eds.), *Professional in distress: Issues, syndromes, and solutions in psychology* (pp. 13–26). Washington, DC: American Psychological Association.

Kimmel, A. J. (2001). Ethical trends in marketing and psychological research. *Ethics and Behavior, 11,* 131–149.

King, P. M. (1986). Formal reasoning in adults: A review and critique. In R. A. Mines & K. S. Kitchener (Eds.), *Adult cognitive development* (pp. 1–21). New York: Praeger.

King, P. M., & Kitchener, K. S. (1994). *Developing reflective judgment: Understanding and promoting intellectual growth and critical thinking in adolescents and adults.* San Francisco: Jossey-Bass.

King, P. M., & Kitchener, K. S. (2002). The reflective judgment model: Twenty years of research. In B. K. Hofer & P. R. Pintrich (Eds.), *Personal Epistemology: The Psychology of Beliefs about Knowledge and Knowing.* Lawrence Erlbaum: Mahwah, N.J.

Kirschstein, R. (2000). Insurance parity for mental health: Cost, access, and quality.

Kitchener, K. S. (1984a). Ethics and counseling psychology: Distinctions and directions. *The Counseling Psychologist, 12,* 15–18.

Kitchener, K. S. (1984b). Intuition, critical evaluation and ethical principles: The foundation for ethical decisions in counseling psychology. *The Counseling Psychologist, 12,* 43–55.

Kitchener, K. S. (1988). Dual role relationships: What makes them so problematic? *Journal of Counseling and Development, 67,* 217–221.

Kitchener, K. S. (1992). Psychologist as teacher and mentor: Affirming ethical values throughout the curriculum. *Professional Psychology: Research and Practice, 23,* 190–195.

Kitchener, K. S. (1992a). Posttherapy relationships: Ever or never? In B. Herlihy & G. Corey (Eds.), *Dual relationships in counseling* (pp. 145–148). Alexandria, VA: American Association for Counseling and Development.

Kitchener, K. S. (1992b). Psychologist as teacher and mentor: Affirming ethical values throughout the curriculum. *Professional Psychology: Research and Practice, 23,* 190–195.

Kitchener, K. S. (1994). Doing good well—The wisdom behind ethical supervision. *Counseling & Human Development, 26*(9), 1–8.

Kitchener, K. S. (1996a). Professional codes of ethics and on-going moral problems in psychology. In W. O'Donahue & R. F. Kitchener (Eds.), *The philosophy of psychology* (pp. 361–370). Thousand Oaks, CA: Sage.

Kitchener, K. S. (1996b, December). The science of psychology with and without virtue. In J. D. Day (Chair), *Considering character: Science, practice and policies.* Symposium conducted to celebrate the appointment of N. M. Meara to The Nancy Reeves Dreux chair of psychology, University of Notre Dame, Notre Dame, IN.

Kitchener, K. S. (1996c). There is more to ethics than principles. *The Counseling Psychologist, 24,* 92–97.

Kitchener, K. S. (1999). *Reconceptualizing responsibilities to students: A feminist perspective.* In M. Brabeck (Ed.), *Feminist ethics.* Washington, DC: American Psychological Association.

Kitchener, K. S., & Anderson, S. K. (2000). Ethical problems in counseling psychology: Old themes— New issues. In S. D. Brown & R. W. Lent (Eds.), *Handbook of counseling psychology* (3rd ed.). New York: Wiley.

Kitchener, K. S., & Barret, B. (2001). Thinking well about doing good in HIV-related practice: A model of ethical analysis. In J. R. Anderson & B. Barret (Eds.), *Ethics in HIV-related psychotherapy.* Washington, DC: American Psychological Association.

Kitchener, K. S., King, P. M., & DeLuca, S. (2006). Development of reflective judgment in adulthood. In C. Hoare (Ed.), *Handbook of Adult Development and Learning.* New York: Oxford.

Kitchener, K. S., & Kitchener, R. F. (1981). The development of natural rationality: Can formal operations account for it? In J. Meacham & M. R. Santilli (Eds.), *Contributions to human development: Social development in youth: Structure and content.* (Vol. 5, pp. 160–181). Basel, Switzerland: Karger.

Kitchener, K. S., & Kitchener, R. F. (2009). Social science research ethics: Historical and philosophical issues. In D. M. Mertens & P. E. Gingsberg (Eds.), *Handbook of Social Science Research Ethics* (pp. 5–22) Thousand Oaks, CA: Sage.

Kitchener, R. F. (1980). Ethical relativism and behavior therapy. *Journal of Consulting and Clinical Psychology, 48,* 1–7.

Kleespies, P. M., Smith, M. R., & Becker, B. R. (1990). Psychology interns as patient suicide survivors: Incidence, impact, and recovery. *Professional Psychology: Research and Practice, 21,* 257–263.

Knapp, S., Gottlieb, M., Berman, J., & Handelsman, M. M. (2007). When laws and ethics collide: What should psychologists do? *Professional Psychology: Research and Practice, 38,* 54–59.

Knapp, S., & VandeCreek, L. (1990). Application of the duty to protect HIV-positive patients. *Professional Psychology: Research and Practice, 21,* 161–166.

Knapp, S., & VandeCreek, L. (2001). Ethical issues in personality assessment in forensic psychology. *Journal of Personality Assessment, 77*(2), 242–254.

Knapp, S., & VandeCreek, L. (2003). An overview of the major changes in the 2002 APA ethics code. *Professional Psychology: Research and Practice, 34*(3), 301–308.

Knapp, S., & VandeCreek, L. D. (2006). *Practical ethics for psychologists: A positive approach.* Washington, DC: American Psychological Association.

Knapp, S., & VandeCreek, L. (2007). When values of different cultures conflict: Ethical decision making in a multicultural context. *Professional Psychology: Research and Practice, 38,* 660–666.

Knapp, S., VandeCreek, L., & Fulero, S. (1993). The attorney-psychologist-client privilege in judicial proceedings. *Psychotherapy in Private Practice, 12,* 1–15.

Kohlberg, L. (1971). From is to ought: How to commit the naturalistic fallacy and get away with it in the study of moral development. In T. Mischel (Ed.), *Cognitive development and epistemology* (pp. 151–235). New York: Academic Press.

Kohlberg, L. (1984). *The psychology of moral development: The nature and validation of moral stages.* San Francisco: Harper & Row.

Kohler, J. (2005, June 1). Attorney, therapist fighting subpoena in court-martial. *Associated Press.*

Kolbert, J. B., Morgan, B., & Brendel, J. M. (2002). Faculty and student perceptions of dual relationships within counselor education: A qualitative analysis. *Counselor Education and Supervision, 41,* 193–206.

Koocher, G. P. (1994). The commerce of professional psychology and the new Ethics Code. *Professional Psychology: Research and Practice, 25,* 355–361.

Koocher, G. P. (1995). Ethics in psychotherapy. In B. Bongar & L. E. Beutler (1995). *Comprehensive textbook of psychotherapy: Theory and practice.* New York: Oxford University Press.

Koocher, G. P. (2008). Ethical challenges in mental health services to children and families. *Journal of Clinical Psychology: In Session, 64,* 601–612.

Koocher, G. P., & Keith-Spiegel, P. C. (1990). *Children, ethics & the law: Professional issues and cases.* Lincoln: University of Nebraska Press.

Koocher, G. P., & Keith-Spiegel, P. C. (2008). *Ethics in psychology and the mental health professions: Standards and cases* (3rd ed.). New York: Oxford University Press.

Korenman, S. G. (1993). Conflicts of interest and the communication of research. *Academic Medicine, 68,* S18–S22.

Korman, M. (1974). National conference on levels and patterns of professional training in psychology: The major themes. *American Psychologist, 29,* 441–449.

Koss, M. P., & Burkhart, B. R. (1989). A conceptual analysis of rape victimization. *Psychology of Women Quarterly, 13,* 27–40.

Koss, M. P., & Shiang, J. (1994). Research on brief therapy. In A. E. Bergin & S. L. Garfield (Eds.), *Handbook of psychotherapy and behavior change* (4th ed., pp. 664–700). New York: Wiley.

Kovacs, A. L. (1984). The increasing malpractice exposure of psychologists. *The Independent Practitioner, 4*(2), 12–14.

Kozlowski, N. F., Rupert, P. A., & Crawford, I. (1998). Psychotherapy with HIV-infected clients: Factors influencing notification of third parties. *Psychotherapy, 35,* 105–115.

Krausz, M., & Meiland, J. W. (Eds.). (1982). *Relativism: Cognitive and moral.* Notre Dame, IN: University of Notre Dame Press.

Krishnamurthy, R., VandeCreek, L., Kaslow, N. J., Tazeau, Y. N., Miville, M. L., Kerns, R. et al. (2004). Achieving competency in psychological assessment: Directions for education and training. *Journal of Clinical Psychology, 60*(7), 725–739.

Kutz, S. I. (1986). Defining "impaired psychologist." *American Psychologist, 41,* 220.

Ladany, N. (2002). Psychotherapy supervision: How dressed is the emperor? *Psychotherapy Bulletin, 37*(4), 14–18.

LaFromboise, T. D., & Foster, S. L. (1989). Ethics in multicultural counseling. In P. Pedersen, J. Draguns, W. Lonner, & J. Trimble (Eds.), *Counseling across cultures* (3rd ed., pp. 115–136). Honolulu: University of Hawaii Press.

Lake, P. (1995). Virginia is not safe for "lovers": The Virginia Supreme Court rejects *Tarasoff* in *Nasser v. Parker. Brooklyn Law Review, 61,* 1285–1298.

Lakeman, R., & FitzGerald, M. (2009). The ethics of suicide research: The views of ethics committee members. *Crisis, 30,* 13–19.

Lakin, M. (1988). *Ethical issues in the psychotherapies.* Oxford, England: Oxford University Press.

Lakin, M. (1994). Morality in group and family therapies: Multiperson therapies and the 1992 Ethics Code. *Professional Psychology: Research and Practice, 25,* 344–348.

Laliotis, D. A., & Grayson, J. H. (1985). Psychologist heal thyself: What is available for the impaired psychologist? *American Psychologist, 40,* 84–89.

Lamb, D. H., & Cantazaro, S. J. (1998). Sexual and nonsexual boundary violations involving psychologists, clients, supervisees and students: Implications for professional practice. *Professional Psychology: Research and Practice, 29,* 498–503.

Lamb, D. H., Catanzaro, S. J., & Moorman, A. S. (2003). Psychologists reflect on their sexual relationships with clients, supervisees, and students: Occurrence, impact, rationales, and collegial intervention. *Professional Psychology: Research and Practice, 34*(1), 102–107.

Lamb, D. H., Catanzaro, S. J., & Moorman, A. S. (2004). A preliminary look at how psychologists identify, evaluate, and proceed when faced with multiple relationship dilemmas. *Professional Psychology: Research and Practice, 35*(3), 248–254.

Lamb, D. H., Clark, C., Drumheller, P., Frizzell, K., & Surrey, L. (1989). Applying *Tarasoff* to AIDS related psychotherapy issues. *Professional Psychology: Research and Practice, 20,* 37–43.

Lamb, D. H., Strand, K. K., Woodburn, J. R., Buchko, K. J., Lewis, J. T., & Kang, J. R. (1994). Sexual and business relationships between therapists and former clients. *Psychotherapy: Theory, Research, Practice, and Training, 31,* 270–277.

Lambert, M. J., & Ogles, B. M. (2004). The efficacy and effectiveness of psychotherapy. In M. J. Lambert (Ed.), *Bergin and Garfield's handbook of psychotherapy and behavior change* (5th ed., pp. 139–193). New York: Wiley.

Lambert, M. J., Garfield, S. L., & Bergin, A. E. (2004). The effectiveness of psychotherapy. In M. J. Lambert (Ed.), *Bergin and Garfield's handbook of psychotherapy and behavior change* (5th ed., pp. 139–193). New York: Wiley.

Lambert, M. J., Whipple, J. L., Hawkins, E. J., Vermeersch, D. A., Nielsen, S. L., & Smart, D. W. (2003). Is it time for clinicians to routinely track patient outcome? A meta-analysis. *Clinical Psychology: Science and Practice, 10,* 288–301.

Lane, P. J., & Spruill, J. (1980). To tell or not to tell: The psychotherapist's dilemma. *Psychotherapy: Theory, Research and Practice, 17*, 202–209.

Langer, C. L. (2011). How I got my wings. In S. K. Anderson & V. A. Middleton, (Eds.), *Explorations in diversity: Examining privilege and oppression in a multicultural society* (2nd ed.), (pp. 121–128). Belmont, CA: Thomson Brooks/Cole Cengage Learning.

Lantz, P., House, J. S., Lepkowski, J. M., Williams, D. R., Mero, R. P., & Chen, M. J. (1998). Socioeconomic factors, health behaviors, and mortality: Results from and nationally representative prospective study of US adults. *JAMA: Journal of the American Medical Association, 279*, 1703–1714.

LaPuma, J., Schiedermayer, D., & Seigler, M. (1995). Ethical issues in managed care. *Trends in Health Care, Law & Ethics, 10*(1–2), 73–77.

LaRoche, M. J., & Turner, C. (2002). At the crossroads: Managed mental health care, the ethics code, and ethnic minorities. *Cultural Diversity and Ethnic Minority Psychology, 8*(3), 187–198.

Larrabee, M. J. (Ed.). (1993). *An ethic of care: Feminist and interdisciplinary perspectives.* New York: Routledge.

Larry P. v. Wilson Riles, 343 F. Supp. 1306 (N.D. Cal. 1972) (preliminary injunction). aff'd 502 F.2d 963 (9th Cir. 1974): No. C-71-2270 RF P (N.D. Cal. 1979).

Lawrence, G., & Kurpius, S. E. R. (2000). Legal and ethical issues involved when counseling minors in nonschool settings. *Journal of Counseling and Development, 78*, 130–136.

Layman, M. J., & McNamara, J. R. (1997). Remediation for ethics violations: Focus on psychotherapists' sexual contact with clients. *Professional Psychology: Research and Practice, 28*, 281–292.

Lazarus, A. A. (1994). How certain boundaries and ethics diminish therapeutic effectiveness. *Ethics and Behavior, 4*, 253–261.

Lazarus, A. A. (2006). Transcending boundaries in psychotherapy. In B. Herlihy & G. Corey (Eds.), *Boundary issues in counseling: Multiple roles and responsibilities* (2nd ed., pp. 16–19). Alexandria, VA: American Counseling Association.

Lazarus, A. A., & Zur, O. (2002). *Dual relationships and psychotherapy.* New York: Springer.

Lee, R. M., & Renzetti, C. M. (1992a). *Researching sensitive topics.* Newbury Park, CA: Sage.

Lee, R. M., & Renzetti, C. M. (1992b). *Socially sensitive research.* Newbury Park, CA: Sage.

Leland, J. (1976). Invasion of the body. *Psychotherapy: Theory, Research and Practice, 13*, 214–218.

Lens, V. (2000). Protecting the confidentiality of the therapeutic relationship: *Jaffee v. Redmond. Social Work, 45*, 273–276.

Lerman, H., & Porter, N. (1990). The contribution of feminism to ethics in psychotherapy. In H. Lerman & N. Porter (Eds.), *Feminist ethics in psychotherapy* (pp. 5–13). New York: Springer.

Lerner, B. (1989). Intelligence and the laws. In R. Linn (Ed.), *Intelligence: Measurement, theory and public policy* (pp. 172–192). Urbana: University of Illinois Press.

Lerner, G. (1993). *The creation of feminist consciousness.* New York: Oxford University Press.

Levine, R. J. (1988). *Ethics and regulation of clinical research.* New Haven, CT: Yale University Press.

Lewis, C. C. (1981). How adolescents approach decisions: Changes over grades seven to twelve and policy implications. *Child Development, 52*, 538–544.

Lewis, J., Arnold, M. S., House, R., & Toporek, R. (2003). Advocacy competencies [Electronic version]. Retrieved Jan. 10, 2010 from http://counseling.org/Publications

Lichtenberg, J. W. (2007). What makes for effective supervision? In search of clinical outcomes. *Professional Psychology: Research and Practice, 38*(3), 275.

Lin, K., Inui, T. S., Kleinman, A. M., & Womack, W. M. (1982). Sociocultural determinants of the help-seeking behavior of patients with mental illness. *Journal of Nervous and Mental Disease, 170*, 78–85.

Liss, M. B. (1994). Child abuse: Is there a mandate for researchers to report? *Ethics and Behavior, 4*, 133–146.

Loftus, E. F. (1986). Experimental psychologist as advocate or impartial educator. *Law & Human Behavior, 10*, 68–78.

Loganbill, C., Hardy, E., & Delworth, U. (1983). Supervision: A conceptual model. *The Counseling Psychologist, 10*, 3–42.

Lubin, B., Hornstra, R. K., Lewis, R. V., & Bechtel, B. S. (1973). Correlates of initial treatment assignment in a community mental health center. *Archives of General Psychiatry, 29*, 497–504.

MacIntyre, A. (1981). *After virtue.* Notre Dame, IN: University of Notre Dame Press.

Macklin, R. (1982). Refusal of psychiatric treatment: Autonomy, competence, and paternalism. In R. B. Edwards (Ed.), *Psychiatry and ethics* (pp. 331–390). Buffalo, NY: Prometheus Books.

Macklin, R. (1995). The ethics of managed care. *Trends in Health Care, Law & Ethics, 10*(1–2), 63–66.

MacNair, R. R. (1992). Ethical dilemmas of child abuse reporting: Implications for mental health counselors. *Journal of Mental Health Counseling, 14,* 127–136.

Maeder, T. (1989, January). Wounded healers. *The Atlantic Monthly,* pp. 37–47.

Mahoney, M. J. (1997). Psychotherapists' personal problems and self-care patterns. *Professional Psychology; Research and Practice, 28,* 14–16.

Mangalmurti, V. S. (1994). Psychotherapists' fear of *Tarasoff:* All in the mind? *Journal of Psychiatry and Law, 22,* 379–409.

Mann, L., Harmoni, R., & Power, C. (1989). Adolescent decision-making: The development of competence. *Journal of Adolescence, 12,* 265–278.

Mann, T. (1994). Informed consent for psychological research: Do subjects comprehend consent forms and understand their legal rights? *Psychological Science, 5,* 140–143.

Maramba, G. G., & Hall, G. C. N. (2002). Meta-analysis of ethnic match as a predictor of dropout, utilization, and level of functioning. *Cultural Diversity and Ethnic Minority Psychology, 8,* 290–297.

Marecek, J. (1995). Gender, politics, and psychology's ways of knowing. *American Psychologist, 50,* 162–163.

Margolin, G. (1982). Ethical and legal considerations in marital and family therapy. *American Psychologist, 37,* 788–801.

Margolin, G., Chien, D., Duman, S. E., Fauchier, A., Gordis, E. B., Oliver, P. et al. (2005). Ethical issues in couple and family research. *Journal of Family Psychology, 19,* 157–167.

Marsh, D. T. (1995, January). Confidentiality and the rights of families: Resolving potential conflicts. *The Pennsylvania Psychologist Update,* pp. 1–3.

Marsh, R. (2005). Evidence-based practice for education? *Educational Psychology, 25,* 701–704.

Masters, W. H., & Johnson, V. E. (1966). *Human sexual response.* New York: Bantam.

Masters, W. H., & Johnson, V. E. (1970). *Human sexual inadequacy.* New York: Bantam.

Masters, W. H., & Johnson, V. E. (1975, May). *Principles of the new sex therapy.* Paper presented at the annual meeting of the American Psychiatric Association, Anaheim, CA.

Matarazzo, J. D. (1986). Computerized clinical psychological test interpretations: Unvalidated plus all mean and no sigma. *American Psychologist, 41,* 14–24.

Mathews, L. L., & Gerrity, D. A. (2002). Therapists; use of boundaries in sexual abuse groups: An exploratory study. *Journal for Specialists in Group Work, 27,* 78–91.

May, W. W. (1990). *Ethics and higher education.* New York: Macmillan.

McAdams, C. R., & Foster, V. A. (2000). Client suicide: Its frequency and impact on counselors. *Journal of Mental Health Counseling, 22,* 107–121.

McCabe, O. L. (2004). Crossing the quality chasm in behavioral health care: The role of evidence-based practice. *Professional Psychology: Research & Practice, 35*(6), 571–579.

McCartney, J. (1966). Overt transference. *Journal of Sex Research, 2,* 227–237.

McGaha, A. C., & Korn, J. H. (1995). The emergence of interest in the ethics of psychological research with humans. *Ethics and Behavior, 5,* 147–160.

McGuire, J., Nieri, D., Abbot, D., Sheridan, K., & Fisher, R. (1995). Do *Tarasoff* principles apply in AIDS-related psychotherapy? Ethical decision making and the role of therapist homophobia and perceived client dangerousness. *Professional Psychology: Research and Practice, 26,* 608–611.

McHugh, M. C., Koeske, R. D., & Frieze, I. H. (1986). Issues to consider in conducting nonsexist psychological research: A guide for researchers. *American Psychologist, 41,* 879–890.

Meara, N. M., & Day, J. D. (2003). Possibilities and challenges for academic psychology: Uncertain science, interpretative conversation, and virtuous community. *American Behavioral Scientist, 47*(4), 459–478.

Meara, N. M., & Schmidt, L. D. (1991). The ethics of researching counseling/therapy processes. In C. E. Watkins, Jr., & L. J. Schneider (Eds.), *Research in counseling* (pp. 237–258). Hillsdale, NJ: Lawrence Erlbaum Associates.

Meara, N. M., Schmidt, L. D., & Day, J. D. (1996). Principles and virtues: A foundation for ethical decisions, policies and character. *The Counseling Psychologist, 24,* 4–77.

Megargee, E. L. (1997). *Megargee's guide to obtaining a psychology internship* (3rd ed.). Washington, DC: Accelerated Development.

Melton, G. B. (1988). Ethical and legal issues in AIDS-related practice. *American Psychologist, 43,* 941–947.

Messick, S. (1995). Validity of psychological assessment: Validation of inferences from persons' responses and performances as scientific inquiry into score meaning. *American Psychologist, 50,* 741–749.

Milgram, S. (1974). *Obedience to authority.* New York: Harper & Row.

Miller, D. J., & Thelen, M. H. (1986). Knowledge and beliefs about confidentiality in psychotherapy. *Professional Psychology: Research and Practice, 17*, 15–19.

Miller, G. M., & Larrabee, M. J. (1995). Sexual intimacy in counselor education and supervision: A national survey. *Counselor Education and Supervision, 34*, 332–343.

Miller, I. J. (1996a). Ethical and liability issues concerning invisible rationing. *Professional Psychology: Research and Practice, 27*, 583–587.

Miller, I. J. (1996b). Managed care is harmful to outpatient mental health services: A call for accountability. *Professional Psychology: Research and Practice, 27*, 349–363.

Miller, I. J. (1996c). Time-limited brief therapy has gone too far: The result is invisible rationing. *Professional Psychology: Research and Practice, 27*, 567–576.

Miller, R. H., & Luft, H. S. (1994). Managed care plan performance since 1980: A literature analysis. *JAMA: Journal of the American Medical Association, 271*, 1512–1519.

Miller, V. A., Drotar, D., & Kodish, E. (2004). Children's competence for assent and consent: A review of empirical findings. *Ethics & Behavior, 14*(3), 255–295.

Miller, V., Drotar, D., Burant, C., & Kodish, E. (2005). Clinician-parent communication during informed consent for pediatric leukemia trails. *Journal of Pediatric Psychology, 30*, 219–229.

Misra, D. (Ed.). (2001). *Women's health databook: A profile of women's health in the United States* (3rd ed.). Washington, DC: Jacobs Institute of Women's Health and the Henry J. Kaiser Family Foundation.

Misra, S. (1992). Is conventional debriefing adequate? An ethical issue in consumer research. *Journal of the Academy of Marketing Science, 20*, 269–273.

Mitchum, N. T. (1987). Developmental play therapy: A treatment approach for child victims of sexual molestation. *Journal of Counseling and Development, 65*, 320–321.

Moleski, S. M., & Kiselica, M. S. (2005). Dual relationships: A continuum ranging from the destructive to the therapeutic. *Journal of Counseling and Development, 83*, 3–11.

Montgomery, S. (1997). *Ethical guidelines for teaching assistants in counseling psychology training programs.* Unpublished manuscript. University of Denver.

Monshi, B., & Zieglmayer, V. (2004). The problem of privacy in transcultural research: Reflections on an ethnographic study in Sri Lanka. *Ethics & Behavior, 14*(3), 305–312.

Morrissey, J. (2005). Training supervision: Professional and ethical considerations. In R. Tribe & J. Morrissey (Eds.), *Handbook of professional and ethical practice for psychologists, counselors and psychotherapists* (pp. 303–316). New York: Brunner-Routledge.

Morrison, C. F. (1989). AIDS: Ethical implications for psychological intervention. *Professional Psychology: Research and Practice, 30*, 166–171.

Morrow, S. L. (2000). First do no harm: Therapist issues in psychotherapy with lesbian, gay, and bisexual clients. In R. M. Perez, K. A. DeBord, & K. J. Bieschke (Eds.), *Handbook of counseling and psychotherapy with lesbian, gay, and bisexual clients* (pp. 137–156). Washington, DC: American Psychological Association.

Murphy, K. R., & Davidshofer, C. O. (2004). *Psychological testing: Principles and applications* (6th ed.). Englewood Cliffs, NJ: Prentice-Hall.

Murray, B. (1998, December). The authorship dilemma: Who gets authorship for what? *APA Monitor,* pp. 1, 31.

Murray, H., Gillese, E., Lennon, M., Mercer, P., & Robinson, M. (1996, December). Ethical principles for college and university teaching. *AAHE Bulletin,* pp. 1–6.

Musca, T. (Producer), & Menendez, R. (Director). (1988). Stand and deliver [Motion picture]. U.S.: Warner Brothers.

Nagy, T. F. (1987, August–September). *Consumer information about psychological decisions.* Paper presented at the 95th Annual Convention of the American Psychological Association, New York, NY.

Nagy, T. F. (2000). *Ethics in plain English: A practical guide for psychologists.* Washington DC: American Psychological Association.

Nathan, P. E. (1986). Unanswered questions about distressed professionals. In R. R. Kilburg, P. E. Nathan, & R. W. Thoreson (Eds.), *Professionals in distress: Issues, syndromes, and solutions in psychology* (pp. 27–36). Washington, DC: American Psychological Association.

Nathan, P. E. (1998). Practice guidelines: Not yet ideal. *American Psychologist, 53*, 290–299.

National Academy of Sciences. (1995). *On being a scientist: Responsible conduct in research.* Washington, DC: National Academy Press.

National Advisory Mental Health Council. (1993). Health care reform for Americans with severe mental illnesses: Report of the National Advisory Mental health Council. *American Journal of Psychiatry, 150,* 1447–1465.

National Advisory Mental Health Council. (1997). *Parity in coverage of mental health services in an era of managed care: An interim report to Congress by the National Advisory Mental Health Council.* Washington, DC: U.S. Department of Health and Human Services.

National Advisory Mental Health Council. (1998). *Parity in financing mental health services: Managed care effects on cost, access, and quality: An interim report to Congress by the National Advisory Mental Health Council.* Washington, DC: U.S. Department of Health and Human Services.

National Association of Social Workers. (2008). *Code of ethics.* Silver Spring, MD: Author.

National Commission for the Protection of Human Subjects of Biomedical and Behavioral Research. (1978a). *The Belmont Report: Ethical principles and guidelines for the protection of human subjects of research* (DHEW Publication No. OS 78–0012). Washington, DC: Government Printing Office.

National Commission for the Protection of Human Subjects of Biomedical and Behavioral Research. (1978b). Institutional review boards: Report and recommendations. *Federal Register, 43,* 56174–56198.

National Institutes of Health. (2003, July 21). *Frequently asked questions of Certificates of Confidentiality.* Retrieved August 1, 2009 from http://grants2.nih.gov/grants/policy/coc/faqs.htm

Navin, S., Beamish, P., & Johnson, G. (1995). Ethical practices of field-based mental health counselor supervisors. *Journal of Mental Health Counseling, 17,* 243–253.

Neimark, E. D. (1982). Adolescent thought: Transition to formal operations. In B. B. Wolman (Ed.), *Handbook of developmental psychology* (pp. 486–502). Englewood Cliffs: NJ: Prentice-Hall.

Newcomer, K. (1990, October 4). Female therapist faces sex charges. *Rocky Mountain News,* local section, p.7.

Newman, A. (1981). Ethical issues in the supervision of psychotherapy. *Psychiatric Forum, 15,* 61–64.

Newman, D. L., & Brown, R. D. (1996). *Applied ethics for program evaluation.* Thousand Oaks, CA: Sage.

Nickel, M. B. (2004). Professional boundaries: The dilemma of dual and multiple relations in rural clinical practice. *Counseling and Clinical Psychology, 1*(1), 17–22.

Nicolai, K. M., & Scott, N. A. (1994). Provision of confidentiality information and its relation to child abuse reporting. *Professional Psychology: Research and Practice, 25,* 154–160.

Nigro, T. (2004). Dual relationships in counseling: A survey of British Columbian counselors. *Canadian Journal of Counseling, 38,* 36–53.

Noddings, N. (1984). *Caring: A feminine approach to ethics and moral education.* Berkeley: University of California Press.

Noel, B., & Watterson, K. (1992). *You must be dreaming,* New York: Poseidon Press.

Noel, M. M. (2008). Sexual misconduct by psychologists: Who reports it? *Dissertation Abstracts International, 68B,* 5975.

Norcross, J. C., Strausser-Kirtland, D., & Missar, C. D. (1988). The processes and outcomes of psychotherapists' personal treatment experiences. *Psychotherapy, 25,* 36–43.

Nowell, D., & Spruill, J. (1993). If it's not absolutely confidential, will information be disclosed? *Professional Psychology: Research and Practice, 24,* 367–369.

Nozick, R. (1968). Moral complications and moral structures. *Natural Law Forum, 13,* 1–50.

Nuremberg Code. (Reprinted in *Science, 143,* 553, 1949/1964.)

O'Connor, M. F. (2001). On the etiology and effective management of professional distress and impairment among psychologists. *Professional Psychology: Research and Practice, 32*(4), 345–350.

O'Leary, E., & Barry, N. (2005). Professional and ethical issues when working with older adults. In R. Tribe & J. Morrissey (Eds.), *Handbook of professional and ethical practice for psychologists, counselors and psychotherapists* (pp. 197–208). New York: Brunner-Routledge.

Olfson, M., & Pincus, H. A. (1994). Outpatient psychotherapy in the United States: I. Volume, costs, and user characteristics. *American Journal of Psychiatry, 151,* 1281–1288.

Oliansky, A. (1991). A confederate's perspective on deception. *Ethics and Behavior, 1,* 253–258.

Orr, P. (1997). Psychology impaired? *Professional Psychology: Research and Practice, 28,* 293–296.

Osborn, C. J. (2004). Seven salutary suggestions for counselor stamina. *Journal of Counseling & Development, 82,* 319–328.

The Oxford English Dictionary. (1989). Oxford, England: Clarendon.

PACE v. Hannon, 506 F. Supp. 831 (N.D. III, 1980).

Pam, A., & Rivera, J. (1995). Sexual pathology and dangerousness from a Thematic Apperception Test protocol. *Professional Psychology: Research and Practice, 26,* 72–77.

Parsi, K. P., Winslade, W. J., & Corcoran, K. (1995). Does confidentiality have a future? The computer-based patient record and managed mental health care. *Trends in Health Care, Law & Ethics, 10*(1–2), 78–82.

Pascarella, E. T., & Terenzini, P. T. (1991). *How college affects students: Findings and insights from twenty years of research.* San Francisco: Jossey-Bass.

Patterson, D., Darley, J., & Elliott, R. (1936). Men, women, and jobs. Minneapolis: University of Minnesota Press.

Patrick, K. D. (1989). Unique ethical dilemmas in counselor training. *Counselor Education and Supervision, 28,* 337–341.

Patton, M. J. (1992). 1991 Division 17 Presidential Address-Counseling psychology and the organized health industry: The hazards of uniformity. *The Counseling Psychologist, 20,* 194–206.

Paxton, C., Lovett, J., & Riggs, M. L. (2001). The nature of professional training and perceptions of adequacy in dealing with sexual feelings in psychotherapy: Experiences of clinical faculty. *Ethics & Behavior, 11*(2), 175–189.

Payton, C. R. (1994). Implications of the 1992 Ethics Code for diverse groups. *Professional Psychology: Research and Practice, 25,* 317–320.

Pedersen, P. B. (1995). Culture–centered ethical guidelines for counselors. In J. G. Ponerotto, J. M. Casas, L. A. Suzuki, & C. M Alexander (Eds.), *Handbook of multicultural counseling* (pp. 34–50). Thousand Oaks, CA: Sage.

Pedersen, P. B. (1997). The cultural context of the American Counseling Association code of ethics. *Journal of Counseling and Development, 76,* 23–28.

Pedersen, P. B., & Marsalla, A. J. (1982). The ethical crisis for cross-cultural counseling and therapy. *Professional Psychology, 13,* 492–500.

Peila-Shuster, J. J. (2011). Ageism: The "-Ism" we will all face one day. In S. K. Anderson & V. A. Middleton (Eds.), *Explorations in diversity: Examining privilege and oppression in a multicultural society* (2nd ed.), (pp. 165–170) Belmont, CA: Thomson Brooks/Cole Cengage Learning.

Pence, G. E. (1984). Recent work on virtues. *American Philosophical Quarterly, 21,* 281–297.

Pence, G. E. (1991). Virtue theory. In P. Singer (Ed.), *A companion to ethics* (pp. 249–258). Oxford, England: Blackwell.

Perez, R. M., Constantine, M. G., & Gerard, P. A. (2000). Individual and institutional productivity of racial and ethnic minority research in the *Journal of Counseling and Psychology. Journal of Counseling Psychology, 47,* 223–228.

Perkins, R. (1991). Therapy for lesbians? The case against. *Feminism and Psychology, 1,* 325–338.

Phelps, R., Eisman, E. J., & Kohout, J. (1998). Psychological practice and managed care: Results of the CAPP practitioner survey. *Professional Psychology: Research and Practice, 29,* 31–36.

Pinals, D. A., Packer, I. K., Fisher, W., & Roy-Bujnowski, K. (2004). Relationship between race and ethnicity and forensic clinical triage dispositions. *Psychiatric Services, 55,* 873–878.

Pipes, R. (1997). Nonsexual relationships between psychotherapists and their former clients: Obligations of psychologists. *Ethics and Behavior, 7,* 27–41.

Pittinger, D. J. (2002). Deception in research: Distinctions and solutions from the perspective of utilitarianism. *Ethics and Behavior, 12*(2), 117–142.

Plato. (1930). *The republic of Plato* (P. Shorey, Trans.). Cambridge, MA: Loeb Classical Library.

Plotkin, R. (1981). When rights collide: Parents, children, and consent to treatment. *Journal of Pediatric Psychology, 6,* 121–130.

Pogrebin, M. R., Poole, E. D., & Martinez, A. D. (1991). *Accounts of professional misdeeds: The sexual exploitation of clients by psychotherapists.* Denver: University of Colorado, Graduate School of Public Affairs.

Pomales, J., Claiborn, C. D., & LaFromboise, T. D. (1986). Effects of Black students' racial identity on perceptions of White counselors varying in cultural sensitivity. *Journal of Counseling Psychology, 33,* 57–61.

Pomerantz, A. M. (2005). Increasingly informed consent: Discussing distinct aspects of psychotherapy at different points in time. *Ethics and Behavior, 15*(4), 351–360.

Pomerantz, A. M., & Handelsman, M. M. (2004). Informed consent revisited: An updated written question format. *Professional Psychology: Research and Practice, 35*(2), 201–205.

Ponterotto, J. G., Fuertes, J. N., & Chen, E. C. (2000). Models of multicultural counseling. In S. D. Brown and R. W. Lent (Eds.), *Handbook of counseling psychology* (3rd ed., pp. 639–669). New York: Wiley.

Pope, K. S. (1988). How clients are harmed by sexual contact with mental health professionals: The syndrome and its prevalence. *Journal of Counseling and Development, 67,* 222–226.

Pope, K. S. (1990). Therapist-patient sexual involvement: A review of the research. *Clinical Psychology Review, 10*, 477–490.

Pope, K. S. (1991). Dual relationships in psychotherapy. *Ethics and Behavior, 1*, 22–34.

Pope, K. S. (1992). Responsibilities in providing psychological test feedback to clients. *Psychological Assessment, 4*, 268–271.

Pope, K. S. (1993). Licensing disciplinary actions for psychologists who have been sexually involved with a client: Some information about offenders. *Professional Psychology: Research and Practice, 24*, 374–377.

Pope, K. S. (1994). *Sexual involvement with therapists: Patient assessment, subsequent therapy, forensics.* Washington, DC: American Psychological Association.

Pope, K. S. (2000). Therapists' sexual feelings and behaviors: Research, trends and quandaries. In L. Szuchman & F. Muscarella (Eds.), *Psychological perspectives on human sexuality* (pp. 603–658). New York: Wiley.

Pope, K. S., & Bouhoutsos, J. C. (1986). *Sexual intimacy between therapists and patients.* New York: Praeger.

Pope, K. S., & Feldman-Summers, S. (1992). National survey of psychologists' sexual and physical abuse history and their evaluation of training and competence in these areas. *Professional Psychology: Research and Practice, 23*, 353–361.

Pope, K. S., & Keith-Spiegel, P. (2008). A practical approach to boundaries in psychotherapy: Making decisions, bypassing blunders, and mending fences. *Journal of Clinical Psychology, 64*, 638–652.

Pope, K. S., Keith-Spiegel, P., & Tabachnick, B. G. (1986). Sexual attraction to clients: The human therapist and the (sometimes) inhuman training system. *American Psychologist, 41*, 147–158.

Pope, K. S., Levenson, H., & Schover, L. (1979). Sexual intimacy in psychology training: Results and implications of a national survey. *American Psychologist, 34*, 682–689.

Pope, K. S., Sonne, J. L., & Greene, B. (2006). *What therapists don't talk about and why: Understanding taboos that hurt us and our clients.* Washington, DC: American Psychological Association.

Pope, K. S., Sonne, J. L., & Holroyd, J. (1993). *Sexual feelings in psychotherapy: Explorations for therapists and therapists-in-training.* Washington, DC: American Psychological Association.

Pope, K. S., & Tabachnick, B. G. (1993). Therapists' anger, hate, fear, and sexual feelings: National survey of therapist responses. *Professional Psychology: Research and Practice, 24*, 142–152.

Pope, K. S., & Tabachnick, B. G. (1994). Therapists as patients: A national survey of psychologists' experiences, problems, and beliefs. *Professional Psychology: Research and Practice, 25*, 247–258.

Pope, K. S., Tabachnick, B. G., & Keith-Spiegel, P. (1987). Ethics of practice: The beliefs and behaviors of psychologist as therapist. *American Psychologist, 42*, 993–1006.

Pope, K. S., & Vasquez, M. J. T. (2007). *Ethics in psychotherapy and counseling: A practical guide* (3rd ed.). San Francisco: Jossey-Bass.

Pope, K. S., & Vetter, V. A. (1992). Ethical dilemmas encountered by members of the American Psychological Association: A national survey. *American Psychologist, 47*, 397–441.

Pope-Davis, D. B., Ligiero, D. P., Liang, C., & Codrington, J. (2001). Fifteen years of the *Journal of Multicultural Counseling and Development*: A content analysis. *Journal of Multicultural Counseling and Development, 29*, 226–238.

Poston, W. S. C., Craine, M., & Atkinson, D. R. (1991). Counselor dissimilarity confrontation, client cultural mistrust, and willingness to self-disclose. *Journal of Multicultural Counseling and Development, 19*, 65–73.

Powell, C. T. (1984). Ethical principles and issues of competence in counseling adolescents. *The Counseling Psychologist, 12*, 57–68.

Prillenltensky, I. (1997). Values, assumptions, and practices: Assessing the moral implications of psychological discourse and action. *American Psychologist, 52*, 517–535.

Public Health. (1996). Confidentiality of alcohol and drug abuse patient record. *Code of Federal Regulations, 42*, 7–31.

Pulakos, J. (1994). Incidental encounters between therapists and clients: The client's perspective. *Professional Psychology: Research and Practice, 25*, 300–303.

Purves, D. (2005). The ethics and responsibilities of record keeping and note taking. In R. Tribe & J. Morrissey (Eds.), *Handbook of professional and ethical practice for psychologists, counselors and psychotherapists* (pp. 105–115). New York: Brunner-Routledge.

Ramsey, P. (1970). *The patient as person.* New Haven, CT; Yale University Press.

Rappaport, B. (1975). Carnal knowledge: What the wisdom of the body has to offer psychotherapy. *Journal of Humanistic Psychology, 15*, 49–70.

Ratanakul, P. (1994). Community and compassion: A Theravada Buddhist looks at principlism. In E. R. DuBose, R. P. Hamel, & L. J. O'Connell (Eds.), *A matter of principles? Ferment in U.S. bioethics* (pp. 121–129). Valley Forge, PA: Trinity Press International.

Ratts, M. J., DeKruyf, L., & Chen-Hayes, S. F. (2007). The ACA advocacy competencies: A social justice advocacy framework for professional school counselors. *Professional School Counseling, 11*(2), 90–97.

Rawls, J. (1971). *A theory of justice.* Cambridge, MA: Harvard University Press.

Reamer, F. G. (1991). AIDS, social work and the "duty to protect." *Social Work, 39,* 56–60.

Regents of the University of California v. Bakke, 438 U.S. 265 (1978).

Remley, T. P., & Herlihy, B. (2010). *Ethical, legal, and professional issues in counseling* (3rd ed.). Upper Saddle River, NJ: Merrill.

Renninger, S. M., Veach, P. M., & Bagdade, P. (2002). Psychologists' knowledge, opinions, and decision-making processes regarding child abuse and neglect reporting laws. *Professional Psychology: Research and Practice, 33,* 19–23.

Rest, J. (1983). Morality. In J. Flavell & E. Markham (Eds.), *Manual of child psychology: Vol. 4. Cognitive development* (pp. 520–629). New York: Wiley.

Rest, J. R. (1994). Background: Theory and research. In J. R. Rest & D. Narvaez (Eds.), *Moral development in the professions: Psychology and applied ethics.* Hillsdale, NJ: Lawrence Erlbaum Associates.

Rhodes, A. E., Goering, P. N., To, T., & Williams, J. I. (2002). Gender and outpatient mental health service use. *Social Science and Medicine, 54,* 1–10.

Richards, D. F. (2003). The central role of informed consent in ethical treatment and research with children. In W. O'Donhue & K. Ferguson (Eds.), *Handbook of professional ethics for psychologists: Issues, questions, and controversies* (pp. 377–389). Thousand Oaks, CA: Sage.

Richardson, F. C. (2003). Virtue ethics, dialogue, and "reverence". *American Behavioral Scientist, 47*(4), 442–458.

Rimler, G. W., & Morrison, R. D. (1993). The ethical impacts of managed care. *Journal of Business Ethics, 12,* 493–501.

Robertson, J., & Fitzgerald, L. F. (1990). The (mis)treatment of men: Effects of client gender role and lifestyle on diagnosis and attribution of pathology. *Journal of Counseling Psychology, 37,* 3–9.

Robinson, W. L., & Reid, P. T. (1985). Sexual intimacies in psychology revisited. *Professional Psychology: Research and Practice, 16,* 512–520.

Rodolfa, E., Bent, R., Eisman, E., Nelson, P., Rehm, L., & Ritchie, P. (2005). A cube model for competency development: Implications for psychology educators and regulators. *Professional Psychology: Research and Practice, 36*(4), 347–254.

Rodolfa, E., Rowen, H., Steier, D., Nicassio, T., & Gordon, J. (1994, Winter). Sexual dilemmas in internship training: What's a good training director to do? *APPIC Newsletter, 19*(2), 1, 22–24.

Rollin, B. E. (2006). *Science and Ethics.* New York: Cambridge University Press.

Rosenbaum, M. (1982). Preface. In M. Rosenbaum (Ed.), *Ethics and values in psychotherapy* (pp. iii–ix). New York: The Free Press.

Rosenhan, D. L., Teitelbaum, T. W., Teitelbaum, K. W., & Davidson, M. (1993). Warning third parties: The ripple effect of *Tarasoff. Pacific Law Journal, 24,* 1165–1232.

Rosenthal, R. (1994). Science and ethics in conducting, analyzing, and reporting psychological research. *Psychological Science, 5,* 127–133.

Ross, A. O. (1958). Confidentiality in child guidance treatment. *Mental Hygiene, 42,* 60–66.

Ross, W. D. (1930). *The right and the good.* Oxford, England: The Clarendon.

Royse, D., & Birge, B. (1987). Homophobia and attitudes towards AIDS patients among medical, nursing, and paramedical students. *Psychological Reports, 61,* 867–870.

Roysircar, G. (2006). Prevention work in schools and with youth: Promoting competence and reducing risks. In R. L. Toporek, L. H. Gerstein, N. A. Fouad, G. Roysircar, & T. Israel (Eds.), *Handbook for Social Justice in Counseling Psychology: Leadership, Vision, and Action.* Thousand Oaks, CA: Sage.

Rubanowitz, D. E. (1987). Public attitudes toward psychotherapist–client confidentiality. *Professional Psychology: Research and Practice, 18,* 613–618.

Rubin, N. J., Bebeau, M., Leigh, I. W., Lichtenberg, J. W., Nelson, P. D., Portnoy, S., et al. (2007). The competency movement within psychology: An historical perspective. *Professional Psychology: Research and Practice, 38*(5), 452–462.

Ruby, J. R., Grimmett, M. A., & Brown, L. L. (2008). Confidentiality: Casual, comfortable, communal. In L.E. Tyson, J.R. Culbreth, & J.A. Harrington (Eds.) *Critical incidents in clinical supervision: Addictions, community, & school counseling* (pp. 123-128). Alexandria, VA: American Counseling Association.

Rudd, M. D., Cukrowicz, K. C., & Bryan, C. J. (2008) Core competencies in suicide risk assessment and management: Implications for supervision. *Training and Education in Professional Psychology, 2,* 219–228.

Rupert, P. A., & Holmes, D. L. (1997). Dual relationships in higher education: Professional and institutional guidelines. *Journal of Higher Education, 68*, 660–678.

Russell, D. (1988) Language and psychotherapy: The influence of nonstandard English in clinical practice. In L. Comas-Diaz & E. Griffith (Eds.), *Clinical guidelines in cross-cultural mental health* (pp. 33–68). New York: Wiley.

Russell, J. E. A., & Adams, D. M. (1997). The changing nature of mentoring in organizations: An introduction to the special issues on mentoring and organizations. *Journal of Vocational Behavior, 51*, 1–14.

Ryan, W. (Ed.). (1969). *Distress in the city: Essays on the design and administration of urban mental health services.* Cleveland, OH: Case Western Reserve University Press.

Rybash, J. M., Roodin, P. A., & Hoyer, W. J. (1995). *Adult development and aging* (3rd ed.). Dubuque, IA: Brown & Benchmark.

Sachs, J. S. (1983). Negative factors in brief psychotherapy: An empirical assessment. *Journal of Consulting and Clinical Psychology, 51*, 577–564.

Sales, B. D., & Folkman, S. (Eds.). (1998). *The ethics of research with human participants* (Draft copy). Washington, DC: American Psychological Association (Board of Scientific Affairs Task Force.)

Sales, B. D., & Shuman, D. W. (1993). Reclaiming the integrity of science in expert witnessing. *Ethics and Behavior, 3*, 223–229.

Salisbury, W. A., & Kinnier, R. T. (1996). Posttermination friendship between counselors and clients. *Journal of Counseling and Development, 74*, 495–500.

Salgo v. Leland Stanford Jr. Univ. Bd. Of Trustees, 154 Cal. App. 2d560, 317 P.2d 170 (1957).

Sanchez, L. M., & Turner, S. M. (2003). Practicing psychology in the era of managed care: Implications for practice and training. *American Psychologist, 58*(2), 116–129.

Sanford, F. H. (1952). A little recent history. *American Psychologist, 7*, 426–428.

Santiago-Rivera, A. L., Talka, K., & Tully, A. W. (2006). Environmental racism: A call to the profession for community intervention and social action. In R. L. Toporek, L. H. Gerstein, N. A. Fouad, G. Roysircar, & T. Israel (Eds.), *Handbook for Social Justice in Counseling Psychology: Leadership, Vision, and Action.* Thousand Oaks, CA: Sage.

Satcher, D. (2009). Mental health: Report of the Surgeon General. Retrieved 12 Jan. 2009 from http://surgeongeneral.gov/library/mentalhealth/home/html

Scarr, S. (1988). Race and gender as psychological variables: Social and ethical issues. *American Psychologist, 43*, 56–59.

Scarr, S. (1989). Protecting general intelligence: Constructs and consequences of interventions. In R. Linn (Ed.), *Intelligence: Measurement, theory, and public policy* (pp. 74–118). Urbana: University of Illinois Press.

Schaeffer, G., Epting, K., Zinn, T., & Buskist, W. (2003). Student and faculty perceptions of effective teaching: A successful replication. *Teaching of Psychology, 30*, 133–136.

Schank, J. A., & Skovholt, T. M. (1997). Dual relationship dilemmas of rural and small-community psychologists, *Professional Psychology: Research and Practice, 28*, 44–49.

Schank, J. A., & Skovholt, T. M. (2006). *Ethical practices in small communities: Challenges and rewards for psychotherapists.* Washington, DC: American Psychological Association.

Scheffler, R. M., & Miller, A. B. (1991). Differences in mental health service utilization among ethnic subpopulations. *International Journal of Law and Psychiatry, 14*, 363–376.

Scherer, D. G. (1991). The capacities of minors to exercise voluntariness in medical treatment decisions. *Law and Human Behavior, 15*, 431–449.

Schiffman, J., Becker, K. D., & Daleiden, E. L. (2006). Evidence-based services in a statewide public mental health system: Do the services fit the problems? *Journal of Clinical Child and Adolescent Psychology, 35*, 13–19.

Schloendorff v. Society of New York Hospital, 211 N.Y. 125, 105 N.E. 92 (1914).

Scholosser, L. Z., & Gelso, C. J. (2001). Measuring the working alliance in advisor-advisee relationships in graduate school. *Journal of Counseling Psychology, 48*, 157–167.

Schmaling, K. B. (2000). Poorly understood conditions. In M. B. Goldman & M. C. Hatch (Eds.), *Women & health* (pp. 1055–1057). San Diego: Academic Press.

Schmidt, L. D. (1986). Some questions about paradoxical interventions. *The Counseling Psychologist, 14*, 309–311.

Schoener, G. R., & Gonsiorek, J. (1988). Assessment and development of rehabilitation plans for counselors who have sexually exploited their clients. *Journal of Counseling and Development, 67*, 227–232.

Schwebel, M., Skorina, J. K., & Schoener, G. (1994). *Assisting impaired psychologists: Program development for state psychological associations* (Rev. ed.). Washington, DC: American Psychological Association.

Schweibert, V. L. (2000). *Mentoring: Creating connected, empowered relationships.* Alexandria, VA: American Counseling Association.

Scott, K. J., Ingram, K. M., Vitanza, S. A., & Smith, N. G. (2000). Training in supervision: A survey of current practices. *The Counseling Psychologist, 28,* 403–422.

Scriven, M. (1982). Professional ethics. *Journal of Higher Education, 53,* 305–317.

Secord, P. F., & Backman, C. W. (1974). *Social psychology.* New York: McGraw-Hill.

Seligman, M. E. (1995). The effectiveness of psychotherapy: The *Consumer Reports* study. *American Psychologist, 50,* 965–974.

Sell, J. M., Gottlieb, M. C., & Schoenfeld, L. (1986). Ethical considerations of social/romantic relationships with present and former clients. *Professional Psychology: Research and Practice, 17,* 504–508.

Seltzer, L. (1986). *Paradoxical strategies in psychotherapy: A comprehensive overview and guidebook.* New York: Wiley.

Sex with ex-clients judged on intent of termination. (1987, July). *APA Monitor,* p. 45.

Shader, R. I. (1970) The walk-in service: An experience in community care. In T. Rothman (Ed.), *Changing patterns in psychiatric care.* New York: Crown.

Sharkin, B. S., & Birky, I. (1992). Incidental encounters between therapists and their clients. *Professional Psychology: Research and Practice, 23,* 326–328.

Shedler, J., & Block, J. (1990). Adolescent drug use and psychological health: A longitudinal study. *American Psychologist, 45*(5), 612–630.

Shepard, M. (1972). *The love treatment: Sexual intimacy between patients and psychotherapists.* New York: Wyden.

Sherman, M. D., & Thelen, M. H. (1998). Distress and professional impairment among psychologists in clinical practice. *Professional Psychology: Research and Practice, 29,* 79–85.

Sherry, P. (1991). Ethical issues in the conduct of supervision. *The Counseling Psychologist, 19,* 566–584.

Sherry, P., Teschendorf, R., Anderson, S. K., & Guzman, F. (1991). Ethical beliefs and behaviors of college counseling center professionals. *Journal of College Student Development, 34*(4), 350-358.

Shoeman, F. (1983, August). Commentary. *Hastings Center Report,* pp. 19-20.

Sieber, J. E. (1992). *Planning ethically responsible research: A guide for students and internal review boards.* Newbury Park, CA: Sage.

Sieber, J. E. (1994). Will the new code help researchers be more ethical? *Professional Psychology: Research and Practice, 25,* 369–375.

Sieber, J. E., Ianauzzo, R., & Rodriguez, B. (1995). Deception methods in psychology: Have they changed in 23 years? *Ethics and Behavior, 5,* 67–85.

Sieber, J. E., & Saks, M. J. (1989). A consensus of subject pool characteristics and policies. *American Psychologist, 44,* 1053–1061.

Sieber, J. E. (2000). Planning research: Basic ethical decision-making. In B. D. Sales & S. Folkman (Eds.), *Ethics in research with human participants* (pp. 13–26). Washington, DC: American Psychological Association.

Sieber, J. E. (2004). Using our best judgment in conducting human research. *Ethics & Behavior, 14*(4), 297–304.

Siegel, M. (1979). Privacy, ethics, and confidentiality. *Professional Psychology: Research and Practice, 10,* 249–258.

Simmons v. United States, 805 F. 2nd 1363 (9th Cir. 1986).

Simon, H. A. (1976). Identifying basic abilities underlying intelligent performance of complex tasks. In L. B. Resnick (Ed.), *The nature of intelligence* (pp. 65–98). Hillsdale, NJ: Lawrence Erlbaum Associates.

Simon, R. I. (1989). Sexual exploitation of patients: How it begins before it happens. *Psychiatric Annals, 19,* 104–112.

Simon, R. I., & Shuman, D. W. (2007). *Clinical manual of psychiatry and law.* Washington, DC: American Psychiatric Association.

Sinclair, C., Poizner, S., Gilmour-Barrett, K., & Randall, D. (1987). The development of a code of ethics for Canadian psychologists. *Canadian Psychology, 28*(1), 1–8.

Slovenko, R. (1992). Undue familiarity or undue damages? *Whittier Law Review, 13,* 643–667

Small, M. A., Lyons, P. M., & Guy, L. S. (2002). Liability issues in child abuse and neglect reporting statutes. *Professional Psychology: Research and Practice, 33,* 13–18.

Smith, C. P. (1983). Research on deception, informed consent and debriefing. In L. Wheeler & P. Shaver (Eds.), *Review of personality and social psychology* (Vol. 4, pp. 297–328). Beverly Hills, CA: Sage.

Smith, D., & Fitzpatrick, M. (1995). Patient-therapist boundary issues: An integrative review of theory and research. *Professional Psychology: Research and Practice, 26,* 499–506.

Smith, M. B. (2000). Moral foundations in research with human participants. In B. D. Sales & S. Folkman (Eds.), *Ethics in research with human participants* (pp. 3–10). Washington, DC: American Psychological Association.

Smith, P. L., & Moss, S. B. (2009). Psychologist impairment: What is it, how can it be prevented, and what can be done to address it? *Clinical Psychology: Science and Practice, 16*(1), 1–15.

Smith-Bell, M., & Winslade, W. J. (1994). Privacy, confidentiality, and privilege in psychotherapeutic relationships. *Journal of Orthopsychiatry, 64,* 180–193.

Snipe, R. M. (1988). Ethical issues in the assessment and treatment of a rational suicidal client. *The Counseling Psychologist, 16,* 128–138.

Snowden, L. R., & Cheung, F. K. (1990). Use of inpatient mental health services by members of ethnic minority groups. *American Psychologist, 45,* 347–355.

Sobocinski, M. R. (1990). Ethical principles in the counseling of gay and lesbian adolescents: Issues of autonomy, competence, and confidentiality. *Professional Psychology: Research and Practice, 21,* 240–247.

Sodowsky, G. R. (1991). Effects of culturally consistent counseling tasks on American and international student observers' perceptions of counselor credibility: A preliminary investigation. *Journal of Counseling and Development, 69,* 253–256.

Somberg, D. R., Stone, G. L., & Claiborn, C. D. (1993), Informed consent: Therapists' beliefs and practices. *Professional Psychology: Research and Practice, 24,* 153–159.

Somer, E., & Nachmani, I. (2005). Constructions of therapist-patient sex: An analysis of retrospective reports by former Israeli patients. *Sexual Abuse: A Journal of Research and Treatment, 17*(1), 47–62.

Somer, E., & Saadon, M. (1999). Therapist-client sex: Clients' retrospective reports. *Professional Psychology: Research and Practice, 30*(5), 504–509.

Sommers-Flanagan, R., Elliott, D., & Sommers-Flanagan, J. (1998). Exploring the edges: Boundaries and breaks. *Ethics and Behavior, 8*(1), 37–48.

Sommers-Flanagan, R. S., & Sommers-Flanagan, R. (2007). *Becoming an ethical helping professional: Cultural and philosophical foundations.* Hoboken, NJ: Wiley & Sons.

Sonne, J. L. (1994). Multiple relationships: Does the new Ethics Code answer the right questions? *Professional Psychology: Research and Practice, 25,* 336–343.

Sonne, J. L., & Pope, K. S. (1991). Treating victims of therapist-patient sexual involvement. *Psychotherapy, 28,* 174–187.

Speight, S. L., & Vera, E. M. (2004). A social justice agenda: Ready, or not? *The Counseling Psychologist, 32,* 109–118.

Spitz, R. (1945). Hospitalism: An inquiry into the genesis of psychiatric conditions in early childhood. *Psychoanalytic Study of the Child, 1.*

Spruill, J., Rozensky, R. H., Stigall, T. T., Vasquez, M., Bingham, R. P., & De Vaney Olvey, C. (2004). Becoming a competent clinician: Basic competencies in intervention. *Journal of Clinical Psychology, 60*(7), 741–754.

Stadler, H. A. (1990). Counselor impairment. In B. Herlihy & L. Golden (Eds.), *Ethical Standards case book.* Alexandria, VA: American Association for Counseling and Development.

Stadler, H. A. (1989). Balancing ethical responsibilities: Reporting child abuse and neglect. *The Counseling Psychologist, 17,* 102–110.

Stadler, H. A., Willing, K. L., Eberhage, M. G., & Ward, W. H. (1988). Impairment: Implications for the counseling profession. *Journal of Counseling and Development, 6,* 258–260.

Stake, J. E., & Oliver, J. (1991). Sexual contact and touching between therapist and client: A survey of psychologists' attitudes and behavior. *Professional Psychology: Research and Practice, 22,* 297–307.

Stanley, B., & Sieber, J. E. (1992). Epilogue. In B. Stanley & J. E. Sieber (Eds.), *Social research on children and adolescents: Ethical issues* (pp. 188–193). Newbury Park, CA: Sage.

Starr, D. S. (2007, February). Medicine and the law: Patient confidentiality vs. threats of violence. *Cortlandt Forum,* 67–68.

Steele, J. M. (2008). Preparing counselors to advocate for social justice: A liberation model. *Counselor Education and Supervision, 48,* 74–85.

Stevenson, S., & Kitchener, K. S. (2001). Ethical issues in the practice of psychology with clients with HIV/AIDS. In J. R. Anderson & B. Barret (Eds.), *Ethics in HIV-related psychotherapy: Clinical decision making in complex cases.* Washington DC: American Psychological Association.

Stewart-Sicking, J. A. (2008). Virtues, values and the good life: Aladair MacIntyre's virtue ethics and its implications for counseling. *Counseling and Values, 52*, 156–171.

Stice, E., & Bearman, S. K. (2004). Body-image and eating disturbances prospectively predict increases in depressive symptoms in adolescent girls: A growth curve analysis. *Developmental Psychology, 37*, 597–607.

Storring, V. (Producer). (1991, November 12). My doctor, my lover [Television documentary]. *Frontline.* Boston, MA: Public Broadcasting Service.

Strasburger, L. H., Jorgenson, L., & Randles, R. (1991). Criminalization of psychotherapist-patient sex. *American Journal of Psychiatry, 148*, 859–863.

Strasburger, L. H., Jorgenson, L., & Sutherland, P (1992). Prevention of psychotherapist sexual misconduct: Avoiding the slippery slope. *American Journal of Psychotherapy, 46*, 544–555.

Stratton, J. S., & Smith, R. D. (2006). Supervision of couples cases. *Psychotherapy: Theory, Research, Practice, Training, 43*, 337–348.

Stromberg, C., & Dellinger, A. (1993). A legal update on malpractice and other professional liability. *The Psychologist's Legal Update, 3*, 3–15.

Sue, D. W., Arredondo, P., & McDavis, R. J. (1992). Multicultural counseling competencies and standards: A call to the profession. *Journal of Counseling and Development, 70*, 477–486.

Sue, D. W., Bernier, J. E., Durran, A., Feinberg, L., Pedersen, P., Smith, E. J. et al. (1982). Position paper: Cross-cultural counseling competencies. *Counseling Psychologist, 10*, 45–52.

Sue, D. W., & Sue, S. (1990). *Counseling the culturally different.* New York: Wiley.

Sue, D. W., Ivey, A., & Pedersen, P. (1996). *A theory of multicultural counseling and therapy.* Pacific Grove, CA: Brooks/Cole.

Sue, S., Kurasaki, K., & Srinivasan, S. (1999). Ethnicity, gender, and cross-cultural issues in clinical research. *Handbook of Research Methods in Clinical Psychology*, 54–71.

Sue, S., Zane, N., & Young, K. (1994). Research on psychotherapy with culturally diverse populations. In A. E. Bergin & S. L. Garfield (Eds.), *Handbook of psychotherapy and behavior change* (pp. 783–820). New York: Wiley.

Sullivan, T., Martin, W. L., Jr., & Handelsman, M. M. (1993). *Professional psychology: Research and Practice, 24*, 160–163.

Sullivan, J. R., Ramirez, E., Rae, W. A., Razo, N. P., & George, C. A. (2002). Factors contributing to breaking confidentiality with adolescent clients: A survey of pediatric psychologists. *Professional Psychology: Research and Practice, 33*, 396–401.

Sussman, L. K., Robins, L. N., & Earls, F. (1987). Treatment-seeking for depression by black and white Americans. *Social Science and Medicine, 24*, 187–196.

Sutter, E., McPherson, R. H., & Geeseman, R. (2002). Contracting for supervision. *Professional Psychology: Research and Practice, 33*(5), 495–498.

Swenson, L. C. (1997). *Psychology and law for the helping profession.* Pacific Grove, CA: Brooks/Cole.

Szasz, T. (1961). *The myth of mental illness.* New York: Dell.

Szasz, T. (1971/1990). The ethics of suicide. In J. Donnelly (Ed.), *Suicide: Right or wrong?* Amherst, NY: Prometheus Books. (Reprinted from *The Antioch Review, 31*, 7–17)

Tabachnick, B., Keith-Spiegel, P., & Pope, K. S. (1991). Ethics of teaching: Beliefs and behaviors of psychologists as educators. *American Psychologist, 46*, 506–515.

Talleyrand, R. M., Chi-Ying Chung, R., & Bemak, F. (2006). Incorporating social justice in counselor training programs: A case study example. In R. L. Toporek, L. H. Gerstein, N. A. Fouad, G.. Roysircar, & T. Israel (Eds.), *Handbook for Social Justice in Counseling Psychology: Leadership, Vision, and Action.* Thousand Oaks, CA: Sage.

Tangney, J. (2000). Training. In B. D. Sales & S. Folkman (Eds.), *Ethics in research with human participants* (pp. 97–105). Washington, DC: American Psychological Association.

Tapp, J. L., Kelman, H., Triandis, H., Wrightsman, L., & Coelho, G. (1974). Advisory principles of ethical considerations in the conduct of cross-cultural research. *International Journal of Psychology, 9*, 240–249.

Tarasoff v. Regents of the University of California, 529 P.2d 553 (Cal. 1974), 551 P.2d 334, 331 (Cal. 1976).

Taylor, P. W. (1978). *Problems of moral philosophy.* Belmont, CA: Wadsworth.

Templeman, T. L. (1989). Dual relationships in rural practices. *Journal of the Oregon Psychological Association, 35*, 12–14.

Texas v. Hopwood, No. 00-1609 (5th Cir. June 5, 2001).

Thomas, J. T. (2007). Informed consent through contracting for supervision: Minimizing risks, enhancing benefits. *Professional Psychology: Research and Practice, 38*(3), 221–231.

Thompson, C. E., Alfred, D. M., Edwards, S. L., & Garcia, P. G. (2006). Transformative endeavors: Implementing Helms's racial identity theory to a school-based heritage project. In R. L. Toporek, L. H. Gerstein, N. A. Fouad, G. Roysircar, & T. Israel (Eds.), *Handbook for Social Justice in Counseling Psychology: Leadership, Vision, and Action*. Thousand Oaks, CA: Sage.

Thompson, C. E., Worthington, R., & Atkinson, D. R. (1994). Counselor content orientation, counselor race, and Black women's cultural mistrust and self-disclosures. *Journal of Counseling Psychology, 41*, 155–161.

Thoreson, R. W., Miller, M., & Krauskopf, C. J. (1989). The distressed psychologist: Prevalence and treatment considerations. *Professional Psychology: Research and Practice, 20*, 153–158.

Thoreson, R. W., Morrow, K. A., Frazier, P. A., & Kerstner, P. L. (1990). Needs and concerns of women in AACD: Preliminary results. Paper presented at the annual convention of the American Association for Counseling and Development, Cincinnati, OH.

Titus, S. L., & Keane, M. A. (1999). Do you understand?: An ethical assessment of researchers' description of the consenting process. *Journal of Clinical Ethics, 7*, 60–68.

Tjelveit, A. C. (1999). *Ethics and values in psychotherapy*. NewYork: Routledge.

Tjelveit, A. C. (2000). There is more to ethics than codes of professional ethics: Social ethics, theoretical ethics, and managed care. *The Counseling Psychologist, 28*, 242–249.

Tjelveit, A. C. (2003). Implicit virtues, divergent goods, multiple communities: Explicitly addressing virtues in the behavioral sciences. *American Behavioral Scientist, 47*(4), 395–414.

Tomcho, T. J., & Foels, R. (2008). Assessing effective teaching of psychology: A meta-analytic integration of learning outcomes. *Teaching of Psychology, 35*(4), 286–296.

Tomm, K. (1993). The ethics of dual relationships. *The California Therapist*, 7–19.

Toporek, R. L., & Williams, R. A. (2006). Ethics and professional issues related to the practice of social justice in counseling psychology. In R. L. Toporek, L. H. Gerstein, N. A. Fouad, G. Roysircar, & T. Israel (Eds.), *Handbook for Social Justice in Counseling Psychology: Leadership, Vision, and Action*. Thousand Oaks, CA: Sage.

Totten, G., Lamb, D. H., & Reeder, G. D. (1990). *Tarasoff* and confidentiality in AIDS-related psychotherapy. *Professional Psychology: Research and Practice, 21*, 155–160.

Toulmin, S. (1950). *An examination of the place of reason in ethics*. Cambridge, England: Cambridge University Press.

Tromskii-Klingshirm, D. M., & Davis, T. E. (2007). Supervisees' perceptions of their clinical supervision: A study of the dual role of clinical and administrative supervisor. *Counselor Education and Supervision, 46*, 294–304.

Turner, S. M., DeMers, S. T., Fox, H. R., & Reed, G. M. (2001). APA's guidelines for test user qualifications. *American Psychologist, 56*, 1099–1113.

Tversky, A., & Kahneman, D. (1981). The framing of decisions and the psychology of choice. *Science, 211*, 453–458.

Tymchuck, A. J., Drapkin, R., Major-Kingsley, S., Ackerman, A. B., Coffman, E. W., & Baum, M. S. (1982). Ethical decision making and psychologists' attitudes toward training in ethics. *Professional Psychology, 13*, 412–421.

United States Census Bureau. (2008, August 14). *An older and more diverse nation by midcentury*. Retrieved September 6, 2010, from http://www.census.gov/newsroom/releases/archives/population/cb08-123.html

U.S. Department of Health and Human Services. (1987). Confidentiality of alcohol and drug abuse patient records. 42 C.F.R. Part 2. *Federal Register, 52*, 21796–21814.

U.S. Department of Health and Human Services. (1988). *Study Findings: Study of National Incidence and Prevalence of Child Abuse and Neglect: 1988*. Bethesda, MD: Westat.

U.S. Department of Health and Human Services. (1994). Policy for protection of human research subjects. In D. N. Bersoff (Ed.), *Ethical conflicts in psychology* (pp. 369–377). Washington, DC: American Psychological Association. (Reprinted from 56FR 28012, 28022, June 18, 1991)

U.S. Public Health Service. (1989). Responsibilities of awardee and applicant institutions for dealing with and reporting possible misconduct in science [Special issue], *NIH Guide for Grants and Contracts, 18*(30).

U.S. Department of Health and Human Services. (2003). *OCR Privacy Brief: Summary of the HIPAA Privacy Rule*. Washington, DC: U.S. Government Printing Office.

U.S. Department of Health and Human Services. (2009). *Child maltreatment: 2007*. Washington, DC: U.S. Government Printing Office.

Vacha-Haase, T., Davenport, D. S., & Kerewsky, S. D. (2004). Problematic students: Gatekeeping practices of academic professional psychology programs. *Professional Psychology: Research and Practice, 35*, 115–122.

VandeCreek, L. (2008). Considering confidentiality within broader theoretical frameworks. *Professional Psychology: Research and Practice, 39*, 372–373.

VandenBos, G. R. (Ed.). (2007). *American Psychological Association dictionary of psychology*. Washington, DC: American Psychological Association.

Vasquez, M. J. T. (1991). Sexual intimacies with clients after termination: Should a prohibition be explicit? *Ethics and Behavior, 1*, 45–61.

Vasquez, M. J. T. (1993). Forward. In K. S. Pope, J. L. Sonne, & J. Holroyd (Eds.), *Sexual feelings in psychotherapy* (pp. ix–xiii). Washington, DC: American Psychological Association.

Vasquez, M. J. T. (1994). Implications of the 1992 ethics code for the practice of individual psychotherapy. *Professional Psychology: Research and Practice, 25*, 321–328.

Vasquez, M. J. T. (1999). Trainee impairment: A response from a feminist/multicultural retired trainer. *The Counseling Psychologist, 27*, 687–692.

Vasquez, M. J. T. (2007). Sometimes a taco is just a taco! *Professional Psychology: Research and Practice, 38*(4), 406–408.

Veatch, R. M. (1981). *A theory of medical ethics*. New York: Basic Books.

Vulcano, B. A. (2007). Extending the generality of the qualities and behaviors constituting effective teaching. *Teaching of Psychology, 34*(2), 114–117.

Walzer, M. (1983). *Spheres of justice: A defense of pluralism and equality*. New York: Basic Books.

Wampold, B. E. (2001). *The great psychotherapy debate*. Mahwah, NJ: Lawrence Erlbaum.

Wampold, B. E., & Bhati, K. S. (2004). Attending to the omissions: A historical examination of evidence-based practice movements. *Professional Psychology: Research and Practice, 35*, 563–570.

Warren, J. I., Murrie, D. C., Chauhan, P., Dietz, P. E., & Morris, J. (2004). Opinion formation in evaluating sanity at the time of the offense: An examination of 5175 pre-trial evaluations. *Behavioral Sciences and the Law, 19*, 171–186.

Watts, R. J. (2004). Integrating social justice and psychology. *The Counseling Psychologist, 32*, 855–865.

Watts, R., Williams, N. C., & Jagers, R. (2003). Sociopolitical development. *American Journal of Community Psychology, 31*, 185–194.

Weber, J. J., Solomon, M., & Bachrach, H. M. (1985). Factors associated with the outcome of psychoanalysis: Report of the Columbia Psychoanalytic Center Research Project (II). *International Review of Psychoanalysis, 12*, 127–141.

Webster's ninth new collegiate dictionary. (1988). Springfield, MA: Merriam-Webster.

Weisberg, J., & Haberman, M. (1989). A therapeutic hugging week in a geriatric facility. *Journal of Gerontological Social Work, 13*, 181–186.

Weithorn, L. A., & Campbell, S. (1982). The competency of children and adolescents to make informed treatment decisions. *Child Development, 53*, 1589–1599.

Weithorn, L. A., & Scherer, D. G. (1994). Children's involvement in research participation decisions: Psychological considerations. In M. A. Grodin & L. H. Glantz (Eds.), *Children as research subjects: Science, ethics, and law* (pp. 133–179). Oxford, England: Oxford University Press.

Welfel, E. R. (1998). *Ethics in counseling and psychotherapy: Standards, research and emerging issues*. Pacific Grove, CA: Brooks/Cole.

Welfel, E. R. (2010). *Ethics in counseling & psychotherapy: Standards, research, & emerging issues* (4th ed.). Belmont, CA: Thomson Brooks/Cole.

Werth, J. L., Jr. (1995). Rational suicide reconsidered: AIDS as an impetus for change. *Death Studies, 19*, 65–80.

Wettstein, R. M. (2005). Quality and quality improvement in forensic mental health evaluations. *Journal of the American Academy of Psychiatry and the Law, 33*, 158–175.

Whiston, S. C., & Emerson, S. (1989). Ethical implications for supervisors in counseling of trainees. *Counselor Education and Supervision, 28*, 318–325.

Widiger, T. A., & Rorer, L. G (1984). The responsible psychotherapist. *American Psychologist, 39*, 503–515.

Wiener, R. L. (1996, June). Affirmative action in public universities: A recent Fifth Circuit Court of Appeals judgment challenges affirmative action plans in state universities. *APA Monitor*, p. 13.

Wilson, D. W., & Donnerstein, W. (1976). Legal and ethical aspects of nonreactive social psychological research: An excursion into the public mind. *American Psychologist, 31*, 765–773.

Wilson, P. F., & Johnson, W. B. (2001). Core virtues for the practice of mentoring. *Journal of Psychology and Theology, 29*, 121–130.

Winokur, S. (1991, August 4). Doctors of desire. *The San Francisco Examiner*, pp. Al, A18–A21.

Wise, E. H. (2007). Informed consent: Complexities and meanings. *Professional Psychology: Research and Practice 38*(2), 182–183.

Wise, T. P. (1978). Where the public peril begins: A survey of psychotherapists to determine the effects of *Tarasoff. Stanford Law Review, 31*, 165–190.

Witt, P. L., Wheeless, L. R., & Allen, M. (2004). A meta-analytical review of the relationship between teacher immediacy and student learning. *Communication Monographs, 71*, 184–207.

Wood, P. K. (1983). Inquiring systems and problem structure: Implications for cognitive development. *Human Development. 26*, 249–265.

Woody, R. H. (1998). Bartering for psychological services. *Professional Psychology: Research and Practice, 29*, 174–178.

Woody, R. H. (2009). Ethical considerations of multiple roles in forensic services. *Ethics and Behavior, 19*(1), 79–87.

World Health Organization. (2000). *World health statistics annual*. Geneva, Switzerland: Author.

World Health Organization. (2002). World report on violence and health. Geneva: WHO.

Worthington, R. L., Mobley, M., Franks, R. P., & Tan, J. A. (2000). Multicultural counseling competencies: Verbal content, counselor attributions, and social desirability. *Journal of Counseling Psychology, 47*, 460–468.

Worthington, R. L., Soth-McNett, A. M., & Moreno, M. V. (2007). Multicultural counseling competencies research: A 20-year content analysis. *Journal of Counseling Psychology, 54*(4), 351–361.

Wrenn, C. G. (1985). Afterword: The culturally encapsulated counselor. In P. Pedersen (Ed.), *Handbook of cross-cultural counseling and therapy* (pp. 323–329). Westport, CT: Greenwood Press.

Wright, R. (1996, June 12). U.S. child poverty rate leads industrial nations. *The Coloradoan*.

Yalof, J., & Brabender, V. (2001). Ethical dilemmas in personality assessment courses: Using the classroom for in vivo training. *Journal of Personality Assessment, 77*(2), 203–213.

Young, I. M. (1990). *Justice and the politics of difference*. Princeton, NJ: Princeton University Press.

Young, I. M. (2000). *Inclusion and democracy*. London: Oxford University Press.

Younggren, J. N. (2002). Ethical decision making an dual relationships. Retrieved February 23, 2010, from http://kspope.com/dual/younggren.php

Younggren, J. N., & Gottlieb, M. C. (2004). Managing risk when contemplating multiple relationships. *Professional Psychology: Research and Practice, 35*(3), 255–260.

Younggren, J. N., & Harris, E. A. (2008). Can you keep a secret? Confidentiality in psychotherapy. *Journal of Clinical Psychology: In Session, 64*, 589–600.

Zeter, H. A. (2011). White out: Privilege and its problems. In S. K. Anderson & V. A. Middleton (Eds.), *Explorations in diversity: Examining privilege and oppression in a multicultural society* (2nd ed.), (pp. 11–24). Belmont, CA: Thomson Brooks/Cole Cengage Learning.

Zipple, A. M., Langle, S., Spaniol, L., & Fisher, H. (1990). Confidentiality and the families' need too know: Strategies for resolving the conflict. *Community Mental Health Journal, 26*, 533–545.

Zur, O. (2007). Boundaries in psychotherapy: Ethical and clinical explorations. Washington, DC: American Psychological Association.

Index